# The Fourth Republic, 1944–1958

JEAN-PIERRE RIOUX

Translated by

GODFREY ROGERS

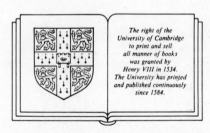

The right of the
University of Cambridge
to print and sell
all manner of books
was granted by
Henry VIII in 1534.
The University has printed
and published continuously
since 1584.

CAMBRIDGE UNIVERSITY PRESS

Cambridge
New York   Port Chester   Melbourne   Sydney

EDITIONS DE
LA MAISON DES SCIENCES DE L'HOMME

Paris

Published by the Press Syndicate of the University of Cambridge
The Pitt Building, Trumpington Street, Cambridge CB2 1RP
40 West 20th Street, New York, NY 10011, USA
10 Stamford Road, Oakleigh, Melbourne 3166, Australia
and Editions de la Maison des Sciences de l'Homme
54 Boulevard Raspail, 75270 Paris Cedex 06

Originally published in French as *La France de la Quatrième République*,
in two volumes, 1980 and 1983
by Editions du Seuil, Paris
and © Editions du Seuil
First published in English by Editions de la Maison des Sciences de
l'Homme and Cambridge University Press 1987 as *The Fourth Republic,
1944–1958*
English translation © Maison des Sciences de l'Homme and
Cambridge University Press 1987
First paperback edition 1989

Printed in Great Britain at The Bath Press, Avon

*British Library cataloguing in publication data*

Rioux, Jeane-Pierre
The Fourth Republic, 1944–1958. – (The
Cambridge history of modern France; 7)
1. France – History – German occupation,
1940–1945   2. France – History – 1945 –
I. Title   II. La France de la Quatrième
République.   *English*
944.082   DC400

*Library of Congress cataloguing in publication data*

Rioux, Jean-Pierre, 1939–
The Fourth Republic, 1944–1958.
(The Cambridge history of modern France; 7)
Translation of: République, la France de la quatrième.
Includes bibliographies and index.
1. France – Politics and government – 1945–1958.
2. France – History – 1945–       I. Title.   II. Series.
DC404.R5413 1987   944.082   86-28403

ISBN 0 521 25238 5   hard covers ✓
ISBN 0 521 38916 X   paperback
ISBN 2 7351 0166 5   hard covers (France only)
ISBN 2 7351 0309 9   paperback (France only)

# Contents

# Maps

# Maps

# Foreword

The author has to confess that in 1944, five years old, he dreamt longingly before the empty sweet jars, but that in 1958, when a student in Paris, he felt qualified to add his voice to those opposing the war in Algeria, a war which painfully marked the political coming of age of his generation. What follows has, inevitably, been influenced by old scores to settle, as well as by happier memories of the period. They alone preclude a pretension to objectivity, an objectivity, moreover, in which the author has, professionally, little faith.

Like the volumes that precede it in the series, this one aspires only to provide a clear account of its subject, as precise as is possible for a period too close to us for all the sources to be available. The reader will judge if it is timely. More than twenty years after 13 May 1958, however, as the heat starts to go out of the polemic, perhaps the Fourth Republic, for so long a skeleton in the cupboard of French political life, can be examined with a fresher eye. The quality of the early works gives some consistency to the exercise. After the special pleading and the invective, the brilliant essays and the parliamentary studies, on which its historiography has been nourished, a larger, more ambitious history can now be attempted; one whose working hypothesis is too obvious for it not to be at least partly correct: the history of France and of the French between 1944 and 1958 cannot be reduced to the political and institutional games so often described.

Having said this, what follows reflects the present imbalance in the work of historians. The period 1944–46 is the best known: consequently, it has been accorded a large place, one its richness in fact justifies. Another imbalance, more regretfully accepted, arises from the fact that more is known about the political organizations and certain economic forces than is about the interaction of the social groups. The framework of *l'Hexagone*, scrupulously respected in the preceding volumes by Henri Dubief and Jean-Pierre Azéma, has less relevance in a global context which saw France torn between Washington, Moscow, and Dien Bien Phu. It has seemed preferable to try to take this change squarely into account, at the risk of shifting familiar perspectives and operating in relatively uncharted areas.

Finally, in part four are the religious, cultural, demographic, social, and regional analyses that the sheer pressure of events in these years has made it necessary to neglect in the earlier sections of the account.

And before relating this troubled and controversial history, let us briefly consider this topicality at its most exciting. By way almost of a prologue stand a few hours of conflict and joyous unity; hours which, if they are not without greatness, are marked by details, tensions, and attitudes that announce some of the difficulties ahead.

On Friday 25 August 1944, around three o'clock, Leclerc and Rol-Tanguy signed the German surrender with von Cholitz. Paris, covered with barricades and still menaced by air raids, was liberated by the popular insurrection and the $2^e$ DB. At four o'clock, General de Gaulle arrived at Montparnasse station, and immediately reprimanded Leclerc for having allowed an FFI colonel to put his signature on the protocol of surrender: the war leader and the political leader were one. At five o'clock, de Gaulle took possession of the War Ministry: as planned for so long, the State was to be restored smoothly, and exactly as before 10 June 1940, the moment of de Gaulle's departure. At 7.30 in the evening, after a stop at the Préfecture de Police, de Gaulle agreed finally to meet the members of the CNR and the Paris Liberation Committee at the Hôtel de Ville, focal point of so many revolutionary episodes. In the emotionally charged atmosphere, the president of the provisional government spelt out his goals, those of pursuing the war and imposing national unity. Republican order was to be the framework for new energies and ambitions, and the Resistance in all its forms had now to ensure the continuity of institutions. Before appearing to the jubilant crowd, de Gaulle dismissed a suggestion that he proclaim the Republic: incarnated by fighting France, it had never ceased to exist. Vichy collapsed silently; its memory was to be swept briskly away.

The following day, in the sunshine of a Saturday afternoon, before the Magnificat and the sniping incident at Notre-Dame, came the confirmation. From the Arc de Triomphe to Concorde, leading Bidault, Leclerc, and the FFI, de Gaulle received the massive popular homage which legitimated his call of 18 June 1940 and the underground struggle. On Sunday 27 August, however, at ten o'clock, de Gaulle, undisputed leader of a nation now freeing itself, had a discreet meeting with Eisenhower: the war continued, and the Allies had still not accorded recognition to the provisional government.

At the same time, the Mathurins Theatre had temporarily withdrawn, in view of the national upheaval, a play by a young author, Albert Camus, whose astringent editorials in *Combat* were starting to make him known to Parisians. The title of the piece, however, was premonitory: *Le Malentendu.*

# Abbreviations

| | |
|---|---|
| ALN | Armée de libération nationale |
| AMGOT | Allied Military Government for Occupied Territories |
| AOF | Afrique de l'Ouest Française |
| APEL | Association des parents d'élèves de l'école libre |
| CANAC | Comité d'action nationale des anciens combattants |
| CAPES | Certificat d'aptitude au professorat de l'enseignment secondaire |
| CDL | Comité départemental de libération |
| CEA | Commissariat à l'énergie atomique |
| CETA | Centre d'étude technique agricole |
| CFLN | Comité français de libération nationale |
| CFTC | Confédération française des travailleurs chrétiens |
| CGA | Confédération générale de l'agriculture |
| CGC | Confédération générale des cadres |
| CGL | Confédération générale du logement |
| CGPME | Confédération générale des petites et moyennes entreprises |
| CGT | Confédération générale du travail |
| CGT-FO | Confédération générale du travail – Force ouvrière |
| CNJA | Centre national des jeunes agriculteurs |
| CNL | Confédération nationale des locataires |
| CNPF | Conseil national du patronat français |
| CNR | Conseil national de la Résistance |
| CNRS | Centre national de la recherche scientifique |
| COFIREP | Compagnie financière de recherches pétrolières |
| COMAC | Commission d'action militaire |
| CREDOC | Centre de recherche et de documentation sur la consommation |
| CRS | Compagnies républicaines de sécurité |
| CUMA | Coopérative d'utilisation du matériel agricole |
| DATAR | Délégation à l'aménagement du territoire et à l'action régionale |
| DPU | Dispositif de protection urbaine |

| | |
|---|---|
| DST | Direction de la surveillance du territoire |
| ECSC | European Coal and Steel Community |
| EDC | European Defence Community |
| EDF | Electricité de France |
| EEC | European Economic Community |
| ENA | Ecole nationale d'administration |
| FDES | Fonds pour le développement économique et sociale |
| FEN | Fédération de l'éducation nationale |
| FFI | Forces françaises de l'intérieur |
| FIDES | Fonds pour le développement économique et sociale des Territoires d'outre-mer |
| FINAREP | Société financière pour la recherche et l'exploitation du pétrole |
| FLN | Front de libération nationale |
| FME | Fonds de modernisation et d'équipement |
| FNSEA | Fédération nationale des syndicats d'exploitants agricoles |
| FO | Force ouvrière |
| FTPF | Francs-tireurs et partisans français |
| GDF | Gaz de France |
| GPRF | Gouvernement provisoire de la République française |
| HLM | Habitation à loyer modéré |
| IFOP | Institut française d'opinion publique |
| IGAME | Inspecteur général de l'administration en mission extraordinaire |
| INRA | Institut national de la recherche agronomique |
| INSEE | Institut national de la statistique et des études économiques |
| JAC | Jeunesse agricole chrétienne |
| JEC | Jeunesse étudiante chrétienne |
| JOC | Jeunesse ouvrière chrétienne |
| MDRM | Mouvement démocratique de la rénovation malgache |
| MLN | Mouvement de libération nationale |
| MNA | Mouvement national algérien |
| MODEF | Mouvement de défense des exploitations familiales |
| MRP | Mouvement républicain populaire |
| MTLD | Mouvement pour le triomphe des libertés démocratiques |
| MUR | Mouvements unis de résistance |
| MURF | Mouvement unifié de la renaissance française |
| NATO | North Atlantic Treaty Organization |
| OCM | Organisation civile et militaire |
| OEEC | Organization for European Economic Co-operation |
| ORA | Organisation de résistance de l'armée |
| PANAMA | Parti national malgache |

| | |
|---|---|
| PCF | Parti communiste français |
| PPA | Parti populaire algérien |
| PPF | Parti populaire français |
| PRL | Parti républicain de la liberté |
| PSA | Parti socialiste autonome |
| PSF | Parti social français |
| PSU | Parti socialiste unifié |
| PTT | Postes télégraphes téléphones |
| RATP | Régie autonome des transports parisiens |
| RDR | Rassemblement démocratique révolutionnaire |
| RGR | Rassemblement des gauches républicaines |
| RPF | Rassemblement du peuple français |
| SAS | Sections administratives spécialisées |
| SAVIEM | SA de véhicules industriels et d'équipements mécaniques |
| SEATO | South East Asia Treaty Organization |
| SEEF | Service des études économiques et financières |
| SFIO | Section française de l'Internationale ouvrière |
| SHAPE | Supreme Headquarters of Allied Powers in Europe |
| SMIG | Salaire minimum interprofessionnel garanti |
| SNCASO | Société nationale de construction aéronautique du Sud-Ouest |
| SNCF | Société nationale des chemins de fer français |
| SNECMA | Société nationale d'étude et de construction de matériel aéronautique |
| SNREPAL | Société nationale de recherches et d'exploitation du pétrole en Algérie |
| SSS | Service de sondages et de statistiques |
| STO | Service du travail obligatoire |
| TCRP | Transport en commun de la région parisienne |
| UDCA | Union de défense des commerçants et artisans |
| UDMA | Union démocratique de Manifeste algérien |
| UDSR | Union démocratique et socialiste de la Résistance |
| UFNA | Union française nord-africaine |
| UGCA | Union générale des commerçants algériens |
| UGEMA | Union générale des étudiants musulmans algériens |
| UGTA | Union générale des travailleurs algériens |
| UGTT | Union générale des travailleurs tunisiens |
| UNAF | Union nationale des associations familiales |
| UNEF | Union nationale des étudiants de France |
| URAS | Union républicaine d'action sociale |
| USRAF | Union pour le salut et le renouveau de l'Algérie française |

PART I

# The needs of the moment, 1944–46

# 1

# Victory

The Liberation of Paris was just one episode in the Allied race to the German frontiers. Until the autumn, swept along by the enthusiasm generated by the breakthrough at Avranches and the landings in Provence, the front continued to lengthen and the liberation of French territory accelerated. British and Canadian forces under Mongomery's orders cleared the Channel region and the Rouen–Lille axis. At Boulogne, Calais, and Dunkirk the German garrisons settled into a tenacious resistance; but Ostend was taken on 8 September and in a flanking movement the American First Army reached Liège: Belgium was liberated. Further to the East, the forces under Patton had crossed the Meuse on 4 September, taking Nancy eleven days later. In the South, after the success of the 15 August landings, the American Seventh Army and FFI forces were clearing the Alpine regions. Sections of the FFI had also gone to reinforce the rapidly advancing B Army under de Lattre de Tassigny.[1] Toulon was taken on 27 August, Marseille and Montpellier, both already freed by the Resistance, followed on 28 and 29 August. Lyon was liberated on 3 September, caught between the Americans who had advanced beyond Grenoble, the FFI who had freed the surrounding area and de Lattre's forces coming up the Rhône valley. On 12 September, after fierce clashes in Burgundy, the forces of 'Overlord' and 'Anvil' met up near Montbard. That French troops of the 2ᵉ DB and the First Army were the first to give one another the accolade there was particularly fitting; so too was the fact that the last of the organized German forces to be caught in the net, the Elster Column, under pressure since Bordeaux, were taken near Issoudun by men of the FFI. By the end of September, France was practically liberated as far as the Vosges. The French regular forces had gone from success to success, while the FFI had been of considerable help in clearing the difficult regions, thus speeding the Allied advance. The swiftness and solidity of the success surprised the experts: Eisenhower had to acknowledge France's military contribution to the struggle. After the completion of mopping-up operations by regular forces and FFI in Brittany – with Brest taken, flattened by bombs – in the Loire,

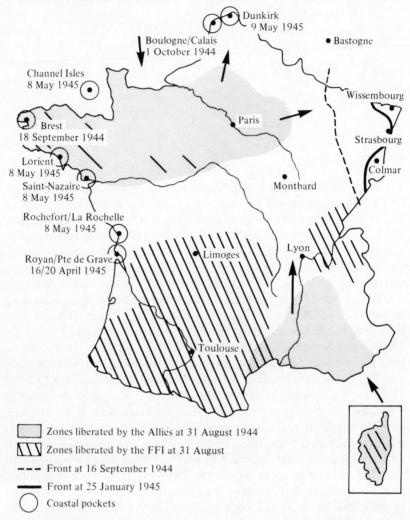

**1 The stages of the Liberation**

the South-West, the Alps and the Jura, only the Atlantic ports and Dunkirk remained as dangerous but effectively neutralized pockets of German resistance.

*Victory delayed*

The speed of the Allied progress had its price. In the rain and mud, and soon the snow, of a particularly severe autumn and winter, the headlong advance came to a virtual standstill. An over-extended front and inadequate supplies – Patton's tanks, for example, were held up by fuel shortages after 30 September – were largely to blame for this. But so too was Eisenhower's hesitancy and the tactical and personal differences between Patton and Montgomery, as well as the hardened resolve of the enemy under von Rundstedt, now staking everything on new weapons and the last, suicidal efforts of the German nation. Unable to open the broad front from the Ruhr to Alsace which would have split the enemy forces and made possible a link-up with the Red Army, the Allies regrouped, organizing and reinforcing their ground forces, still benefiting, weather permitting, from total mastery of the air. In the North, after the failure of the Arnhem operation, Montgomery had to be content with clearing the mouth of the Scheldt. The Americans did not take Aix-la-Chapelle until 21 October, advancing slowly and with difficulty along the Siegfried Line, not freeing the region of Metz until mid-December.

The French forces stood out well from this generally gloomy situation. Those under de Lattre regrouped between the Vosges and Switzerland, absorbing the FFI forces to relieve the frozen and exhausted colonial soldiers. De Lattre then swept past the Vosges into upper Alsace, taking the Germans from behind, reached the Rhine and managed to liberate Mulhouse on 20 November before running up against stiff resistance at Colmar. Leclerc's $2^e$ DB forces, now detached from the American Seventh Army, displayed similar energy as they raced down from the Vosges further to the north. With their taking of Strasbourg on 23 November the pledge made at Koufra was honoured: the liberation of the city symbolized the recovery of national unity, offering a foretaste of final victory, as well as restoring, for the moment at least, the prestige of an army upon which the scars of 1940 were still visible. However, individual exploits of this kind could not conceal the fact that the war as a whole was stagnating. True, the provisional government was able to exploit the delay to consolidate its authority within France, and hence its authority in dealing with the Allies; but these long months of waiting and sacrifice weakened the nation still further, complicating already acute economic and human problems, fostering apathy and delusion.

The difficulties and disappointments were compounded when the Germans launched their counter-attack in the depths of winter. The V1 and V2 rockets were still a threat, and the atomic weapon was close. The Americans responded with saturation bombing of Germany and by rapidly stepping up their own atomic research programme, strengthening still further the industrial character of their war effort. The German offensives in the Ardennes and Alsace of December and January took the Allies by surprise, forcing them to dig in at Bastogne, determined to hold the road to Antwerp at all cost. But Hitler's final gamble failed – and at Yalta the fate of the German people (and some others) was already being settled. The

Germans held on tenaciously at their frontiers, however, and it was only after fierce fighting that the French First Army and an American force overran Colmar on 9 February. The whole frontier, from Lauterbourg to the Saar, was finally clear on 20 March, with, by a nice irony, the very last battles for French soil taking place on the site of the Maginot Line. But on 30 March, urged on by de Gaulle, de Lattre was over the Rhine and heading for Karlsruhe: the German campaign which would end at Berchtesgaden and on the Danube had begun. The ultimate humiliation for Germany came on 8 May 1945, when de Lattre, not only a French general but a full member of the victorious alliance, came to receive the German surrender from Keitel. With the capitulation in the hours which followed of the remaining coastal pockets of German resistance, the freeing of French territory was complete. France had made a major contribution to her own liberation, and by her efforts had earned herself a place among the victors. Yet the conflict had lasted much longer than expected: in addition to penalizing the error – frequently made during the successes of the summer – of confusing liberation with victory, it had worsened the already bleak situation in France. The news of the German surrender was of course greeted with singing and dancing in the streets, but the joy was tinged with a certain hopelessness; as Simone de Beauvoir commented gloomily: 'Cette fin ressemblait à une morte'.[2] Coming on top of the existing problems, the burden of the war had helped to deaden opinion.

### 'US go home'

Repeated references in the press and in official statements to the question of the conduct of the war and relations with the Allies, in particular with the Americans,[3] had left little doubt as to the uncertainty surrounding France's role and status in the alliance. And on each occasion a crisis arose it was de Gaulle alone who reasserted France's right to a position of equality among the Allies – without the broader political or collective opinions having had an opportunity to express themselves in the usual way. De Gaulle's increasingly personal hold on this area of power had received tacit public approval during the war, not least from a recognition that it was necessary. For under the ordinance of 4 April 1944, de Gaulle was overall military leader as well as President of the provisional government; flanked by Diethelm, Commissioner for the War, and Marshal Juin, chief of National Defence forces since August, de Gaulle presided over the Committee of National Defence, where the final decision was his.

De Gaulle was well aware of the political implications of military dependence, but he was equally aware that only the United States could provide the arms and supplies the French forces needed. All the French units were thus placed on the American troop list and subject to inspections and constraints – something that was often a source of resentment, especially among *maquisards* and colonial troops unfamiliar with American military methods and discipline. And in fact, despite an important increase in numbers, the French forces received no additional help: the Pentagon had not planned for France's new eagerness. From September 1944, then, the government was set on rebuilding a national armaments industry, though shortages meant that output did not reach a level sufficient to equip one division per month until May 1945. In the meantime, the only solution lay with making do and improvisation.

Tensions with the Allies came to a head more quickly at the level of politics. After several years of close contact with de Gaulle, Churchill and Eden understood his character and appreciated his determination to win the war; the agreements of 30 June cleared up the remaining sources of friction with the British. The Soviet leadership was now cautious in its approach, in marked contrast to its resolute attitude in 1943 when it had been the first to recognize the CFLN; but it was unwilling to antagonize the Americans in the final stages of the war when crucial decisions were being made over the post-war settlement. It was then with Roosevelt and Eisenhower that the troubles arose. The American leadership had in fact been making concessions for several months under pressure from de Gaulle. After the General's speech on D-Day, Eisenhower had had to admit the military usefulness of the FFI under Kœnig: in the battlefield the Americans quickly came to appreciate the value of these highly unconventional soldiers. Furthermore, the Vichy régime had melted away without a struggle, and at every stage of the advance, from Bayeux to Paris, the legitimacy of the Gaullist authority was confirmed and increased. When the GIs arrived it was often to find Gaullist administrators already in charge, the officers of the military liaison services of Boislambert easing the early frictions which inevitably resulted. The threat of an Allied Government of Occupation thus receded. Roosevelt had to give way, and on 6 July de Gaulle was received in Washington as the head of the French state, a visit which gave him his first great success with public opinion in the United States and Canada. Not that the Americans had abandoned their belief that the future of France would be settled only after the final victory; indeed, Roosevelt went as far as to delegate to Eisenhower responsibility for deciding whether or not liberated territories 'deserved' civil administrations. But the pressure of events finally convinced the American leadership that de Gaulle's attitude was an accurate reflection of opinion in France. On 25 August agreements were reached over the civil administration, the currency – avoiding the flooding of the country with American 'francs' – press censorship, and on the fate of materials captured from the Germans. In addition, Eisenhower had agreed to allow the 2ᵉ DB to break away to head for Paris.[4] After a final consideration of the by now overwhelming evidence, the Allies gave official recognition to the provisional government on 23 September.

But many practical problems remained. Acknowledged as the political victor, de Gaulle was now ready to make the sacrifices necessary for the successful prosecution of the war. Thus agreements were also made on 25 August with the Allied High Command which stipulated that final authority over the French forces lay with the Americans, that over-excitable FFI members would be placed on the reserve, and that the distribution of German materials captured by the French forces would be decided by American officials. Yet the political advantage now lay clearly on the French side: an exchange of letters between de Gaulle and Eisenhower of 6 and 13 September even hinted strongly at the possibility of territorial concessions for the French forces penetrating into Germany. The bases of the understanding between the two governments and the two leaders were clear: the military and material stakes were such that France accepted freely the discipline of the Allies; politically, however, French sovereignty was henceforth inviolable.

The logic of this relationship made it necessary, though by no means easier, to accept with dignified resignation the 100 000 victims of Allied action, and to contain outrage when, for example, Royan was 'accidentally' razed by bombers returning from the Ruhr. The shortcomings of the American aid had to be accepted, for in the first six months after the landings only 200 000 of the promised 700 000 tonnes of supplies in fact arrived. There had to be acceptance also that for as long as the conflict continued, war supplies and petrol had absolute priority, and that control of the main road network had to be relinquished. It was perhaps inevitable that all this, compounded by the policy of requisitioning, should have generated resentment and even hostility among the civilian population and the often poorly informed CDLs. A campaign of liaison and explanation was launched using hastily recruited English-speakers;[5] François Coulet led a delegation charged with helping in the regulation of these sensitive issues, complying as far as possible with the distribution of labour and supplies wanted by the Americans; but balancing the demands of impatient officers with the anxieties of local civilian officials was always a delicate task. The war and the presence of a huge army brought the usual problems and incidents: spy scares, the hardships of the rations system, the vexed question of the treatment of German prisoners, unruliness, petty crime, and prostitution. Tension mounted as the French people discovered that America was not just candy and cigarettes; in the spring of 1945 the 'US go home' graffiti multiplied and there began to be talk of the 'nouveaux occupants', while the American press contained stories about French ingratitude. Yet it would be unrealistic to take this changing view of the Americans for a sign of deep ill-feeling. Behind the daily hardships and frictions the population remained profoundly grateful to its liberators, while finding new self-confidence and encouragement in de Gaulle's steadfast defence of French sovereignty.[6]

Not that the French authorities remained deaf to the grievances. Diplomatic channels were frequently used to protest over unfair requisitioning, unruliness among the troops, encroachment on local civilian authority, as well as over the visible reluctance of the Allies to devote resources to clearing out the pockets of German resistance on the coasts. But this readiness to complain was tempered by an awareness that persistent grumbling over issues of secondary importance was out of place in the tense wartime conditions, particularly given the scale of the military aid being provided. Having said this, when French sovereignty was at stake, de Gaulle was ready to provoke and manipulate an open crisis in order to achieve his goals.

This was clear in the conflict which arose in June 1945 over the Alpine frontiers. When the Germans and Italians surrendered on 2 May, the Alpine Army detachment of General Doyen swept through the passes to occupy the Aosta valley almost as far as Turin. Roosevelt's successor, Truman, ignorant of the long-standing dispute between France and Italy over these border regions, and increasingly worried by the general situation in Italy, demanded the withdrawal of the French forces to the 1939 borders. De Gaulle promptly ordered the consolidation of the new positions, while making moves to secure a diplomatic solution. Under this, Tende, Brigue, and the passes remained French,[7] though Truman's angry suspension of supplies to the French troops forced the abandonment of other claims in the Aosta region after 7 June.

Much more important was the Strasbourg affair.[8] Eisenhower, alerted of an imminent German attack on Alsace at the end of 1944, and making a careful distinction between the military and the political, planned to abandon the city. But when the German offensive began on 1 January, de Gaulle, strongly supported by Marshal Juin, ordered de Lattre to defend Strasbourg without further reference to his American superiors. De Gaulle was convinced, correctly it turned out, that the first fine weather, by restoring air supremacy to the Allies, would bring the German advance to a halt. He played Churchill off against Roosevelt, and insisted on the purely political dimension of the affair. After a stormy meeting of the military leaders, de Gaulle met Eisenhower on 3 January; he argued for the strict subordination of military force to the political objectives of States, and concluded with a threat to close all roads to Allied convoys if the First Army was denied adequate supplies. Weakly backed by Washington, anxious to avoid any extra risks in the middle of the battle, Eisenhower gave way: the views he had expressed to Churchill in February 1944 as to France's limited future capacity for independent action had been handsomely refuted.[9]

There can be no doubt that after these difficult months the French people were immensely satisfied with their country's new-found independence. There is no doubt either that they gave de Gaulle the credit for a moral and political victory which crowned the military successes. Was there not perhaps an element of self-deception in their confidence? In March 1945, 67 per cent had serious claims on the left bank of the Rhine, and 70 per cent approved de Gaulle's refusal of Roosevelt's invitation to meet him in Algiers. In December 1944, well before the final victory, 64 per cent already considered that France had recovered her place among the great powers; and a month later, 87 per cent were in favour of a further call-up of troops. In spite of moral and physical exhaustion, the country readily accepted a muster of its depleted resources to support the Allies in the final effort. With such strong faith in de Gaulle and his government's ability to win for France her share of the victory, the diplomatic struggle for a place among the great powers was sure of solid popular support.[10]

## The problems of the army

The same confidence is hard to detect in the relationship between the nation and its army. Here, the ravages of a protracted war combined with the divisions and exhaustion of the country to postpone the sorts of fundamental changes hoped for by the Resistance and by those who remembered the tragic scenes of June 1940.

The bulk of the regular troops came from overseas, and French public opinion had at best a hazy knowledge of the circumstances in which their recruitment and training had gone on in London, Algiers and, with the exception of Indo-China, throughout the French Empire. Thanks to the efforts of de Gaulle, Giraud, and Jean Monnet in Washington, eight divisions or approximately 300 000 men had been equipped by the Allies since 1943. These divisions had been in the thick of the fiercest fighting since landing with the Allies, and were now severely depleted and close to exhaustion. The necessary reinforcements had to come either from a call-up of young men in metropolitan France (and since 20 June 1944 the provisional government had stressed that the general mobilization of 1939 was still in force), or by integration of active FFI units. Such an increase in the number of French troops would upset the careful plans of the American experts, but it was welcome to de Gaulle, aware that military strength would count for much in the final assessment of the country's position.

Immediate recourse to the FFI was thus essential, military necessity finally coinciding with their own eagerness. The Resistance within France had always taken for granted that the underground struggle would finish in the open. And they were determined that this would be the occasion to create a new French army, one loyal to the Republic, better led and trained by officers open to democratic ideas, with a role to play in the general education of the young, and a contribution to make to the forming of new national élites. Indeed, on the strength of this somewhat vague consensus some were ready to declare the war *populaire*, to call for a masive purge of the discredited officers, and heap extravagant praise on the patriotism of local militia, held to embody widespread aspirations to reshape French society. The Communists were especially keen to deploy this argument, seeing in the structures of the Resistance – the FFIs, and within them the FTPF, and the COMAC – the instruments for exercising political pressure and a means of preserving zones of influence. The example of the FTP Colonel Guingouin in Limoges, refusing to hand over authority to the general assigned to what he considered to be his personal fief, is well known. But for one such case there were countless other Communists whose chief concern was simply to train the flood of eleventh-hour recruits and dispatch to the front those still eager to fight.

Just how reasonable is it to speak of a patriotic war analogous to the *levée en masse* of the Year II? Of the 400 000 men the FFIs could realistically have mobilized in September 1944, a maximum of 120 000 were actually integrated into the regular forces of the landings, to which can be added the 20 000 men of the 27th Alpine Infantry Division, plus the FFI units that concentrated their efforts on the German coastal garrisons. The figure is both low and high: low, if the notion of a widespread 'rush to the front' is accredited; high, when one considers that those involved were young – too young, according to some officers – typically around twenty, and were from the reduced population of the inter-war years. It is incontestable, however, that an important part of French youth was ready to fight.[11]

Orders to leave were not long in coming. Juin and the General Staff were charged on 26 August with incorporating all the FFI groups and volunteers as quickly as possible, and the FFI command structures were abolished by decree on 19 September: right from the start, and as de Gaulle took care to stress during his first visit to the provinces, the new forces had to be absorbed into the regular army. But putting this into practice proved harder than expected: the sheer numbers involved surprised the government and worried the Americans. Individual volunteers could be coped with, but the arrival of entire units, each attached to its own leaders, identity and experiences, and with basically civilian attitudes, posed unexpected problems. Among the officers of the French African Army the reaction was one of surprise and often resentment. Many of these officers had been cut off from metropolitan France since 1940 or 1942; unfamiliar with guerrilla warfare methods, they were already alarmed by the disorder and anarchy that seemed to them to reign there now. They responded unfavourably to the influx of eager but undisciplined recruits, some of whom were even political activists: considerable firmness would clearly be needed to teach these dowdy and sometimes refractory heroes the principles of line fighting.

A total of 289 groups, ranging in size from commando patrols to entire divisions, had to be hastily formed into 113 units of battalion strength. The new recruits were extremely heterogeneous – by age, social background, political commitment, and region; for example, the brigade of Alsace-Lorraine under Malraux, Jacquot, and Chamson, mixed Alsatians and peasants from the South-West in ever-growing numbers.[12] Once the obviously unsuitable had been eliminated, the remainder had to be fed and clothed, taught discipline under fire, the use of new weapons and the rudiments of logistics, and from them the future NCOs had to be selected and trained. Against the background of the war's unpredictable course and the control of supplies by the Americans, it was perhaps inevitable that the result, born of military necessity and political expediency, should have been improvised, hybrid, and lacking any overall unity. The new forces quickly became a troublesome source of embarrassment to the General Staff. With a few fortunate exceptions the marriage of old and new was rarely a happy one,[13] and in too many cases a determination to chase out the enemy was all that the disparate elements had in common. The amalgam had clearly failed and, among the FFI men, hopes of creating a new army faded. After the crossing of the Rhine patriotic ardour cooled and public interest declined, and the war became an affair for the professionals.[14] And as long as the general political situation remained uncertain the government hesitated, and did little in fact to encourage the integration of the Resistance leaders into the traditional hierarchy.

After the victory, in a climate of general disappointment, priority was given instead to reform of the existing military structures. The French army had become unwieldy and top-heavy. Eighteen divisions certainly constituted a sop to national pride, but the land army alone had 38 500 officers for 1 300 000 men. Moreover, this sprawling officer corps was composed of very different and often rival groups: veterans of 1939–40, officers from the African Army, from de Gaulle's France Libre, FFI leaders, returning prisoners; even the so-called *naphtalinés* retired by Pétain in 1942 were now hoping to get back on the ladder of promotion. There was clearly an urgent need for streamlining. Yet the *épuration* in the army was mild: roughly 700 officers were actually dismissed, with early retirements and discreet reinstatements later. The brunt of the pruning operation was in fact borne by the FFI officers, who now returned to civilian life disappointed by their failure to secure worthwhile careers in the army, and embittered by the obstruction they had encountered. From 25 000 at the Liberation, their number had fallen to 4000 by 1947. True, the military hierarchy was streamlined – in the land army, for example, the number of officers was down to 22 000 by 1946 – but the new blood the Resistance would have brought in had not been exploited. The result was apathy and routine.

The issue was obviously closed, and except in December 1945 there was to be no major parliamentary debate on the army. True, there was talk among officials of the creation of a rapid intervention force – a notion dear to de Gaulle and one that would reappear in the Fifth Republic's *force de frappe* – and the cult of the commando was carefully nurtured in the units. But on the fundamental questions, such as the function of military service or the place of the army in French society, nothing was settled. Indeed, the ordinance of 4 January 1946 merely confirmed the traditional structures of the army and its role as the unquestioning instrument of French foreign policy. The impressive units involved in the victory were cut back, then disbanded, and demobilization was pushed quickly to completion: by the end of 1945 the land army had only 610 000 men, a year later just 460 000, and its best forces were already being sent to Indo-China or the German garrisons. The priority was no longer a military one, of course, and if in principle favourable to a far-reaching reform of the army, all the political forces agreed that the necessary resources could not be spared in the difficult period of reconstruction. With low pay, poor material, slashed budgets, and depressed morale, the army sank back into complacency and inertia. Having failed to tap the fresh energies of the Resistance forces, the army was once again becoming isolated from the nation. The colonial wars and inadequate means would do the rest.

### The return from the camps

The return of the prisoners and deportees liberated by the Allies, and France's participation, albeit relatively modest, in the massive flows of refugees which washed across Europe, formed a bitter-sweet epilogue to the victory. That this story is still little known, reduced typically to eye-witness accounts, is perhaps significant. For a long time the national conscience found it hard to come to terms with the memory of the innumerable anonymous victims and martyrs, while at the time there was an often pathetic contrast between the incredulity of public opinion and the joy of the survivors and their families.

The statistics, though hard to establish, are grim. The government estimated at 1.2 million the number still held as prisoners of war in the camps.[15] Of approximately 200 000 people deported from France, 75 000 were *déportés raciaux*, almost all of them Jews; 63 000 were political prisoners, including 41 000 held for Resistance activities; and another 50 000 were common criminals. In addition, more than 700 000 Frenchmen had been working in German factories, requisitioned by the STO in most cases, mixed with volunteers and the participants in the *Relève*, Laval's scheme whereby skilled labour was traded for French POWs. To those in the camps have to be added the 200 000 from Alsace and Lorraine drafted into the German forces. The 2.5 million refugees included those from Alsace and Lorraine, and evacuees from the prohibited areas and battle zones of the coastal regions, along with foreigners of seventeen nationalities, uprooted or in flight, all victims of a decade-long nightmare. A total then of approximately 5 million individuals in search of countries, homes, and identities.

Responsibility for them fell to the Ministry of Prisoners, Deportees, and Refugees, a post taken up in the autumn of 1944 by Henry Frenai, founder of *Combat*; and the official efforts were supplemented by the Red Cross and various national and international bodies. Frenai faced a difficult and uncertain situation: if the war continued his task was to help the survivors to hold on, to make the waiting easier to endure; but at the same time, should the war end quickly he had to be ready to cope with an influx of returning survivors. The logistics of the exercise were daunting: with queries from families to be answered, official missions organized for the front, scarce supplies and transport found, funds obtained to provide immediate financial assistance to the survivors (and this without endangering future pension rights), and liaison services set up with the Allies. Meanwhile, those returning had to be met and looked after, subjected to medical inspections, issued with new documents, and of course scrutinized for those using the general confusion to cover the traces of a compromising political past.[16]

The position in Germany was desperate. Expectant tension had been mounting since the D-Day landings: in the famines, heavy bombardments, and sudden pulling back of the camps, prisoners became the helpless victims of the war's final convulsions. In some cases they liberated themselves; most waited for the arrival of the Allies; others, abandoned by their guards and fearful of evacuation to the East by the remaining Nazis or the Red Army, fled westward; thousands perished on the way. In the concentration camps there was worse. The return of the first survivors in February 1945, freed from Auschwitz by the Soviets, and the arrival via Switzerland of those from Ravensbrück at the beginning of April, revealed the awful inaccuracy of the idea which had prevailed in France up until then concerning the Holocaust.[17] Yet the Allies launched no commando operations to liberate the remaining camps or to help those trying to free themselves. The opening of Buchenwald, Dora, Dachau, Mauthausen and Belsen at the end of April exposed the full extent of the horror: amidst the typhus, repression, daily agony, and mass graves the unthinkable took on a ghastly human visage. For the survivors – just 3 per cent of the Jews, perhaps 20 per cent of the others, fewer than 40 000 in all – there awaited the awesome task of restoring life to bodies and personalities forever scarred by their ordeal.

In Paris and at the frontiers a total of 23 000 officials and volunteers manned twenty reception centres, each capable of 'processing' up to 40 000 people daily. The feeding and clothing of the refugees posed problems during the winter, but most had reached their homes by the summer. Next, in mixed groups by air and rail, came the prisoners and deportees. Apart from a few over-publicised early difficulties, the great majority were looked after and helped home without excessive delays or obvious injustices. In June the one-millionth freed prisoner was dealt with, and in December, its job over, Frenai's ministry was dismantled. The outstanding questions had already been taken in hand by the various associations of victims and ex-prisoners, and were settled, albeit extremely slowly, by the Ministry of Ex-Servicemen.

The full account of the social reintegration of the survivors has yet to be written.[18] At the time public attention was drawn only to the political dimension of the problem; for on the eve of elections the large numbers of prisoners and survivors constituted a significant electoral force. This was the consideration behind the fierce campaign against Frenai by the Communists in May and June 1945, and, conversely, the public denunciation of Soviet reluctance to free the prisoners from the east of the Elbe. The survivors themselves, though somewhat overwhelmed by this polemic, were certainly intent on getting speedy recognition for their rights and claims, but only a small minority really succeeded. The major political personalities of the deportation readjusted quickly and well, but all the others had to come to terms slowly and painfully with the realities of an unfamiliar domestic wartime experience.[19] Thus to their sufferings could be opposed those under the Occupation; for their shattered hopes there was the zeal of the Resistance, and for their lost years and physical exhaustion they discovered a victorious younger generation which had lifted the shame of their defeat. Disorientated socially, politically, and emotionally, uncertain of their place in the future, the survivors of the camps felt disappointment, bitterness, and anger. The practical problems they faced were manifold: rediscovering a family life which had perhaps changed greatly, the difficulty of getting back into a profession, the need to re-create a social position. And such basically private sentiments and griefs could scarcely find a coherent social or political expression. The final outcome was commonly a happy one, but it would be unrealistic to imagine that all was forgotten or repaired. Not, however, that their experience had been an entirely negative one; the opportunities to observe an industry and agriculture so different from those in France, the human and cultural contacts, and the spiritual awakenings were not to be forgotten either. Tribute must be paid to the silent determination of the survivors; their often heroic efforts to pick up the threads of ordinary everyday lives bear witness to a simple but brave desire: that of escaping from the past, not in order to forget but simply in order to live again.

Lastly, there is the collective service these thousands of witnesses performed for their country. The sight of prisoners in worn and outdated uniforms, of skeletal figures with bulging eyes, weighing 40 kilos, the faces of oppressed and oppressors which appeared in the press and exhibitions – all produced a profound impact on public opinion. Thanks to them, and to the stories told in countless French families, several generations would forget neither the war nor the Nazi horror.

# 2

# Survival

'As the tide retreated it suddenly exposed, from one end to another, the mutilated body of France' noted de Gaulle.[1] Shattered and exhausted in its victory, the nation now faced severe constraints. For the people as for the government, day-to-day survival became the overriding obsession.

## The human losses

No price can be put on the blood and suffering of the war. In statistical terms however, and as Table 1 makes clear, the human toll was only half what it had been in 1914–18,[2] a difference readily appreciable from war memorials throughout France. With cynicism one can observe that since civilian casualties were heavier than those of the military the losses were, in terms of age and sex, more 'equitably' distributed. Similarly, the collective obligations to victims were lighter: 214 000 war pensions to invalids, widows, orphans, and parents in 1950, compared with 2 450 000 in 1934.[3] Finally in this vein, one can note that if the demographic stagnation of the 1920s and 1930s had persisted, the resulting deficit of births would have exceeded one million; as it was, the upsurge of fertility from 1942, though barely perceived even after the Liberation, in fact served to limit the shortfall.[4]

Nevertheless, even if the level of births and deaths was almost in balance by 1943, in the short term the loss of 1.5 million people exacerbated the long-standing and well-known demographic sluggishness. According to a hastily conducted census of March 1946, the population of metropolitan France was 40 503 000 – the same as at the end of the nineteenth century and over a million fewer than in 1936. Still, the trend had been reversed, and from 1943 a small surplus of births over deaths was registered. But while this optimistic development may have stimulated social and political zeal, it made even more urgent the task facing the authorities of quickly lifting the constraints of the immediate post-war period in order to take full advantage of the now promising demographic conditions and encourage the upward movement in the birth rate.

Table 1: *The human losses*

| | |
|---|---:|
| Servicemen killed in action or dead from wounds | 170 000 |
| 92 000 in 1939–40; 58 000 from 1940 to 1945; 20 000 FFI | |
| Dead in enemy hands | 280 000 |
| 40 000 prisoners, 60 000 political deportees, 100 000 *déportés raciaux*, | |
| 40 000 Alsaciens–Lorrains conscripted into the German forces | |
| Civilian victims | 150 000 |
| 60 000 in bombings, 60 000 in fighting and atrocities, | |
| 30 000 executions | |
| Deficit of births to natural deaths of which 300 000 due to raised | 530 000 |
| wartime mortality | |
| Emigration | 320 000 |
| 300 000 foreigners, 20 000 French | |
| | 1 450 000 |

For the moment this meant providing food, clothing, and heating, reducing the mortality rates among the young and old, and drawing up the final balance sheet of the problems. Official figures released in March 1945 showed that 70 per cent of men and 55 per cent of women had lost weight, while in the cities one in three children had problems of growth.[5] The effects of wartime hardship were visible on those in the J1, J2, and J3 age groups between 1938 and 1948, marking them off physically from their better-nourished juniors.[6] Not until the mid 1950s did French youth begin to get noticeably stronger and better built. And of course there were the mental and psychological costs to be measured: memories of deaths and bombings, traumas of scattered families, studies hopelessly disrupted, all the frustrations and anxieties of the generation of the *zazous*. The solution to these problems was above all economic: in the conditions of 1944 only economic growth and the prospect of a normal standard of living would offer hope for the future to a younger generation badly scarred by its ordeal, and allow the demographic revival to develop.

### The strangled economy

To begin with then, solutions to the human problems had to come from the economy. Yet it was here that the legacy of the war was the most brutal, far more so than in 1918. The most visible losses, of buildings, were immense, with entire regions devastated.[7] Seventy-four *départements* had been touched by the war, compared with thirteen in 1914–18; a quarter of all buildings had been destroyed, compared wtih 9 per cent in 1914–18; and a million families were homeless. After damage on this scale to a building stock that was already mediocre and inadequate before the war, priority clearly had to go to the construction of housing and commercial and administrative buildings. Yet the losses of productive capital made this impossible. All the official reports on the war damage underlined the enormousness of the task, and in 1946 the Ministry of Reconstruction estimated the cost of a return to normality at 4900 milliard francs, the equivalent of between two and three years' pre-war national income.[8]

The most serious destruction, threatening to choke the entire economy, was to the transport system. The railways had suffered especially badly from the fighting and bombings, as well as from the sabotage campaign waged by the Resistance. Of the pre-war network's 40 000 km only 18 000 km remained serviceable, and this in unconnected sections; 115 of the 300 major stations had been destroyed, as had 24 of the principal marshalling yards and 1900 strategic constructions. Only one locomotive in six was in working order, one goods wagon in three, and one carriage in two: the Paris–Strasbourg journey took more than fifteen hours. Repairs to track and rolling-stock, however makeshift, were vital in the weeks following liberation if economic suffocation were to be avoided. And not least since the road network, responsible before the war for the equivalent of two-thirds of rail traffic, was in ruins. With 7500 bridges down, any sizeable river constituted a major obstacle, though 1500 were hastily re-built to allow a minimum of essential traffic. Early estimates put the cost of reconstructing the road network at an impossible 20 per cent of the State's budget for 1945. Moreover, with only one lorry in five having sur-vived requisitioning and conversion to gas, and with petrol so scarce, the immediate value of the roads was slight. Fortunately, the inland water-way network and the merchant marine were less seriously affected; from 1945 the former was carrying 40 per cent of its pre-war traffic, while the merchant fleet, part of the Allied shipping pool until 1946, was able to offer roughly a third of its 1939 capacity. The paralysis of road and rail transport gave the canals and merchant marine a new importance; but most of the equipment was old, unable to meet the demands placed on it now, and the near total destruction of the main Atlantic ports posed a serious obstacle to the handling of cargoes. Overall, the breakdown of the transport system served to fragment the national market, encouraging hoarding and the unofficial distributive networks, something which in turn forced the government, often against its will, to exercise an even greater local and sectorial control.

The second great difficulty was the shortage of coal, the major source of energy at this time. In 1938, France's 212 mines (125 in the North, 12 in the East, and 75 in the Centre and Midi), their productivity depressed by poor technology and the multiplicity of concessions, had managed to pro-duce 47 million tonnes. France was the world's largest importer of coal, purchasing nearly one-third of her total requirements. The massive requisitioning for Germany's needs during the Occupation had seen France supplied at only 65 per cent of the pre-war level;[9] domestic consumption shrank, industry faced shortages, stocks were run down, the machinery wore out, and the irreducible needs of the large coal consumers, the gas and electricity industries and the SNCF, were growing, forcing them to operate at unsafe levels. The cumulative effects of poor diet, falling real incomes, and the struggles against the *occupant* had taken a heavy toll on the workforce. Between 1938 and the autumn of 1944, the number of miners fell from 240 000 to 205 000; over the same period total daily output slumped from 156 000 to 67 000 tonnes, and per capita output from 1220 to 674 kg. Drastic action was needed, for the repercussions of this double exhaustion of men and equipment were alarming. Coal imports were blocked: 23 million tonnes of coal had been imported in 1938, but in 1946 it was only with great difficulty that France obtained 10 millions, half coming from the United States and 3 millions from Germany. In 1945, French industry disposed of 40 million tonnes of coal, compared with 67 millions in 1938. Thus, for example, the metallurgical industry of Lorraine, relatively unscathed by the destruction but highly dependent on imported coal and coke, could resume production at only a fraction of pre-war levels: 58 000 tonnes in December 1944, compared with a monthly output of 500 000 in 1938. Partly then from necessity, though partly also due to the irresponsibility of the owners, already eager to concentrate on lucrative exports, the industry neglected the efforts at reorganization and investment being made in other branches of the metallurgical and engineering industries. Denied adequate and suitable raw materials these in turn stagnated. The vicious circle was complete. To avoid company closures and to meet the priority needs of the SNCF, it was domestic consumption of coal, gas and electricity which for a long time to come had to bear the brunt of the shortages, while it was from an exhausted and increasingly demoralized workforce that further efforts and sacrifices were demanded.

The picture was sombre in many other respects. During the war the newest machine tools had been taken to Germany; those left had an average age of twenty-five, thus adding to an existing weakness of French industry. Agriculture was short of machines and fertilizers. In the long wait for victory and the return from the camps, and despite the use of 510 000 German prisoners of war, there was a severe labour shortage. Foreign workers, such as the Poles from the Nord and Lorraine, were now returning home; and immigration, in spite of the measures since 1932 to encourage it, was still on a modest scale.[10] It was now that the effects of the 1914–18 war on the active population of France became fully apparent. Lastly, the pressure for a rise in wages, blocked during the war, and with wages now hopelessly inadequate, could not be contained for long.

In all then, France contained a fragmented market, a shattered industry, an exhausted workforce and strong aspirations for improved standards of living. Coming into a context dominated by chronic economic difficulties since 1931, the war had exacerbated structural imbalances and multiplied urgent tasks for the future. The index of industrial production offers possibly the most powerful statistical statement of the economic drama: for a base of 100 in 1938, this stood at 38 in 1944, and at just 29 for a base of 100 in 1929.

In this weakness lay the threat of a permanent and structural inflation, one born of the widening gulf between faltering supplies and a buoyant demand. Inflation had been a feature of the French economy since 1936, but had accelerated dramatically during the Occupation. Like Vichy, the Germans allowed prices to soar, preferring a short-term appeasement of the mounting discontent of producers, sellers, and wage-earners, attempting where possible to correct the growing disparity between official prices and those of the black market. The summer of 1944 was of course the moment to meet the cost of this and embark on a fresh, possibly daring, policy.[11] Yet it was impossible to tackle the structural causes of the inflation until the economy as a whole had been put in order. A delayed consequence of the wartime abuses, mirroring and aggravating the shortages and injustices of the Liberation period, the inflation now in fact put down deep roots in the French economy. Already a serious problem for the government in the autumn of 1944, the inflation was to be a major historical factor for many years to come.

Inflation made it even harder to support the financial and monetary constraint which was the other essential feature of the immediate post-war period. This constraint served in fact as the link between the problems which collectively were responsible for the economic strangulation:

1. Between 1938 and the Liberation, wholesale prices had multiplied by 2.5, and by 3.5 in 1945; retail prices had at least quadrupled, while the average cost of living – the black market excluded! – had tripled. On an index of 100 for 1938, wages stood at 163 in 1944, their lag behind official prices increasing each month. But unfreezing wages or prices would inevitably set off a new inflation.

2. The needs were such that a long-term disequilibrium in the balance of trade was unavoidable. The first reliable statistics, those for the second half of 1945, showed imports to be worth 34 milliard francs for exports of just 7 milliard. Dependence on imports, swollen by coal, vital manufactured goods, and food meant that a long-term policy to favour a renewal of stocks and capital goods had to be forgone simply in order to meet immediate needs. To this was added the decline of invisible export earnings from shipping, overseas investments, sales of patents, and tourism. A loan was thus indispensable, and it would have to come from the United States. But

this obvious solution was complicated by France's chronic weakness as a potential borrower, and by the singular strength of the dollar since the Bretton–Woods agreements.[12]

3. Borrowing was also necessary to cover the deficit in public finances. The deficit in 1944 was 300 milliard francs, with receipts covering only 30 per cent of expenditure. The following year, with a civil budget of 289 milliard and 172 milliard for the war effort, the shortfall was 207 milliard francs.[13] The combination of accumulated deficits and unavoidable new expenditure made inevitable a ballooning of the public debt: it increased fourfold, passing from 445 milliard francs in 1939 to 1680 by the end of 1944, to 1874 a year later and to 1942 by March 1946. The only hope for a slow-down here came from the increasing place in the enormous total of free loans from the Banque de France and short-term debt (low-interest Treasury bonds in particular). In fact, interest and liquidation payments more than doubled, rising from 15 milliard francs in 1939 to 30 milliard in 1945 and to 37 milliard in 1946. True, as a debtor and tax collector the State did benefit from inflation, and the part of tax revenues in the servicing of the debt fell from 23 to 12 per cent. But this small bonus did not remove the initial handicap.

4. The monetary situation was also serious. Hopes that this would improve with the end of the 'Occupation charges' and unfavourable exchange agreements imposed by Germany were quickly dissipated by the burden of military expenditure in the last stages of the war and the contraction of tax revenues due to the stagnation of the economy. The reserves had fallen from 97 milliard francs in 1939 to 80 milliard by September 1944, and to 65 milliard a year later, and now bore little relation to the overall money supply in circulation. The proliferation of paper money, greatly disproportionate to the growth of bank holdings and postal deposits, was the sign and source of a potentially massive inflation. From 129 milliard francs in 1939, the note issue had swollen to 558 milliard by May 1944, and reached 623 milliard in October.[14] At the prevailing price and production levels, however, only 150 milliard were required for the needs it was possible to satisfy. In the absence of anything to buy, the remaining 400 milliard were being hoarded by individuals – in rural washtubs it was popularly alleged. At the first opportunity this colossal sum, greater than the national product, would flood into circulation, setting off a huge inflation. Having struggled so hard to resist the AMGOT money, the government clearly could not risk precipitating a collapse of the currency now by allowing a return to free market conditions. A prompt 80 per cent reduction in the money supply was in fact required, but with communications disrupted and order uncertainly restored this would be a hazardous operation to attempt.

In this difficult context – with both expenditure and the note issue increasing, a need to restore an equilibrium between prices, incomes and investment, and with the budget, the debt, and the currency all unstable – would the final choice be one between loans and inflation, between controls and liberalism? No doubt improvisation was the most appropriate course for the moment, but these choices would have soon to be faced.

## The obsession with food supplies

The most glaring difficulties and the greatest discontent arose over the question of food supplies. The provision of necessities quickly became the touchstone of the government's popularity, especially among the urban population. That there were misunderstandings and frictions was inevitable, since on this issue the authorities had only a very slender margin for manoeuvre.

To a country which imported nearly one-tenth of its food in 1938 the war had come as a brutal shock, familiarizing the people with shortages and poor diet, forcing it to live *au ras des rutabagas*.[15] However, during the long period of restrictions and price controls one comforting belief had taken deep root; since German requisitioning of at least half of France's food production was responsible for the shortages, it followed that victory would bring the return of abundance. The appeal of this simplistic argument (one that the broadcasts from London and the underground press had not dared, perhaps, to counter too directly) remained strong, much to the dismay of the government and the commissaires de la République.[16] Other ingrained reflexes and attitudes persisted: fraud, for example, for so long synonymous with a patriotic duty *vis-à-vis* the *occupant* and officialdom, had become almost second nature; similarly, the thriving black market was popularly taken as proof of the existence of ample stocks. In its hardship, the population failed to grasp that the *débrouillardise* (resourcefulness) it employed to compensate for the meagreness of the official rations merely served to fuel a black market which made a nonsense of the controls and reinforced inequalities.[17] For the profiteers and swindlers were of course only too pleased to make up for the shortcomings of the official rations. Price controls and suppression of frauds succeeded in eliminating some of the more flagrant abuses, but they were of little use against the basic law of the market: the people wanted fuel, food, and clothing that the economy simply could not provide consistently or in quantity.

The rations were meagre, falling below basic physiological needs for the poorest members of the urban population. Given that the minimum daily requirement, depending on age, sex and occupation, is in the order of 2400 calories, the size alone of the official rations goes a long way to explaining the attraction of, and perhaps even the necessity for, the black market: just 900 calories per adult in Paris in August 1944, 1210 in September, and 1515 in May 1945.[18] To obtain them there was the endless queuing, and often kowtowing to shopkeepers to whom the system of ration cards bound entire families.[19] Once the official rations were finished, almost any means were acceptable to reach and if possible cross the 2000 calorie threshold: barter, parcels from relatives, arrangements with shopkeepers, visits to 'friendly' farms, gardens and discreet *élevages*, and 'mutual aid' between neighbours or workmates. But the almost picturesque impression all this can create must not obscure the fact that for the isolated and poor the reality was often quite desperately bleak. Whatever the value of the 'extras' to be had by one means or another, there can be no doubt that the population experienced considerable hardship – of a basic daily fat requirement of 78 grammes they obtained only 15; of 40 grammes of meat they in fact got 24; and for parents of small children the daily hunt for milk remained a nightmare until 1948. Self-sufficiency and improvisation were the natural accompaniments to a food market dominated for so long by selfishness and the brute force of money.

Why did the shortages persist? The official statistics are unreliable guides here, with a large part of production beyond all control. Moreover, even if supplies could have been found, the disruption of the transport system made their rational distribution impossible; in the autumn of 1944, for example, nineteen trains of 600 tonnes would have been needed to get an extra kilo of potatoes to each Parisian household. Improvement depended in fact on the restoration of a truly national market and an efficient transport system, as well as on a central authority capable of regulating prices and distribution.[20]

Explanations for the contraction in food supplies are not hard to find, however. The agricultural balance sheet of the war was grim, with serious labour losses,[21] scarcities of imported fertilizers, and large areas ravaged by the fighting. Three million hectares of farming land had gone out of cultivation; yields of cereals, potatoes, and grapes were down by between 25 and 40 per cent in 1945. Mechanization, feeble before the war, was now at a standstill; handicapped by the shortages of raw materials and spare parts the agricultural machinery industry could meet only 20 per cent of needs, while existing machines fell victim to the fuel shortages. And wartime slaughtering and German requisitioning had taken a heavy toll on reserves of animal power; the number of horses, for example, had dropped from 2.2 million in 1938 to 1.5 million in 1944. Between September and December 1944, 3000 new machines were hastily imported from the United States to work the most fertile lands;[22] but shortages existed at every level, and even when the machines were available a lack of apparently minor items, sulphur for the vines or string for baling, could bring work to a standstill.

To this have to be added the consequences of the severe winter of 1944–5 and the disastrous frosts of spring 1945, as well as the continued block on significant imports of textiles, oils and colonial products.[23] The declared grain harvest for 1945 was one-third down on that of 1944 (and barely half of the pre-war level), the potato crop was 20 per cent down, and the number of cattle had fallen by 4 per cent: a one-third shortfall of bread, meat, butter, and milk could thus be expected. Only with the better harvest of 1946 was a precarious balance restored.

The statistical dimensions of the problem have, however, to be placed in their monetary and social contexts. It was clearly hard to persuade the peasants to declare and sell their produce at the official prices when the black marketeers were coming to them with much more lucrative offers. Moreover, in the sense that the producers had little chance of obtaining in exchange the machines and manufactured goods so badly needed on the farms, their reluctance to sell was understandable. In most cases it was the peasant diet which remained generous, with only the surplus finding its way onto the black market.[24] Here was the inspiration for the endless press campaigns denouncing rural egoism and profiteering. And indeed, agricultural incomes had fallen only slightly, recovering their pre-war level by 1946. Rural reserves were large: on a base of 100 for 1938, deposits with the Crédit Agricole stood at 743 in December 1944, and at 1717 two years later. Part of this new wealth had of course come from the profits of the black market. But it was also due to the widespread enforced conversion of capital into cash;[25] a reduced expenditure on materials and fertilizers and the impossibility of buying new machinery had necessarily increased the liquidity of farms; once normal conditions returned this artificial liquidity would be absorbed by the long overdue investment. In the meantime, however, the delay accentuated the regional and social disparities in French agriculture. From 1944 to 1947 the large, efficient farms of the Paris basin and the North were the only ones to be allocated the scarce materials, and they benefited the most when, for example, tractor sales were de-controlled in the summer of 1948. These were the farms where output was the most responsive to investment, and it was clearly to them that resources had to be directed if significant increases in food output were to be realized quickly.

The small- and medium-sized farmers, however, outdistanced in the race to invest, saw their savings eroded by inflation before they could obtain the new materials. The full implications of the handicap acquired now were to become apparent during the battle for agricultural productivity of the 1950s.

Not surprisingly, these subtleties were lost on urban public opinion, quick to see all farmers as hoarders and profiteers getting rich from the hunger of others. For their part, the farmers, resentful of this hostility to them, resisted the controls and began to organize their protest.[26] The issue quickly became a political one. The Socialists, with Tanguy-Prigent as Minister of Agriculture, controlled the new Confédération Générale de l'Agriculture (CGA) which was formed in the Resistance and responsible for purging the agricultural organizations which had supported Vichy's Corporation Paysanne.[27] Anxious to consolidate the position of the Left in a traditionally hostile milieu from which the Right and Centre had been temporarily eliminated, the CGA leadership adopted an accommodating attitude to the basically corporatist demands of the farmers, even going so far as to threaten a general food strike if the ceilings for agricultural prices and incomes were not raised: a terrible threat, taken very seriously by the authorities in the summer of 1945.[28]

The response from the government to the difficulties was a highly empirical policy of limited long-term effectiveness. Unable to control the volume of imports while the war lasted and the normal circuits were disrupted, or restrain the upsurge of demand at the end of the Occupation, and powerless, finally, over the problem of agricultural output, the government had to be content simply to avoid the disaster a return to free market conditions would inevitably unleash. This consideration underlay the severe and soon unpopular aspects of its policy: price controls, vigorous requisitioning of urgent supplies by prefects and commissaires de la République, the repression of fraud, plus the embarrassed attempts to explain to public opinion why it was necessary to maintain and, from 1945 to 1949, renew the ration card system. Application of this policy was often difficult: the position of the central authority still seemed unsteady, and its local representatives were readier to bow to popular pressure for immediate action. The men on the spot were of course acutely aware of the political dimension of the food question: the CDLs were using the shortages to attack the authorities in Paris, and the Patriotic Militia and the Communists were engaged in an often unruly hunt for profiteers, real or supposed. In short, hunger was behind the tension and unrest mounting in the provinces.

A report from the Nord in March 1945 observed: 'the complaints are numerous and bitter; the milk is too watery and turns before it can be boiled, the bread is inedible, the soap simply disgusting; ... Families are alarmed by the knowledge that for six days of the week they have only bread to give their children, and just 60 grammes of meat on the seventh day.'

In Lyon the tensions had the character of a deep social conflict, the maximum monthly fat ration of 100 grammes available to the workers contrasting starkly with the abundance of the black market and the opulent restaurants. For Christmas 1944 the commissaire de la République, Yves Farge, rounded up provisions from the luxury establishments for distribution to the sick and wounded of the Alpine Division and to the workers rebuilding the city's bridges. At the important demonstration called by the CGT for 11 March 1945 to spur the government to action the banners carried a simple but eloquent slogan: 'Nos gosses ont faim.' A quarter of the workers of the Fouga Company at Béziers had deserted the factories in December 1944 to hunt for food. At Marseille and on the Côte d'Azur rations were well below the national average. In March 1945, of the 15 000 litres of milk needed daily only 4000 were distributed, and here again the contrast with the flourishing and well-stocked black market was blatant; Ramadier, the Minister of Provisions, was noisily booed during a visit to the region in December 1944.[29]

The confusion and chaos thus fuelled the impatience. The shortages opposed town to country, and the regions of monoculture and those isolated by the disruption of transport to those of the Paris basin, Brittany, and the Centre, regions which had suffered less than others but whose energies were now harnessed to feeding Paris. The food question acquired heavy social undertones, multiplying the divisions in the country and enabling the CGT and the Communists to ferment agitation. Moreover, it had a detrimental effect on the political situation, for the government had no coherent long-term policy: firmness was essential, yet too-harsh controls would simply drive food and necessities off the market altogether. At the same time, however, the government could not ignore political realities; concessions did have to be made, sometimes inopportunely. Thus on 29 August 1945, as part of the election campaign, it was decided that bread controls would be abolished on 1 November; but the poor harvest forced their reintroduction on 28 December, with an even further reduction of the adult ration to 300 grammes a day.[30]

This maladroit move unleashed a wave of protests, with strikes at Laon, Le Creusot, Nantes and in Normandy, the looting of bakeries, while at Tours the *préfecture* was stormed and the new ration cards ritually burnt. According to an opinion poll of January 1945, 40 per cent of the population blamed the shortages on the government while 37 per cent invoked the general conditions, and in the towns the proportions were 50 and 33 per cent respectively. That this was a judgement born of distress is clear from the fact that the same poll revealed wide differences over the remedies to be adopted.[31] In January 1946, 49 per cent still gave the satisfaction of basic daily needs as their principal concern, compared with 26 per cent for health, and 15 per cent for money: proportions which were to remain unchanged until 1949. This durable and legitimate obsession explains the storms of popular indignation regularly provoked by the exposure of the petty frauds born of hardship, by the least sign of hesitancy on the part of the authorities, and, above all, by the scandals, all covered at length by a press eager to help its circulation by posing as the vigilant guardian of the public interest.[32]

It is, then, the scandals and the *faits divers*, the chorus of complaints and the empiricism of the government's approach which monopolize attention. But what of the underlying social and economic realities? The action of the various social groups involved in production at this time remains largely unexplored,[33] but all the available evidence suggests that their solidarities and self-interest contributed to the blockages, inflation, and shortages. This was certainly the case in agriculture but applies equally to other branches of the economy. The *corporatisme* of Vichy, the culmination in fact of a long development, was deeply ingrained, so much so as to render often superficial and irrelevant the debate over *dirigisme* versus liberalism which preoccupied the public authorities. Vichy's Comités d'organisation, hastily transformed into Offices professionnels, retained for the moment their influence and personnel. But their abolition in April 1946 left the way clear for the employers' unions of the CNPF, reconstituted in December 1945. The return to free trade unions for workers and employers alike, however desired or necessary, could not but weigh heavily on production by providing the framework for professional and sectorial resistance to the collective exhortations of the State. Survival clearly required a redrawing of the rules both of production and of those governing the social interaction of all involved in it.

# 3

# The purges

When, in *Combat* of 24 August 1944, Albert Camus wrote, 'This difficult birth is that of a revolution', he was expressing the belief held by all in the Resistance, namely that the bloodshed would be the prelude to sweeping changes and future justice. Just a year later and in the same columns, on 30 August 1945, Camus reflected bitterly on the disappointment of these hopes. The experience of the *épuration*, the process whereby collaborators and those compromised with the Vichy régime were punished and removed from positions of authority, had shown that 'the path of simple justice is hard to find'. This uncomfortable truth was to haunt the national conscience and trouble political life.[1]

## *The summary executions*

It was with an attitude which veered between hope and apprehension that the bulk of the population had followed the excesses of the bloody round of guerrilla attacks and reprisals under way since the winter of 1940/1. Indeed, the wave of denunciations which submerged the authorities in autumn 1944 reflected in part the sudden surfacing of long-repressed fears in the relief of the Liberation. The targets for the violence were members of the Milice, officials of the Légion, PPF militants, profiteers, informers, and traitors; executed, with or without an appearance before a *maquisard* court martial, in reply to the massacres committed by the forces of repression. To them were added the victims of private feuds and banditry and, above all, the local rivalries within the Resistance itself. These excesses worried the leadership; as early as 1943 the CNR condemned the publication of blacklists, and in February 1944 the radio in London and Algiers ordered that violence be directed only against *miliciens*, informers, and Doriot's followers.

This restraint had to be maintained in the confusion which reigned from June to September of 1944. Of course, absolute priority still went to the struggle against the enemy, and the FFIs argued that any help to the German forces, even indirect, constituted a wartime treason punishable by

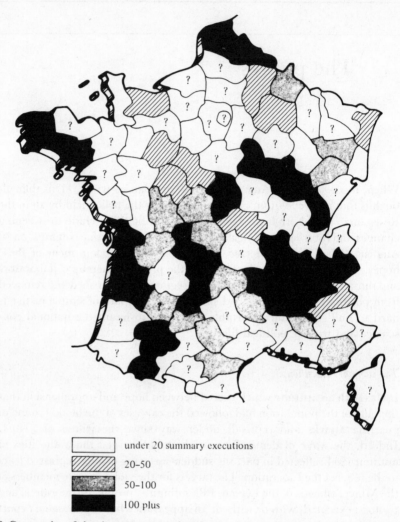

2 Geography of the *épuration*: executions
*Source: L'Histoire,* 5 October 1978, p. 27.

under 20 summary executions
20–50
50–100
100 plus

death. Informers, *miliciens*, and double agents were the chief victims. This
accounts for the high number of summary executions in the *départements*
where the armed struggle still raged (see Map 2): the North and West, the
Massif Central, Aquitaine, the Toulouse region, in the Rhône valley, the
Alpes, Jura, Côte d'Or, and the Yonne. But the directives to the FFI leaders
and the CDLs from Algiers and the CNR make clear the existence of real
fears that events could get out of control.

Such fears were justified by the nature of incidents and the volatility of local conditions. Jeering crowds, swastikas daubed on the houses of known traitors, the shaving of heads of women compromised with the enemy, kidnappings and imprisonment could all easily be the preliminaries to public or private executions. Moreover, it was not unknown for the FFI units and the new local authorities to be implicated in the organization of popular protest and in the dissimulation of acts of summary vengeance. The first tasks, then, were to protect the suspects until they could appear before the special courts planned by the provisional governments and to put a stop to the court martials, the military tribunals of the FFI and the 'tribunaux populaires'. From the beginning of September the commissaires de la République, the prefects and the CDLs began reorganizing the forces of the Sûreté which were to make the arrests, and set up the commissions charged with collecting evidence on the suspects. In fact, the unofficial *épuration* associated with the armed struggle was quickly brought under control. When it did reappear this was due either to the unforeseeable course of the war itself, as after the German counter-offensive of winter 1944–5 in the Ardennes, or to acts of pure banditry, like the 'maquis' of Le Coz whose terrorizing of the region of Loche was not stamped out until 21 October.[2] Nonetheless, the tension was real, fostering a climate of fear, with stories of mass graves beginning to circulate at the end of August.

Not surprisingly, the *résistants*, who set such store by speedy justice as the prelude to national reconstruction, along with all the eleventh-hour patriots, were among the first to be alarmed by the delays in setting up the various courts, the Chambres civiques and the High Court of Justice. These did not start to function until the autumn, and in the meantime the pressure of local opinion was such that the most serious cases had to be dealt with by the military tribunals. However, a scrupulous application of articles 75 and 83 of the Penal Code condemning collusion with the enemy and acts detrimental to the national defence, plus the new punishment of *indignité nationale* (a loss of civil rights and a confiscation of property), corresponded closely to the unanimous wishes of the government, including the Communists, something clear from the restrained attitude of Marcel Willard, now First General Secretary at the Ministry of Justice. Speaking at Evreux on 8 October, de Gaulle spelt out his priorities clearly: clemency was necessary in order to reassure the Allies, to win the war, and to start the work of reconstruction as soon as possible. This belief in the need to curb the *épuration* was reflected in his systematic granting of pardons to the women, minors, and unimportant figures condemned to death. Yet some members of the Resistance had misgivings about this indulgent version of justice under which 73 per cent of death sentences were commuted. In fact, the *épuration* was already revealing its capacity to create a serious unease in the national conscience.

The foreign press had done much to inflame passions over the question. On 11 September 1944, the German newspaper, *Tages Post*, asserted that

9000 executions had already been carried out in Paris. And the Allied press was scarcely more responsible in its approach; in April 1946, *The American Mercury* estimated at 50 000 the number killed by the Communists in the South-East alone. But French officials also added to the confusion which was ultimately to benefit the enemies of the Resistance. After all, exaggerating the extent of the disorder may have made it easier to convince the populations of the need to accept the new authority; it was the Socialist Minister of the Interior, A. Tixier, who mentioned a figure of 105 000 victims to Colonel Passy in February 1945, having omitted to deduct from this all those killed by the Milice and the Germans.

Serious figures only came with the return to peace. Two official inquiries, carried out by the intelligence services and the gendarmerie in March 1946 and November 1948, and whose accuracy has been confirmed by the American historian Peter Novick, give a total of 9673 executions, of which 5234 occurred before the landings; of the remaining 4439, 3114 were without trials, 1325 with. A still more accurate inquiry by the gendarmerie in 1952 arrived at a total of 10 882 executions, 8867 of which were directly attributable to the Resistance, 5143 occurring before the landings and 3724 after. The almost identical figure of 10 842 was given by General de Gaulle in his *Mémoires de guerre*, published in 1959.[3] The same year, however, Robert Aron's *Histoire de la Libération de la France* contested the official figures; using an inquiry of December 1958 and sensational eyewitness accounts, Aron put the number of summary executions at 30 000–40 000, a figure he maintained in his *Histoire de l'épuration*, without having questioned sufficiently the validity of belated research which ignored important urban centres and mixed the victims of both sides.

Today, an inquiry conducted by the Comité d'histoire de la Deuxième Guerre mondiale makes it possible to accept as free of serious errors the figure of 9000 summary executions, to which can be added the 767 executions after trial; in all, then, roughly 10 000 Frenchmen paid the supreme penalty;[4] a figure which, however distressing, is far removed from that put forward by Aron or by the exaggerated reports common at the time. Three-quarters of the executions occurred before the landings or during the fighting; the remainder were born of impatience at the slowness of official justice. Agricultural workers, small farmers, and artisans all came off worse than industrial workers and *cadres*, to whom the anonymity of cities and large towns afforded some protection from denunciation and capture.

*Justice steps in*

There is no doubt that the number of victims would have been much higher but for the prompt intervention by the authorities. Armed with police powers under the ordinance of 29 February 1944, the commissaires de la République

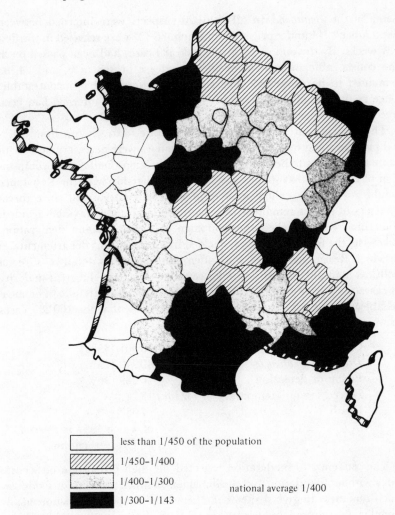

less than 1/450 of the population

1/450–1/400

1/400–1/300        national average 1/400

1/300–1/143

3 Geography of the *épuration*: cases before the courts
  *Source: L'Histoire*, 5 October 1978, p. 27.

began making protective arrests and interning suspects from the beginning of September, sometimes against the wishes of the CDLs. They also set up the Commissions de vérification that were to examine the cases and decide on release or referral to the courts. A considerable number of lives were saved by these measures. Conditions in the internment camps were not always ideal, particularly in the large and overcrowded ones, such as Schirmeck (Bas-Rhin) or La Noé (Haute-Garonne); but there were no grounds for the comparisons with the concentration camps made by opponents of the *épuration*.[5] In all, 126 020 suspects were interned between September 1944 and April 1945, of whom 36 377 were released in the first few weeks. By the end of April 1945, 86 589 cases had been passed on to the courts, able in turn to decide on release or sentence, and 24 383 remained to be examined. The success of internment is incontestable, since at the end of the operation 55 per cent of those interned had been freed and 45 per cent passed on to the courts.

The regular courts were able then to operate relatively free from external pressures and impatience.[6] Certain changes were necessary here, with some magistrates to be dismissed and modifications made in the composition of courts so that judges used to dealing harshly with the Resistance would not now be called upon to judge collaborators. But since three-quarters of judges remained in office this could not always be avoided, something which fuelled the campaign of scepticism and denigration. Likewise, the forming of juries, decided by Commissions départementales in which Resistance groups were often influential, was not always free of political manipulation or desire for revenge, though in the great majority of cases the jurors performed their task honestly and carefully. The most reliable statement of the verdicts and sentences, that for 160 287 cases examined by 31 December 1948, reads thus:

| | |
|---|---|
| Charges dropped or acquittal | 73 501 (45%) |
| *Dégradation nationale* | 40 249 (25%) |
| Prison or detention | 26 289 (16%) |
| Forced labour (temporary or for life) | 13 211 (8%) |
| Death | 7 037 (4%) |
| | of which 4397 *in absentia*, |
| | and 767 executions |

The tendency to moderation reflected the high proportion of accusations without foundation and the flimsiness of much prosecution evidence. Such readiness to give suspects the benefit of doubt was not universally popular: the autumn and winter brought attacks on prisons and lynchings of freed prisoners, without the authorities always being able to intervene in time.[7] The geography of the court activity (see Map 3) forms, naturally, the mirror-image of that of the summary executions; that is, weak in the regions where a maximum *épuration* had already been achieved by the summary executions, but above the national average (1 in 400 of the population) in all the important urban zones where anonymity had offered suspects an initial protection. Alsace was the exception to this rule, both for the number of cases and the severity of the verdicts, since the court of Colmar was not set up until the city's liberation by the Allies, and it then had to deal with the flood of cases from the neighbouring regions. Paris, for all the notoriety of its collaboration, does not disrupt this overall pattern, having slightly more cases than the average, fewer death sentences, and more acquittals.

However, these observations should not obscure the fact that the French people at the time raised questions only over the delays in the proceedings and showed massive interest only for the appearance before the High Court or the provincial courts of prominent figures. Thus the trials of Pétain, Laval, Suarez, Henri Béraud, Brassillach, Jean Hérold-Paquis, Bonny, and Lafont, excitedly covered by the press and radio, tended to monopolize attention to the exclusion of all the other, less spectacular, cases.[8] Indeed, as far as the mass of ordinary accused were concerned it seems certain that the families of their victims and the Resistance only succeeded in mobilizing opinion between October and December 1944.

The attitude which took root during 1945 was a combination of impatience and lassitude. This was clear from the resurgence of protest and violence in the summer, when the efforts of a still-active minority were reinforced by the demands from the returning prisoners and deportees for explanations, rekindling the campaign of the Front national. Yet this was a protest without clear objectives or direction, an explosion of anger over the shortcomings of a justice which dealt harshly with the minor figures and staged show trials of the leaders while allowing notorious culprits to go free. Questions about the nature and role of the *épuration* did now begin to be asked, but general interest in the issue had already been sapped by the long wait for victory, pushed into the background by the hardships and disillusionment of daily life at the end of a severe winter. The remaining condemned were gradually forgotten, their cases of interest only to their families and a minority press which specialized in the exaltation of their martyrdom. By December 1948, 69 per cent of those condemned had been released, and the dismantling of the special courts in January 1951 was barely registered by public opinion. At the time of the vote on the law of amnesty of 6 August 1953, fewer than 1 per cent of the condemned were still being held.

## The failure of the collective purges

An examination of the incidence of the *épuration* yields some valuable social information. The most severely punished were the unimportant and poor. The wealthy and influential could employ the best lawyers, drag out the proceedings, get their case transferred to another *département*, find favourable witnesses, and invoke in their defence secret help given to the Resistance, help made all the more valuable of course by virtue of their social position. At Valenciennes,[9] for example, the court acquitted one-third of employers and one-quarter of artisans, shopkeepers, members of the liberal professions, soldiers, and policemen, compared with only one-tenth of peasants, workers, and employees. Furthermore, the different categories of collaboration drew different degrees of severity: military collaboration brought convictions in 90 per cent of cases, political collaboration in 50 per cent, and economic collaboration in 33 per cent. Yet it was in the first category that the working-class youths were concentrated; unemployed or hard-up, they had been the most susceptible to the appeal of the Milice or *doriotisme*. Indeed, all the evidence available today confirms that far from being the brutal application of a socially inspired 'People's Justice', the *épuration* was in fact more indulgent towards the notables than the underlings, and less hard on the well-established members of society than on the young.

At the time, however, opinion was only convinced of this by the failure of the purges of the Civil Service, the liberal professions, and the companies. On the administration there is little information; no general inquiry has ever been published, and the defence of those involved was extremely well organized, and elicited great discretion from the press. The administrative tribunals showed considerable leniency: a number of officials who might then have feared for the future still occupy positions of great responsibility today. Lists of those to be punished had been drawn up before the Liberation, and an ordinance of 27 June 1944 defined the cases to be sanctioned as those involving help to the enemy, hindrance of the war effort, restriction of public liberties, and the obtaining of personal gain from the application of the Vichy régime's measures. And all the efforts of the government favoured a very narrow application of these criteria; as de Gaulle declared in July, there could be no question of 'sweeping aside the vast majority of the State's servants'. Under a new ordinance of 10 October, the CDLs were empowered to set up Commissions d'enquête and Jurys d'honneur; but of the 50 000 cases they prepared the commissaires de la République passed only 11 343 on to the relevant ministries, where a strong *esprit de corps* worked in favour of clemency in most cases. Thorough in the police force (in the region of Rennes, for example, there were 95 sanctions for 1548 cases examined), the purge was limited in the army, the Ministries of the Interior, Foreign Affairs, and Colonies, and weak everywhere else. By 1950 the reinstatement of the officials who had been punished or suspended was almost complete. Not surprisingly, the continued presence of local officials whose actions and loyalties were suspect in the eyes of the population was a source of discontent; in December 1944, 65 per cent considered the purge of the administration to be insufficient.[10] Yet the official argument was a powerful one: the *épuration* had to be curbed in the interests of returning to order and overcoming the material problems; the restoration of the State had priority in the struggle to survive and to stand up to the Allies.

The same argument was used over the *épuration* of companies and the professions. Local committees did investigate industry and commerce, recommending sanctions to the commissaires de la République; but the final say rested with the national commission. And the numerous conflicts which arose between the CDLs and the economic inspectors and officials of the Finance Ministry – deliberately slow in examining accounts – held up the initial sanctions and hastened decisions from Paris. Thus after 16 March 1945 the Resistance organizations were forbidden to interfere in the *épuration économique*. Henceforth it was extremely weak: intent upon defending production, the authorities were determined to prevent further disruption to companies. This overriding priority explains, for example, why the same companies that had profited from the construction of the Atlantic defences during the Occupation now undertook the rebuilding of the shattered transport system. Only the press, which had been both a symbol of the Collaboration and a decisive arm of the Resistance, was brought under strict control, subject to economic, professional, and political *épuration*, with confiscations and sensational trials of owners and editors. But this was an exception, and in the other professions, including those most closely involved in the corporative reforms of Vichy, prosecutions were rare, confined to a few dozen individuals among the doctors, engineers, and *experts*. How, after all, could it ever be proved that the members of such groups, the *cadres* of the nation, had profited from German power in order to exercise a social authority which was naturally theirs? Personalities from the world of entertainment and the arts were the only ones to be offered up to popular condemnation, a concession to opinion hard to resist given, for example, that 56 per cent of Parisians approved the arrest of Sacha Guitry in September 1944.[11]

This leniency provoked reactions. The half-heartedness of official efforts to recover illicit profits led to attacks on known profiteers during the winter of 1944/5. At Lyon and in the Mediterranean regions the idea of proceeding from patriotic justice to social justice had its advocates. Companies were sequestered, often with the consent of the commissaires de la République, or placed under provisional administrators backed by the CDLs and trade unions: Neptune at Sète, Fouga at Béziers, the mines of Alès, Berliet at Lyon, and twenty-two companies at Marseille. This threat of 'sovietization' prompted swift action from the government, but the restoration of order was slow, not complete until 1947 for companies like Berliet. Of course, impatience for changes of this kind gave the nationalizations of 1945 a symbolic value as fulfilments of popular justice, an aspect the authorities were careful to emphasize in the case of Renault or the mines of the Nord-Pas-de-Calais for example. But in reality these were calculated decisions: part of a national strategy. An immediate and widespread collective appropriation could not be tolerated; as P.-H. Teitgen cried to the Assembly: 'I have not the right to use the *épuration* to carry out structural reforms.'[12]

Little by little, then, the *épuration* is reduced to its true proportions. The *gros* suffered less from it than the accomplices and small fry; those responsible for carrying it out gradually lost their enthusiasm; the mistakes, iniquities, and loopholes left justice discredited. The social and economic structures had proved resilient to pressure, and the State had asserted its exclusive right to modify them: behind the apparent upheaval the clear outline of the status quo can already be seen.[13] The idea, current at the time, of a ferocious and unrelenting popular justice exacting a heavy toll of the nation's élite is clearly untenable. As a painful epilogue to the civil war which had raged since 1940 the *épuration* in France was moderate, much more so than in Belgium, Holland, Norway, and Denmark.

### Forgetting the scale of the crime

At the time, however, denunciation of the excesses of the *épuration* quickly became the basis of an energetic campaign by a hitherto demoralized Right. Preaching from the pulpit of Notre-Dame de Paris on Palm Sunday 1945, Father Panici stigmatized the most ardent *épurateurs* as the 'disciples of the Germans'. With their liberty and property menaced, erstwhile advocates of the New Order and the National Revolution began to organize, mobilizing their influence and contacts, setting up a press to defend and whiten their reputations. Now was born the sinister legend of the *épuration*, one of bloodshed and massacres whose victims were the middle classes and the nation's natural leaders, a legend which exploited the language of the recent nightmare: camps, torture, betrayal, and destruction. It was reinforced by the testimonies and publicly aired doubts over the *épuration* from such genuine *résistants* as Colonel Rémy, Jean-Louis Vigier, and Hubert Beuve-Méry. Imperceptibly, the accused progressed from contesting their judges to arguing openly that their actions had been the correct ones. The upsurge of popular protest in the summer of 1945 fuelled the campaign of denigration. In 1946, the weekly *Paroles françaises* of former *résistant* André Mutter began specializing in the defence and rehabilitation of the *épurés*; the cause soon attracted others – *Ecrits de Paris, Aspects de la France*, and *Rivarol*[14] – all intent on using this theme as the basis for a new 'national opposition' to resist an anarchic democracy manipulated by Communism. In a best-selling pamphlet published in 1948, abbé Desgranges condemned the new sin of '*résistantialisme*'.[15]

This campaign would probably have come to nothing if some of its criticisms had not been accredited by the *résistants* themselves. Mauriac and Camus did battle in the columns of *Le Figaro* and *Combat* over the respective merits of Justice and Charity, with Camus being forced finally to recognize that his was the weaker case.[16] The state of the country, the demands of the Allies, the delayed victory, and the attitude of the political parties all contributed to dissipate the revolutionary hopes the CNR programme had fostered in some quarters: the difficulties and injustices of the *épuration* served to drive home this disappointment. A sterile polemic raged, culminating in 1951 with Jean Paulhan's *Lettre aux directeurs de la Résistance*.[17] On the one hand was the fact that in the regions where the Resistance had led mass risings in summer 1944, like Brittany and the Limousin, a brutal but definitive *épuration* had received overwhelming acceptance; on the other, however, that the hesitations, delays, and injustices were evidence of the failure of a popular resistance. The character of the *épuration* in fact exposed the weaknesses of the Resistance, pointing up the gulf between its hopes and reality and the fragility of a morality divorced from politics.

Others (in particular during the Cold War) pointed an accusing finger at the FTPFs, instigators of an unruly popular justice which could have opened the door to wholesale expropriation and Communism. Since 1941 the Communist Party had indeed called for 'a French victory in which no trace of the treason will remain', for a massive but rapid and just *épuration*. But the Party did not envisage a revolutionary outcome, and was very well aware that it would be blamed for any generalized disorder, something that would immediately re-form an anticommunist opposition capable of isolating the Party and destroying its national image. The purges were of course necessary, but if the democracy to which the Communist Party hoped to bring new blood was to be restored they had to be moderate. Here, perhaps, lies the paradox of the *épuration*: not only did it enable part of the Right to regroup but it went a long way to isolating the Resistance within the nation. Most of all, it helped to shut the Communists in precisely the political ghetto the entire Resistance had wanted to destroy, a development the Cold War was to reinforce. This contradiction started to emerge in 1945: after 1947 the 'Popular justice' of 1944 became synonymous for many with 'Communist justice'.

This helps to explain the ease with which the outcome sought by the government was accepted. Aware that weakness now would be fatal, de Gaulle's government, backed by all the Resistance, including the Communists, was intent on rebuilding a State based on national unity, on recovering dignity for France, and on harnessing the nation's energies to the task of reconstruction. Of course, honour required that those responsible for the disaster be punished severely and at the highest levels. But at the same time the people had to be persuaded that the immediate needs had absolute priority. Thus responsibility for the purges had to reside with the courts, and indulgence was made to serve policy. By rekindling partisan passions a generalized settling of scores would rapidly undermine the fragile national unity built up since 18 June 1940, while the resulting chaos

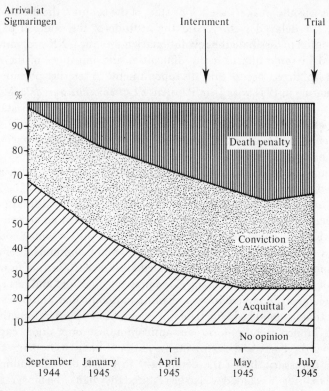

1 French opinion and Marshal Pétain

*Source:* based on results of opinion polls published in the *Bulletin de l'IFOP*,
October 1944–August 1945.

would justify intervention by the Allies. What honour clearly did not require was the dismembering of the administration and institutions from
which it was hoped to erase the traces of the Vichy interlude. Conciliation
and indulgence would contribute to the creation of unity and greatness.
The State was the source of all legitimate authority, and it repudiated
disorder. In short, the end to the *épuration* was imposed by necessity: that of
survival and reconstruction. It was the priority of getting the nation back to
work and consolidating the State which brought a general pardon for the
errors of the past.

This approach was based on realism. An opinion poll of May 1944
revealed that while 20 per cent were supporting the Resistance in one way
or another and that 28 per cent wanted to see a popular repression, 44 per
cent were in fact looking to the State to restrain the popular initiatives and
60 per cent had an eventual breakdown of order as their main worry. A
clear majority was thus ready to accept the official proposals for the return

to normalcy: a punishment of the most notorious collaborators, but with a clear distinction drawn between the high priests of La France Allemande and those who had merely implemented the National Revolution (in September 58 per cent even refused to accept that Pétain could be tried and punished). It was thus a punishment from above, without an examination of the deeper social implications, which brought the period of vengeance to a close. From the autumn, however, as weariness and indifference took hold and the refusals to give an opinion multiplied, so the sternest gaze became fixed on the expiatory victims.

The case of Pétain is the best illustration of this. As Fig. 1 makes clear, neither Sigmaringen nor Pétain's return to France had any impact on an increasingly severe popular judgement. It was as if the persistent difficulties and the never-ending war made it necessary to harden one's verdict on the past; to consider Vichy as having been more than just an episode; to see 1940 as having inflicted lasting damage on the country; and to argue as a result that the figure most clearly identified with a policy based on acceptance of this should bear, alone, the responsibility.[18] The *épuration* seems then to have focused discontent, serving, rightly or wrongly, as a safety valve for the tensions born of the shortages, the black market, and a daily life of humiliation and hardship for which no end was in sight.

Between the extremes of brutal punishment and irresponsible leniency, perhaps no real justice was possible while the population as a whole refused to submit to a searching self-examination. A punitive justice had dealt with the leaders and those swept along by the disorder and panic: but only a coherent political justice might have been able to come to grips with the institutions, groups, and ideologies outside of which these individuals and their actions were meaningless. The method adopted for the Nuremberg Trials, that of first defining the crime, then proceeding to punish the guilty, was not used for the *épuration* in France. Consequently the fundamental questions, such as what exactly identified a collaborator, or what was the nature of the links between the Collaboration and the National Revolution, were not posed. Instead, a view of the Resistance as the sole source of legitimacy and of its struggle as the foundation of the new régime was accepted without a serious examination of the social context of the Vichy period; the dimension of the crime was reduced to that of the offence itself, and the political failure to the treason alone. By opting for a prompt return to order the new leadership rejected the task of reflection these issues required. Was it, for example, possible to judge an individual member of the Milice without judging Vichy as a whole? Or the presenter of Radio Paris without bringing the nature of the broadcasting itself into question? Could one, in short, punish the offence without a searching examination of the economic, social, and political bases of the system which had allowed it to take place?

Such an examination would have required treating Vichy and the Collaboration as social phenomena, a readiness to admit that the Resistance was the work of a small minority, and a willingness to probe deeply to find the reasons for this situation. Without a recognition of the collective character of the crime, where was the chain of responsibility to be severed? As Sartre observed: 'These four years were a long impotent dream of unity.'[19] The Resistance, faithful to the tradition of 1789, had indeed dreamt of completing the work of national unity. Yet the reality made it clear that such hopes had little future: for both collaboration and Vichy had been based on a silent and massive acquiescence.[20]

Indeed, one can ask if the population as a whole was quite as innocent in its attitude to the victims of the *épuration* as it cared to believe. In 1943, General de Gaulle had promised that France would need to know vengeance. Yet after 1944 the desire for vengeance foundered amidst the reticence of the nation. Was this not in part because too severe a judgement on those involved in the Occupation implied a judgement on everyone? Having rejected this course, the people accepted instead a Republic whose divisions were more recognizably its own. As Jean-Marie Domenach noted, 'it was as if one were frightened by the sheer scale of the crime'.[21]

# 4

# Restoration

Fourteenth July 1944. Normandy, the beach at Courseulles. General de Gaulle gave a final piece of advice to François Coulet, the first commissaire de la République to exercise authority over part of the liberated territory: 'Do not give them politics, they do not want it.' Speaking on the radio on 29 August – echoing his speech of 25 July to the Consultative Assembly, anticipating that of 12 September at the Palais de Chaillot to all the officials of the Resistance and the State – de Gaulle declared: '. . . the people have decided, by instinct and reason, to satisfy the two conditions without which nothing can be achieved: order and effort. Republican order, under the only true authority, that of the State; concerted effort, to allow a legal and peaceful construction of the basis for renewal.'[1]

## The return to order

The Liberation opened a period of political tension. What it did not do was to initiate a revolutionary challenge to the consensus forged between the newly united nation and the authority that was necessary for the urgent tasks ahead, those of victory, survival, the closing of the Vichy interlude, and reconstruction. The exercise of power was not always straightforward in this period, but no attempt was under way to subvert it. This interregnum was not insurrectional: it was legitimated by the continuation of the war, by the wait for elections, and by republican and patriotic continuity. The collapse of Vichy and its administration removed all reactionary opposition, and the AMGOT threat had been averted: acceptance of what was necessary was aided by this absence of an alternative. And although political preparations were certainly being made for the future, the choice was not to be between revolution and reaction but rather between the degrees of reforming zeal the new State would institutionalize.[2]

Those involved knew that the future course had been settled well before the landings. Since September 1941 efforts in London, Algiers, and within France had been geared towards the creation of a centralized French authority capable of assuming direction of the liberated nation peacefully and smoothly. A series of legal measures had prepared for this.[3] The institutional framework was ready; for its installation the CFLN (which became the GPRF or provisional government on 2 June) had chosen dependable men from among the loyal followers of Jean Moulin, each appointment being carefully vetted by the Comité général d'études, a sort of underground Conseil d'Etat composed of nine republican jurists. The arrival of the new men and their assumption of responsibilities had been organized since before June by Alexandre Parodi, the government's general delegate in France. Parodi scrupulously applied the advice of de Gaulle: the struggle of the Resistance was vital for national survival, but above the Resistance and its actions stood the authority of the State, and it was in the latter's name that officials were to speak and act.[4]

The key figures of the new administrative structure, replacing Vichy's regional prefects, were the commissaires de la République. Their mission was clear: to establish as quickly as possible and by whatever means a legal authority to confront the various *de facto* authorities. Under Parodi's orders, they were the mandated representatives of the provisional government, sent out to inform and guide public opinion and to uphold order and legality; they were open to dialogue, negotiating with the fighters, directing the prefects, sub-prefects, and civil authorities. Above all, however, they had to safeguard a national consensus which was no longer simply that of the Resistance itself; the Jacobin conception of the State they incarnated was to be a vital counter to the fragmentation of the country. Thus at every level of the hierarchy were appointed men committed to the reconstruction of the machinery of the State in its pre-war forms, a move seen by some as 'republican vigilance', by others as the return to power of the *haute bourgeoisie*.[5] In short, the State charged its servants with protecting the general interest in the face of possible disorder.

It would be a mistake to see this as an arbitrary or machiavellian decision. The measures were in fact accepted by the CNR with only a few grumbles. Francis Closon, the head of its CDL Commission and the representative of de Gaulle and d'Astier, had fought since summer 1943 to ensure for the various Liberation committees – which issued from the underground struggle and on which all the Resistance groups were represented – a full part both in and after the Liberation, able to act as brakes on popular impatience and screens behind which the officials could operate. In April 1944 it was finally acknowledged that this hierarchy of committees, topped by the CNR itself, could in no sense be considered as a 'parallel power' or 'soviet'. On D-Day and during the national insurrection the CDLs took a leading role, determined to save the nation from 'l'effroi du néant'.[6] After the insurrection their task was that of pacifying the population, of preparing the way for the State's officials, aiding the prefects though without surrendering any of their power to them, and remaining as provisional consultative bodies to replace the former Conseils généraux.

These measures for unity had the unanimous backing of the political parties, anxious to have a say in the aftermath of the war and unconditional in their support for de Gaulle.[7] The clandestine SFIO and the Christian Democrats were still too weak not to grasp such an opportunity to reinsert themselves in the national current, while the other parties, Radicals, Democratic Alliance, and Republican Alliance had been revived merely to accept decisions over which they could have no influence. The CNR, in its 'Instructions pour la libération du territoire' of 15 March 1944 – better known subsequently as the CNR programme – had organized its military directives around the theme of obedience to the CDLs and FFI leadership, condemning all divisive initiatives, and concluding with a call for national unity centred on the CFLN and its president, General de Gaulle.[8] Lastly, and decisively, the Communist Party threw its weight behind the measures. Grenier and Billoux had been brought onto the CFLN in Algiers in April, in order, as Billoux put it, to give the government 'a greater legitimacy to speak and act in the name of France'.[9] On the CNR where they were predominant and at every level of the Resistance, the Communists made concessions to hasten the victory and justify their return in force to the forefront of political debate. Thus in spite of hesitations among its deputies in Algiers and the armed groups in France, the Communist Party accepted in fact to be under-represented in the administration now being set up;[10] likewise, it accepted that the insurrection and the general strike organized by the CGT have a purely military objective. This Front national tactic was rigidly adhered to until the victory, something over which no one had any doubts, neither de Gaulle and his entourage, nor the commissaires de la République. Indeed, it was in distinctly Gaullian terms that Duclos called upon the Party's Central Committee on 31 August for 'a policy of mobilization of all the forces for that war that France must pursue if she is to figure tomorrow among the great nations'. With its reintroduction of political parties into national life, the emphasis on the continuity of the State and the submission to military goals and government authority, a strong atmosphere of 'Union sacrée' pervades this carefully ordered interregnum.

The composition of the government of 'Unanimité nationale' formed on 9 September and presided over by de Gaulle confirms this impression. A former President of the Senate under the Third Republic, Jean Jeanneney, who, though not active in the Resistance, had first been contacted by de Gaulle in May 1942, became Minister of State charged with reorganizing the public authorities: republican continuity was assured by respect for the past. The President of the CNR, Georges Bidault, became Minister of Foreign Affairs, while a Socialist with strong Gaullist sympathies, Adrien

Tixier, was Minister of the Interior. The Communists received two portfolios, Aviation to FTPF leader Charles Tillon and Public Health to François Billoux.[11] The overall result was a subtle mixture of party politicians (two Communists, four Socialists, three MRP, three Radicals and one Moderate) and nine non-party members; the two currents of the Resistance were present, with one-third of its members from metropolitan France and two-thirds from Algiers; and the generations were mixed, with newcomers and experts rubbing shoulders with experienced parliamentarians. This then was the team whose efforts had now to be concentrated on the triple objectives of 'la guerre, le rang, l'Etat'.[12]

The immediate task of restoring the State and a centralized authority was complicated by the fact that in the former southern zone the CDLs had already overstepped their powers; suspending Vichyite officials, carrying out searches, sometimes being involved in the arrests and summary executions. Some newly appointed prefects arrived to find the *préfecture* occupied by the CDL leadership; elsewhere, commissaires and prefects had to exploit their personal political commitments to assert themselves. At Limoges, for example, liberated by Guingouin's men on 21 August, the Communist prefect, Jean Chaintron, helped by the CDL and its leader, Pastor Chaudier, restored order gently to a region menaced by a wave of bloody reprisals, and where 'popular democracies' had sprung up in the rural areas since their liberation by the maquis several months earlier. In the Auvergne, commissaire Henry Ingrand, former regional chief of the MUR, was in charge by the end of July, bringing the maquis under control and calming the fears of the authorities in Paris. The arrival of Emmanuel d'Astier, commissaire à l'Intérieur, the skill of Jacques Bounin, and the quickly restored discipline of the Communists brought a gradual easing of tension in the Languedoc. In the Ain, however, commissaire Yves Farge ordered the arrest on 18 September of Colonel Romans-Petit, leader of the FFI forces responsible for the liberation of the *département*, for having illegally exercised the powers of the prefect of Lyon. Finally, at Toulouse, relations remained very delicate for a long while between commissaire Pierre Bertaux, the CDL, and the FFI leader Colonel Ravanel.[13]

Tensions of this kind were generally absent from the former northern zone. The CDLs, which had played a more limited role in the underground here, accepted the authority of the prefects with little protest. The CDL of the Ille-et-Vilaine, for example, whose meeting of 21 August had been presided over by de Gaulle himself, was attuned to the everyday worries of the population, bombarded the prefect with 4000 resolutions in a single year, yet was quickly forced to recognize that it had no popular following.[14] Apart from the incidents during the *épuration*, the regions of the West, the Loire, the North, and the East experienced few serious difficulties.[15] During the winter of 1944/5 it became clear to the officials of the central authority that these CDLs were no longer representative of general opinion; with their momentum failing they were reduced to the role of somewhat aimless centres of discussion for veterans of the conflicts. The CDLs certainly helped to amplify and articulate complaints over the hardships of daily life; but with essentially urban membership (only 8.6 per cent of peasants), marked left-wing colouring, and the preponderance of Communists among them, they were less and less representative of the country or even of the Resistance, itself a heterogeneous minority.

The rapid restoration of order was also helped by General de Gaulle's visits to the provinces. The first of these (14–18 September), to the peripheral regions, Lyon, Marseille, Toulouse, Bordeaux, and Orléans, allowed him to gauge his popularity, to chide and convince disgruntled *résistants* and to encourage members of the administration; that of October, to Normandy and his native city of Lille, brought him face to face with the misery and destruction: de Gaulle's presence contributed everywhere to the consolidation of national unity. By the beginning of the autumn the administration's mastery of the situation was apparent; the *préfectures* were operating, municipal delegations were set up in the communes until elections could be held, and the stormy CDL meetings were boycotted by the officials of the State. Tribute could certainly be paid in December to the Resistance's role as 'the regenerator of the institutions'; but the fact was that against the regional and minority aspirations it had articulated, the *département* had been restored as the framework of political and administrative life; and power was centralized in Paris.

Any remaining doubts as to the final outcome were dispelled by the affair of the Patriotic Militia. This had been set up by the CNR on 15 March 1944, and the statute of 10 August defined it as a police force under the orders of the Liberation Committees. During and after the insurrection its task was to replace the FFI men leaving for the front, to combat the black market and sabotage by the 'Fifth Column', and to unmask traitors. The militia was in fact the armed force of the Resistance, one capable of bringing a very direct physical pressure to bear on the agents of central authority. During the Liberation its action was indistinguishable from that of the FFI, a confusion which worried many elements of the Resistance.[16] After the insurrection, and depending on local conditions, the militia worked with the official police force (now being purged, and outnumbered by three to one), its ranks swollen with eleventh-hour *résistants* and FFI members reluctant to join the army. Authority over the militia was uncertain, shifting between the CNR, local authorities, and Communist officials, the last especially interested in it as the potential base for a mass movement.

Strengthened by the official recognition from the Allies on 23 October (itself an acknowledgement of the return to order accomplished since

D-Day) and aware of public unease over the militia, the government took action. On 28 October, just a few days before a CNR meeting to formalize the militia, it decided on the disarming of all civilian groups: henceforth any FFI member not engaged in the regular army was suspended and holders of firearms were subject to the normal laws of the Republic. The decision provoked noisy protests from the CNR and sections of the press close to the Resistance, sparing de Gaulle but quick to attack the government. Nonetheless, on 31 October it was confirmed that all firearms were to be surrendered to the police or gendarmerie. Jacques Duclos denounced the move as a conspiracy of the 'trusts' against the Republic; the CNR went ahead and voted the statute for the militia on 4 November; and some local committees, notably in Paris, ordered armed patrols to be carried out in open defiance of the authorities. The government replied on 8 December with an announcement of the creation of the Compagnies républicaines de sécurité (CRS), hoping thus to absorb the disaffected energies. And the Communist Party abandoned its hitherto strenuous defence of the militia after the return of Maurice Thorez from his wartime exile in Moscow on 27 November. With his 1940 condemnation for desertion amnestied by de Gaulle – currently negotiating with Stalin – Thorez could now recover his leadership of the Party in France. Addressing the Central Committee at Ivry on 21 January 1945, the Communist leader made a special point of reminding those present that 'all the irregular armed groups cannot be maintained any longer'. By February–March 1945 the problem of the militia was settled, their arms either surrendered or forgotten. With the militia disbanded, the Resistance could no longer mobilize, an outcome greeted with approval, it seems, by public opinion.[17]

### The failure of the Resistance Party

With hindsight it is clear that the battle for order was quickly won. On the basis of the press and contemporary declarations, however, it is not hard to form the impression that revolutionary change was imminent. And it is certain that many people experienced these months as a clear break with the past, just as for others they were the prelude to subversion. The moment was indeed unique in French political history: the Right had collapsed with Vichy, and the Left, invested with all the moral authority of the Resistance, was now the natural spokesman for the national interest. The expectations of change that the unity of the struggle had fostered were embodied in the CNR programme of 15 March 1944, which soon acquired the status of a charter for the future. As *Combat* had urged on 21 August 1944, 'the word liberation must be taken in its broadest possible sense', and for many the newspaper's subtitle, 'De la Résistance à la Révolution', stood as a statement of intent.[18]

The CNR programme in fact laid down that the Resistance would remain united after the Liberation to oversee the sweeping economic and social reforms. The programme's ambitious economic objectives included the dismantling of the 'feudal empires' of money and finance, a planning-based growth to ensure general prosperity, worker participation, and strategic nationalizations. In the social domain the programme proclaimed the right to work and retirement, as well as to leisure, culture, and education; there was a project for a Social Security system, and real incomes and employment were to be protected. Finally, the Resistance was to provide the first members of the constantly renewed élite of merit whose task would be to guide the people towards a 'République nouvelle'. In short, the programme promised a combination of liberty and justice, crossing political liberalism with socialist economics.

This programme, nurtured in the atmosphere of patriotic fraternity, had unanimous support from the Resistance, and its themes were echoed on all sides: by de Gaulle, the political parties, and the movements that had issued from the Resistance. There was a willingness to explain its vital choices to the nation. An almost missionary zeal, of young men come to politics through the underground, or of their elders with a recovered taste for civic idealism, motivated the new press which had ousted, often quite literally, that discredited during the Occupation.[19] In spite of paper shortages and the readership's preoccupation with news of the subsistence crisis, large circulations and a singleness of tone made this new press a powerful instrument of civic education.[20] The radio, with new personnel under Jean Guignebert, managed to shake off an unfortunate wartime reputation and made its contribution to the debate; the State's monopoly was consolidated, regional structures were developed, and radio now completed its conquest of French homes without sacrificing its new standards.[21] With the importance of mass communications now recognized, their control became a political question. This consideration, plus that of recovering an international audience after the return to order, lay behind the government's financial and political support for *Le Monde*, launched by Hubert Beuve-Méry in December 1944. With its independent and critical approach this unique newspaper was to take the place occupied by *Le Temps* before the war as the organ of information for the economic, political, and administrative élites.[22]

The scope of politics was widening in other, less familiar areas. The greater role of women, with the provisions crisis and the ordinance of 21 April granting them the vote in municipal elections, was the logical sequel to their place in the Resistance struggle. Street demonstrations and protest movements were expressions of this force, which was moreover, one that only the Communists proved able to harness consistently. Widespread aspirations to culture and leisure, along the lines traced by the Popular

Front and recognized by the CNR programme, also contributed to a heightening of political awareness. At Grenoble, for example, the Peuple et Culture movement, which issued from the maquis of the Vercors, expressed a notion of justice, a desire for greater self-determination, and a regional consciousness. Culture and politics merged at more popular levels; in the press, at public meetings, and in the Comités d'entreprise; Jean Guéhenno was charged with encouraging this development at the Ministry of Education. The output of reviews was particularly rich at this time: intellectuals argued over the rights of the individual, for and against the class struggle, defined their positions *vis-à-vis* Marxism, attempted to come to terms with contemporary problems. The message seemed at last to have found an audience and its bearers a place of responsibility; Jean-Paul Sartre's introduction to the first issue of *Les Temps modernes* of 1 October 1945 stood as a manifesto: 'The distant goal we set ourselves is that of a liberation.'[23]

Was power really shifting? Were partisan divisions really being eclipsed? The sheer range of ambitious subjects treated in the press – economics, education, work, defence, empire, global strategy, mass culture and, invariably, the need for new élites – certainly seems to bear witness to a readiness for far-reaching change. A faith in the power of consensus alone to break the old habits and reshape politics was bolstered by the apparent magnitude of the task ahead, by a view of post-Liberation France as a kind of social and political vacant lot;[24] indeed, it was now that the tenacious myth of a massive Resistance movement, which had left France cleansed and pure, grew up. The appeal of this was understandable: after October 1944 it would have been hard for anyone to question, let alone deny, a patriotic attachment to the values of the Resistance. Commitment or *engagement* of this sort acquired a visible prestige, offering a collective absolution, reducing the past to a straightforward victory of heroism. To judge from the articles in *Combat*, probably the most effective spokesman for this attitude – declaiming against mediocrity, demanding an end to the power of monied interests – the Resistance seemed assured of a permanent place in French political life.

In reality, however, the doctrinal foundations were weak. A vague and poorly thought out *travaillisme* (Labour socialism) received considerable attention, and was enthusiastically hailed as an alternative to both the 'République bourgeoise' and the Soviet model. This middle way between capitalism and Marxism excited the founders of *Défense de la France* and the OCM, men like Philippe Vianney and Georges Izard, attracted the Christians and Socialists, and was probably not far removed from what a majority of the population actually wanted to see. But it failed to find an audience among the decision-makers, and remained without practical political importance. In the CNR the political parties reigned supreme; the

CDLs were weak and divided; the Front national already seemed to be controlled by the Communists; and the government refused to embark on long-term policies until elections had been held. There remained only the MLN; in September this presented itself as a bridge between the government and the people, and in October it proposed a fusion of all the non-party forces, including the Front national. But any hopes this may have raised were quickly disappointed, for by November the political parties had already begun to reassert themselves.

With the founding of the Mouvement républicain populaire (MRP), whose inaugural congress was held on 26 November, the political energies of Roman Catholics at last found an intelligent and promising outlet. A long tradition of French liberal Catholic thought, from Lamennais to Marc Sangnier, which before the war had developed in the Parti démocrate populaire, the Jeune République movement, and in *L'Aube*, now took a significant political form. The circumstances were favourable: the eclipse of the traditional Right encouraged a realignment of its electorates towards a Christian Democracy more closely attuned to the prevailing mood. The Catholic hierarchy, acutely aware of the opprobrium it had earned by enthusiastic support for Vichy's National Revolution, and anxious now to concentrate on the urgent pastoral tasks, quickly gave its blessing to a movement which offered a solution to the old problem of relations between the Church and the Republic and which would allow Catholics access to the highest levels of the new régime. Female suffrage and support from the clergy enhanced the new party's electoral prospects, while doctrinal modernity and its founders' prestige as Resistance leaders and confidants of de Gaulle – Maurice Schumann, Georges Bidault, François de Menthon, and P.–H. Teitgen – gave the MRP an obvious place in post-war France. Filling a historical vacuum in French democracy, posing as the party of loyalty to de Gaulle, able to count on the support of the Catholic CFTC, and with a flexible and effective structure modelled on that of the Communist Party, the MRP made spectacular progress. By 1945 the only important new political party of the post-war period had more than 100 000 members.[25] Its leader, Georges Bidault, was confident of realizing his ambition: to remain independent of the too-secular SFIO and ignore the woolly *travaillisme*, and to make the MRP the only political force capable of matching the Communists.

The SFIO for its part did not conceal its ambition to become the principal political party in France.[26] Apart from slight internal changes (organization was modified, discipline was tightened, and links with the federations were strengthened) and a rigorous purging of its ranks, the SFIO was reconstituted on the pre-war lines. But the dynamic clandestine leadership under Daniel Mayer was retained and, despite the absence of Léon Blum who did not return from deportation until May 1945, the party's congress of November 1944 renewed the offer to the Communists of talks over the organic unity the two parties had achieved during the Resistance struggle, as well as exploring the possibilities for a broad-based social democratic party. The Socialists supported de Gaulle, confident in their ability to push him towards faster structural reforms or to suggest a programme for government.[27] There remained of course the strategic dilemma over relations with the Communists: should the Socialists work for a union of all the Left, or for one of the non-Communist Left? But the prospects for the future looked bright. Militant activity revived in the autumn; the party's social bases were shown to be intact; the SFIO bastions of the North, Bouches-du-Rhône, and the South-West were reconstituted; and the affiliated professional, youth and cultural organizations recovered. And climbing membership figures reinforced the optimism.[28]

At the same time, the political parties smothered at the Liberation were also reviving. The Republican Federation of the Seine met in February 1945, attracting former members of de La Rocque's PSF, Français Libres, and a few 'independent' Radicals. The Radicals held a 'mini-congress' in December 1944; they were still extremely isolated and had few militants, even if the prestige of Jean Zay did much to offset past errors. But Radicalism had deep roots in French political life and was far from dead; the Radicals presented their own lists in the elections, determined to fight for the maintenance of the 1875 constitutional laws.

The consequences of this return in force of the political parties could already be felt in the embryonic parliamentary life the government tolerated to the provisional Consultative Assembly. Transferred from Algiers to Paris and enlarged by ordinance in October to admit representatives of the internal Resistance, the Consultative Assembly was meeting from 7 November. The entire political spectrum was present: 148 members from the Resistance, parties, associations, and movements in metropolitan France, 40 representatives from overseas and the external Resistance, and 60 members from the Assembly elected in 1936. The Assembly kept its President from Algiers, the Socialist Félix Gouin, and operated along classic parliamentary lines. From December, however, the tone of debate hardened; true, the Assembly still gave ovations to de Gaulle, his ministers or news of fresh victories, but questioning over supplies, the alliances, the *épuration* and nationalization became noticeably more insistent and probing. The government's honeymoon period was in fact over, and although de Gaulle could safely ignore some of the subsequent results, there were unmistakable signs that parliamentary life was reviving.

The Resistance movements on the other hand were losing momentum, effectively by-passed in this reconstitution of political life around the traditional structures of parties, Assembly, and government. Their long-term prospects had been weakening since January–February 1945 with the onset of disillusionment over the *épuration* and the difficulties of everyday life. The MLN's first national congress of 23–28 January 1945 was to be decisive. The essential question was simple: should the CNR programme be the basis for continuing work with the parties and unions in order to align the non-Communists behind social democratic objectives? Or, as the Communists wanted, should all the members of the Resistance, including the Front national, fuse together, accepting the tactic of an unconditional union of the entire underground? Preliminary regional congresses in Lyon and Paris had given contradictory answers, and the OCM offered its services while the Socialists and Communists discussed a common programme. In the sessions of the congress the Communists and their allies confronted a disparate but determined socialist Left. A debate which opposed Pierre Hervé, director of *Action*, a weekly linked to the Communist Party, and André Malraux, just returned from the fighting in Alsace, went in favour of the latter. By 250 votes to 119, the MLN rejected fusion with the Front national. Unity of the Resistance required a specific objective: without this a purely political logic had triumphed. The 1200 participants at the Front national's congress on 3 February enthusiastically proclaimed the 'Renaissance française' and gave a large echo to the Communists' proposals, but had to acknowledge the rupture with the Socialist Left and hasten their own movement's alignment with the PCF. The grandiosely named 'Etats généraux de la Renaissance française' of 14 July, suffused with historical allusions and for which *cahiers de doléances* had been prepared, brought the CNR and CDLs together by an evocation of shared experience, but the proposals were of clearly Communist inspiration. And in the meantime the MLN had broken up, its 500 000 members either dispersed among the existing political parties or abandoning militant activity altogether. A minority joined with the Front national to form the Mouvement unifié de la Résistance française (MURF) which after July became a simple appendage of the Communist Party.[29] The majority set about organizing a federation to embrace Libération-Nord, the OCM, Ceux de la Résistance, Libérés et Fédérés, the SFIO and, if possible, Jeune République, which had not joined the MRP. Faced with the departure of the Socialists, a handful of those left founded the Union démocratique et socialiste de la Résistance (UDSR) on 25 June; here finally was a political party issued directly from the Resistance, but it was tiny and soon had to conclude an electoral alliance with the SFIO.[30]

Political life had been reconstituted along its old lines, and the parties had demonstrated their ability to absorb the new men. Those who had hoped for something different were disappointed: they had failed to appreciate the extent of the constraints, and had put too much faith in the value of a denunciation of existing political traditions and habits to open the way for an alternative. This failure of the avant-garde was closely mirrored by the onset of weariness and indifference among the population: in December 1944, 47 per cent had found the Resistance's place in political life too limited; yet just three months later, in March 1945, 53 per cent were without an opinion on the CNR programme; in April only 12 per cent wanted the Resistance to found a new political party, whereas 79 per cent saw it merely as a patriotic movement which could, if necessary, make a contribution to the efforts of the existing parties.[31] Alienation, abdication of responsibility, claimed the disappointed. The great strength of de Gaulle and the Communists, however, was to have understood that a return to the Republic would be enough to satisfy the population.

### The Communist strategy

This was a period of rapid change for the French Communist Party. From 380 000 in January 1945 its membership had risen to around 800 000 by the end of 1946: the PCF not only recovered its pre-war audience but established itself as the principal political party in France. The Party's organization and methods had evolved; the underground struggle brought a renewal of personnel in the Party machine; the events of autumn 1944 allowed techniques of mobilization and propaganda to be perfected, showing the value of meetings, petitions, and delegations.[32] The Party's ability to strike deep chords in French society, important since 1936, was taken a stage further; the press under its control, for example, doubled its 1939 circulation, and with ten million copies in 1946 accounted for between 20 and 25 per cent of the national circulation. Strike strategy had been perfected, and it was during the war that the Communist Party completed its takeover of the CGT leadership. The Party also proved adept at infiltrating and affiliating mass movements: this was clear from 1945 for the Front national, for the Union des femmes françaises which mobilized on the theme of provisions, and for the Union des jeunesses républicaines de France, as well as for a wide range of cultural associations and organizations of ex-servicemen and former deportees. These efforts bore fruit in the elections: the Communist Party attracted one voter in four and won control of major municipal strongholds.

In addition, there was the moral credit the Party had accumulated during the war. The 'parti des fusillés',[33] as it now styled itself, could point to its impressive record of Resistance and patriotism – one further enhanced by the current prestige of the Red Army,[34] to develop to the full its reinsertion in the nation. Indeed, it was on moral rather than doctrinal grounds that the PCF now made its most powerful appeal;[35] in the name of the sacrifices it had made and its role in hastening the Liberation, the PCF now sat as permanent judge on the other political parties, as the incarnation of the purity of the Resistance struggle. The importance of this

stance should not be underestimated: the PCF now set itself up as spokesman for the poor and the pure, wielding a moral advantage worth more
than all the theories.

The Communist Party was present at all levels of public life. It was a
party of government, with ministers whose loyalty to the State was unconditional; it was central to parliamentary life in general and to the parliamentary Left in particular; it was the focal point for the militants active in
the CDLs and the organizations of the Front national; and it was present in
every French commune. True, it is not certain that the Communists were
generally perceived to be the principal political force;[36] after all, much of
the intense political activity of the period stemmed precisely from a desire
to limit the place they occupied. But the sheer size of the PCF was striking,
and the political education of a young generation was profoundly marked
by the solidity of its moral and revolutionary appeal.

The Communist Party's strategy was based on an appreciation of the
global context of the struggle against Fascism and the benefits offered by
the Front national framework. Liberated France, it concluded, could not be
considered ripe for revolution.[37] The meetings of the Allies which
culminated at Yalta in February 1945 had not placed France in the zone of
Soviet influence. Consequently, the duty of the PCF lay in reinforcing the
national unity around de Gaulle in order to intensify the struggle against
Hitler, thus easing the pressure on the Soviet Union by forcing a redep-
loyment of German forces to the West, and in working to create a liberated
France strong enough to contain Anglo–Saxon ambitions to hegemony.
Legality, patriotism, and unity were thus the keynotes of the Party's
strategy. De Gaulle was of course an ideological enemy, but his capacity to
generate national unity made him the most effective agent of the strategy:
subversion and double-talk were excluded by the commitment to de
Gaulle. The goals laid down by the PCF Central Committee on 31 August –
'To liberate France, to punish the traitors, to let the people be heard' – were
those of the CNR programme. Indeed, the Communist Party scarcely
required a programme of its own: 'We must hold national unity dearer than
what we ourselves cherish', urged Thorez.[38] This sacrifice of short-term
partisan objectives in the national interest added still more credibility to
the Party's image as the guardian of the values and virtues of the
Resistance; it allowed the Party to denounce *travaillisme* as divisive, and to
participate in the government while continuing to encourage extensive
militant activity. The tasks of the moment – an anti-monopolist union, the
restoration of the republican State, and the assertion of national independence – would lay the bases for future democratic progress. In short, installed in its patriotic role, the PCF intended to make the most of the
exceptional circumstances, not to set up a 'dual power' in French society,
but to secure a number of tactical advantages.

Application of this strategy was not always straightforward. In September and October 1944, the war and the isolation of the regions complicated relations between the base and the leadership. Local figures, like Guingouin in the Limousin, had acquired considerable personal authority over the areas they had helped to liberate. Moreover, the leadership seemed divided: Thorez strove to impose the Soviet analysis from Moscow, but in Algiers those around Billoux and Grenier did not hesitate to criticize de Gaulle, and their leader, the influential André Marty, had spoken of the need for a 'strong and democratic power'. The leader of the clandestine Communist Party in France, Jacques Duclos, seemed closer to Thorez, but he could not ignore the views of those in Algiers. The divisions, both geographical and between leadership and base, were apparent over the role of the CDLs and in the affair of the militia. Little would have been needed to convince many grassroot militants that a violent revolutionary struggle was imminent.[39]

But the Communists were too deeply immersed in society not to measure the scale of the material priorities. At the same time, order began to be restored within the Party, and after the return of Maurice Thorez, his popularity undiminished, the uncertainties and divergences ceased.[40] With the weakness of the country so obvious, the need for discipline was understood as well as accepted. The war was continuing, de Gaulle had not mastered all the problems, and elections were approaching. Without abandoning its overall strategy the Party made a few tactical adjustments, switching the emphasis from national unity to unity of the Left, negotiating from a position of strength with the SFIO and the remnants of the Radicals over a Popular Front tactic. This changed approach testified of course to the failure of the union of the Resistance, but confirmed the Party's capacity to reunite: it now dominated the Left. The PCF had grasped that the real battle of the future was that for reconstruction: this would clearly strengthen the position of the party of the workers, forcing de Gaulle and the Socialists to obtain its co-operation. The PCF had successfully passed the test of the return to the Republic, no doubt the only political victory to count in the eyes of the leadership.[41]

### 'Tout se relâche'

The municipal elections of April–May 1945 provided the parties with their first test and pointed up the imprint of the past on the political system. De Gaulle's announcement to the Assembly on 2 March of his refusal to lead a 'parti unique' left the way clear for the parties. Against the background of the war-weary and exhausted nation, even the old quarrel over education was revived, monopolizing energies and attention and polarizing opinion along the Left–Right division. Since September 1944, the Ligue de l'enseignment and the Syndicat national des instituteurs, both dissolved by Vichy, had been demanding revenge in the form of a nationalization of all teaching and an end to subsidies for Church schools. The education quarrel had clearly lost none of its ability to unite an otherwise divided Left;[42] and the Communists pushed the Socialists to adopt a hard line on the issue in order to deepen the isolation of the MRP. In November 1944, the government had simply renewed the subsidies to the Church schools until the start of the next academic year. But a commission set up to examine the problem failed to find a satisfactory long-term solution, and on 28 March 1945, encouraged by the Communists, the Consultative Assembly voted an immediate end to the subsidies by a large majority. The secular shibboleth had united the Left and provided a serious basis for hopes of a new Popular Front. De Gaulle could afford to ignore this, but the tension was visible, isolating him already from the parties.[43]

The elections, fought under the sign of the union of the Resistance, had to be held even before the return of the prisoners in order to clarify a difficult situation; the provisional municipal delegations were unstable and local conflicts and injustices remained. For the government these elections were the first test of popular loyalty to the institutions of the Resistance; for the parties, however, they were an opportunity to flex new muscles and to reconsider their strategies on the basis of the results. In the first round, on 29 April, the Liberation Committees were completely crushed, the MRP made an unexpected breakthrough, the Radicals and Moderates declined, and the PCF dominated the Left. As always in these elections the results owed much to purely local conditions, but the party leaderships were able to draw the obvious conclusions. In the first round, the PCF had profited from the union of the Left to emerge at its head; in the second round, therefore, it sought to isolate a principal opponent and favour a Popular Front solution. Classed with the Right over the secular principle, the MRP now came under violent attack: 'Machine à Ramasser les Pétainistes' or 'Mensonge, Réaction, Perfidie' were typical slogans of the campaign against it. In the second round the MRP lost ground, winning only 477 communes, compared with roughly 15 600 to the Moderates, 6400 to the Radicals, 4100 to the Socialists and 1400 for the PCF: the MRP's experience provided a pertinent warning to de Gaulle.[44]

After the elections, in the political calm of the summer, the PCF and the CGT worked to encourage a revival of the traditional republican forces, the Radicals and the Ligue des droits de l'homme,[45] mobilizing on the Jacobin theme and the battle for production. The negotiations with the Socialists over organic unity came to nothing: an article by Duclos in *L'Humanité* of 12 June paid a glowing tribute to the achievements of the Soviet Union and reiterated the Party's commitment to follow the example set by Lenin and Stalin. The SFIO congress in August thus recognized that further discussion was pointless, although the same congress's insistence on loyalty to Marxist principles disappointed Léon Blum; re-established as leader and, through the pages of *Le Populaire*, as mentor of the party, Blum had hoped to convince the militants of the need for a modern socialism of the kind he had outlined in *A l'échelle humaine* in 1941. But if fusion was unattainable, faith in unity of action persisted: thus on 23 August, in response to a call from the CGT, the old Délégation des gauches was re-formed. Grouping Communists, Socialists, trade-unionists, and members of the Ligue des droits de l'homme, this was to orchestrate the opposition to de Gaulle over the constitutional project and the elections.

The ordinance of 21 April 1944 laid down that a Constituent Assembly be elected within a year of the Liberation. With Germany defeated and the prisoners returning, the government decided that the time had come to hold the elections. There was disagreement, however, over the procedure to be adopted. Ignoring the protests of the Communists, Radicals, and the CGT who invoked the anti-plebiscitary tradition of the Republic, and against the wishes of the Consultative Assembly's commission, de Gaulle succeeded in imposing a preliminary referendum. The electorate (which now included twelve million women) had two questions to answer: the first was on whether or not the Assembly elected was to be a Constituent Assembly; the second involved approval or rejection of the government's proposals for the period before the new Constitution came into force. Replying No to the first question amounted to a return to the Third Republic; a No response to the second question would set up a completely sovereign Assembly, one in which the Communists were likely to have the upper hand. The government proposals at stake in the second question (which became the law of 2 November 1945) limited the work of the new Assembly to seven months, stipulated that the final project be submitted to a referendum and that in the meantime the government could only be brought down by an absolute majority in a vote of censure. In spite of the attachment of the Radicals to the two-round single-member elections of the Third Republic, a single-round proportional representation was easily accepted as being a more equitable system. It had the advantage of strengthening the party leaderships, alone responsible for establishing lists of candidates, and of avoiding too sharp a Left–Right polarization. The only disagreement arose over the decision to use the *département* as the framework for the elections and over the method of calculating the 'remainders' in the system of proportional representation;[46] on each point, however, de Gaulle imposed his views, leaving the parties to argue among themselves.

De Gaulle, of course, called for affirmative replies to both questions in the referendum, although he did not give his public backing to any list in the elections held the same day. The Communists, counting on the Front

Table 2: *Elections to the Constituent Assembly, 21 October 1945. Electors: 24 626 000; votes: 19 170 000 (77%)*

|  | Votes | % | Seats | Seats in 1936 |
|---|---|---|---|---|
| PCF | 5 011 000 | 26.1 | 148 | 72 |
| MRP | 4 937 000 | 25.6 | 143 | – |
| SFIO | 4 711 000 | 24.6 | 135 | 153 |
| Moderates | 2 785 000 | 14.4 | 65 | 228 |
| Radicals | 1 725 000 | 9.3 | 31 | 145 |

national, the MURF and the CGT after both Socialists and Radicals had refused to join them on a common list, campaigned for a Yes–No response; the SFIO and UDSR, the MRP, and the Moderates all supported the double affirmative; the Radicals alone called for the No–No outcome. The national unanimity of just a few months earlier was forgotten: the parties were eager to go before the electorate, and the campaign was enthusiastic and hard-fought.

Participation in the referendum of 21 October 1945 was average, lower than in 1936, with a 20 per cent abstention rate. As expected, 96 per cent of the voters replied Yes to the first question: an overwhelming rejection of the Third Republic, a régime too closely identified with the defeat of 1940. On the second question, however, the response was more ambiguous; 12.3 million voted Yes, but the No still attracted 6.2 million votes, an important figure, one that reflected the influence of the Communists. In all then, a considerable personal victory for de Gaulle, a relative failure for the Communists – unable to maintain discipline on the question of the sovereign Assembly – and the collapse of the Radicals. But these conclusions have to be strongly nuanced in the light of the elections to the Constituent Assembly held the same day: for as the results for the main parties make clear (Table 2), the electorate had swung sharply to the Left.

The results contained two potential majorities. The basis for a tripartite alliance was emerging: the Communists, MRP, and Socialists between them accounted for more than three-quarters of the votes cast and over 80 per cent of the seats. The alternative was a new Popular Front: even without the support of the Radicals the Communists and Socialists had an absolute majority. In either case the Communists would be in a strong position; with twice as many seats as in 1936 their success was striking, even if not quite the landslide predicted during the campaign. Not only had the PCF retained its strongholds in the industrial regions north of the Loire and in Mediterranean France, but, and thanks to the Resistance and the maquis, it was now established as a major political force in less developed and rural regions, such as the Centre. Compared with this the Socialists were in a much weaker position; their advance had been less spectacular in terms of votes and, caught between minor gains from the Radicals and heavy losses to the PCF, they won fewer seats than in 1936. And the geography of support for the SFIO had shifted, progressing in the areas of the Right but contracting in the traditional strongholds of the Left; its support was now more national but socially less homogeneous. Contrary to Blum's optimistic predictions, the Socialists had not taken the commanding position, a failure which led to fierce criticism of the leadership by the militants. Overshadowed by the PCF, the SFIO was not attracted by the prospect of a Popular Front in which, unlike in 1936, it would now be the weaker partner. And not least since the eclipse of the Radicals was almost total; only local prestige and an absence of opposition from the Right had enabled them to conserve a few pockets of influence; but this sharp contraction in the traditional source of majorities brought instability to the Left and to the parliamentary system as a whole. The second lesson of these elections, and their only innovation, was the rise of the MRP. Solidly implanted in the Catholic regions of the West and East, it had nonetheless won support in the large industrial centres and to the south of the Loire, acquiring a genuinely national audience. Against the background of the Communist advance, the disarray of the Moderates and the vacuum on the Right meant of course that the MRP attracted a conservative electorate and followers of de Gaulle, who were quick to see it as the only bulwark against the 'Marxist bloc': as its secular opponents had hoped, the MRP emerged as strongly identified with the Right. But the new party was not completely frustrated in its initial objectives: the Right had opposed it in seventy-one of ninety-four constituencies; nearly a quarter of its electorate came from the Centre or Left, largely thanks to the efforts of the Christian Democrats before the war; finally, the MRP had captured the largest share of the new electorate, notably among the women.

This first election was, then, a demonstration of continuities and of the extent to which political life had been reconstituted along traditional lines. Indeed, the map of political opinion was now based more than ever on the single and irreducible criterion of religious practice.[47] However, both the Resistance and the CNR programme had made an impact, albeit an indirect one: there were many new parliamentarians, come to politics through the underground struggle; there was a greater homogeneity in the geography of opinion, thanks to the introduction by the MRP of notions of political and social renovation into the Centre and Right. Aspirations toward renewal and for a break with the ideologies of the past were thus clearly expressed. But a conflict over responsibility for realizing them was already developing between de Gaulle and the parties: within a few weeks the rupture would be accomplished. The Communists no longer concealed their hostility to de Gaulle, who for his part was not prepared to concede to the growing demands of the parties in the Assembly. As he summed up the situation: 'Tout se relâche'.

The activities of the Communists in the Délégation des gauches, the source of post-election speculation about a common programme for governing, reinforced the SFIO in its refusal of a concertation of the Left which would isolate the MRP. Faced with this the PCF could only wait, its leadership apparently recognizing that de Gaulle's 'dictatorship' precluded all possibility of a negotiated majority. However, in its capacity as principal political party the PCF proceeded to lay claim to the presidency of the Assembly and to important posts in the government, seeking to organize the debate around itself. This move was frustrated by the insistence of the SFIO and the MRP on the necessity of both a tripartite majority and de Gaulle's presence at the head of the government; they succeeded in this, obtaining the election of a Socialist, Félix Gouin, to the presidency of the Assembly and the unanimous re-election of de Gaulle as leader of the government on 13 November. De Gaulle's steadfast refusal to allow the Communists any of the three key posts – Foreign Affairs, Interior, and National Defence – provoked the furious indignation of the 'parti des fusillés'. But it accepted a compromise solution on 21 November; under this Thorez became a Minister of State, the disputed Defence portfolio was split between Charles Tillon at Armaments and Edmond Michelet (MRP) at Armies; Billoux, Marcel Paul, and Ambroise Croizat received National Economy, Industrial Production, and Labour, all of secondary importance in de Gaulle's eyes; while Bidault and Tixier remained at Foreign Affairs and the Interior. Significant in this episode was that the continued presence of de Gaulle at the head of the government was due to the SFIO and MRP: the legitimacy de Gaulle incarnated was now under the protection of the political parties.

The incompatibility between the constitutional projects of the Assembly and those of de Gaulle soon became apparent. For its part, the Assembly was determined to have complete control over the preparation of the text to go before the people; the Assembly's commission, headed by François de Menthon, did not disguise its hostility to de Gaulle's proposals. The steady worsening of the relations between government and Assembly came to a climax on 30 December during a vote on military expenditure. The Socialists, backed by the Communists, decided to make a stand: despite Vincent Auriol's efforts on behalf of the government to avert the crisis, André Philip for the Socialists demanded a 20 per cent reduction in military expenditure. Only a compromise proposal from the UDSR allowed confidence to be saved, postponing further discussion until 15 February, but on condition that the government had by then deposed military projects acceptable to the Assembly. This was the final straw for de Gaulle:[48] on 20

January 1946, after several days of morose reflection, the General assembled the ministers and announced his resignation. The departure of de Gaulle did not produce a sharp reaction in public opinion;[49] and it eased the reconstitution of political life on the bases he rejected. From his retreat at Marly, de Gaulle awaited the calls for his return he believed would soon come, posing already as the solution to the expected difficulties. His achievement was impressive: the State had been restored in its previous form; the essential parts of the CNR programme had been realized; a national unity born in the Resistance had been enlarged. At the same time, however, de Gaulle had to recognize that the system of elections, parties, and Assembly he had restored no longer required his authority to function. With the ending of the war, the consensus incarnated by de Gaulle had disintegrated: his refusal to become either a dictator or a party leader meant that he was left isolated and unheeded. What remained was an incontestable personal legitimacy, triumphantly acknowledged on the Champs-Elysées on 26 August 1944, but which since had failed to find a political expression: from now on this was to lie at the root of the complex relationship between de Gaulle and the nation. As he reflected: 'My popularity was like a fund from which the disappointments would be paid.'[50]

# 5

# Production

One message was hammered home with insistence in the workplace, by the press and radio, by the authorities: production had to increase. Over this imperative was fought what came to be known as the 'troisième bataille de France', one whose rhetoric called for effort, duty, and patriotism. 'Soldiers of the Reconstruction, let us try to equal our elders, those of the Revolution, who, in rags and tatters, led France on the path of greatness', urged a typical propaganda pamphlet of the time.[1] Nor was it just rhetoric: these months were in fact marked by an atmosphere of disciplined effort in the enthusiasm of recovered liberty. An increase of output would allow the supply problems to be surmounted, the bottlenecks eased, the destruction repaired, and monetary stability restored. And, as the CNR programme had promised, reconstruction was to be accompanied by far-reaching economic and social reform.

The political forces were fully mobilized. The SFIO and the MRP gave their support, though their audience for this theme was limited. For his part, de Gaulle acknowledged that the economy had a contribution to make to national greatness.[2] On 10 September 1944, Benoît Frachon launched 'la grande bataille de la production' in the name of the CGT.[3] The Communist Party threw its weight totally and continuously behind the efforts which were to lay the foundations for the 'renaissance national-ale': at the meetings of the Central Committee of 31 August 1944 and 21 January 1945, as in the PCF's programme for government of 1946, absolute priority went to the economy.[4] Speaking in the mining regions of the Nord on 21 July 1945, Thorez defined production as the highest class duty of the French worker and identified increased output as the weapon with which to defeat the forces of reaction. At the same time, the Right of powerful economic and financial interests was keeping its head down. The employers – whose conspicuous absence from the Resistance de Gaulle had not hesitated brutally to underline – were in disarray. The way was open for change. Under cover of reconstruction, with the 'trusts' neutralized and the workforce galvanized, the State extended its role, grappling with the financial problems, becoming directly involved in production, and assuming responsibility for modifying the balance of social power.

*Living with inflation*

The government's margin for manoeuvre in these early months was slender: production would take many months to revive and the threat of inflation was ever-present. Yet the character of the early measures would clearly be decisive for the subsequent course. Some, like Pierre Mendès France, head of the new Ministry of National Economy, along with the Socialists Tixier, Philip and Moch, argued for an immediate laying of the foundations of a planned economy with a strong nationalized sector. An opposing view, one defended, for example, by Pleven, now Minister of Finance, was that nothing be done until the State was stronger and elections had been held. For their part, the Communists demanded that the interests of the working class be given priority.

The hardening of positions and the first conflict came over the monetary question. Wages, whose real value had declined under Vichy, had to be increased. In Algiers the government had decided to empower the commissaires de la République to negotiate new wage levels in their regions. This had produced abrupt increases of 50 per cent on average; and similar-sized increases in family allowances in October 1944 and in the wages of civil servants in January 1945 generalized the upward revision of incomes. Conversely, prices were frozen and industrial subsidies were maintained. Much of the framework of production erected by Vichy was in fact retained: the Comités d'organisation were simply transformed into Offices professionnels, and the Délégation générale à l'équipement national was absorbed into the Ministry of National Economy.[5] While this waiting policy certainly aggravated the budgetary difficulties (subsidies alone accounted for 85 milliard francs or 20 per cent of expenditure in 1945), it had the advantage of avoiding a brutal widening of the gap between prices and incomes, between production costs and retail prices, at the same time as allowing staged planning to be tried and favouring the reival of production. For Mendès France this was to be the task of his Ministry of National Economy alone, taking priority over the Ministry of Finance, working in a medium-term perspective of two years, and refusing to be deflected from this by the immediate problems.

But the bases of this policy were gradually undermined. In October 1944, for example, pressure from the CGA led to an increase in agricultural prices. And in November, at the insistence of the Ministry of Finance and against the wishes of Mendès France, a large loan issue was made. With this the government showed that it favoured classic measures based on calls to confidence in preference to an authoritarian reduction in the money supply, despite the fact that the latter was at the same time proving effective in Belgium. The loan was in fact a great success, bringing in 164 milliard and reducing the notes in circulation from 642 milliard in April to 572 milliard by Christmas. Nonetheless, in spite of a press campaign, the efforts to recover illegal profits remained half-hearted, the black market persisted, and the affluence of those who had obviously done well out of the war contrasted sharply with the sacrifices being demanded of the workforce. Sensing that 'this deep consensus between a government which knows what it wants and a nation which knows where it is being led' was absent,[6] Mendès France offered his resignation on 18 January 1945, but de Gaulle refused to accept it. The arguments of Mendès France's opponents were not, however, negligible: while the war and hunger continued, unpopularity could be dangerous; until the dynamism of the nationalized sector had been established it would be imprudent to alienate the employers and risk a contraction of production and private investment.

The trial of strength between the two views, between rigour and liberalism, came in February over the question of the new banknotes, now arrived from the United States and Great Britain. Mendès France and Moch called for a delay and a limit to their exchange – partly to facilitate a general survey of bank accounts, partly to restrain personal expenditure. Pleven, on the other hand, backed by the government and public opinion, advocated an immediate and straightforward one-to-one exchange of the new for the old notes. Fears of a slow-down in production, as had occurred in Belgium, and an unwillingness to upset the peasants, led to the adoption of Pleven's solution on 29 March. Mendès France was isolated, without the backing of a major party, weakly supported by the Socialists, abandoned by the MRP, and bitterly attacked by the Communists eager to echo popular grievances and staking all on production. His resignation on 5 April was accompanied by the publication of a long and bitter letter in which he asked whether the new Republic was really going to be based on a policy which favoured the selfish and greedy at the expense of the weak. De Gaulle's response was to point to the weakness of the country as a reason for not creating further upheaval, and to restate his belief that the next few months would bring an improvement.[7]

This conflict was more than one of experts and ministers: at stake were two different views of the future. Mendès France, in the name of the hopes of the younger elements present in the Resistance, rejected the inflationary course because of its implications for future change. He acknowledged that in the short term inflation would lubricate the social frictions; but he saw too that in the long run it would reinforce the status quo. Under the stimulus of inflation, investment could be abandoned to the conventional market forces, thus strengthening the traditional relationship between capital and labour. The deflation advocated by Mendès France – temporary: he was too good a Keynesian not to recognize that inflation would be useful once production had been launched – was to be the opportunity for the introduction of planning based on the public and controlled sectors, with surveillance of the private sector. In this perspective, the current shortages were actually beneficial; putting a premium on rational choices, favouring public investment, and enabling reconstruction, modernization, and the assault on the 'trusts' to be combined. Opposed to Mendès France were, in addition to Pleven, Lacoste, Socialist Minister of Industrial Production; René Mayer, spokesman for the financial interests; Courtin; and Monick, Governor of the Banque de France. They argued that recovery and growth would be anti-inflationary, that investment could be financed through the normal channels of credit and loans, and that the balance between prices and wages could be fixed by decree.[8] The future was to prove them wrong, but at the time it was their view which received the all-important backing of de Gaulle and the Communists. With hindsight it is clear that the future course was settled in spring 1945; however, this certainty should not obscure the fact that – *sur le tas* – concessions to those actually engaged in the struggle for production seemed indispensable if morale and energies were to be sustained.

After the departure of Mendès France, de Gaulle allowed Pleven to add the Ministry of National Economy to his Finance portfolio. The orthodoxy of the rue de Rivoli triumphed completely, and although small-scale plans were drawn up for particular sectors of the economy, no attempt was made to co-ordinate their application. The exchange of banknotes in June went smoothly, and was followed in July by a tax of 'national solidarity' on capital which brought the note circulation down to 440 milliard francs and slightly increased the mass of non-convertible forms and Treasury bonds. But prices had already started to rise. With imports increasing and the elections making concessions necessary, control of agricultural prices was relaxed. And social pressures could no longer be ignored: the strongly hierarchical wage structure negotiated in April by the Minister of Labour, Alexandre Parodi, failed to avoid either the explosion of wages or the disparities between the regions and the sexes. Indeed, at the end of the year the government had to return calamitously to some aspects of the policy it had rejected in April, with heavy subsidies to stabilize the prices of necessities. Worse, the revival of exports was being stifled by the difference between French and foreign prices, the debt was becoming unmanageable and the reserves were emptying: on 25 December the franc was finally devalued, losing more than half its value.[9] The solution adopted underlined France's weakness, even if it served to channel her subsequent borrowing demands more directly to the new International Monetary Fund.

These palliative measures had little impact on the inflation. The black market was as tempting as ever and the budget deficit continued to grow. There had, however, been a significant change in the relationship between

Table 3: (a) *Monthly indices (base 100 in 1938) of prices, incomes and cost of living, 1944–50\**

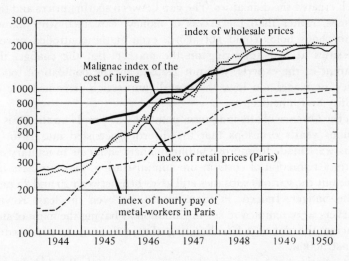

(b) *Half-yearly indices (base 100 in 1938) of incomes, cost of living and purchasing power of incomes (Paris), 1945–49\*\**

|  | weekly wages | | cost of living | purchasing power of weekly wages | |
|---|---|---|---|---|---|
|  | net | with social transfers |  | net | with social transfers |
| 1945 April | 322 | 356 | 590 | 55 | 60 |
| 1945 October | 365 | 403 | 650 | 56 | 62 |
| 1946 April | 402 | 443 | 700 | 57 | 63 |
| 1946 October | 548 | 620 | 950 | 58 | 65 |
| 1947 April | 617 | 698 | 960 | 64 | 73 |
| 1947 October | 760 | 868 | 1250 | 61 | 69 |
| 1948 April | 1014 | 1167 | 1360 | 75 | 86 |
| 1948 October | 1227 | 1436 | 1530 | 80 | 94 |
| 1949 April | 1234 | 1443 | 1600 | 77 | 90 |
| 1949 October | 1272 | 1487 | 1650 | 77 | 90 |

\* *Source:* G. Dupeux, *La France de 1945 à 1965*, Colin, 1969, p. 30. (The Malignac index takes black market prices into account).

\*\* *Source: Mouvement économique en France de 1944 à 1957*, Imprimerie nationale/PUF, 1958, p. 118.

supply and demand of which the inflation was a symptom. With the revival of production it was less the scarcity of produce than its price which created the difficulties. The gap between soaring prices and trailing incomes, rather than the excess of money, explained why many low-income households could not afford, even at the controlled prices, the necessities at last appearing on the market. But the change, though apparent to the experts, was not grasped by the population: too much money or wages too low, the overall impression remained one of inequality and injustice.

In the absence of any long-term policy it was simply on the basis of the previous year's decisions that the disorder persisted into 1946. True, efforts were made to improve public finance, with cuts in military expenditure, a reduction of costs in the administration, and increases in taxation; but the various subsidies still absorbed between 20 and 25 per cent of the budget. Indeed, in these conditions even the least Keynesian observers were tempted to see the inflation as having the merit of steadily reducing the deficit while boosting the revenues urgently needed for reconstruction.

Negotiations to try to halt the wage–price spiral all failed. In spite of the efforts by the Gouin government in February, the so-called Palais-Royal talks had to be opened in the middle of the summer election period. The trade unions demanded an overall 25 per cent wage increase and pressed for a minimum wage and sliding scale, while for the employers the reconstituted CNPF showed its ability for tough bargaining. The settlement finally reached for October by the Bidault government merely confirmed wage increases in excess of 25 per cent. Industrial and agricultural prices soon followed of course, climbing by an average of 50 per cent in the second half of the year. Not until December, when it was too late, did the Blum government attempt to break the vicious circle by imposing an overall 5 per cent price reduction.

Can the gravity of the situation be exaggerated? Was the inflation not simply an inevitable consequence of the revival of production? The dismantling of the war economy aggravated the distortions between agricultural and industrial prices and favoured the production of capital goods at the expense of consumption. Coming in this context, the inflation's positive effect was to increase the value of stocks and widen profit margins, helping to avoid widespread bankruptcies among the less efficient companies, at the same time as stimulating investment and even employment.[10] On the other hand, however, the inflation pointed up the State's failure to arbitrate between the powerful interest groups and the trade unions, its powerlessness to uphold a semblance of justice over food prices, and its inability to restore confidence in the franc. Above all, and this despite the nationalizations and the creation of the Plan on 3 January

1946, there is the fact that the inflationary instability of prices re-established the market economy on one of its natural bases, that characterized by anarchic competition, injustice and, before long, social tensions. The solutions offered by inflation in fact prevented an invigorating shake-up of the economy's productive structures, mitigated the stimulative effects of the new public sector, and contributed to a gradual restoration of precisely the kind of unbridled capitalism anathematized in the CNR programme. Setting up a directed economy implies control of prices: but who at the time was prepared to confront the French public with this certainty? The liberalism adopted instead had the result of reinstalling the competitive impulse at the heart of the economy: the inflation thus stands as a weighty corrective to all the talk of planning and modernization. But could this have been avoided, given that throughout these crucial months the shortages gave such a strong position to those with something to sell?

## Nationalization

A view widely held by members of the Resistance was that the liberation of France would be complete only with the ousting of the 'trusts', a convenient formulation which captured the public's imagination. At the Comité général d'études, René Courtin had drawn up a long report recommending nationalization both to punish the treason of the bourgeois élites of before the war and to provide a framework for the development of a new élite to serve the nation.[11] Very similar themes were explored in the CNR programme, and the left-wing parties were quick to see them as the means for granting the workforce a greater voice in the system of production. In his Chaillot address of 12 September 1944, de Gaulle, though not excluding the principle of free enterprise, acknowledged that the principal sources of wealth had to return to the nation. But while the need for nationalization was thus broadly accepted, the strategic question of the public sector's future role received little serious attention.

Indeed, although the measures taken at this time are often presented as parts of a carefully prepared project, they are in fact more realistically considered as responses to the pressure of events. In this perspective two quite distinct phases can be indentified: the first, of winter 1944–5; the second, from December 1945 to May 1946.

The government had taken over the coalfields of the Nord and Pas-de-Calais on 27 September 1944, suspending the presidents and directors of the companies. An ordinance of 13 December created the Houillères nationales du Nord et du Pas-de-Calais; a decree appointed a new director and a consultative committee, one-third of whose members were drawn from the trade unions, and funds were made available by the State. These measures were imposed by necessity: the urgently needed production of coal could not recommence without the agreement of the miners and their unions, who refused to work under the former directors who had organized requisitioning for the Germans. There were overtly political motives for the sequestration of Louis Renault's factories on 4 October: nationalization, by the ordinance of 16 January, was a punishment for economic collaboration with the Germans. The form of the nationalization was original, however; having seized the factories without compensation, the State dissolved the former company on 15 November and set up in its place the Régie nationale des usines Renault; although under the authority of the Ministry of Industrial Production, the new firm was financially independent and run by its own director and a board composed of representatives of the State, the consumers, and the staff. In fact, the death of Louis Renault on the eve of his trial had removed any final scruples and opened the way for complete confiscation. For the merchant fleet, on the other hand, the ordinance of 18 December 1944 merely extended Vichy's measures concerning the requisition and control of transport by the State; nationalization here came through the acquisition of majority stakes in the companies with compensation for the shareholders. In the case of Gnome et Rhône, aircraft engine manufacturers who had worked for the Germans, the ordinance of 29 May 1945 did not alter the structure and operation of the company; the State simply replaced the compensated shareholders at the head of the new company, the Société nationale d'études et de construction de matériel aéronautique (SNECMA). The same approach was used for air traffic, under the State's control since September 1944 as part of the war effort; this was nationalized on 26 June 1945, with the State taking shares in the various companies, which were regrouped in 1948 to form Air France. In each of these cases, then, empirical solutions were adopted with the aim of restoring production quickly in the vital sectors of transport, fuel, engines, machinery, and vehicles. No coherent legal framework was established, no attempt was made to codify either the compensation procedures or future strategies; speed was the sole imperative.

Nationalization was not the only solution to the problems of production. Some companies had been occupied since the Liberation, their sequestrated property the object of openly collectivist ambitions, often involving worker control. This was the case for the Paris transport network, where pressure from the trade unions and the CDL resulted in a municipal takeover of the TCRP and the creation of the RATP. In Lyon, where Marius Berliet was arrested on 4 September, Yves Farge appointed a communist engineer to run the confiscated Berliet factories; this was the start of a novel social experiment, one based on the active participation of the employees grouped in 'Comités patriotiques d'entreprise'.[12] In Marseille, the requisition of fifteen major companies secured the backing of the trade unions for enabling a return to work in the badly damaged city and formed the framework for an experiment which lasted until 1948. There were similar ambitions and outcomes at the mines of Alès and the Fouga factories in Béziers.[13] In each case, under local pressure from the trade unions and the Resistance, the commissaires de la République gave their blessing to these acts of 'révolution économique' which satisfied the new élites, postponing for later the question of compensation to the owners and allowing the experiments in worker control to progress. The reasons for this – tactical concessions or shared enthusiasms – mattered little: by giving their approval to a *fait accompli* the authorities were able to hasten the revival of production without recourse to nationalization.

A more coherent approach underlay the second phase of nationalization. The lively parliamentary debates this provoked bore witness to a more penetrating analysis of the role of the public sector and State intervention in the economy. Under pressure from the Consultative Assembly, Pleven had to promise in July 1945 that the major nationalizations detailed in the CNR programme would be carried out before the end of the year. In fact, the de Gaulle government realized only one, but its successor completed the rest of the programme. The controversial nationalization of banking and credit was achieved with the law of 2 December 1945. Under this complicated piece of legislation the State became the sole shareholder in the Banque de France and in the four principal deposit banks. However, after a confrontation between de Gaulle and the Left, the latter pressing for a complete control of credit and investment, the commercial banks escaped nationalization; under the solution adopted, the State merely obtained representatives with a right of veto in each of the banks. A Conseil national du crédit was established to advise the minister, its views carrying authority also for the private banking sector. Finally, the Commission de contrôle des banques set up by Vichy retained its task of watching over the levels of reserves covering deposits and credit. But the outcome clearly reflected the changed balance of political force: the choice of ministry to oversee the banking system, a task the Left had hoped would go to that of National Economy, in fact remained with the government; and the increasingly artificial distinction between deposit and commercial banks was formally maintained. The State now had effective control over credit, but its long-term capacity to direct investment was limited.

Nationalization of the insurance companies on 25 April 1946 revealed similar ambiguities. The dispersal of portfolios between more than 900 companies dominated by eleven groups, and the obvious international ramifications, made this a delicate operation. But the measures taken, affecting the thirty-four firms who between them accounted for over 60 per cent of the enormous capital held by the insurance companies, betrayed the hesitancy of the legislators. Only the Communists had called for complete nationalization; the other parties wavered, torn between favouring the interests of the policy-holders or those of the State, strongly tempted by the size of the reserves at stake. Conversely, nationalization of the gas and electricity industries, realized by the law of 8 April 1946 and prepared by the Communist Minister of Industrial Production, Marcel Paul, demonstrated an unequivocal resolve to assume total control of this vital sector. Differences arose here, however, over the structures to be established. The Communists argued for a single company, but the other parties were daunted by the sheer complexity of a production and distribution to meet industrial, domestic, and collective needs and by the diversity of the existing companies. The solution adopted set up two public corporations, the EDF and GDF, each with a monopoly of production and distribution, supervised by the Ministry of Industry but financially autonomous. A number of exceptions were made: small gas plants, the cokeries of the mines, and bottled and natural gas for the GDF; the power stations of the mines, the SNCF, the iron and steel industries, and the hydroelectric installations of the Rhône for the EDF. And distribution was to be organized later on a regional basis, using the schedules left by the former suppliers. The result was sprawling and unwieldy: but what was essential had been achieved; to satisfy the growing energy demand which was the key to production. The same rationale lay behind the law of 17 March 1946 which extended the regional measures on coal of 1944 to cover output of all combustible minerals, setting up a national company, the Charbonnages de France, to oversee nine subsidiaries in the mining basins.

Both phases of nationalization reflect the weight of circumstances. Time was short and output had to increase: the struggle for economic survival stimulated the latent *dirigiste* instincts of the State, and nationalization was the result. The same imperative was decisive in the choice of leaders for the new public sector, drawn in fact from among the existing and experienced managers in each industry and from the body of high officials which had taken shape under Vichy. Recruiting a new élite from the trade unions, as was tried with some success by Socialist and Communist administrators, notably at the EDF, would in most cases have taken too long. Thus, despite the efforts of Marcel Paul in this sense, the new managerial élite was not drawn principally from the Resistance: once again the rapid return to order imposed continuity. This appointment of experts from the public and private sectors did much to lay the foundations of a future technocratic power. The Régie Renault offers a good illustration of this. Robert Lacoste had originally intended to appoint trade-unionists and CGT officials, like Emile Perrin, to its management. But Lacoste's solution was rejected: instead a classic industrialist, Pierre Lefaucheux, former member of the Comité général d'études and an ardent defender of a dynamic capitalism against creeping *étatisme*, was appointed to run the company. He quickly gave proof of his independence: ignoring instructions from the Plan to concentrate on heavy goods vehicles, he launched the Renault 4 CV in October 1946. Production of this successful car began in August 1947 on American-style assembly lines, and was shortly followed by the introduction of automated machines which were to revolutionize mass production methods.[14] The urgent need to produce was at the origin of a nationalized sector open to innovation and able to make good use of heavy investment. Not surprisingly, it soon became the favoured destination of American aid for reconstruction.

The role of political objectives connected with nationalization is harder to gauge. The themes of an anti-capitalist rejuvenation were in fact mingled with the postulates of a technocratic planning.[15] For the Communists, the CGT and many of the workers directly affected, the extension of the public sector was to be an irreversible step, the source of hopes that labour, the decisive factor in the revival of production, would soon receive its just political rewards. The PCF thus abandoned its traditional hostility to nationalization, an attitude still present in the 1935 discussions of the Popular Front programme. But its new analysis was superficial. Combining the Jacobin heritage with respect for the Soviet model, the PCF was at pains to stress that nationalization was in no sense a socialist measure, but merely a development of traditional republican policies to strengthen democracy and increase the nation's economic independence and prosperity. The new favourable attitude was thus accompanied by no serious reflection over the role the nationalized industries would have in the evolution of monopoly capitalism or in a nascent technocracy.[16] True, without the efforts of the Communists in the government, the Assembly, and in the companies themselves, the changeover would certainly have been less straightforward and less complete; but their analysis led them to defend with success a version of nationalization which was closely tied to the State. The contribution to the battle for output was incontestable, but in the process the streamlining of the State suffered.

The Socialists were no less committed to output, but they saw nationalization as a genuine step towards the socialization of the economy and hence as part of the transition to socialism. In the tradition of Albert Thomas and the *planistes* of the 1930s, they argued for the autonomy of the nationalized companies *vis-à-vis* the State, both in matters of production and marketing and in their control, where the community as a whole was to be represented alongside personnel. This version of nationalization with a high degree of autonomy came under strong attack from the PCF, and the CGT was rocked by the debate. For their part, the MRP and CFTC also favoured autonomy for the public companies, but in fact saw this as a means to strengthen the capacity of the nominally neutral State to act as arbiter. Indeed, the logic of their approach enabled them to support de Gaulle over compensation to the former owners, to back the Communists over the authority of the State, while joining the Socialists over the desirability of financial and administrative autonomy! Finally, de Gaulle, though receptive to the *étatisme* of the Communists' proposals, firmly resisted the use of nationalization as a punishment, rejected spoliation, and was opposed to tight control by the trade unions.

There were important divergences, then, over the definition of long-term objectives as well as over details: by 1946 the ambiguities were increasingly obvious. For example, thanks to the concerted vigilance of de Gaulle and the MRP and the SFIO, the compensation procedures were favourable to the former shareholders. Yet to meet the obligations thus created, the new national companies were too often forced to make large bond issues, at the risk of exhausting their reserves with interest and capital repayments and, above all, of weakening their capacity for investment. Likewise, the diversity of their juridical statutes reduced the coherence of the public sector as a whole. The statute of *régie* gave Renault and the RATP considerable autonomy but reinforced the position of the managing director appointed by the government; the SNECMA and Air France were mixed participation companies; the EDF, the GDF, and the Charbonnages de France had the status of national corporations whose presidents were elected internally by the Conseil d'administration, subject only to approval by the government. In theory, each Conseil d'administration was composed of representatives of the State, consumers, and personnel: workers and managers; in practice, however, representatives of personnel were always in a minority, those of the State dominated thanks to their control of finance, while the 'consumers' were often spokesmen for the major industrial customers of the nationalized industries. Lastly, overall policy for the public sector remained extremely vague. Initially, no doubt, such flexibility favoured the rapid recovery of output; in the longer term, however, the dispersal of ministerial responsibilities in the absence of a strong Ministry of National Economy and the importance of Treasury experts in setting pricing policies, tended to limit the contribution of the public sector to the economy. Nonetheless, to begin with, until 1947, its vanguard role in one new domain helped to form a favourable overall judgement of its performance: for the public sector became the showcase for the government's social policy.

### The 'New Deal'

The moment was in effect propitious for social reforms touching both family life and the workplace. The ambitions of the CNR programme, the complexion of the parliamentary majority, de Gaulle's own enthusiasm for participation, the eclipse of the *patronat*, and the new vitality of the trade unions: for a few months all the circumstances favoured action to relieve the bitter atmosphere of social revenge which had dominated since autumn 1936.

The ordinance of 22 February 1945 making the creation of comités d'entreprise (works councils) obligatory in all companies employing 100 or more workers was an attempt to bring far-reaching changes to the heart of the productive system. The principle had been recognized in cabinet on 29 September 1944: a stop had to be put to the 'gestions sauvages', repetitions of Berliet had to be avoided. The measures were an extension of the 1936 law on staff representation, but also took into account the achievements of the comités sociaux set up by Vichy. The comités d'entreprise, elected from lists drawn up for the first round by the trade unions, were to be convened once a month by the employers; they were to control the *oeuvres sociales* (welfare and social activities) of the firm, something already prepared for by Vichy's *Chartre du travail*; they could examine the company's accounts (to the horror of the employers who claimed secrecy to be vital for competition), were to receive reports on the company's progress and could ask questions. Although primarily consultative bodies, the comités d'entreprise would become – so it was claimed by the Socialists and Communists – an important instrument within the private sector of the new directed economy.

The reality was both more modest and more ambiguous. The employer's monopoly of direction and decision-making was untouched; in many cases the views expressed by the comités d'entreprise were simply ignored; their role was typically limited to that of running the various *oeuvres sociales*. Furthermore, the demands of the workforce could henceforth be formulated only by its elected representatives. Thus in spite of the high claims made for them, the task of the comités d'entreprise was basically one of co-operation: they served in fact to institutionalize – entirely consistent in this respect with the ambitions of 1936 – trade union activity. Under the law of 16 May 1946, the measures were extended to cover private and public companies employing fifty or more workers; that of 23 December 1946 re-established collective bargaining, though stipulated that the negotiation of wages and differentials by branch remained the responsibility of the Ministry of Labour. The social progress realized within companies by these measures, this 'révolution par la loi', was less than had been hoped for, and only the public sector respected scrupulously the letter and spirit of the new legislation.

The return to free trade unions, on the other hand, satisfied one of the ambitions of the Resistance at the same time as maintaining a minimal organizational framework around production. The government in Algiers had abolished Vichy's *Chartre du travail* on 27 July 1944, restoring property and rights to the trade unions in existence in September 1939 and returning in effect to the labour legislation of 1884 and 1920. However, special commissions were set up to organize the *épuration* in the trade unions, and a close watch was maintained over the employers' and agricultural organizations whose sympathies were the most suspect. Furthermore, a circular of 28 May 1945 from Parodi announced that free trade unions of suitable size would henceforth be considered by the public authorities as representative bodies, the main criteria for recognition being the union's wartime record and its diligence in the application of the new social legislation. The sense of these developments is clear: the trade unions were now free, but they were in danger of losing their liberty of action by becoming the unquestioning instruments of the State's policies for reconstruction. The role of the trade unions was increasingly one of official and compulsory dialogue, of support for a social policy in whose elaboration they had no part.

Here too, however, the immediate problems overshadowed the long-term risks. Working-class trade-unionism, reconstituted in the clandestine struggle and represented on the CNR, assumed its new responsibilities without hesitation. The CGT, openly active since 27 August 1944, was under the firm leadership of Benoît Frachon, and Léon Jouhaux did not recover the post of Secretary-General until his return from Germany in May 1945. The decision of the Confederal Bureau on 5 September (by 89 to 45 votes) to split the post of Secretary-General between Frachon and Jouhaux was a clear sign of the extent and effectiveness of the infiltration of the CGT achieved by the Communists during the Resistance and since the Liberation.[17] Not that this development created difficulties with the government; relations between the CGT, and the Socialists and Communists now in the government, such as Lacoste and Croizat, were excellent; the CGT did not hesitate to throw all its forces into the battle for production. The union's strength grew accordingly: the Popular Front records were broken, and by the end of 1945 more than 5 million membership cards had been issued. True, this inflation of numbers was no remedy for the chronic weakness and division of French working-class trade-unionism; but the notion of representativity and the commitment to the policies of reconstruction fixed the unions in the role of acknowledged social partners, responsible for disciplining the workforce.

One newer feature in this circumstantial unanimity was the enthusiasm at all levels of the economy for organization and legal representation, an aspiration born in the 1930s and one that Vichy had attempted to satisfy. In spite of the boost given to unity by the underground struggle, the CFTC, with just 700000 members, continued to offer its own Christian Democrat version of working-class trade-unionism, and definitively rejected fusion with the CGT in September 1945. Similar aspirations among managerial staff resulted in the creation of an ambitious Confédération générale des cadres (CGC) on 15 October 1944, to which the Ministry of Labour was forced to grant representative status in summer 1946. In October 1946, after a series of strikes, civil servants finally obtained the right to trade unions, as well as a general statute for public sector employment drawn up by Thorez on lines proposed by the CGT.[18] Lastly, with Vichy's Corporation Paysanne dissolved, the pre-war agricultural organizations merged on 2 October 1944 to form the Confédération générale de l'agriculture (CGA),[19] whose initial aims, as we have seen, were to orchestrate opposition to pressure from the authorities and to bargain over support for policies of reconstruction. Within agriculture, the *métayers* and *fermiers*, backed by the left-wing parties, obtained a degree of satisfaction, with the law of 13 April 1946 setting a nine-year minimum for tenancies and giving juridical recognition for the first time to the crucial practical distinction between the farm and the land on which it stood. Here too, however, aspirations for change were satisfied in a well-prepared context, in this case by the law of 4 September 1943.

Where were the employers in this ferment? In fact, a temporary eclipse was the price the *patronat* now paid for a deep involvement in Vichy's National Revolution and for a conspicuous absence from the Resistance. Under pressure from the legislators, faced with the problems of production, and with an extremely limited political audience, the employers renounced organized action, and withdrew into isolated and piecemeal negotiation. De Gaulle and Parodi soon became uneasy over their silence and in October 1944 tried to fill the vacuum by appointing Étienne Villey to set up a Commission de représentation patronale.[20] From his side, Lacoste was making similar efforts to re-establish contact, creating a Commission consultative pour l'aide aux entreprises. But both bodies, too obviously linked to the government, met with a cool reception from the employers. A few of the more progressive elements did, however, begin to participate in some of the other new structures being set up (such as the Ecole nationale d'administration (ENA) or the Comité central des prix), establishing contact here with the top officials responsible for running the public sector and preparing the Plan. Nonetheless, for several months the dominant attitude among the employers was one of distrust and isolation that no amount of pressure could alter.

The myth of the *patronat* as drastically weakened and deliberately excluded from dialogue at this time has, however, to be discarded. The most powerful interests, it is true, did adopt a prudent low profile. But, for example, the Confédération générale des petites et moyennes entreprises (CGPME) of Léon Gingembre quickly revealed its ability to mobilize the discontent of the retailers and small employers. From October 1944 the CGPME was active in organizing their resistance to the authoritarian economic controls; in January 1945, faced with the threat of a total collapse of distribution networks, the government was forced to grant it official recognition. Likewise, the Jeunes patrons organization was reconstituted. And finally, on the eve of the October 1945 elections, the most powerful economic interests broke their self-imposed silence. The giants of petrol, metallurgy, engineering, electricity, mining, and retailing, names like Serrigny, Mercier, Peyerimhoff, and Wendel, began organizing strategy and electoral funds, listening now to the views of the semi-official commissions. A liaison committee called a meeting for 21 December 1945: at this the CNPF was formed, which adopted its official statutes six months later. The old structure, under which the productive and distributive sectors were grouped together, was retained; and the CNPF's principal leaders, Pierre Ricard and Georges Villiers, adopted a relaxed approach, co-operating over the new legislation and the Plan. What is clear, however, is the extent to which the productive imperative had overcome initial hesitations and the rapid way in which, all things considered, the *patronat* had re-formed its official representative body and pressure groups: when conditions changed it would recover its pugnacity. At every level of the social hierarchy then, and with varying degrees of enthusiasm, the battle for production brought into being a solid range of spokesmen, representatives, and pressure groups.

Post-war France's 'New Deal' was cemented by an important innovation, one intended to transform the condition of the workers and to give complete meaning to the policy of social justice: an ambitious Social Security system. The 'revolution' which for many was to follow the Liberation did, with this system, touch the everyday lives of a large section of the population.

The first steps had been taken with two ordinances of 30 December 1944 to raise contributions. Two further ordinances (4 and 19 October 1945) regrouped all the existing insurance schemes into a single organization and made adherence to Social Security obligatory for all wage-earners; reciprocal agreements were to allow foreign workers to participate. The insurance contributions were set at 6 per cent of the wage for the worker and 10 per cent for the employer; family allowance contributions were fixed at a uniform level of 12 per cent; the threshold wage for contributions by the wage-earners was set at a low level. The worker's share was deducted at source and sent with that of the employer to the Social Security office in each *département*. The cover was to be truly national, with a network of regional and national offices set up to compensate for disparities between regions or professions. From the outset the Social Security system covered sickness, old age, handicap, death, and accidents at work (and from October 1946 the last, along with occupational diseases, were charged to the employer alone). Approximately 9 million Frenchmen and their families were directly affected by the introduction of daily sickness allowances, an 80 per cent reimbursement of medical costs, the right to a pension in excess of 20 per cent of the highest wage, and a death insurance scheme. And from August 1946 the Social Security offices took over the running of the various family benefits (maternity, single-income, and nursing allowances) now available to all and at the same level. The only payments not to come under their control were those for unemployment, which remained the responsibility of the State. Subsequent measures were still more ambitious: the Croizat law of 22 May 1946 prepared the way for obligatory social insurance for all, and in September, somewhat over-confidently given the economic realities, 1 January 1947 was set as the date for making the old age insurance cover general. Lastly, the principle of the control of the system by the contributors themselves through elected administrators was accepted in July 1946, after a proposal to confine the running of the Social Security offices to the trade unions alone had foundered on stiff opposition from the CGC and the MRP.[21]

Inevitably it took time to make the system comprehensive: cover for all non-wage-earners did not finally come until August 1967! There were administrative difficulties, imbalances, and delays; the general system co-existed with a variety of autonomous schemes – in the mines, the EDF, and for civil servants; family allowances became independent again under a law of 21 February 1949 imposed by the MRP which distinguished policy over the family from social security; and the old age insurance scheme had to be overhauled in January 1948 before it could be extended the following year to cover 15 million individuals. Artisans, peasants, retailers, and managers were prominent among the social groups who refused the obligatory principle or clung to a corporative system. Moreover, with the employers' contributions rising faster than in neighbouring countries a pause was necessary until output had risen. Above all, there was the inbuilt weakness of a system which treated the symptoms while doing little to attack the causes, a system whose rapidly rising expenditure simply reflected the widespread aspirations to greater well-being and better health. Yet in spite of these shortcomings the main ambitions of 1945 had been realized. The new system was based on the principle of *solidarité* (that is, contributions were not simply totalized to the credit of individuals but were immediately made available to all the members); it was on its way to becoming comprehensive; it was run democratically, with the State merely overseeing its operation and meeting the unavoidable early deficits. Finally, with contributions proportional to incomes but payments the same for all, the system made significant social transfers possible: collective obligation thus became an element of a redistributive economic and social policy. By 1949 payments of one sort or another from the Social Security system represented 12 per cent of gross household incomes.

In conclusion, however, it is worth bearing in mind that neither the advances in social policy nor the stronger organizational framework around producers could compensate for the damaging effects of inflation, or dissimulate the scale of the immediate problems. The battle for production was long and hard, and the beneficial effects of redistribution and the public sector were slow to be felt. The first Plan was not approved and financed until January 1947; until then its experts could only collect information and advise on the most urgent priorities. Labour shortages persisted, and the inflation continued its insidious work of demoralization, upsetting fore-casts, reinforcing inequalities, and fuelling social unrest. True, by 1947 industrial output reached its 1938 level, labour productivity was rising, and the economy appeared to have recovered its suppleness and dynamism. But this more optimistic picture had a darker social side: between 1944 and 1948 the average working week increased from 40 to 45 hours; the pur-chasing power of wages was between 20 and 25 per cent down on pre-war levels and had dropped by 30 per cent since the Liberation.[22]

# 6

# France in the world

Military victory did not remove the question mark which hung over the future position of France among the nations of the world. This uncertainty was only increased by the growing awareness of the extent to which even France's internal affairs were now shaped by forces beyond her control. Henceforth, this consideration was to haunt French foreign policy. True, the attitude of haughty independence adopted by de Gaulle was comforting for a population preoccupied with material difficulties and the domestic political situation. But alone it scarcely constituted a durable solution to the question of the position of a seriously weakened and diminished France in a post-war world dominated by the superpowers, nor to that over the future of her Empire.

*Greatness without means*

De Gaulle, of course, had no hesitation and subordinated his entire policy to the pursuit of greatness for France. His goals were threefold. First, to restore a French presence in all the areas where France had exercised sovereignty in 1939. Secondly, to participate fully at every stage of the post-war settlement. Thirdly, to secure a definitive curtailment of Germany's potential for harm. His methods had not changed since London and Algiers: compensating for weakness with intransigence, taking decisions alone, and exploiting the least incident to expose long-term objectives. His diplomacy, in the tradition of Bismark, favoured situations where a balance of force was decisive and where obstinacy on the essential points could if necessary be combined with trickery. De Gaulle's undisputed position as national leader in the months after the Liberation enabled him to impose his objectives, setting both the tone and the direction of future policy.

His efforts to recover greatness for France encountered no opposition from the political forces. The CNR programme took for granted that France's universal mission required power and glory, though gave little guidance on how they were to be exercised. The antifascism of the Resistance embraced a hope for a fraternal and democratic Europe in which France, as in 1848, would lead the way. This period was in fact marked by an upsurge of nationalism, providing a welcome diversion from the humiliation of everyday life, and one to which all shades of political opinion, including the Communists, contributed. This explains why de Gaulle's departure was not followed by any radical shift in French foreign policy: the objectives he had set went unquestioned, and Georges Bidault and the MRP were the guarantors of continuity in the approach to foreign affairs.[1] Not that conditions favoured a serious reappraisal of French foreign policy. Public opinion remained blissfully ignorant of France's diminished international stature, the inexperienced parliamentarians were unfamiliar with the diplomatic procedures and realities, and the political parties paid surprisingly little attention to foreign policy. There was a tendency to be satisfied with rhetoric and the taking of small revenges. Indeed, in many respects the prevailing attitude is reminiscent of that over the *épuration*, a collective refusal to confront a possibly unpalatable reality.[2]

A number of early episodes revealed both the scale of French ambitions and the limits to their realization. Churchill had a rapturous greeting in Paris on 11 November 1944, but the talks failed to uncover a basis for an Anglo-French alliance, and de Gaulle had no difficulty in avoiding being drawn into too close a relationship with the most European but the weakest of the three great powers. Conversely, he had high hopes for an alliance with the Soviet Union. After all, the USSR had been the first of the powers to recognize the France Libre movement back in the difficult days of September 1941: de Gaulle saw in such an alliance the means to isolate Germany definitively and to lend weight to French diplomacy *vis-à-vis* Roosevelt and Churchill. As is clear from his *Mémoires de guerre*, de Gaulle attached considerable importance to his meeting with Stalin in Moscow at the beginning of December,[3] and it may well have influenced the loyalty of the Communists in France. In diplomatic terms, however, the outcome was meagre: the security pact signed on 10 December merely echoed those of 1892 and 1936; de Gaulle acknowledged Soviet ambitions in Eastern Europe, tacitly accepted the setting of Germany's eastern border on the Oder–Neisse line while refusing to commit himself over the Polish question. But in return he failed to get firm Soviet support for his German policy: at Yalta a few weeks later Stalin did not conceal from Roosevelt that he had found the French leader lacking in realism. For his part, de Gaulle had no doubts that Roosevelt alone was responsible for the open exclusion of France from the conference; a conviction which accounted for his brusque rejection of the American leader's invitation to meet him in Algiers in February 1945, arguing that the head of the provisional government could not accept being 'summoned to part of the national territory by a foreign Head of State'.[4] Reticence and tension towards the English-speaking Allies and unconditional openness towards the Soviet Union appear, then, as the keynotes of French foreign policy in the months immediately after liberation.

Not surprisingly, then, it was the German question which monopolized French attention.[5] At the time of Yalta and Hiroshima this was presented to domestic opinion as the central issue of the day.[6] The French position, nurtured on memories of 1815 and 1919, was unequivocal. Germany had to abandon pretensions to a centralized Reich so obviously prone to expansionist urges. French authority was to be established on the left bank of the Rhine and in the Saar. These territorial inroads on the hereditary enemy were to be completed by an internationalization of the Ruhr and by heavy reparations in coal, machines, and money. Finally, the diplomatic settlement would be cemented by the presence of French forces in the contested territories.

This policy, one of fragmenting a nation in order to make it democratic, at the same time as exploiting it economically, one which saw Nazism as the natural culmination of the entire German national experience, made the French position at the Nuremberg Trials a delicate one. Whatever the skill of the French jurists, it was hard to argue for the punishment of a whole people while denying it the physical means for moral repentance! On the other hand, the hard-headed French approach came to terms easily with the military occupation of a number of zones originally accorded to the Americans and British in Berlin, the Saar, the Palatinate, the Southern Rhineland, then in Baden, Wurtemburg, and Hesse. Disregarding the historical realities of the southern Länder, the French took over areas which, given the behaviour of de Lattre's troops, only Great Britain and the United States were willing to grant them. Indeed, Stalin, whose gains in the East were not contested, refused to give up any of his Berlin zone. However, these territorial gains, along with the various economic and financial compensations (the Paris Conference of November–December 1945 accorded France 20 per cent of the total reparations) were in fact the last concessions France would obtain from the Allies. From now on, the Allies held firm over the fundamental questions of a decentralized Germany, the internationalization of the Ruhr, and the annexation of the Rhineland. The Americans, anxious not to see Germany slide under Soviet influence, were already providing extensive material aid to avoid complete chaos in the defeated country and from September 1946 were actively committed to German economic and political reconstruction. At the Moscow Conference in March 1947, France had to bow to this outcome.

That the French policy had failed is hardly surprising. The legitimacy de Gaulle bestowed on French policy after the Liberation must not be underestimated, but a glance at the chronology is sufficient to show that France owed her place in the international settlement above all to the goodwill of Great Britain and the United States. In October 1944, for example, France was not invited to the Dumbarton Oaks talks where the bases for the United Nations Organization were prepared, though the Allies agreed to grant her a seat on the Security Council. Similarly, it was Churchill who informed de Gaulle in Paris on 11 November that France would in fact be allowed to sit on the European Consultative Committee, which, however, had just completed its first task, that of defining the three zones and a statute for Berlin. France was absent from the crucial conferences of 1945 at Yalta, San Francisco, and Potsdam, and hence had no voice in the decisions which marked the future of the whole of Europe. Even her role of occupying power France owed to Churchill's persistent pleading of her case. Ostensibly, of course, the outcome was encouraging: from the autumn of 1945 France participated in the regular meetings of the Allied Foreign Ministers and she had a full right of veto in the United Nations. But if France was offered the role of a superpower her ability to fill it looked doubtful.

France had now to seek a solution to her economic difficulties through American dollar diplomacy. The United States brought the lend-lease contracts to an end on 21 August 1945. Under the terms of the Bretton–Woods agreements, debtor nations were henceforth obliged to seek loans from the dollar-dominated International Monetary Fund and the International Bank for Reconstruction and Development. True, France obtained the inclusion of the Saar in the French currency zone and the possibility of paying in francs for Iraqi petrol. But in December 1945 the French government was forced to ask for a 550 million dollar loan from the Export–Import Bank to finance essential purchases of machines and raw materials. In return, of course, came the first French concessions over the question of a centralized German administration.[7] The Gouin government sent Léon Blum, Emmanuel Monick, and Jean Monnet to Washington in spring 1946 to plead the French monetary, economic, and social case. The Blum-Byrnes agreements of 28 May which resulted made the war debt interest-free and allowed its total to be added to the loans for use in reconstruction. In return for this important help, however, the French negotiators had, in addition to giving some far from socialist reassurances over the role of nationalization, to promise free access to the French market for American products.[8] In spite of Blum's assertions to the contrary, it is not unrealistic to see this as the start of a major realignment in French diplomatic and economic positions. The pursuit of greatness had given way to an extremely one-sided financial and economic bargaining which left little doubt as to France's impoverished status.

*What future for the Empire?*

The appetite for greatness was no better served by the Empire. It had made a capital contribution to the victory, accepting heavy human sacrifices,

European and native, mobilizing its financial and material resources, and providing the Allies with important air and naval bases. Consequently, the Empire seemed certain to make a contribution to France's new struggle, that for the restoration of her rank among the nations of the world: the imperial mystique was now carried to a level rarely equalled in the history of French colonialism. But evolution in the overseas territories was too advanced, economic and financial exploitation was too strong and the global context of colonialism too profoundly altered for this comforting illusion to endure for long.[9] Acceptance of the reality was to prove difficult, even tragic, and did not come until much time and many opportunities had been lost.

A brief look at the recent past is necessary to understand this evolution. Whereas Vichy's propaganda had presented the Empire as holding hope for the future, de Gaulle, taking a diametrically opposed position, had condemned the armistice by insisting on the importance of the French colonies to the Allied effort in a conflict soon to become global. For its part, the strongly Jacobin antifascism of the Resistance within France (and including the Communists) had produced a consensus over the colonies: the extension to the overseas territories of the Republican liberties recovered by the population of metropolitan France would, it was claimed, assure the future of a rejuvenated Empire. If little attention was given to the notion of the community of peoples, that of a democratic France with 100 million equal citizens was exalted.

These intentions, more liberal than emancipatory, were discussed at the Brazzaville Conference at the end of January 1944 attended by the colonial governors, the administrators of the Maghreb territories, and members of the Consultative Assembly in Algiers.[10] The purpose of the Brazzaville Conference was not to examine the wishes of the colonial peoples themselves, but merely to consider future relations between metropolitan France and her Empire. De Gaulle declared that progress in French Africa would only come if the people could 'raise themselves little by little to a level where they could participate in running their own affairs'. But the Conference's work and discussions revealed the hesitations and contradictions which were to shape the future. The Conference braved the wrath of the commercial and colonial lobbies with its recommendations for an end to forced labour, changes in customs laws, industrial development, and a massive education effort. It angered many civil servants and *colons* with proposals for a Federal Assembly respectful of local life and liberties, and by its rejection of a centralized imperial administration. Lastly, of course, the Conference aroused high hopes among the colonial peoples. Yet its participants continued to hesitate between the traditional French colonial ideal of assimilation and the new notion of federation. Furthermore, the liberalism of the Conference's recommendations sat uneasily with the basic principle laid down at the start of its work and reiterated at the end, namely that 'the civilizing mission accomplished by France in the colonies precludes any idea of autonomy and all possibility of evolution outside the French imperial bloc. Self-government, even in the distant future, is out of the question.' More than ever, 'the political authority of France is to be exercised with precision and rigour over all the territory of her Empire'.

Still, despite these ambivalences, Brazzaville had recognized the principle of a Federal Union or French Federation, something de Gaulle was at pains to stress in Washington on 10 July. By March 1945 a number of high colonial officials and the ministers Pleven and then Giacobbi had accepted the notion of the integration of the colonized territories and states into a sovereign 'French Union'. The dynamic of the proposed Union was to come from the extension to the overseas territories of French Republican principles. A series of legal measures prepared the new structure. An ordinance of 7 March 1944 established equality between French and Muslims for public employment in Algeria. The same ordinance opened the first electoral college, that of the French, to 70 000 Muslims, and placed all the Algerians aged over 21, a total of 1.5 million voters, in a second college responsible for electing the local assemblies in which the proportion of Muslims was raised to two-fifths. In September 1945 this reformed two-college system was extended to all the overseas territories. The reforms continued, somewhat pell-mell: the principle of representation of all the colonies in the Constituent Assembly (August 1946), complete juridical assimilation for Oceania (March 1945), the granting of *département* status to Martinique, Guadeloupe, Guiana, and Réunion (19 March 1946), the abolition of forced labour and the promise of an overhaul of colonial law. What remained unclear, however, was whether this reforming zeal was in preparation for the assimilation or emancipation of the colonies.

The ambiguity was not resolved and the French Union established by the Constitution of 1946 bore its imprint. The juridical and political structures of this complex framework for French influence were the source of lengthy discussion and revisions, particularly after the rejection of the first constitutional project on 5 May 1946, and came to occupy an important place in the domestic political debate (see Chapter 7). The sixty-four overseas parliamentarians participated actively in the preparatory work, and without adopting any violently nationalistic positions. But they were unable to prevent the meeting of the 'états généraux de la colonisation française' in the summer of 1946, which mobilized the representatives of the conservative forces of metropolitan France and the powerful colonial interest groups. Moreover, in the second Constituent Assembly, which voted on the project presented by the Socialist Marius Moutet, the Left no longer had the majority.[11] Instead of providing a flexible general framework whose details could have been decided later by an overseas Assembly elected on universal suffrage – a solution rejected by the then premier, Georges Bidault – the outcome was a rigid and definitive structure handed down from Paris.

The Preamble to the new Constitution affirmed confidently that France would never use her force against the liberty of another people.[12] Yet its three final paragraphs dealing with the French Union were confused and contradictory. Was the equality they proclaimed one between groups or between individuals? Did they offer full French citizenship to all the colonial peoples, or merely a federation of equal peoples? And to what extent was a full equality of rights compatible with the 'traditional mission' of France which, to the satisfaction of Radicals and Moderates, was reiterated here in terms reminiscent of nineteenth-century colonialism? Some of these uncertainties were clarified in Title VIII of the Constitution, but this in turn established the profound distinctions upon which the new French Union was in fact to rest. The first element of the French Union was the 'indivisible' French Republic; this was composed of metropolitan France, Algeria (promised a special statute), the overseas *départements* and territories (the former colonies). These were to elect representatives to the French Parliament and were placed under the authority of the government in Paris. The second category of membership of the French Union was that of the associated states and territories; their populations would have citizenship not of France but of the French Union. However, the status of the associated states within the Union was determined by the nature of their existing formal relationship with France: thus for Tunisia, Morocco, Indo-China, and the territories under United Nations mandates, nothing had in fact changed. The central institutions of the French Union – its president (a position held automatically by the president of the Republic), the High Council, and the Assembly[13] – were given only minor advisory or consultative functions: real legislative power remained with the French Parliament, where, not surprisingly, the overseas representatives were soon to focus their energies. Federation, self-government, and eventual emancipation had all been rejected: in their place, metropolitan France imposed a French Union which, for all the possibility of evolution offered in article 75 of the Constitution, merely attempted to integrate the former colonies with France while offering the other members of the Empire a hollow associative status. Tightly corseted in the constitutional framework, evidence of a refusal to recognize a rapidly evolving reality, the French Union risked early atrophy.

The dangers became clear when the new structure had to confront growing aspirations to national independence it could neither satisfy nor contain. Compared with those of Great Britain and the Netherlands, France's approach in this field already seemed outdated. Behind this lay a failure to measure the change wrought on the colonial context by the war. To begin with there was the powerful stimulus the struggle against Fascism had given to national patriotisms, particularly among members of the colonial forces. Secondly, the war had undermined the unity of the French Empire: Vichy and France Libre had disputed the African and Levantine territories; North Africa had been the theatre for the triangular conflicts between de Gaulle, Giraud, and the Americans; and Indo-China had remained deeply isolated. Thirdly, the prestige of metropolitan France had suffered, damaged by the defeat of 1940 and not improved by the *attentiste* attitude of many colonial administrators during the struggle between the followers of Pétain and France Libre. Moreover, the indigenous nationalist movements had received open support from the Americans; as early as July 1940 the United States was pressing for the establishment of collective trusteeships over the European colonies, and in May 1942, with the backing of the Soviet Union, put forward the principle of their internationalization. Lastly, the nationalists were encouraged by the opportunities for rapid change offered by the presence of foreign forces in the French territories.

In Black Africa these developments remained discreet up to the electoral and constitutional debates of 1945–6. But the subsequent disappointment with the terms of the French Union was responsible for the creation of the Rassemblement démocratique africain, founded by Houphouët-Boigny, which grouped most of the African representatives. At the first congress at Bamako in October 1946, the movement announced its rejection of assimilation, a purely tactical acceptance of the French Union, and looked ahead to a democratic struggle of a united Africa. Similar conditions in Madagascar allowed the Mouvement démocratique de rénovation malgache to build up its authority.

For the moment, however, North Africa was the only area to attract serious attention. Here, the local rulers had exploited the confused situation in Algiers to try to recover some of their authority,[14] taking the risk, albeit with American approval, of encouraging the independence movements. In Tunisia, the Neo-Destour nationalists, although deprived of the imprisoned Bourguiba's leadership, were getting stronger. After a rejection of all reforms by Resident-General Esteva, Moncef Bey formed a government of 'nationalistes pacifiques' under Chenik on 31 December 1942, attempting at the same time to resist German and Italian pressures. In May 1943, with the approval of the Allies, the French authorities in Algiers deposed the Bey, replacing him with a puppet ruler to implement their orders. The episode was important: by violating the La Marsa agreements the France Libre leadership had shown itself to be as unworthy of confidence as Vichy. The lesson was not lost on the Neo-Destour nationalists. Bourguiba, released in April 1943, was back at their head, having successfully resisted Italian attempts to label him as an ally of Mussolini. The Neo-Destour rejected the timid reforms of February 1945, argued its case in the Arab League and at the United Nations, and enlarged its popular following with the creation of a powerful Muslim trade union, the Union générale du travail tunisien (UGTT). There were similar developments in Morocco, where the meeting between Roosevelt and Sultan Ben Youssef at Anfa in January 1943 had bestowed a legitimacy on nationalist aspirations and appetites for reform. From January 1944, all the Moroccan nationalists were united in the Istiqal party which demanded an end to the French protectorate. After violent incidents in February the Istiqal leaders were imprisoned, but nothing was done about tackling the cause of the unrest. A policy of gradual reform in Morocco was henceforth refused by both the Istiqal nationalists and the European settlers.

In Algeria, the imperatives of the war effort had forced the French authorities in March 1943 to accept a Manifeste du peuple algérien drawn up by Ferhat Abbas. Although marking a move away from the principle of assimilation, the Manifesto's proposals were moderate, pointing to Algeria's contribution to the war to call for a Muslim Assembly and an undertaking to negotiate a federal statute for the country. Here, in fact, was a clear demonstration of the war's unifying impact, in this case on an Algerian nationalism historically divided between the urban and working-class Parti du peuple algérian (PPA) of Messali Hadj, the Islamic nationalism of the Ulémas, and an indigenous bourgeoisie hitherto attracted by assimilation but now ready to support Ferhat Abbas. In June the Muslim notabilities and representatives joined a more extreme demand for an autonomous Algerian state to the Manifesto. Faced with this concerted pressure, Georges Catroux, the Governor-General appointed by the CFLN, and de Gaulle, in his Constantine speech of 12 December, offered substantial reforms, proposals which resulted in the ordinance of 7 March 1944. But it was already too late: on 14 March the Association des amis du Manifeste et de la liberté (AML) was set up to organize nationalists of all persuasions behind Abbas. From now on, largely thanks to the dynamism of the PPA militants, the demands were for 'an autonomous Algerian Republic federated to a renovated French Republic'.

Against the background of a seriously weakened Algerian economy, severe hardship among the Muslims, and the drawing up of the war's human balance-sheet, the nationalist message began to penetrate the masses for the first time. And it was the radicalism of the PPA with its demands for an Algerian government, rather than the federalism advocated by Ferhat Abbas, which made most headway. The French authorities seemed oblivious to this profound evolution in opinion. On 25 April 1945 they took the risk of deporting Messali Hadj, by now an uncontested and charismatic popular leader. Protests occurred on 1 May, and in several areas the victory celebrations of 8 May degenerated into rioting. At Sétif twenty-nine Europeans were killed after clashes between the police and approximately 10 000 Muslim demonstrators carrying nationalist banners and flags. From Sétif the violence spread out to the surrounding country-side, where attacks on farms, officials, and public buildings left a hundred dead. Less than 5 per cent of the Constantine region's population had been involved in the troubles and those responsible for the rural massacres were clearly not all nationalist militants, though a conspiracy of some sort may well have been at the root of the outburst. The bloodshed at Sétif showed that an open rupture between the two sides could occur. In the eyes of many Muslims this was made inevitable by the ferocity of the French repression. Under cover of martial law and backed from the sea and air, units of Senegalese, Foreign Legionnaires, and European militia devastated the region, leaving between 6000 and 8000 Muslims dead.[15] In spite of the warnings sounded by Albert Camus,[16] opinion in metropolitan France was poorly informed over this butchery; for the two communities in Algeria, however, the memory of the Sétif explosion and its repression was never erased. The efforts of the liberal Governor, Chataigneau, were ruined before they had begun. The extent to which the tragic incident had poisoned Franco-Algerian relations was clear from the bitterness of the scenes at the Constituent Assembly more than a year later, on 22 August 1946, when a moderate text providing for Algerian autonomy was pre-sented by the Union démocratique du Manifeste algérien (UDMA), the party founded by Ferhat Abbas in the wake of the repression. Abbas believed that he was still in control, but both Messali's Mouvement pour le triomphe des libertés démocratiques (MTLD) and the Algerian Commun-ist Party now had no difficulty recovering solid followings. From now on, dialogue in Algeria was difficult, overshadowed by the bloody memory of Sétif, invested with symbolic value as a genuine but failed attempt at national insurrection.[17]

### The point of no return in Indo-China

In Indo-China the dialogue had already broken down. The hesitations and contradictions of French imperial policy had brought the situation there to a critical point: the Fourth Republic inherited the forlorn war which followed. Although only dimly perceived by the French public, the prob-lems of Indo-China had never ceased to hold official attention and were extensively covered by the press. The initial French intentions had seemed promising: from December 1943 the CFLN was planning to grant Indo-China institutions of its own, and the Brazzaville Conference had addressed its first message to 'captive Indo-China'. But just two years later, on 8 December 1945, Jean Sainteny, commissaire de la République in the Tonkin, was writing thus: 'We have to fight with nothing, without support, without leadership, without a goal.'[18] These were the conditions which condemned France to wage a hopeless and anachronistic war, one which, even before the war in Algeria, brought discredit upon the régime's founders.

The Japanese takeover in Indo-China on 9 March 1945 was the catalyst for the reaction whose complexity was never fully grasped in Paris. In the space of a few hours, the Japanese eliminated the French administration and forces that Admiral Decoux had kept in Vichy's sphere of influence since 1940. They gladly left Bao Dai and Sihanouk to proclaim the independence of Vietnam and Cambodia on 11 March: with the end of the war only weeks away, the Japanese in effect passed to the nationalists the task of eliminating Europeans from the peninsular. The response from the provisional government on 24 March 1945, promising local liberties inside the projected French Union but maintaining a governor-general, though consistent with the spirit of Brazzaville, was doubly inappropriate to the circumstances in Indo-China. Not only did the proposals fall well short of popular expectations, but France was totally incapable of intervening to impose them. Paris in fact had misread the situation, failing to see beyond the Japanese and Bao Dai to the growing strength of the nationalist forces. The nationalists had begun the difficult job of organization in 1941 with the creation of an Independence Front, the Vietminh. The Communists under Ho Chi Minh were prominent in this, mobilizing on the theme of the patriotic struggle against both French and Japanese Fascism. In the conflict against Vichy and the Japanese, the Vietminh forces, backed by the Americans and the Chinese of Chiang Kai-shek, reinforced Giap's guerrilla campaign, establishing a firm hold in the mountains of the Tonkin on the border with China. The Kuomingtang Chinese were in fact supporting the non-Communist nationalists, but could not contest the popularity and leadership of Ho Chi Minh. Sainteny's skilful negotiations with the Vietminh, in which he suggested that independence would be possible in a few years, succeeded in isolating Bao Dai in the summer of 1945 at the moment of the Japanese collapse. In August the Vietminh forces became the Army of National Liberation; a general insurrection was launched, with People's Committees set up in rural areas. Emperor Bao Dai abdicated on 25 August, and the Vietminh, invoking the principles of 1789 and the San Francisco Charter, proclaimed an independent Republic of Vietnam in Hanoi on 2 December. The united front strategy had triumphed: democrats, nationalists, Catholics, and Buddhists joined the Communists in the government of National Unity formed by Ho Chi Minh. The new régime had the blessing of Bao Dai and of the victorious Chinese, whose armies were supporting the conservative Vietnamese nationalists.

France might have been expected to act at this point to impose her wishes. That she did not was because of a decision taken by the Allies at Potsdam in which she had had no part. At Potsdam it was decided to partition Indo-China along the 16th parallel, with the Chinese receiving the Japanese surrender to the north of it, the British to the south. For the moment, then, France was excluded. De Gaulle could do nothing but wait for the end of the fighting in Germany before dispatching Leclerc's forces to Indo-China; and this without a reconsideration of the project for an Indo-Chinese Federation within the French Union, a project now quite clearly overtaken by events. Leclerc took command of the meagre forces in Indo-China on 16 August; the following day, another Gaullist, Admiral Thierry d'Argenlieu, was named High Commissioner at Saigon. Their mission was to ignore the *de facto* authorities, restore French authority by any means, and impose the terms of the 24 March proposals.

A French physical presence was indeed quickly re-established. The British left the Cochin China province without delay; Leclerc made a triumphant entry to Saigon on 5 October, and his armoured forces carried out a successful clearing-up operation in the South; Cambodia and Laos both hastened to restore their relations with France. D'Argenlieu, convinced that the Vietminh were no longer a problem in the South, turned on the Vichyite administrators and *colons*, taxing them remorselessly with 'collaboration'; he also revived the committees of native notabilities, a classic instrument of French colonial rule. In the North, however, Leclerc realized that force alone was not sufficient to consolidate the French position. Negotiations were needed with Ho Chi Minh and the Chinese, and this time serious attention had to be paid to the basic demands of the nationalists: national independence and the territorial union of the provinces of Tonkin, Annam, and Cochin China. To gain time, and without considering the full implications, Paris accepted this solution. On 28 February 1946, in return for France's surrender of her concessions at Shanghai, Tientsin, Hangchow, and Canton, China agreed to hand over to Leclerc's forces in the Tonkin province, though continuing to give discreet support to Ho Chi Minh, currently negotiating with Sainteny. Agreement was reached between them on 6 March. Sainteny and Leclerc, exploiting the success of the latter's forces, had persuaded the Gouin government to leave them a free hand to conclude a quick settlement which would put the non-Communists back in power in the North before Giap could unleash a generalized insurrection of the Communists. Ho Chi Minh had also sought to gain time, accepting the French peace proposals in preference to a Chinese presence. Under the 6 March agreement, the Vietnam government accepted the presence of the French army for five years; the question of the three provinces was to be settled by plebiscite; and the Republic of Vietnam, with an ambiguous 'Free State' status, would join the new Indo-Chinese Federation, itself a part of the French Union. With Ho Chi Minh's concession over these two crucial points the future in Indo-China seemed clearer.

Within a few months, however, Thierry d'Argenlieu, supported by the Gaullists and not repudiated by de Gaulle, had condemned the new settlement. D'Argenlieu attacked the 6 March agreement as a new Munich, arguing that the former colony of Cochin China, purged of Communists, could not be treated in the same way as Annam and Tonkin. Naturally, such arguments found support among the powerful financial and colonial interests and in certain sections of the French press; the Right and the MRP were quickly convinced; the issue divided the SFIO and weakened the position of its Minister for Overseas France, Marius Moutet. The logic of the attack was that of the old colonial principle of divide and rule: isolating Cochin China from Vietminh influence would allow metropolitan France to tighten its grip on the Indo-Chinese Federation; some went further, arguing that setting up a régime of loyal notabilities in Saigon would provide the base for an eventual French recovery of the entire peninsular. It was on d'Argenlieu's initiative that an autonomous Republic of Cochin China was suddenly proclaimed on 1 June 1946 and a puppet régime installed. The news reached Ho Chi Minh the next day – in the aircraft taking the Vietminh delegation to Paris for talks whose main object was to have been the future of the three provinces! Gouin resigned on 12 June after the rejection of the first constitutional project, but without having had the courage to disavow d'Argenlieu's action. Georges Bidault, who succeeded him on 19 June, was determined that the 6 March text should represent the maximum French concessions to the Vietminh, having been influenced by a letter from Leclerc to Maurice Schumann which asserted that France had won and that Ho Chi Minh could henceforth be considered as 'un grand ennemi'.[19] The Fontainebleau Conference was thus doomed to failure: the uneasy *modus vivendi* signed by Moutet and Ho Chi Minh on 14 September did no more than leave the door open for future discussions.

By now the partisans of war on each side were preparing. Still acting on his own initiative, d'Argenlieu proceeded to elaborate a federal structure around Cochin China from which the North was excluded. Faced with the progress of the nationalist maquis, the administrators, *colons*, and the army were already speaking of the need to inflict a severe lesson on the Vietminh. Meanwhile in Hanoi, the pro-Chinese faction was eclipsed and the hardline Communists were organizing the guerrilla struggle against the French forces. A noisy press campaign in France in autumn 1946 denounced a policy of 'abandon' which, it was claimed, would imperil the entire French Union. The MRP and the Radicals acquiesced, the SFIO seemed struck by paralysis, and the Communists remained tight-lipped. In this atmosphere of confusion and mounting tension, the inevitable occurred. On 23 November, in reply to attacks on French garrisons and the first murders of Europeans, and with the consent of Bidault and the local authorities, French forces bombarded and cleared the strategic port of Haiphong, at a cost of approximately 6000 dead. A telegram sent by Ho Chi Minh on 15 December to his former colleague Léon Blum – who in the meantime had become premier and who was then personally favourable to fresh discussion towards independence[20] – was held up in Saigon for eleven days by members of d'Argenlieu's entourage. By the time it reached Blum it was scarcely relevant: Giap's forces had struck in Hanoi on 19 December, leaving more than 200 dead. Ho Chi Minh returned to the underground, declaring that the goal was now to drive the French out of Indo-China using all available means. Blum, his conscience as torn as it had been over events in Spain in the summer of 1936, agreed to the sending of French reinforcements. And with this was set in motion the fatal mechanism of escalation, to be so important later in Algeria: that based on the principle of no negotiation before definitive military victory.

Hesitating between firmness and concession, continuing a Gaullist policy of French presence which failed to take into account either the realities of the post-war context or the strength of nationalist sentiment, and unable to secure obedience from its military and civil representatives, the Republic became embroiled in a hopeless war. Its policy and actions were soon to drive the people of Indo-China into the arms of the Vietminh. In metropolitan France as in the rest of the world, what was to become the 'Dirty War' had opened the first chapter of its 'Dreyfus Affair'.[21]

# The Republic of the lesser evil, 1946–52

# 7

# The parties take charge

The resignation of General de Gaulle on 20 January 1946 brought a profound change to the political landscape. With his departure the task of leading France out of the difficult interregnum devolved upon the political parties of the majority. The Assembly had acquired an incontestable legitimacy from the two consultations of autumn 1945, and its members at least had no doubt that the electorates had delegated their authority to the parties. The enthusiasm and energy these deployed in tackling the question of the Constitution bore witness to a full and conscientious assumption of this responsibility. At the same time, however, the political and parliamentary practices which now became current, both in government and in the elaboration of the Constitution, already had disturbing implications for the character and efficiency of the régime in gestation.

## The tripartite system

That the Communists, Socialists, and the MRP were the true masters of the situation had been clear since 21 October 1945. De Gaulle had drawn the obvious personal conclusion: the coalition of the three parties formed after his departure merely gave formal expression to this established political reality. All three agreed on the need to act quickly – to avoid a power vacuum which would emphasize still further the rupture between de Gaulle and his successors. Yet, as the formation of the second provisional government demonstrated, a coalition of the three major parties was to require a sometimes difficult subordination of inclination to interest. The Communist Party was intent on obtaining a share of power commensurate with its status as the principal political party; it proposed Thorez for the premiership, accepting the risk of exciting the already vigorous anticommunism of its partners. The SFIO, fearing an eventual slide into a People's Democracy, persisted in its refusal to join the PCF in a Popular Front and called instead for a three-party alliance. Thus the 'Marxist' parties, though they had a clear electoral majority between them, in effect left the outcome in the hands of the Christian Democrats of the MRP. These hesitated for two days, grappling with the dilemma presented to them by de Gaulle's resignation. Leaving the government through loyalty to the General would certainly strengthen the position of the MRP at the head of the opposition; but was it prudent or consistent with the ideals of the Resistance to thus abandon the nation to a government of the Marxist Left? The MRP finally opted to join a coalition, on the condition that it be headed by a Socialist. Its decision may well have been influenced by the intervention of General Billotte, a member of the General Staff, who warned Maurice Schumann of the likelihood of immediate military, economic, and diplomatic reprisals from the United States in the case of Thorez becoming premier.[1]

Clear in the reaching of this compromise is the distortion of the democratic process: responsibility for the decision had shifted first from the elected Assembly to the government itself, then from there to the caucuses of the political parties. The tripartite alliance was in fact accepted in the absence of an alternative. The Communists refused an alliance with the MRP, just as the Socialists and the MRP refused one with the Communists; none of the partners wanted to be identified individually with the unpopular measures which would have to be taken, yet with elections approaching none was prepared to be out of office. Thus far from being an agreement to govern, the tripartite protocol signed on 24 January 1946 was simply an arrangement for cohabitation, an uneasy armed truce between the three parliamentary monoliths. The solidarity postulated by *tripartisme* was one of convenience rather than conviction, something clear from the painstaking attention devoted to the sharing out of the portfolios; the promise made by the partners to refrain from criticism and controversy pointed up rather than concealed the conflict which underlay the alliance. Leadership went therefore to the weakest partner, the Socialists, in the person of Félix Gouin, President of the Constituent Assembly, and this after the Communists had rejected Vincent Auriol in favour of someone believed to be closer to their views on the Constitution.

After his investiture by the Assembly on 23 January, Gouin left the parties to share out the portfolios as they thought fit. Not surprisingly, the team which received the Assembly's vote of confidence six days later was a faithful reflection of the alliance: seven Socialists, six MRP, and six Communists. The vice-presidencies of the Council of Ministers were divided between Maurice Thorez and Francisque Gay (MRP); Foreign Affairs remained with the MRP; the Communists kept the portfolios of Labour and Production; the Socialists retained those of Agriculture, Overseas, and Education. The three parties were ready to abandon the two least popular posts – Provisions and Finance – to political outsiders, and the former went to an experienced administrator, Longchambon. But Finance was harder to place; the Radical Party, excluded from power, forbade Mendès France to accept, and the post was finally taken by the Socialists, being added to

that of Economy in the hands of André Philip, an advocate moreover of
Mendès France's policies. Auriol, who had replaced Gouin as President of
the Assembly, delivered a strong speech on 31 January 1946 extolling the
virtues of opposition in a democracy: yet for many observers the problem
was less one of the opposition than that of where exactly power now lay.
With Gouin? At the Palais-Bourbon? In reality, the power was already in
the hands of the three parties, each of which was seeking to impose its
views and build up its ministerial strongholds.

In these conditions it was hardly surprising that *tripartisme* produced a
constitutional project likely to favour its own position and future. The 24
January protocol had said nothing about the Constitution, and the
government did not intervene in its elaboration. As de Gaulle had
indicated the previous autumn, this was to be the responsibility of the
Assembly alone, something which now meant the political parties. Under
the law of 2 November 1945 – itself a kind of pre-Constitution defining the
work of the Constituent Assembly and its relationship with the government – the Constitutional Commission under André Philip had been at
work since 4 December on the project which had to be presented to the
electorate within a seven-month deadline. The Commission's lively debates were of a high intellectual standard, examining the relative merits of
English democracy, the American presidential system, the Assembly-
based régime, exploring the themes of the rights of man, the separation of
powers, and 'absolute democracy'.[2] Its final project was close to the
wishes of the Socialists and Communists.

The experience of the Third Republic and the numerous projects for
constitutional reform published before the war all pointed to the necessity
of curbing the power of Parliament and restoring a strong executive, at the
same time as initiating a far-reaching reform of the structures of the State.
The desirability of change along these lines had been agreed upon by
figures as dissimilar as Tardieu, in *La Réforme de l'Etat* (1934), and Léon
Blum, in *A l'échelle humaine* (1945). Yet the conditions now were not
favourable to such reforms. Memories of Vichy's contempt for representative democracy were strong and did much to enhance the creden-
tials of a parliamentary system as the true expression of both pluralistic
democracy and a Jacobin tradition of union and innovation. Furthermore,
the hovering presence of de Gaulle, strongly suspected of Caesarism by
the Left, reinforced distrust of authoritarianism and a strong executive.
Yet these fears had to be balanced against those produced by the prospect
of an all-powerful Communist Party dominating a large and easily manipulated Assembly. Finally, it is important to appreciate that many
members of the Constituent Assembly in fact drew little or no distinction
between national sovereignty itself and the democratic expression of that
sovereignty by the major political parties; parties which were sensitive to

popular opinion and equipped to articulate its aspirations. Viewed in
this light, it seemed obvious that the masses – whose entry into
twentieth-century politics had been manipulated by single-party Fascism – would now assume their responsibilities in a pluralistic
framework organized around the political parties. Moreover, it would be
unrealistic to ignore the extent to which the apparent stability of *tripartisme* overcame reservations concerning the problem which was in fact to
plague the Fourth Republic: parliamentary majorities. For those involved in the tripartite experiment, whose partners accounted, after all,
for three-quarters of the electorate, it seemed to guarantee solid majorities, permitting changes of policy without drastic electoral or parliamentary upheavals. In short, there was a strong and perhaps pardonable
temptation to institutionalize what already seemed close to the ideal.

Of course, agreement over this did not remove the scope for self-
interest. The Communists, for example, argued against the separation of
powers and for a unicameral régime; popular sovereignty would be exercised by the elected representatives alone, without intermediaries or a
supreme arbiter, the President of the Republic being retained in a purely
honorific role. The Communist project for the Constitution, deposed on
23 November 1945, provided for the recall of deputies, an Assembly
elected on proportional representation, and the members of which would
exercise a close control over the government. This would provide the
basis for the 'advanced democracy' which Thorez presented as the goal
for the future in an interview to *The Times* on 17 November 1946. The
Socialists saw through this manoeuvre, but were sufficiently hostile to
the personal power incarnated by de Gaulle that they backed the Communists over unicameralism and the supremacy of the parliamentary
majority, disagreeing among themselves over the details. Guy Mollet, a
rising figure in the SFIO, argued in the Commission for the full prerogatives of the Assembly and the parties; Auriol, on the other hand,
though still playing the conciliator between the different groups, defended Blum's ideas on the desirability of a stable majority with a legislative mandate, and on the democratic value of the referendum. Faced
with the Left's agreement over the basic points, the MRP argued for an
independent and strong executive, a President of the Republic armed
with real powers, and a second chamber to counterbalance the influence
of the popularly elected Assembly. This position allowed the MRP to
strengthen its image as a bulwark against the Communists, coming
close, so it thought, to de Gaulle's views. But it was in a minority; and
when François de Menthon resigned as Reporter-General of the Constitutional Commission on 2 April after the rejection of the MRP's proposals he was replaced by Pierre Cot, a progressive close to the PCF. It
was Cot who brought to completion a project satisfactory to the

Socialists and Communists, which was finally adopted by the Assembly on 19 April by 309 to 249 votes.[3]

The text opened with a comprehensive declaration of political, economic, and social rights. This drew its inspiration from the ideals of the Resistance, as well as from the projects of the Ligue des droits de l'homme whose members were prominent on the Commission. It was innovatory in substituting the People for the Nation as the source of sovereignty; by recognizing the right to resist oppression; and by guaranteeing to all citizens – of both sexes now – education, vocational training, essential needs, and the right of strike and association. The cornerstone of the constitutional structure detailed in the subsequent sections of the text was the National Assembly. This was to be a single chamber, elected for five years, and alone responsible for the election of the President of the Council and the President of the Republic, the latter retained after an unexpected alliance between the PCF and the MRP on the Commission. The Assembly was given unlimited powers – the mechanisms for its dissolution were deliberately complex and hard to apply; and the principle of the legislative mandate had not been admitted. In the *départements* the prefects lost some of their powers to the Conseils généraux. No special provisions were made for the French Union. In short, it was an Assembly-based régime in which the political parties would exercise sovereignty, a perpetuation in fact of the system which had functioned since 2 November 1945.

To widespread surprise the referendum of 5 May 1946 rejected this project. With 10.5 million for to 9.4 million against, it was the first time in French electoral history that a referendum had produced a negative result. Several factors explain this unexpected and unprecedented outcome. Doubts over the wisdom of a unicameral system in which an omnipotent but unwieldy Assembly was likely to fall under Communist control had certainly coincided with a rising tide of anticommunism. There was also the fact that for the first time a referendum was held without a prestigious figure to intervene in favour of the Yes vote: for de Gaulle had maintained his silence. The campaign was a confused one, dominated by the clashes between the MRP and the Communists. For the socialists and Communists, both closely identified with the text, the result of the referendum was their first defeat since the Liberation. The MRP, on the other hand, hailed the outcome as a victory for itself, seeing in the No vote a proof that a defence of freedoms was a viable electoral platform, one which would allow the party to consolidate its electorate. This reasoning was sound: an opinion poll conducted after the vote in May showed that among those who had voted against the text, half had done so from hostility to the Communists and to defend freedoms, compared with only 22 per cent because the text seemed a bad one and 10 per cent from party loyalties. Of course, the new female electorate had made a decisive contribution to the negative

Table 4: *Elections to the Constituent Assembly, 2 June 1946. Electorate: 24 696 989; votes: 19 881 339 (80.5%)*

|                               | votes        | % vote | seats | change (on 1945) |
|-------------------------------|--------------|--------|-------|------------------|
| PCF                           | 5 243 325*   | 26.4   | 146   | −2               |
| MRP                           | 5 614 254    | 28.2   | 161   | +18              |
| SFIO                          | 4 234 114    | 21.3   | 115   | −20              |
| Radicals–RGR                  | 2 203 288    | 11.1   | 37    | +6               |
| Independents, PRL, Moderates  | 2 586 358    | 13     | 63    | −2               |

* The figure includes 44 000 votes obtained by the ten Trotskyist lists. The extreme Left hostile to Stalin maintained its 1945 position: a minority inside the working classes was impatient, and a part of the Communist electorate rejected the 'class collaboration' of the PCF.

result; nonetheless, the outcome was a clear indication that the French electorate was once again divided into two roughly equal blocs, a division determined by an acceptance or rejection of a Communist-dominated Left.

The elections of the second Constituent Assembly on 2 June 1946 (Table 4) confirmed the lesson of the referendum. The MRP – most closely identified with the No vote – advanced; the Communists held firm; the SFIO lost ground; and the Radicals and Moderates began to climb back from the disaster of 1945.

### The turning-point of summer 1946

This striking of a new balance of electoral force marks a watershed in the political history of the post-war period, one whose significance exceeded that of the constitutional issue which had provoked it. The total of nearly 9.5 million votes – compared with 10.4 million for the heterogeneous bloc of Radicals, MRP, Independents and right-wing parties – meant that the Socialist–Communist Left no longer had the majority in France. True, the MRP continued to pay lip-service to *tripartisme*; it would be unwise to take the new development as proof of the end of the Resistance period and of a massive reappearance of the Left–Right cleavage in French political life. But an important realignment of opinion was certainly taking place. Henceforth, the defence of traditional Republican liberties and anticommunism were electorally profitable themes. They would provide a solid foundation for an alternative majority, this time of the Centre-Left and Right – the so-called Third Force – a majority likely to be based on the MRP.

For the moment there was an uneasy hiatus: on the one hand, the tripartite alliance, intact but crippled by its ideological divisions; on the other, the looming Third Force solution. The SFIO was in a particularly difficult position, having alienated both sides by its failure to choose between a union of the Left, that is, with the PCF, and a broader, national union in the spirit of the Resistance. The latter solution was possible with de Gaulle, but became unworkable after his departure and the emergence of the MRP to monopolize the Gaullist electorate and slogans. On all the important issues – liberties, social justice, peace, and collective security – the SFIO's campaign had proved less effective than those of its rivals; as a result it lost more than 10 per cent of its 1945 electorate, now dispersed between the PCF, the MRP, and the Radicals. Disappointed, the party's militants swung leftwards, seeking the remedy in the Marxist doctrinal sources and in dreams of working-class unity. At the SFIO congress in August, the leadership under Daniel Mayer was outvoted, despite strong support from Blum, still hoping for a doctrinal renewal and an original social approach. An opposition grouped around Guy Mollet, an obscure militant who had become deputy and mayor of Arras after a distinguished Resistance service in the OCM, rejected what it saw as the 'radicalization' of the party, denounced the concessions to the middle classes and the timidity of the proposed structural reforms; offering in their place a Marxism of a pronounced *guesdiste* hue. The congress gave Blum a warm reception but refused to accept his policy proposals, and Daniel Mayer's 'rapport moral' was rejected. The unexpected election of Guy Mollet as Secretary-General on 4 September announced the SFIO's response to its electoral setback: a swing to the Left, a closing of the ranks, and a return to the traditional doctrinal sources. The tone hardened *vis-à-vis* the other partners in the tripartite alliance: the secular shibboleth guaranteed hostility towards the MRP, while an open rejection of the Soviet model was to be the party's weapon in an intensified ideological struggle against the PCF.

While the Socialists were thus weakened, the groups and parties smothered at the Liberation were, on the contrary, emerging from their long silence. Partly as a reaction to the triumvirate of the monoliths, the Right and Centre of French politics showed increasing signs of life, basing their recovery on the theme of Republican liberties and a denunciation of the excesses of the *épuration*. Michel Clemenceau's PRL maintained its position, hopeful of becoming the core from which a new right-wing bloc would develop. Other small groups – the Alliance démocratique of Flandin, the independent republicans, and Paul Antier's Parti paysan – also held firm, resisting the MRP's encroachment onto the Right's electorates. More original, however, were the developments at the Centre. Here, a newer political personnel was emerging, one hostile to *tripartisme* and encouraged by the victory of the No vote in the referendum, an outcome for which it claimed much of the credit. At the Radical Party's congress of April 1946, the Neo-Radicals – like Émile Roche, Martinaud-Déplat, Henri Queuille,

René Mayer, and Jean-Paul David – who had been hostile to the Popular Front before the war, ousted the advocates of union with the Left. The defeated faction – led by Pierre Cot, Albert Bayet, and Jacques Kayser – set up the Rassemblement des gauches républicaines (RGR), a broad-based electoral coalition of the non-Marxist Left and various currents of moderate opinion which brought together veterans of the Third Republic and younger talents issued from the Resistance. Indeed, under the RGR's expansive electoral umbrella the UDSR, all that remained of the great 'Resistance Party', had to fight alongside erstwhile supporters of La Rocque, the Socialistes indépendantes of Paul Faure, and unreconstructed right-wingers.

Far more spectacular than these stirrings on the Right and Centre was the return of General de Gaulle to political debate. He broke his six-month silence on 16 June at Bayeux – the anniversary of the town's liberation – with a vigorous attack on the constitutional draft. De Gaulle had revealed the basic premiss of his constitutional analysis to André Philip, the chairman of the Constitutional Commission, as early as 1 January 1946, asking bluntly: 'Does one want a government which governs, or an omnipotent Assembly which chooses a government to implement its will?'[4] Although he had taken no part in the referendum campaign, de Gaulle now claimed the No result as a personal victory, as further evidence of his special relationship with the popular will. De Gaulle's arguments were familiar: the French propensity for partisan quarrels, inflamed by the political parties, had produced a stalemate; new institutions were now needed to curb this 'perpetual political ebullience' and save the prestige and authority of the State. Much of what came to be known as the 'Bayeux Constitution' was classic – bicameralism, the virtues of a Senate, the separation of powers, and ministerial responsibility. The novelty of de Gaulle's proposals lay in the role of the President of the Republic; he was to stand above the parties, no longer simply their delegate; he was to be elected by a college larger than Parliament, making him President of the French Union as well as of the Republic. But de Gaulle was still thinking in terms of an efficient parliamentary system. Thus the President of the Republic was responsible for choosing a government capable of reconciling the general interest with the orientation expressed in Parliament. The policy and work of the government were to be directed by the premier, nominated by and in close contact with the President of the Republic; fidelity to the policies promised during the elections was to be watched over by Parliament. The tasks of the Head of State were to ensure continuity, to arbitrate, to guarantee national independence; and he had the right to consult the nation directly in moments of crisis. The 'Bayeux Constitution' clearly accorded a large role to the Head of State, but its opponents were mistaken in claiming that it would introduce Bonapartism or a presidential system; in fact, and as Léon

Blum pointed out,[5] its logic was rather that of the Second Republic or the American Constitution. And there is no evidence that de Gaulle had serious thoughts or ambitions in those directions. Indeed, at no time during the Fourth Republic did he reply to the question left unanswered at Bayeux, namely that of the source of the exceptional sovereignty and right of arbitrage he proposed to give the Head of State: perhaps 18 June 1940 and 26 August 1944 were still too close for de Gaulle to thus acknowledge that even his legitimacy might require a textual justification? At the time, however, with the tripartite alliance faltering and the electoral prospects so encouraging, it was no doubt inevitable that some members of de Gaulle's entourage should have seen the 'Bayeux Constitution' as the rallying-point for a new political movement; one aloof of course from the political parties, but ready nonetheless to accept an immediate parliamentary position. At the end of July, the enthusiastic René Capitant founded, without great success, the Union gaulliste pour la IV$^e$ République.

While the Gaullist threat began to take shape in the summer of 1946 the parties of the majority continued to cling to the advantages of the tripartite system. The Communists had not abandoned their plans for union with the SFIO. The MRP, aware of its likely future difficulties, was hoping for an eventual alliance with the Socialists against the Right and the PCF, and was thus reluctant to force its potential ally into a Popular Front with the Communists by breaking the alliance now. As for the Socialists themselves, they were too insecure to contemplate giving up the meagre powers of arbitrage they could still exercise within the alliance. The bankruptcy of *tripartisme* was obvious, the shortcomings in economic and foreign policy glaring; but the partners were intent on extracting the maximum advantage from the alliance in the next elections, after which it could be discarded.

The façade of unity had thus to be maintained for a little longer. The MRP's leader, Georges Bidault, secured the investiture of his variation on the familiar coalition theme on 26 June – although, significantly, not before having explored the possibility of an all-MRP solution with SFIO backing. The changes in the composition of the team were minor, merely registering the outcome of the elections; the MRP gained slightly, placing Robert Schuman at Finance and François de Menthon at National Economy; Provisions still went to an outsider, this time Yves Farge. While the new government handled everyday business and tried to cope with the rising tide of economic and social unrest, the Assembly returned to the question of the Constitution. The Constitutional Commission, now chaired by Paul Coste-Floret, had a slender margin for manoeuvre; attempting to reconcile a need to abandon the institutions of the Third Republic with the fact that a project which did precisely this had just been rejected; and it had now to work in the shadow of the 'Bayeux Constitution'. In fact, the elections had not disrupted the parliamentary majority sufficiently for the Commission to

Table 5: *Referendum of 13 October 1946. Electorate: 24 905 538*

|  |  | % of electorate |
| --- | --- | --- |
| Votes | 16 793 143 | 67.4 |
| Abstentions | 7 775 893 | 31.2 |
| Spoilt papers | 336 502 | 1.4 |
| 'Yes' | 9 002 287 | 36.1 |
| 'No' | 7 790 856 | 31.3 |

produce more than a slightly amended version of the 'Cot Constitution', revised simply to satisfy the new balance of interests. After another round of delicate arbitration and conciliation by Auriol, still President of the Assembly, the new text was adopted by 440 to 106 votes on 30 September. Under its terms, the President of the Republic recovered some of the powers amputated by the previous project; the bicameral principle was admitted with the creation of a Council of the Republic; and the French Union was extensively redefined in a more conservative sense, reducing its federal aspects. De Gaulle had stongly condemned this compromise project at Epinal on 22 September. An embarrassed and confused MRP was thus left to defend its text alone. The Communists and Socialists gave their support, but without enthusiasm and chiefly out of hostility to de Gaulle.

The uncertainties and divisions within and between the parties of the majority were perceived by the general public. In the referendum of 13 October (Table 5) it chose indifferently between the Yes called for by the members of the tripartite alliance and the No demanded by de Gaulle, the Radicals, and the parties of the Right.

De Gaulle had caused more than 5 million votes to desert the tripartite alliance; but without being able to alter the referendum's outcome. The MRP's electorate had split; the efforts of the Left in favour of the Yes response had been ineffective; and the Moderates had demonstrated their potential. Yet neither de Gaulle nor the parties had cause to rejoice: nearly 4 million of those who had voted in May and June had gone to swell the ranks of the abstentionists, repudiating both the text and the system of party rule of which it was the expression.[6] De Gaulle was to deride the Constitution as having been 'accepted by 9 million, refused by 8 million, and ignored by 8 million'. The most widespread reaction to the Fourth Republic's founding text was thus one of apathy or hostility: only time would show if this was a temporary protest, born, for example, of economic hardship, or evidence of an already profound disillusionment and disaffection.

*Launching the Republic*

The new Constitution appeared to break with the past, opening with a generous Preamble which incorporated many of the principles laid down in the first project. But we have already seen the ambiguities this in fact created over the French Union. An examination of the Fourth Republic's constitutional structures raises a number of further questions.

Parliament (articles 5 to 25) was composed of two chambers: the National Assembly and the Council of the Republic. But this was in reality an extremely lop-sided bicameralism. The National Assembly was elected for five years,[7] and it exercised sovereignty in the name of the People. The Assembly was responsible for fixing its own procedures and timetable, and its permanent commissions were to scrutinize all proposed legislation, controlling debate in the sessions of the Assembly. All legislative power was held by the Assembly, a power it could not delegate – an important point since it precluded the issue of *décrets-lois*, a systematic arm of government in the 1930s. The cornerstone of the constitutional edifice was thus a powerful and unfettered National Assembly; in comparison, the second chamber, the Council of the Republic, was very feeble. The originality of its title reflected the desire to break with the unpopular Senate of the Third Republic, though the retention of a second chamber had been imposed by the outcome of the first referendum. The intention of the Constitution's makers had clearly been to create an essentially deliberative second chamber, one whose views could in practice be ignored. The law of 27 October 1946 establishing the rules for its composition – 315 members, elected indirectly from local collectivities – was of sufficient complexity to ensure that elections to the Council of the Republic were unlikely to generate serious public interest.[8] A second law, voted at Queuille's instigation on 28 September 1948, was to fix their mandate at six years, with half the members renewed every three years, and returned to the electoral college of the Third Republic's Senate. The weak and constrained second chamber, in which rural and small-town France were over-represented, had quite obviously been conceived merely as a sop to the doubts over full unicameralism expressed in the first referendum. More important in the eyes of the Constitution's architects was the new Economic Council. This was composed of representatives of the trade unions, the employers, and other interest groups; its task was to advise the Assembly on economic and social matters, and on the Plan.

The new Constitution bore witness to the widespread reluctance to leave too much power in the hands of a strong executive. The role of the President of the Republic was less than under the 1875 constitutional laws. Like his Third Republic predecessors, the President was elected for seven years by Parliament united in congress at Versailles and he was eligible for one further term of office; but unlike them he did not control military and civil appointments and his acts had to be countersigned by the President of the Council and one minister. However, his considerable moral authority could be exercised in the Council of Ministers, in international negotiations, on the Council of the Judiciary, and in his *ex officio* role as President of the French Union. The presidency thus defined would allow a strong personality considerable scope for action within the terms of the Constitution; but it also made conflict likely with the figure who was in fact responsible for national policy, the President of the Council or Premier. After his designation by the President of the Republic, the premier was to seek the confidence of the Assembly for a particular programme. Thus, and in contrast to the 1875 laws, the new Constitution provided for a leader committed to a specific policy, a leader moreover who had to obtain a parliamentary majority in conditions broadly similar to those of a legislative mandate. As if to underline the importance attached to this procedure, the investiture required an absolute majority of the 626 members of the Assembly, irrespective of the number voting.

From whichever angle it is considered, the Constitution of the Fourth Republic invariably leads back to the control exercised by the National Assembly. Much more powerful than the Council of the Republic, important in the election of the Head of State, with full responsibility for laws and budgets, the Assembly in effect controlled the government: and this without any of the effective counterweights characteristic of an authentic parliamentary régime. Indeed, the fact that the Assemblies of the Fourth Republic did not have to resort to censure motions could be taken as evidence of the extent of their control over governments. Conversely, the motion of confidence deposed by the government – decided upon in cabinet, voted after a day of reflection, requiring an absolute majority, and marking the rupture of the investiture – became an all-too-common feature of parliamentary life; and many premiers, sensing the mood of the parties, resigned without even setting the official mechanisms in motion. Government was vulnerable: the Assembly, on the other hand, was well protected, the mechanism for its dissolution complex and hard to set in operation. The Assembly could not be dissolved in the first eighteen months of its life; thenceforward, two votes of no confidence had to have occurred in a subsequent eighteen-month period before the decree of dissolution could be signed by the Council of Ministers. Finally, as a further instance of the Assembly's undisputed authority, during the electoral period following a dissolution, the interim government would be directed by the President of the Assembly, a new Minister of the Interior would be appointed by the Assembly's Bureau, and each group or party present in the Assembly, but not in the government, would designate a Minister of State. Obviously, no government was ever likely to take such a risk: dissolution, far from being automatic as in a genuinely parliamentary system, was something to be avoided at all costs.

What the new Constitution in fact proposed was *gouvernement d'assemblée* – that is, an omnipotent Assembly, dominated of course by the political parties, which itself assumed the functions of government. This outcome simply reflected the political conditions in which the project had been elaborated. The Constitution's architects did not doubt that *tripartisme* was evidence of the new maturity in French politics, created by the experiences of the war and the Resistance; a new maturity which entrusted representation to the care of the political parties, now strong, efficient, and few in number. The Constitution of the Fourth Republic bears witness to two beliefs widely held at the time of its elaboration; first, that the situation of 1945–6 had prepared France for a long period of constructive stability; secondly, that modernity required the organization of democracy by mass political parties. With hindsight these beliefs may seem bold or naive; at the time, however, they were an accurate reflection of an optimism which, as we have seen, the Resistance had invested with credibility, evidence in fact of a genuine and patriotic resolve to complete at last France's political modernization.

The sudden and massive injection of partisan ideology into a body politic notoriously slow to evolve was, perhaps, at the origin of the incomprehension which developed between the electorate and the political parties. The transition, against the background of severe economic hardship, from the humiliation and suffering of the recent past to an exaltation of civic activism and organized democracy, was too brutal. The result was bewilderment and a return to the more familiar political symbols and attitudes of the past. The opinion polls – largely ignored by politicians at the time – suggest that the results of the referenda owed more to the circumstances in which they were held than they did to the content of the projects at stake; in July 1945, for example, nearly 40 per cent would have been satisfied with a slightly modified version of the 1875 régime. And indeed, when the cacophony of partisan politics is ignored, it is a wholehearted desire to be governed which emerges most consistently from the deeper strata of French opinion: thus in November 1945, 50 per cent wanted a President elected by universal suffrage; in March 1946, 48 per cent wanted the President to have a significant political role. Of course, time was short and the Constitution's makers had to act quickly. In their haste, however, they institutionalized the *décalage* which already existed between the ferment of the parties and these deep-seated yearnings for stability.

With the Constitution at last adopted, elections had now to be held to the National Assembly. On 10 November 1946, in a deteriorating social climate, an apathetic electorate returned yet again to the polls. And the elections compounded the fundamental problem outlined above: for the

Table 6: *Elections to the National Assembly, 10 November 1946.*
*Electorate: 25 053 233; votes: 19 203 060 (76.6%). Abstentions and spoilt papers:*
*5 850 173 (23.4%)*

|  | votes | % of votes | seats | change |
|---|---|---|---|---|
| PCF | 5 524 799 | 28.8 | 165 | +19 |
| MRP | 5 053 084 | 26.3 | 158 | − 3 |
| SFIO | 3 480 773 | 18.1 | 91 | −24 |
| Independents | 2 953 692 | 15.4 | 76 | +13 |
| Radicals | 2 190 712 | 11.4 | 54 | +17 |

beginning of the new régime coincided with the break-up of the tripartite
system of which it was the fruit.

Abstention was both high, 22 per cent, and geographically and socially
homogeneous, a clear sign of the electorate's growing weariness (Table 6).
The division of French opinion into two blocs deepened, with that of the
Left now in a clear minority. The Radicals and the various Right-wing
groups stabilized their shares of the votes, although Capitant's Gaullist
formation failed to make headway. In spite of its divisions, the MRP,
fighting on a slogan of 'Bidault sans Thorez', recovered much of the ground
lost in the referendum. On the Left, the SFIO continued its slide, while the
Communist Party was able to advance slightly to recover its place as the
principal political party.

The parties of the tripartite alliance were still in the majority, but their
increasingly open divisions made it impossible to maintain the fiction of
coalition rule. To the MRP's slogan of 'Bidault sans Thorez' the PCF
opposed that of 'Thorez sans Bidault'; but the candidature of Thorez was
defeated. It fell to the SFIO to break the impasse. Recognizing that coalition was impossible, Léon Blum emerged from retirement to form a single-
party team on 16 November 1946; it was obviously a short-term solution,
though one with considerable social and overseas achievements to its
credit. The elections to the Council of the Republic (24 November and 8
December) were a triumph for the two principal and now openly antagon-
istic parties. The PCF and MRP obtained 61 and 62 seats respectively,
compared with 37 for the SFIO, 35 for the RGR, and 20 for the Independents and PRL. It was logical therefore that the MRP's candidate, Champetier de Ribes, should defeat the Communist Georges Marrane, supported
*in extremis* by the Socialists, in the elections for the Council's President.

The electoral college to choose the Fourth Republic's first President was
now complete. Vincent Auriol was elected at the first round at Versailles on
16 January 1947, obtaining 452 votes against 242 for Champetier de Ribes
and 60 for a Moderate, Michel Clemenceau. Auriol, a Socialist and the

skilled compromiser of 1946, had no intention of being a mere figurehead and was determined to use to the full the margin for manoeuvre the new Constitution afforded the President. On 21 January 1947, however, Edouard Herriot succeeded Auriol as President of the National Assembly, thus recovering his position of before the war, a potent symbol of continuity between the Third and Fourth Republics. After the resignation of Blum, Auriol designated another veteran parliamentarian, Paul Ramadier, the former Minister of Provisions. Ramadier formed a quadripartite alliance in which the members of the tripartite alliance were joined by the Radicals, the UDSR, and the Independents. The parties, however, were not slow to assert their authority: seven days after his unanimous investiture on 21 January, Ramadier, like Gouin before him, accepted questioning in the Assembly over the composition of his team, which culminated in a vote of confidence initiated by the leaders of the majority groups. Auriol was the only one to draw attention to the fact that this practice, so reminiscent of the Third Republic, was contrary to the new Constitution.[9]

# 8

# The double fracture of 1947

The year 1947 had a particular importance in France, for it was here that the brutal confrontations of what de Gaulle was to describe as the 'année terrible' left possibly their deepest scars. Of the two ruptures which occurred, the first, that of the beginnings of the Cold War and decolonization, was beyond French control; reduced to the rank of second-class power, France was merely carried along by international developments, although the policies she chose to follow may be criticized on several counts. For the second rupture, however, marked by the departure of the Communists from the Ramadier government and the rapid heightening of social tensions, she bore a far heavier responsibility. With hindsight it is clear that much of the subsequent history of the Fourth Republic was set by the events of 1947.

## The start of the Cold War

Tension between the United States and the Soviet Union had been growing throughout 1946. The former's possession of the atomic weapon did not compensate for the strength of the Red Army's conventional forces; Stalin's intentions were ambiguous; in Greece, Iran, and in Eastern Europe the future of the Yalta settlement looked uncertain. At Fulton on 5 March, Churchill warned for the first time of the 'Iron Curtain' which, from Stettin on the Baltic to Trieste on the Adriatic, had descended across Europe; speaking in Zurich on 19 September, he argued that European unity was vital to guarantee liberty and security. The purpose of such warnings was clear: to counter the likely isolationist urges of the United States.

The American response to the situation and to European fears was the 'Truman doctrine'. From January 1947, the American President abandoned the policy based on confidence in Stalin advocated by Henry Wallace and went back to the camp of the 'hawks' – James Forrestal, Dean Acheson, and George Kennan. The warnings of the Kremlin-watchers and the Pentagon were henceforth listened to; General Marshall was appointed Secretary of State. The logic of the American policy of containment that was developed at this time ran as follows: for the peoples of Eastern Europe it was too late, their liberation would spark off a new global conflict; instead, efforts had to be concentrated on containing Stalin and preventing the 'Free World' from slipping into his camp. Since the nations of Southern and Western Europe were on the front line of this conflict, the United States would help them recover the economic and political stability necessary to ward off the Communist menace. This reasoning lay behind the policy Truman presented to Congress on 12 March. There was to be financial, diplomatic, and military aid for Greece and Turkey, the former torn by civil war, the latter threatened on her northern borders; and similar aid was envisaged for the other nations menaced by totalitarianism, among which France figured prominently. The American analysis of the situation in France was summed up by Acheson on 22 February thus: with four Communists in the government, one holding the vital Defence portfolio;[1] with one-third of the electorate voting for the PCF; with the trade unions, factories, and military either controlled or infiltrated by the Communists; and with a worsening economic and social climate – a Soviet takeover could occur at any moment.

The failure of the Moscow Conference of March–April lent force to this analysis. The breach was not yet irreparable, but on all the important points – the peace treaties with Germany and Austria, reductions in the occupying forces, reparations, frontiers, the German government – the Conference had failed to reach agreement. The Soviets' displeasure at the Truman doctrine was obvious, as was their determination to extract the maximum economic advantage from the occupied zones, including the Ruhr, whilst continuing to hold out for a united Germany. Bidault repeated the familiar French proposals, but the political decentralization of Germany was clearly a lost cause, and the Allies were already making concessions to Germany over her coal output and the reconstruction of her heavy industries. Furthermore, the only positive points for France, the placing of the Saar in the French economic orbit, and that over coal imports, were decided by the Western Allies alone. The future power blocs were starting to take shape.

Imperceptibly then, France was being drawn into the Western camp. A friendship treaty with Britain signed at Dunkirk in March breathed new life into the Entente Cordiale. But it was with the announcement in June of the Marshall Aid programme that the westwards attraction became irresistible. The American Secretary of State had recognized that Europe's needs far exceeded her means; he saw too that the resulting 'dollar gap' would ultimately damage American commercial interests. The solution he offered was a massive programme of free and unconditional aid to run from 2 April 1948 to 30 June 1952 which was to help to restore conditions of peace and stability in Europe. The avowed aims of Marshall Aid were to combat hunger and chaos, regardless of national frontiers and political doctrines, and the Soviet zone was not excluded from the offer. But subsequent American declarations, notably by Acheson, hinted strongly that priority would in fact be given to countries struggling to defend their democratic institutions against totalitarian pressure. Such views found a strong echo in France, where the MRP, the Radicals, the Moderates, and some Socialists were beginning to ask whether a country which kept Communists in its government could reasonably hope to receive significant amounts of American aid. This consideration was an important factor in the dismissal of Communists from the governments of several European countries – Belgium, Luxembourg, France, and Italy – which occurred between March and May 1947.

In the French context the Marshall offer was doubly opportune, giving a further stimulus to the Third Force option at the same time as promising relief from the economic and social difficulties which were most likely to benefit the Communists. The growth in output and modernization laid down in the Monnet Plan was going to require massive imports, estimated at 11 milliard dollars until 1949. Equilibrium had to be restored to the commercial balance, and public finances brought under control, if aid was to be usefully distributed and France's international monetary commitments honoured. Jean Monnet recognized in the spring of 1947 that external aid was vital if the immediate problems were to be overcome and the Plan's targets met without hopelessly compromising the future. By the summer only 240 million dollars remained from previous loans with which to meet an estimated 450 million dollar deficit for imported grain, coal, petrol, and raw materials. The Marshall offer came to a country forced in August to reduce the bread ration to 200 grammes – 75 grammes less than at the worst point of the war – and to suspend its imports due to the lack of dollars to pay for them. On the other hand, of course, material problems of this magnitude hardly favoured a long and careful examination of the ideological constraints implicit in the American offer. France's endless economic and social difficulties provided advocates of alignment in the Western camp with what was no doubt their most powerful argument.

The position of France in the Cold War's Western camp was thus less a result of deliberate choice than of the need to seize the only means of economic survival being offered to her. Only the most far-sighted observers, such as Jean Monnet,[2] drew attention to the rupture this necessary but irreversible decision would lead to. True, the British and French agreed on 17 June not to reply to the American offer before consulting Moscow, but the Paris Conference attended by Molotov broke up on 2 July without reaching an agreement. Moscow had insisted that American aid go only to victims of Nazi Germany, and was increasingly violent in its attacks on 'American imperialism'. Faced with the East's stance, the 'free' nations of Western Europe were left with little real choice. From July to September, again in Paris, the hardening of the blocs went a stage further as the 'Sixteen' finalized their acceptance of the American aid,[3] Soviet hostility forcing both Finland and Czechoslovakia to refuse. The European Economic Commissions now began their work; the customs union of the sixteen nations was set up; contacts with Washington multiplied: the camp of what Moscow denounced as 'imperialist lackeys' took shape.

The beginning of the Cold War marked the definitive failure of French policy over Germany; accepting Marshall Aid meant abandoning pretensions to German resources and territory. During 1947, Bidault had to give way on each of the points stubbornly defended by de Gaulle: autonomy for the Rhineland and Ruhr; acceptance of the Anglo-American joint zone and its sovereignty over the French sector in order to better resist the Soviets. In return, however, France was left control of the Saar, allowed to erect a tariff wall around it and introduce the franc, take the region's coal for French industry, and appoint a High Commissioner to watch over its relations with Germany. Soviet threats over the Saar at the London Conference changed nothing; France was by now solidly anchored in the Western camp; she would soon have to accept the idea of a West Germany separated from the East and bolstered by American economic aid.

French docility over these points was rewarded handsomely. The concession over the Saar made defeat over the Ruhr easier to accept; and although the coal problem was not settled, American aid meant that coal could at least be purchased. Better still, Marshall Aid gave a vital boost to the Monnet Plan, severely handicapped by the economic and social crisis until autumn 1947. The United States also met the needs of the transitional period until the Marshall Plan came into operation. France received approximately 60 per cent of this interim aid, to be added to the loans from the Import–Export Bank, Treasury advances, and restituted Nazi loot. These dollars enabled France to pay for the essential purchases and to hold on until the Marshall Aid arrived. Thus even before the Cold War began in earnest the French position was fixed; indeed, the creation of the Cominform in October 1947 was interpreted merely as the predictable Soviet response to the Marshall Plan. Not, however, that the ideological conflict went unnoticed by the general public: the presence of the PCF ensured that it would reverberate at every level of French domestic politics.

*Early problems for the French Union*

On 15 August 1947, India and Pakistan obtained their independence in the framework of the new British Commonwealth – Burma, Ceylon, and Malaysia were soon to follow the same course; in Indonesia the project for an independent federal structure was progressing. These successful steps by Great Britain and the Netherlands towards the decolonization of their empires throw into unhappily sharp contrast the experience of France in the same field. Unable to give authority to the unwieldy French Union, France pursued inconsistent and short-sighted policies, and became enmeshed in a war in Indo-China.

French policy in Madagascar bore many of the repressive traits visible later in Algeria. Post-war conditions there were grave, with widespread famine, a black market, and the persistence of nominally illegal forced labour. Initially, however, the chances for a peaceful settlement seemed good. The Mouvement démocratique de la rénovation malgache (MDRM) had progressed steadily since its foundation in February 1946. It was successful in the local elections of January 1947 and, thanks to an energetic Comité franco-malgache, had solid support among progressive opinion in mainland France. The MDRM had now approximately 30 000 members, and controlled the trade unions; it had also taken the lead over the violent nationalist secret societies, the Jina and the Panama (the Parti national malgache, underground since 1941), and for a while it looked as if the MDRM might be able to guide even the most extreme elements towards a peaceful settlement within the French Union. But this was to reckon without the tension which had been mounting since the autumn of 1946; incidents and provocations were increasingly common; activist cells were being formed, often on the initiative of former NCOs of the French colonial forces. An insurrection broke out in the night of 29–30 March 1947;[4] although it failed to become general, guerrilla fighters were quickly entrenched in the south and the centre of the upland regions. By the time the rebels' poor supplies and lack of leadership had brought their defeat in December 1948 approximately 550 Europeans and 1900 natives had been killed. Military and political unpreparedness and overconfidence in American intervention on their behalf condemned the rebels to failure; but not before they had succeeded in mobilizing the Madagascan cultural and ethnic values and symbols in the service of nationalism, an achievement with which the progressive urban élites who later led the country to independence had to come to terms.

Reaction on the French side had many of the disquieting aspects already seen in Indo-China: an administration easily swayed by powerful colonial interests, a press screaming for revenge, and military encroachment onto civil authority. And as in Indo-China, military victory was preferred to negotiation. An expeditionary force of 18 000 men arrived in April; the repression which followed was of an exceptional ferocity – the official figures acknowledge 89 000 natives killed. Crack forces – the 'paras' and Foreign Legionnaires – were left a free hand to comb the bush, practising psychological warfare, torture, and summary executions; vigilante groups were set up; the native populations were uprooted.[5] After this savagery by both sides – but in which the French technical superiority was devastating – the barrier of hostility and mutual incomprehension was impenetrable. Paris held the MDRM alone responsible and punished it accordingly. The Malagasy deputies were imprisoned and their Movement dissolved after the French Parliament, with the exception of the Communists and some overseas deputies, voted to lift their immunity in June and August, and this without hearing their case. A solidarity meeting was held on 5 June, and the deputies' barrister, Pierre Stibbe, launched a vain campaign in their defence.[6] On the island the High Commissioners Marcel de Coppet and, from 1948, Pierre de Chevigné struggled to restrain the worst excesses of hardline settler opinion, now orchestrated by the Ligue des intérêts franco-malgaches. But the atmosphere in Madagascar was irretrievably poisoned, and dialogue with the westernized nationalist élite had been broken.

Dialogue and long-term policy were equally absent from French North Africa. The situation in Morocco had begun to deteriorate: in Tangier on 10 April, Sultan Ben Youssef departed from his previously vetted speech, omitting the customary homage to France and adding a paragraph extolling the virtues of the Arab League. The controversy that ensued resulted in the dismissal of the liberal Resident-General Eric Labonne, responsible for significant economic improvements. The appointment of General Juin as his successor on 15 June was welcomed by the *colons*, but brought closer a showdown with the Istiqal nationalists. In Tunisia, underground agitation was gaining momentum. The reforms hoped for by the Resident, Jean Mons, came to almost nothing; French officials continued to cling to the system of direct administration. A strike at Sfax called by the UGTT to protest over low wages degenerated into rioting on 5 August; only the sang-froid of the troops allowed the number of victims to be limited to twenty-nine. Meanwhile, Arab nationalism was finding increasingly strident spokesmen. After escaping from Réunion, where he had been held by France since 1926, the veteran rebel Abd El Krim arrived in Cairo on 31 May 1947. In January 1948 he joined with Allal El Fassi and Bourguiba to set up the North African Liberation Committee. From now on the Arab League's intention of giving direct help to Maghreb nationalism was clear, as was the likelihood of the cases being taken to the United Nations.

In Algeria a surer grasp of the war's impact and a more objective approach to the social situation appeared to offer the bases for a far-sighted French policy. But although trade and investment were indeed recovering, other aspects of the Algerian economy were less encouraging; native agriculture remained at the mercy of drought; prices soared and wages stagnated. Among the Muslim population the demographic problems were acute:[7] the annual natural increase exceeded 2 per cent (150 000); infant mortality was massive; sanitation mediocre; the daily ration was fixed at just 1520 calories; a poorly qualified workforce fuelled a steady exodus to metropolitan France.

It was into this context of agrarian, economic, and demographic problems that the long-promised Algerian statute came, finally adopted by the Assembly on 27 August 1947. The long and difficult debate had involved four projects. That of the government, presented by the Minister of the Interior, Depreux, offered Algeria departmental status, with a governor-general to represent Paris and an Algerian Assembly working with him to look after specifically Algerian interests. The Communist project involved associate membership of the French Union, stopping short of independence but granting the Algerian Assembly wider powers than those proposed by the government. A third project, that of the Socialists – grateful for an opportunity thus to distance themselves from their colleagues in the government! – limited the powers of the Assembly but replaced the governor-general with a minister resident in Algiers. Lastly, the Muslim deputies from Algeria, also divided amongst themselves, hesitated between a rejection of all discussion until the people had been consulted, and demands for a sovereign Assembly within the French Union. The government was forced to take into account SFIO and MRP wishes, as well as some of the demands made by the groups of the rapidly coalescing Third Force – the Radicals, the UDSR, and the Independents. De Gaulle added to the confusion by going back on the terms of the ordinance of 7 March 1944 and the law of 5 October 1946; he now advocated a strict separation of the Muslim and European electoral colleges – disappointing the Muslims but exciting settler opinion, as reflected in the RPF's successes in the overseas territories.[8] A protracted but uninspired debate, in which adroit manoeuvring by Ramadier was needed to head off repeated ministerial crises, was concerned chiefly with the composition of the respective electoral colleges and the means of ensuring a 'loyal' majority in the Algerian Assembly. The much-amended government project was accepted at the end of August and promulgated on 20 September 1947.

Under the new statute, Algeria was divided into *départements*, each with its own structures and nominal financial autonomy. The *départements* were placed under an all-powerful governor-general, the direct representative in Algiers of the French government and responsible to the Minister of the Interior. The governor-general had authority over the prefects and the local administrations, with the exception of Justice and Education for the Europeans. The only original structures were the Assembly itself and a six-member council of government – a rubber-stamp body between the governor-general and the Assembly. This last was carefully divided into two colleges of sixty members; the first elected by the 460 000 citizens of French status, plus the 58 000 assimilated Muslims; the second by 1 400 000 unassimilated Algerians. The Assembly had minimal financial powers; it was to assure the application of French legislation in Algeria, and was to nominate six representatives to the Assembly of the French Union. The text also opened the way for the suppression of the unpopular and wholly undemocratic *communes mixtes* and an end to the special régime for the Saharan regions; a future female suffrage and an education programme in French and Arabic were also announced. The statute marked a departure, albeit a very modest one, from the principle of assimilation. Yet what seemed an honorable compromise in Paris satisfied neither side in Algeria: the colonial élite considered it a disgrace, and the Muslims remained indifferent.

For in fact the initative in Algeria was already shifting to the side of the nationalists. The MTLD, under the strong leadership of Messali Hadj, freed in October 1946, scored notable successes in the general elections of November 1946 and in the municipal elections of October 1947; the UDMA of Ferhat Abbas was also progressing; and the Algerian Communist Party, having thrown off the tutelage of the PCF in a spectacular change of strategy in the summer of 1946, was building new support and momentum on the themes of the Algerian cultural identity and the nationalist struggle.[9] These nationalist advances robbed the French project of much of its potential relevance; even without them, however, it is questionable whether a wholehearted or honest application of the statute was ever in fact envisaged. On 11 February 1948, the liberal Governor, Yves Chataigneau – detested by the Europeans in Algeria and attacked from inside the Schuman cabinet by René Mayer, Minister of Finance and deputy for the Algerian constituency of Constantine – was replaced by Marcel-Edmond Naegelen, a Socialist with strong Jacobin views. Naegelen's appointment was a victory for the *colons* and heralded a return to authoritarian policies. On his orders the hounding of the nationalists now began in earnest; no efforts were spared to secure 'good' results in the approaching elections. Against a background of renewed violence from the Messalist nationalists, the French authorities indulged in systematic electoral manipulation, vetting candidates and falsifying results.[10] The outcome of the 11 April elections surpassed the hopes of even Naegelen and the Europeans: in the first college the Right, the Centre, and the RPF crushed the Socialists and Communists, obtaining fifty-four of the sixty seats; in the second college the candidates of the administration 'won' forty-one of the sixty seats, with just nine for the MTLD, eight to the UDMA, and two for the Socialists. This result helps to explain of course why the Algerian statute was quite simply forgotten; the *communes mixtes* remained, and the proposals for agrarian, educational, and social reforms were stillborn. As for Algerian elections, until 1958 their 'loyal' outcome was never to pose a problem for the French administration in Algeria. Apparently oblivious to the explosive economic, demographic, and social situation, the French authorities continued as before. In Algeria then, the policies of the Third Force had made dialogue impossible, succeeding only in convincing the nationalists of the futility of action within the law.

The position was graver still in Indo-China. A policy marked by pre-varication and deceit destroyed the last chances for negotiation, divided the Vietnamese people, and fuelled the conflict. After the Hanoi attack of 19 December 1946 the Indo-Chinese problem became increasingly entangled with French domestic politics. The Socialists and Communists remained favourable to negotiations, but the MRP and the Right were determined to use the 'treason of 19 December' as a pretext for breaking off all dialogue with the Vietnamese government. Moutet was dispatched to Hanoi at the beginning of January, but deliberately avoided contact with Ho Chi Minh (in fact a message from the Vietnamese leader was not communicated to him); to d'Argenlieu's satisfaction, Moutet concluded that the restoration of order was the precondition for negotiation; and Leclerc, already discour-aged, refused to take over. From now on French policy was concerned only to recover the military initiative and to find alternative spokesmen among the nationalists and Catholics to oppose to the Vietminh. The strategic axes and the major towns of Hanoi, Hué, and Nam Dinh were cleared by armoured forces – but control of the jungle was abandoned to the guerril-las. By the middle of March 1947 the French General Staff, having lost all contact with the Vietminh regular forces, felt able to declare order restored. It was at this point that the interaction between domestic and overseas politics again became apparent. Further military credits for Indo-China were voted by the Assembly on 22 March, but the issue had split the Communists from the rest of the government. Four days previously the Communist Minister of Defence, Billoux, had refused to be associated with an official tribute to the French forces in Indo-China, and Thorez had left the government benches. Angered by what he saw as insubordination from his ministers, Ramadier now, in fact, decided to break with the Communists.

This development of course strengthened the opponents of negotiation, deepening Ho Chi Minh's isolation still further – rumours of his death were even encouraged by the French side. Between 21 December and 5 March he had made seven calls for an immediate ceasefire: all went unanswered. The departure of the Communists from the government on 5 May completed his isolation, depriving him of support inside the cabinet. True, the headstrong d'Argenlieu had been replaced on 5 March by Bollaert, a Radical with Gaullist sympathies, but traces of the former's policies remained. The military was pressing for an anti-guerrilla campaign based on extensive – and costly – patrolling of the territory; now the first armed outposts in the bush were built. The administration and *colons* of the South kept up their pressure through an anti-Marxist Front de l'Union nationale du Vietnam, clamouring for a union of the three provinces. Such hopes were encouraged by the French authorities in order to get the Front's support for the solution which was in fact taking shape on the French side – the restoration of Emperor Bao Dai. In France the SFIO continued to waver; the MRP, now firmly in control with Paul Coste-Floret at the Ministry of War, announced a definitive military victory and the elimination of the Vietminh; and the hardliners received another boost with the launching of de Gaulle's RPF. This domestic political context left Bollaert little room for manoeuvre in the negotiations: on the one hand an insistence that the French Union was the only acceptable framework for a settlement – on the other a steadfast refusal to recognize Ho Chi Minh's government as representative.

To a renewed call from Ho Chi Minh on 26 April for an immediate ceasefire and fresh talks, Paul Mus replied by laying down impossibly severe and humiliating conditions that the Vietminh could never accept. On 19 July, worried by the growing international stature of Bao Dai and by signs of weariness among the population, Ho Chi Minh removed Giap and brought more non-Communists into his government; a few days later he offered to co-operate with Bao Dai. Neither concession produced a change in the French position, one whose familiar premiss Bollaert summed up by affirming that settlement was impossible before an end to 'this insane guerrilla action'. All talk of independence was anathema – Bidault furiously crossed out the word in the draft of Bollaert's Hadong policy speech of 10 September. In Indo-China as in France, the Third Force was intent on excluding the Communists from all negotiations. Faced with Ho Chi Minh and the non-Communist nationalists, the French government, Bollaert, the military, and the colonial administration concentrated all their efforts on bolstering Bao Dai's position. The idea of an Indo-Chinese Federation was abandoned. The logic and price of anticommunism was clear: what had been so strenuously refused to Ho Chi Minh at Fontainbleau, a united Vietnam, was now to be handed to Bao Dai, a figure widely recognized to be weak. This was the solution finally embodied in the Along Bay agreement of 5 June 1948. By then, however, after General Valluy's major autumn offensive had failed to engage the Vietminh in the open, the 'dirty war' was well established.

Madagascar, Algeria, and Indo-China: in each case dialogue with the nationalists had been broken; in each case the French Union had started badly. French policy had been shown to be tied to the evolution of domestic politics, an evolution dictated by the logic of anticommunism. The blusterers continued to applaud each 'definitive' military pacification; the pessimists worried about the scarcity of potential interlocutors. No Associated States had been found to participate when the

Assembly of the French Union met for the first time at Versailles on 10 December 1947. Like the elections which had guaranteed its 'loyal' composition, the Assembly was already a hollow sham.

## The Republic alone

To these failings overseas were added serious difficulties within France. In the space of a few months the Republic which claimed descent from the Resistance became estranged from its two principal sources of legitimacy: Communism and Gaullism. This brutal rupture, predictable from the convulsions of *tripartisme*, rocked the nation as it faced a deepening economic and social crisis.

The economic situation was indeed alarming, for in 1947 the cost of the previous year's short-sighted policies had to be met. Rationing, the black market, and the failure to block wages caused prices to soar. The forecasts for 1947 were dramatic: the public sector (State expenditure, Social Security, and local charges) accounted for half the national income. A commission was hastily set up to make drastic cuts in subsidies and defence expenditure, and reduce employment in the swollen public sector. Hopes were being pinned on a revival of output. But this required stable prices: in a belated attempt to break the vicious circle of wage and price increases, Blum and Philip imposed an overall 10 per cent reduction in prices, to be effected in two steps of 5 per cent each, in January and March. Their deflationary experiment failed: the winter was hard, the population hungry and impatient; there were bottlenecks in raw materials, energy, and labour; the commercial balance deteriorated and the currency reserves dwindled. In the spring, with output down by at least 10 per cent, came mounting unrest in industry and pressure from groups like the CGPME; the reserves were exhausted, and American credit had to be used on day-to-day expenditure rather than for reconstruction. Ramadier's uncertain grasp on economics was visible in a policy which lurched between liberalism and *dirigisme*; authorizing, for example, a 20 per cent increase in meat prices in February at the moment when the second stage of the price reduction was to be implemented! Finally, the grain harvest was destroyed by frost, and with the farmers again withholding supplies, the food stocks were running low.

There were bread riots in May in the regions of the Centre. Bakers in Paris were closed on Sundays. The bread ration was reduced to 250 grammes, then to 200 grammes in September. The combined moral authorities of President Auriol, Cardinal Suhard, Pastor Bœgner, and the Chief Rabbi had to be mobilized in a campaign to persuade the rural communities to make a greater effort.

And wage demands could not be ignored. After a strike of the Paris press came a partial strike at the Renault factories. This was called by a Trotskyite minority on 25 April, but it was widely followed and had to be quickly taken in hand by an embarrassed CGT.[11] May Day saw large demonstrations throughout France; in Paris, Thorez and Frachon made no attempt to restrain the crowd on the place de la Concorde from booing the Socialist Minister of Labour, Daniel Mayer. The strike of the Renault metal-workers ended on 16 May after substantial increases had been awarded, and was followed by threats of action by gas, electricity, and railway workers. An agreement of 23 May between Mayer and the CGT raised the basic minimum wage and disguised the resulting general increases as productivity bonuses. Between January and July the money supply rose by 40 per cent and wages by 47 per cent; over the same period wholesale prices increased by 91 per cent and retail prices by 93 per cent. Yet in spite of this drastic erosion of purchasing power, Ramadier persisted in his claims that the upsurge of strike action – which from June marked the collapse of the Blum experiment – was engineered by the Communists.

In reality, several factors were present in the unrest of spring 1947. An increased belligerence on the part of the CGT was real enough; it reflected the Communist leadership's alarm at the signs of impatience among the workforce – the danger of which was clear from the support for the Trotskyite initiative at Renault – and at the anticommunist stirrings within the union itself. The CGT militants knew that something concrete now had to be shown for the industrial peace the union had guaranteed since 1944 in the name of reconstruction.[12] The government was in part responsible for heightening tension by its extensive use of the press and radio to denounce scandals and conspiracies, and to make highly charged appeals for calm. The Joanovici affair, for example, concerning a metal merchant who had made a fortune selling metal to the Germans at the same time as funding a Resistance movement, filled the press and led to the suspension of a prefect of police; or the Hardy affair, involving a *résistant* whose sensational trial showed him to have been at the origin of Jean Moulin's capture; the iniquities of the *épuration*: all helped to tarnish the image of the Resistance. The anticommunist scares multiplied; an extensive Communist infiltration of the Ministry of Ex-Servicemen was uncovered; rumours spread of an 'International brigade' being formed in France, and of secret arms stocks; Depreux warned of a 'nouveau 6 Février', and Auriol took very seriously the alarmist reports of the security forces. From March onwards, in an atmosphere of increasing tension between Moscow and Washington, the notion of an imminent Communist takeover made rapid progress – on Ramadier's personal authority the new Head of the General Staff, General Revers, placed the reliable forces of order on a state of alert.

This was not the only threat to the régime for, at the same time, de Gaulle's opposition began to take a dangerous new form. He had had ample time to reflect on the tactical error of retiring in January 1946 – France had managed without him. In February 1947, convinced that a new global conflict was close and that Communist infiltration had reached a critical point, he decided to found a new movement, the Rassemblement du peuple français (RPF). Two speeches, one at Bruneval on 30 March, the other at Strasbourg a week later, laid the bases for his new resistance to an 'illegitimate' régime. The themes of the Gaullist message were familiar, although their tone had hardened. For the economy, the role of the State had to be reduced and the spirit of free enterprise encouraged. Gaullist social reflection was limited to developing a closer association of capital and labour to form a bulwark against collectivism. For the colonies, the generosity of Brazzaville was replaced by a strong insistence on continued French presence within the framework of the French Union. Lastly, a strong and independent France was to remain outside of the two blocs that were taking shape, although her commitment to the West was emphasized. Formally constituted on 14 April, the new movement had a broad appeal: to former members of the Resistance; to erstwhile *travaillistes* who remembered the 'social' ordinances of 1944–5; and above all, thanks to the stress on patriotism, freedom, and anticommunism, there was a vast clientele to be recruited from the MRP, the Centre, and the Right – from workers through to apprehensive bourgeois who had supported Vichy; plus of course all the Gaullist faithfuls. As Malraux, charged with RPF propaganda, was to quip about the new movement's catch-all composition: 'Le RPF, c'est le métro.' In spite of an immediate and unanimous condemnation of de Gaulle's initiative by the three majority parties (who promptly forbade their adherents double membership), and the stated intention of the RPF not to become just another political party, the new movement grew spectacularly: 810 000 requests for membership by 1 May; perhaps a million members by the end of December.[13]

The question now was to see if the mushrooming of the RPF would produce a defensive response from the members of the tripartite alliance, a closing of ranks in order to combat the Gaullist threat. There was no shortage of calls from the Communists for 'Republican vigilance' against the new Louis Napoleon; calls echoed by the SFIO leadership, and by Ramadier who warned against placing hopes in a 'Supreme Saviour'. The MRP, although the most directly threatened of the three parties in electoral terms, was more cautious in its criticism, but could not conceal that it was badly shaken by the irruption of the Gaullist alternative. For the moment, however, the attitude of the Communists was ambiguous. The Communist ministers seem to have underestimated the hostility that the economic and political crisis and this new Gaullism in fact focused on them. Until mid-March they repeatedly argued, often against members of their own party, that to break the ruling coalition would precipitate France into the

American camp; insisting, for example, that Bidault enjoyed their full confidence to negotiate in Moscow. True, the debate over Indo-China had left Ramadier at least in no doubt that the Communists could not be in both the government and the Opposition; but even at the end of the Moscow Conference their future course was not fixed: the Party's leadership remained uncertain as to Stalin's strategy. On the other hand, however, there is no doubt that the wave of strikes, by producing the familiar defensive response, did much to influence the PCF's attitude. In danger of losing the initiative to the groups of the extreme Left, the PCF had quickly to reassert its authority in the trade unions and in strike action if it was to preserve the influence which, since 1936, had established the Communist Party in its unique spokesman-of-the-working-class role.[14] And such a role was clearly incompatible with a continued endorsement of the Ramadier government's policies on prices and wages by the Communist Ministers. More, then, than either Indo-China or Madagascar it was the social question which determined the attitude of the PCF – it was government policy on price and wage controls which moved Thorez to his most violent outbursts in the cabinet during the final weeks. Not only was the Communist Party in a contradictory position, but its failure to come to terms with the rapidly evolving domestic and international situation underlined painfully the absence of long-term policy which had handicapped the PCF since the Liberation.

The decision to dismiss the Communist ministers on 5 May 1947 was Ramadier's alone, the logical conclusion to draw from the Communist refusal the previous day to vote confidence in the government's economic and social policy. The Communists had not intended to resign from the government and their summary dismissal took them by surprise; indeed, Georges Marrane, Minister of Health, who was a member of the Council of the Republic and thus not directly involved, waited twenty-four hours before following his comrades out of the government. Nor was the incident followed by an immediate and hostile reaction; later in May, and in June, Duclos made conciliatory declarations; and the Party Congress at Strasbourg called merely for the formation of a democratic government in which the Communists would occupy their rightful place.

In fact, it was not until much later, in the autumn, that the dismissal of the Communist ministers received its full ideological interpretation. At the time they reacted calmly; their departure, particularly that of Thorez, was not without dignity, reaffirming in their final speeches a determination to defend the interests of the French working class. And until its position in Stalin's Cold War strategy became known, this stance was to serve the PCF well, preventing it from becoming merely another element of the Opposition; preserving its electoral potential while leaving the way open for an eventual return to power. The Socialists had of course taken a considerable risk, that of cutting themselves off from the working class by breaking with the party most closely identified with it, and ruining in the process all hopes for a union of the Left. Ramadier and the parliamentary group had presented the SFIO with the *fait accompli* – some, notably Guy Mollet, opposed Ramadier and Blum, and argued that the Socialists should also leave office. After a stormy session of the National Council on 6 May, the SFIO decided by 2529 to 2125 votes in favour of remaining in power, adding only the condition that this not depend on a reactionary majority. What had seemed inconceivable at the Liberation had in fact happened – the Socialists now agreed to govern without the Communists. No doubt their decision had been influenced by the urgent need to defend the régime against the double challenge of the Communists and Gaullists; no doubt either, however, that this decision marked a turning-point in the history of their party.

Thanks to the small majority in the SFIO's 6 May vote, the way for the Third Force was now open. De Gaulle for his part had taken the responsibility of attacking a legitimate régime and beginning a new resistance. The tripartite alliance was in ruins. The conditions of its collapse were the same as of its creation: a crisis whose outcome was settled by the political parties acting in what they perceived to be the national interest – the electorate had not been asked for its opinion.

## The 'great fear' of autumn 1947

Against a background of mounting Cold War tension and acute industrial unrest since the spring, the deterioration accelerated. The Ramadier government's days were numbered since 5 May 1947: under pressure from the SFIO leadership, lukewarmly supported by Auriol, and without a coherent economic and social policy, it simply drifted. Efforts at controlling prices succeeded only in driving produce off the market; wage increases conceded sector by sector rekindled the inflation. Robert Schuman, Minister of Finance, called for orthodox budgetary policies and an end to subsidies; André Philip advocated a *dirigiste* approach. Ramadier refused to arbitrate; on 4 July he dismissed as of purely academic interest the debate over liberalism versus intervention, reiterating his faith in a common-sensical pragmatism. The conditions of daily life were becoming desperate. In September domestic coal production fell, the price of imports rose; grain was scarce after the poor harvest; a kilo of potatoes supposed to cost 9 francs typically sold for between 16 and 20; shortages of bread and sugar led to rioting at Verdun and Le Mans. Auriol noted grimly for 15 September: 'The unrest is close to panic ... the government appears to lack the means to get its authority respected.'[15]

The strikes spread swiftly, first in the public sector, then to metallurgy, the banks, the big stores, and transport. A vicious circle had in fact developed: no sooner were the strikes of May and June settled with an 11 per cent agreement between the CGT and the CNPF than a comparable increase was demanded for the public sector, which in its turn provoked renewed demands in the private sector. Although the CGT tried where possible to take the unrest in hand, the impetus for action usually came from the workforce. The demands were narrowly economic – for a raising of low wages, productivity bonuses, parity between the public and private sectors – and reflected widespread anxieties over food and supplies. The government repudiated the 11 per cent settlement of the summer and continued to struggle to impose the arbitrations of the Joint Commissions, helped in its efforts by Daniel Mayer's contacts with the trade unions. But finally, in October, it was forced to concede the 11 per cent award in the public sector, as well as a generous revision of differentials.

The industrial unrest fostered fears of subversion. A conspiracy uncovered in the summer revealed that Vichy sympathizers with extensive contacts among industrialists and the military were preparing an armed defence against a possible Communist takeover. Developments in Eastern Europe added to the tension; Petkov, leader of the Bulgarian Peasant Party, was hanged on 16 August; the opposition parties in Poland and Hungary were eliminated; Moscow was tightening its grip in Eastern Europe. And Stalin's Cold War strategy for the Communists of Western Europe was at last made clear. A secret meeting of the leaders of the nine European Communist Parties held at Szlarska-Poreba in Poland (22–27 September) prepared the launching of the Cominform and gave official form to the policy of hostile blocs. It was during these discussions that Djilas and Zdanov made a violent attack on the policies followed by the French and Italian Communists since the Liberation. Dumbfounded and defensive but finally penitent, Duclos and Fajon had to admit their Party's error, that of having believed in the efficacy of a parliamentary and governmental action, of having thus been a 'witless lackey of imperialism'. The repercussions of the new Soviet analysis were not slow to be felt in France: from October the PCF moved into open opposition. Meanwhile, de Gaulle continued to announce the coming global catastrophe, adopting an increasingly extreme anticommunism. On 27 July at Rennes he denounced the PCF as a 'party of separatists' whose sole purpose was to further the interests of the Soviet Union and its satellites. And he was no less severe towards the political parties, incapable of confronting the Communist menace, concerned only with their own interests: at Vincennes on 5 October he attacked all 'the little parties who were absorbed in the intrigues of their own little world'.[16] The RPF began to organize, building itself an important place in the political system it affected to despise. At the end of August a parliamentary intergroup of forty-one deputies was formed, and lists were drawn up of candidates to be presented under the Rassemblement's patronage in the October municipal elections.

These elections in fact crystallized the crisis. The campaign was a hard one, with violent incidents involving Gaullists and Communists. The RPF developed rapidly, tempting the parliamentarians and perfecting its methods of mass meetings. The campaign revealed to the Communists the extent of their isolation and the disastrous impact of the Polish conference. The RPF's electoral breakthrough was spectacular, capturing 38 per cent of the vote; the advances were especially important in the large urban centres, allowing it to take control of Bordeaux, Rennes, and Strasbourg, and dominating the Paris municipality, now led by the General's brother, Pierre de Gaulle. However, the movement had not always been careful in its choice of candidates, and the results showed that its electorates were already further to the Right than were its leaders. Predictably then, the Gaullist surge had a particularly serious effect on the MRP, now reduced to 10 per cent of the vote, and this concentrated in the Catholic strongholds of Alsace and Brittany; these elections in fact marked the start of the MRP's decline and the end of its ambitions to become a great popular party. The Left remained stable; the Socialists resisted the Gaullist and Communist assaults; the PCF, reaping the benefits of its stance as the champion of working-class interests, consolidated its share of the vote at 30 per cent. And the naming of mayors by the councils in the days immediately following the elections amplified the swing to the Right, confirming the strength of the anticommunist positions. Electorally then, France was now divided into three roughly equal parts: the Gaullists, the Communists, and the parties of the future Third Force. The tripartite alliance was completely lifeless: the future course depended now on the Radicals and Moderates.

In terms of parliamentary arithmetic the subtraction of 165 Communists and 40 Gaullists excluded all tripartite solution. The investiture of a government required 314 votes: yet the MRP and Socialists between them had only 249 – to form a Third Force they would need the support of 100-odd Radicals and Moderates. In the municipal elections, however, these had either supported the RPF or had not presented candidates against it; the survival of the régime hung, then, on their refusal now to provoke the dissolution of the Assembly – something de Gaulle demanded in an imperious ultimatum on 27 October. Several considerations were present in their rejection of this course: the advantages to them of proportional representation – for the RPF was known to favour a return to a straight majority system – the Communist danger; and the obvious attractions of power. With their decision to back a Third Force solution the balance of French politics settled at the Centre: de Gaulle had miscalculated, at least for the moment. Ramadier reshuffled his cabinet on 22 October, acknowledging the new balance of force by removing André

Philip, Tanguy-Prigent, and Moutet; Agriculture, a key post given the food crisis, went to an Independent, Marcel Roclore; and Robert Schuman remained at Finance. The vote of investiture on 30 October was secured by just twenty votes. With the UDSR in disarray, the MRP divided and the Radicals recovering quickly inside the RGR, the Centrists could look forward to taking power.

Ramadier's exhausted government, openly condemned by Guy Mollet, hung on for a little longer. But its replacement had to occur without a break – with social unrest mounting and two-thirds of the electorate known to be hostile, the parties of the Third Force were understandably reluctant to face the test of new elections. Blum, backed by Auriol and Mollet, attempted to obtain the investiture on 21 November but was defeated by nine votes – all from the Centre. The power of the Right and the Centre to arbitrate was in fact absolute; and as Blum's humiliating experience had shown, they did not intend to make any concessions, least of all over anticommunism. The logical sequel, a shift to the Centre-Right, occurred the following day, when Robert Schuman secured the investiture by a large majority. Schuman had support from the Radicals and Independents as well as from his own MRP, was unopposed by the Socialists, and was able to reassure even the Gaullists. He formed a large MRP-based team, one which included most of the major figures of the years to come.[17] Nonetheless, the appetites of those responsible for the change had not all obtained satisfaction, and the distribution of ministerial portfolios had already pointed up what was to be a major weakness of the Third Force's composite parliamentary majorities. For between the investiture of Schuman himself and the vote of confidence in his team on 27 November, 90 votes deserted Schuman. It was of course no coincidence that among the defections were 32 from the PRL, 11 UDSR, 12 Independents, and 8 Radicals.[18]

For the moment, however, Schuman, a devout Catholic from Lorraine, inspired confidence; so too did his appointment of Jules Moch, a firm and methodical Socialist, as Minister of the Interior. The urgent task awaiting Moch was that of restoring order in a situation close to insurrection; for a third wave of strikes, in November and December, took the form of overtly political conflicts. An increase in tram fares, decided by Marseille's new RPF municipality, provoked a general strike in the city, degenerating into rioting on 10–12 December. The restoration of order by the CRS – in which the Communists were numerous – was slow and unenthusiastic; the mayor, Callini, was injured; public buildings were occupied and bars pillaged; and a young Communist was killed.[19] On 15 November a strike broke out among the miners of the Houillères du Nord after the resignation of the president, Duquet, and the dismissal of Delfosse, an administrator and prominent CGT official. The bitter conflict opposed the CGT-organized miners, exhausted by their efforts in the battle for production but galvanized for this new resistance, to the CRS and then to troops soon sent in by Moch.[20] The mining regions were placed under virtual military occupation, the atmosphere poisoned by the provocations and brutality of the often ill-disciplined forces of order. Violence on the other side broke the unity of the strike, setting 'rouges' against 'jaunes', opposing Communists to Socialists. On 3 December the derailment of the Paris–Tourcoing Express left twenty-one dead, the last in a long series of anonymous acts of sabotage in the region. Rival meetings were held under the protection of PCF and RPF 'heavies'; rumours of the approaching Communist bid for power multiplied. And strikes spread again to metallurgy, textiles, chemicals, food, building, transport, and the public services. With the setting up on 28 November of a Central Strike Committee by the twenty CGT federations by now involved in the action, the prospect of an insurrectional general strike seemed to move closer.[21]

The response of the government to this threat to the régime was to order a complete mobilization of the forces of order, calling out the reserves and conscripts, and giving unanimous backing to the brutal resolve of the Minister of the Interior. On 4 December, after a tumultuous debate lasting six days, the government secured the passage of a series of emergency measures of 'Republican defence', including a guarantee of the right to work.[22] However, the defeat of the strike movement owed less to the actions of the authorities than to the growing opposition it encountered among the moderate and non-Communist elements of the workforce. From 15 November, the initial anger subsided; resistance to Communist intimidation strengthened; workers began demanding secret ballots for the continuation of strikes, and pickets were deliberately confronted. Calls for an end to the strikes and for talks came from the independent trade unions, the CFTC, and the Force Ouvrière groups of the CGT. With this waning of enthusiasm, the way was open for the forces of order to evacuate the occupied factories and for the setting-up of official arbitration procedures. Outbreaks of concerted violence occurred at the start of November at Saint-Etienne, Béziers, Nice, and Valence; but the general strike movement was faltering. The CGT leadership sensed the mood changing, and talks with Daniel Mayer resulted in the calling of a general return to work on 10 December. The Republic of Auriol and Schuman had been saved; and the working class, whether from exhaustion, wisdom, or disenchantment, returned, confused and divided, to production.

This upsurge of unrest raises, of course, the question of the Communist Party's objectives. And despite the very different context, the reply is strikingly similar to that of three years previously: the PCF had faithfully implemented the Cominform's strategy, one whose aim, whatever the Party's opponents and even some of its militants believed, was not an insurrectional one. Under this strategy the task of the PCF was to mobilize

French opinion on the theme of national sovereignty, thus contributing to the resistance to American domination of Europe. In short then: yes to agitation; no to subversion. From the end of October, when the PCF's attitude was one of open opposition and Duclos had violently attacked the Marshall Plan, the Party leadership worked continuously to avoid a loss of control which could lead to an attempted insurrection. This general Cold War strategy of the Socialist bloc was in fact well-suited to the French context. The policy of 'advanced democracy' was not abandoned, merely shelved; the patriotism of the Resistance and the Liberation was harnessed to the struggle for national independence *vis-à-vis* the United States. And although the programmed pugnacity of the autumn lacked an immediate objective it allowed the PCF to reconcile the demands of Moscow with a defence of the gains it had made in France since 1936. That it protected the PCF's electoral potential was clear from the municipal elections of October; it also helped to forge a new generation of party militants and officials; and it enabled the effectiveness of the links with the labour movement to be confirmed and strike strategy refined. As in 1944–5, then, the goal of the Party leaders in making an ideological about-turn, as in ordering the aimless unrest, was clear: to preserve the Party and to deepen its identification with the interests of the nation and the working class.[23]

Not only was this a dangerous game but it proved a bad calculation – for the confrontations of 1947 split the French trade union movement. True, the crisis had had the merit of making clear to all the sense of developments since 1936. The decisive place of the strongly unionized public sector in the conflict reflected the evolution in the role of the State; henceforth, the trade unions were increasingly to act as pressure groups on the public authorities, for their part often less willing to cede than the employers or the CNPF. In the process, however, the violence and anti-communist hysteria had torn apart the fragile *syndicaliste* ideology which traditionally masked the political divergences within the trade-union movement. At their second national conference on 18 December, the Force Ouvrière groups decided to break from the CGT and form an independent movement. The patient work of organizing anticommunist energies, often within Socialist groups in firms, that had been under way since 1938 and in full flood since autumn 1946, had thus culminated in rupture.

Under Léon Jouhaux's leadership, the new union of FO–CGT was formally constituted in April 1948; the newcomer, funded to a large extent by the American unions and even the CIA, was welcomed by the SFIO.[24] Another development was the creation of the powerful Fédération de l'éducation nationale (FEN), influenced by the Syndicat national des instituteurs, and committed to a defence of the secular principle in the education system and the *œuvres sociales* of its members. Aware, however, of the weakness a division would produce, the FEN refused to take sides in the new rupture, adopting instead a position of 'provisional' autonomy.[25]

The spectacular and far-reaching split in the historically weak French trade union movement came as the working class, exhausted and demoralized after a year of struggles, relapsed into silence. The political leaders of the Fourth Republic already seemed too preoccupied with the intricate parliamentary manoeuvres for the Third Force coalition to recognize this new quiescence as a cause for concern. On a more positive note, the political minority which controlled the parliamentary solutions could at least congratulate itself on having successfully warded off the double threat to the régime, and on having broken out of the alarming spiral of social unrest and fear. Little remained now of the ethos of the Liberation; those condemned as ideologically bankrupt just a few years earlier had triumphed, and were eager to show that they held a valid alternative to both Communism and Gaullism. One part of this alternative was now to involve leading France firmly into the Cold War's Western camp.

# 9

# France under the American umbrella

The period from 1948 to 1952 brought no healing of the divisions opened in 1947. The Cold War intensified and the great power blocs hardened their positions; in preparation, so it often seemed, for the final confrontation. For in France, as elsewhere, these years were overshadowed by fears of a generalized and suicidal global conflict. The spectacular events which punctuated this difficult period are familiar: the Prague takeover in February 1948; the purges and executions in Eastern Europe; the Berlin blockade from June 1948 to May 1949; the partition of Germany and the birth of the Atlantic Alliance. Outside Europe, the period was that of McCarthy in the United States, the advance of Communism in China and Indo-China, and, finally, open war in Korea from June 1950 to November 1951. And in the background was the awesome menace of the American and Soviet atomic weapons.

Not that all was negative. Indeed, this tense global context stimulated some unexpectedly positive developments in France. A place under the American economic and military umbrella, in fact, led to serious reflection on the nature of the Atlantic commitment and on national independence; and French fears of a German revival prompted initiatives for European unity rather than the traditional defensive reaction. A considerably improved material position fostered a relative euphoria among the population, helping to dissipate the accumulated anxieties of the previous decade; domestic opinion remained effectively insulated from external developments. As a result, tension rose less sharply in France, and alignments there were less automatic than in other countries; even if there was conflict in Indo-China as an increasingly insistent reminder of the unpalatable reality.

## The American umbrella

The choices made in 1947 meant that French security and prosperity were now dependent on American aid, something quickly demonstrated by the stimulative effects of the Marshall Plan. As we have seen, the interim aid from the United States ensured an improvement in supplies of petrol, coal, and grain, easing conditions during the winter and bringing the end of restrictions nearer. The new Economic Co-operation Administration (ECA) responsible for administering the Marshall Plan set up its missions in the European capitals; the team in Paris, though careful to avoid open interference in the running of French foreign affairs, gave decisive backing to Jean Monnet, Commissioner for the Plan. That there was direct American intervention in the economic and administrative life of the nation is thus undeniable; and the parliamentary debate of 28 June on the ratification of the agreement had made clear the risks of 'colonization' present in the American aid proposals, with their stipulations concerning financial stability, protection for American firms seeking to invest in France, and the ban on exports of strategic goods to the East. American aid fixed France in the commercial orbit of the West, one which was liberal in its ideology and practice, but sharply delimited in the new geography of the balance of world power.

The economic advantages were too important to ignore, however. The impact on internal reconstruction and modernization will be examined later, but the sheer size of American aid has to be underlined, not least because of its clear implications for the conduct of French diplomacy. Between April 1948 and January 1952, France received 2629 million dollars, of which 2122 million were free grants. The French share in fact represented 20.2 per cent of the total American aid to Europe, compared with 24.4 per cent for Great Britain, but only 11 per cent for Italy and 10.1 per cent for West Germany. Moreover, France had the largest share of the free grants (23.8 per cent), a compensation no doubt for her diplomatic concessions over the German question and in recognition of her efforts in favour of European reconstruction. And not only did these dollars – which represented 48 per cent of the resources of the Fonds de modernization et d'équipement for the same period – come at the critical moment to boost investment and planning,[1] but American control of their distribution within the economy was minimal, left in fact to French officials to decide. With industrial output rising and trade reviving, the closing of the 'dollar gap', and the modernization of production, the economic benefits directly attributable to Marshall Aid were incontestable.

This certainty makes even more surprising the French reluctance to acknowledge the advantages of American aid. Before examining the reasons for the French reticence it is worth considering the disappointment of French hopes to extend to all the recipients of Marshall Aid the benefits of the Monnet Plan in the form of a common programme for European recovery. Tentative steps were taken in this direction; the Organization for European Economic Cooperation (OEEC) was created in Paris on 16 April 1948 and set up at the Chateau de la Muette, grouping (in accordance with

American wishes) the sixteen nations who had accepted the American offer, and joined by the future West Germany on 31 October 1949. But it soon became clear that the Europeans were divided and that as a result the ECAs would have to operate in strictly national frameworks. In particular, the Labour government in Great Britain was determined to avoid too close ties with the Third Force and Christian Democrat governments of France, Italy and, soon, Federal Germany, preferring instead to negotiate directly with the United States, and still hoping to make sterling the dominant currency in Europe. In a similar spirit, the Benelux countries proved unwilling to share the benefits of their recent economic union. French hopes had been premature, and although a young disciple of Monnet, Robert Marjolin, became General Secretary of the OEEC, Paul-Henri Spaak was appointed General Director in October 1948. The new organization's structures were weak, and its experts and planners were continually hamstrung by their respective national governments; decisions taken unanimously by its Council of Ministers were not binding on any member whose representatives had abstained from the vote. In short, the OEEC was never given any of the supranational authority with which it might have been able to negotiate on more equal terms with Washington. Consequently it was never able to impose a coherent plan for European reconstruction: a Belgian initiative of February 1949 was fruitless; in April it became clear that Anglo-French economic union was chimerical; in 1950 the Petsche, Stikker, and Pella plans for European investment came to nothing, as did those of 1952 on transport and agriculture. Successive initiatives ran foul of national interests, as in the rejection of a customs union by Great Britain, anxious to preserve her privileged relations with the Commonwealth.

On the positive side however, the OEEC made an important contribution to the liberation of exchanges. Taking advantage of the necessary readjustment of parities following the devaluation of sterling in September 1949, the OEEC secured the adoption of a code which, whilst not disturbing customs duties, committed the members to the suppression of the exchange quotas in common use since the crisis of the 1930s; from 1951 the quotas on three-quarters of all imports were abolished. Still more encouraging was the creation in July 1950 of the European Payments Union to facilitate compensatory payments between the central banks of the member states, and the automatic issue of credits in units of account. Embracing the franc and sterling zones, this clearing body made a significant contribution to the refinement of commercial policies, as well as fostering a European financial solidarity to oppose to the IMF and American investors, even if the orientation of credit and investment continued to resist effective control.[2] Much of the responsibility for these early failures lay with Great Britain; but the chronic inflation in France – exacerbated by the cost of the war in Indo-China and by the rise in raw material prices triggered by the Korean War – was also an obstacle to further progress.

In fact, however, French reticence stemmed less from the economic implications of American aid than from the system of military alliance which came in its wake. A seriously weakened Europe and a France with her best forces already fighting in Indo-China had little real choice when the conditions of the Cold War necessitated a rapid solution in the military domain. The feeble European structures of the OEEC and the Council of Europe were now hastily capped by an Atlantic framework within which the American involvement in Europe took an overtly military form.

The original offer from the Americans had included no such commitment; at the end of 1947 they made their aid conditional simply on the development of genuine co-operation between the free nations of Europe. In fact, the initiatives came not from the United States but from Europe, where Bevin and Bidault were already seeking American military support, no longer against Germany but to resist the Soviet threat. The two countries had very different conceptions of the aims of European construction; the British, by Bevin's declaration of 22 January 1948, still favoured a formal political union and judged the American physical presence to be an adequate safeguard against future German aggression; the French, on the other hand, wanted a more ambitious federal structural for Europe, one capable of resisting alignment with either of the great power blocs, and in which France would have an important role. But these differences and hesitations were quickly forgotten in the rapid increase in East–West tension which followed the Soviet takeover in Czechoslovakia on 20 February. On 17 March the Brussels Pact was signed for fifty years. It set up the Western Union, a Council of the Foreign Ministers of France, Great Britain, and the Benelux countries; it was in fact a military pact providing for automatic assistance in the event of aggression against one of its signatories in Europe or overseas; there was also a project to extend the terms of the Pact to the economic, social, and cultural domains. A permanent committee of ambassadors and experts in London prepared the details; from the summer, a Combined General Staff of the five members was operational at Fontainebleau under Montgomery and with de Lattre in command of the ground forces. No one, however, was under any illusions; the most the nine British, French, and Belgian divisions could hope to do in the case of a conflict with the Soviet Union would be to attempt to hold the Red Army's forces at the Rhine: from the beginning it was clear that only the Americans could inject the Brussels Pact with credibility, that in effect a European defence had to be an Atlantic defence.

An American response to European needs was not slow in coming. The Vandenberg resolution, voted by the Senate on 11 June, authorized the American government to conclude military alliances in peacetime outside the American continent, marking an important departure from isolationism and being the harbinger of an expansionist policy. The timeliness of the new American attitude was dramatically demonstrated by the Soviet blockade of Berlin which began on 22 June. The blockade and the massive air-lift operation it necessitated until May 1949 added a fresh urgency to negotiations between Washington and the members of the Brussels Pact. The talks were long, with difficulties over the cost of arms, the place of the overseas territories in a future defence system and, above all, over the question of automatic intervention. The re-election of Truman in November allowed the obstacles to be overcome and on 4 April 1949 the North Atlantic Treaty was signed in Washington between the United States, Canada, the Five, and Italy, plus Norway, Denmark, Iceland, and Portugal, joined in 1952 by Greece and Turkey. Although the new Treaty was presented to opinion in Europe as a desirable complement to the Brussels Pact, it in fact made it redundant. The efforts of Bidault and of Schuman, his successor at the Quai d'Orsay in July 1948, efforts concentrated on securing American support, had been rewarded; henceforth the United States accepted that American security was inseparable from that of Europe.

Yet in spite of its recognition for this principle the North Atlantic Treaty left a number of questions in suspense. Article 5 excluded automatic intervention in the event of an attack, the State Department having insisted on the sovereignty of Congress alone to decide on American intervention. French diplomacy for its part left unanswered the delicate question of the Treaty's compatibility with the Franco-Soviet Pact of December 1944. And serious ambiguity surrounded the likely future relations between the nascent Atlantic community and the European alternative currently taking shape.[3] For the Treaty created the structures which formed the basis of the North Atlantic Treaty Organization (NATO); in addition to its executive body, the Council of Ministers, there was a Council of Deputies, a Council of Economic and Financial Defence, and from 1950 a Council of Military Production. Above all, however, it rendered completely redundant the Defence Committee of the Brussels Pact; the defence budgets of the signatories and of the Western Union were subordinated to the plans for an Atlantic defence; from 20 December 1949 the members of the Brussels Pact had, in effect, to transfer their military charges to NATO. The increase in tension due to the Korean War accelerated the process still further; the twelve NATO divisions and 1000 aircraft stationed in Europe seemed slight in comparison with the twenty-seven divisions and 6000 aircraft of the Soviet Union. French diplomacy now joined those calling for a vigorous defence of Europe, ready to accept that a military commitment accompany Marshall Aid; there remained, however, the thorny problem of the Pentagon's insistence that German troops be integrated into the combined forces of the Atlantic alliance. In the spring of 1951 the NATO General Staff became operational, and the Supreme Headquarters of Allied Powers in Europe (SHAPE) was set up at Rocquencourt near Versailles, with Juin taking command of the forces for the central zone.[4] The threat of a generalized global conflict had robbed the purely European context of its relevance: the American 'umbrella' was complete. From now on the strategy of NATO was to create a 'shield' of conventional forces in Europe strong enough to withstand an initial Soviet attack; at this point, argued the theorists of deterrent strategy, escalation to the 'major attack' would be restrained by the known atomic strike potential of the United States Air Force.

Presented in these terms, with one treaty succeeding another under the relentless pressure of the events in Prague, Berlin, and Korea, the Third Force policy-makers appear to have let themselves be drawn resignedly and without resistance into the American Cold War camp. Viewed from this angle the French alignment acknowledged the logic of anticommunism coupled with the weakness of the political parties. This was certainly the interpretation advanced by the Communists and Gaullists; thus for the PCF and its fellow-travellers[5] (soon to be joined by the faction excluded from the SFIO), national independence was synonymous with resistance to 'colonization' by the Americans; the Marshall Plan and NATO enslaved Europe to the United States and abandoned France to the capitalist 'trusts' and the excesses of anticommunist hysteria.[6] And this analysis, with its strongly patriotic undertones, would probably have been echoed by the Gaullists but for the fact of their own anticommunism, which led them finally to accept the Atlantic alignment as a necessary evil. However, this often violent opposition did not have deep enough roots in public opinion to present a serious challenge to the proponents of an Atlantic alignment and European unity; that is, the MRP, firmly in control of French foreign policy; the bulk of the Socialists, alarmed by the developments in Eastern Europe; plus of course the Radicals, the Moderates and the Right. In other words, all the elements of Third Force governments.

The relative ease with which these groups were able to impose their views has, however, to be balanced against what is known about French opinion at the time. The opinion polls show that between 1948 and 1952 there were widespread hopes of preserving a large measure of French independence within the Western alliance; efforts for European unity certainly had the support of a majority of Frenchmen, but opinion was visibly hostile to unconditional commitment to one camp. Thus in July 1949, when Marshall Aid was at its height, opinion was already divided; 25 per cent were favourable, 20 per cent less favourable, 23 per cent unfavourable or hostile, and 22 per cent had no opinion; a majority already expressed an indifference that could easily turn to hostility. And the doubts increased when the American aid acquired a full-blown military character; in September 1952, and contrary to the sense of all the treaties, 45 per cent thought that France should take no part in a war between the United States and the Soviet Union; 36 per cent were prepared to support the United States, and only 4 per cent the Soviet Union.[7] Quite clearly, then, the divisions of opinion over this crucial question in no way corresponded to the partisan divisions of France: the Communist electorate would not support the Soviet Union, but nor on the other hand were the pro-American parties assured of a massive consensus.

Yet this deep-seated desire for non-alignment was never at the forefront of popular preoccupations, and it failed to find a clear political expression. This absence of a party political outlet explains why the debate over neutrality remained confined to narrow intellectual and political circles. The basic premiss of the neutralist argument, namely that German rearmament was the inescapable implication of the Atlantic alliance, was of course incontestable; and a long series of articles in *Le Monde* between April 1948 and September 1950 developed the theme of French neutrality and non-alignment. But neutrality never found a wider audience and the debate was limited to the pages of the left-wing non-party press. The neutralist arguments lacked concrete objectives and looked unrealistic; in political terms, a defence of peace implied making common cause with the Communists; and in practical terms, a meaningful non-alignment would require an independent military effort clearly beyond French means.[8] That the silent majority did not mobilize for the independence it in fact favoured left the way clear for the Third Force governments, even affording them a margin of manoeuvre to make initiatives.

## Initiatives over Europe

The German question and moves for European unity were the two, complementary, bases of an original and positive French diplomacy conducted by the MRP. With a right to a major say in the future of Germany acknowledged by her partners, France was strongly placed to influence the making of alliances and to mould the future of Europe. Whatever the claims of their opponents, the governments of the Third Force took full and sometimes far-sighted advantage of this privileged position.

The point of departure here was a recognition of the progress of aspirations for European unity and of the new conditions that the Cold War offered for their realization. The struggle against Fascism had injected new life into the ideal of a united and democratic Europe, a notion previously discredited by the European 'New Order' of the Nazis. After 1945 a growing awareness of the diminished place of Europe in international affairs had mobilized a variety of disparate political, economic, and intellectual groups, many of which issued from the Resistance. These groups provided a forum for the debate on European unity; in December 1947 they decided to co-ordinate their efforts. Political encouragement in this sense was not lacking; de Gaulle had expressed cautious approval in September 1945; Van Zeeland had consistently pleaded for a federal Europe; and in Zurich on 19 September 1946, Churchill had spoken of Great Britain's hopes for a united Europe in which France and Germany would at last be reconciled. Such aspirations acquired a new relevance with the start of the Cold War and the launching of policies for economic reconstruction in Europe. The Congress of the Hague, which brought the different movements together in May 1948, discussed projects for a European Charter of Human Rights, a Supreme Court of Justice, and a European Assembly. The European Movement, founded as a result in October 1948, was presided over by Churchill, Blum, Spaak, and De Gasperi; it organized a campaign of opinion, studied a variety of political, economic, and cultural projects, and acted as a pressure group on governments. Such pressure was scarcely necessary in France; as early as 19 July 1948 Bidault had suggested that the signatories of the Brussels Pact examine a project for economic union and a European Assembly. And in spite of British reticence, the members agreed to set up a consultative European Assembly that was to provide a forum for debate and a framework for ministerial and parliamentary contact and co-operation.

The Council of Europe set up at Strasbourg on 5 May 1949 was, in fact, the first international organization born of a wholly European initiative; its statutes gave a large place to an invocation of the shared European ideals of civilization, development, and liberties. The founding members, the Five plus Italy, Denmark, Sweden, Norway, and Ireland, were joined in 1949 by Greece, Turkey, and Iceland, then by the Saar and Federal Germany in 1950 and 1951: the self-consciously democratic character of the members precluded admission of Spain and Portugal. However, the idealistic enthusiasm of the summer of 1949 was short-lived; the economic domain was quite clearly dominated by the OEEC and dollar aid; the most important cultural projects were already in the hands of the United Nations and UNESCO; above all, the creation of a European political authority with real powers was quickly seen to be unattainable. In the Consultative Assembly – where the deputies, designated by their national Parliaments, were grouped by political complexion rather than by nationality – initiatives from France, Italy, Belgium, and Holland which might have laid the bases for European federalism were consistently blocked by the British and Scandinavians. The Assembly certainly helped familiarize politicians with the idea of joint action, and it could sign conventions and suggest detailed projects to governments. But the Committee of Ministers, a body insisted upon by the British, could and did veto any measure likely to encroach on the sovereignty of national Parliaments and governments. Any remaining hopes that European unity might be forged in the Assembly at Strasbourg were dashed when Paul-Henri Spaak, its first and highly enthusiastic President, resigned amidst general popular indifference on 10 December 1951.

With the exception of the Communists, who had refused to ratify the creation of the Council of Europe and who moreover were not invited to sit on it, the experiment at Strasbourg was followed closely by the political parties in France. The limitations had quickly been perceived, and there was a recognition that the German question constituted a particularly serious obstacle to further progress. Among the politicians of the Third Force the conviction was gaining ground that the severe policy towards Germany, initiated by de Gaulle and continued by Bidault, might be self-defeating, the surest way, in fact, of rekindling German nationalism. Furthermore, the Cold War had changed the priorities, raising serious doubts as to the wisdom of a prolonged humiliation of a defeated country which was now the front line of European defence against the Soviet menace. Lengthy talks in London (23 February–1 June 1948) produced a compromise between the United States, Great Britain, and France on a statute for the occupied zones and on the summoning of a German Constituent Assembly; at the same talks France had to abandon definitively her plan for the political separation of the Ruhr and the internationalization of its industries. The Berlin blockade, that put a stop to all serious negotiation between the Three and the Soviet Union, despite the spectacular Soviet proposals of June 1949, further underlined the urgency of the economic and political reconstruction of Germany that was now under way. Agreements of April 1949 in Washington led to the creation in September of the German Federal Republic, Konrad Adenauer becoming its first Chancellor: with the creation of the German Democratic Republic on the other side of the Iron Curtain on 7 October, the hopes for German unification vanished. Under the Petersburg agreements of 22 November the Federal Republic agreed to refuse all militarization but obtained in return important concessions over the economy and national sovereignty, and reparations to the Allies were ended. Faced with the determination of the United States and Great Britain to see a rapid reconstruction of West Germany, France could do little. Obstinate and ill-humoured bargaining brought her satisfaction only over the Saar, politically autonomous since 1947, but whose entire coal production went to France from 1 April 1949. However, by an agreement of 3 March 1950 France had to accept a reduction in the powers of her High Commissioner in the Saar; the Bonn Government wanted a customs union and was already demanding the return of the region to Germany.

The credit for breaking out of the impasse created by the Saar problem and the failure of European political unity went to Robert Schuman. For Schuman, an experienced parliamentarian, stigmatized by the Communists as a 'Boche' because of his roots in Lorraine, the Germanophobia of the Third Republic was anachronistic, whilst the solutions it produced – enforced demilitarization of Germany, international authority in the Ruhr, annexation and economic exploitation of the Saar – were illusory. What was required according to Schuman was a moral rehabilitation to help Germany become genuinely democratic, and from France a readiness to co-operate sincerely and on an equal footing with the traditional enemy.[9] In the spring of 1950 several factors increased the need for the kind of fresh approach advocated by Schuman. The Americans were looking for signs of Europe's willingness to overcome her problems. A crisis of over-production was looming in the steel industry – indicative of the failure of the OEEC – where the stubborn attachment of the European producers to cartel arrangements frustrated the work of the experts. There were hopes also that a demonstration of European unity and dynamism might ease international tension. And there was the domestic political situation to consider: the Indo-Chinese problem was serious, the Socialists had left the government in February, social tension was high and the elections were close. Schuman correctly perceived that this set of circumstances gave an enormous diplomatic value to the project for a European Coal and Steel Authority drawn up by Jean Monnet and his team and presented to him on 29 April. Schuman acted quickly; securing the reluctant consent of the premier, Georges Bidault; side-stepping the officials of the Quai d'Orsay and the representatives of the industries involved; ignoring the British completely but seeking and obtaining the backing of Adenauer and Acheson; the French Parliament was not consulted, and the cabinet gave its approval without having had time to examine the proposals closely: Schuman made public the French project at the Quai d'Orsay on 9 May 1950.[10]

The project involved placing the entire French and German outputs of coal and steel under a single High Authority within an organization open to the other European countries. The common market for these two major products, unencumbered by customs duties, would favour modernization and eliminate the unprofitable and inefficient producers; planning would be facilitated without recourse to nationalization and without bowing to the wishes of the largest producers; executive decisions in the industries were to be taken by the High Authority, composed of independent figures appointed by the governments. Apart from its originality, the great strength of the Schuman Plan lay in acknowledging that a European unity which began at the highest political level had failed, and to offer instead a more modest but profound integration from below, through the economy: as Jean Monnet's text asserted prophetically, the project would establish 'the first solid bases for the European federation essential for the preservation of peace'.

The project was immediately condemned by the Soviet Union, but welcomed by the United States who saw it as removing the main obstacle to the German reconstruction essential for the security of the Atlantic bloc. All the European countries were favourable, with the exception of Great Britain where the Labour government refused to place the newly nationalized iron and coal industries into such open competition. Political opinion in France was more nuanced. The CGT and the Communists saw it as an anti-Soviet manoeuvre, and drew attention to the risks of unemployment associated with rationalization. De Gaulle denounced it for its overly supranational character. The Socialists had reservations about the emerging Europe of the Christian Democrats – Schuman, Adenauer, and De Gasperi – but gave a mild support.[11] The Radicals were divided, and the Independents, from a combination of Germanophobia and hostility to intervention in the economy, were against. Only the MRP, Schuman's own party, was wholeheartedly in favour. The most determined opposition, however, came from the iron and steel producers: backed by the CNPF they had hoped to organize their own lucrative cartels. It was the backing of the nationalized industries – the Charbonnages de France, then the SNCF and the Régie Renault, all important consumers of steel – which allowed Schuman and the planners to surmount this opposition.

From June 1950 six governments were committed to accept the principle of the project: Paris, Bonn, Rome, Brussels, the Hague, and Luxembourg. The most serious obstacle, the cartels in the German iron and steel industry, was overcome in the negotiations, expertly conducted by Jean Monnet. The treaty setting up the European Coal and Steel Community (ECSC) was signed in Paris on 18 April 1951. Major decisions affecting the future of the industries required approval by a Council of Ministers, and an Assembly of Deputies and a Court had controlling and arbitration responsibilities. But the High Authority retained a broad scope for initiative, and the ECSC was in fact close to the project unveiled on 9 May 1950, even if the outbreak of the Korean War dashed the original hopes that it might contribute to an easing of international tension. In spite of concerted opposition from the Communists and Gaullists, the treaty was ratified in December, thanks to Paul Reynaud's rallying of the Independents. The High Authority was established in Luxembourg on 10 August 1952 with, appropriately enough, Jean Monnet at its head, and the common European market for coal and steel was operational from 1953. The realization of the French project was a considerable personal victory for Robert Schuman and an important contribution to the cause of European unity.

The community formula of the Schuman Plan was applied less successfully to the thorny problem of German rearmament. Time was short: the

Korean War shattered illusions over neutrality, and the speed of West Germany's economic and political recovery took the hardliners and the undecided on the French side by surprise. The nations of Western Europe were under pressure to take part from the United States, fighting Communism in the name of the United Nations; in August 1950 France sent a battalion to the Korean conflict, and this without being able to participate fully in either decisions over the conduct of the war or in the talks which brought the conflict to an end in the autumn of 1951. Within the Atlantic camp, however, France was coming under pressure from all those calling for a German contribution to the common defence: Churchill, Adenauer, the Assembly in Strasbourg, and Acheson, who on 12 September 1950 at the conference of the Three in New York stated unequivocally his determination to see the Germans armed by the following autumn. The dilemma faced by France was acute: should she bow to American pressure and abandon the hopes of the Liberation by accepting a German defence for Europe, and this when the best French forces were engaged in Indo-China? Or should she resist and risk provoking a crisis within NATO when a generalized conflict seemed imminent?

To gain time and recover the initiative Pleven, now premier, presented the National Assembly on 24 October 1950 with a plan for a European military community. This was the twin of the Schuman Plan (its elaboration had been supervised by Jean Monnet), and it applied to the problem of arms the same principles being tried for coal and steel. The new project involved the creation of a European Army under a European Minister of Defence controlled in turn by a European Assembly; both the military budget and the arms programmes would be common, and the national forces would be integrated from a very low level of command upwards. The scheme was ingenious, and with integrated recruitment, supranational logistics, and common defence objectives it removed for a time the spectre of a German army and organized the debate around a French initiative. Its fundamental weakness undoubtedly lay in the attempt to create a common European Army for a Europe whose political immaturity and disunity was obvious. Certainly in France the project was at the origin of long-lasting and serious difficulties. Once again the Communists and Gaullists united in an outright opposition, but all shades of French political opinion were agreed to resist the reconstruction of a German army and General Staff. And the response elsewhere was equally nuanced; the White House, the Pentagon, and NATO, all stressed the project's lack of realism and did not conceal their irritation. However, the consistent French rejection over the next few months of any alternative which involved the formation of independent German units, plus Bonn's rallying to the French proposals, finally led Washington to consider the Pleven Plan as the only workable solution to the problem of how to re-arm the Germans without exciting French fears;[12] and General

Eisenhower, the NATO Supreme Commander from April 1951, let himself be convinced of this by Jean Monnet. Against a background of eased international tension after the signing of the Korean armistice at Pam Mun Jon, the French project slowly won official acceptance.

In the course of laborious discussions begun in February 1951, the main stumbling-blocks – the size of the integrated units, the degree of supranationality, and the hostility of the British – were gradually overcome. A year later a fragile agreement was concluded in Paris; under it the units were fixed at approximately 13 000 men; supplies and arms would be common but recruitment, training, and control of the reserves remained national responsibilities; the joint structures (a Commissariat modelled on the High Authority of the ECSC, a Council of Ministers and a Court of Justice) were given limited powers. Indeed, the guiding principle of the proposed European army was more obviously coalition than genuine integration. These, then, were the bases for the treaty creating the European Defence Community signed in Paris on 27 May 1952, after approval by the Bundestag and the members of the Atlantic Pact. The final outcome was unsatisfactory to France on several counts: first, the twelve German divisions (compared with fourteen French), even if commanded by non-Germans, amounted in fact to a German army; secondly, the length of stay of the British and American forces in Europe was not specified; thirdly, the shared structures were weak and the proposal for a common Defence Minister had been dropped. And the contradictions were glaring at the level of the supreme command, placed in the ambit of NATO and thus automatically going to an American: from its inception, the European Defence Community (EDC) was firmly installed under the shelter of the American umbrella. West Germany was now completely free of the victors of 1945, and the weak EDC looked likely to become a simple tool of American policy.

The European military union of the Pleven Plan suffered, then, from similar ambiguities and defects as the projects for economic and political union. That the French Parliament perceived the dangers was clear from the slender majority by which it authorized Edgar Faure's government to negotiate the Treaty of Paris in February 1952. Final ratification was far from certain, and French opinion was already being inflamed by simplistic arguments for or against the EDC. The protracted quarrel that in fact followed was a severe reprimand for the five years in which French policy over Europe had been daring, courageous, but without popular support.

*Impotence overseas*

The French initiatives for Europe and the Atlantic Community were undermined by the problems overseas, where the absence of a long-term policy left the course of developments more than ever at the mercy of events. True, the institutional framework was in place, and Vincent Auriol was a conscientious President of the French Union. But, without a policy, the governments were content merely to expedite day-to-day affairs, confronting the problems as and when they arose. The MRP duo of Coste–Floret – immovable during five ministries – and Letourneau dominated Overseas Affairs, and their uninspired example was followed by the Independent Jacquinot after the 1951 elections. Only François Mitterrand, the UDSR minister in the Pleven and Queuille cabinets from July 1950 to July 1951, attempted to inform public opinion in France and seek fresh bases for dialogue in Black Africa by re-establishing contact with the leaders of the Rassemblement démocratique africain (RDA); his efforts ran up against deeply engrained habits of imperial administration and economic exploitation, and foundered amidst widespread indifference.[13] It was as if a tacit consensus had developed not to confront the problems of decolonization, to ignore the examples of India and Indonesia, and to disregard the ever-widening economic gulf between the members of the French Union and metropolitan France. As a result the French 'colonies' remained what they had always been, refuges for capital, a fall-back in case of panic, and the object of a haphazard distribution of public funds. Thus investment flowed again to the AOF, Morocco continued to receive French capital throughout the Korean crisis, and approximately 50 milliard francs were distributed each year – through the Fonds d'investissement pour le développement économique et sociale des Territoires d'outre-mer (FIDES) created in April 1946 – but without any noticeable impact on the development of the recipients.

The gathering storm in North Africa received only scant and superficial attention. In Tunisia, where the failure of the 1947 reforms was obvious, the death in exile at Pau of Bey Moncef in September 1948 left Lamine Bey as the legitimate sovereign and undisputed spokesman for the Tunisian nation. In the absence of a political intiative from Paris the Tunisian nationalists now progressed rapidly, encouraged by the return of Bourguiba in September 1949. They supported the Bey's negotiations with Paris in which he pleaded with Auriol for an evolution of the Protectorate to a statute of Co-operation. A seven-point plan presented by Bourguiba in Paris in April 1950 found support among the Socialists and Communists and even dented the general apathy; and a way out of the impasse seemed to appear when on 10 June Schuman defined the mission of Périllier, the successsor to Jean Mons, as that of 'leading Tunisia towards the full development of her resources and towards the independence that is the ultimate goal for all the territories of the French Union'.[14] But the Bidault government was powerless to impose such good intentions on the French community in Tunisia, quick to mobilize against all change in the status quo let alone a transition to independence. Schuman's remarks sparked off a violent outcry from the Right and Centre, the military, and the metropolitan press sympathetic to the *colons*; a campaign of opposition which forced the government to retract and abandon its conciliatory approach in the autumn. From this climb-down by Paris the Neo-Destour nationalists and the UGTT drew the conclusion that the stakes had been raised. Serious troubles soon occurred, with rioting at Enfidaville on 25 November. In 1951, despite some administrative reform in February, the Bey increasingly called for complete national sovereignty for Tunisia; his ministers took the Tunisian case to the United Nations which now began calling for talks to start. By the beginning of 1952, with the Neo-Destour committed to independence and the French of Tunisia organized to resist all change, and with a rising tide of terrorism and counter-terrorism, it was obvious that Paris had lost the initiative.

In Morocco, where Resident General Juin was left a completely free hand by Paris, friction developed when the Sultan rejected a programme of reforms which would have led to co-sovereignty. The position of Sultan Ben Youssef was delicate – open to dismissal by the Resident General, pushed by the Istiqal nationalists to go beyond his 10 April 1947 speech, and under pressure from the powerful local leaders and interests hostile to the central power. An open confrontation was made even more likely by the steady economic and social deterioration since 1948 and by the harsh repression of nationalists and Communists. During an official voyage to France in October 1950 the Sultan failed to convince Auriol of the urgency of transforming the Protectorate status. In December Juin forced the removal of the nationalists from the Moroccan Council of Government; in January he increased the pressure still further by encouraging a local leader, the docile Pasha of Marrakesh, Thami El Glaoui, to head internal opposition to the Sultan, demanding that he repudiate the Istiqal nationalists in the name of Moroccan traditionalism. The weak and divided Pleven cabinet did not interfere, and when Auriol refused to back the Sultan the latter was forced to comply with Juin's demands in order to save his throne. The effect on Moroccan opinion of this imperious French attitude was disastrous, uniting all the nationalists in a Moroccan National Front and stimulating the animosity of the Arab League. The recall of Juin in August 1951 solved nothing, for he in effect chose his own successor, General Guillaume, who proved as undiplomatic and ineffective as himself. The Arab States now took the Moroccan affair to the United Nations. The Sultan issued a memorandum on 20 March 1952, calling for a new national government and reforms: Paris rejected the proposals, but could suggest no alternative. The strikes and protests which followed added to the tension of the uneasy stalemate.

For the moment, however, the signs of approaching troubles in North Africa were overshadowed by the already grave problems of the war in

Indo-China, whose tragic dimensions were at last beginning to percolate through to the French public. The contradictions of the Along Bay agreement of June 1948 restoring Bao Dai quickly became apparent. The MRP clung to the terms of this settlement, a prisoner of outdated notions of power and nationalism, although the SFIO was ready to back the more republican General Xuan, now head of the government. Bao Dai's great feat had been to obtain from Paris what it had refused to Ho Chi Minh, that is, the promise of independence and a union of the three disputed provinces. Yet Paris was no longer in a position to impose this solution on the military and *colons* in Indo-China, or on their vociferous pressure groups within France. In the summer of 1948 the André Marie government was pressured into refusing Bao Dai first the Cochin China province, then the transfer of services controlled by the French colonial administration. Indeed, the result of the short-sighted MRP policy followed by the French governments was to systematically undermine the position of the French protégé; the new sovereign finally took power in March–April 1949, but only after much procrastination on both sides; around the newly independent Vietnam were hastily set up associated states of the French Union with negligible sovereignty, Laos in July 1949, Cambodia in November; and above all, the military defeats and press campaigns destroyed Bao Dai's standing in Vietnamese opinion. Hopes for a peaceful settlement were dismissed; the Americans who supported the new ruler were already pessimistic for the future. The rupture between the new Vietnam and the Communist government of the North was welcomed, despite the fact that this thrust Ho Chi Minh more firmly than ever into the arms of the Chinese Communists. Visibly powerless to govern the country, unable to raise an army or even stamp out the lucrative speculation on the national currency, Bao Dai was quite obviously a French puppet. In its slow decline the corrupt and illegitimate régime of Bao Dai, despised even by the French army to which it owed its survival, destroyed the last chances for a nationalist solution in Vietnam. The right-wing Vietnamese patriots were already looking to the United States for help, whilst those on the Left were turning to the Vietminh.

And even the hopes for a military solution were fading. Until the spring of 1949, when each side still expected a political solution, the military position had, it is true, been stabilized. But the guerrilla activity was well established; attacks on French convoys were frequent, requiring reinforced protection of the main arteries. The Vietminh were solidly entrenched in the Tonkin, and in Cochin China Gallieni's tactics based on isolated posts in the countryside were extended. Such tactics were inappropriate against the guerrilla fighters, perfectly at home in the rural areas and among the native population, and the results were disappointing. Delays for supplies and mail, the dangerous patrols, and dependence on locally recruited forces, all caused morale to suffer; and, too often, the soldiers marooned at the posts, facing the invisible enemy for weeks on end, could be saved only by the speedy arrival of an armoured brigade when the 'Viets' launched their final night-time attack. Short of men, with a divided High Command and inappropriate methods, the French expeditionary force was fast becoming bogged down. And there was no end in sight to the war. On the contrary, the strong offensive launched by Giap in the Tonkin in March 1949 showed that despite supply problems the Vietminh was ready to seize the vital new opportunity offered it by the victory of Mao in China. General Revers, Head of the General Staff, now hastily dispatched to inspect the position, drew the obvious conclusion: definitive military victory was unattainable, but France had to hold on until the inevitable American intervention. For Indo-China was in fact to be the test of the solidarity of the recently signed Atlantic Pact. In this task, holding on for a little longer, the French forces were successful, repelling a Vietminh offensive on the South in the winter of 1949–50 and bringing the Tonkin Delta under solid military control.

With the events of the summer of 1950, the start of United States military aid to France in Indo-China and the war in Korea, this ana-chronistic colonial war suddenly became part of the international crusade against Communism. For Paris, the General Staff, and Saigon, the oppor-tunity was a godsend; immobility could now be presented as tenacity; there were American arms and money; and the support of the Soviet Union and Communist China for Ho Chi Minh even invested Bao Dai with a semblance of legitimacy. This development was accelerated by the French military disasters of the autumn; in the north of the Tonkin province the Vietminh went on the offensive, capturing the French out-posts guarding the frontier with China, and whose planned evacuation had been delayed for months due to Carpentier's hesitations. Then in September Dong Khé fell, in October it was the turn of Cao Bang, then Langson. Entire French brigades were wiped out, and with the defences of the North pierced, the Delta and Hanoi were threatened. In a desperate attempt to halt the slide to a disastrous humiliation, de Lattre was ap-pointed to command in Indo-China. His prestige and charisma injected new energy into the demoralized French forces; on 18 January 1951 the Vietminh drive on Hanoi was stopped at Vinh Yen; and in June, having lost the struggle in the heavily fortified Delta, Giap abandoned battle tactics and sent his men back to the guerrilla combat. The situation was saved but – and as de Lattre was well aware – far from solved. To defend Vietnam against international Communism the French and Vietnamese forces would need American arms and resources. De Lattre went to Washington in September, convinced the Americans of the importance of the French struggle in Indo-China and secured an increase in military aid; at the end of October the American Chief of Staff went to Saigon to inspect personally the Indo-Chinese front.

American arms and money eased the crippling burden of the war for France: of the 830 milliard francs spent between 1945 and 1951 almost one-third came from the United States. Lavish consignments of armoured cars, aircraft, and trucks arrived to equip the French expeditionary force and the new Vietnamese army; this last under French control but which Bao Dai hoped to make an instrument of independence. And for the moment at least the American 'advisers' did not demand a say in the use to which their aid was put. Without the dynamism and flair of de Lattre – he died on 11 January 1952 – the extent of France's humiliation in Indo-China was to become only more apparent. The French forces, just 54 000 officers and volunteers, were submerged in the mass of colonial troops and Legionnaires of the expeditionary force (120 000) and the Vietnamese forces (260 000). Suffering heavy losses, increasingly bitter, and believing themselves forgotten, they either lost faith in the war they were fighting or retreated into a desperate anticommunism. Now absorbing more than 40 per cent of the Defence budget, the war in Indo-China had an undeniable impact on the political life of metropolitan France; it failed, however, to affect deeply a public barely aware of this painful demonstration before the world of France's weakness and dependence on the United States.

# 10

# The Third Force

Surveying the French political scene each year in his preface to *L'Année politique*, André Siegfried altered little of his basic analysis between 1948 and 1952. Since 1934, ran the argument, France had been in turmoil, with her political life dominated by the confrontation of opposing doctrines; this turmoil had now abated, and a politics based on attachment to principles had given way to one based on a rejection of extremes: the Third Force. And it is indeed the Third Force, with its endlessly reiterated aim of saving the régime from the extremists and its glorification of good sense and balance and moderation, which sets the somewhat muted tone to these years; in sombre contrast to the bright but by now rapidly fading hopes of the Liberation period. Perhaps its caution was justified; after all, the Gaullists and Communists, who between them held a potential electoral majority in the country, both claimed to want to destroy the régime. For the Republic – with its shrunken social and political bases, and defended by a parliamentary majority artificially crystallized around the Centre by the events of 1947 – *attentisme* became both a tactic and the only practical policy.

Detailing the long list of ministries and the crises from which they issued certainly points up the fragility of the system.[1] Yet against this has to be weighed the important continuities of personnel, for many figures held the same key posts in successive administrations; and, of course, there was a continuity implicit in the Third Force's stubborn defence of the status quo. Nor, finally, should one forget that broader developments were favouring a repudiation of extremes: as economic conditions improved and stability returned, so appetites for violent partisan conflicts appeared to wane.

## The extremists in the majority

The exclusion of the Communist Party undoubtedly fostered this indifference to partisan conflict. An attitude of docile and even proud loyalty to Stalin restored to the PCF the 'foreign party' label it had managed to shake off in the about-turn of 1934. And although obedience to Cominform orders meant that exclusion was not unwelcome to the Party, the virulent and all-pervading anticommunism of the Cold War period guaranteed that its isolation would continue. The result was a sterile stalemate: to retain its identity the PCF had to distance itself from the reality of the French context; yet in doing this, in faithfully applying Moscow's orders, the Party was clearly unable to develop the kind of policy relevant to France which would have brought this internal exile to an end. At the Party's Twelfth Congress at Gennevilliers in April 1950 Thorez reiterated the Cominform doctrine on which the PCF's attitude was henceforth based: the preservation of a fragile world peace increasingly menaced by the enemies of the Soviet Union was the principal objective, and the task of the PCF was to mobilize energies in France to this end. From this followed logically the second objective, that of the 'national struggle' to resist American 'imperialism' and its instrument in France, the SFIO, the 'party of Washington'. The pertinence of this analysis was, at the very least, questionable, given first that Socialist support for the Third Force was already weakening, and secondly that the greater part of the French population considered the threat of war to have receded and the real danger to come now from Communism.[2]

The reaction of the PCF to the events of 1948 in fact set the tone for the whole of this period. After the Prague takeover in February, for example, the Party leadership solemnly greeted the 'great victory of Czech democracy', whilst *L'Humanité* rushed to draw the contrast between the Czech people's eager new commitment to the great task of reconstruction and France's continued descent into misery and crisis, a decline welcomed of course by Blum.[3] The logic and tone were identical after the Cominform's condemnation in June of Tito's schism in Yugoslavia and over the bloody purges in the popular democracies of Eastern Europe. At the same time, however, the Communist Party was determined to protect its greatest asset: its image as the champion of the French working class. The violent strike by miners in the autumn of 1948 – in the middle of the Berlin crisis and negotiations over the coalfields of the Ruhr – provided the occasion to test and reinforce this image. In an already difficult social context, marked by strikes in metallurgy, transport, and the public sector, the PCF embarked on a calculated manoeuvre to show the muscle of the working-class movement and throw it into the opposition to French alignment in the Atlantic bloc. Measures taken by Robert Lacoste, Socialist Minister of Industry in the Queuille ministry, over absenteeism and overmanning in the mines, plus moves against a worker co-operative at Beaumont-en-Artois, provided the pretext for the strike. The Communist leadership of the CGT mining federation reacted sharply, voting strike action from 4 October by a large majority. In spite of a climb-down by the government and the administration of the mines, the CGT went ahead with the action, similar to that of the previous year; action clearly unsuited to the French context, but opportune for the Cominform strategy.

Abandoned by the other trade unions, the Communists of the CGT organized the strike and picketing in all the mining basins; many recovered the reflexes and methods of the Resistance when confronted by the 60 000 CRS and troops immediately mobilized against the 15 000 strikers by Jules Moch, the Socialist Minister of the Interior. The CGT leadership attacked the Marshall Plan, while in the besieged and bitterly defended mining regions the targets were the militants of Force Ouvrière, Socialists, and 'jaunes'. The strike's subversive character was strengthened with the decision on 16 October to call out the safety teams from the mines; four days later the CGT launched a campaign to extend the action to the railways and to organize financial support for the strikers. But this met with little success; only the dockers gave their support and the transport workers and metal-workers refused to join the action; and funds were now running low. By the beginning of November the failure of the strike was clear; a brutal reconquest of the mining basins using tanks and armoured cars, that left two dead in the Loire and the Gard, was completed on 2 November; the official return to work was ordered on 29 November: 'You are tomorrow's victors', promised *L'Humanité*. The strike left an atmosphere of bitter anger in the mining regions; the exceptional brutality of the repression had done more than the exhortations of the union leadership to forge worker unity; and the 2000 dismissals which followed the end of the strike in the mines bore witness to the Third Force's resolve to curb the Communist threat once and for all, much to the relief of an apprehensive bourgeoisie. But the handling of the strike in the mines had lost the Republic the support of the working class, even if its enthusiasm for such violent 'tactical' action had suffered in the process.

The consequences for the Communist Party were no less negative. This brutal social confrontation made it even harder to imagine a French government breaking with the United States, just as it was now hard to believe that the Communists had a long-term policy for France. The PCF's isolation was deeper than ever; its enemies now claimed that the insurrection the Communists appeared to dream of would require Soviet tanks to succeed; the PCF had exhausted its resources in a deliberate test of its ability to mobilize the working class through the trade unions; the democratic efforts of a decade had been ruined, and the PCF now entered the grim era of uncompromising Stalinism. True, the Party still had its role as the spokesman of the working class, but the impact of its political action was less certain. Until 1952 efforts here bore little fruit. Demonstrations against American imperialism, protests over the war in Indo-China, militancy in factories, verbal and often physical confrontations with the various 'class enemies' (particularly violent with the militants of the RPF), as well as the hostile stance in the Assembly[4] – all came to nothing. The illness of Thorez, his departure for the Soviet Union in November 1950, and the interim leadership of Duclos and Fajon, deepened the Party's inertia; between 1947 and 1952, the leadership admitted a fall in membership from approximately 900 000 to 500 000.[5] But its adversaries were mistaken to claim victory: as the 1951 elections showed, with one elector in four ready to vote for it, the PCF's electoral potential was almost unchanged. This resilience testified to the massive social implantation of the Party. Through the activities of its numerous affiliated organizations the PCF retained an audience among precisely those sections of the population increasingly disillusioned with the traditional 'bourgeois' political system with which the Republic was identified. This Communist 'counter-society' was present and active at every level of local life, supporting the efforts of the Party's militants, spreading news and information, able, finally, to mobilize the electorate under even the worst conditions. In a difficult period for the Party, organizers of associations, trade unionists, and elected officials, all tireless advocates of improved material conditions and the defence of the interests of the weakest members of society, were an invaluable source of prestige.

In addition to the manifest shortcomings in domestic politics the Party's position was scarcely helped by its struggles on the intellectual front and its support for peace movements and decolonization. The importance of these struggles should not be exaggerated; although they have been described at length by discontented Party intellectuals and former fellow-travellers, their genuinely popular appeal was extremely limited. The bulk of the population remained indifferent to the views of the writers, artists, and philosophers involved; the associations which mobilized behind Pablo Picasso's Dove of Peace emblem attracted very few workers, peasants, or employees; and if a 'Cold War culture' was indeed created at this time its implications were not clearly perceived until after 1952.[6] In this domain the PCF was almost certainly better placed than the mediocrity of its intellectual arsenal appears to suggest, but the absence of a long-term policy remained a handicap, one for which invective was no solution.

Communist intellectuals were especially active in the various peace organizations. The Mouvement de la paix, founded at Wroclaw (Poland) in August 1948, had as its objective the mobilizing of mass support behind the pacifist, progressive, and communist intelligentsia of the West;[7] at the first International Congress of the Partisans de la paix, held at Paris in April 1949 after a massive propaganda effort by the Communists, Ehrenbourg, Yves Farge, and Aragon joined Joliot-Curie, the movement's president, in a vigorous condemnation of the arms race, colonialism, and American imperialism. The recruitment of the progressive intelligentsia to this new antifascist crusade was paralleled by the final decline of neutralism as an issue for militant action; the feeble Rassemblement démo-cratique révolutionnaire founded by Sartre and Rousset in 1948 collapsed, and the campaigns in *Le Monde* and *L'Observateur* had, as we have seen, little impact. Communist domination prevented the Mouvement de la paix from building a broad-based appeal and in 1950 it had only 72 000 members, although the campaign in favour of the Stockholm appeal against the atomic bomb that drew millions of signatures, laced with violent attacks on Tito and the Socialist lackeys of the United States, gave a welcome boost to its activities from March 1950.[8]

A slightly more promising theme for the Party's action was anti-colonialism, where opposition to the war in Indo-China allowed it to at least reduce its Cold War isolation. The potential value of this cause was demonstrated by the Henri Martin affair involving a sailor condemned in 1950 and again in 1951 for having campaigned against the war and openly expressing his sympathies for the Vietnamese resistance. The PCF and the CGT took up his defence from the start, although he was not released until August 1953, and then only after the affair had mobilized Sartre, numerous non-Communist intellectuals, and the Ligue des droits de l'homme.[9]

The stance of the French Communist Party in the ideological combat of the Cold War lost it the support of many intellectuals whose favour it had held in 1944. With the positions of the opposing camps no longer open to modification through argument, dialogue gave way to a bitter and sterile exchange of accusations. Just a few weeks after the founding of the Mouvement de la paix, the Lyssenko affair demonstrated to many the willingness of the PCF to sacrifice the truth in order to accept Stalinist orthodoxy, in this case on progress in biology, even if Jacques Monod and Marcel Prenant salvaged some honour for the French Party.[10] Then, from January to April 1949, the action brought by Kravchenko, author of a best-selling attack on the Soviet system, *J'ai choisi la liberté*, against *Les Lettres françaises*, saw the celebrities of the progressive élite come forward to self-confidently refute the accuations of Stalinist crimes. Kravchenko won his case, but the complacency of the intellectuals shocked many, whilst the incessant anticommunist attacks of the press and radio seemed justified to a large section of public opinion.[11] The scenario and consequences were similar in December 1950 over the case brought by David Rousset against *Les Lettres françaises* concerning the existence of Soviet concentration camps.

The struggle against Tito and the need to justify the purges in Eastern Europe only tightened Stalinist discipline, bringing sharper and sharper attacks from the PCF's most experienced and effective polemicists, Wurmser, Kanapa, Garaudy, and Daix. And it was now in fact that the fellow-travellers began to desert; Sartre broke with the PCF for a time in January 1950 over the question of the camps; the following year brought a denunciation of the trials from Camus in *L'Homme révolté*; Merleau-Ponty now adopted an increasingly critical attitude to the developments on the other side of the Iron Curtain; others, such as Vercors, Cassou, and Martin-Chauffier, departed without a fuss. And 1950 also saw the Third Force step up its anticommunist pressure, dismissing Joliot-Curie as head of the Atomic Energy Commission, revoking the powers of Communist mayors in Paris. The two most consequential organs of progressive opinion, *Les Temps modernes* and *Esprit*, began to have doubts over their earlier loyalties; the former under Sartre retreated into two years of silence, whilst Mounier and his team abandoned their indulgent attitude towards the PCF.[12] The Party's isolation was at its deepest; the efforts of a decade to woo the intellectuals were destroyed in the space of a few months. From December 1949 the attitude of the PCF was increasingly defensive and inward-looking; dialogue was closed; henceforth the Party's ideological coherence was narrowly defined in the pages of *La Nouvelle Critique*; the faithful adjusted to a strict diet of social realism. On this front it was not until the end of the Korean War, the campaign in favour of Henri Martin, and the demonstrations against General Ridgway in May 1952 that dialogue, halting and difficult, began to reappear.

Compared with the PCF the other major opposition to the Third Force, organized Gaullism, was ill-adapted to strengthening or even maintaining its position during this difficult period. There is, however, a danger of anachronism when assessing the fortunes of the RPF at this time. The subsequent electoral decline of the Rassemblement should not, for example, obscure the fact that the system of *apparentements* was largely to blame for its reduced parliamentary representation in 1951; nor should the long period in the political wilderness and the recourse to a very solitary de Gaulle in 1958 give the impression that without its leader the RPF lacked all ideological and organizational consistence. Such a conclusion would be premature: at the beginning of 1948 the RPF had over a million members and was capable of rivalling the Communist Party by the variety and dynamism of its militant activity – the Third Force was not mistaken in considering the RPF as its principal adversary.

The momentum of the RPF's launch was in fact sustained. De Gaulle made several nation-wide tours, boosting morale and gauging opinion for himself, making superb use of the mass meetings expertly stage-managed by Malraux and Soustelle. Much was made of the truly national and apolitical character of the movement; it was repeatedly stressed that the RPF was not concerned to win seats for itself or to form coalitions, but wanted instead to free France from the dictatorship of the political parties. The RPF's ambition to become an authentic popular movement allowed it to place a great emphasis on the need for new forms of democracy based on deeper involvement of the citizens through consultation and participation. Although its opponents did not hesitate to class the RPF with the Right or extreme Right (with the fascist Right according to the Communists), it was in fact closer to the Bonapartist tradition in French political history, one which defies straightforward definition in terms of the familiar Left–Right division. Its structures had little in common with those of the established political parties; there were no local committees to select candidates, just loosely formed groups in different regions and professions, the accent being on the value of personal contacts rather than rigid formal structures. The impetus came of course from the top, in the person of de Gaulle; then the members of the Council of Direction and the staff of the rue de Solferino headquarters, named by him; relayed in turn by energetic delegates in the regions and *départements*.[13] The local Councils and the National Council elected by the membership had little direct influence on the RPF's activities and the National Conferences, the first of which was held at Marseille in April 1948, bore little likeness to the congresses of the political parties, and were the occasion for solemn appeals for patriotic efforts by the French people rather than an opportunity for discussion and policy-making.

Although the Socialists, the MRP, and the Radicals had all forbidden their adherents membership of the RPF, many of its members in fact saw their action in the Rassemblement as transcending partisan politics and felt no conflict of loyalties in dividing their energies between the RPF and their original party: the chances were thus good for building up a grassroots following. The RPF was successful in some new domains; its monthly *Liberté de l'esprit* launched in February 1949 under the editorship of Claude Mauriac, although of limited doctrinal originality, captured, thanks to its serious reporting and the prestige of its contributors – Jean Paulhan, Roger Caillois, Gaëtan Picon, Raymond Aron – an important audience in the worlds of learning and the arts dominated by the Left since the Liberation. Above all there was the familiar Gaullist theme of the association of capital and labour, revived by the General at Saint-Étienne in January 1948, reiterated at each May Day meeting, and the object of a proposed law repeatedly put forward between March 1950 and December 1952.[14] This idea was the springboard for RPF efforts in the factories, and several hundred 'Action ouvrière' groups were set up. Initiatives in the social domain were completed by some original work among student groups, ex-servicemen, and family associations.

However, over the months the early high hopes gradually faded. The RPF obtained 58 of the 320 seats in the elections to the Council of the Republic in November 1948, but the coherence of the Gaullist group was weakened by the presence in its ranks of Moderates and Radicals. The Rassemblement's strong showing in the cantonal elections of March 1949, when it took 32 per cent of the votes and a third of the posts, certainly boosted morale, but there was a worryingly high proportion of double candidatures. And the Third Force still held what was in fact the trump card: the ability to gain time by postponing the legislative elections. The RPF leaders, somewhat smugly installed in their self-appointed role as the only alternative to the Communists, were forced to wait, counting on militant activity to maintain enthusiasm and momentum. Yet without an electoral deadline on which energies could be focused, this was not an easy task; nor was it even certain that the elections would bring a decisive outcome, not least since the RPF was fighting on two fronts, against the Communists but also against the Third Force. By the summer of 1949 signs of impatience and discouragement were visible; as Malraux is reported to have summed up the situation: 'General de Gaulle has led us to the Rubicon, but to go fishing from its bank.' The local groups resented subordination to Paris; the leadership was increasingly infiltrated by Radical, MRP, and right-wing parliamentarians; the RPF weekly, *Le Rassemblement*, was losing its readership; funds were running low. De Gaulle himself, forbidden on the radio and frequently the victim of official obstruction and even humiliation in the course of his tours, continued to believe that mobilization was compatible with inactivity, and staked the future of the RPF on his personal prestige. Yet the contradictions of the Rassemblement's position were inescapable. How could support for the Atlantic alliance be squared with a championship of national independence? Was it realistic or electorally prudent to go on announcing an imminent global catastrophe when popular aspirations were so clearly to peace and prosperity? Just how credible was the claim to stand for a fraternity transcending partisan divisions when the RPF militants so rarely hesitated to use physical force against the 'rouges'? How could the rhetoric of the association of capital and labour be reconciled with the obvious indifference of the employers and an overt hostility towards the CGT? And there was the problem of the Rassemblement itself: could such a disparate movement really be run on tight, almost military lines? The year of 1950 was a difficult one for the RPF; its leadership squabbled, money was scarce, and the meetings and rallies attracted smaller audiences. A solemn appeal from the General on 17 August on national defence fell flat. On the eve of the 1951 elections, membership had fallen to 350 000, its press was moribund, and in many cases the local groups too readily accorded their backing to candidates interested primarily in securing the prestigious and electorally invaluable label of official Gaullist approval. As the difficulties multiplied it began to look as if the Rassemblement might have come too late, out of place in France's new-found peace.

## The Centrist alternative

The response of the Third Force to the double threat of Communism and Gaullism was a straightforward one of survival: to save the régime, and hence itself, from the extremist alternatives of popular democracy or dictatorship, time was essential. This was to be used to weaken the extremist opposition: on the one hand maximum use was to be made of the conditions of the Cold War to perpetuate and deepen the isolation of the Communists, whilst on the other the supporters of de Gaulle had to be wooed back to the parties of the Third Force. One way of gaining time was to push back electoral deadlines, as in the postponement of the cantonal elections scheduled for October 1948 to March 1949. And since the extremists were in the majority there could be no dissolution of the Assembly: a uniquely parliamentary solution involving a change of government had to be found for each crisis. It was in the course of the recurrent crises, however, that the bases of the Third Force majorities shifted slowly rightwards, first to the Centre, then to the Centre-Right. As we have already seen, without the 165 Communist votes, the Socialists and MRP together could not muster the 314 votes required for the investiture of a premier. Initially, the necessary balance was held by the Radicals and Moderates, who as a result were able to control the Centre-Left cabinets. Then, when Socialist support weakened, the balance shifted further to the right in order to find the necessary extra votes from the Independents, control thus passing to the Centre-Right. Clearly any premier could be brought down by a handful of deputies or by a disciplined splinter group: in spite of this vulnerability, however, if dissolution were to be avoided the majority would have to re-form shortly afterwards. As André Siegfried observed, for all its apparent instability the Third Force system had an inbuilt self-correcting mechanism, each crisis containing in effect the elements for its own resolution.[15]

Politics in this situation was concerned, as Queuille remarked, 'not to solve problems but to silence those who posed them,' the main thing being to remain in power by evading the issues. All the cabinets of this period were broadly identical in composition, containing one-third Socialists, one-third MRP, and one-third Radicals and Moderates: the premiers were interchangeable – Ramadier for the Socialists, Schuman or Bidault for the MRP, Queuille or André Marie in the case of the Radicals, and Pleven for the UDSR. The inescapable need to form coalitions, despite increasingly divergent programmes, led the parties to negotiate majorities for specific problems once the position in the Assembly had reached deadlock and dissolution loomed. On the education question, for example, the Socialists and Radicals, attached to a secular State monopoly, were outnumbered by a broad majority extending from the MRP to the Right, committed to defend the *école libre*. Over the economy, however, the Radicals made common cause with the Right in an ardent advocacy of liberalism, successfully counterbalancing the MRP and SFIO who favoured a more *dirigiste* approach. Undoubtedly the weakest piece in this complicated game of parliamentary chess was the SFIO, torn between its support for the Third Force and a concern not to slide too far rightwards. This dilemma of the

SFIO was at the origin of numerous ministerial crises; Schuman's defeat in July 1948 was the result of SFIO anxieties over the education question and military credits for Indo-China; hostility to the liberal financial projects of the Independents and Paul Reynaud, now at Finance, led Blum and the Socialist ministers to precipitate the fall of the André Marie ministry in August; differences over prices and incomes policy and the defence of civil servants moved them similarly to bring down Queuille in 1949, Bidault in June 1950, and Queuille again in July. The MRP, Radicals, and Moderates made less frequent but equally effective use of the same weapon, quickly blocking Schuman in September 1948 when he attempted to appoint a Socialist, Christian Pineau, to Finance, and Pleven in February 1951 over the electoral system to be employed for the next legislative elections. Only Queuille was sufficiently adroit and effective to satisfy everyone between September 1948 and October 1949; his achievement was considerable, stabilizing the franc, halting the advance of the RPF in the cantonal elections and those to the Council of the Republic, holding off the PCF, and, with 389 days in office, establishing the legislature's record for ministerial longevity.

Behind the apparently endless succession of premiers and cabinets – each change meticulously regulated by the parliamentarians but of decreasing interest to the general public – an important change was occurring in the distribution of political force. As the 1951 elections sharply pointed up, the 'idéologues' were losing ground; the uninspiring reality of rule from the Centre in effect robbed the MRP and the Socialists of the doctrinal originality they had acquired in the Resistance and the Liberation. As far as the MRP was concerned, its claims to be the party of loyalty to de Gaulle and of resistance to the Communists collapsed with the emergence of the RPF – many of its voters went over, secretly or openly to the new Gaullist movement. Increasingly compromised with the Right, the MRP's attraction as an original and innovative party faded; what had once seemed a fresh party fighting for a dynamic new Republic now looked simply like the mainstay of a cautious Christian Democracy. The MRP's stance over the education question lost it secular support, and the pro-European cause it espoused had little popular appeal. It still had strong backing among women, managers, the liberal professions, and civil servants; but support among the young, workers, and peasants was contracting; and as the MRP's electoral audience became concentrated in the middle classes so it encountered progressively stiffer competition from the Radicals, the RPF, and the Right. The MRP's decline was dramatic, the number of active militants falling from almost 100 000 in 1947 to 50 000 in 1948, finally stabilizing at roughly 25 000 in 1950. True, there was still a place in the political spectrum for the MRP, but it was no longer a privileged vehicle for the hopes of the Liberation.[16]

The MRP's main Third Force partners, the Socialists, were experiencing a similar loss of identity. The divisions between the party militants, the SFIO leadership, and the parliamentary group were growing. The decision to support the Third Force quickly led to internal difficulties: the various Socialist youth organizations, suspected of Trotskyist leanings, disappeared; combined militant action with the RDR or RPF was forbidden in 1948; the 'Bataille socialiste' group was expelled. Moreover, on each of the major issues the Socialists were caught off balance: after the Prague takeover their anticommunism was too fierce to make alliance possible with the PCF; Ramadier and Moutet were both too deeply implicated in the outbreak of the war in Indo-China for the Socialists' repeated calls for fresh talks with Ho Chi Minh to have much credibility; their commitment to the Atlantic alliance and to the ideal of European unity prevented them from immediately adopting a strong opposition to German rearmament. Humiliated and weak, unreliable in their support of governments, the Socialists played a smaller and smaller role in decision-making. The failure of Jules Moch – backed by Blum and Auriol for the investiture on 14 October 1949 but forced to renounce after three days of unsuccessful attempts to construct a cabinet – put an end to Socialist hopes of leading a government. They participated aimlessly in the governments which succeeded Moch's dismal experience, counting on the presence of Daniel Mayer at the Ministry of Labour to preserve something of their image as a party of the working class. They withdrew from government in February 1950, only to return in July, losing the Ministry of the Interior but obtaining the appointment of Guy Mollet, under pressure as SFIO General Secretary, as Minister for Relations with the Council of Europe in the Pleven cabinet. The death of Léon Blum in March 1950 only added to the SFIO's difficulties: the party's social base was shrinking, its press declining, and membership falling – 280 000 in 1947, 190 000 in 1949, barely 130 000 in 1951.

If the Third Force experiment worked against the interests of the MRP and the Socialists, it favoured the groups and individuals of the Third Republic who had seemed largely discredited in 1944; that is, the Radicals and the Right. The Radicals were now an indispensable source of majorities in the Assembly; they even recovered electoral success, first in 1948 when the RGR of which they were the principal element became the strongest group in the Council of the Republic, then with the performance of their local figures in the following year's cantonal elections. The presence of the RPF and the question of double membership posed some problems, but with Herriot presiding over the Assembly, Monnerville presiding over the Council of the Republic, and the re-emergence of Daladier, the veterans of the Third Republic had successfully completed their return to the corridors of power. And the Radicals were less than ever a party of the Left: the

'Neo-Radicalism' first aired at the Radical Congress of 1946 and that had the favour of Martinaud-Déplat, Bernard Lafay, and Emile Hugues, combined a defence of free enterprise and the market economy with hostility to state intervention, nationalization, and 'oppressive' social protection; whilst alignment with the Atlantic and European camps, plus a ready ear for the colonialist arguments of the Algerian lobby led by Borgeaud and René Mayer, set the tone for foreign affairs. In short, a Radicalism barely distinguishable from the Centre-Right or Right and which like them found in anticommunism a minimal ideological colouring for its programme; indeed, the virulently anticommunist 'Paix et liberté' movement was run by a Radical, Jean-Paul David.[17] Acceptance of electoral funds from the CNPF and a compromise over the secular principle under André Marie completed Radicalism's abandonment of the tenets of the old Belleville programme.

There were unmistakable signs of vitality still further to the right. Here, Louis Marin's Fédération républicaine, Pierre-Etienne Flandin's Alliance démocratique, and even the PRL, had all failed to make serious headway before 1948, a reflection of an ideological and personal bankruptcy and lack of contact with post-war realities. On the fringes, the Pétainistes had been active since April 1948, orchestrating demands for the Marshal's amnesty and, after his death in July 1951, for rehabilitation and the return of his remains to France; but their lists, the Indépendant républicains headed by Maître Isorni and Admiral Decoux, obtained only a meagre token success in the 1951 elections.[18] And in fact innovation came not from the conservative Right regretful of such a dubious past, but from a liberal Right armed with an efficient organization and a concise and coherent programme capable of rallying the diverse currents of the Right.[19] Circumstances favoured this development: the Centre-Left was eager to secure the support of the Right against the RPF; and the education controversy, economic recovery, and financial orthodoxy were all good subjects for this liberal Right's blend of commonsense arguments and a defence of liberties. The first stage of the return in force of the Right was marked by the entry into the André Marie government of Paul Reynaud as Minister of Finance – henceforth Reynaud was the pivotal figure for all the right-wing deputies. His appointment was complemented by that of an Independent, René Coty, to the Ministry of Reconstruction, Joseph Laniel of the PRL as Under-Secretary of State for National Economy, and Maurice Petsche, a Peasant member, as Secretary of State for the Budget. These appointments confirmed the Third Force's willingness to help all its potential supporters; they also signalled the access of the Right to control of economic and financial policy, albeit for the moment under the leadership of a Radical. Thus the presence of Petsche at the Ministry of Finance from September 1948 to July 1951 was to do much to reassure business and commercial interests, and marked the end of the *dirigiste* experiments of the Liberation. The second stage of the return in force of the Right came with the founding of the Centre national des indépendants under Roger Duchet, begun in the summer of 1948 and formally constituted in January 1949. This flexible structure brought together the traditional Right of Flandin, unreconstructed Vichyites, what was left of the PRL, and the Independents; with an electoral machine generously fuelled by funds from the employers this group quickly established itself as an important element in the Third Force's parliamentary arithmetic. Just before the 1951 elections the Peasant Group of Paul Antier decided to join forces with Duchet, and on 15 February 1951 the Centre national des indépendants et paysans (CNIP) was formed. Rivalries and disagreements persisted of course; but from now on, a liberal Right, fighting on the theme of the defence of liberties, had a serious electoral potential.

Nor was the audience for this liberal Right confined to parliamentary circles: sections of the press and intelligentsia, sympathetic to its ideas and often already deeply affected by the Gaullist phenomenon, realigned or reappeared; combative anti-Marxist currents, traditionalist or not, could now express themselves more easily.[20] The Action française held on doggedly for the release of Maurras in April 1952; apologists for Vichy found an outlet in *Écrits de Paris*; the lively weekly *Arts* and the review *La Table ronde* founded in 1949 specialized in no-holds-barred attacks on the leading figures of the progressive Left; and the launching of *Rivarol* in January 1951 provided the various currents of the Right with a forum in the tradition of *Gringoire*. These developments were in fact echoed throughout the press, where 'moderate' views now seemed to enjoy the greatest success; the left-wing daily press of Paris declined, while the circulations of *L'Aurore*, *Le Figaro*, *Le Parisien libéré*, and *France-Soir* rose as the stridency of the Liberation was abandoned.

## The verdict of 1951

It would be misleading, however, to define the Third Force and explain its failure uniquely in terms of playing for time and the realignments occurring beneath the surface of French political life. The use of delaying tactics carried risks as well as advantages, and as the 1951 elections showed, leaving problems in suspense did not make them go away.

The months leading up to the elections saw confidence in the régime shaken by a series of scandals. In March 1950 the parliamentary inquiry into the 'scandale des vins' which had dragged on since the end of 1946 finally cleared Félix Gouin, but members of his entourage and SFIO hangers-on were incriminated; the affair of the 'bons d'Arras', not in fact dealt with until May 1952, revealed the corruption of a Gaullist deputy,

Antoine de Récy; there were widespread rumours about the involvement of prominent political figures in the lucrative speculations on the Vietnamese currency. Above all, the so-called 'affaire des généraux' rocked public opinion, disgraced the army, and provided powerful ammunition for the enemies of the régime.[21] By August–September 1949 it was clear that the secret report by General Revers on the situation in Indo-China had been leaked – copies circulated in Paris and extracts had even been broadcast by the Vietminh radio. Suspicion settled on Peyré, a close confidant of Generals Revers and Mast, who appeared to have betrayed his position of trust for political ends. Senior officers and parliamentarians were implicated; clumsy attempts to smother the affair brought swift denunciations from the RPF and PCF (the latter demanding in vain that Jules Moch be arraigned before the High Court); others alleged that the MRP Minister for Overseas France, Coste-Floret, had engineered the whole affair to discredit the opponents of his policy over Indo-China. Whatever the truth, this and the other scandals, along with the political machinations, leaks, and sensational press coverage which accompanied them, earned all those involved a harsh judgement from the general public, one that rebounded inevitably on the régime itself.

This background only added to the extreme caution with which the Third Force prepared to face the electorate. After six months of discussion over electoral reform (eight different projects were successively rejected on 21 February 1951!), involving an open conflict between the Assembly and the Council of the Republic, the latter in favour of a return to a majority system, it was Queuille who finally secured the passage of a new electoral law on 9 May 1951. The new law retained proportional representation but modified it with a system of *apparentements* or associations; under this, different lists could combine before the elections, not on their programmes but for the counting of the votes and the final distribution of seats. Applicable only for lists presented in at least thirty constituencies, that is, those of the national parties, the system of *apparentements* was quite clearly a device designed to help the Centre-Left and Centre-Right obtain the necessary electoral quota, take the major share of the redistributed votes and, in the case of an absolute majority, all the seats: completely contrary in this respect to the principle of proportional representation. As a further precaution, the Parisian constituencies of Seine and Seine-et-Oise, where the RPF and PCF were strong, were excluded from the *apparentement* system. Even if such ruthless electoral manipulation to secure a Third Force majority could still be held to be compatible with democratic principles, the character of the election campaign itself dispelled any possible doubts that the principal aim was to block the Gaullists and, above all, the Communists. For if the PCF could be weakened it would be possible to continue with the policies followed since 1948 without having to fracture the Gaullist bloc or shift too far rightwards; while halting the RPF advance would leave all the options open for the future. Indeed, the system of *apparentements* constituted the ideological testament of the Third Force: first rally together all those who wished to defend the régime of the Fourth Republic, lead them to an electoral victory, and then, after the elections, decide on majorities and policies.

Predictably, the Communists refused to make any *apparentements* – it would moreover have been impossible for them to find willing partners. De Gaulle insisted that the RPF also remain aloof from association with other parties, often to the disappointment of RPF candidates compromised on the Centre and Right in their constituencies.[22] Of the ninety-five constituencies subject to the new rule, *apparentements* were formed in eighty-seven (of which thirty-six were total between the SFIO, MRP, RGR, and Independents). In most cases the *apparentements*, typically of two or three, were shaped by local circumstances, without the national party organizations being able to impose either discipline or a minimum of doctrinal convergence. The Communists fought the elections on the issue of national independence; the Gaullists counter-attacked with a virulent anticommunism and their familiar arguments of impending global catastrophe. The other parties adopted moderate and vaguer arguments, offering a cautious survey of achievements but mindful above all of tailoring their positions to suit local conditions.

The first thing to note about the outcome of the elections of 17 June 1951 (Table 7) is that the system of *apparentements* worked everywhere as its Third Force architects had intended – in thirty-nine constituencies the joint lists took all the seats.[23] With 54.7 per cent of the votes, the three partners of the defunct tripartite alliance could congratulate themselves on being in the majority. Yet the régime's opponents, Communists and Gaullists, had between then almost half (47.7 per cent) the votes; and an unfavourable judgement on the régime was no doubt a common motive for abstention. The main lessons of the election were a swing in favour of the Right, stability for the Left, and a strong Gaullist push. All the parties suffered to some extent from the mushrooming of the RPF: in spite of the *apparentements* the Rassemblement obtained more than four million votes, taking a million from the Left, two million from the Centre and Right, and seducing the abstentionists.[24] And although the landslide hoped for by de Gaulle had not occurred, the geography of Gaullist support – strong to the north of a line from Bordeaux to Belfort, present in the East and West, advancing in the working-class areas in and around Paris – lent weight to the RPF's claim to stand above the traditional cleavages of French political opinion. As intended, the system of *apparentements* had a dramatic impact on the PCF, robbing it of 42 per cent of its deputies: behind this brutal decline in parliamentary representation, however, the PCF's electorate was almost

Table 7: *Elections of 17 June 1951*

1. *Results*

| | | |
|---|---|---|
| Electorate | 24 530 523 | |
| Votes | 18 966 967 (77.3%) | |
| Abstentions and spoilt papers | 5 563 556 (22.7%) | |

| | votes | seats |
|---|---|---|
| PCF | 4 939 380 (26%) | 95 (−70) |
| RPF | 4 122 696 (21.7%) | 106 |
| SFIO | 2 894 001 (15.3%) | 95 (+4) |
| Independents and Moderates | 2 563 782 (13.5%) | 87 (+11) |
| MRP | 2 534 105 (13.4%) | 84 (−74) |
| RGR | 1 913 003 (10.1%) | 77 (+23) |

2. *Some sociological breakdowns of vote in %*

| | PCF | SFIO | RGR | MRP | RPF | Moderates |
|---|---|---|---|---|---|---|
| Workers | 47.8 | 14.8 | 4.4 | 11.5 | 15.9 | 5.6 |
| Employees | 23 | 11 | 2 | 24 | 28 | 7 |
| Civil Servants | 20 | 33 | 15 | 7 | 10 | 15 |
| Peasants | 17 | 11 | 17 | 12 | 22 | 22 |

*Sources:* C. Leleu, *Géographie des élections françaises depuis 1936*, PUF, 1971, p. 76; *Partis politiques et classes sociales en France*, ed. M. Duverger, Colin, 1955, *passim*; *Sondages*, March 1952.

stable, having fallen by only 600 000, and the Party's bastions of working-class support were in fact stronger than ever. Far behind the two opposition monoliths came the four roughly equal parties who shared the votes of those loyal to the régime. The great victim of the elections was the MRP, losing half its electorate and half its deputies, partly due to the progress of the Radicals and Moderates, but above all as a result of the Gaullist push. In the areas of the East and West the Catholic electorate had abandoned the MRP; the traditional distribution of the middle-class vote, so disrupted in 1944, had been re-established. The position of the SFIO was less serious, but the slow haemorrhage continued – more than two million votes had now been lost since 1945. The minor advances the SFIO was able to make at the expense of the Communists in the conservative rural regions were far outweighed by its losses to the Gaullists; support for the SFIO was increasingly confined to the traditional strongholds of the Midi and the North, dependent on the prestige of local figures and benefiting from the weakness of the Radicals. The remaining votes were shared by the coalition of Radicals and Independents thrown together by the system of *apparente-*

*ments*, and whose discreet political ascension the elections confirmed: the Radicals were predominant in the South-West; the Independents in the Centre and East. Overall then, the elections had shown that the old rallying call of 'défense républicaine' was still effective, notably among the rural voters, whose loyalty had compensated for the urban victories of the Republic's enemies; and the system of *apparentements* had not struck people as being too disgraceful. In short, the Third Force appeared to have been saved.[25]

Yet nothing was solved. Six formations of almost equal parliamentary strength now sat in what Queuille named the 'assemblée hexagonale'. Although the parliamentary regression of the Communists had eased tension, there was now the problem created by the irruption of the Gaullists: the four groups that had used the *apparentements* were in fact obliged to continue their marriage of electoral convenience in the new Assembly. This posed enormous problems, since over the intractable education question and economic policy only three-way alliances were possible: the Socialists were committed to defend *laïcité* in education, the Independents were liberal in economics, and the future of the MRP was increasingly uncertain. The new legislature began badly. It was not until 10 August, after a month-long crisis, that Pleven managed to form a government; this was backed by the MRP, Radicals, and Independents; the Socialists voted the investiture but decided not to participate in the government. It looked, then, as if a 'Fourth Force' solution based on the Radicals and Independents might be emerging. True, there could be no stable majority to govern, but the possibility remained of negotiating fresh majorities problem by problem.

Any chances Pleven might have had were ruined with the prompt resuscitation by the RPF of the parliamentary conflict over the education question. The old problem had in fact been simmering for some time, and was now to give a conclusive demonstration of the centrality of the clerical–anticlerical quarrel to the political history of contemporary France.[26] Vichy's subsidies to the Catholic schools had been abolished in the summer of 1945: complete *laïcité* was implicit in the return to Republican legality, although it is worth noting that in 1946 proposals to introduce the principle of freedom of choice in education were only narrowly rejected by the two Constituent bodies. Since then, inflation had aggravated the financial difficulties of the private schools; meetings, the creation of parents' associations, and, notably in the West, protests by the bishops, testified to the growing unrest. Hopes that a reasonable compromise solution might be found, not least in view of the urgent practical problems facing the country, evaporated in the flare-up of the quarrel after the unexpected nationalization on 16 May 1948 of the Catholic schools previously owned by the mining companies, the issue having united the Socialists and Communists against the government. A few days later, on 23 May, an anodyne decree from the MRP Under-Secretary for Public Health, Mme Poinso-Chapuis, providing help to needy families irrespective of the status of the schools their children attended, provoked a storm in the Assembly and an outcry from the press; in spite of approval by the Conseil d'Etat, this measure was never in fact applied. Discontent among the defenders of the *école libre* was now running high; with, of course, the petitions and parliamentary questions over fund-raising activities, taxes, and municipal subsidies to schools acquiring a huge importance thanks to the *laïc* camp's sensitivity over these minor points. Some of the heat did go out of the conflict during the first Queuille ministry, only to return in April 1950 with a fresh campaign led by the bishops, and threats of a tax strike. Passions were calmed thanks to behind-the-scenes negotiations involving Rome, and an all-party commission was set up to find a reasonable solution. This sat between October 1950 and May 1951, its conclusions providing further timely ammunition for the campaign. The likely impact on public opinion of this incessant political squabbling may be judged from the fact that between 1945 and 1951 the proportion of the population favourable to the *école libre* had risen from 23 to 46 per cent.

The education quarrel thus inflamed provided the Gaullists with an ideal opportunity to flex their new parliamentary muscles, and to devastating effect. The issue had been partly to blame for the damaging ministerial crisis between June and August 1951, and with the creation of an Association parlementaire pour la liberté de l'enseignement the potential majorities in the Assembly were already seriously compromised. Two projects were presented to the Assembly; the first, from the government, that became the *loi Marie*, proposed an extension of grants for secondary education to the private schools; the second, of parliamentary inspiration, presented by an MRP deputy, Barangé, provided a modest annual subsidy – 3000 francs, barely 100 francs at 1980 price levels – to all families with children attending a primary school regardless of its status. In fact, a very small share of this, roughly one-sixth, was to go to the private schools. After a month of impassioned debate, lasting from 21 August to 21 September, both projects were finally adopted, voted by a coalition of the MRP, the Moderates, the RPF, and a section of the Radicals. But while the financial consequences were slight, the political implications were enormous: for with the secular SFIO thus detached from the 'clerical' MRP, the Third Force was fatally weakened. In scoring this, its first victory, the RPF had shown itself to be the basis for a new potential majority of the Centre-Right.

After this success the Gaullist deputies returned of course to the opposition, and Jacques Soustelle was confident of being able to maintain their discipline. Already, however, the strains of perpetual opposition were starting to be felt; some RPF deputies, loyal to de Gaulle but under pressure from their electorates, were increasingly tempted by the prospect of changing the régime from within. The shortcomings of constructing new majorities issue by issue were clear to all. The Pleven cabinet's incomes policy, for example, was voted by the PCF, SFIO, MRP, and RPF but rejected by the Radicals and the Right; the Schuman Plan, on the other hand, was ratified by all except the RPF and the Communists; and, finally, it was the abrupt withdrawal of Socialist support over financial policy that brought Pleven down in January 1952. A Radical, Edgar Faure, now took on the difficult task of finding economic measures acceptable to both Socialists and Moderates, but was forced to admit defeat in February after a month of exhausting efforts to hold his majority together.[27]

The Third Force was patently incapable of producing durable majorities. At Auriol's request, Paul Reynaud tested the remaining options; his failure led him to the inevitable conclusion: since a Centre-Left majority with Socialist support was impossible the solution would have to be found on the Centre-Right with RPF backing. The accuracy of this conclusion was confirmed by the unexpected investiture of Antoine Pinay on 6 March 1952, secured with 324 votes in favour, 206 against and 89 abstentions: for although most of the Gaullist group obeyed the call to abstain, it was the defection of twenty-seven of its members, led by Frédéric-Dupont, which allowed Pinay to reach and cross the vital 314 vote threshold. Their defection in fact marked the start of the absorption of the already crumbling RPF into the system of the parties, and hence an unblocking of the situation on the Right of the political spectrum. This reversal for de Gaulle was paralleled by the rise to power and, soon, to popularity of a former member of Pétain's Conseil national: with the investiture of Antoine Pinay the period opened in 1944 was well and truly closed.

# 11

# Reconstruction and modernization

By 1946, the State had the means, and in the work of reconstruction the opportunity, to set up an *économie concertée*, striking a new and more or less pragmatic balance between liberalism and intervention. The public sector had a vital contribution to make in the struggle for output and investment; the Social Security system made it possible to distribute a larger share of the national income to the workforce; while stronger unionization and organization of the economic groups promised a better collective discipline, even if this was inevitably undermined by the slide in real incomes. It was to co-ordinate the means to the desired ends, to overcome resistance and ease friction, that the Plan was created. The Plan established priorities and stimulated ambition, looking beyond the immediate task of post-war reconstruction to identify the long-term national choice as the stark one between modernization or decline.

## The ambitions of the First Plan

In the autumn of 1945, a small team led by Jean Monnet received the backing of de Gaulle to begin work of research, consultations, and meetings; a summary of its preliminary conclusions was placed before the General on 4 December.[1] On 3 January 1946, without the Assembly having been consulted, a decree brought into being what was ambitiously announced as 'a first overall plan for the modernization and economic equipment of metropolitan and overseas France'. The stated aims of the First Plan were the development of national production and external trade, especially in those areas where the French position was strongest; to increase productivity; to ensure full employment; to improve living standards and the quality of the environment and collective life in general. Jean Monnet, appointed Commissioner for the Plan, and flanked by the Planning Council made up of ministers and experts, was given a completely free hand to make general proposals and work directly with the relevant ministries, responsible personally to the head of the government.

Perhaps the first point to make about Monnet's team concerns its size:

the Plan's small headquarters near Sainte-Clotilde never had more than thirty full-time chargés de mission, and their task was, in fact, to mobilize and co-ordinate expertise from the exterior within the framework of the objectives set down in the Plan. Its members were drawn from a number of fields; the technical services were run by Etienne Hirsch, a mining engineer previously in charge of organizing arms and supplies for France Libre; another key figure was Robert Marjolin, an academic who had headed the French purchasing mission to the United States and worked at the Ministry of National Economy under Mendès France, before leaving the Plan for a European career in 1948; another academic, philosopher turned economist Pierre Uri; statistical skills came from Jean Vergeot, a member of Sauvy's team; Paul Delouvrier, the chief adviser to Pleven, was responsible for the financing of the Plan; Jean-François Gravier concentrated on the regional dimension of the Plan; finally, Félix Gaillard directed the Plan's staff. At the centre of course was Jean Monnet; his approach can best be summed up as one of intuitive and lucid empiricism, the fruit of his long experience in the cognac trade, the English-speaking business Community, and international institutions. Monnet's conception of the Plan was based on the techniques of industrial mobilization he had observed and implemented during the war as a member of Allied committees, and as the CFLN's commissaire for armaments, reconstruction, and provisions in 1943. Indeed, when Monnet and his team are compared with pre-war *planistes* like Raoul Dautry, or with Lacoste's entourage, who dreamed of vigorous intervention and selective planning to overcome the crisis and shortages, it is clear that the Monnet Plan was not of strongly *dirigiste* inspiration, nor were its architects the most fervent advocates of action by the State.

One of the Plan's major assets was the availability to its experts of a new and reliable statistical apparatus. Much of the groundwork for improvements in this field had in fact been laid by Vichy: the acute wartime shortages had been an obvious incentive to greater accuracy and the projects for post-war reconstruction had entailed the compilation of comprehensive statistical files, and by 1943 the concept of 'national accounting' had developed. After the war, largely thanks to the activities of the Plan, this approach was to progress at the expense of the former, more narrowly statistical one.[2] The angle of vision thus broadened to give an overall view of the economy; economic forecasting, albeit a still far from exact science, gained acceptance and aroused the interest of the politicians. In March 1950 research on national income was entrusted to a committee of experts, and shortly afterwards the Ministry of Finance established its own Service d'études économiques et financières; François Bloch-Lainé appointed Claude Gruson to lead this, who with Simon Nora and Jean Serisé set up what became the official economic forecasting service. Progress was also being made in the field of statistics: the INSEE was set up on

27 April 1946, initially as part of the Ministry of National Economy but later autonomous; headed by François-Louis Closon, former commissaire de la République at Lille, the INSEE took on the task of setting up files on companies, before concentrating its attention on demography and patterns of consumption. Lastly, a team at the Ministry of Industry initiated the collection of essential information from the professions. These advances were consolidated by the law of 7 June 1951 which established the principle of obligatory, centralized, and confidential gathering of statistics, even if the collection from the employers had to be left in the hands of the CNPF. Clearly then, the deficiencies of information were being overcome, and by the early 1950s a general accounting model of the French economy was operational.

Scientific research also received active encouragement, partly thanks to an awareness of modern technology's contribution to economic recovery, but also from the desire to preserve a degree of independence for the future *vis-à-vis* the United States.[3] The task of the CNRS, reorganized on 2 November 1945, was to compensate for the shortcomings of research in the universities, to train researchers, and foster international contacts; although the results in the field of applied science were disappointing, the CNRS did much to save French science from a slow decline. In October 1945 the Atomic Research Commission was charged with applying the latest atomic research to the national defence, and until 1951 was responsible for the French nuclear programme. Here, as at the CNRS, Frédéric Joliot-Curie supervised the formation of a new generation of researchers and co-ordinated the early successes: these included the putting into action of 'Zoé', the first European atomic pile on 15 December 1948; the start of work at the Saclay research station in the summer of 1949; and in 1952 the first plan for the development of atomic energy was voted. Lastly, the Institut national d'études démographiques, founded in October 1945 under the direction of Alfred Sauvy, was already deeply involved in studying the mechanism of the French demographic renewal and analysing the needs and wants of the population.[4]

The as yet deficient efforts in applied research received an important stimulus from the public sector. The INRA, created in March 1946, grappled with the problems of extending mass-production methods to agriculture; researchers at the PTT worked on the modernization of communications technology, experimenting already with electronics and television; researchers of the official aeronautical body had begun work on the Caravelle; and the SNCF and EDF, under Louis Armand and Pierre Massé, were both modernizing their plant in close collaboration with Monnet's experts. Inevitably, the results of these early efforts were uneven, and the co-ordination was not always successful; but the enthusiasm was real, and the impetus created was undeniable. Another important development, though with less immediate consequences, was the setting up of the Ecole nationale de l'administration (ENA), founded on 9 October 1945 as a training college for top civil servants and administrators. The ENA, the brainchild of Michel Debré, sought to 'meritocratize' recruitment to the highest echelons of the French administration, the so-called 'grands corps', instilling dynamism and coherence into a class of competent administrators, one which might cushion the State from some of the failings of the political parties. A broad range of subjects was taught at the ENA, but the largest element was economics of a pronounced Keynesian flavour; although the ENA's first graduates did not reach positions of high responsibility until the 1950s, they were all strongly influenced by the teaching of Mendès France, Jean Fourastié, and Pierre Uri, on the role of investment, growth and, of course, the Plan.

The skill of the Monnet team lay above all in involving in the preparation of the Plan those who would in fact be responsible for its implementation. Eighteen 'modernization commissions', each with between thirty and fifty members, met regularly at the Plan's headquarters. The commissions brought together a wide range of employers, trade unionists, experts, and civil servants; in all, nearly a thousand representatives were involved at this stage, accepting the subordination of their corporate interests to the task of solving common problems. This pooling of expertise and experience in the service of the national interest gave an incontestable authority to the projects of the planners, helping to remove possible obstacles to the Plan's application. It was virtually without discussion that the Blum cabinet adopted the Monnet Plan in January 1947.

The basic premiss of the Plan, expressed in the *Données statistiques sur la situation de la France au début de 1946* it published, and in Pierre Uri's September 1947 report on progress to date, was an identification of the constrictive *malthusianisme* that underlay France's poor economic performance. The Plan's experts argued that France had fallen behind demographically and economically; it was this backwardness which was at the origin of the recurrent balance of payments crises, the social conflicts, and the depressed standards of living. The structural failings of the French economy were manifested in a whole series of problems: low productivity of labour, outdated technology, over-cautious entrepreneurs,[5] plethoric distribution networks, excessive administrative costs, and a too-ready recourse to protectionism. True, the Plan conceded, output had revived since the Liberation, targets for individual sectors could be reached, and reconstruction would no doubt alleviate some of the problems. But the Plan looked beyond this, arguing that a straightforward return to the pre-war situation was not enough, that unless accompanied by a thoroughgoing modernization, French reconstruction would be of no more than limited effectiveness. To correct this, postulated the Plan, required only a slight modification of the objectives set in 1944: on the one hand, the public sector would remain at reasonable proportions and the trade unions would ensure co-operation in the efforts to increase productivity; on the other, the action of the State in the economy would be concentrated less on price levels than on credit and investment; the benefits of competition were acknowledged and help from outside France was to be sought. In short, to the unbridled individualism responsible for the *malthusianisme* that characterized the French economy, the Plan opposed concerted action and incentives. The sterile *dirigisme* versus liberalism debate was side-stepped: decisions remained the responsibility of those directly involved, but these responsibilities carried an obligation to work with the other social partners to agree on common targets and on the most effective ways of attaining them.[6]

The Monnet Plan more frequently evoked continuities between the 1950s and 1930s than it did aspirations to break with the past associated with the Liberation period. The public sector had acquired an undeniable importance, but capitalism would not now be pushed back any further; intervention by the State might be necessary to surmount the immediate problems of distribution and shortages, but the long-term health of the economy depended on co-operation between the State and companies, a co-operation it was the Plan's task to foster. The Soviet model was thus rejected: instead, the Plan wanted France to confront – though not in a spirit of blinkered economic nationalism – the challenge of international trade dominated by the United States. Since incomes from overseas investments and the French Union faced an inevitable decline, efforts had to be concentrated on exports: it was this emphasis on international trade which necessitated frequent revisions of the Plan and constant scrutiny of the all-important dollar exchange. The Monnet Plan quite deliberately ignored the unresolved problems of supplies and housing, focusing instead on that of heavy investment; the question of agricultural production received little attention compared with that of the construction of a dynamic modern economy capable of meeting international competition and dominating Europe.[7] Self-consciously distanced from the everyday obsessions of living standards and rebuilding, inflation and consumption, the Plan concentrated on output, productivity, modernization, growth, and competition, drawing lessons for the future from the failures of the past.

More concretely, the Plan identified the priorities for France. Originally to run from 1947 to 1950, the Plan was in fact extended to 1952 so that its end coincided with that of Marshall Aid. The objective was to combine increased production with modernization, setting as a target the reaching of the best pre-war level of output, that of 1929, by 1949, and exceeding it by 25 per cent the following year. The Plan laid down the preconditions for success: consignments of German coal, lower costs of production, increased incentives to labour mobility, and foreign financial aid – it was to secure the last that Monnet joined Blum in Washington in March 1947 to present his proposals and negotiate the funds. The Plan gave absolute priority to six sectors: coal, production of which had to increase from 47 to 65 million tonnes; electricity, output of which was to rise from 23 to 37 milliard kW/h.; steel, where production was to grow from 4 to 10 million tonnes; cement, transport, and agricultural machinery; and to these six basic industries were added fuels and chemical fertilizers. Moreover, output in all sectors was to increase significantly and exports had to double. Compliance with the Plan was compulsory for the public sector; for the private sector the government offered guaranteed supplies of controlled primary materials to producers who agreed to follow the Plan's guidelines for output and productivity.

The main obstacle to the success of the Plan looked likely to be financial. In spite of Delouvrier's efforts the targets set by the Plan were, on paper at least, financially unattainable; the total investment required was enormous, amounting to roughly a quarter of French national income.[8] Monnet, however, refused to be deterred, preferring to launch the Plan and let it prove itself in action. He was careful, for example, to cultivate American support for his project, stressing its Atlantic and European framework; he was careful too in the choice of personnel for the purchasing expeditions for primary materials and machine tools, dispatching only the most dynamic employers, officials, and experts on the study trips, exchanges, and productivity missions. When in 1947 the Plan was seriously menaced by inflation (see Chapter 9), Marshall Aid came to its timely rescue. At the same time, savings and self-financing were encouraged; the State helped over short-term difficulties with subsidies and tax reliefs, and the nationalized banks were mobilized in support of the Plan. The inflation was now actually welcome, giving buoyancy to the money supply and easing liquidity problems. From 1948 the available resources were channelled through the Fonds de modernization et d'équipement (FME); this drew 53 per cent of its funds from American aid in the first year, 72 per cent in 1949, 53 per cent in the following year, and 16 per cent in 1951, an annual average of 48 per cent. The financial obstacle had been overcome: Monnet's leap in the dark was vindicated. The mechanism of the distribution of American Aid (Table 8 and diagram) enabled the State to play a major role in the financial execution of the Plan; it provided 51 per cent of total investments in 1947, 58 per cent in 1948, almost 62 per cent in 1949, and 57 per cent in 1950. Of approximately 3800 milliard francs worth of investment between 1947 and 1952 (at 1954 prices), 2000 milliard came from the resources of the public sector or from private companies (through self-financing, bank loans and savings), 240 milliard came from the State as subsidies and tax relief, and 1560 milliard took the form of loans to companies from the FME. Strongly backed by the Treasury and nationalized

Table 8: *Distribution of the exchange value of Marshall Aid, 1948–51*
(*as % of total*)

| | |
|---|---|
| Charbonnages de France | 14 |
| EDF: 22.16; GDF: 0.83 | 22.99 |
| SNCF | 5.50 |
| Compagnie nationale du Rhône | 1.71 |
| Reconstruction of housing | 9.16 |
| Construction of housing | 3.64 |
| Reconstruction of agricultural, industrial, and commercial concerns | 5.88 |
| Reconstruction of merchant and fishing fleets | 2.05 |
| Loans to agriculture | 7.35 |
| Loans to private industry | 8.34 |
| Saar | 0.99 |
| Algeria: 3.21; Morocco and Tunisia: 2.56 | 5.77 |
| Other overseas territories | 1.69 |
| Armaments production | 4.78 |
| Reduction of ceiling of provisional advances to Treasury from the Bank of France | 3.42 |
| Reduction of public debt | 2.73 |

*Source: Le Monde,* 4–5 June 1967.

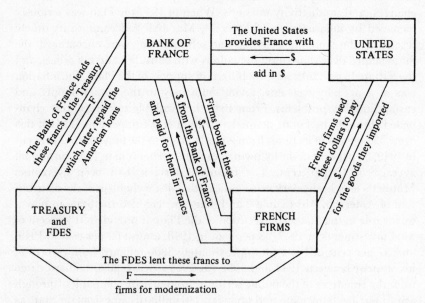

2  The mechanism of Marshall Aid

*Source:* J. Guyard, *Le Miracle français*, Seuil, 1965, p. 20

Table 9: *Estimates of national income and industrial production*

| | National income | | Industrial production |
|---|---|---|---|
| | milliard 1938 francs | index | index |
| 1929 | 453 | 119 | 133 |
| – | – | – | – |
| 1938 | 380 | 100 | 100 |
| – | – | – | – |
| 1944 | 191 | 50 | 38 |
| 1945 | 207 | 54 | 50 |
| 1946 | 315 | 83 | 84 |
| 1947 | 341 | 90 | 99 |
| 1948 | 366 | 96 | 113 |
| 1949 | 414 | 109 | 122 |
| 1950 | 448 | 118 | 129 |
| 1951 | 477 | 126 | 143 |
| 1952 | 490 | 129 | 145 |
| 1953 | 505 | 133 | 146 |
| – | – | – | – |
| 1958 | 636 | 167 | 213 |

*Source: Annuaire statistique de la France, rétrospectif,* Imprimerie nationale/PUF, 1961, p. 365, and A. Sauvy, 'Rapport sur le revenu national', *JO, Avis et rapports du Conseil économique,* 7 April 1954.

banks, the Plan was thus able to direct consistently the strategic investments of this period, a factor of decisive importance for its realization.[9]

*Progress of the Plan*

By 1952 the successes were manifest, with 1929 levels of production reached and then bettered. The rhythm of recovery was less regular than anticipated, and several hasty readjustments had been necessary: nevertheless, the Plan had contributed to the raising of the gross national product of 1953 to a level 39 per cent higher than in 1946 and 19 per cent superior to the 1938 level. With an average annual growth rate of 4.5 per cent the French post-war economic recovery was less spectacular than the 'miracles' in Federal Germany or Italy. But industrial output was growing by a steady and sustainable 7 per cent per annum, even if it was in fact only 12 per cent higher than the level of 1929, well short of the 25 per cent originally planned (see Table 9). And not only were the scars of the war and its aftermath healing, but modernization was progressing.

The progress here owed much to the Plan's careful selection of priorities and the obstinacy with which they had been pursued (see Table 10). The

Table 10: *The priorities of the first plan*

| | | 1929 | 1938 | 1944 | 1945 | 1946 | 1947 | 1948 | 1949 | 1950 | 1951 | 1952 | Targets of Plan met to: |
|---|---|---|---|---|---|---|---|---|---|---|---|---|---|
| Coal | million tonnes | 54.9 | 47.5 | 26.5 | 35 | 49.2 | 47.3 | 45.1 | 53 | 52.5 | 54.9 | 57.3 | 96% |
| Electricity | milliard kW/h | 15.4 | 19.9 | 16 | 18.3 | 22.8 | 25.8 | 28.8 | 29.3 | 33 | 38.1 | 40.5 | 95% |
| Steel | million tonnes | 9.7 | 6.1 | – | 1.6 | 4.4 | 5.7 | 7.2 | 9.1 | 8.6 | 9.8 | 10.8 | 87% |
| Cement | million tonnes | 4.3 | 3.7 | – | 1.5 | 3.3 | 3.8 | 5.3 | 6.4 | 7.2 | 8.1 | 8.6 | 101% |
| Tractors | thousands | – | 1.8 | – | 0.5 | 1.9 | 4.2 | 12.4 | 17.3 | 14.2 | 16 | 26.1 | 85% |
| Rail traffic | milliard km units | 70 | 48.6 | 24.6 | 43.9 | 63.9 | 68.2 | 71.9 | 70.6 | 65.3 | 73.5 | 72.6 | – |
| Crude petrol treated | million tonnes | 0.8 | 5.8 | – | 0.2 | 2.3 | 5 | 8.2 | 11.5 | 14.5 | 18.4 | 21.4 | 105% |
| Nitrate fertilizers | thousand tonnes | – | 196 | – | – | 148 | 176 | 190 | 229 | 259 | 287 | 288 | 127% |

*Source: Annuaire statistique de la France, rétrospectif,* Imprimerie nationale/PUF, 1961, *passim.*

work of modernization associated with the Plan captured public imagination; the understandably triumphal tone of the planners announcing the latest successes echoed through the cinema newsreels, the press, and in speeches of politicians. Praise was heaped on the miners and metal-workers; the meeting of targets for cement and electricity production were occasions for celebration; the population was invited to admire the new French rolling-stock and the feats of French engineering, or marvel at the natural gas discoveries at Lacq.

Behind this infectious enthusiasm lay solid achievements. Two-thirds of the total investment had in fact gone to the basic industries and capital goods production, and it was in these areas of high return that the public sector concentrated its efforts. The results for energy and transport were especially encouraging. The initial target of 65 million tonnes of coal had proved over-optimistic, but a revised figure of 60 million was almost reached, and daily output per miner rose from 1229 kg before the war to 1307 kg; and thanks to mechanization, better uses for waste products, a regrouping of the richer mines, and an improved statute for miners in 1946, some of the more structural problems faced by the coal industry, those of depth, thin seams, and labour shortages, were overcome. The nationalized electricity industry (EDF) was in the vanguard of the planning experiment; the Plan's targets, revised upwards in this case, were reached to a level of 95 per cent. The hydroelectric programme in particular received massive investments and supplies of raw materials; work was begun on a total of seventy sites, on the Rhône and the Rhine, in the Alps and Pyrénées, and in the Massif Central. The old thermal stations had of course to be kept in operation for the time being and there were serious shortfalls between 1950 and 1952, and domestic consumption was heavily sacrified in favour of industrial users. But laws passed in 1951 and 1952 allowed the investments of the Second plan to be brought forward so that work could begin immediately on all the projected dams and power stations. There was spectacular progress too in the refining of petroleum products, and although France was still dependent on the Middle East for 92 per cent of supplies, national needs were now covered. Overall, the total energy supplies in 1952 were 33 per cent higher than in 1938, 52 per cent greater than in 1946. This promising balance sheet was marred only by the rapidly growing dependence on imports (equal to 37 per cent of French energy needs before the war and already standing at 32 per cent) and the fact that energy available per capita in France was appreciably lower than in either Federal Germany or Great Britain.

The transport services, so badly damaged at the end of the war, were quickly rebuilt. Equipped with better and more powerful rolling-stock, the SNCF was already handling a greater volume of traffic than in 1929, and the rail network's modernization and electrification were both progressing.

Like the EDF and the mines, the SNCF did much for the prestige of the public sector, for example, pioneering attempts to co-ordinate rail services with road and water transports; one result of this impressive performance was permission in August 1951 to abandon the uniform distance tariff responsible for distorting operating costs. Equally characteristic of this vigorous reconstruction were the reopening of the ports and the rebuilding of the French merchant fleet, as well as early moves towards the creation of a road and motorway network – notably the autoroute de l'Ouest out of Paris – with the setting up in December 1951 of an official agency for road construction and investment.

The balance sheet is more nuanced in the case of the iron and steel industries. To begin with, until 1948, the difficult social climate and fears of nationalization had inhibited many of the owners from making new investment. The most dynamic companies, however, did take advantage of the facilities offered by the Plan. Thus the Société des forges et aciéries du Nord et de l'Est and the Denain et Anzin company – merged in 1948 to form Usinor, the second largest French iron and steel producer – had ordered two wide-band continuous hammer forges from the United States in April 1947, both of which were paid for entirely by the FME; set up at Denain and Florange, the American equipment was completed with three new lines and modernized blast furnaces. Thus, by the time the ECSC was launched, the French industry had caught up with its European competitors, although its technology was only that of the American industry in 1929. The Plan's targets were almost reached – 10.8 million tonnes rather than 12.5 million – and the introduction of electrification and the Martin method of steel production were actually ahead of schedule. Against this, however, has to be set the fact that dependence on coke remained greater than forecast, productivity did not rise as much as intended (72 tonnes per worker a year rather than the 80 tonnes planned for), and reorganization of the companies involved proved slow and difficult. On the whole the owners did well, taking the aids and credits offered them, securing the right in 1951 to make their own loan issues and to join together within the future ECSC; they invoked the low level of overall demand to justify their refusal to practise vertical integration of the increasingly moribund processing industries, arguing instead for a return to the traditional policy of lucrative exports of semi-finished products. The Plan's modernization commission relented over this, and by 1950 30 per cent of production was exported; and the Sollac sheet-metal producers co-operative, set up in Lorraine at the end of 1948 at the prompting of the giant De Wendel group, in effect protected the weakest companies from competitive pressures to restructure and modernize. Decisions were in fact already being taken to forgo investments which would have raised the industry's productive capacity to 15 million tonnes.[10]

The most acute bottlenecks of 1945, coal and transport, had been eased, and although labour shortages persisted, immigration from North Africa encouraged hopes for an improvement here too. Unemployment was practically non-existent; and the smaller active population was making considerable extra efforts – the average working week was 45 hours, but a 48-hour week was common in the priority sectors. The Plan had been successful in channelling energies in the required direction. What it had failed to do, however, was prevent new bottlenecks forming, this time at the level of consumption. Between 1938 and 1950 the real value of household incomes rose by only 2.4 per cent. Food supplies were no longer a preoccupation, but mass consumption had yet to take off. Items of consumption actually fell from 81 to 72 per cent of total domestic production, inversely proportional in fact to the extension of administrative control, exports, and fixed capital formation.[11]

Many essential products were in short or barely adequate supply (see Table 11). Output in the metallurgical, textile, and electrical industries was consistently oriented towards the companies producing equipment and capital goods. Two vital sectors in particular lagged behind: building and agriculture. In the former the shortages of labour and investment (only 13 per cent of the Plan's total) meant that while housing construction in the devastated regions was usually sufficient, a general housing crisis was already developing; the demand for newer, larger, and better housing was to go unsatisfied for many years. Agriculture, receiving a mere 8 per cent of the Plan's investment, was even worse off; food production was scarcely higher than in 1938, with an average increase of 8 per cent rather than the 16 per cent hoped for. The year of 1949, marked by a disastrous drought which caused production to fall by 20 per cent, gave a brutal reminder of the artificiality of the agrarian prosperity during the wartime hardships. True, the urban population no longer faced rationing, but agricultural production remained chronically inelastic and wholesale prices were slumping: it was now, with the rest of the nation already absorbed by the adventure of industrial modernization, that the farmers became aware of their technical backwardness. By 1952, two out of five farmers had incomes inferior to the national minimum (SMIG); a disparity soon reflected in the resumption of a heavy *exode rural*, with between 100 000 and 150 000 leaving the countryside each year. The differences in productivity were growing, not only between France and her neighbours (from 1 to 1.6 on average) but between the French regions (from 0.4 to 2 between Savoie and Oise). Yet apart from tractors, too heavy for most farms, and chemical fertilizers, the Plan had little to offer for these problems. Handicapped financially as a result of their unproductive saving and the ravages of inflation, the majority of French farmers were unable to respond to the challenge of modernization. The most powerful and best organized, influential in the FNSEA and with strong parliamentary pressure groups, reacted to the situation with a

Table 11: *Output of some consumption items*

|  | 1938 | 1946 | 1949 | 1952 |
|---|---|---|---|---|
| **Meat** | | | | |
| million tonnes | 1.69 | 1.25 | 1.86 | 2.06 |
| **Milk** | | | | |
| tonnes | 133 000 | 103 000 | 132 000 | 150 000 |
| **Wine** | | | | |
| million hectolitres | 60.3 | 36.2 | 42.9 | 53.9 |
| **Refined sugar** | | | | |
| tonnes | 723 000 | – | 632 000 | 669 000 |
| **Potatoes** | | | | |
| million quintals | 156.7 (average 1929–1938) | 98.8 | 96.5 | 110.7 |
| **Shoes** | | | | |
| million pairs | 69.1 | 40.6 | 46.5 | 70.5 |
| **Clothing fabrics** | | | | |
| tonnes | 50 000 | 30 100 | 54 200 | 41 500 |
| **Household soap** | | | | |
| tonnes | 229 000 | – | 137 100 | 144 200 |
| **Crockery** | | | | |
| tonnes | 51 000 | 19 000 | 54 000 | 51 000 |
| **Newsprint** | | | | |
| tonnes | 357 000 | 122 000 | 243 000 | 287 000 |
| **Cigarettes** | | | | |
| million packets | 640 | 792 | 1 105 | 1 421 |
| **Radio sets (declared)** | | | | |
| millions | 4.7 | 5.6 | 6.4 | 7.9 |
| Private cars | 183 000 | 11 900 | 115 800 | 303 600 |
| Completed homes | 80 000 | – | 56 000 | 83 900 |

*Source: Annuaire statistique de la France, rétrospectif, Imprimerie nationale/PUF, 1961, passim.*

vigorous defence of the status quo. Thus, in spite of widespread sugar shortages around 1948, the beet producers of Picardy continued as before, safe in the knowledge that a third of their crop would be purchased by the State for turning into low-quality alcohol or burnt; likewise the large grain producers to the north of the Loire, who received the lion's share of the subsidies, hoarded the harvests until prices rose. French agriculture was in fact entering a difficult period, one marked by the vital structural changes of the 'silent revolution' and punctuated by outbursts of bitter anger from their casualties.

This strongly nuanced balance sheet of the First Plan would be incomplete if it failed to take into account the efforts of the individuals and communities most directly involved in the task of reconstruction. It closes therefore with a brief survey of two regions deeply concerned by post-war reconstruction: Normandy and Lorraine.

Conditions in Normandy at the end of the fighting are familiar (see Chapter 2, note 7). In October 1944 the State, acting through the Ministry of Reconstruction and Town Planning, assumed responsibility for the reconstruction of the devastated region, accepting the cost of rebuilding and guaranteeing the replacement of all that had been lost. Each victim became the owner of Treasury bonds for war damage, for the most part estimated and distributed efficiently and equitably. The State encouraged the victims to form co-operatives and associations for reconstruction, at the same time as accelerating the rationalization of urban and rural property structures, supporting the efforts of the local authorities, and dispatching competent planners and architects to the region. In 1948, when the clearing up and the recuperation of materials was complete, and the mined areas had been cleared, the plans went into action. Five years later, 29 per cent of houses and other buildings had been reconstructed, and in the small towns and villages the often highly successful job of rebuilding was finished. Progress in the larger towns and cities was slower; Auguste Perret's plans for the centre of Le Havre had barely begun to be executed, and Rouen was still a sprawling encampment of temporary accommodation. Choices had had to be made, and initially at least priority had been given to capital projects; labour had to be recruited for the work of rebuilding, the ports had to be cleared and restored, and agriculture had to be modernized. By the early 1950s the results were visible: three-quarters of the farms in Normandy had been modernized, the port of Le Havre was fully operational, and the lower valley of the Seine was reaping the benefits of the expanding trade in petroleum products. Not only had the worst of Normandy's war damage been repaired, but the region had taken a decisive step on the path of modernization.[12]

Recovery in Lorraine was closely linked to the mobilization of the region's natural and human resources. The coal industry, for example, was systematically favoured by the Plan; the mines were quickly restored, reaching their pre-war level of output by March 1947. A programme of mechanization (involving new cutters and conveyor belts), accessible seams, the prompt recruitment of an Algerian workforce to replace the departed Poles, the perfection of the Carling process for coke manufacture, advances in organic chemistry, plus an imaginative policy from the public sector working in concert with the iron and steel producers – all guaranteed the Lorraine an important place in the future ECSC. Similar policies, again featuring significant mechanization, were adopted for the exploitation of the region's iron ore deposits, the richest in Europe, while, as we have seen, the iron and steel industry now managed to make up for many of the opportunities missed in the past. The Sollac plant in the valley of the

Fensch, between Hayange and Thionville, offering 9000 jobs, was approaching completion in 1952, standing as a symbol of confidence in the region's future. And the traditional industries of Lorraine (pottery, glass, and brewing) were healthy; the region was demographically dynamic and its towns were growing. Indeed, the enthusiasm generated by these aspects of the recovery led to an overlooking of some of the structural problems of the region, such as the weakness of light industry, inadequate housing for workers, and the generally mediocre physical and educational condition of the population. For the moment, however, as yet untroubled by competition from the Saar, and investing massively and confidently in the future of Europe and its heavy industries, Lorraine could be held up for general admiration as an example of successful reconstruction.[13]

### The return of the liberals

The achievements of the Monnet Plan were, then, considerable: the shortages and bottlenecks were being overcome, the structural rigidities eased, and the capital-intensive bases for modernization laid. The Plan's emphasis on consultation and the pragmatism of its leading figures reassured the private sector, while the promise and then the reality of stability and improved living standards secured the co-operation of the workforce in the struggle for higher productivity. The great paradox of this period, however, lies in the fact that the ambitions of the Plan, and the assumptions and calculations on which they rested, could so easily be turned against the *dirigistes* by the advocates of a return to economic liberalism, the logical accompaniment to the new abundance.[14] The political context, both in France, with the establishment of the Third Force, and outside, with the striking of Atlantic and European stances, was increasingly to favour the arguments of the liberals.

The impetus for this shift in attitudes came from the recovery programme drawn up in December 1947 by René Mayer, Minister of Finance in the Schuman cabinet, and adopted in January 1948. The reasoning behind this was unambiguous; France was living beyond her means, consumption was outstripping the capacity to produce or import: to restore an equilibrium and to eradicate the threat of galloping inflation once and for all, purchasing power had to be reduced, and the economy based on the free play of market forces gradually restored at the expense of the directed economy. And against the background of a difficult social and monetary context this severe but still essentially circumstantial criticism of price controls, subsidies, and abusive manipulation of the tax system would finally give rise to a full structural analysis of the French economy, one presented in the first reports of the Commission des comptes de la nation examining in 1953 the experience of the preceding years. Based on assumptions identical to those of the Plan, the future course was set: weight had to be shed from the top-heavy and rigid sectors of the economy, such as small-scale retailing and agriculture; all branches of industry were to compete on the sole criterion of efficiency; the protected and unproductive sectors were to make way for a rejuvenated market economy in which movements of prices, wages, and labour would be unhindered. Savings were to be mobilized productively, and in future the funds for investment would come from the national and international banks rather than from self-financing. Lastly, exchange controls and restrictions were to be eliminated from the Atlantic and European markets. Henceforth, then, the recovery was to come through economic liberalism: competition was to be the price for expansion and well-being: the collectivist aspirations of the Liberation were definitively repudiated: a quick return of confidence among the *patronat* could be looked forward to.[15]

This plan for stability, one whose logic can in fact be seen to mark the end of a period, was soon put into practice by the advocates of a return to a free and competitive economy; first by Mayer himself, then by his successors at the Ministry of Finance, Paul Reynaud and Maurice Petsche. In the spring of 1948 Mayer introduced a compulsory loan in the form of a levy on revenues and profits, reduced demand sharply to control inflation, and blocked all wage increases; while on the monetary front the 5000 franc notes were withdrawn from circulation and free markets restored for gold and foreign exchange. By the summer the gap between agricultural and industrial prices had been narrowed and inflation checked: stability seemed to have returned, and this at the moment when the Marshall Aid began arriving in full. To compensate for the inadequacy of savings and to finance reconstruction (the American funds were, as we have seen, directed in priority to equipment), classic measures were adopted: cuts in public expenditure, a successfully floated government loan in January 1949, advances from the Banque de France, and increased taxes. A fiscal reform introduced in the autumn of 1948 under Queuille caused the revenue from direct taxation to grow from 263 milliard francs in 1948 to 356 milliard in the following year, and to 554 milliard in 1950, an increase of approximately 50 per cent at constant values; and indirect taxation was also increased. The effect on the State's finances was considerable; whereas budget revenues covered 64 per cent of expenditure in 1948 the figure stood at 77 per cent in 1950. Between January 1945 and January 1951 the debt rose only from 1674 to 2845 milliard francs, a fall in real terms of 70 per cent when the full impact of the devaluations and inflation is taken into account: budgetary balance became possible again. The last general increase in wages (15 per cent) negotiated with the State's approval came in September 1948, and the government was able to stifle the wave of strikes of October–November 1948 without having to make further concessions.

Economic recovery and American aid were the bases for the relative calm that reigned from January 1949 to June 1950, a stability popularly attributed to Queuille. Bread rations were abolished in January; those for chocolate, milk, fats, and textiles, in March–April; on 30 November 1949 prices were freed and the administrative structures for rationing and controls dismantled. The international financial instability caused by the fluctuations of sterling resulted in a devaluation of the franc,[16] but exports responded vigorously, their value climbing from 1040 million dollars in 1947 to 1880 million in 1950; the commercial balance was re-established, its deficit shrinking over the same period from 1451 million dollars to 78 million. Marshall Aid and credits from the IMF (a total of almost 2500 million dollars) allowed both the current and overall accounts to be righted: of course, dependence on Washington increased, but this was accepted as the price of stability and domestic recovery. It was into this confidence-inspiring context that the law of 11 Februrary 1950 came, bringing a return to free collective bargaining: from now on wages were to be freely negotiated between unions and employers; the arbitration mechanisms developed since 1936 practically vanished; the role of government was now limited to the fixing of the minimum wage (SMIG), based on a typical family budget and from 1952 indexed to prices on a sliding scale. The strikes in the spring of 1950 did not challenge this return to the laws of supply and demand in the labour market, and part of the lag was made up the following year by negotiation. In fact the period of major industrial and social conflicts was over: the State – which had controlled wages without ever having mastered prices – in effect stood down; with this abdication the balance swung conclusively against the wage-earners; for whereas retail prices had increased eighteenfold from 1938 to 1950, wages over the same period had increased only tenfold.

The outbreak of the Korean War on 25 June 1950 temporarily dampened hopes that a liberal market economy would bring expansion and stability. The war quickly caused levels of international demand to rise and prices of imported raw materials to soar, while diverting resources to armament production. France was not insulated from these developments; her expansion was still too fragile and exports too weak for the impact on prices and the franc not to be quickly felt. Widespread fears of a generalized war stimulated heavy forward purchasing, the balances deteriorated, capital sought refuge investments, and political life was disrupted. Against its will the State was forced to intervene; in 1951 almost a third of its resources were devoted to investment, and the extended Monnet Plan was now able to prove itself as a producer of capital equipment. However, the Treasury had to find the funds for this activity, and the inevitable recourse was to the printing of money. A large unbacked note issue was injected into the economy,[17] with a predictable effect on price levels: at the end of 1951 wholesale prices had risen by 45 per cent and retail prices by 38 per cent; over the same period the SMIG progressed by only 15 per cent and the real purchasing power of wage-earners in fact fell by 20 per cent.

The crisis was exacerbated by the fragility of the economic recovery and social peace obtained within the framework of the Plan. Cost-push inflation now took over from the demand-pull inflation, and although calm had returned to world markets by the autumn of 1951, French prices continued to rise until January 1952. Attempts to streamline budgets were undermined by the growing burden of the war in Indo-China. Furthermore, the taking of effective countermeasures was made difficult by the domestic political context – in the long controversy that now developed over the economic policies to be adopted, none of the parties, all mindful of their potential majorities, were prepared to call for increased taxation, while the Left was also fighting to protect the public sector and the Social Security system from the attacks of the liberals. The impasse was finally broken by the Pinay stabilization; yet again the inflation had exposed the impotence of both liberal and *dirigiste* economic policies, imposing instead a political solution that involved unexpected methods. The inflation penalized France in the European and global contexts at precisely the moment when the ECSC and the OEEC were acquiring real significance. One result was a glaring minus on the balance-sheet of the first experiment with planning; the Plan had quite clearly failed to prevent France acquiring the European record for inflation. And this failure fuelled other doubts over the experiment: what, for example, was the true value of a Plan which seemed to have restored the French economy simply in order then to throw it into the cold bath of competition of a regenerated capitalism? Clearly, the secret of matching economic policies to circumstances remained an elusive one. In the absence of a steady and self-sustaining growth, stimulating the economy merely stoked up inflation, deflation produced recession, while investment could still only be obtained at the expense of consumption.

An economy reeling under successive waves of inflation, unresolved structural problems, and the uncertain mastery of the liberals now in charge, could all provide grounds for disappointment or unease. Yet to these could be opposed one massively optimistic development: the sustained demographic revival of France. Between January 1946 and January 1951, the population grew from 40.1 million to 42.1 million; the French birth-rate, so long a cause for concern, was now buoyant, exceeding 21 per thousand in 1947, stabilizing subsequently at 19 per thousand, the second highest in Europe. Against the often difficult background of reconstruction, with its hardships and extra effort,[18] the 860 000 babies born each year were a very tangible proof of confidence in the future.

# Conclusion to parts I and II

In March 1951, an engineer, father of six, wrote longingly: 'Ah! Si je pouvais avoir ma 2 CV.' His letter caught the attention of the Citroën sales department and provided the basis for a publicity campaign.[1] It would not be out of place at the head of the balance-sheet of these years of reconstruction. The long months of shortages were over and a new ease was in the air, a feeling that mass consumption was just around the corner. Since 1948, though still dazed by a decade of crisis, France could begin, not without pride, to count her locomotives and babies, and appetites for the fruits of sustained economic growth were already being whetted. After the crisis, the war, and the deprivations, a repaired economy was at last starting to offer fresh hopes and open new horizons. The virtues of the free market were now sung on all sides; Antoine Pinay incarnated the new climate of confidence for savings; the conventional wisdom of the lesser evil had triumphed. Is this to say, then, that the regenerative energies of 1944 were illusory or that they had been led astray?

It is undeniable that the politicians had recognized the chronic weaknesses of the French economy. The analysis of this, developing since the 1930s, had imposed itself after the war: 'La modernization ou la mort', cried René Pleven. Undeniable also is that fresh men and groups had been left a free hand to make good use of the new resources available to the State since 1944 in order to prod a hitherto paralysed free market capitalism back into life and to entice the producers out of their *malthusianisme* with handsome subsidies. Jean Monnet had been listened to by both de Gaulle and Schuman, and, for a time at least, by Wendel. The sheer urgency of the post-war period's problems had in fact massively validated the familiar criticisms of the shortcomings. The Plan had co-ordinated the task of surmounting the shortages as quickly as possible, at the same time as realizing its main ambition: the modernization of the part of the productive sector whose role was to be greatest in the future. To this end, moreover, the class struggle had been left on one side, at least until 1947: technocrats of the public sector, open-minded industrialists, responsible trade unionists, and the ruling parties of the Left, all consistently backed by the efforts of the workforce, had, together, won the battles for production and modernization.

Yet to listen to René Mayer, Maurice Petsche, or the steel masters a little later, and to consider the mechanisms of the ECSC or the character of France's external exchanges within the Atlantic bloc or the French Union, the return in force of capitalism is patent. And this is in fact the conclusion now of many involved closely at the time: 'récupération' affirms François Bloch-Lainé; 'restauration' argues Claude Bourdet.[2] Had the Resistance and the modernization been simply to allow the *patronat* to reap the full benefits of the dynamic growth of the 1950s? Had the *dirigisme* of the Liberation period served merely to ease the transition to a free enterprise economy rejuvenated by its contact with the United States?[3] In the construction of housing, in the buying up of titles issued from the flimsy Resistance press, in the speculation on the Vietnamese currency, and in the scandals, powerful interests and small swindlers alike were not slow to get to work. Had it really been necessary at the same time to sacrifice mass consumption in order to rebuild a strong productive machine, one taken in hand by the nationalized sector but under whose shelter private firms had been able to restore profit margins which allowed them to recover their lucrative investments? As Georges Boris observed bitterly: 'Instead of the demolition of capitalism and the work of socialist construction which were meant to have begun, it seems that we have only been able to erect a wall of defence, a rampart against the onslaught of a super monopoly capitalism that has risen rapidly from the ruins of traditional capitalism.'[4] Feeble reformist, is the riposte of those who now argue that in 1945 'the State had safeguarded the future chances for a breakthrough by monopolistic finance capital.'[5] Without attempting to judge between these interpretations, one can nonetheless observe that the Liberation did not destroy the 'trusts' it had fulminated against, and that the new public sector appears to have played a decisive role afterwards in safeguarding and restructuring capitalism. However, without reliable studies on the transfers effected by the public sector to the private sector, or on the evolution of investment and profit branch by branch, not only are firm conclusions impossible but little can be understood of the nature of wage conflicts or of the interaction of the various social groups.[6]

The detailed evolution of incomes is also little known. It is certain, however, that between 1944 and 1952 producers and sellers were consistently advantaged and held up well to the inflation. They actually outnumbered wage-earners at this time – 13 million compared with 8 million – and satisfaction of their appetite for security and stability was why the political balance settled so solidly at the Centre. Farmers in prosperous regions, retailers – witness the proliferation of small shops after the Liberation – the liberal professions, and manufacturers, had all been able to come to terms relatively easily with the black market, just as they were to profit fully from the return to free prices after 1949, while using inflation to reduce their debts. The authorities were at pains not to give these groups any cause for discontent, even if, in the background, the trend to concentration that accompanied modernization was already threatening small business men. Indeed, with the promise of a stable currency and the repudiation of all fiscal policy which might have damaged their interests, everything was in fact done to reassure these groups. And in this respect the governments of the Liberation period differed little from their successors.

For their part, the wage-earners were just as consistently disadvantaged. True, they had obtained serious new guarantees at the Liberation: substantial wage increases, indexed wage scales, trade unions with important new powers and, above all, a Social Security system that was both democratically run and largely paid for by the employers. Against these advances, however, stands the fact that they were heavily penalized by the long control of wages at the time when inflation was causing retail prices to soar: the wage-earners were left far behind in this spiral. The political content of the strikes of 1947 and 1948 is of course undeniable, but there were clearly solid economic reasons for the difficult social climate that reigned until 1949. Indeed, it was as if the most determined forces of the Resistance lost on every front. The patriotic efforts of the workforce were resolutely harnessed in the productive struggle vital for the community as a whole, yet from which they reaped only meagre advantages – this, moreover, as the exploitative private sector was reviving. Similarly, an enthusiasm to promote social policy in fact hastened the integration of the trade unions and workers into class co-operation, even collaboration, through the comités d'enterprise, the commissions of the Plan, and the social transfers. As for the policy of the Communists, it had contributed to begin with to the restoration of a State in which the world of labour was little represented, and then, after 1947, to the isolation of an important section of the working class from national life.

Is it, then, to the familiar lament for the failure of the Resistance that one must return? The literature of recrimination and apology is vast – the Resistance has been 'painstakingly divorced from the history of its own epoch'.[7] Weakness, suicide from within, attack from without? The variations on the basic theme are endless, with responsibility attributed variously to de Gaulle, to the Communists, to the United States, or to the Soviet Union, the opportunity to denounce the power of capital, the political parties who betrayed the idealism of the Resistance, or the naïvety of the heroes themselves. What such arguments have in common, wherever they finally place the blame, lies in casting the Resistance in a role it had never been capable of filling. Their appeal, of course, is understandable: many résistants were slow to abandon their hopes, and the myth of the Resistance, one that the post-war cinema, for example, did much to forge, held an irresistible attraction for the population at large. Yet with authentic *résistants* continuing to believe that they had been betrayed,[8] and with so expansive an alibi of civic heroism accessible to a population that had, in the vast majority, simply acquiesced in Vichy and the Occupation, it is clear that the Resistance had become a currency in too free a circulation for its value not to fall sharply.

Of course, it can be argued that the CNR programme had not been fully implemented, or that the cultural ferment left traces, or that without de Gaulle or Stalin the seeds would have borne richer fruit. Our view would be that it is time to finish with such pious wishful thinking. How, after all, is it possible to ignore the fact that the *résistants* were now prominent in the parties, movements, and *rassemblements*? And that they were reconstructing political life in its old framework? Or not to see that the *résistants*, joined for the occasion by figures with less glorious pasts, were now leading this 'jeu des partis' from which the Fourth Republic was ultimately to perish? Or, of course, that they were at the vanguard of the work of modernization? More generally, is it reasonable to suppose that membership of the Resistance bestowed a durable guarantee of infallible political lucidity and progressivism? With hindsight, the example already being offered by certain Socialist and MRP politicians over Indo-China and Madagascar provides some food for thought as regards this last point. Those involved in the Resistance had believed that their commitment had an ideological force of its own which transcended the struggle. But once the unanimity of summer 1944 had evaporated they had to face the fact that only their personal heroism remained; that, more than anything else, France longed for calm; and that the Third Force drew its strength precisely from its refusal of all ideological combat. In this respect the *après-guerre* period gave a painful demonstration of something that is abundantly clear to the historian today, namely that the Resistance was, above all, a Jacobin reflex, one of patriotic unity.[9] Must one conclude that the Resistance had been nothing more than this? After all, its few thousand active members could never have accomplished a profound regeneration of France on their own. Having said this, however, to recognize the just proportions of the Resistance is in no way to diminish its greatness.

Unless, if failure there was, it is not to the overwhelming majority of Frenchmen that it must be attributed. For, rather than a hypothetical 'defeat' of the Resistance, what is really striking is the obstinacy – one the experience of the *épuration* made clear – with which France refused to look herself squarely in the face; as if the three shocks of 1936, 1938, and 1940 had broken some inner mainspring of French society, one whose tension had previously been maintained by the weight of collective ambitions. Those who lament this decline of great causes would do well to remember the nature and scale of the urgencies and constraints, so serious and so persistent, and whose presence has been felt throughout the account of these years. France was the only nation to receive the full impact of all the major shocks of the post-war period: devastation, monetary crisis, the aftermath of a civil war, social problems and, above all, the Cold War and decolonization. At each stage, determination and effort had transformed these constraints into imperatives for action: the achievements were considerable. It was thus, in small steps, almost haphazardly, that were set up an original planning experiment, an embryonic Welfare State, a political framework which, in metropolitan France at least, respected democracy, and a social life that offered a little more to the workers. Piecemeal, for better or for worse, some individuals had been able to influence the course of events in this period: Thorez, Auriol, Schuman, Monnet, Pleven, and others whose action is less familiar. Lastly, of course, de Gaulle, unperturbed by the doubts and conflicts of the internal Resistance, the *rassembleur*, determined in his quest for national grandeur. De Gaulle was responsible for the restoration of the State on its former lines, but also for launching modernization; it was de Gaulle who rebuked the great powers, but who allowed the irreversible to develop in Indo-China; it was de Gaulle, finally, who failed once he was no longer the war leader, but who conserved intact a unique capacity for direct dialogue with the nation in times of crisis.

The proudly victorious nation of 1945 was, however, no longer capable of assuming a role henceforth dictated beyond the frontiers of *l'Hexagone*: coming to terms with this uncomfortable truth was to prove difficult and slow. Marshall, Zdanov, and Ho Chi Minh had all, in their different ways, pushed back the authority of French governments, who could then only accept the inevitable. By their inability to grasp the extent and significance of the changes in the overseas and global contexts, the political leaders were like the people which, having refused since 1945 to judge itself, was already casting envious eyes forward to the fruits of expansion. The page is turned: what point is there in dwelling on the past? Before moving on from the *après-guerre*, however, one last doubt remains: is it possible that from 1944 to 1952 France merely persisted in the same humiliating stagnation that had moved Bernanos to anger since Munich? As he claimed at Christmas 1946: 'The France of the Liberation has failed like its predecessor. Perhaps this is because they are one and the same'.[10]

# PART III

# The Republic in decline, 1952–58

# 12

# Governing without choosing

Between the investiture by surprise of Antoine Pinay in March 1952, and that by necessity of Pierre Mendès France in June 1954, the Right, back in power, was confident that it governed a bourgeois France. Moderates and Independents, Radicals and the MRP, joined now by the Gaullists – who, de Gaulle cruelly underlined, 'vont à la soupe' – completed the sweeping away of the Third Force, an outcome predictable from the result of the 1951 elections and confirmed by the SFIO going over to the opposition in January 1952. The Right's brand of liberalism was well suited to the buoyant economic situation, able to satisfy both the needs of modernity and the interests of conservatism. Economic growth was welcome, savings were defended, pressure groups operated with a cynical openness, and 'la France profonde' began to let out its belt after the hardships of the *après-guerre* years. Indifferent to the conflict of ideologies and the party squabbles, though acutely sensitive to the personalization of power,[1] the population was concerned chiefly with the protection of its living standards, seduced by the emerging Welfare State and the fruits of expansion. But while the population was more an observer than a participant, it nonetheless passed a severe judgement on the *immobilistes* who treated its quiescence as a guarantee of their own freedom of action. The governed democracy was in fact in a crisis of inactivity, with the energies of the representative régime increasingly absorbed by its own procedural mechanisms.

This provincial Right, so concerned with French interests, fell victim to the changes in the global power context. From 1953, the death of Stalin and the reaching of a nuclear balance brought an easing of international tension and opened the way for a policy of 'peaceful co-existence' between East and West. At the same time, decolonization accelerated. The policies of the Third Force and the assumptions on which they were based crumbled, without alternatives being found. With the end of the Cold War, Pleven's European Army became less indispensable; and a fear of Communism was no longer enough to explain the progress of nationalism in North Africa, nor did it avoid a rout in Indo-China. From the shelving of the EDC to the disaster at Dien Bien Phu, impotence and a refusal to choose were draped with chauvinistic cant.

## Monsieur Pinay, 'Français moyen'

It was to general surprise that the investiture was voted to Antoine Pinay on 6 March 1952. Pinay had first come to the attention of Vincent Auriol as a prudent Minister of Public Works; although Auriol had initially counted on Pinay's failure as a way of preparing for a new Centre–Left coalition under Queuille, the successful halt to inflation that defused the Communist agitation and restored popularity to the régime soon brought Pinay the full confidence and co-operation of the President.[2] The Radicals and UDSR had accepted to vote for Pinay, certain that their candidate would soon replace him. The leaders of the MRP, ignoring the doubts of the grassroots militants, took the risk of becoming the left flank of Pinay's Centre–Right coalition: the presence of Robert Schuman at the Quai d'Orsay, Pierre Pflimlin at Overseas Affairs and Jean Letourneau at Associated States guaranteed the continuity of the MRP's policies on Europe and the colonies. The Communists, Socialists, and most of the Gaullists were hostile. The support for Pinay had come from the Right, the vital extra votes needed for the investiture provided by the twenty-seven right-wingers who defected from the RPF under the leadership of Frédéric-Dupont. Pinay, a leader of the Alliance démocratique and a friend of Flandin, had the outlook of a liberal *orléaniste*; he was hostile to the *dirigistes* and scathing about the 'sottises' of the Liberation and the technocrats of the new public sector; a leather manufacturer from Saint-Chamond was soon to establish a reputation as a new Poincaré. With the Communists and Gaullists neutralized the Third Force appeared to have triumphed. In reality, however, denied the support of the SFIO and increasingly at the mercy of a handful of office-seeking Centrists, the Third Force had collapsed, leaving the way clear for the Right, now drawing support from as far to the left of the political spectrum as the MRP and Radicals, and looking likely to engulf the RPF.

The great strength of Pinay, who took for himself the unpopular Finance portfolio, lay in offering commonsense policies and presenting his in fact highly empirical liberalism as a defence of the consumer. To tackle inflation and halt the spiral of wages and prices Pinay adopted psychological weapons; to stabilize the franc he sought to reassure holders of capital; while to balance the budget and avoid bankruptcy he preferred cutting expenditure to raising new taxes. There was certainly nothing startingly new about these policies – the approach was that of any level-headed business man. Yet Pinay was far from being an economic or financial naïf; the high-powered brains trust assembled around him since 1948 was to keep the new premier well-informed and to lend authority to his appeals to public opinion.[3] Economic and financial orthodoxy in the person of Jacques Rueff, former adviser to Poincaré, praised the Pinay experiment, and the CNPF was enthusiastic. The experienced and reassuring figure of Pinay seemed to symbolize the successful marriage of the classic liberalism of before the war to the dynamic mechanisms of neo-capitalism. Speaking in his region, at Saint-Etienne on 21 September 1952, Pinay summed up his personal approach thus: 'Order in finance is accompanied by order in the exchange markets, monetary order by order in the economy, and order in the State itself by order in the behaviour of its members.'[4]

Pinay's conservative economic policy, with its accent on saving and 'good housekeeping' in economic affairs, and its reduction of credit and investment, could never have succeeded in the overheated economic conditions and ideological turmoil of the preceding period. And its success now was in fact purely circumstantial, the result of improvements in the international economy; after two years of expansion related to the Korean War boom of 1950–1, output and trade were slowing down, raw material prices sinking, and industrial investment contracting. The great chance for Pinay was to have come to power at the moment when the effects of this cooling down in the international economy were beginning to be felt in France. French prices now followed the general downward trend – on a base of 100 for 1949, wholesale prices levelled out at 144 in the second half of 1952, falling back to 143 the following year and to 135 in 1954–5; the impact on retail prices was less marked but reflected the same trend, 145 in 1952, 143 in 1953–4, and 145 in 1955. Not until 1957 did the chronic price inflation, so characteristic of the post-war period, reappear. Not surprisingly, the credit for this very welcome economic and political success offset a considerably less impressive record in other fields; the accumulated political, diplomatic, and colonial blunders of the period appeared to be of distinctly secondary importance when compared with the stabilization of prices under Pinay. And although damaging to sellers in general and to shopkeepers in particular, stable prices satisfied the needs of the growing numbers of wage-earners, providing a solid basis for the higher living standards that the expansion was to bring. The opinion polls conducted by the IFOP leave no doubt that stability of prices was widely perceived to be the major issue of the day – by 57 per cent of those questioned in September 1951, 46 per cent in April 1956, and 58 per cent in January 1958 – a preoccupation which must be interpreted as a sign of rising popular expectations, one which completely overshadowed the questions of world peace, the European Defence Community, or Algeria.[5]

In effect, then, the economic and financial measures of the Pinay experiment simply took advantage of the changes in the broader international economic context, while encouraging the popular belief that

France could overcome the difficulties by her own efforts. An overall public spending budget of 3500 milliard francs was reduced by 110 milliard, advances from the Banque de France were refused, and 100 milliard francs worth of public investment was blocked until it could be paid for from receipts. Thus, while the deficit was indeed slightly reduced and this without recourse to new taxes, total expenditure by the State was now considerably higher than in 1951; public administration remained a big spender, playing, willingly or not, a counter-cyclical role in the economy.[6] The drying up of funds within companies and the lower levels of investment that reduced the overall demand for credit were in fact what brought the inflation down: in spite of Pinay's assertions to the contrary, financial stability was a consequence of the slow-down in the economy, not its cause.[7] Moreover, the efforts to counter inflation were reinforced by the adoption of a sliding scale for wages indexed to prices – introduced by a longstanding opponent of the principle – which was well received by the unions and guaranteed a large degree of social and industrial peace. Conversely, the amnesty on tax fraud, though popular with industrialists and the wealthy, did little for revenues and served to channel the energies of the tax inspectors towards easier targets, notably the already struggling small shopkeeprs: the seeds of Poujadism were being sown by this inopportune policy.

The centrepiece of this collection of empirical and not totally coherent measures was the loan of May 1952 on which Pinay hung his name and based his popularity. With highly attractive terms – including a return of 3.5 per cent, capital indexed to the price of gold,[8] exemption from taxation and death duties – the loan proved to be the most solid launched by the French State in the twentieth century. Although its success, with 428 milliard subscribed between 26 May and 17 July, disappointed initial hopes – bringing in only 34 of the 2000 tonnes of gold estimated to be in the hands of individuals, but consolidating the titles of many previous loans – the loan's gradual absorption up to 1973 earned it an unparalleled reputation. Small savers and wealthy investors alike were to congratulate themselves for many years to come on their great chance of 1952, and incalculable death duties were avoided thanks to the quickly acquired habit of 'mettre en Pinay avant de mettre en bière'. But such long-term fame was no answer to immediate problems; the Pinay government was forced to borrow from Swiss banks, introduce a price freeze in the autumn, and even begin to encroach upon the Welfare State. And it was over this last, with a proposal to transfer 0.75 per cent of family allowance funds, that the MRP – so sensitive over the question of social security – brought Pinay down on 22 December. In fact this was merely a pretext, for the MRP was seeking to protect Schuman from criticism for his ineffective handling of foreign policy: but the issue chosen was nevertheless significant, underlining the contradictions of this transitional period in which the *dirigiste* instincts of the recent past co-existed uneasily with those of the unexpectedly revived liberalism.

To its credit the Pinay experiment had successfully taken advantage of the circumstances favouring stability to curb domestic consumption, to rekindle enthusiasm for savings, balancing supply and demand while they were slack, in preparation for the great expansion of the years ahead. Pinay had made his appeal to the broadest possible consensus, bypassing Parliament and the parties to go directly to the nation and its millions of consumers. Some of the methods used were traditional; committees of notables in the *départements* gave their solemn blessing to the loan; Pinay received delegations and corporative representatives, encouraging them in their efforts, reminding them of their civic responsibilities over prices. More original and more important was the harnessing of the modern means of persuasion; radio and television, the latter still in its infancy, were used to reach the public directly; modern marketing techniques were employed, such as in the 'défense du franc' operation in which the big stores promoted low-priced articles with tricoloured publicity. As for the deputies, they had to face the vote of confidence on Fridays, before facing their constituents at the weekend when they were invariably reminded of popular esteem for Pinay as the defender of purchasing power and savings. Pinay attained a degree of personal popularity rare for a premier of the Fourth Republic – in April, at the Foire de Lyon, the crowd greeted him with enthusiastic cries of 'Tenez bon, monsieur Pinay' – and one which was to last into the Fifth Republic. For the first time, the fall of a premier was deplored by a majority of the population.[9]

Doubtless the balance-sheet of the Pinay experiment is not as strongly positive as collective memory would have it.[10] Some investments were lost definitively, unproductive hoarding was encouraged, there were important deficits on the commercial balances, and the budget remained deliberately unbalanced – for in practice Pinay was as close to Keynes as he was to Poincaré. Finally, the slow-down in the economy pushed unemployment up to 48 000 in December 1952, compared with 31 000 the previous year. But the halt to inflation and the temporary return of confidence in the régime were inestimable assets, a durable protection from criticism over other, less positive aspects of domestic policy. This was clear from the test of strength engaged with the Communists in May 1952. Two Radical ministers, Brune at the Interior, and the party's powerful General Secretary, Martinaud-Déplat at Justice, were intent on putting a stop to Communist subversion, strongly backed in their efforts by the 'Paix et liberté' movement, the secret police networks of Dides and the prefect of police, Jean Baylot.[11] The PCF at this time, under the leadership of Duclos while Thorez convalesced in Moscow, was energetically implementing Stalin's orders on the anticolonial struggle and resistance to American imperialism. Working through the CGT and the Mouvement de la Paix, the Communists were, for example, disrupting supplies to Indo-China from the French ports. The arrival in Paris of General Ridgway – newly appointed Commander of the Allied Forces in Europe, and accused of using biological warfare in Korea – was the occasion for a large demonstration on 28 May organized by the Party. The demonstration was marked by violent incidents, in the course of which an Algerian was killed, and on the same evening Jacques Duclos was arrested. Two pigeons were found in his car, and Brune immediately claimed that they were carrier-pigeons, part of a Communist plot to subvert the State.[12] The accusation made the authorities look ridiculous, but the entire episode came as a severe shock to the Communist Party; several of its leaders were arrested,[13] and the CGT proved unable to organize action for their release. The methods and goals of Pinay had been misunderstood; the Communists now faced a witch-hunt in the administration and the Party's rank and file was in disarray. It was only through the application of methods more familiar in Eastern Europe, with the exclusion in the autumn of both André Marty and Charles Tillon from the leadership,[14] that the PCF recovered its internal discipline and direction. There could be no doubt now that the Resistance period was closed. Never had the Communists been so isolated in public opinion, or so obviously paralysed by their loyalty to Stalin's strategy. Anticommunism had an easy target, and under the Right this became an arm of government.

There was no real challenge from the other potential source of opposition, the by now disintegrating RPF. The right-wing dissidents had aired their grievances to a contemptuous de Gaulle in June, and the gradual reconciliation of the parliamentary Gaullists to the 'system' of the political parties was in fact well under way. The Rassemblement's leadership vacillated, its press collapsed, and enthusiasm and membership ebbed away. Clearly then, the domestic political context, though disturbed, posed no serious threat to the Right in power: it was over the intractable EDC question and the French Union that Pinay lost his majority, much, as we have seen, to public disapproval. Pinay's successors, a Radical, René Mayer (January–May 1953), and a PRL, Joseph Laniel (June 1953–June 1954), the former a Paris businessman, the latter an industrialist from Normandy, never attained Pinay's popularity, though like him both fell over external issues. Both, however, learnt from Pinay the value of wooing public opinion with moderate policies and an assiduous attention to the cult of higher living standards. For it was this question which remained at the forefront of popular preoccupations until 1954. Were the French people in fact prepared to reopen old wounds and make painful choices? Or could a Cassandra-like figure have persuaded them to face up to the inevitable? The questions are perhaps futile; for in 1952, when opinion did express itself clearly, it opted simply for the safeguard and improvement of its well-being.

## Shelving the EDC

This overriding domestic priority makes it hard to assess the real impact on public opinion of the quarrel over the European Defence Community, a quarrel which touched many raw nerves and provided a brutal demonstration of the weaknesses of the system of government. Did this skeleton in the cupboard provide the basis for a new Dreyfus affair, as was claimed at the time?[15] Or was it not just a partisan agitation, a quarrel confined to an élite? Only archival-based research into the deeper strata of public opinion would enable a choice to be made between the various conflicting interpretations of the reactions to the French initiative over European defence fathered by Robert Schuman and René Pleven.

The agreements signed at Bonn and Paris (26–27 May 1952) recognized the international sovereignty of West Germany and brought the EDC into existence. In signing for France the Pinay government fulfilled the mission the Assembly had originally given to Edgar Faure in February by the slender majority of 327 votes to 287. But after the signing of the treaty there remained the problem of ratification, and a fresh parliamentary debate was necessary before France could be irrevocably committed to the EDC. However, until the summer of 1954 a curious inactivity on the diplomatic front blocked all solution, while the previous favourable majority disintegrated and a vast quarrel came to dominate opinion. Thus on the one hand there were niggardly technical advances – to the extent that the other partners, all of whom with the exception of Italy had ratified the treaty within the time limits, began to have serious doubts over French willingness to find a reasonable solution – while on the other raged a sensationalized and moralistic controversy; the EDC question became more deeply than ever enmeshed in the conflicts and stalemates of French domestic politics. It was, for example, commonplace to claim that all the dramatic problems of the post-war period and the Cold War were still explosively combined in this one issue – the reunification and rearmament of Germany, the future of the European projects launched by the ECSC, the defence of Western Europe and the free world from a foreseeable Soviet attack: in short, all the problems the EDC had been set up to deal with (see Chapter 9). In reality, however, the national and international context had changed, and the contending parties were gradually forced to modify their positions and adopt new arguments. The end of the conflict in Korea, the easing of international tension, the death of Stalin, and the new Soviet leadership's calls for negotiation and disarmament – all made a Soviet attack look less likely. Why then, argued its opponents, hurry to ratify a treaty of increasingly doubtful relevance? And particularly given that, with the threat from the Red Army reduced, the EDC issue inevitably tended to focus attention on the two points where French weakness had been clear since 1944: American hegemony and the revival of Germany.

The labyrinthine complexity of the dealings surrounding the EDC treaty should not obscure the fact that in diplomatic and parliamentary terms they simply maintained a virtual standstill. They can be summarized in three stages:

1. From February to December 1952, under Pinay and then Schuman, the treaty was not put before the French Parliament. Officially, this was because the treaty was incomplete and failed to provide all the necessary guarantees; the parliamentary debate in February had brought to the surface belated French anxieties over the durability of the American military commitment in Europe, as well as over the British attitude and the relative strength of the French contingents. In addition, it was common knowledge that the combined NATO headquarters set up by Eisenhower planned to deploy twelve German divisions in the European force – to get her project accepted, France had already conceded over most of the details of its military organization. In order to gain time, France now called for still more detailed clarifications and extra clauses, hoping – despite the obvious incompatability of the two objectives – to broaden the solidarities between the Allies without at the same time increasing the supranational character of the military instrument to be created. These, then, were the official reasons for the delay. Unofficially, however, the stalling was a result of the government's dependence of the votes of the defecting RPF deputies who, though they had voted it into office, remained loyal to de Gaulle in their hostility to the EDC. The increasingly vociferous opposition, in private and in public, of de Gaulle and Auriol, plus the split that occurred among the Radicals – so important for the forming of majorities – once Herriot and Daladier had united in a common opposition to the EDC, were sufficient to immobilize the entire issue.

2. From January to November 1953, the inactivity stemmed from the changes in the structure of the majority in the Assembly, changes confirmed by the entry of RPF ministers in the Laniel government. The control exercised by the deputies over governments was now tighter than ever. Mayer had to make a public undertaking not to pose the question of confidence over the taboo subject of the EDC, and to concentrate even more intensely than had Pinay on the details of the agreements. This he did; with the lukewarm support of Bidault, now back at the Quai d'Orsay, where he showed himself to be less of an enthusiast for the EDC than Schuman had been. Against a background of mounting impatience in London and Washington, the question of the margin of independence to be enjoyed by France

within the French Union was revived, as was the old problem of the Saar. By now the text of the treaty was so complex (132 articles) and so bloated with annexes that only a handful of specialists was in fact capable of meaningful negotiation. Yet French and international opinion continued to oscillate between hilarity and indignation over such issues as the colour of the soldiers' headgear or the hunting and fishing rights of the combined garrisons! Nor did Mayer reap the fruits of his compliance with the wishes of the Assembly: he was brought down by the Gaullists in May 1953, punished in fact for having dared to believe a solution to be within his grasp.[16] Meanwhile, the parliamentary committees of National Defence and Foreign Affairs had already been careful to appoint reporters known to be hostile to the EDC project, General Kœnig, and Jules Moch.

Under Laniel, who succeeded Mayer in June and whose ministry was a volatile mixture of supporters and opponents of the treaty – the MRP members held in check by the Gaullists, while the Independents, UDSR, and Radicals squabbled among themselves – everything concerning the EDC was quietly forgotten until the parliamentary debate of 17–27 November. Under increasing pressure from the United States (Foster Dulles was to speak in December of drastic revision of alliances if the French procrastination continued) and in order to prepare for the meeting of the Three in Bermuda that was to precede a meeting of the four Foreign Ministers planned for Berlin, serious discussion of the EDC could be postponed no longer. At the end of a protracted round of oratorical sparring, from which the only thing to emerge was a long plea in favour that an exhausted Bidault could not deliver and which had to be read by Maurice Schumann to the obviously uninterested Assembly, Laniel received simply the vaguest possible mandate to continue to work towards European unity. Clearly, none of the entrenched positions had shifted; the humiliating rebukes and threats this outcome earned for France from Eisenhower and Churchill at the Bermuda Conference served merely to strengthen the anti-American stance of the opponents of the EDC.

3. From November 1953 to April 1954, proposals to settle the question of the Saar by means of a referendum and the clarification of the conditions for British participation in the defence of Europe were increasingly overshadowed by the situation in Indo-China. Undeterred, Bidault put forward two further conditions for the treaty's ratification: a clarification of the aims of the new Soviet leadership and a peace settlement in Indo-China. The wretched EDC project now weighed more heavily than ever on French domestic politics: the hostility of the Gaullists weakened the position of many 'Europeans' on the Right, and helped forge a common front with the Socialists and Communists, pushing the MRP towards the opposition – the majority which would bring Mendès France to power was already taking shape. In the absence of an acceptable alternative the race

was now on to kill off the EDC once and for all. Thus at the same time that Bidault was attempting to convince the Berlin Conference that ratification was imminent, Moch and Kœnig condemned the treaty as being 'completely ineffective', and the Gaullist ministers, led by General Corni-glion-Molinier, stepped up their pressure in the cabinet. On 31 March, Marshal Juin threw his weight into the struggle with a strong denunciation of the EDC project, something for which he was subsequently repri-manded. But the damage was done, and for the demonstrators who jostled Laniel and Pleven at the Arc de Triomphe on 4 April 1954 Juin's name was added to the combatants in Indo-China. However, these were the final skirmishes in the struggle, for all attention was now focused on Indo-China and the Geneva Conference.

Why should there have been so many delays? The simple fact is that whereas the majorities favourable to the EDC – and who made govern-ments – were increasingly fragile, their opponents – who brought down governments – remained as determined and active as ever. Thus a govern-ment's only hope of survival lay in shelving the EDC treaty. Moreover, as we have seen, the changed international context meant that the EDC no longer stood as a coherent reponse to Moscow but simply as a shakey framework of guarantees and precautions, and this at a time when the easing of international tension and the growing exchanges between the European 'miracle' economies were making such a framework less and less necessary. Time, clearly, was against the defenders of the treaty, weakened and demoralized, and no longer able to invoke the urgency of a reply to the Soviet threat. Among them only the MRP held up well, easily able to weather the attacks of its dissidents such as Léo Hamon, Charles d'Aragon, and Robert Buron, and too wholeheartedly committed to the cause not to easily influence the arguments of the entire pro-EDC camp. The reduced risk of war, they claimed, was not a sufficient reason to refuse German rearmament; for the United States would not maintain its forces in Europe indefinitely; and only a Franco-German reconciliation embodied in the EDC would cement the European political structure. They of course welcomed the efforts of Spaak and De Gasperi to place the European army inside a strong European political structure by means of article 38 of the treaty, which allowed for an increase in the supranational powers of the European Assembly. Yet such thinking was ahead of its time – with the exception of a small number of convinced Europeans, such as those in France grouped around Jean Monnet, neither French public opinion nor the political parties were ready for the 'United States of the Six'. And thus the principal argument available to the treaty's defenders, that of 'the EDC or the Wehrmacht', slowly became one of a lesser evil.[17] If Europe was impossible, it was argued, at least adopt the EDC to guarantee the Atlantic alliance: after all, did not victory in Indo-China depend on American aid?

This argument, whose good sense was underlined by Raymond Aron in *Le Figaro* and Jules Romains in *L'Aurore*, appealed to a broad spectrum of the Right favourable to the Atlantic and European alignments, from Reynaud to Laniel, as well as to a large section of the Radicals, led by Queuille, Martinaud-Déplat, Gaillard, Mayer, and Bourgès-Maunoury. At the same time, however, this argument could easily be turned against those who invoked it: with too much anticommunism, too strong a portrayal of the anti-EDC camp as the allies of the Kremlin, and an exaggerated confidence in the democratic virtues of Germany, the opposition would not find it hard to present the members of the pro-EDC camp as the new *'munichois'* or even as the new *'collaborateurs'* ready to deny France all independence of action.

The opponents of the EDC also had to modify their arguments. Until the death of Stalin and the troubles in East Berlin, and carried along by a hatred of Bolshevism and Soviet expansionism, the EDC enjoyed a considerable favour in opinion. Its only adversaries of note were the Gaullists and the Communists, the former from attachment to an ideal of European national identities strong enough to counter American and British hegemony, the latter from obedience to Moscow. But with the approach of peaceful co-existence and the growing American impatience to settle the affair, this slender consensus needed to develop new themes if it were to grow into a broad coalition capable of defeating the EDC. The themes found were those of the defence of national independence *vis-à-vis* a revengeful Germany and a rejection of American imperialism. Once again the PCF and the Gaullists were at the heart of this new *'résistance'* to all the potential *'vichystes'*. Drawing up the catalogue of Washington's perfidy and defending the memory of the victims of Nazism were familiar tasks for the Communists; the European Army, claimed the PCF, would simply be a tool of the Pentagon and a haven for unreconstructed SS men. The Communists threw all their forces into the struggle against the EDC, conscious, perhaps, that this return to the sources of French national honour would help to rid them of the 'foreign party' label and facilitate their reinsertion in political life. De Gaulle for his part, vigorously backed by Jacques Soustelle and Michel Debré, developed the themes he was to make his own under the Fifth Republic, denouncing the pro-Europeans as unpatriotic and blinded by their own idealism, railing against French submission in the Atlantic camp, where, moreover, only NATO and not the feeble EDC assured the effectiveness sought by the United States. For de Gaulle, the struggle against the EDC was of course a magnificent opportunity, one likely to make Gaullism a genuinely popular political force at the very moment when the RPF was disintegrating.

This energetic hostile reaction from the opposition of the time of the Third Force served to galvanize many of those hitherto indifferent or apathetic over the EDC. Thus the former advocates of neutralism began to campaign, and *Le Monde* now became the most influential organ of opposition to the EDC.[18] The 'progressisme' of the Liberation, recovered from the shock of the Cold War period, found an effective vehicle in the *Combat* of Claude Bourdet, as well as in *France-Observateur* and *Libération*. Left-wing Catholic opinion was mobilized by *Témoignage chrétien*; strict secular opinion by the Ligue des droits de l'homme under Emile Kahn. The cause built up a following among students, trade unionists, and militants: indeed, it was in the struggle against the EDC as much as in that of anticolonialism that the 'nouvelle gauche' acquired identity and coherence. A major split appeared in the SFIO, where the party's strongly pro-European majority favourable to the EDC, led by Mollet, Jacquet, Pineau, and Defferre, was confronted with a determined left-wing minority, grouped around Daniel Mayer, Moch, Savary, Lejeune, Lacoste, Pivert, and Verdier – all key figures from the SFIO in the underground. The issue provoked fierce debates in congresses and meetings, with the pro-EDC majority obtaining only a limited success by wielding the old spectre of Soviet expansionism. The conflict was intense, and although Mollet retained control of the party machine he was unable to prevent a split in the parliamentary group and serious unrest among the SFIO rank-and-file militants.[19]

The quarrel over the EDC, for so long confined to political and diplomatic circles, gradually spread to broader sections of the public. As it did so it became entangled with other issues and conflicts; with, for example, the clerical–anticlerical argument when the EDC was presented as an instrument of the Europe of the Christian Democrats; or with economic nationalism, when interest groups tried to arouse public opinion over the ruin of the French iron and steel producers by the ECSC and the threat to the French arms industry from the German economic 'miracle'. The EDC controversy divided the political forces still further, readjusting the balance between them. It disturbed the upper levels of the French administration, whose members were alarmed or angered by the extent of ministerial vacillation and where the notion of unquestioning obedience was clearly compromised by a quarrel which stirred the consciences of many top officials who had been in the Resistance. Even the French army was contaminated.[20] True, the forces in Indo-China and North Africa maintained their silence, but in the garrisons in France and Germany there was a mounting and increasingly vocal opposition to the EDC, one nurtured on ideas of national honour, on anxieties over careers, and on hatred for the traditional enemy. Efforts by Generals Ely, Stehlin, Béthouard, and Larminat to offer a loyal and intelligent defence (widely diffused by the *Revue militaire d'information*), were overshadowed by the hostility and prestige of Kœnig, Monsabert and, above all, Marshal Juin. And these last were encouraged by their impatient and recalcitrant junior officers, many of whom acquired their first experience of psychological action and a taste for direct pressure on the political authority in the controversy over the EDC.

By endlessly reiterating arguments which at bottom revolved around a possible future war with Germany, the EDC quarrel helped bring to the surface a past which had been dismissed, perhaps too hastily, in 1945. This vigorous battle over the collective memory was fuelled by a topicality which focused attention on the recent nightmare. Thus the trial at Bordeaux in January–February 1953 of the members of the SS 'Das Reich' division responsible for the atrocities committed at Oradour-sur-Glane and Tulle in June 1944 seemed to demonstrate the kind of crimes a German army was capable of. That the Alsaciens among the condemned – forcibly conscripted into the Wehrmacht during the war – were immediately pardoned by the French Parliament was revealing of the wish not to see the old wounds reopened: Alsace and the Limousin were both discontented, but for exactly opposite reasons. Similarly, the case of the Finaly children, taken from their adoptive French parents by their family in Israel, rekindled memories of a drama experienced by one French family in two in 1939–45. Finally, the execution in June of the Rosenbergs, martyrs to McCarthyism, provoked an outcry from the opponents of the EDC. Such powerful emotive images could not but strike deep chords in a nation which since 1944 had put its faith in the healing powers of a collective amnesia (see Chapter 3), yet which seemed to have lost none of its appetite for impassioned controversies.

This stirring of the collective conscience, and the revival of instincts of nationalism and self-preservation, tended of course to inflame the quarrel over the EDC. After all, in July 1954, 83 per cent believed the German atrocities in the last war to have been neither minimized nor exaggerated, 61 per cent feared a reopening of the concentration camps, and 45 per cent preferred that a still suspect Germany be kept weak and unarmed.[21] Not, however, that this reawakening of painful memories worked massively and decisively in favour of the anti-EDC camp; the European ideal had a serious popular appeal, and the argument that the EDC would in fact neutralize German militarism was widely accredited. According to the opinion polls, views on the issue scarcely altered between September 1951 and February 1955, with 42–43 per cent in favour of a European Army, 26–22 per cent hostile, and 32–35 per cent giving no answer. In fact, this stability of opinion reflected the widespread indecision and ignorance that surrounded the question. Many, for example, believed that with the treaty signed the EDC was already operational; others, more concerned simply with the protection of living standards, were content to delegate their civic responsibilities to the nation's political and moral élites. Indeed, it is possible that public

Table 12: *The French and EDC*

| in % | May 1953[a] | July 1954[b] | 19–22 August 1954[c] | 23–30 August 1954 | 31 August–8 September 1954 | January 1955[d] |
|---|---|---|---|---|---|---|
| for | 30 | 19 | 21 | 14 | 16 | 36 |
| on balance for | | 17 | 16 | 17 | 18 | |
| on balance against | | 11 | 12 | 12 | 11 | |
| against | 21 | 20 | 22 | 24 | 22 | 32 |
| undecided or no answer | 49 | 33 | 29 | 33 | 33 | 32 |

[a] 'If a referendum were held on the treaty project, as it now stands before the Assembly, would you vote for or against?', poll conducted 28 April–10 May 1953, *Sondages*, 2, 1953 (supplement), p. 9, published in November 1953.
[b] 'Attitude to the EDC', *Sondages*, 1–2, 1958, p. 139.
[c] 'Attitude to the EDC', poll on 'Opinion and the national awareness', of 19 August–8 September 1954, *Sondages*, 4, 1954, published in *France-Soir* and *Le Monde* of 14–15 October 1954.
[d] 'If you had had to vote on the Paris Accords, would you have voted for or against?', poll on 'Opinion and the Mendès France government', of 15–30 January 1955, *Sondages*, 1, 1955, p. 28.

opinion was either calmer or more confused than the vociferousness of the politicians and interested parties would suggest. Thus in July 1954, on the eve of the final impassioned outburst that closed the debate, 36 per cent were favourable to the EDC, compared with 31 per cent hostile, while 33 per cent were still without an opinion.[22] Such figures scarcely point to a fissuring of French opinion into blocs like that caused by the Dreyfus affair.[23] Having said this, it would be a mistake to dismiss the quarrel over the EDC as a completely artificial one, as a mere storm in the perennially agitated parliamentary teacup. It did after all help to bring about a major change in the political landscape in June 1954 with the coming to power of Mendès France. And striking additional proof of its real significance was provided after 1958, indeed throughout the Fifth Republic, by the remarkable consistency with which the same two camps re-formed over the questions of European unity and the Atlantic Alliance. The arguments and positions forged in the confused quarrel over the EDC, itself born of fears of a new war, were long to outlive the circumstances which had produced them.[24]

Table 12 (*cont.*)

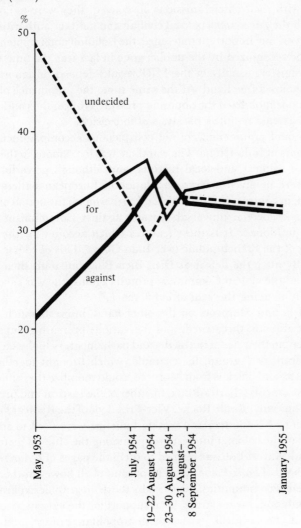

*From Cap Bon to Dien Bien Phu*

Overseas, a wait-and-see attitude and the search for a middle way were increasingly relied upon to hold together a French Union from which, with the exception of Black Africa, all hopes for positive evolution seemed to have evaporated. Having lost the long-term initiative, Paris used force to deal with emergencies in Tunisia and Morocco, and proved unable to avoid a humiliating defeat for its army in Indo-China. Governments were no more successful than before in getting their wishes obeyed: poorly or belatedly informed – something clear from many passages in Auriol's *Journal* – and with their official missions obstructed, they were too often presented with the *fait accompli* of local civilian and military authorities. There was, however, one important difference: the isolation and impotence began at last to be recognized by the public; gone in fact was the time when the relevant minister, usually of the MRP, could depend on ignorance and apathy to enjoy a free hand. At the same time, the imminence of decisive confrontations mobilized the opposing pressure groups, thus adding to the already weakened régime's paralysis of indecision.

Pressure and argument were not conspicuous accompaniments to the developments in Indo-China. The war there was too remote, in the hands of professional soldiers and local recruits, and although powerful colonial interests were involved a large population of European settlers was not threatened, in contrast to North Africa. Furthermore, the notion of a purely Asiatic arena for the universal crusade against Communism was not seriously questioned. It is these features which account for the singular unconcern of the French public over Indo-China. This of course changed dramatically after the defeat at Dien Bien Phu, but until then only the scandals and the violent Communist protests against the war succeeded in occasionally piercing the wall of indifference.[25]

In Tunisia and Moroco, on the other hand, interests much closer to home were directly threatened, and the various pressure groups quickly proved adept in their use of the media and parliamentary lobby tactics. The 'Présence française' group, for example, which brought together *colons*, industrialists, and officials from Morocco, could mobilize the influence and prestige of François Charles-Roux, member of the Institut and president of the Suez Company, Emile Roche, Vice-President of the Radical Party, and Marshal Juin. Newsletters and weekly bulletins were used to spread the arguments of the colonial interest groups among the élites of metropolitan France, and Marcel Boussac opened to them the pages of *L'Aurore*, Marcel Dassault those of *Paris-Presse*. Most important of all however, the presence of large French communities, menaced by the demographic explosion of the native population, meant strong local support for the various associations, branches of the political parties of metropolitan France, and colonial defence bodies.[26]

An important element in the crisis was the apparent inability of the political parties in France to come to terms with the historical phenomenon of decolonization: with the exception of the PCF, determined but isolated, not one of them took an openly anticolonial position. As a result, the newer and more far-sighted forces of opinion were formed and acted outside of the party political system. Thus to the pressure of the conservative colonial lobbyists there responded a moral and intellectual opposition to colonialism, an opposition linked, for example, to the *progressisme* or neutralism recently rejuvenated, as we have seen, by the quarrel over the EDC. The anticolonial struggle gradually became the main objective of *France-Observateur*, founded in 1950, where Claude Bourdet, Hector de Galard, and Roger Stephane led journalists who had come from *Combat, Libération,* and *Action.*[27] A commitment to the same cause was clearly visible behind the proclaimed objectivity of *Le Monde,* and was the principal factor in the launching of *L'Express* in May 1953. The most original development, however, was the convergence of this anticolonialism inspired by human rights with that of organized Christian opinion. Already present in the pages of *Réforme, Témoignage chrétien,* and *Esprit,* this theme was now taken up by a significant part of the Catholic hierarchy, backed by Rome, no longer committed exclusively to the outmoded narrow missionary approach to the question that was still aired in *La France catholique.* Also influenced by this new Christian reflection on the colonial question were the Mission de France, the various Catholic youth movements, and the Centre Catholique des Intellectuels Français, the last choosing 'Colonialisme et conscience chrétienne' as the subject for its 1953 conference. The full significance of such a shift in Catholic attitudes can be appreciated when one considers the place occupied by Catholicism in the training of the young and the formation of élites. The change was consolidated with the founding by Robert Barrat and Roger Stephane in June 1953 of the 'France-Maghreb' movement, one to which François Mauriac gave his prestige and active support.[28] Disparate and initially predominantly Parisian, this brought together journalists and intellectuals, students and teachers, trade unionists and managers, Communists and Christians; and put modern press techniques to good use for its weekly journals. It made incontestable progress in public opinion, and this in a non-partisan atmosphere reminiscent for some of the Liberation period; indeed, one of its members, General Catroux, a disciple of Lyautey, was sometimes given space in even *Le Figaro* to present the liberal case.

This new dimension to the debate added to the already considerable confusion of the major political parties. The MRP, so deeply implicated in the conduct of foreign policy, was particularly badly shaken by this offensive from an active Catholic minority. It split, rejecting the principle of autonomy, but favouring reforms; from May 1951 the MRP ministers had to face attacks from the party's youth movements, and numerous militants and officials linked to Action catholique, such as Léo Hamon, Robert Burron, and Félix Lacambre, made public their criticisms. The SFIO, though disturbed by the 'feudal' aspects of Moroccan nationalism, was closely attentive to the situation in Tunisia and was in fact favourable to an evolution towards independence. True, the arguments of someone like Charles-André Julien, specialist on Maghreb history and former adviser to

Blum, were not always to the liking of the party bosses, but the militants of the Tunisian Socialist Federation, under the dynamic leadership of Dr Cohen-Hadria, had a considerable influence inside the party machine.[29] Moreover, for the moment the minority in the SFIO opposed to the EDC had the good sense not to try to mix its struggle with that over attitudes and policies to the overseas territories; this, plus the secular stance of Bourguiba and the strong links between the Tunisian unions and Force Ouvrière all worked in favour of SFIO support for the Tunisian cause, the most recognizably 'French' of the North African nationalisms. Freed of the responsibility of office, the Socialists seemed able to present themselves once again as a force for change and innovation on this issue. Conversely, the position of the Radicals accurately encapsulates the contradictions experienced by the French political class over the colonial question. Thus while individuals like Pierre Mendès France and Edgar Faure remained open to argument, the all-powerful Martinaud-Déplat, who held a variety of ministerial posts between January 1952 and June 1954, combined an unflinching anti-communism with a deep hatred for Maghreb nationalism. He controlled the Radical Party's North African Federations, whose numbers were swelling now with worried white settlers, and courted the wealthy colonial interests, represented in the party by René Mayer, deputy for Constantine, senator Borgeaud of Algiers, and his colleague Colonna from Tunisia. Clearly the legacy of Caillaux was not threatened here, and since the Radicals were now considerably more important in the forming of governing coalitions than either the MRP or SFIO their attitude of aggressive impotence weighed heavily in the policy-making balance.

What Bourguiba described as 'an era of repression and resistance' opened in Tunisia with the Pleven government's negative response to Chenik on 15 December 1951 over the memorandum outlining the evolution towards Tunisian autonomy. The notion of co-sovereignty was not completely dismissed, but Paris was at pains to underline the inviolability of the French protectorate over Tunisia. The Neo-Destour nationalists, modernized and reinforced with popular support from the UGTT of Ferhat Hached, were now resolved to make no concessions. The replacement in January 1952 of the liberal Resident, Périllier, by Jean de Hautecloque, greeted with jubilation by a European community whipped up by the press and the counter-terrorist groups, brought the trial of strength between France and the nationalists closer. Having banned the Neo-Destour congress planned for 16 January, de Hautecloque had to use the French forces of General Garbay to crush the general strike and riots which followed; between 28 January and 1 February, this repressive action left more than 200 civilians dead in the Cap Bon area. Chenik and three other ministers, whose dismissal the Bey had refused, were arrested and deported on de Hautecloque's orders on 25 March. But the puppet government of loyal local officials under Baccouche, though acceptable to the French of Tunisia, was clearly incapable of breaking the impasse: the Bey now refused to approve all measures and projects from Paris; Bourguiba was deported. In this stalemate situation the advantage gradually passed to the Tunisian side. In August the Bey formed what amounted to an alternative government made up of nationalist notables; the assassination of Ferhat Hached on 5 December by counter-terrorists had the effect of immediately strengthening anti-French opinion at the United Nations – where the opposition included the United States this time – where the debate closed with a reminder of Tunisian capacities for self-government. Events in Tunisia were clearly no longer under French control. Only 8 per cent of the Tunisians and 46 per cent of the *colons* took part in the local elections of 3 May 1953, and even the Tunisian Socialist Federation had supported the boycott. The tide of violence rose relentlessly, with the 'Main rouge' organization confronting the nationalist terrorists in the towns, while in the rural areas armed bands of *fellaghas* (tribesmen) created a climate of perpetual insecurity. The Laniel cabinet did finally replace de Hautecloque by the more conciliatory Voizard, but the Destour nationalists merely increased their demands, rejecting out of hand the programme of reforms put forward in March 1954 by the new Mzali cabinet. Isolated and discouraged, Mzali resigned on 17 June: in the chaos that now reigned in Tunisia the choice was the stark one between open war or negotiations with Bourguiba.

The Tunisian drama rebounded directly on developments in Morocco. Here the final crisis began with the French rejection on 29 March 1952 of a memorandum on possible reforms from the Sultan. A general strike called by the Istiqal unions for 7 December 1952 to protest over the assassination of Ferhat Hached in Tunisia revealed the depth of the antagonism; the strike degenerated into rioting, with lynchings and murders on both sides, military repression, and dozens of deaths. After this outburst, General Guillaume, a disciple of Juin and in fact named by the latter to succeed him as Resident-General in Morocco, proceeded to purge and dismiss all the local notables suspected of nationalist sympathies, arguing that the unrest was part of a vast conspiracy of international Communism, and began dealings with El Glaoui, the aged pasha of Marrakesh. By early 1953 Guillaume's policy had succeeded in removing most of the opposition's leaders. The colonial pressure group in France, led by Juin and Martinaud-Déplat and using *L'Aurore* as its mouthpiece,[30] now put into action the scheme it had long nurtured to depose Sultan Ben Youssef, suspect to the colonialists since his Tangier speech of 1947. As in 1951, El Glaoui was at the centre of the plan – Juin paid a glowing tribute to him in his address to the Académie française on 25 June[31] – details of which were finalized in Paris during the summer of 1953. Between 13 and 19 August, El Glaoui called his followers together, summoned his candidate, Moulay Arafa, from Fez, had him named as the new Iman, and dispatched his forces to encircle Rabat. General Guillaume paid little attention to the official instructions from Bidault asking him to restrain El Glaoui;[32] with the capital surrounded, the press controlled, and no signs of a likely popular reaction, the plan went ahead smoothly. On 20 August, Sultan Ben Youssef, by now a completely isolated figure, was arrested by Guillaume and immediately deported to Corsica, then to Madagascar, while on the same day Moulay Arafa was proclaimed as the new Sultan. Fearful of civil war in Morocco if this *fait accompli* did not receive prompt official recognition, Laniel and Bidault weakly underwrote Guillaume's action. In the divided cabinet the only protests came from Edgar Faure and François Mitterrand, and the latter, already opposed to French policy in Tunisia, resigned. The 'Présence française' pressure group had triumphed: on the surface the situation seemed calm. Yet by riding roughshod over the Treaty of Fez of 1912, France had given Moroccan nationalism a martyr and a hope for the future in the person of the deposed Ben Youssef: by September Morocco was again troubled by violent incidents.

The position in Indo-China was of course far worse and, for France at least, a costly and increasingly unpopular war was fast moving towards its climax. With deepening involvement by the United States on one side and growing aid to the Vietminh from Communist China on the other, the conflict's international character had developed steadily since 1950. France was now on the front line of the defence of the free world, and her colonial war was integrated into Washington's policy of containment in the Far East and the Pacific. Between June 1950 and May 1954, according to the figures presented to the American Senate, United States aid to France totalled 3.6 milliard dollars, or 80 per cent of the overall cost of the war. These figures were disputed by the French governments, keen to receive more help but anxious to avoid direct intervention by the American advisers in its distribution or in the conduct of the war. The French governments argued ceaselessly for greater unconditional aid, adopting a strict bargaining tone which conflicted somewhat with the great stress placed at the same time on the heavy national sacrifices being made by France, claiming that the allies were supporting no more than half the cost of the war. And indeed military expenditure between 1952 and 1955 did account for roughly a third of the French budget, compared with a quarter under normal conditions. But the French case in favour of more American assistance was increasingly unconvincing: greater but always unconditional aid would make of France a pillar of NATO and an effective front line of the Cold War; in return she would ratify the EDC, eliminate the Communist menace from North Africa and Black Africa, and safeguard Indo-China. They were arguments which, as the Communists were not slow to point out, could all too easily be summarized as: French and native lives in return for American dollars. Arguments also to which Eisenhower, Dulles, and the Pentagon's experts were less and less receptive: the Korean War ended in July 1952, international tension was easing, and there was an awareness that American and British economic interests would be very well protected by the Indochinese Associated States without the need to conserve the rickety framework of the French Union: all that prevented them from pulling out was the Chinese threat. The risk for France was clear: accepting an internationalization of the conflict without any guarantee of having a decisive role in an eventual negotiated settlement, for the extent of American aid already ensured a considerable say for the United States in such an outcome. Moreover, the likely long-term advantages for France looked increasingly slight – the Associated States of Vietnam, Laos, and Cambodia had all been told repeatedly that crushing the Vietminh would be the prelude to the end of French tutelage, and hence an end in fact to the ambitions of the French Union. In short, France was fighting a war in which she could gain nothing, one in which success would probably mean an end to the French presence in Indo-China, the main principle the war had been fought to uphold! As General Navarre concluded wryly: 'In continuing to fight alone, we were risking our own necks to safeguard the interest of others.'[33]

This growing inconsistency of French objectives was paralleled by the increasingly half-hearted commitment to the war itself. As early as October 1950 Pierre Mendès France had posed the choice in unequivocal terms – either go all out for a military victory, something that would require a tripling of troops and funds, or negotiate with Ho Chi Minh. Yet neither of these alternatives was acceptable to the Right, the first because of its strict budgetary policies and the need to maintain troops in the already troubled North African territories, the second from anticommunism and obedience to Washington. Again and again, ignoring the views of military experts like Generals Blanc and Lechères, these governments refused to make available the resources necessary for a French military victory in Indo-China. And they seemed even to want to ignore the sacrifices being made by the French expeditionary forces; from 1948 the lists of honours awarded in the Indo-Chinese campaign were no longer published in the *Journal officiel*, and although a law of July 1952 finally accorded the status of war veterans to the soldiers of Indo-China it was not in fact applied until after the French defeat. Increasingly demoralized by their exhausting struggle against an invisible enemy, the French forces harboured a bitter contempt for the administrators and politicians in Paris. A lack of long-term policy, steady subordination to the logic of the conflict's internationalization – which would lead to the Geneva Conference – and disillusionment among the combatants: perhaps the only truly coherent element in the French position was in implacable hatred for Ho Chi Minh; France did not even reply to an offer from him for fresh negotiations made through the Swedish newspaper

*Expressen* on 29 November 1953: on 20 November French paratroops had been dropped on Dien Bien Phu for yet another 'definitive' assault on the Vietminh.

De Lattre had correctly realized that until greater political and military aid arrived it was essential to hold the positions and block the Tonkin Delta. After his death on 11 January 1952, however, his successors, Salan and then Navarre in May 1953, had to come to terms with the fact that this aid was still not adequate, that their forces were becoming bogged down, and that an extension of the conflict was imminent. With the fall of Sam-Neua on 13 April 1953 the way into Laos and hence into Thailand was open to the Vietminh – and this at a time when their Chinese and Soviet aid was visibly more regular and more effective. These developments ruined Navarre's initial plan to progressively hand over control of the cleared southern zone to Bao Dai's Vietnamese army, thus leaving his own forces free to regroup in the northern zone before provoking the Vietminh into what for it would be a fatal battle in open country. The Vietminh's advance into Laos brought a proposal from Foster Dulles for an internationalization of the conflict; this the Mayer government refused, though in fact it was only thanks to intervention by American air forces that Laos was saved. In reality Giap had taken the initiative in deliberately stepping up the conflict near the borders of Laos, thus drawing the fighting away from the strong French bases on the Delta. The trap worked. Disregarding the warnings of Chiefs of Staff Ely and Blanc and of the airmen, Navarre and above all Cogny, responsible for the North Vietnam zone, decided to solve the problem of access to Laos with the traditional methods of colonial warfare, by setting up a single fortified base. Dien Bien Phu, a hollow 9 km wide and 16 km long near the border with Laos, which had been occupied in November by six paratroop battalions, was chosen as the site on 3 December. To arguments that Dien Bien Phu was encircled by mountains in which the enemy could hide, was more than 300 km north-west of Hanoi, that all its supplies and reinforcements would have to be flown in, and that it would tie down large numbers of men – to these arguments the enthusiastic Cogny replied that the Vietminh would not be able to transport its materials and that only insignificant groups would be able to skirt this otherwise obligatory point of passage. An airlift of American Dakotas brought the materials for what was built up into a formidable entrenched camp, equipped with support posts and a modern communications network, the entire operation conceived and executed like a textbook military exercise, and command of which went to Colonel de Castries. The bellicose declarations to the press that accompanied the construction of the camp did not, however, dispel the doubts of the experts and observers, nor those, belated, of Navarre himself. But it was too late now, for the decisive battle had begun.[34]

General Giap was to win the battle of Dien Bien Phu by systematically demonstrating each of the French assumptions to have been mistaken. Aware that a victory would be of great importance in the international negotiations that were starting, Giap threw his best forces into the struggle, while maintaining a harassing action in the Delta. Each night brought intense activity by thousands of guerrilla fighters and natives, opening jungle routes invisible to French air cover, bringing in supplies and equipment, establishing firing-posts in the hills around the camp, inaccessible to French artillery. The fate of Dien Bien Phu was in fact sealed from the start of the massed Vietminh attack on 15 March 1954 – the airstrip was put out of action, the outlying forward support posts were taken in ferocious surprise attacks, and de Castries was unable to use his reserves for the counterattack. Denied adequate reinforcements, amidst the wounded and the scattered materials, the 10 000 defenders of Dien Bien Phu (of seventeen nationalities) held on during a month of terrible fighting, pinned down at the bottom of the hollow. But the outcome no longer depended on their heroic resistance: throughout April a projected relief operation involving massive American air power to smash Giap's lines was delayed by France's allies, then definitively abandoned on 25 April after a categorical refusal from Churchill – with the solution of the Indo-China conflict now in the hands of the diplomats at Geneva, Dien Bien Phu fell to the Vietminh on 7 May 1954.

The shock of the defeat was enormous. The Vietminh had lost nearly 8000 men and had 15 000 wounded or missing. But the French expeditionary force had abandoned seventeen of its best battalions (between 6 and 9 per cent of its forces), with 1500 dead on the evening of the final assault, and 4000 seriously wounded, many of whom would not survive. Nearly 12 000 soldiers of the French Union had been taken prisoner, of whom more than 7000 were never to return from the terrible prison camps.[35] Among them were several hundred French officers – at the hands of their Vietminh captors they were now to learn the techniques of torture and brainwashing, measure for themselves the impact of psychological warfare, and reflect bitterly on the ingratitude of the Republic which had abandoned them. The French army was humiliated,[36] and the civilian population was alarmed: in a very real sense the Fourth Republic had itself suffered a mortal blow at Dien Bien Phu.[37]

In the immediate aftermath of Dien Bien Phu the expeditionary force half-heartedly resisted the offensive in the Delta that followed the disaster, while among the Vietnamese forces morale collapsed completely. Each night now the Haiphong–Hanoi artery was cut by the enemy: each morning it had to be reopened by the armoured forces. Navarre could no longer guarantee to save Hanoi. In France, where the exhausted Laniel government had obtained a stay of execution from the Assembly, reluctant to provoke a ministerial crisis as the international negotiations got under way, the slow agony of Dien Bien Phu was the subject of feverish press and radio coverage. The inevitable outcome confirmed the French public in its belief that the real choice was between negotiation or abandonment.[38] At the Geneva Conference, planned since those of Bermuda and Berlin and opened on 26 April, the Vietminh and its Soviet and Chinese allies now held the trump card which would determine its outcome: for Giap and his men had won the greatest, and in fact the only, pitched battle in the history of decolonization.

### 'Nous sommes en 1788'

The disaster in Indo-China struck a political leadership already over-whelmed from all sides – so much so that its weakness now began to under-mine the régime itself. These years of economic consolidation saw the development of a popular alienation and disaffection which was to con-tribute so much to the collapse of the Fourth Republic. Among participants and observers alike, there was a growing awareness of the problem, and of the dangers it created. Thus Hubert Beuve-Méry, editor of *Le Monde*, pointed to the widespread sense of being duped by the politicians, and to the disenchantment and latent hostility this fostered;[39] or Paul Reynaud, for whom France was 'l'homme malade de l'Europe'; or Mendès France, who concluded ominously: 'Nous sommes en 1788.'[40] And in fact, with hindsight, it is clear that many of the elements present in the final crisis of the Fourth Republic were taking shape in the second half of 1953.

One danger came from mounting popular impatience, which found ex-pression in the social unrest of the summer; unrest that was by no means incompatible with the aspirations to stability and greater well-being already described. Behind this lay the fact that France was now facing the consequences of the Pinay stabilization. The budget deficit, though reduced, persisted – 769 milliard francs in 1952, 698 in 1953, 346 in 1954, 507 in 1955 – a source of concern to the economic liberals in power. Yet given the burden of the war in Indo-China and the unjust tax system – the latter necessary to reassure the holders of capital but responsible for a stagnation of receipts – this was unavoidable. In the absence of a readiness to tackle the deep-seated causes of the imbalance, governments were thrown back on familiar expedients; from 1952 to 1955 bankruptcy was avoided only thanks to frequent 'exceptional' advances from the Banque de France. The persistent external trade deficit exhausted the reserves of strong cur-rencies and along with the domestic deficit increased France's dependence on capital and American loans. This twofold deficit maintained the dangers of inflation and caused an unproductive expansion of the money supply in circulation, while control of credit and investment depressed the economy, exacerbated the difficulties of the retailers, and increased the likelihood of unemployment. In the spring of 1953, for the first time since the Liberation, the number of registered unemployed approached 100 000; farmers were hit by slumping food prices; and in their hardship the retailers looked back with envy to the days of inflation and easy profits. A survey conducted by the INSEE showed that 25 per cent of employees earned less than 20 000 francs a month (the SMIG or minimum wage was currently fixed at that figure), while 60 per cent had less than 30 000 francs; particularly badly off were the employees of the State. This then was the disturbing economic background against which the crisis developed.

First the shopkeepers: on 22 July, in the small town of Saint-Céré in the Lot, Pierre Poujade, a stationer, organized his fellow tradesmen in resistance to the tax inspectors (the detested 'polyvalents') who, according to the protesters, spared the wealthy and influential – the 'gros' – to concentrate instead on the modest and vulnerable – the 'petits'.[41] Throughout the summer of 1953, groups of Poujade's supporters went to the aid of similar victims of fiscal pressure in the *départements* of the Centre and the South-West. In November the Union de défense des commerçants et artisans (UDCA) was founded, and its militants obtained their first success in December by wresting control of the chambre de commerce of Cahors from the 'notables' of Gingembre's CGPME. What quickly came to be known as 'Poujadism' was launched – with the backing of the Communists it embarked on a campaign of noisy opposition to a régime it denounced as 'oppressive' and 'rotten'. On 28 July the endemic agitation of the wine-growers of the Midi took a particularly violent turn, with road blocks and barricades to protest against imports of Algerian wine and to protect wine prices. This dramatic episode, in which *préfectures* were besieged and the Languedoc was cut off from the rest of France by the CRS forces, offered in fact a foretaste of the very extensive rural unrest which was to accompany the 'silent revolution' of the 1950s. After the wine-growers it was the turn of the cattle-rearers; on 12 October fourteen *départements* of the Centre and the West were paralysed by producers protesting over low prices for livestock. The official agricultural union, the FNSEA, was increasingly repudiated by its activist minorities, and in September a splinter organization, the so-called 'Comité de Guéret' had been formed in the Massif Central; this was behind the October action and was to be the driving force in the MODEF movement for the defence of small family farming. The final outburst of the summer of 1953 saw the State – in its capacity as employer – come under direct attack in a general strike of the public sector which brought France to a virtual standstill.

The public sector strike began in the postal service, quiet since 1946, but where the cumulative effects of an expanding volume of mail, an extension of services, inadequate staffing, a failure to modernize, and repeated economy measures had brought the employees to the end of their patience.[42] The strike spread rapidly: on 7 August, just two days after it had started in the Bordeaux sorting-office, the strike was almost general in the public sector, with the SNCF, the RATP, and EDF–GDF all involved and the mines and metal industry threatened; two million workers were on strike, and there were almost four million strikers by 15 August. At the origin of the action was the Force Ouvrière union, but with rapid rallying to the cause by the CGT – anxious to forget its difficulties of the previous year – the union movement presented a solid front. The strike turned into a trial of strength when the Laniel government, in contravention of the 1946 statute for the public sector, attempted to introduce requisition measures, and declared its rejection of the strike on 12 August. Was this strike action as spontaneous as it was widely believed to be at the time? The initial impetus undoubtedly came from the rank-and-file militants of Force Ouvrière, strongly influenced by revolutionary syndicalist doctrines, and the strikers themselves were readier to claim inspiration from 1936 than from 1947. The exhaustion of the workforce was certainly one factor in the action; the strike provided a welcome opportunity for the release of pent-up tensions – it was not without significance that the strikes occurred at the moment when so many French families were on holiday. The strike movement was not unpopular: in spite of the enormous disruption caused at the peak of the holiday season there were no serious incidents between strikers and those deprived of public transport. Nor were the strikes marked by violence, occupation, or demonstration; and although the country was in effect paralysed, the population was not alarmed by possible subversion or by the activities of the Communists as had so clearly been the case in 1947–8. Indeed, that the strikes of 1953 have failed to hold a large place in the collective memory is a reflection of the fact that they were less the product of a vast social confrontation than of the purely circumstantial crisis experienced by the régime itself.

It is then in the political domain that the significance of the strikes has to be sought. Under Pinay the Force Ouvrière unions of the PTT had in fact refined their bargaining methods *vis-à-vis* government: what provoked the recourse to strike action was the announcement on 4 August of the *décrets-lois* drawn up by Edgar Faure, Minister of Finance in the new Laniel cabinet. Taken on 10 August, part of a package of special powers accorded to the new government by the Assembly before it too dispersed for the summer holidays, the measures included further stringent economies in the public sector, and in particular a reduction of employment and a raising of the retirement age for public employees. Those affected immediately condemned the proposals as unilateral, contrary to the 1946 statute, and totally unacceptable. However, the animosity of the strikers was directed less against the person of Laniel than against the system of *gouvernement d'assemblée* now widely perceived to be responsible for the maladministration. It is this which accounts for the antiparliamentarian current present in the demands of the strikers – an ironical resolution from the postal workers in the Manche, for example, solemnly declared the return of the deputies to their work in the Assembly to be more important than that of the strikers to theirs, asking for the requisition measures to be applied to the deputies.[43] From 9 August, under pressure from the unions, the Socialists and Communists began demanding the recall of Parliament: Herriot had to use underhand methods to spare the parliamentarians such an embarrassingly public discussion of where responsibility actually lay, and in fact the deputies of the majority were not to air their views until 6 October.[44] Meanwhile, on 25 August, the strike movement had ended. The government promised that the measures would not be applied in the PTT. The various unions involved had negotiated separately, outbidding one another in demonstrations of their representative character and aptitude for responsible dialogue – something hard to imagine a few years earlier. Salaries and staffing were to be increased: the strikers returned to work. It was clear to all, however, that the State was no longer the arbiter it had been in 1936 and that the elected representatives had refused to assume their responsibilities. By its response to this summer of unrest the Fourth Republic had in fact lost the support of millions of working people whose hopes for a better future it had once embodied.

It was, then, with a growing sense of disillusionment that the people followed the succession of political crises which laid bare the extent of the system's decay. The 36-day governmental interregnum of June–July 1953, the longest under the Fourth Republic, made clear the impossibility of obtaining stable majorities from the Assembly elected in 1951. The passing of the SFIO to the opposition and the divisions of the MRP and the Radicals simply reinforced the logic of the electoral outcome: the Right remained in control of the parliamentary solutions – even if some by-election results already appeared to indicate a swing back to the Centre-Left among the electorate. To exploit its position fully and lastingly, however, the Right needed the votes of the Gaullists, to begin with the handful of defectors, then, gradually, the bulk of the RPF deputies. Yet the position of these was increasingly precarious; in May, drawing the obvious lesson from RPF defeats in the municipal elections,[45] de Gaulle had withdrawn his personal support from the RPF deputies and given them their parliamentary liberty. Gaullism – whose leader had already begun his 'traversée du désert' and whose deputies now sat as the Union républicaine d'action sociale (URAS) – was thus of no more than limited use in the forming of majorities. The advantage seemed then to lie with the Independents, Peasants, and Moderates, who in terms of parliamentary arithmetic ought to have been able to form successful coalitions with the MRP, the Radicals and the UDSR. In practice, however, even these majorities could not be stable, since on every major issue these groups were divided not only between, but within themselves.

The René Mayer ministry lasted just nineteen weeks. At the start of the crisis begun by Mayer's resignation on 21 May 1953, both Guy Mollet and André Diethelm (RPF) refused to form governments. President Auriol, alarmed for some time now by the developments, publicly denounced this systematic RPF and Socialist opposition which, along with the more discreet opposition of the Communists, prevented the parliamentary system from operating and was clearly weakening the Republic. In vain. Paul Reynaud was proposed, but was too favourable to the EDC and deliberately ruined his chances by demanding immediate constitutional reform if elected. Bidault's attempt for the investiture failed by just one vote. André Marie, Radical, could not get unanimous support even from within his own party. And Pinay abandoned his attempt. A meeting of party leaders and former premiers called by Auriol could offer no solution to the deadlock. The crisis had entered its second month when the exhausted Assembly finally produced a majority for the investiture of Joseph Laniel. The support was of course composite, from the Right and the Gaullists, but also from the MRP and the Radicals. Laniel was the protégé of Reynaud not of Flandin; a former member of the CNR he was less marked by the past than Pinay – to whom he was opposed – and the Independents and Peasants recognized in him a new vehicle for the same policies. The Gaullists were naturally delighted to be in a government at last, while the MRP, angered by what it considered too sharp an intervention by Auriol in the crisis, derived some satisfaction from voting for a candidate known not to have the confidence of the Elysée. Finally, the Radicals could congratulate themselves on placing Queuille, Martinaud-Déplat, Edgar Faure, and André Marie in the government. It was clear from the crisis that a Socialist, an MRP, a Radical, a Gaullist, and an Independent, were all, individually, unable to secure a majority: it was clear from the outcome that the Right could not dominate the parliamentary solutions indefinitely. The politicians were well aware of the appalling effect the protracted parliamentary deadlock had produced on the public, several top officials had made known their exasperation, and there had even been rumours of a military coup. One episode stands out, however, from this depressing overall picture – the attempted investiture, between those of Reynaud and Bidault, of Mendès France. After sharply reminding the Assembly that 'Gouverner, c'est choisir' he went on to outline a vigorous emergency policy, the one he was in fact to apply in 1954. The impression this energetic plain speaking had on the Assembly was clear from the voting that followed – just 119 hostile (of which 100 were Communists) and 202 abstentions. Although Mendès France fell 13 votes short of the 314 necessary for the investiture, he had won an incontestable moral victory, one that would not be forgotten quickly.

The exceptional crisis of 1953 was brutal proof that on every major issue – economic and social policy, the EDC, North Africa, and Indo-China – no majority existed to appoint an individual capable of carrying a clear and consistent policy to its conclusion. True, as André Siegfried pointed out, majorities could certainly be found when each of the familiar problems was taken in isolation; but taken together they precluded any stable majority with which to govern.[46] In this helpless fragmentation of energies the tendency to *gouvernement d'assemblée* was of course strengthened: the political parties chose – and ultimately controlled – the premier; government was increasingly run on parliamentary lines; power came to be exercised almost in rotation, with each change accompanied by a judicious redistribution of ministerial portfolios between the interested groups – all of which had predictably unfortunate consequences for decision-making and the administration. Some of the more clear-sighted parliamentarians already hoped for a revision of the Constitution. Yet was it realistic to suppose that the solution lay in adjustments to the constitutional texts?

The Republic's chronic indecision was held up for public exhibition during the election of Auriol's successor. The choice was of course a narrowly political one. The Parliament which met in Congress at Versailles in December 1953 scrutinized each candidate's stance over Indo-China, on economic policy, in the education debate, and, most of all, over the EDC; it refused first to swing to the Right – the initial favourite, Laniel, was rejected;[47] or then to the Left – Naegelen, hostile to the EDC and backed by the Communists, was in turn rejected. More serious preparatory discussions might have avoided some of the twelve ballots which had to be held before the Republic chose its President. The surprise victor to emerge from this laborious and discouraging spectacle was a Norman and a traditional republican; he was an experienced parliamentarian who, due to illness, had not taken part in the decisive vote on the EDC; he was of the Right – an Independent – without being too clerical; his *bonhomie* and moral integrity were to make him a popular President: in the choice of René Coty the Fourth Republic of 1953 had, after all, only been faithful to itself.

# 13

## The impossible renewal

Joseph Laniel was brought down on 12 June 1954, for having failed to avoid Dien Bien Phu or to settle any of the outstanding problems. Laniel was succeeded by the author of the indictment of his government, Pierre Mendès France. The new premier's reputation was that of a 'liquidator': in the single summer of political grace accorded him by the Assembly, Mendès France did indeed liquidate the problems which had so paralysed his predecessors. Yet beyond his subsequent defeat, and in what came, no doubt prematurely, to be known as 'Mendésisme', was encapsulated the whole question of whether the Republic was capable of renewal, of adapting itself to the needs of a rapidly modernizing nation. The few months during which Mendès France held power were marked by optimism, when thoughts at last turned to the future. They were ended brutally by the crisis in Algeria, which brought a return to the familiar impotence.

### The summer of grace for Mendès France

The investiture of Mendès France as premier on 17 June 1954 broke with the established parliamentary practices of the Fourth Republic in several ways. It was not preceded by the usual succession of attempted investitures by the leaders of the various groups in the Assembly: instead there was a direct appeal from President Coty to Mendès France, whose sensational speech of the previous year had not been forgotten. Nor was there the familiar bargaining over portfolios with the party bosses: instead there were consultations with members of the administration, military experts, and union leaders, which persuaded Mendès France of the need to act quickly. His speech to the Assembly offered leadership and commitment to a coherent policy rather than undertakings not to touch certain taboo questions. The investiture, that Mendès France insisted be unconditional, and that required 314 votes to succeed, was secured by a handsome margin, with 419 in favour, 47 against, and 143 abstentions. In this large majority were the Socialists, wholehearted in their support; the Radicals more divided over the choice of Mendès France than they appeared; the UDSR;

224

the Gaullists, under their new title of 'Republicains sociaux'; the Independents from the overseas constituencies, plus a few deputies of the Right. Also present in the majority were the votes of the Communists and Progressistes (a small group close to the PCF), voting in favour of an investiture for the first time since 1947 and thus marking their reinsertion into the political debate, although Mendès France, wary of a manoeuvre and anxious not to tie his hands in the Geneva talks, in fact refused to consider their 99 votes as contributing to his final majority. The Right was resolutely hostile, aware that this new majority was based on a repudiation of its policies. The MRP, committed to defend the policies of Bidault, the European initiatives, and French interests overseas, abstained from the vote, making clear from the start, through the voice of a young deputy for Seine-Inférieure, Jean Lecanuet, its reservations and likely hostility to the new government: the attitude of the MRP towards Mendès France was in fact to alternate between halfhearted support and bitter opposition, with the emphasis increasingly on the latter as time went on. Ostensibly then the positions were clear: an opposition that was defined by a defence of the policies of the past; a new majority, present in embryo in the struggle against the EDC, was now united by the conviction that those responsible for Dien Bien Phu could not represent France at the Geneva talks, that the time had come for the problems to be solved rather than shelved, and that the country was looking for a change. Yet whatever the strength of such convictions this was nevertheless a composite majority, one forged under the pressure of exceptional circumstances[1] – the old handicap of constructing majorities problem by problem had not vanished and the volatile parliamentary arithmetic of 1951–2 could still operate. Moreover, many of the votes that made up the new majority were attracted more by the emergency measures than by the long-term views that might lie behind them, seduced by the coherence of the policy but potentially divided on the means for its realization. From the outset then, the victory of Mendès France was marked by ambiguity.

What had certainly mobilized support was the incisive diagnosis of the ills and the drastic remedies proposed. At his investiture Mendès France presented what amounted to a breakneck timetable for resolving the immediate problems, under which the Indo-China affair was to be settled and a plan for economic recovery drawn up by 20 July, and the EDC voted on before the autumn. For the execution of this part of his programme Mendès France demanded absolute and unconditional support; he would succeed or resign. Then, when these obstacles had been cleared, was to come a comprehensive policy of economic and social progress for reconstruction, a policy for friendly co-existence in the overseas territories, and a specifically French stance in international affairs. The bases of this programme of coherent short- and medium-term policies had been published as an 'Appel à la jeunesse' in *L'Express* on 14 May 1954 (and it was to reappear in *La République moderne* of 1962). Fundamental to it was that the sterile divisions of the past – Left–Right, secular–clerical, liberal–*dirigiste*, East–West – had to be forgotten; they belonged to the period opened by the crisis of the 1930s and were irrelevant in the new period opened by détente and the neo-capitalism of the 1950s. Emphasis was placed on the benefits of controlled economic growth, a dynamic public sector, and progress in science and modern thought.[2] The *ad hoc* approach imposed by the problems since 1944 had now to make way for policies to construct a strong and dynamic France that could be entrusted to the next generation. This collection of themes and ambitions, those of an impatient techno-cracy tempered by a Radicalism that looked back to Alain, scarcely constituted a coherent doctrine and what came to be known as 'Mendésisme' in fact took shape only slowly. But its immediate impact was far from negligible – not surprisingly a section of the younger gener-ation was enthusiastic, attracted by the prospect of an end to the inter-minable arguing over the past that would open the way for the creation of a modern democracy. On the other hand, it was unlikely to provoke the same response at the Palais Bourbon: the parliamentary majority which had brought Mendès France to power was more appreciative of the energy and severity he deployed to clear the immediate political obstacles than of ambitious and far-reaching plans for the reconstruction of France – the plans of someone who in his investiture speeches of 1953 and 1954 had laid claim to a triple political heritage: of Poincaré for financial rigour, of Blum for social action, and of de Gaulle for the preservation of national independence and the exaltation of the State.[3]

The team selected by Mendès France bore witness to the new ambition and style of government. Mendès France himself took the key Foreign Affairs portfolio, operating for the moment from the Quai d'Orsay rather than Matignon.[4] With him he brought his own team of loyal colleagues and advisers, many of whom were to have brilliant careers under the Fifth Republic. In charge of the staff and responsible for the elaboration of policy material and reports was a long-standing friend, Georges Boris, director of *La Lumière* before the war and adviser to Léon Blum. Dipolomacy was the responsibility of Philippe Baudet, Jean-Marie Soutou, and Claude Cheysson; André Pelabon, Jacques Juillet, Michel Jobert, and Léone Georges-Picot for internal affairs and the secretariat; Simon Nora, Jacques Marchandise, Jean Serisé, and Jean Saint-Geours, for economic affairs; while the presence of Jean-Jacques Servan-Schreiber provided a link with the world of the press and the intelligentsia. The composition of the new government, complete by 18 June – Mendès France made known to de Gaulle the importance he attached to this symbolic date – reflected the same criteria. It was small, sixteen members rather than the usual twenty-two; it was fresh, only four ministers of the Laniel government were retained and none of the major figures of the past years were present; and its average age was low, thanks notably to the presence of François Mitterrand at the Ministry of the Interior, Jacques Chaban-Delmas at Public Works, and Christian Fouchet at Tunisian and Moroccan Affairs. The familiar carve-up of portfolios between each of the parties of the majority did not take place, the accent being placed on personal contact and competence rather than on party membership – something illustrated by the appointment of the MRP Robert Buron, against the wishes of his party, to the Ministry of Overseas France. The advantage had certainly shifted in favour of the majority of 17 June, but there were some continuities: Edgar Faure remained at Finance,[5] the Radical, Berthoin, symbolized the attachment to the secular principle at Education; and Guy La Chambre at Associated States stood for continuity with the political personnel of the Third Republic. Finally, the Républicains sociaux made an important appearance in the government, with four key posts including that of National Defence under General Kœnig. In short, at all levels of the executive Mendès France had sought to balance youth and experience, harnessing ability and efficiency in the service of the State. This team now had the four-week truce its leader had secured from the Assembly in which to obtain the all-important first results on which it would be judged by the parliamentarians and public opinion. It was in order to convince and woo the latter that Mendès France gave the first of his soon-to-be-famous weekly radio talks on 19 June.

The most pressing problem was Indo-China, and it was on the Geneva negotiations that Mendès France now concentrated his attention. Strongly backed by Ambassador Jean Chauvel and thanks to the repeated stressing of the finality of the 20 July deadline, Mendès France was to realize the considerable exploit of showing that even the defeated can sometimes present their victors with an ultimatum.[6] Exploiting the groundwork prepared by Bidault, Mendès France convinced all present at Geneva – Eden and Dulles for the allies, Molotov, Chou En-lai, and Pham Van Dong for the Vietminh – that France was ready to send extra forces to Indo-China if a settlement was not reached before the deadline expired.[7] While this pressure certainly speeded up the negotiations it did nothing to remove the basic ambiguity of the French position: for the need to hold out some hope to Bao Dai – represented at Geneva and perhaps already resigned to American support for the South[8] – made it impossible to explore the solution favoured by Pham Van Dong, that of a united Vietnam freely associated with the French Union and which might have best served French interests. And in fact priority went to obtaining a ceasefire rather than to finding a durable political solution; it was decided to dissociate the cases of Laos and Cambodia and an agreement was reached on the supervision of the truce. In a harrowing last-minute race against the clock, and under pressure from Molotov, Eden, and Chou En Lai, the two outstanding problems were overcome: as in Korea, the partition would be along the seventeenth parallel (the Vietminh had control almost to the thirteenth parallel) and free elections to settle the future of the divided country were to be held under international control two years after the ceasefire. On 21 July the armistice for Vietnam, Laos, and Cambodia was signed and their independence recognized. The achievement was considerable: just a few weeks after the crushing military defeat at Dien Bien Phu, Mendès France had obtained what was by any standard the least unfavourable settlement, one which gave the régime of South Vietnam under Ngo Dinh Diem time to prove itself while sparing the French expeditionary force further losses. With the French evacuation from Indo-China a few months later six years of 'dirty war' came to an end. These years had claimed 92 000 lives from France and the French Union, cost more than 3000 milliard francs, and had done much to worsen relations between the Republic and its army.[9] The Geneva settlement was greeted with relief by French opinion, and even *Le Figaro* acknowledged the service Mendès France had rendered the nation.

To the success over Indo-China was quickly added another, the result of secret preparations initiated at Geneva. On 31 July 1954 Mendès France, accompanied by Fouchet and Marshal Juin (whose important support Mendès France had carefully cultivated), made a spectacular surprise visit to Tunis. Two phrases from Mendès' speech at the Bey's Palace of Carthage were widely reported and aroused immediate enthusiasm among the Tunisian population. He declared that France recognized the internal autonomy of Tunisia and was ready to transfer the exercise of sovereignty to the Tunisian people and institutions. These propositions in fact contained little that was new; it was rather their tone and timing and their dramatic presentation which struck an encouraging note; France appeared finally to have chosen. As before, the public were kept informed, and the press was favourable. Behind the 'Carthage declaration' in fact lay careful diplomatic preparations begun at Geneva, where contact had been established with friends of Bourguiba. General Boyer de Latour was appointed Resident-General in Tunisia, and charged with opening negotiations with the *fellaghas* and preparing for a transfer of powers to a representative Tunisian government, one that was to include the Destour nationalists.[10] A noisy campaign by the hastily organized 'France-Tunisie' parliamentary pressure group led by Colonna and Jean Médecin, mayor of Nice, was ignored, and on 10 August, after a final unsuccessful attack in the Assembly from Martinaud-Déplat, the deputies – with the exception of the MRP and the Right – voted heavily in favour of this new liberal policy in Tunisia.

After peace in Indo-China and a renewal of dialogue in Tunisia there remained the European Defence Community as a stumbling-block to the lauching of a new French foreign policy. Mendès France was well aware of this and was eager to see it removed as quickly as the others. His approach to the EDC question – like that of his entourage – was, however, strangely and uncharacteristically hesitant; the consistently detached and open-minded attitude he adopted to an issue which divided French political opinion so sharply bears witness in fact to his real uncertainty as to what the outcome should be, an uncertainty increased perhaps by the knowledge that the changed international context made the EDC of only secondary importance. In June 1953, like his predecessors, he had been in favour of negotiating a new Treaty of Paris, one that would be more flexible without becoming unworkable. By August 1954, however, realizing that France was completely isolated among the allies, he had come to the conclusion that a decision one way or the other was necessary to break the stalemate, something which would at least allow France to speak with greater authority in the future within the Atlantic alliance and make it possible to encourage fresh moves for European unity. This ambivalent attitude to-wards the EDC was reflected in the composition of his cabinet, which included both supporters and opponents of the projects. Mendès France now turned to two of these, Bourgès-Maunoury and General Kœnig, the one favourable and the other hostile, asking them to re-examine the entire EDC issue from a disinterested angle. The results were disappointing, mere changes of detail – over veto rights, the supranational dimension, and the stationing of troops – and for which the impetus had come from Mendès France himself. But his subsequent call for five additional protocols was rejected outright by the allies. Against a background of mounting pressure from the United States, the Brussels Conference of 19–23 August saw the Five refuse any further modifications to the project, one that was, after all, originally a French initiative; and the pro-EDC camp in France increased its pressure, with Robert Schuman and André Philip denouncing Mendès France's policy in *Le Figaro* and *Franc-Tireur* just as the conference was opening.

Discouraged, Mendès France was now ready to abandon the EDC as a lost cause, and he decided not to engage his government's responsibility before Parliament over the project it had simply inherited. The risks were indeed serious: three Gaullist ministers hostile to the EDC – Kœnig, Chaban-Delmas, and Lemaire – resigned on 13 August, only to return in September after the Treaty's rejection had provoked the resignation on 31 August of three pro-EDC ministers – Bourgès-Maunoury, Claudius-Petit, and Hugues; an episode which exposed the fragility of Mendès France's composite majority, pointing already to the difficulties ahead. The arguments over the EDC had been exhausted, France was unpopular with her allies, and the executive had remained neutral. Moreover, the EDC had not even been the subject of a final parliamentary debate, for on 29–30 August the Assembly voted by 319 to 264 to adopt the 'question préalable', a procedural motion which effectively closed the highly charged session without a discussion. On this note of anticlimax the EDC was dead. In February 1952 it had had a favourable majority of 40 votes; in August 1954 a majority of 55 was against: the slightness of the difference reflects the intensity of the quarrel and the rigidity of the positions it produced; it suggested that the issue would leave traces in French political life. Decisive in the final outcome had been the split among the Socialists, with 53 voting in favour and 50 opposed. The MRP was outraged, qualifying the result as the 'crime du 30 août' – from now on the hostility, indeed hatred, of some of the MRP leaders for Mendès France was bottomless, and would join with that of the colonial Right for whom he was the 'bradeur d'Empire'.

However, having resolved in a few weeks the three problems which had paralysed his predecessors and done so much to weaken the Republic, Mendès France was at the height of his popularity both at home and abroad. That he was accorded the special economic powers on 10 August is evidence that the deputies also considered the 'contract' of 17 June to have been fully honoured. An exceptional national consensus, even broader than that for Pinay, now worked in favour of Mendès France. His supporters, led by *L'Express*, were ecstatic; the entire *progressiste* and anti-EDC press was enthusiastic; and even the opposition press was, for the moment at least, not unfavourably disposed towards the new government and its leader. The Saturday evening radio broadcasts that Mendès France made a regular feature of his ministry found a large audience, capturing public imagination with their sincere and single-minded tone and message in a way that perhaps no one had done since de Gaulle, encouraging by their energy and conviction hopes that a new democracy might indeed be possible. International opinion was also impressed – Foster Dulles was reported to have described the French premier as a 'superman' – while for the French public, Mendès France quickly became 'Mendès', then simply 'PMF'. More importantly, this support for a leader was issued directly from the sources of sovereignty, short-circuiting to a large extent both Parliament and even the political parties. This was clear from the results of an opinion poll conducted at the end of the summer of 1954: among the electorates of the parties in Mendès France's majority, the proportion of those satisfied was 78 per cent for the Socialists, 85 per cent for the Radicals, and 60 per cent for the Gaullists; more surprising were the findings among the electorates whose party loyalties might have been expected to produce an unfavourable verdict: for the Moderates and the Right the proportion of satisfied was 63 per cent, for the MRP 60 per cent, and for the Communists 40 per cent.[11] Not only did the parliamentary majority for Mendès France have a genuinely popular basis, but the potential opposition to him was partisan and unrepresentative. The Gaullist and Communist threats had been defused, the most urgent of the overseas problems and the intractable EDC quarrel had been settled, and the government had a solid popular audience. The future of the régime at last began to look brighter. The question now would be to see if this broad popular and political consensus was evidence of a real determination to continue on the course hoped for by Mendès France himself, or was not simply the expression of a widespread but inevitably temporary sense of relief.

## The sound of sharpening knives

The period of grace for Mendès France was short-lived. Almost immediately after the dramatic successes of the summer the arguing began again and confidence waned, and this as some of the less fortunate implications of the earlier haste became apparent. The new direction in French foreign policy that Geneva, Tunis, and Brussels appeared to herald did not go unchallenged. After the rejection of the EDC there were fears of a too-rigid attitude *vis-à-vis* Washington; concern was voiced in some quarters over the influence exercised by Georges Boris, with suggestions that he was a dangerous Gaullist and that his strong views on East–West détente were responsible, variously, for the premier's alleged anglophilia and pro-Soviet stance; there was the alarm caused by one of his government's first acts, a refusal to follow the United Fruit's trade embargo on progressive President Arbez's new régime in Guatamala which was believed to threaten American interests, and France's referral of the affair to the Security Council on 21 June.

That Mendès France was going to have to modify his original ambitions and expectations was soon clear from the nature of developments in Indo-China. The mission to Hanoi of Jean Sainteny, the experienced negotiator of 1946, was fruitless, and the policy of co-operation with North Vietnam and steps towards recognition of Communist China came to nothing. In the South, on the other hand, France was forced to adopt an accommodating attitude to American views and objectives in order to avoid further damage to the Western Alliance already shaken by the rejection of the EDC. Thus in mid-August France declared that she would join the South-East Asia Treaty Organization (SEATO) that was to form the basis of the American policy of containment of Communism in this region of the world. This commitment in effect precluded all action – with France as the obvious intermediary – to reconcile the two Vietnams. Emperor Bao Dai was now neglected in favour of Ngo Dinh Diem, the new head of government openly backed by the United States. The situation evolved rapidly. On 8 September the Manila defence pact creating SEATO was signed; on 28 September, Diem demanded a faster evacuation of the French forces; the following day anti-Vietminh agreements were made between General Ely and the Pentagon advisers in Saigon; on 3 November, General Collins was appointed as the White House's special representative in South Vietnam; and on 13 December the United States became formally associated with the French military effort. From 1 January 1955 American aid to France for Indo-China was cut by three-quarters, the last civilian responsibilities were transferred to Diem, and the French expeditionary force began its evacuation that would be complete by April 1956. From now on the burden of Indo-China was entirely Washington's: France had withdrawn completely and without honour – just a few months had been sufficient to dissipate the hopes built up at Geneva of injecting new life into the French Union in Indo-China and of a genuine and uninterrupted dialogue in the Far East.[12]

Similarly, the rapid solution to the German rearmament question – one that the rejection of the EDC had looked likely to delay for a long while – did less than might have been expected to enhance the diplomatic prestige of Mendès France. On 22 August, Mendès France had been able to convince Adenauer that the Paris–Bonn axis was to be the basis of his European policy. This commitment explains why, ignoring the attacks and possible pitfalls, he responded so positively to an initiative from Eden to revive the Western Union of the Brussels Pact, originally set up in 1948 to counter the German threat. The international conference held in London was in fact the opportunity for Italy and Germany to join the Pact's original signatories – a neat solution which offered the double advantage of establishing a degree of European control over the future German army and, since Great Britain was a member of the Brussels Pact, of settling the thorny question of British participation in the defence of Europe. In the course of delicate but optimistic negotiations during September and October, the success of which owed much to the efforts of Mendès France, Eden agreed to maintain British troops on the continent and Adenauer renounced all manufacture of atomic weapons on German territory.

Foster Dulles gave his approval, satisfied that this new solution – considerably less supranational than the EDC – did not compromise the overall authority of the NATO Command. The agreements were concluded in London on 3 October, then re-examined and signed in Paris on 23 October. The Paris Accords secured German approval on the end of the allied zones of occupation, the canalization of the Moselle, and the settling of the future of the Saar by means of a referendum. More importantly, they brought Italy and Germany into the Western European Union of the Brussels Pact; the Council and Assembly of the Union were to encourage disarmament and supervise the particular accords with Great Britain and Germany (over the stationing of troops and the manufacture of certain arms). The signatories could keep independent forces overseas, while over questions of the integration of divisions and decisions on tactics, logistics, and strategy, all the European forces were placed under the authority of SHAPE. However, with Federal Germany now accorded a greater degree of sovereignty than was recognized by the 1952 agreement, adhering directly to the Atlantic Alliance and with no troops outside Europe, it was clear that the Paris Accords had in fact created a German army integrated into NATO.

Not surprisingly, it was this aspect of the agreement which dominated the debate on ratification in the French Assembly of 24–30 December. Only after invoking the survival of his government was Mendès France finally able to get the Paris Accords ratified, by the slender margin of 287 to 260, with 74 abstentions. The Communists, consistent in their hostility to any new German army, now joined the opposition; but all the other parties were divided by the issue, the government losing the votes of many Socialists, Radicals, and Gaullists; and the MRP persisted in its opposition. The entire debate was anachronistic. Many parliamentarians had genuine hopes for disarmament, détente, and European harmony; yet many others rejected these same hopes in the name of the Resistance. And the inconsistency implicit in ratification was glaring: having rejected the EDC, were the deputies now to accept the entry of Germany into the Atlantic Alliance, precisely the outcome France had been seeking to avoid when she launched the EDC in 1951? By ratifying the Paris Accords the French Parliament in effect adopted the solution Washington had advocated since 1950! True, France had at last demonstrated her loyalty to the Atlantic Alliance; but only by an impossibly tortuous route and at the cost of enormous collective bitterness ten years after the end of the war, a bitterness moreover that was now likely to rebound in Parliament on the government responsible for reopening the wound.[13]

The climate of confidence had in fact deteriorated sharply since September. Writing in his 'Bloc-notes' column in *L'Express* François Mauriac pointed to the widespread bewilderment and exasperation of public opinion at the rising tide of hostility to the government, at what he described as the increasingly audible sound of 'couteaux qui s'aiguisent'.[14] Ever since Geneva and Tunis, organized anticommunist opinion had been in uproar, accusing the premier of having betrayed the Atlantic Alliance and of being intent on making France the Soviet bridgehead in the West. A virulent campaign by *Rivarol* and a press of scandal sheets attacked the 'progressisme' of Boris and Nora and the 'neutralisme' of the 'juif Mendès'. It is against this increasingly poisoned background that the so-called 'affaire des fuites' has to be considered. This had begun under the Laniel government, but it did not develop into a full-blown scandal until after Mendès France had come to power, when his Interior Minister, François Mitterrand, was accused of leaking French defence secrets to the PCF and hence to Moscow. Jean Mons, former Resident-General in Tunisia and at this time Secretary of the Committee of National Defence was subsequently condemned for having leaked the reports of the Committee, only to be cleared two years later when two of his subordinates, both of left-wing sympathies, were exposed as the real source of the leaks.[15] It was clear however that the culprits had been manipulated by the French security forces, drawn into a conspiracy involving double agents, passing to them documents that were 'treated' so as to appear to implicate a senior member of the government: the hostile fingers pointed accusingly at the Minister of the Interior. Before Mitterrand's inocence in the 'affaire des fuites' could be established he was made the victim of ferocious parliamentary attacks from the Right and of a campaign of smears and innuendo in which he was accused pell-mell of being a traitor, a homosexual, of encouraging Communist subversion; and was held responsible for the French defeats in Indo-China. With hindsight the significance of this complex imbroglio, many details of which are still obscure, lies in revealing the extent of the régime's internal decay: there was powerful political protection for many of those actively involved; the role and loyalties of the secret services were open to serious questioning; the conspirators had links with several of the political parties (not all of which were of the Right), with dubious organizations like 'Paix et liberté', and with the American intelligence services; clear too in this confluence of anticommunism with the colonial Right's implacable hatred for the 'bradeur' were the depths to which some politicians were prepared to stoop in order to discredit their adversaries. At the time the 'affaire des fuites' was a personal tragedy for Mitterrand, although Mendès France was to remain unwavering in his support for his Interior Minister. It is certain moreover that the doubts repeatedly and quite deliberately cast on the integrity of members of his government constituted a serious handicap for the French premier in international negotiations. And Mendès France was left in no doubt as to the breadth of hostility the Right was now capable of orchestrating against him: at the end of the debate in the Assembly over the 'affaire des fuites' he won the vote of confidence with a slender majority, just 287 to 249, losing the votes of eleven Radicals.

Mendès France was aware of the insidious damage episodes of this kind could cause – in his speech he spoke of the 'usure' of authority – and concluded the wretched debate on the 'affaire des fuites' with an impassioned call for an end to the 'régime de l'intoxication lente', repeating his appeal for a political renewal that would allow energies to be devoted to tackling the real problems faced by France. From October, however, there were growing signs that the determination necessary for such a renewal did not exist; to begin with, not even in his own party. At the Radical Party Congress in Marseille, Mendès France had received warm praise from Herriot, but was powerless to prevent Martinaud-Déplat being elected to the administrative presidency of the party in preference to Daladier. The former thus retained his control of the party machine and the manipulation of the mandates; and many Radicals were already distinctly cool towards *Mendésisme*, readier in fact to rally around René Mayer in an opposition to the new North African policy. The signs were no more encouraging among the other groups in the majority. The strongly pro-EDC Socialist leader, Guy Mollet, refused to agree to a proposal that six Socialists enter the government. Certainly suspicious and probably jealous of Mendès France, Mollet was intent on consolidating his hold over the SFIO deputies and in particular over the personalities who had dared to oppose him with the minority.[16] Out of determination to reinforce the internal discipline of the SFIO party machine, Mollet in fact blocked the solution which might have done much to strengthen the position of the government, and helped instead to persuade its opponents that the SFIO would not commit itself to support Mendès France indefinitely. Lastly, de Gaulle was prepared to give no more than qualified personal support; true, he agreed that his meeting with Mendès France on 13 October be known publicly, and he did praise the energy and resolve of the premier, even agreeing with most of his policies; but he would go no further, and while the Gaullists in the Assembly were now free to develop the very real affinities that existed between Gaullism and *Mendésisme*, de Gaulle himself refused to abandon his position on the political sidelines.

Nor did constitutional reform – the necessity of which had been a subject for discussion since 1950 – look likely to open the way for the sort of fundamental changes Mendès France had called for. Indeed, Mendès France's personal convictions left him little faith in textual tinkering as a panacea for deep-rooted political ills, attaching importance rather to the harnessing of new energies and to changing attitudes. He persevered nonetheless in a wearying parliamentary struggle that culminated in the constitutional law of 7 December 1954 – one of such limited impact that it was quickly baptized the 'réformette'.[17] It was clear from the struggle and its outcome the extent to which weakness and instability were now accepted as almost intrinsic features of the parliamentary system. Thus a proposal allowing the investiture to be secured by a simple majority – a tacit recognition of the chronic difficulty of finding broad-based majorities – encountered little opposition; neither did one providing for the presentation of all the ministers before the investiture debate – thus giving even greater scope for horse-trading over the distribution of portfolios. Conversely, the proposal to give the Council of the Republic the legislative powers of the Third Republic's Senate, including the right to initiate laws, was secured by only two votes. And on the two crucial points – the right of dissolution and electoral reform – Mendès France was unable to impose his views. True, it was agreed that in future the premier could assure the interim in the event of a dissolution; but the one change which would have done most to strengthen the position of the executive, the notion of a legislative mandate or contract between the Assembly and the government – a development Mendès France had pointed to in his 17 June speech – was rejected by the deputies. Lastly, a proposal for a return to smaller constituencies (the *scrutin d'arrondissement*), something the Radicals had called for since the Liberation, was easily repulsed. The experience over the 'réformette' showed that the key to political renewal did not lie in changes to the constitutional texts: and by pursuing the issue Mendès France had lost a little more of his parliamentary support.

Even economic and social policy, the domain where the competence of de Gaulle's former Minister of National Economy was perhaps disputed the least, did nothing to stem the tide of hostility.[18] In fact, there was little time to act here; not until a final ministerial reshuffle of 20 January 1955 had moved Robert Buron to Finance and Edgar Faure to Foreign Affairs was Mendès France at last free to co-ordinate the elaboration of a long-term policy for this area. With inflation under control and economic growth revived, there was moreover a general complacency over this aspect of the government's action. In the minds of many deputies the special economic powers accorded on 10 August in the euphoria that followed Geneva were merely an extension to the spring of 1955 of the eighteen-month plan drawn up by Edgar Faure under the Laniel government.

In fact, an innovative modern policy was embarked upon, with the full co-operation of the Finance Ministry. Now that economic growth was steady the priority was to accelerate it still further by concentrating on the weakest points of the economy: regional development, industrial reconversion, and the modernization of agriculture. Approximately 120 decrees – many of whose long-term repercussions under the Fifth Republic deserve closer study – formed the framework for this policy of active public support for the economy; a policy which could be backed, at least for the moment, by solid financial measures thanks to the funds released by the end of the year in Indo-China. For agriculture came cheap loans, price support schemes for milk and meat producers, encouragement for industrial crops such as maize and colza, and a programme of conversion to fruit and rice production in the wine-growing regions of the Languedoc. In the industrial sector there were measures to favour company restructuring and the beginnings of a policy to improve the training of the workforce, efforts spearheaded by the nationalized firms which, following the example of Renault, the authorities wanted to make the showcase of France's new economic dynamism. Policies, then, of encouragement and support, with the emphasis deliberately placed on the creation of an efficient market economy capable of performing well in international competition. There were conflicting political reactions: *néo-capitalisme*, intoned the Communists; intolerable *dirigisme*, shrieked the Right and the employers. But in fact, with only a few months in which to act, the question of long-term economic modernization was not to become a major issue in the public debate.

The beginnings of an innovative social policy met with a similarly muted or indifferent response. Moves were made to establish regular contractual bargaining with the trade unions; loans for the construction of municipal housing were doubled, with 350 000 new homes per year set as the target in an attempt to make up the accumulated shortfall; and an ambitious programme for education and scientific research was launched, with, for its goals, the construction of 14 000 new classrooms and the recruitment of 12 000 teachers in six months, plus reforms in the universities and a stimulus to nuclear research.[19] These far-sighted measures generated little enthusiasm among the parliamentarians; on the other hand, an anti-alcohol campaign launched in the interest of public health provoked an immediate hostile response. With decrees of 20 November restricting the privileges of the *bouilleurs de cru* (home-distillers), tighter controls over both licensing and the sales of the most noxious of the distillations available on the market, the government opened a Pandora's box of vested interests and parliamentary opposition. Action in this field was long overdue; as deputy for a Norman constituency since 1932, Mendès France had first-hand knowledge of the ravages caused by alcoholism in rural France.[20] He did not hesitate now to attach his name to the campaign against alcohol abuse, allowing *L'Express* to make much of his liking for milk and publicizing his views on the desirability of distributing milk to schoolchildren. The issue was an explosive one, mobilizing the *bouilleurs de cru*, the agricultural organizations of the FNSEA, the lobby groups, and entire communities in some regions. Pressure was brought to bear on deputies from rural constituencies in a campaign of strenuous opposition to measures whose success, it was claimed, spelt certain national decline. Pierre Poujade, by now a rapidly rising figure, soon proved himself as the most accomplished champion of this noisy resistance, lacing his rabble-rousing tirades against the policies of 'Mendès-lolo' with eulogies of wine's wholesome qualities, and thinly veiled anti-Semitic attacks on the premier and his unpatriotic taste for milk. And not all parliamentarians were unreceptive to Poujade's venomous rhetoric.

This fracas weakened but did not bring down the government: the final crisis came over the much more serious problems in North Africa. In Tunisia the momentum created by the 'Carthage declaration' had been lost, and the hostility of the French community and the colonial administration, plus divisions between conciliators and extremists within the Destour movement, threatened to bring the negotiations to a standstill.

Repeated efforts by Fouchet, Boyer de Latour, and Mendès France himself were necessary before the Tunisian government eventually managed to conclude a cease-fire agreement with the *fellaghas* on 22 November. But in January 1955, with the situation still tense, the general negotiations got under way again, having now to deal only with the vital questions of the control of the police and the stationing of French troops in the henceforth internally autonomous country. The position in Morocco was much more difficult – the 'Carthage declaration' had not produced the positive effect hoped for and tension and violence had continued to mount. An official inquiry conducted by Vincent Monteil revealed the extent to which detained nationalists were mistreated in the prisons, and the new Resident-General, Francis Lacoste, was unable to loosen the colonial lobby's hold on the police and administration. In addition, Mendès France's position over the Moroccan problem was not entirely free of ambiguity; at once reluctant to raise directly the question of the exiled Sultan's return – an initiative likely to have had an effect similar to that of the 'Carthage declaration' in Tunisia – and convinced that in 'feudal' Morocco the evolution towards internal autonomy would have to be very gradual. With this approach he satisfied neither side: the delay disappointed his supporters in the 'France-Maghreb' movement, whereas the Right and the MRP saw it as a stalling tactic, a prelude to the 'abandonment' foreshadowed by his Tunisian policy.

It was in Algeria, quite without warning, that the storm broke. On 1 November 1954, a wave of violence involving seventy incidents in thirty places, most of them in the Kabylie and Aurès regions, left eight dead, among them a young French schoolteacher, Guy Monnerot. Although caught completely unawares, the police quickly established that the obviously co-ordinated attacks were the first stages of an armed insurrection planned by an organization unknown to them, the Comité révolutionnaire d'unité et d'action (CRUA); on 10 October this group had founded a Front de libération nationale (FLN), whose objectives were unlimited revolution and independence for Algeria. The response from Mendès France and Mitterrand was to meet force with force, immediately dispatching reinforcements of CRS and paratroopers to Algeria, outlawing the MTLD of Messali Hadj and rounding up its militants. As yet no one spoke of war, but the signs of contagion were obvious: after Tunisia and Morocco it was the turn of Algeria. No serious attempt was made to analyse the deeper causes of the rebellion – the 'banditry' in fact brought from the Mendès France government a determination matched only by that of the hostile coalition now intent on bringing it down. On 12 November, Mendès France announced to the Assembly that there would be no compromise with rebels who threatened the peace of France and the security of the Republic; Mitterrand declared that 'L'Algérie c'est la

France' and reaffirmed the government's determination to uphold the authority of Parliament, the Constitution, and the rule of law over the whole of French territory, 'des Flandres au Congo'.[21] Between November and January, French military forces in Algeria were increased from 57 000 to 83 000, roughly 2000 suspects were arrested, and a plan of reform was prepared that would allow the revised 1947 statute to be applied at last. And on 25 January, as the French forces launched a vast operation in Kabylie, Jacques Soustelle, a liberal, was appointed Governor-General in Algeria. In Soustelle, a Gaullist and senior figure of the RPF, an opponent of the EDC, a distinguished ethnologist, and a left-wing intellectual, the government could feel confident of satisfying the members of the majority.

Hopes that this show of firmness might reassure those who, having applauded at the time of the 'Carthage declaration', were now highly alarmed by the developments in Algeria, were in vain: instead it served merely to crystallize all the discontents and hatreds held in suspension since Geneva. It was now, for example, that reports began to circulate that Bidault had been on the point of securing a far better settlement in Indo-China; there were accusations that the rejection of the EDC had been on Moscow's orders; allegations that the reports of French torture in Morocco were the work of the traitors in the government. René Mayer, deputy for Constantine, now had little trouble in uniting all the currents of opposition to Mendès France – the anticommunists, the pro-EDC camp, the MRP, the colonial pressure groups, the vested interests the government had offended – fuelling the hostility with misleading speculations over the government's intentions in Algeria, suggesting, for example, that Mitterrand planned changes to the *communes-mixtes* which would mean an end to European political supremacy.[22] On the evening of 5 February 1955, at the end of a debate on North Africa, the government was defeated by 319 to 273 votes, with 22 abstentions. Voting for Mendès France were the Socialists, the UDSR, two-thirds of the Radicals and Gaullists, and a few Moderates; in the hostile coalition were the Communists, the MRP, the Right and the Moderates, seventeen Gaullists, and twenty Radicals led by René Mayer. When the result was announced, Mendès France, in defiance of parliamentary custom, mounted the tribune of the Assembly to reply to those who had brought down his government; drowned out by an angry commotion from the Communists, the MRP, and the Right, he could do little more than state his belief that 'men come and go, national needs remain'. The 230-day experiment to inject the machinery of the State with dynamism was over: an opinion poll conducted at the time showed that 53 per cent believed the Mendès France government to have done a better job than its prodecessors.[23] Of course, hopes for a political renewal did not vanish completely on 6 February; the question now was to see whether *Mendésisme* was possible without Mendès

France. For the moment, however, with the benefit of exceptionally favourable economic conditions, the Fourth Republic could safely afford to indulge its taste for parliamentary games.

### At the eye of the storm

The fall of Mendès France was followed by the long ministerial crisis of February 1955. President Coty knew that the solution still lay with the divided Radicals, and to lead a new Centrist government he favoured the competent and adaptable Edgar Faure, capable of continuing the existing policies without arousing an impossible hostility in the Assembly. Yet passing directly from Mendès France to his fellow Radical Faure was clearly out of the question: the various groups responsible for bringing down the government had first to be given an opportunity to present their alternatives. That the support for Mendès France had indeed been an exceptional episode in the life of the Assembly was clear from the parliamentary manoeuvres which filled this interregnum – manoeuvres made even more absorbing, though no less futile, for those involved by the constitutional 'réformette' under which the absolute majority of 314 votes was no longer required for the investiture of a government. In quick succession then came an attempt by Pinay – rejected by the MRP, the SFIO, and the Radicals – by Pierre Pflimlin, too pro-EDC and MRP to be acceptable to the SFIO and the Gaullists; finally, by the Socialists with Christian Pineau – whose efforts to revive the Centre-Left solution were blocked by the Right and the Gaullists. Now that all the contenders had tried and failed, Coty's original solution could be accepted: Edgar Faure received the investiture on 23 February by 369 to 210 votes, backed by everyone except the Communists and Socialists. Faure had reverted to the practice of negotiating directly with the groups in the Assembly before the investiture and the ministry he formed was a judicious mixture of the elements in his majority. The MRP, savouring its revenge on Mendès France, placed Pflimlin at Finance, Schuman at Justice, Teitgen at Overseas, and Bacon at Labour; the Républicains sociaux had four portfolios, including Defence, left in the hands of Kœnig; the Radicals also had four, with Bourgès-Maunoury at Interior; while the Right obtained five, with, notably, Antoine Pinay at the Quai d'Orsay. As an exercise in political compromise or *dosage*, the Faure cabinet could not be faulted. Nor was the outcome an undesirable one: power now went to an experienced figure, one well placed for the last two years to understand the aspirations of the French people to stability and peace, and who was sufficiently supple to elevate their satisfaction to the status of an alternative political consensus based on 'means' rather than 'ideals'. Like Mendès France, Faure realized that for the bulk of the population sharing the fruits of expansion and economic modernization, with better standards of living, improved amenities, and more social services, counted for more than questions over the Atlantic Alliance, Europe, Germany, and colonial wars. New policies for détente, peace, co-operation, and exchange were therefore required. Where Faure differed from his predecessor, however, was in being ready to try to wean the politicians gradually and painlessly away from the old quarrels.

This classic ministry and its conservative leader had the good fortune to come to power at a moment when, despite persisting bottlenecks and archaisms, awareness of change and the role of modernization grew rapidly. In the space of a few months some of the most striking signs of the developments that were changing the face of France became apparent – the dam at Donzère-Mondragon went into service, the oil pipeline linking Paris to the lower Seine was completed, petrol from Parentis went onto the market, Pierre Dreyfus and Louis Armand modernized Renault and the SNCF, the metallurgical industries were progressing, scientific research was buoyant, atomic energy seemed near, and the first graduates of the ENA were about to come to grips with the practical problems of the administration. Economic growth was rising by 5 per cent a year, national income had grown by 25 per cent between 1952 and 1955; trade was expanding, notably in the most dynamic sectors, and in 1955, for the first time since the war, the commercial balance was positive. And higher demand in turn stimulated production; increased currency earnings eased the budgetary imbalance, reducing the humiliation of the search for foreign loans and advances. True, these sorts of changes were not without victims – victims for whom Poujade was already the champion – but the signs of material progress were now unmistakable.

Armed with renewed special economic powers, the Faure government favoured these developments with policies that continued those of Mendès France. The Second Plan, for the period 1954–7, presented by Jean Monnet's successor Etienne Hirsch, was voted on 27 May 1955. More flexible and with more diversified finances than the First Plan, it was an accurate reflection of the general evolution, giving priority to energy, regional development, and the provision of education, sanitation, and social amenities. Programmes were voted for telecommunications, the merchant marine, and the electrification of the railways, while the project to canalize the Moselle went to an advanced stage of planning. Help for agriculture was maintained, and an official body (the Fonds de garantie mutuelle) was set up in May to organize markets and exports. For industry the emphasis was placed on encouraging essential mergers, and the new Fonds pour le développement économique et sociale (FDES) provided a better allocation of loans. A housing policy drawn up by Roger Duchet enabled the construction of new homes to finally reach 240 000 in 1955 and in fact prepared the way for the major urban development schemes of the years to come. Rounding off this collection of measures was the beginning of a fiscal reform which, even if it did not eliminate the fraud and injustice, favoured companies wishing to make investments (decree of 17 September), as well as trying to calm the retailers by increasing tax reliefs and reducing in June local taxes and taxes on turnover and added value (TVA). These policies had an appreciable international dimension. In July the European Payments Union was enlarged, while a Franco-German agreement of August accelerated the reductions of quotas and the moves towards free trade in Western Europe begun in January. At the Messina Conference in June, France had figured prominently among the members of the ECSC enthusiastic to follow up proposals from the Benelux countries for a broader European economic union – the Common Market was taking shape and this time the initiative was not immediately condemned by the French employers. In short then, the State concentrated its efforts on encouraging the success of a rejuvenated capitalism, both at home and internationally, striking a balance between intervention and liberalism, with the nationalized sector conserving its role of leadership and example, and with the Plan to keep a look out for eventual difficulties.

The social consequences of this economic dynamism were not slow to be felt. True, a resurgence of demand–pull inflation was already apparent; true also that inequalities persisted and that some sectors lagged noticeably behind others. This was clear from the summer of violent conflicts in the shipbuilding industries of the Loire-Inférieure. Shrunken real incomes, the structural difficulties of the naval construction industry, and the merging of the shipyards of the Loire and Penthoët were the factors behind the unrest at Saint-Nazaire and Nantes. The union movement here was strong and militant, dominated by the CGT and FO but with the CFTC also able to play a significant role. The tension finally eased in October with salary increases of 22 per cent at Saint-Nazaire and of 12–15 per cent at Nantes, but this only after a wave of go-slow strikes, brutal CRS repression of riots, abortive conciliations, and an intransigent attitude from the employers: the six weeks of acute social conflicts left an indelible mark in the memory of the workforce and the communities involved.[24] However, this unrest did not spread – its confinement to one sector and one region bears witness to the economic conditions which were now on the whole favourable to wage-earners.

This quiescence owed much to the fact that the public sector, so decisive in any movement of widespread unrest, was now calm. The troubles of 1953 had resulted in a major restoration of purchasing power among workers in the public sector, implemented in July 1955 with increases of 14 per cent for wages and 18 per cent for pensions, increases made possible by the easing of the difficulties in public finances. Of particular importance, actual and potential, was the agreement signed at Renault on 15 September. The basis of this was contractual, with the two sides agreeing that during two years all possible means of conciliation would be used before the recourse to strikes or lock-outs; in return came a guaranteed 4 per cent annual wage increase and recognition for the gains already acquired (three weeks holiday with pay, pension rights, sick pay, and paid bank holidays). Prepared by the technocrats of the public sector, the Renault agreement was favourably received by the unions (with the exception of the CGT which denounced it as a ploy to curb the militancy of the working classes), by the more open-minded elements of the CNPF, and by the Faure government. There were hopes that this example from a major nationalized company of an intelligent contractual approach to wage negotiations – a landmark in the history of chronically poor French industrial relations – would serve as a model for similar agreements in the private sector.

Coming after the unrest of 1953 and the urgent measures of 1954, the steady diffusion of growth's economic and social benefits fostered a climate of peace and optimism in 1955. The Faure government was able to take advantage of this favourable domestic context to attend to other, more problematic issues. The general improvement in the European economies now began to find a clearer political expression. Since the Messina Conference, an intergovernmental committee of experts under Paul-Henri Spaak was hard at work examining the details of a general European Common Market and a European Community for the peaceful uses of atomic energy – work which had gone ahead without France raising the familiar obstacle of the supranational character of the future institutions. The committee's findings were the basis for the successful Venice Conference of May 1956, the final stage in fact before the conclusion of the Treaty of Rome the following year. And there was a significant amelioration in Franco-German relations; Faure and Pinay secured the ratification of the Paris Accords on 30 March from the Council of the Republic; France came to terms with German reticence over the new statute for the Saar; and there was a mutual recognition that the partition of Germany was likely to be lasting and that it probably actually contributed to stability between the two power blocs. More generally, the question of Austrian independence was settled in May, and there were other signs which made détente appear a credible policy. The Geneva Conference in July saw Eisenhower and Bulganin make efforts to find acceptable compromises; Krushchev was reconciled with Tito; and the Soviet Union multiplied its calls for disarmament and allayed American anxieties over the Far East. These developments strengthened French diplomacy's growing conviction that a new era in international relations had indeed dawned, one in which peaceful co-existence and co-operation were the most realistic policies for France. This was the lesson to be drawn from the entry in force of the Third

World to the international stage marked by the Bandoeng Conference of Afro-Asian States in April. Or from the course of events in Indo-China, where the Diem government, completely subservient to the United States, and having repudiated the Geneva settlement, was now procrastinating over the elections: the overthrow of Emperor Bao Dai in June brought hardly any reaction from France.

In Tunisia and Morocco this new positive attitude was to lead eventually to solutions which were both the least costly for France and the most promising for the future. And here Edgar Faure even borrowed some of his predecessor's energetic style to hasten the outcome. His dramatic meeting with Bourguiba at Matignon on 21 April saved the negotiations over Tunisia that were once again in danger of becoming bogged down. On 3 June he signed a series of conventions with the leader of the Tunisian government, Tahar Ben Ammar; in addition to establishing the internal autonomy of Tunisia, these protected the rights of the European community, provided for a French military presence at Bizerte and a say for France in Tunisian diplomacy and defence policy, and this without blocking the now foreseeable evolution towards independence. In the space of a few weeks Bourguiba returned in triumph to Tunis, the French Parliament gave its massive approval to the agreements, and colonial pressure groups bowed to the inevitable. The virtues of this painless decolonization were widely recognized, and the way was now open for a peaceful co-operation in the line traced by the 'Carthage declaration'.[25]

The same logic encountered considerably more difficulties in its application to the crisis in Morocco. Faure, extremely hostile to Arafa but anxious not to antagonize conservative opinion already on the defensive and present in his cabinet, proceeded cautiously but purposefully towards his goal, choosing as his representative Georges Izard, counsel to the Sultan and an active member of 'France-Maghreb'. He refused to be forced into hasty action by the wave of violence which shook Morocco in June, with more than 800 incidents and in which the liberal industrialist and press magnate Lemaigre-Dubreuil was assassinated, using it instead as the opportunity to appoint the dependable Gilbert Grandval as Resident-General on 20 June. Fully backed by Faure, Grandval took vigorous steps to halt the slide: El Glaoui was boycotted, undisciplined members of the administration were dismissed, the 'Présence française' agitators were expelled, and the police was purged of its blatantly pro-European elements. Grandval, having braved the attacks of which he was the object, announced his conclusion on 1 August: only the quick return of the exiled Sultan would restore peace to Morocco. However, Faure continued to steer his prudent middle course, curbing the zeal of the Resident-General but resisting the conflicting pressures on him – from inside the divided cabinet, from the military in Morocco, from 'France-Maghreb', from Marshal Juin. A team of experts under Jacques Duhamel was charged with secret negotiations towards a settlement. Fresh violence, urban and, for the first time, rural, erupted in Morocco on 20 August 1955, the second anniversary of the Sultan's deposition, with the massacre of more than fifty Europeans. In the wake of this Grandval was replaced by Boyer de Latour, strongly influenced by Marshal Juin and quickly outwitted by the European community in Rabat. But the pressure from Faure's representatives on Arafa to abdicate in favour of a Council of the Throne, the preliminary to the return of the Sultan, was now successful. And although the Gaullist ministers Raymond Triboulet and General Kœnig resigned on 6 October, the colonial hardliners, fearful of another upsurge of violence in Morocco, did not set in motion the mechanism for bringing down the government. Against a background of growing concern at the United Nations over the situation in Morocco, Faure's liberal solution slowly but surely took shape: on 25 October El Glaoui himself pledged allegiance to Ben Youssef.

A joint declaration defining future relations between France and Morocco, based on the vague but mutually acceptable formula of 'l'indépendance dans l'interdépendance', was signed by Ben Youssef in Paris on 6 November. It was as Sultan Mohammed V that the exile of Madagascar returned in triumph to Rabat on 16 November. Final recognition of Moroccan independence came on 2 March 1956 (under the Mollet government), and on 15 June a similar convention was concluded between France and Tunisia. In November France sponsored the entry of the two new states to the United Nations, and opened with them a policy of co-operation.

This outcome was of course entirely consistent with the evolution of the post-war world. To secure it, however, had required considerable skill and determination from Mendès France and Faure: and in the process the latter's parliamentary majority had proved as fragile as that of his predecessor. On 9 October, during a difficult debate over Morocco, the Faure government was saved only by a move from the Socialists: the Right and the Gaullists now deserted the government, whereas the Socialists and Communists approved its Moroccan policy. In more stable circumstances this support might have formed the basis of a new majority, but developments in Algeria and in metropolitan France were now to shatter the peace and show that political renewal had not survived the summer.

### 'Mendésisme' or 'Poujadisme'?

If one were attempting to identify what was really at stake during these first, relatively peaceful months of the Faure government, when the policy successes began to accumulate and social tension fell, it could, with only slight exaggeration, be summed up as the conflict between *Mendésisme* and *Poujadisme*. For it was on the outcome of this struggle that the success or failure of political renewal hung; this was the real issue of the moment and one that the war in Algeria served merely to obscure and ultimately to smother completely.

What, then, was 'Mendésisme'? In its broadest sense it could be defined as loyalty to the ideas of Mendès France. And the most important of these was the urgent need to extend to French political life some of the modernization that was beginning to have such a momentous impact on French economy and society. Hopes that such a change might be possible could find encouragement in developments in the Radical Party which, under Herriot, had elected Mendès France to the vice-presidency in May 1955 and appeared to accept his ideas as the bases for its own regeneration. Yet the hopes generated by *Mendésisme* were multiform – there was a sense in which it was all things to all men, a danger that it would overstep the framework of Radicalism and strict parliamentarianism envisaged by Mendès France himself. The impatient enthusiasm of some of his younger followers and the sometimes exaggerated approach of the team at *L'Express* point to the ways in which Mendès France could be handicapped by his most fervent supporters. Indeed, on a number of occasions Mendès France expressed public irritation at being identified with positions which went far beyond his utterances as a Radical, as a economic expert, or as a lecturer at the ENA. In short, Mendès France risked becoming a prisoner of the doctrine that carried his name. And the ambiguities were only multiplied by the importance that the doctrine acquired at many levels of political, economic, and administrative life under the Fifth Republic and among the new Left of the political clubs or the PSU of the 1960s. What it never became, however, was an organized political force: just as there could be no Gaullism without de Gaulle, so there could be no *Mendésisme* without Mendès France. In one sense perhaps this was not the fatal shortcoming it seems: so closely did *Mendésisme* echo the moods and needs of the period that its message in fact frequently transcended the more obvious political differences. Thus Edgar Faure, though a political opponent of Mendès France, adopted policies directly inspired by *Mendésisme*, and others were to draw on its themes to enrich other, more familiar areas of the French political landscape. That *Mendésisme* influenced the attitudes and choices of an entire generation is incontestable. Especially receptive were élite groups and future decision-makers; for many of these its mixture of technocracy and Republican democracy, the rejection of the sterile divisions of the past (including the class struggle), and the emphasis placed equally on the public sector and on free investment, all seemed to offer a real alternative to stagnation and immobility. The ambiguities of *Mendésisme* make it hard to pinpoint exactly where its appeal was concentrated, but a general profile of its audience would certainly include the following: urban rather than rural; in the tertiary sector rather than among manual workers; in the middle-class groups benefiting from expansion and change rather than among the groups facing decline; and, surprisingly given the secularism of Mendès France, strong among the Christian youth movements. To the profile could be added, possibly as a failing, that *Mendésisme* proved consistently better at identifying problems than at acting upon the political mechanisms for their resolution. Among the most important themes that entered the arena of debate under the label of *Mendésisme* were the need for a State that was both modern and socially just; a respect for democracy and, related to this, the priority of public opinion over the political parties; a rejection of Communism; a support for the struggles of colonial peoples and a call for international co-operation; and, naturally, the return to power of Mendès France. The profile would be incomplete without considering those whose animosity and hatred *Mendésisme* aroused: the defenders of a traditional France untouched by modernization; the strict Marxists and the unrepentant liberals; the enemies of the Progressistes; the imperialists; the 'BOF' – the groups in French society, popularly identified with the petty tradesmen (BOF = *beurre, œufs, et fromages*), who had done well out of the war and the provisions crisis; and, unfailingly, the anti-Semites.

The modernity that found a champion in Mendès France, and that Edgar Faure had for a time looked able to introduce gradually into the political system, provoked a massive and hydra-headed opposition. At the root of the disparate coalition of resistance to modernity lay less a hatred of progress *per se*; rather, a desire to assure a future for existing positions and privileges. For the economic and social change associated with modernization was eroding the position of hitherto prominent groups in French society, robbing them, in the process, of their political audience. It is this which explains their hurried – in some cases almost desperate – mobilization of any theme likely to make their voices heard: antiparliamentarianism, hostility to Paris and the technocrats, protest over taxation, a defence of *l'Algérie française*. The most conspicuous and best known of these agitations was Poujadism, and it illustrates the essential characteristics of the other, often more discreet resistances to change of these years.[26]

In the two years since its beginnings at Saint-Céré in the summer of 1953, Pierre Poujade's protest had gained real momentum, with the holding of mass meetings, carrying out raids on tax offices, and infiltrating professional organizations. Poujade had proved himself as an effective orator and a canny populist leader; he presented his protest almost as a moral crusade, protesting loyalty to a Republic of 'good sense', though ready to employ tactics of street agitation reminiscent of those used by the *ligueurs* between the wars. Trailing in Poujade's wake were the Communists, ever attentive to popular discontent (the PCF did not condemn the movement until the autumn of 1955), some small groups of the extreme Right, Gaullist militants disappointed by the RPF's compromise with the parliamentary system, and the defenders of *l'Algérie fran-ȼaise*. By far the most important, however, were the 3 million-odd self-employed – for the most part shopkeepers, artisans, and small farmers – who flocked to Poujade's meetings and formed the bulk of his electorate. The revolt of these last was born of economic growth. Until the 1950s a buoyant demand and persistent shortages had encouraged an artificial expansion of the service sector of the French economy. This expansion had been particularly strong in retailing: 100 000 new shops had opened each year since 1940; by 1954 they numbered 1.3 million, occupying 2 240 000 persons of whom 1 250 000 were paid employees. These shops, usually small family concerns, had low turnovers but generous profit margins, and owed their success to inflation, which made it possible to anticipate on price increases; indeed, for many of them this was a period of considerable prosperity. Around 1952, however, conditions began to turn against the retailers: restrictions came to an end, goods were beginning to flood onto a market in which demand was still not fully rekindled, there were the first signs of the changes in production which were to revolutionize distribution and prepare for the supermarkets, and, above all, inflation ended. For the most vulnerable of the retailers the consequences were dramatic. True, the era of bulk purchasing had not yet arrived, but the choice available to consumers was widening, and with prices stagnant the small retailers could no longer cover their inevitable losses. Under these conditions taxation quickly became an insupportable burden and the most obvious target for protest. Although the roots of the Poujadist revolt lay in long-term economic change, the movement had anti-fiscal objectives, borrowing, for example, from the themes of the Ligue des contribuables of the 1930s. And in fact Poujadism can be situated in a long tradition in French history of resistance to taxation and the administration in Paris. The decision by the Mendès France government on 14 August 1954 to accept in a finance bill the so-called Dorey amendment allowing for the imprisonment of anyone who resisted tax inspection only increased the anti-fiscal dimension of the protest. This inopportune measure hardened the resolve of all those who had experienced the humiliation of the often brutal inspections by the 'polyvalents', the reduction of tax relief, and the clamp-down on fiscal fraud. Conditions were ripe for the revolt to spread.

This phase of the Poujadist revolt was in fact short-lived. With the return of inflation in 1956 and especially in 1957, this time by demand, conditions swung back in favour of the retailers, enabling them to cover their losses, pay their taxes, and even forget the genuine fiscal injustice of which they had often been victims; in spite of efforts by Edgar Faure, this quelling of agitation over the tax system in fact put an end to hopes for significant fiscal reform under the Fourth Republic. The Poujadist movement had, never-theless, drawn attention to the resentment and panic of a backward France in danger of being swept away by modernization; the France – as André Siegfried put it – of those 'who struggle noisily, with the frantic gestures of drowning men'.[27] Support for Poujadism was concentrated to the south of a line from Saint-Malo to Geneva, that is in the economically stagnant re-gions, those worst hit by rural depopulation – the 'désert français' – where Poujade's message found ready audiences in the shops, family firms, work-shops, and cafés of the declining small towns and *bourgades*. And to this France of the Poujadists could be opposed the modern France of the North, the demographic vitality of the important urban agglomerations, the large impersonal companies and corporations, the administration and the technocrats, and, naturally, Paris. Born of a powerlessness to stem the tide of modernization, Poujade's revolt was backward-looking, invoking the glories of France and the uncomplicated patriotism of the pre-1914 primary school, coming close to Vichy with its exaltation of a social life based on the family and the small community, a way of life now under attack from the technocrats, the tax inspectors, and the politicians.

This mobilization of the casualties of economic growth and their sincere if confused evocation of the past was not wholly antipathetic: no doubt today many of the Poujadist themes would be looked on with favour by the ecologists. At the time, however, Poujade alarmed the French political classes and certainly helped to point up many of the failings of the 'system'. For the progressive intelligentsia of Paris he was a Fascist – 'Poujadolf' was the name *L'Express* gave him – and in evidence there was his xenophobia, his rantings against homosexuals, and his overtly anti-Semitic attacks on Mendès France; and around Poujade naturally gravitated the extremist groups now ready to use force against the régime of the 'bradeurs d'Empire'. But the charge was off-target: Poujade's great popular appeal was not based on Fascist leanings, but rather on his combination of a hostility to the parliamentary system, an almost naive faith in a benevolent Republic and in the value of plain speaking to confound the politicians or 'vendus'. On 24 January 1955, 100 000 provincials converged on the Porte de Versailles in response to Poujade's call; in February he held a capacity audience at the Vel' d'Hiv' spellbound; and on 18 March he was actually in the Assembly to harangue the deputies in an attempt to get the Dorey amendment repealed. But whatever his opponents might claim, Poujade's ambitions did not include a *putsch*: in the autumn of 1955 his programme was as strong on populist causes as it was weak on remedies, with only vague calls for the 'Etats généraux' to be summoned, the abolition of the divisive political parties, and the harmony of all social groups in a 'frater-nité française' in which the ideal would be the self-employed.

No doubt the excesses of Poujadism contributed to a heightening of national tension; no doubt either that its appeal was a dangerously irresponsible and negative one.[28] Having said this, the fact remains that Poujadism did focus attention on what were after all the real issues of the moment: the chronic weakness of the Republic of the political parties, the fact that modernization had victims as well as benefits, and that a far-reaching change in the political system was necessary to restore confidence. The Poujadists, however, could do little. Given the firmness of the régime's response to violence and intimidation since 1947 their agitation was likely to remain volatile but verbal, while in the long run a return of economic conditions favourable to the shopkeepers and self-employed would bring the movement to a standstill. That Poujade's movement did not stagnate and then fade away was due to its mobilization of a major new cause: Algeria. With the defence of *l'Algérie française*, taken up in earnest after the Poujadist congress at Algiers in November 1954, Poujade had a powerful new rallying cry, one which touched widespread and deep-seated anxieties, allowing him to capture the attention of social groups otherwise unreceptive to his message, and to consolidate his protest. In doing so Poujade helped to preclude all calm reflection on the subject of political renewal. The question of whether in 1955, without the Algerian drama, the political system of the Fourth Republic could have been stabilized and the effects of modernization digested painlessly cannot be answered. What is certain is that Algeria reintroduced into French political life exactly the sorts of urgent pressures that Geneva had been thought to relieve, reinforcing the contradictions and highlighting the weaknesses of the 'politics of the lesser evil'. Not only did the Algerian problem come to overshadow all others, but it postponed all attempts at renewal.

The signs of deterioration in Algeria were unmistakable. A resurgence of terrorism in March had led to the declaration of a state of emergency on 3 April, strengthening law-and-order measures and transferring considerable civil authority to the military in the troubled areas. The rebellion was still far from general, but the apparent indifference of the population in fact encouraged the FLN to launch the classic cycle of terrorism and repression of revolutionary guerrilla warfare; it improved its recruitment and refused to develop the tentative contacts made by Soustelle's emissaries, such as Germaine Tillion and Vincent Monteil, who had to abandon their efforts. Important reinforcements arrived, taking the total French forces in Algeria to more than 100 000 men by the summer of 1955. But the heavy motorized units were only really suitable for protecting the roads and strategic points, and as yet there was no systematic patrolling of the countryside. With hindsight the situation in the summer of 1955, when both sides marked time, was not irretrievable. The official French policy of integration, under which Algeria was considered an integral part of France and the linguistic, cultural, and religious specificity of the Algerian population recognized, was embodied in an ambitious and not unattractive plan announced on 1 June. Although opposed to Soustelle's policy, the Europeans in Algeria were not yet mobilized by desperation or anger, and good relations between the two communities were still possible. In short, the war in Algeria had not yet assumed the character of an out-and-out political, religious, and popular struggle. The turning-point was reached with the general insurrection which broke out in the region between Constantine, Philippeville, and Guelma on 20 August. At El Halia and Ain Abid, 123 Europeans, among them women and children, were savagely massacred in an outburst of popular agitation that had been assiduously cultivated by the FLN commandos of the Northern Constantine Wilaya. More than anything else this appalling episode served to drive a wedge between the European and Muslim communities, just, of course, as the FLN had intended. The Philippeville massacre was ruthlessly avenged, with 1273 'rebels' killed, according to French sources, 12 000 according to the FLN. The effect on the liberal Soustelle was dramatic: profoundly shaken by the savagery and realizing that the FLN had secured its first crucial victory he now swung sharply into the camp of unlimited repression. The tragic circle was complete: with all Muslims henceforth regarded by one side as potential rebels, and the FLN seen by the other to be waging the holy war of the *moudjahidin*, the trial of strength had begun.

It was generally believed in Paris that with the reforms ready the simplest solution would be to implement the modified 1947 statute as quickly as possible. In September the French government reiterated its determination to hold onto Algeria and to persevere with the policy of integration. But if there was a growing awareness that the time had gone when reforms could simply be handed down to Algeria, the question now was that of finding someone with whom they could be negotiated. The bases for dialogue with the Algerians were fast disappearing: on 26 September, sixty-one Muslim members of the Algerian Assembly announced their rejection of the principle of integration; the moderate Ferhat Abbas rallied to the FLN cause; and the nationalists embarrassed France by raising the Algerian question at the United Nations. At the same time that Albert Camus was calling in vain for a 'trêve du sang' in *L'Express*, the first French paratroop divisions were already waging a counter-guerrilla campaign in the Aurès mountains; patrols were stepped up, the state of emergency was prolonged and extended to the whole of Algeria, and the reserves were called up. France was determined that there could be no compromise with those responsible for Philippeville: the impasse was total. In October the French Assembly debated interminably over Algeria, but failed to define a coherent long-term policy, rejecting secession, finding assimilation too dangerous, and recognizing that integration was in fact unworkable. Among officials in

Paris and Algiers the by now familiar conclusion was quickly reached: a 'pacification' was the precondition to reforms.

This climate of unease and deadlock brought the Faure government to an end. Faure was convinced that faced with such grave problems the exhausted Assembly, close to the end of its mandate, was incapable of innovating or making the necessary decisions, and on 20 October he proposed to bring forward the legislative elections scheduled for June 1956. The confused rumpus that followed left no doubt that the 'system' had relapsed into its former bad habits. The political parties, unprepared for an election campaign, were caught unawares by Faure's proposal; some immediately sought to make electoral reform the condition for advancing the elections, without the Socialists and Communists being able to block the manoeuvre. The electorate was the bewildered and alienated spectator of a frenzied activity among the politicians, with, in the space of a few days, Mendès France battling against Edgar Faure for control of the Radical Party, the government fighting over proposals for a completely proportional representation, the Assembly voting then rejecting a return to *scrutin d'arrondissement*, bitter arguments over constituency boundaries, and an endless shunting of projects between the Assembly and the Council of the Republic. Although uneasy at the prospect of facing the electorate, a majority did finally accept early elections, but was ready to use the slightest pretext to bring down the Faure government before any project of electoral reform could be voted: on 29 November it failed to win a motion of confidence. However, having been defeated by 318 to 218 votes (thanks to a 'miscalculation' in the opposition's parliamentary arithmetic!), Faure could invoke article 51 of the Constitution which allowed for the Assembly to be dissolved if two governments had fallen by absolute majorities in the preceding eighteen months. Thus, on 2 December, for the first time since 16 May 1877 – a no-less sensitive date in the annals of the Republic – the Assembly was dissolved. Among those who furiously proclaimed their fidelity to the traditions of the Republic, Faure's decision to proceed with the dissolution earned him a reputation as the latter-day de Broglie, and led in fact to his exclusion from the Radical Party.

What, on the eve of the elections, was the Assembly's record? Five years had been wasted in exhausting efforts to find impossible majorities; by abandoning the EDC it had previously accepted, the Assembly was responsible for the régime's most serious diplomatic setback; faced with problems overseas it had retreated in unprincipled disorder; worst of all, the Assembly had quite clearly failed to adapt the parliamentary system to the needs of modern France. Its hostility towards genuinely popular leaders like Pinay and Mendès France had accentuated the failings of a system conceived when three monolithic political parties held a solid majority, a system moreover that was intolerant of popular exasperation at its futile parliamentary arithmetic. Faure believed that with early elections he could outdistance both Mendès France and Poujade, hoping to strengthen the Centre-Right majority which had in the end arbitrated over all the major issues and assumed responsibility for the failings. Perhaps the public was favourable to the dissolution which gave it an opportunity to register its views; at the same time, however, it could scarcely be indifferent to Poujade's electoral call to 'Sortez les sortants!'[29] The electorate was not being asked to pronounce upon political renewal for there had been none: instead it was to deliver a verdict on *gouvernement d'assemblée* and express its desire to see the Algerian question settled as quickly as possible.

## 14

# The Algerian snare

The French electorate was to be consulted at last. The brevity of the preparations – less than three weeks – in the middle of a hard winter, helped to fix the candidates in their *départements*, where the campaign was hard-fought and highly political. For the first time the pace was set by the modern media rather than the press, with the exception of *L'Express*. The national and peripheral radio stations outdid each other in the enthusiasm of their coverage, and some candidates even made a more sophisticated use of television.[1]

This animation reflected a widespread awareness of what was at stake in the elections, as well as the hunger for direct debate, and could perhaps be taken as an indication of the vitality of French democracy. Having said this, there were signs that instead of dominating the elections the political parties were themselves dominated, unable to inject the debate with vigorous or original arguments.

*The elections of 2 January 1956*

The major parties that had commanded French political life since the Liberation all entered the 1956 campaign weakened. The Communist Party, only recently emerged from its long torpor of the Cold War, had to its credit the demonstration of its better parliamentary instincts provided by the investiture of Mendès France and its contribution to the clearing of the EDC issue. The internal position of the Party was improving; the generation of militants of the Resistance period had been removed from positions of authority after the Marty-Tillon affair and after the exclusion of Lecœur in April 1954; and from December 1955, Maurice Thorez was back at the head of the Party after his return from the Soviet Union and the long months of convalescence in France. The slide in membership had been halted since 1954, stabilizing at the quite encouraging level of approximately 160 000 members, 38 per cent of whom were workers, distributed between 19 000 cells of varying degrees of activity. However, if the PCF could reasonably hope to have consolidated its following, its electoral arguments inspired less confidence. Thorez, disorientated before the changes in the Soviet leadership and the new policy of détente, backing Molotov against Krushchev, had become locked in a polemic over the economic and social conditions in France, in which his arguments seemed directly inspired by the final writings of Stalin. In the spring of 1955, to refute Ramadier, Mendès France and, so it seemed to many, the facts, he published a pamphlet in which he defended the thesis of the 'relative and absolute pauperization of the proletariat', demonstrating that popular purchasing power was at 40 per cent of its pre-war level, that the average working day was 15 per cent longer, and consumption of coal, meat, and cotton was lower among the working classes than in 1900.[2] This pessimistic analysis, stubbornly defended throughout the summer of 1955, widely diffused and simplified inside the Party and the CGT, inevitably raised doubts as to the theoretical competence of the PCF and its grasp on the economic and social realities of France in 1955. Furthermore, preoccupied with hostility to the United States and opposition to German rearmament, the Party failed to exploit fully the Algerian question. The PCF certainly devoted more serious attention to the issue than the other parties, but its position remained ambiguous: the special powers and repression were loudly denounced and negotiations were called for repeatedly, yet the role of the Algerian Communist Party was consistently exaggerated while that of the FLN was practically ignored, and the future place of Algeria in the French Union was solemnly reiterated. Handicapped by this uncertain grasp on developments in Algeria, the PCF's propositions remained vague and confused; and to reinforce its credibility as a potential party of government it could only fall back on the old notion of a Popular Front or a 'Front unique' with the Socialists – a variation on 1935 modified in the light of the experience of 1947.

This overture was promptly repulsed by the Socialists, also weakened but certainly reluctant to form an alliance with the 'Parti de l'Est'. The SFIO membership crisis had in fact continued; with 110 000 members it had just its strength of 1935; and this was an ageing membership (70 per cent over forty) in which the predominance of officials and the middle classes was more marked than ever, albeit still flanked by the working-class and agricultural bastions of the North and the Midi. The SFIO youth movements had practically disappeared, recruitment was stagnant, the affiliated bodies and organizations were moribund, and, in spite of Force Ouvrière, contacts with the trade unions were weak. The SFIO was nowhere near rivalling the powerful Social Democratic parties of Federal Germany or Scandinavia, and seemed unlikely to be able to tap the fresher energies mobilized by *Mendésisme*.[3] Debate over theory and policy was almost non-existent, with only *La Revue socialiste*, directed by the historian Ernest Labrousse and expounding a mild-mannered eclecticism, to assume the heritage of Jaurès and Blum. The party dissipated its energies in internal squabbling, absorbed by the old quarrels of majority and minority factions, with the all-powerful General Secretary, Guy Mollet, himself the symbol of outdated loyalties, playing the role of peacemaker.[4] More positively, however, the SFIO still had a solid group of experienced parliamentarians; increasingly torn between the safety of the familiar arguments and positions and embarking on the adventure of the new, they no longer hesitated, after six years of sterile opposition, to denounce Communism; an ambitious social policy was promised; for Algeria they opposed what Mollet described as 'une guerre imbécile et sans issue', and sought a solution in cautious recognition of the 'personnalité algérienne'.

Far graver was the position of the MRP. With a membership of barely 50 000, in which the proportion of workers, peasants, and artisans had fallen as that of officials, managers, and the liberal professions had risen, the MRP was popular only in name.[5] Its meagre youth movements were disaffected; its trade unionists were increasingly seduced by *Mendésisme*; its leading parliamentary figures were compromised with the Right; former ministers had abandoned it. The electoral verdict looked likely to be severe for a party which, as Mauriac cruelly put it, was no more than 'le tramway nommé pouvoir'. And the MRP's arguments were implausible, trying to convince its electorate that the party's rightwards shift had in fact halted the advance of reaction, that the Mendès France government had been the most conservative of the legislature, and that the outgoing majority was alone capable of making initiatives. To sum up, each of the monoliths was struggling: the Communists uncertainly stable, the Socialists ageing and hesitant, and the MRP already in a state of advanced decay. After a decade little remained of the Fourth Republic's founding fathers' hopes to consolidate and regenerate democracy by basing it on three powerful parties deeply rooted in French society.

The parties which had not been members of the tripartite alliance were also facing difficulties. The RPF was a very pale shadow of the force which had once seemed to menace the existence of the Republic. It had ceased all parliamentary and electoral activity in May 1953, because, according to de Gaulle, the system had become too unstable and the climate too base for positive action to succeed. Its press had all but vanished, and the rue de Solferino headquarters were deserted. And the attitude of de Gaulle was not always consistent, notably over decolonization, with, for example, a simultaneous support for Grandval and Kœnig. De Gaulle now devoted his time to writing his *Mémoires de guerre* and travelling in the French Union, announcing in July 1955 that he was no longer interested in politics. On 14 September, the RPF was suspended, though not formally dissolved, de Gaulle merely keeping a few trusted contacts and confidants. After this the Républicains sociaux (as the Gaullist deputies became) had to struggle to preserve their parliamentary identity, continuing to condemn the system in which they participated, continuing to call for a far-reaching reform of the State some of them still dreamt of destroying. For their part, the Radicals, though now at the centre of the political stage, were irreparably split by *Mendésisme*. The hostile faction, calling itself the Rassemblement des gauches républicaines (RGR) and led by Edgar Faure, could use all the means available to an outgoing government to bolster its campaign, fought on the slogan of 'Changer, en persévérant'. Confronting the RGR – especially in Paris, though more flexible and accommodating in the provinces – were the members and deputies of the Radical Party behind Mendès France, re-animating what was left of the networks of electoral committees, sometimes able to draw on the energies of youthful enthusiasts from among the readers of *L'Express*. Among the Right, the supporters of Pinay and Laniel were grouped in the Union des indépendants et paysans led by Roger Duchet, its progress closely followed by a sympathetic René Coty. Financed mainly by the CNPF and the agricultural and colonial lobbies, this mobilized its faithful electoral clientele with the routine Communist scare, denouncing Mendès France and glorifying the Pinay stabilization. However, this moderate Right was in turn outflanked by the action of Poujade and by the resurgence of a hardline Right, the latter loosely organized around Tixier-Vignancour and fighting in the name of *l'Algérie française*. It is clear then that the groups which had drawn the Third Force gradually rightwards were also powerless now to propose anything new to the electorate.

This failure of the political parties to introduce original issues or themes into the election campaign left the way open for the marginal groups more closely attuned to public opinion. Poujade's lively campaign, which attracted a great deal of coverage, allowed him to develop his image as a real threat to the régime of 'chaos and betrayal', castigating pell-mell the 'fossils' of the SFIO, the 'Judases' of the MRP, Mendès France, the 'maggots' of Gaullism, and the electoral catch-alls of the RGR and 'Pinay-la-Honte'. Poujade's attitude to the parliamentary system was certainly ambiguous, wishing to arm a 'purified' Republic with new powers at the same time as claiming to protect the citizens against the abuse of power: in reality, however, his nominally apolitical appeal embraced all the themes the parliamentary Right was loath to exploit openly – xenophobia, the virulent nationalism of *l'Algérie française*, the defence of the 'petits' against the might of Jewish capital. The candidates on Poujade's 'Union et Fraternité française' lists offered little that was concrete, just the by now familiar promise to fight against the 'trusts' and the 'gang of parasites': as a political programme it was slight, but it would be sufficient to dislodge many of the outgoing deputies.

The response of Mendès France, pushed by Jean-Jacques Servan-Schreiber and *L'Express* (that invented the formula), consisted of launching a 'Front républicain'. In a few days this had won the support of the SFIO under Mollet, François Mitterrand and the members of the UDSR hostile to Pleven, and Jacques Chaban-Delmas seeking to hold part of the Gaullist group together. Hastily formed, this disparate coalition – with the Phrygian cap as its symbol and *L'Express* (appearing daily during the campaign) to encourage its efforts and monitor the opinion polls – was able to agree on a minimal programme of a negotiated peace settlement in Algeria, social progress, and modernization of France, to oppose to the 'majority of Dien Bien Phu'. Working in favour of this coalition was its appeal to the young, its support in the press, a gift for formulas and for popularizing the essential themes of *Mendésisme* or the 'nouvelle gauche'. And, above all, public opinion was on its side, favourable to this coalition of the modern Left from which the Communists were absent and confident in its natural leader, Mendès France. At the close of the election campaign, 37 per cent of the electorate wanted the Front républicain to win, compared with 24 per cent for the outgoing majority, and 13 per cent for the Popular Front solution proposed by the Communists; 27 per cent wanted to see Mendès France as the new premier, as against 8 per cent for Pinay, 6 per cent for Edgar Faure, 3 per cent for Thorez, and 2 per cent each for Mollet and Poujade.[6] Working against the Front républicain was the vagueness of its brief programme and its lack of control over its members, each of whose party machines was determined to pursue its own interests in the event of victory.

With hindsight one might be tempted to consider the 1956 election campaign uniquely in terms of the Algerian drama: the opinion polls suggest that the reality was more complex. True, 25 per cent did consider North Africa as the major problem to be settled, but 15 per cent still gave priority to the familiar material problems of wages and purchasing power, while 9 per cent hoped for an improvement in East–West relations, 5 per cent wanted better housing, and 5 per cent monetary stability.[7] This diversity of popular preoccupations tended to favour the action of pressure groups with specific demands, at the same time as penalizing the political parties with their hierarchies of issues drawn up by the party headquarters; it also suggests the electoral irrelevance of much that appeared in the press during the campaign, such as the endless calls for national recovery. This confusion of objectives was mirrored by the struggle itself, also confused and open to several interpretations. The outgoing governmental majority, for example, on the defensive, appeared to be fighting only the Front républicain: behind the party quarrels, however, another struggle was discernible, that which opposed the forces capable of touching opinion directly, *Mendésisme* and *Poujadisme*. And since the 1956 election was fought under the 1951 electoral law, the situation was further complicated by the system of *apparentements*; these were less common than in 1951 – 44 on the Left, 58

Table 13: *The elections of 2 January 1956*

|                        | Votes                | Seats        |
|------------------------|----------------------|--------------|
| PCF                    | 5 503 491 (25.8%)    | 146 (+51)    |
| SFIO                   | 3 366 371 (15.8%)    | 89 (− 6)     |
| Radicals               | 3 049 503 (14.3%)    | 70 (− 7)     |
| MRP                    | 2 407 197 (11.3%)    | 71 (−13)     |
| Independents           |                      |              |
| and Moderates          | 3 572 565 (16.8%)    | 100 (+13)    |
| Poujadists             | 2 476 038 (11.6%)    | 51           |
| Gaullists              | 927 937 ( 4.4%)      | 17 (−89)     |
| Electors               | 26 770 895           |              |
| Votes                  | 21 303 102 (79.6%)   |              |
| Abstentions and        |                      |              |
| spoilt votes           | 5 467 793 (20.4%)    |              |

*Source:* C. Leleu, *Géographie des élections françaises depuis* 1936, PUF, 1971, p. 79.

on the Right – and their distribution was only poorly controlled by the leaderships of the Front républicain and the Poujadists; they ought, in theory, to have favoured the parties of government *vis-à-vis* the supposedly extra-parliamentary forces, the Communists and the Poujadists. In this confused context it was scarcely surprising that the electorate, which had the impression of being consulted merely in order to shuffle the parliamentary cards in preparation for another five years of complicated manoeuvres at the Assembly, expressed itself less clearly than had been hoped for.

That the outcome of the election of 2 January 1956 was equivocal (see results in Table 13) did not reflect apathy among the electorate; the electorate was relatively young, with 500 000 new voters, and participation was high; indeed, 1.5 million citizens had themselves hastily registered on the electoral lists. The confusion stemmed rather from the number of combinations for governing the vote made possible, for once again no clear majority had emerged. In absolute terms, the Right, with a total of 10.9 million votes, had a lead of 500 000 over the Left. But the Left–Right division was no longer the decisive one around which majorities were formed: each party in fact acted independently, and each coalition depended on the intentions of its members. By far the greatest surprise was the spectacular breakthrough of the Poujadists, winning 2.5 million votes and fifty-one deputies; they could now either try to disrupt parliamentary life or reinforce a future coalition of the Right. Predictably, their support was strongest among the apprehensive populations of the stagnant regions south of the line from Saint-Malo to Geneva. However, in spite of this the Poujadist deputies were not sufficiently numerous to block the work of the

Static and dynamic France in the elections of 2 January 1956

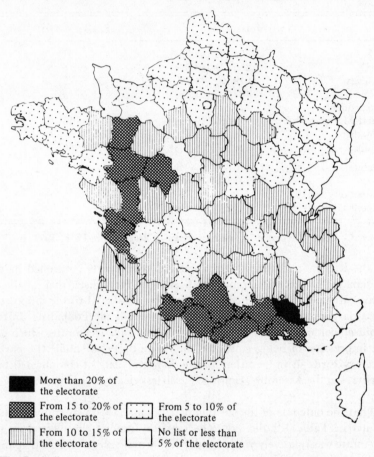

More than 20% of
the electorate

From 15 to 20% of        From 5 to 10% of
the electorate           the electorate

From 10 to 15% of        No list or less than
the electorate           5% of the electorate

4  The Poujadist votes
   *Source: L'Histoire*, 32 (1981), p. 13.

Assembly, and their leader was reluctant to bind his hands by forming
hasty alliances. The aimless activism of the Poujadists would, moreover,
soon exhaust itself in the presence of a strong government capable of satisfying the partisans of *l'Algérie française* and restoring the prestige of the Republic in the eyes of Poujade's electorate. The success of the Poujadists was
nevertheless worrying: one voter in ten had indeed wanted to dislodge the
'sortants' and, perhaps, the régime itself.[8] The other isolated group, the
Communists, had held up well, attracting one voter in four. The PCF
recovered the votes of those who had abandoned it for the RPF in 1951, and
it had condemned Poujade in strong enough terms not to be threatened or
compromised on this score. The PCF remained the principal political force

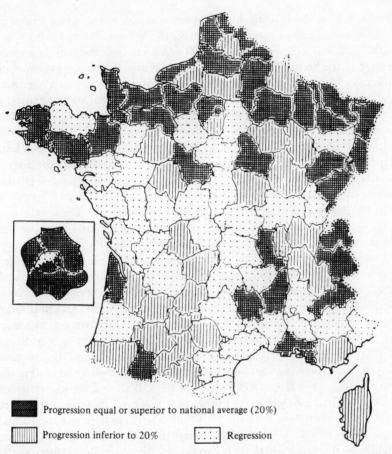

Progression equal or superior to national average (20%)

Progression inferior to 20%     Regression

5 Evolution of percentage of votes favourable to the parties of the Front républicain, 1951–6 inclusive

Source: F. Goguel, *Chroniques électorales. La Quatrième République*, Presses de la FNSP, 1981, p. 163.

in the country, and since it was no longer the main target for the other parties it suffered less than in 1951 from the system of *apparentements*. With the same share of the vote as in 1951 the PCF got back the fifty deputies denied it then by the electoral law.

The second real surprise of the elections was the way in which the Poujadist breakthrough had effectively robbed the outgoing Centre–Right coalition of the expected benefits of the *apparentements*; a system of almost complete proportional representation had in fact operated. Many Moderates were beaten by small margins, overtaken by supporters of Mendès France or Poujade; and many reliable deputies from the overseas territories were also missing, for it had been decided not to hold elections in the troubled Algerian context. However, the 'sortants' were far from defeated: with one vote in three, and 200 deputies, and over a million votes more than the Front républicain, they could reasonably aspire to power, or rather could have done if the arithmetic of the Assembly had not been against them. For now that the Poujadists had made their startling entry, a coalition of Independents, the MRP, and a handful of Gaullists and Radicals could no longer form a majority. The position of the MRP was even more alarming than in 1951; 13 per cent of its electorate had been lost, dispersed between the Front républicain, the Poujadists, and the Right. Finally, as expected, Gaullism all but disappeared as an organized parliamentary force, taking barely one vote in twenty, and scattering 80 per cent of its 1951 electorate over the rest of the political spectrum. The conclusion, then, seemed obvious: the Front républicain was the only more or less coherent group capable of forming a majority with which to govern.

Was this in fact a victory for the Front républicain and Mendès France? An electorate unfamiliar with the workings of the Assembly thought so, and it was certainly hailed as such by *L'Express*, quick to announce the 'New Deal'. The electoral ascendancy of *Mendésisme* was clear, securing more than a million votes for the Radical lists, notably in the Paris region and in the modern dynamic regions of the North and East, whereas traditional rural Radicalism had fallen victim to the Poujadists. Behind this advance were the votes of many Catholics,[9] and the association with Mendès France had certainly been electorally fruitful for the UDSR and the Républicains sociaux of Chaban-Delmas. On their own, however, these successes were insufficient, and it was from the SFIO that the decisive extra support had come. The Socialists had in fact halted their decline, even progressing slightly in the cases where their candidates were seen to be closer to the Front républicain than to the traditional positions. Yet, with 28 per cent of the vote, the coalition which was supposed to have swept Mendès France to power had only 170 deputies; and even if the Popular Front solution with the Communists had not been rejected it was impossible now given that approximately 300 deputies were needed to form a government. The elections had failed, once again, to produce a clear majority; once again an artificial one would have to be constructed. The 'system' had triumphed, returning the responsibility for forming a government to the political parties and dashing the remaining hopes for *Mendésisme*. This outcome was received unfavourably by the public: many were to remember their disappointment in 1958.[10]

Clear signs of a new vigour had, nevertheless, come from the Left of French politics, and the eighty-nine SFIO deputies were now the arbiters of the confused situation. President Coty concluded that Guy Mollet was the only possible choice for the new legislature's first premier, even if the

Poujadists might play the same role of arbiter for a subsequent coalition of the Right. On 26 January, Coty – giving, with hindsight, the lie to those who considered the President of the Fourth Republic to have little real influence on the course of events – charged Mollet with forming a government. Three weeks of meticulous political preparation had in fact cleared the field for Mollet:[11] the outgoing majority had had to acknowledge its inability to govern, though Edgar Faure and the MRP were already proposing their support for a future majority that would exclude the Poujadists and the Communists; the Radicals had rejected both the Popular Front and 'Union Nationale' solutions; and Mendès France, more mindful of the violent opposition he would encounter from former defenders of the EDC than of the genuine popular support he would have enjoyed, declined to insist on the premiership. Thus it was the SFIO leader, Guy Mollet, strongly backed by his party, who formed the new government. The Mollet team, laboriously put together,[12] was voted triumphantly into office on 5 February by 420 deputies, the 83 abstentions and 71 votes against coming from the Right and the Poujadists.[13] Apart from the Socialists and Radicals, the Communists had rallied to Mollet, seeing their support for him as a vote against the continuation of the war in Algeria; while a majority of the MRP and Gaullists had been won over by the allusion in the investiture speech to 'l'union indissoluble entre l'Algérie et la France': a contradiction, if it existed at this stage, was not perceived by the Assembly. No one, however, could be in any doubt that Mollet's first task was to exorcize the Algerian spectre.

## Tomatoes from Algiers

There was little in the appointment of Guy Mollet to make the Europeans in Algeria uneasy. His declarations on Algeria during the election campaign had consisted of the same generalities and reluctance to confront the real questions as those of the other parties. The Front républicain, like the outgoing majority, rejected outright the idea of eventual independence for Algeria, just as it rejected all direct negotiation with the rebels. Support for the policy of integration was half-hearted, a possible federal solution had aroused varying degrees of interest, but only the Communists had argued that sooner or later negotiations would have to be opened with the authentic representatives of the Algerian people. This vagueness of propositions over Algeria was of course mirrored by the election results: the new government had received a massive responsibility without clear instructions from the electorate as to how it should be discharged. The originality of the Front républicain's proposals for Algeria had lain in the promise of free elections with a single electoral college, modernization of the economic

structures, and agrarian reforms, the future premier undertaking to supervise personally the implementation of these measures which, it was
believed, would extinguish the conflict. Guy Mollet retained some of these
*Mendésiste* themes, but innovated by appointing a minister resident in Algeria, responsible for implementing policy from Paris. And with General
Catroux, former Governor-General in 1943–4, responsible for the successful policy of reconciliation in Morocco, a disciple of Lyautey and with
impeccable republican loyalties, Mollet appeared to have made a
promising choice. It was to announce Catroux's appointment and to hold
talks that Mollet decided to go in person to Algiers on 6 February.

In Algiers, however, where Soustelle had been given a triumphant send-
off by the Europeans when he left for Paris on 2 February, the opposition to
Mollet was already preparing. European opinion in Algeria took a dim
view of the new government in which the second figure was *le bradeur*, and
whose Justice Minister, Mitterrand, had previously done so much mischief
at the Overseas Ministry; worse, supervised elections had been promised
for Algeria, and Mollet was widely believed to be already negotiating
secretly with the FLN murderers. For the activists of the European community it was too much: the liberal Catroux, they decided, had to be
resisted; the time had come for Algiers to impose its wishes on Paris. At the
head of the popular agitation in Algiers was a Comité d'entente of ex-
servicemen; this was composed mainly of veterans of the African and
Italian campaigns, of the First French Army, and of 1914–18; members of
Leclerc's forces and Gaullists were rare; indeed, former sympathies were
more likely to have been with General Giraud, if not with Vichy. Few
Muslims were involved ('fraternization' was not yet encouraged), but
rather a section of the modest *pied-noir* population, for the most part
workers, artisans, shopkeepers, and petty officials, many of whom traditionally voted for the Left. By 5 February, with the atmosphere in Algiers
tense, these groups were assembling, ready to demonstrate to Mollet their
anxieties, the depth of their attachment to Algeria, and their hatred for the
*bradeurs*. Manoeuvring discreetly in the background were those already looking to the future and in whose hands – as events of twenty-seven months
later were to show – this angry and apprehensive crowd was to be an
effective instrument of political pressure. Among them were the mayors,
acting for the powerful colonial interests, and led by Amédée Froger; a few
academics from the faculties of law and economics, such as Lambert and
Bousquet; a student action committee led by Pierre Lagaillarde; the tiny
Union française nord-africaine (UFNA) led by the fanatical Robert
Martel; the local Poujadist chiefs, such as the café-owner Joseph Ortiz and
the restaurateur Roger Goutalier; plus a handful of determined Gaullists
grouped around Maître Biaggi. These influential figures, formed into a
Comité de défense de l'Algérie française and already dreaming of a *coup*

*d'état*, were adept at manipulating the ex-servicemen and the mass of the *pied-noir* population, and proved dependable new allies for the extreme Right in metropolitan France.

Events moved quickly on 6 February. The official procession from the airport was greeted in silence by the Muslim population; once in Algiers, however, Mollet found himself confronted with an angry European mob. During the wreath-laying ceremony at the war memorial the security forces lost control, and the French premier was pelted with tomatoes, rotten eggs, and abuse; it was only with great difficulty and considerable personal courage that he managed to reach the safety of the Palais d'Eté. Mollet was badly shaken by the experience, not least since he, a life-long Socialist, was the victim of what appeared to be a truly popular action. Anxious to avoid civil war, and under pressure from Lambert, prefect of Oran, and Cuttoli, Secretary to the Governor-General, he gave way: the appointment of Catroux was abandoned. The French government had given way to the Algiers mob. The same evening, intoxicated by this first success, the followers of Martel, having failed in an attempt to capture Mollet, tore up the gardens of the Palais d'Eté.

The consequences of the capitulation in Algiers were soon felt. After both Savary and Defferre had refused the post, Robert Lacoste was appointed to replace Catroux as minister resident in Algeria. Lacoste was a tough SFIO boss, on the right-wing of the party, and had entered politics through the trade union movement and the Resistance. A bluff no-nonsense party politician, Lacoste had little time for ideology and moral scruples; he knew nothing of Algeria, but was not indifferent to the past glories of French imperialism. Once in Algeria he proceeded to cajole the military and surrounded himself with a team of undistinguished advisers (with the exception of the prefect Chaussade, spiritual father of the Fifth Republic's Constantine Plan). Indeed, Lacoste's approach was very much that of an imperial proconsul, loudly affirming his determination to fight on two fronts: first, against the rebels, ready, in his famous phrase, to fight until the 'dernier quart d'heure'; secondly, to break the economic stranglehold of the great colonial interests, responsible for native misery and disdainful of the ordinary *pied-noir* populations. And with Guy Mollet understandably reluctant to return to Algeria, Lacoste was left a free hand to implement the Mollet government's Algerian policy, now corrected in the light of the events in Algiers and presented to the Assembly on 16 February. The Europeans had to be appeased: what he discreetly referred to as the 'douloureuse manifestation' had, Mollet claimed, enabled him to understand the strength of their attachment to France and their legitimate fears for the future. He promised them that they would not be abandoned, that independence for Algeria was out of the question. True, an Algerian identity obviously existed and was recognized, but the historical and ethnic bases of Algerian nationalism were strenuously denied. And the notion of an Algerian State was categorically rejected: Algeria was a province of France, and as such 8 million Muslims could never expect to prevail over 1.5 million Europeans. The links between France and Algeria, reiterated Mollet, were indissoluble. Mollet had settled on a middle course, one which exploited the uncertainties of public opinion and recalled the former policy of integration, hoping to satisfy the Muslims while retaining the confidence of the Europeans. And if the future remained as hazy as ever, the middle-term objectives were now clear, summed up in the soon to be familiar trio of ceasefire, elections, discussions. This approach comforted both sides. To begin with the Left, because the definitive solution was to come not from Paris but from negotiations with the elected representatives of the Algerian people, even if, significantly, there was no mention now of the project for a single electoral college. While on the other hand, since the restoration of order was made the precondition for elections, the timetable for a political settlement was sufficiently vague to reassure the partisans of *l'Algérie française*. Meanwhile, in the wait for the democratic solution in an unspecified future, the French government would continue to wage war against the rebels at the same time as striving to modernize Algeria's economic structures.[14]

The about-turn was brutal. All those who, just a few weeks earlier, had voted for the Front républicain in the belief that it would end the war in Algeria had now to face the fact that peace was no longer part of the policy. Accusations of weakness, impotence, and betrayal were not slow in coming, particularly from the activist minorities and younger voters, harsh in their judgement on what they stigmatized as 'national-molletisme'. But their anger was not shared by the public as a whole, nor by the political parties. Mollet in fact had massive support for his policy in Algeria; the granting of sweeping special powers to his government was voted by 455 deputies, with just 76 Poujadists and Moderates (including Paul Reynaud) voting against. Under these, Mollet and Lacoste were empowered to govern by decree in Algeria, and authorized to take whatever measures they considered necessary for the restoration of order. In return for this surrender of its legislative sovereignty and the potential threat to democratic safeguards in Algeria, the Assembly was offered, and accepted, merely the familiar assurance, repeated by the project's Socialist reporter, Montalat, that the objective was simply the restoration of conditions suitable for the holding of negotiations and elections. The deputies seemed oblivious to the danger, apparently satisfied by a debate which saw Jacques Soustelle claim that defeating the fanaticism of the FLN would restore French power and avoid another Sedan, and Guy Mollet invoke the memory of Léon Blum to defend this new *loi-cadre*. Even the Communists voted the special powers, albeit with strong reservations.[15] They had denounced the 'Fascist conspiracy' of

6 February, and were increasingly to call for talks to be opened with the representatives of the Algerian movements and fighters; but, on the other hand, they still nurtured hopes for a Popular Front with the Socialists, and it was for this tactical consideration, swayed finally it seems by Thorez, that the Communist deputies decided not to condemn openly what they in fact opposed.[16]

Not, however, that the policy consisted solely of repression. Armed with a political support which was, for all its nuances, almost unanimous, the Mollet government's ambitions for Algeria included reform and construction. And the growing hostility of the Communists within France actually helped the government by lending credibility to the official view of the rebellion as the work of international Communism and Third World progressives. The resignation of Mendès France as Minister of State on 23 May in protest over an Algerian policy he considered inappropriate and unworkable had little effect. The other Radical ministers remained in the government, and with *Mendésisme* now clearly losing momentum the Radical Party was swinging away from it towards positions more favourable to *l'Algérie française*. Only Defferre, Savary, and Mitterrand were left to voice protests from time to time in the cabinet. Within the SFIO an opposition led by Daniel Mayer, Oreste Rosenfeld, André Philip, and Roger Quilliot could do no more than persuade the party's Lille congress in July to accept the 'double front' thesis, according to which the struggle against the 'ultras' was given the same priority as that against the rebels, an argument to which the MRP also rallied. As for the Moderates, the Right, and the revived extreme Right, they of course adopted an attitude of benign neutrality towards this stern Algerian policy of a government of the Left. In Algeria, Lacoste expelled a few troublemakers, and sent some of the more turbulent law students to calm down in isolated postings; he even went through the motions of attacking the entrenched economic interests, such as Blachette's concession on the alfa. But Lacoste was anxious to secure European acceptance for his reforms, and the struggle on this 'second front' was not pursued. His reforms, most of which went no further than the ambitions of the 1947 statute, included the opening of the lower reaches of the civil service to Muslims, a reorganization of local administration, better wages, a programme for housing and schools, and the creation of eight new *départements*. Behind these measures lay the hope of creating a new Muslim élite, one favourable to France and with whom it would be possible to negotiate in the future. But as always these efforts foundered amidst the opposition of the powerful colonial interests. Thus the ambitious agrarian reform (decrees of 20 March and 25 April) providing for the expropriation and redistribution of estates of more than 50 hectares failed miserably; in spite of the troubles, the gulf between European and native agriculture continued to widen. As the FLN did not fail to point out, real power in

Algeria lay with the great *colons* and the notables who served their interests, a classic colonial situation the Socialists of metropolitan France were visibly powerless to change.

Imperceptibly, the Mollet government and its minister resident in Algeria became locked into an all-out war. The diplomatic front had not been ignored. Christian Pineau had attempted a direct approach to Nasser in Cairo, and Guy Mollet went in person to Moscow to secure Krushchev's neutrality. Furthermore, between April and September talks were held in Yugoslavia and Italy with FLN emissaries. These contacts were far from being negative, but on each occasion they ran up against the question of the ceasefire, the precondition for elections for France, a recognition of the representative status of the FLN, and the first step towards independence for the Algerians. But in fact the logic of the military struggle was already sweeping all other considerations aside. Heavy reinforcements arrived, much to the satisfaction of the military, now under Salan's command and worried by the intensification of FLN activity and the spread of insecurity to the Oran region. Since August 1955, either by recall or by lengthening the service for the conscripts of 1952 and 1953, the French forces in Algeria had been increased to 200 000. In six months the Mollet government managed to double this number, taking the political risk and the moral responsibility of involving the whole country in the war by sending young conscripts to Algeria. Thanks to a partial recall of the conscripts of 1951–4 and an extension of military service from eighteen to twenty-seven months, the numbers were increased to 400 000 by July and to roughly 450 000 by the summer of 1957. With these new forces – the largest deployment of French troops outside France since 1830 – a systematic patrolling of the entire Algerian territory at last became possible; this, it was believed, would contain the rebels, isolate them from the population, and force them to surrender. The mobilization of young conscripts for the war in Algeria did not go unchallenged in France, with the Communists, militants of the extreme Left, and Christian pacifists encouraging the resistance. Incidents at Rouen and in the Landes in the autumn of 1955, when some conscripts had refused to leave, probably owed more to deplorable barrack conditions than to hostility to the war, but between April and June 1956 the protests became general. Angry and emotional scenes occurred at embarkation points and railway stations, with women lying on the tracks to prevent troop trains leaving. The PCF was particularly active in this protest, using its contacts in the trade unions and its affiliated bodies to organize petitions, industrial action, and demonstrations. But this agitation came to little. By the summer of 1956 the prevailing attitude among the conscripts was visibly one of apathetic resignation, an attitude moreover which echoed that of the public at large.[17]

Acceptance of the war was only encouraged by the fact that throughout

1956 the FLN won fresh national and international support. On 22 April, the UDMA leaders, Ferhat Abbas and Ahmed Francis, with those of the Oulémas, arrived In Cairo. Their rallying to the cause brought the FLN valuable support among the moral, religious, and bourgeois élites, which included experienced diplomats and politicians. The Algerian Communist Party finally recognized the futility of its solitary action, and on 1 July invited its combatants to go over to the ALN (although those who did were treated with great suspicion, despite, for example, the exploit of Maillot who had deserted in April with an arms convoy, or the courage under torture of individuals like Henri Alleg and, later, Maurice Audin). And the old struggle between the MNA of Messali Hadj and the FLN now turned decisively in favour of the latter; the last of the Messalist armed bands were tracked down by Krim and Amirouche or denounced to the authorities, some even receiving a precarious protection from the French forces. This fratricidal conflict was to reach its terrible climax on 28 May 1957 when an FLN unit massacred 300 men of the Melouza *douar* suspected of collaboration with the MNA. In France, where partisans of Messali were numerous among the immigrant Algerian workers, the settling of scores between activists of the warring factions became intense in all the large towns and cities, and was responsible for several thousand deaths up to 1958. These crimes, all vigorously exploited by the French propaganda services, heightened the atmosphere of terror surrounding the struggle, reinforcing the hold of the ALN over the Algerian population. This was clear from the increasing difficulties faced by the French forces in their search for information on the rebels: the recourse to torture now became indispensable, if not justified. There was also a change in FLN strategy: in response to the Messalists and the Communists, its trade union activities were developed; the Union générale des travailleurs algériens (UGTA) was built up until it was capable of organizing spectacular strikes in the towns, the UGCA was created to group together the tradesmen, and the UGEMA for the students. Support for the FLN among the urban population now grew rapidly, whereas it remained often patchy in the countryside, the regions of the Algérois and Oranais lagging behind the Constantinois, the Kabylie, and the South.

Partly due to these developments, the nationalist movement now acquired a more concrete and detailed programme, the result of a secret meeting of all the rebel leaders inside Algeria held in the Soummam valley in August 1956.[18] At the Soummam Conference the fighters in Algeria, led by Abbane Ramdane, asserted their predominance over the chiefs in Cairo, notably with the establishment of the principle of collective leadership for the movement. Other important consequences of the Soummam Conference were the secularization of the nationalist movement, providing the struggle instead with a more revolutionary and Third World tone and vocabulary, the restructuring of the FLN politico-military organization based on the Wilayas, and the fixing of the movement's priority goal as the creation of an Algerian State. The outcome of the Soummam Conference marked the ascendancy of the nationalist intellectuals over the peasant soldiers, of the Kabyles over the Arabs, and of the combatants over the diplomats in Cairo; it was perhaps inevitable that it should have been contested from within the FLN, notably by Ben Bella and Krim. Abbane was in fact executed in Morocco early in 1958, and later experience taught the leaders in the *djebel* (bush) to be wary of the theoreticians and the wisdom of co-operation with the 'palace revolutionaries'. Nonetheless, the principle of collective leadership and the goals set by the Soummam Conference were retained as basic elements of the FLN's struggle. This new political maturity and coherence of the nationalist movement soon bore fruit at the international level.[19] Moscow, it is true, maintained a cautious attitude towards the FLN, but FLN diplomats, encouraged by the growing doubts of the authorities and public opinion in the United States over French action in Algeria, managed to get the Algerian question placed on the agenda of the eleventh session of the United Nations in November. And in July, at Brioni, Nasser, Tito, and Nehru had given an unequivocal affirmation of Algeria's right to independence. Meanwhile, support from Tunisia and Morocco was taking increasingly concrete forms, with offers of training and rest facilities for ALN fighters and help with the transport of supplies and arms, these often purchased from the popular democracies of Eastern Europe. And in the background, Nasser's Egypt, hostile to the victors of the Soummam Conference but hopeful of leading the Arab awakening around the Mediterranean, gladly offered the leaders of Algerian revolution hospitality in Cairo.

In this transformed and unfavourable context France could do little more than persevere with her long-term efforts and wait upon events. The French army at least had no doubts. It had come to see the war against the rebels as the means for redeeming the disgraces accumulated since June 1940, hanging its honour on a defence of the French presence in Algeria, flattered in its role of upholder of justice and order by the politicians of metropolitan France. And after Indo-China the army knew how to dress its combat in Algeria with a degree of modernity. Officers like General Chassin and Colonel Lacheroy, familiar with the doctrines and methods of Giap, argued that in periods of détente the forces of international Communism advanced stealthily but surely, fuelling colonial revolutions and injecting them with Marxist ideology: yesterday, Indo-China; today, Algeria. The mission of the French army in Algeria was then to defend the free world from an insidious subversion. This reasoning dictated the methods to be used. It was essential to isolate the rebels from the civilian population they hoped to win over by terror and indoctrination. To teams of élite troops went the task of eliminating the guerrilla bands, launching daring raids into previously encircled and, if necessary, bombed areas. The French paratroops excelled at this aspect of the struggle; galvanized by a morality of uncomplicated heroism, always effective in action, the 'paras' became the idols of the European community. The other, less glorious but in the long-run equally important, duties fell to the mass of ordinary units, swollen with conscript soldiers. To these went the often difficult defence of the strategic axes, the routine patrols, helping to locate and pin down the enemy. The garrisons and isolated posts also had the day-to-day tasks of controlling the civilian population, combing the camps and villages, checking identity papers, conducting searches in the slums. Brutal and above all repetitive, this side of the military effort in Algeria did much to lose France the sympathies of entire communities, swinging opinion inexorably in favour of the ALN.

Attempts were made to halt the slide. Techniques of psychological warfare, perfected by Lacheroy, were tried, with anti-FLN talks, pamphlets, films and cartoons, but without great success. A policy of emptying the rural areas, moving whole villages to camps, proved equally ineffective. Really positive results were in fact only achieved with a continuous French presence among the native population. The best illustration of the results that could be obtained with this approach, one which allowed the effects of the war to be gradually effaced, was the work of the Sections administratives specialisées (SAS) in the countryside and, to a lesser extent, that of the Sections administratives urbaines (SAU) in the towns.[20] Usually commanded by experienced native affairs officers, these units harnessed the civilian skills of the young French conscripts – artisans, farmers, teachers, nurses – to provide schools and clinics, to arbitrate in local affairs, to perform numerous small services to the native population, working, of course, in the purest colonial tradition of paternalistic action. The great strength of the SAS lay in building up direct contact and confidence with the inhabitants of the villages and *douars*, offering through their action an image of France other than that of military repression. Indeed, the FLN itself admitted to having severe difficulties in overcoming the genuine Franco-Algerian harmony created by this more positive side of French policy.

Given time, initiatives of this kind might have borne more fruit. But unforeseeable developments now occurred which made a peaceful solution for Algeria remoter than ever. Conclusive proof of Nasser's aid to the rebels came on 16 October 1956, when a French naval search of the *Athos*, a cargo vessel coming from Egypt, revealed an arms shipment. The following week, on 22 October, a Moroccan plane taking four major rebel leaders – Ben Bella, Boudiaf, Ait Ahmed, and Khider – from Rabat to Tunis for an important Maghreb solidarity conference with Bourguiba and Mohammed V landed instead at Algiers, where its passengers were immediately arrested. The plane's French pilot had in fact obeyed instructions from the military authorities in Algiers under Air-Marshal Frandon to change his destination. The only member of the government to have been contacted by telephone from Algiers during the weekend was Max Lejeune, Secretary of State with responsibility for the armed forces in Algeria. Mollet, not informed until the operation was over, decided to underwrite the act of piracy, bowing in effect to the *fait accompli* of the military in Algiers. The incident brought furious protests from the Sultan of Morocco, who did not intervene to prevent the massacre of thirty Europeans at Meknès in reprisal; Alain Savary, Secretary of State for Tunisian and Moroccan Affairs, resigned, as did Pierre de Leusse, the new French ambassador in Tunisia. In vain: the Mollet government, apparently a victim of its own wishful thinking, now hailed the exploit as having demonstrated, notably to Cairo, the strength of French resolve, and having left the FLN leaderless. In reality, however, not only had the capture of the nationalist leaders ruined the chances for negotiation, but it opened the way for the extreme elements of the FLN in Algeria to take the lead.

### Suez and Budapest

With the Suez expedition the Mollet government thought it had found a perfect opportunity to weaken the troublesome Egyptian leader and strike the FLN at its nerve centre in Cairo. Between 22 and 24 October, at the same time as the capture of Ben Bella, a secret meeting with Ben Gurion was taking place at Sèvres to finalize the details of a combined military operation against Egypt by France, Great Britain, and Israel. A French government led by the Socialists now prepared the final act of gunboat diplomacy in the Near East: the patriots of the Second International unwittingly took up where the imperialists had left off.[21]

The Suez affair had begun on 26 July, with Nasser's annuncement to an ecstatic crowd in Alexandria of the nationalization of the Suez Canal. Since coming to power in February 1954, Nasser had skilfully negotiated the withdrawal of the British garrisons from Egypt, adopted a policy of pan-Arabism and violent hostility to Zionism, and in September 1955 had concluded arms deals with Czechoslovakia and the Soviet Union. In fact, the Western bloc's strenuous rejection of a Soviet role in the Near East, a region whose status quo it had guaranteed since May 1950, allowed Nasser to exploit the tension between the two camps. An attempt by the United States to unite the moderate elements in the Pact of Baghdad in December 1955, seen by Nasser as a challenge to Arab solidarity, plus the American refusal on 19 July 1956 to participate with the Soviet Union, Great Britain, and the World Bank in the financing of the giant Aswam dam project for the Upper Nile, completed the Egyptian leadership's realignment away from the West. Its answer was to appropriate the Canal revenues to finance Egypt's independence and modernization.

Nasser's action brought a muted response from Washington. The Suez Canal was of only limited economic and strategic importance to the United States; Dulles, sick, and Eisenhower, preoccupied with his re-election campaign, were in fact content to monitor Soviet intentions and offer occasional encouragement to the principal protagonists. It was left then to France and Great Britain, pushed by Israel, to take action. Mollet, the Socialist, now joined Eden, the Conservative, in a defence of the capitalist interests of the Suez Canal shareholders (to whom, moreover, Nasser had promised a fair compensation). If for Great Britain this was the occasion to defend the last vestiges of her influence in the Near East, for France the motives were a mixture of historical justification and the pressure of events in Algeria. The Suez expedition may have caused dissension within the Mollet government. Christian Pineau, Minister of Foreign Affairs, who had made efforts to cultivate support among Third World leaders, in fact had· a reasonable opinion of Nasser, and was to claim later that Algeria had not been for him the decisive consideration.[22] On the other hand, Bourgès-Maunoury, Minister of National Defence, and his adviser, Abel Thomas,[23] strongly backed by Lacoste, Max Lejeune, and the military, saw in Nasser an agent of international Communism, an accomplice of the FLN, a neo-Nazi, and an anti-Semite. Guy Mollet, himself strongly anglophile, came down on the side of those hostile to Nasser·and in favour of concerted action against him. What they hoped to see in Egypt was a modern secular régime, with Nasser replaced by, for example, Neguib (responsible for the overthrow of Farouk), and an Arab League won over to a responsible nationalism and freed of Muslim fanaticism. Memories of the concentration camps and the Resistance were still strong among the French political leadership, and there was a considerable sympathy for the young Jewish State, pursuing its Socialist experiment based on the kibbutz movement. Strong also were memories of Munich, which had split the SFIO and weakened France, and made a fresh capitulation even harder to accept. And indeed, the Egyptian leader was widely regarded almost as a new Hitler, a view accredited by the presence and influence in Egypt of several former Nazis, as well as by the expansionist Arab nationalism expounded by Nasser in his *Philosophie de la Révolution*, that *L'Express* had made known in France. With the exception of the press close to the Communist Party, all the major French newspapers denounced Nasser's action as totalitarian bluff. And all accepted the ultimate argument of the politicians, summed up characteristically by Robert Lacoste: 'One French division in Egypt is worth four divisions in Algeria.'

The ambitions then were clear: eliminate the Egyptian obstacle to a quicker solution in Algeria, thus protecting French troops; destroy the prestige of Nasser in the Arab world; and, in the process, restore France to the status of a great power capable of imposing her will. From 28 July, in the same underground headquarters in London used to prepare the D-Day assaults, a combined Franco-British team drew up a plan for landings at Port Said and Alexandria. 'Operation Musketeer' was backed up by increased secret French arms supplies to Israel, and by the launching of a carefully timed Israeli attack in Sinai. Meanwhile, against a background of mounting pressure from the Canal's users, the UN Security Council would, it was hoped, continue to hesitate, paralysed by the Soviet veto and United States indecision. The team at Sèvres settled the details of the operation in October; on 30 October an ultimatum was issued calling on both Israel and Egypt to pull back from the Canal zone to their original positions; the expected Egyptian refusal provided the pretext for the Anglo-French intervention. The British shelled the Egyptian airfields on 1 November, and on 5 November (six days later than planned, so poor was co-ordination between the allies), and after the fleet had bombarded the strategic installations, French and British paratroopers landed successfully at Port Fouad and Port Said. However, less than 48 hours later, and in sight of Ismailia, the Franco-British forces received orders from their governments to abandon all action. Among the rapidly advancing forces, as among the Israelis who had also routed Nasser's troops, jubilation turned to bitter disappointment as the Suez expedition came to its miserable close.[24]

At the origin of this fiasco was the change in the attitude of the superpowers. The United Nations had in fact quickly pronounced in favour of an immediate ceasefire and international arbitration, while on the evening of 5 November, a Soviet ultimatum called on Paris and London to abandon their action, hinting strongly at reprisals against them involving nuclear missiles. More important still was the reaction from the United States. Eisenhower, now re-elected to the White House, had been surprised by the brutality of the European intervention in the Near East; he had no desire to see the United States become involved in a conflict of this kind in such a sensitive area that was clearly subject to Soviet ambitions. On 5 November he let it be known that the Europeans could not count on American petrol to replace that of the Gulf, lost due to the closure of the Canal, a serious threat at a moment when petrol restrictions were already necessary and panic food buying had begun. And, above all, the American President struck the alliance at its weakest point by allowing a run on sterling to develop. Eden, already under attack from the Labour opposition, gave way before this double pressure on 6 November, and resigned shortly afterwards. Informed by telephone from London of the British decision, the French authorities could only follow suit a few hours later. The following day the United Nations decided to send its forces to the Canal zone while negotiations under Dag Hammarskjöld began again. Israel, though bolstered by the victory in Sinai, had aligned herself unequivocally with the Western

imperial powers and had inflicted a bitter and not to be forgotten humiliation on Arab progressivisim. France and Great Britain both emerged
discredited and weakened from the episode: their place in the Near East
was now taken by the Soviet Union and the United States. At the time,
however, the French authorities appeared to consider the adventure a partial success, blaming the final outcome on the United States. When, on 20
December, confidence in the Mollet government was renewed by 325 votes
to 210, the Assembly itself seemed ready to believe that the shame of
Munich had indeed been redeemed, that the future in Algeria had been
preserved, and that Israel was now safe.

This was a fair reflection of the popular verdict on the episode. For
although 58 per cent had condemned Nasser in August for the nationalization of the Canal, the public in France remained considerably less involved and less volatile over the Suez affair than in Britain. Due partly, it is
true, to a highly favourable media campaign and government control of the
news services, the Suez expedition appeared to have genuine popular
support, with only the Communists denouncing the bluster and abuse
which surrounded it.[25] Having said this, the polls conducted by the IFOP
show that diplomatic solutions were strongly and consistently hoped for;[26]
and, on 3 November, only 44 per cent of Parisians against 37 per cent
approved of the raid (a result confirmed by a national poll in March 1957).
The predominant reaction then was neither jingoism nor unbridled
'national-molletisme', just a short-lived and resentful nationalism: Suez
was no more than a small break in the general bewilderment and discouragement of the French people, faced with painful international realities and
the war in Algeria. The politicians for their part ought, perhaps, to have
paid more attention to the polls of the time: Guy Mollet's personal
popularity, after attaining a peak of 37 per cent 'satisfied' in March 1956,
fell to 30 per cent in July, before reaching its low point of 20 per cent a year
later.[27]

The end of 1956 was marked also by the rumble of Soviet tanks. Indeed,
France and Great Britain had counted on the troubles in the popular
democracies of Eastern Europe to neutralize the Soviet Union during their
Suez adventure. The assumption had proved incorrect. Krushchev had not
been ready to give way, and the sudden return to a Cold War climate added
to difficulties in France. On the evening of 7 November, a few hours after the
order had been given to halt the action in Egypt, thousands of Parisians
held a violent demonstration outside the Communist Party headquarters,
rue Le Peletier, attempted to ransack the offices of *L'Humanité*, and clashed
with the police and a Communist counter-demonstration led by Raymond
Guyot and Jeannette Vermeersch. Elements of the extreme Right were
certainly responsible for fanning the agitation, but the great majority of
those present for this night of violence on the streets of Paris were there

simply to protest their impotent anger over the crushing of the Budapest rising on 4 November by the Red Army's tanks. The prestige of the Soviet Union had never been so low; nor, as a result, had the PCF ever been so detested and isolated:[28] it now paid dearly for a total submission to all the turns of Moscow's policy. In Poland, the Kremlin had grudgingly allowed the former 'Titoist' Gomulka to take control, hoping thus to check an already advanced revolt within the Party. But in Hungary, where Rakasi had been unable to introduce essential reforms during Stalin's lifetime, a more popular and overtly anti-Soviet revolt was met with force. The revolt was bloodily crushed by the Red Army, and its leader, the liberal Communist Imre Nagy, was replaced by Kadar.[29] The drastic repercussions for the PCF of its haste to applaud the Soviet intervention, hailed without hesitation as a victory for Leninism, were quickly felt, the more so since the French public had been kept well informed of the Hungarian drama, notably by the commercial radio stations frustrated by the military censorship over the Suez expedition. Many Party memberships were not renewed at the beginning of 1957, numerous Party intellectuals protested or resigned, and the PCF suffered a huge loss of prestige among fellow-travellers and sections of the public sympathetic since 1944 to the Resistance record and moral appeal of the 'Parti des fusillés. The rupture of Sartre with the Mouvement de la Paix provided a spectacular example of this disaffection. And indeed, for the first time since the Liberation, ex-Communists now became a significant feature of the French political landscape, reinforcing, in particular, the opposition to the war in Algeria. It was on the ruin of 'Progressisme' that a new intellectual Left was to attempt to construct an alternative Socialism.

The PCF was now heavily penalized for its apparent inability to accept that Stalin was dead. The shakiness of the Party's grasp on the economic and social realities of modern France has already been seen in the 1956 election campaign. To this can be added its failure to understand the evolution in moral standards and behaviour, something clear from its campaign against birth-control, vigorously led by Thorez's wife. Above all, however, there was the French Party leadership's stubborn denial of the destalinization which had begun with Krushchev's secret report denouncing Stalin's crimes, read to the Twentieth Congress of the Soviet Communist Party on 25 February.[30] Some European Communists, such as the Italian leader, Togliatti, were prompt to acknowledge the report, and *Le Monde* began its publication in France on 6 March. Yet the French delegation to Moscow – Thorez, Duclos, Fajon, and Doize – despite having heard the full report, at first persisted in a denial of its authenticity, then refused to confirm its existence before the Party's Political Bureau until 19 June. And even then the French Party's militants were only presented with the watered-down version published by *Pravda* on 12

July.[31] Thorez, still hesitating between Molotov and Krushchev, was clearly uneasy at the prospect of exposing and repudiating all the Soviet errors he had so calmly accepted since 1930. The Budapest drama in fact completed an unfortunate evolution in the history of the French Communist Party. Placed on the defensive, the PCF now lost the benefits of its partial reinsertion in national political life; its hopes for a united front or a Popular Front majority in the new Assembly were ruined; and it chose to accept weakness and isolation. In the eyes of many, this attitude of the Communist Party, along with that of the SFIO, solid in its support for the policies of Guy Mollet, was to do much to discredit the traditional Left.

## The balance sheet of 'Molletisme'

To the credit of the Mollet government, however, stands a refusal to allow the Algerian drama to absorb all its energies, and an attempt to implement policies of recognizably Socialist inspiration. And what better demonstration of good intentions, what more certain way of rallying the faithful, than with the resuscitation in the first weeks of the new government of the perennial clerical–anticlerical quarrel over education? An agitated press campaign and a series of meetings were launched; the 'scandal' of the Marie-Barangé law was denounced, the possibility of nationalizing teaching was discussed, and the old question of reserving public funds for State schools was mooted again.[32] but the offensive came to little, running up against opposition from the UDSR and, of course, the MRP. It was in fact quietly forgotten in the furore over Suez and Budapest; discussion of the Cartier report recommending the law's abrogation was called for in the Assembly on 25 October, only to be ignored on 8 November as a result of a procedural motion introduced by the MRP. This was not the only backward glance. Nostalgia for a united working-class movement, albeit now somewhat soured by anticommunism, was stirred in May with the visit of an official SFIO delegation to Moscow, the first since the Congress of Tours. Mollet and Pineau also made the pilgrimage in May; their talks failed to produce any Soviet undertaking over disarmament, but they returned with Moscow's solemn blessing for the 'liberal spirit' in which they envisaged a solution for the Algeria problem.

There were tangible achievements on the European front. The SFIO position was that with the EDC out of the way the development of a European community would foster internationalism and contribute to world stability. Mollet even gave his official backing to the Comité d'action pour les Etats-Unis d'Europe of Jean Monnet. Construction of European political unity was for the moment impossible – Great Britain had repulsed all initiatives from the Six since 1953, and the French

Socialists, whose anglophile sympathies we have seen over Suez, were re-luctant to act without her; consequently, progress had to come through greater economic and scientific co-operation. Encouraged by the mounting successes of the ECSC, talks for a European community for the peaceful development of atomic energy were held under Spaak and Pineau; in July 1956, the French assembly accepted the Euratom project. This co-oper-ation in peaceful atomic research – open to all, hence eventually to Great Britain – did not prevent France aspiring to possess atomic weapons, even if she was bound not to produce any until 1961. Technical and military preparations now began in earnest. On 30 November, the Atomic Energy Commission was charged with supplying the plutonium, a plan for con-struction was drawn up by General Ailleret, and the Saharan site of Reg-gane was chosen in July 1957; and at the same time, General Blanc, Chief of General Staff, set up the Javelot brigade, the precursor of modern nuc-lear-armed divisions. France of course did get her bomb, an incontestable heritage the Fifth Republic acknowledged only with reluctance. The diffi-cult question of the Saar was finally settled by the Franco-German agree-ment signed at Luxembourg on 5 June 1956; under this the region returned officially to Federal Germany on 1 January 1957, the French government having ignored the concerted howls of protest from Communists, Gaullists, and even some Socialists and liberal industrialists still fighting the battles of the past. Proof of the Mollet government's grasp on the changed realities of international competition came with its deliberate reopening of discus-sions at the Venice Conference in May 1956, and the signing in Rome on 27 March 1957 of the treaties setting up the Euratom and the European Economic Community (EEC) or Common Market. The Rome agreement was ratified without difficulty by the French Assembly on 10 July.[33] The treaty, creating a customs union in which free circulation of labour and goods between the six was planned for 1 January 1958, was by no means perfect; it offended *dirigiste* sensibilities, including those within the SFIO; and there remained important practical problems, such as the need to protect French agriculture, provide for the integration of the overseas territories, and, of course, leave the way open for British entry. Nonethe-less, to its supranational features and the latitude it left big business could be opposed the generous scope it allowed to national policies. And, after all, was it not essential to avoid the fragmentation of Western Europe and the drawing of Germany towards the East? Moreover, might not an active and united European neutrality *vis-à-vis* the superpowers ultimately favour the emergence of a realistic and mature European Socialism? Clearly these could be no more than long-term gambles on the future – but they were taken consciously, with an awareness of what was at stake.

With a similar timeliness the Mollet government might have been able to use policy over the French Union to redeem some of the failings of its

Algerian policy. Following the course traced by Mendès France and Edgar Faure, amiable negotiations led by Alain Savary resulted in an agreement granting recognition of Morocco's prerogatives as a sovereign State on 28 May 1956, even if the Algerian drama was to complicate their application. Likewise, after Bourguiba had been received on 2 February with the honours of a Head of State, independence for Tunisia came on 20 March, with the questions of the French garrison at Bizerte and the defence of the frontier with Algeria to be settled later. In both cases, the French negotiators under Alain Savary had shown considerable skill and flexibility, and had preserved reasonable chances for future co-operation. In the same positive vein – which stood France in good stead with the international authorities increasingly concerned by the Algerian affair – was the *loi-cadre* for the French Union prepared by Gaston Defferre, who, having distinguished himself by an openness and readiness to negotiate over Indo-China, was now Minister for the Overseas Territories. The Defferre *loi-cadre*, promulgated on 23 June, established throughout the French Union a direct universal suffrage and single electoral college – that is, precisely what France still hesitated to accord to Algeria. The indigenous political élites, many of them experienced and trusted figures in the political life of mainland France since the Liberation, now led an orderly and smooth transition in many parts of the French Union: Togoland moved towards autonomy, Madagascar prepared for independence, an African university was set up at Dakar, and a common organization for the Saharan territories settled contentions over frontiers and safeguarded France's interest in the petrol of the regions.[34] This relatively trouble-free passage of Black Africa towards independence, an evolution the French Community of the Fifth Republic would accelerate, even fostered hopes in some quarters for seeing a French equivalent of the British Commonwealth.

The socialist ambitions of the Mollet government naturally led to the promotion of an energetic economic and social policy inside France. An enlarged and centralized Ministry of Economic affairs, now with a total of eight Secretaries of State, and headed by Ramadier after Lacoste's appointment to Algeria, was created to foster economic growth and investment, and stimulate the public sector and the Plan, all in an enthusiastic Keynesian atmosphere and with a relaxed approach to budgetary balance and personal competence. A former trade-unionist, Albert Gazier, took charge of both Labour and Public Health at the Ministry of Social Affairs, with responsibility for extending the advantages of the Welfare State to the least privileged members of French society. The economic legacy inherited from the Faure government was by no means faultless: the budget deficit was considerable, inflation had reappeared, the franc was vulnerable, and there was a danger of imbalance on the external exchanges. However, the general economic conditions were favourable, and with a growth in industrial output of 10 per cent in 1956 and 9 per cent the following year, Mollet was left with a reasonable margin for manoeuvre. Faithful to the ambitions of the Popular Front and building on the example set by Renault, a third week of paid holidays for employees was introduced on 28 February 1956, a move which stimulated popular forms of tourism, such as caravanning, and whetted appetites for foreign travel among the better off. Changes were made to the system of tax allowances by region to encourage industrial decentralization and to help reduce the growing disparity in standards of living between Paris and the provinces. Of particular importance was the creation of the Fonds national de solidarité, the first step towards a comprehensive provision for the old, a welcome antidote to the otherwise shabby treatment of those at the end of their working lives. Run by the Caisse des dépôts, this scheme was financed by a 10 per cent increase in income tax, levies on speculations on the stock exchange and land-holdings, and, above all, by the introduction of the famous *vignette* (tax disc) for cars. The sum of 32 000 francs a year now made available to the needy old, the sick, and the handicapped, was not a great deal, but it was an important start. Indeed, the resistance the project encountered speaks volumes for its significance. The right-wing majority in the Council of the Republic was resolutely hostile; against a background of grumbles and protests from tax-payers, it led to an interminable shunting of the project between the two Chambers, necessitated the posing of the question of confidence seven times, and in fact delayed the adoption of the project until June.

And this was not all. To the consternation of its opponents, especially the Independents, alarmed by this wave of socialist legislation and *étatisme*, the Mollet government continued to table projects and was at work on others for the future. A number of these followed in rapid parliamentary succession. Bernard Chochoy's *loi-cadre* on housing, responsible for 320 000 housing starts in 1956, tried to industrialize and streamline the building trades; the construction of municipal housing and low-cost homes was given priority over luxury flats and home-ownership, and there were efforts to improve rural housing. Another *loi-cadre* dealt with agriculture; this sought to stabilize agricultural incomes, favour the dissemination of technical knowledge, and was responsible for the launch of the co-operatives for farm equipment and machinery (CUMA), as well as improving social security for workers in the agricultural sector. A plan providing aid for the development of Brittany was approved on 18 May, and was in fact to serve as the model for subsequent policies for regional development. Individual projects included the tidal power station on the river Rance, the nuclear station at Avoine, and the Moselle Canal. Lastly, considerable efforts were made in education, with the minister, René Billières, giving priority to technical training, and beginning the reform with an extension of schooling, changes in the syllabus structure to favour career choices, and moves to make teaching methods more flexible. Other projects of the Mollet government which might have come to fruition included an overhaul of the fiscal system with the introduction of local taxes, a constitutional reform of the French Union, compulsory arbitration in industrial disputes, new powers for the Comités d'enterprise, and a higher reimbursement of medical charges. Shortage of funds meant that this series of reforms had soon to be abandoned. Behind the apparent diversity of the projects can, however, be discerned a genuine aspiration to economic modernization and social justice, one whose legacy was received, almost unacknowledged, by the Fifth Republic.

For once again, and to the self-righteous astonishment of the Left in power, the obstacle was financial. It was not of domestic origin. Indeed, the economic situation in metropolitan France probably posed no more of a danger to public finances under Mollet than it had under Pinay or Faure. True, stability of agricultural prices was threatened by the terrible frosts of 1956; but tax revenues still covered three-quarters of expenditure, and there was a good chance that Ramadier's budget for 1957 would have reduced the deficit. His loan issues of June and September 1956 were taken up without difficulty, and wages were under control, albeit thanks in part to a dubious manipulation of the sliding scale index (wholesale prices rising only from 141 to 143 between January 1956 and April 1957). The cause of the failure was in fact the war in Algeria; this was the financial burden which ruined all the long-term projects; its setbacks which overshadowed, in every sense, the whole of Guy Mollet's policy. In effect, the departure of the conscripts to Algeria in 1956 deprived the French economy of 200 000 of its youngest and most dynamic workers. From this point onwards, the imbalance of supply and demand steadily worsened; the shortfall represented roughly 1.5 per cent of gross national product; demand–pull inflation reappeared; and the cycle of deepening deficits had begun. Henceforth demand could only be met by increased imports, thus swelling the commercial deficit (413 milliard francs in 1956), and upsetting the overall balance of accounts. The 300 milliard francs of additional military expenditure made it impossible to find the 350 milliard judged necessary to pay for the government's economic and social policies. In spite of heroic efforts by Ramadier, the budget deficit, which had averaged 650 milliard from 1952 to 1956, grew to 925 milliard in 1956, and was to exceed 1100 milliard in 1957. French foreign exchange reserves dwindled, and the franc came under pressure as soon as the extra imports – notably expensive petrol during the Suez crisis and war materials – had to be paid for. Output certainly continued to grow, but the public purse haemorrhaged uncontrollably: in short, the Mollet government sacrificed the success of its ambitious social policy to a stubborn pursuit of the war in Algeria.

And at the same time it destroyed its own majority. In the confusion of public opinion and the uncertainty of the other political parties, Mollet could count on a broad coalition of negative support from all those who, though hostile to his domestic policies, rejected independence and even negotiation in Algeria. Yet with the weakening of the franc, the ruining of the budget, the pursuit of a programme of social reform, and the attacks on privileges, his government mobilized the opposition of those otherwise prepared to support it over Algeria. This was the lesson to be drawn from a by-election held in Paris in January, when an Independent highly favourable to *l'Algérie française* obtained a massive success, with the candidates of the Left divided, and the Mendésiste and even Pierre Poujade coming nowhere. The same phenomenon was observed in May during a by-election at Lyon. The spring of 1957 saw discontent growing, exploited by the Moderates and the Right: against the widespread appointment of Socialists to positions of high responsibility in the State; against Ramadier's fiscal reforms; against the reform of the medical profession planned by Gazier; and against Mollet himself, now also under attack within the SFIO. A disparate coalition of Communists, Poujadists, and seventy-five Moderates and Radicals finally brought down the Mollet government on 21 May 1957, ostensibly over its financial policy. The pretext was unimportant. The longest-lived ministry of the Fourth Republic had succumbed to exhaustion – which stemmed from its failure to remove the irresponsible ambiguity it had fostered since 6 February 1956. Elected to bring peace in Algeria, the Mollet government had not only deepened the conflict in Algeria, but had brought the entire French nation into it. Powerless to impose decent and realistic negotiations on Algiers, it had also failed to convince the hardliners who had supported it for so long of the need to at least place the French economy on a war footing; visibly at the mercy of events and dragged down by its mistakes, it failed on every front. Nor was the verdict on it merely a political one: the Mollet government was condemned for a moral failure. It is at this level that the inevitable return to the events in Algeria must now be considered.

The situation in Algeria at the end of 1956 was difficult, complicated by the Suez affair, and with the potential benefits of systematic patrolling still not fully apparent. From October onwards, roughly 3000 incidents occurred each month. Control of the population was tighter and more brutal than ever, but the ambushes continued. Above all, the FLN now concentrated its action in the towns, generating a climate of hatred and suffering which in turn encouraged counter-terrorism and pitched battles.[35] Responsible for the change in nationalist strategy was Abbane Ramdane; he believed that by focusing its efforts on Algiers the FLN would demonstrate the strength of its hold over the population and open the final phase of the struggle for national liberation. Into action now went the terrorist networks set up in the city by Yacef Saadi and his commandos, who, having successfully resisted a vast police operation of 26 May 1956, had cleared the Algiers Kasbah of much of its organized crime and were responsible for the working of the nationalists' parallel politico-administrative structures and fund-raising. In August, in retaliation for the rue de Thèbes attack by European activists and in application of the decisions taken at the Soummam Conference, they began operating in the European quarters of Algiers. The FLN's campaign of indiscriminate urban terrorism became general in September. Bombs exploded on 30 September at two crowded city centre cafés, the Milk Bar and the Cafétéria, killing four and wounding fifty-two, among them many children. In November and December, against this background of mounting violence, came a school strike and then a general strike. The Europeans of Algiers responded on 29 December, during the funeral of Amédée Froger, killed the previous day by Ali la Pointe, with a terrible anti-Muslim pogrom. It was to break this spiral of violence and fear and to sabotage the unlimited general strike of Muslims in preparation that, on 7 January 1957, Lacoste handed over full responsibility and power for the restoration of order to General Massu and his Tenth Paratroop Division, just returned from Egypt.[36] The 'battle of Algiers' had begun.

It ended in October 1957 with victory for the French forces. All the local FLN leaders were dead or imprisoned, the terrorist networks had been smashed, and some Muslims had rallied to the side of the forces of order. Massu had set up efficient patrolling of the entire city, isolating the Muslim quarters, and establishing tight control over their inhabitants. Then, operating in small, ruthless, and well-equipped groups, the paras had gone in: combing the Algiers Kasbah, carrying out searches, recruiting informers, hunting suspects – the effectiveness of their action measured by the steady fall in the number of bombings. And to help them there was torture, which now became a basic instrument of the French struggle against the terrorists; carried out in specially established centres or at the Villa Susini, interrogation under torture was indispensable to obtain the information without which the battle of Algiers could not have been won.[37] In one sense, however, this proved a pyrrhic victory; for the widespread use of torture, accepted by the authorities of the Republic – Paul Teitgen, General Secretary of the Algiers police, was one of the few to protest by giving his resignation[38] – in fact raised the first serious doubts in a hitherto untroubled French public as to the legitimacy of the war in Algeria. In France, to stifle the reports and protests which fuelled such doubts, the Mollet government resorted to increasingly frequent press seizures, and practised a heavy censorship on the journalists of the French national radio. Finally, in April, as a sop to the activists and to reassure the general public, it agreed to set up an imposingly named Commission permanente de sauvegarde des droits et libertés individuelles; this was in fact little more than a cynical gesture on the part of the authorities,[39] but with it the handful of protesting intellectuals so despised by Lacoste had obtained a symbolic first victory in this new Dreyfus Affair. Disquieting evidence of the methods being employed in Algeria was steadily accumulating. Henri Marrou, historian at the Sorbonne, expressed his shame and unease for France and the Republic in an important article in *Le Monde* of 5 April 1956; the harrowing testimony of Jean Muller, a former lorry driver killed in the fighting, was published by the *Cahiers du témoignage chrétien* on 15 February 1957; the Comité de résistance spirituelle published a collection of eyewitness accounts, *Des rappelés témoignent*, in March; René Capitant protested publicly after the death under torture of his former student, Ali Boumendjel; and there were many others.[40] And each protest, each voice raised in alarm, added insistence to the fundamental questions it was increasingly hard to ignore. What was the value of a Republic whose deeds contradicted the principles of the Resistance from which it claimed to derive its legitimacy? What, moreover, was the moral authority of the Socialist-led government which allowed the Republic to succumb in this way? These questions had already received one answer; from Algiers, in the cry of the European crowd at the funeral of Froger: 'l'Armée au pouvoir!'

## 15

# The collapse

Félix Gouin, breaking a ten-year silence on 9 October 1957, expressed his unease: 'What is striking is the apathy, the almost total indifference of the public. It is evidence of a grave disaffection from the parliamentary régime. Were this to find itself in danger, would it have any more defence than had the Second Republic faced with the *coup d'état* of 1851?' Fears for the future of the Fourth Republic were growing. Its prospects certainly looked slight: the Assembly and the political parties were unable to turn the verdict of universal suffrage into a stable majority for government, the population was disaffected, and difficulties were multiplying. Trapped and powerless, the Republic crumbled, as much weakened from within as attacked from without. On 9 December 1957, a senior imperial administrator, Robert Delavignette, who resigned from the Commission de sauvegarde set up by the Mollet government, prophesied: 'The most serious, it seems to me, is not just the atrocities, but the fact that the State is destroying itself. In Algeria we are witnessing the decomposition of the State, and this gangrene is threatening the nation as a whole.'[1] The Algerian snare was tightening.

*The question*

On 21 May 1957, a purely circumstantial parliamentary majority, lacking both cohesion and a programme, brought down the minority coalition which had held power for more than a year and whose electoral commitments had not been honoured. This was the point of no return, beyond which the popular will counted for little and events took charge. In the crisis that followed the fall of the Mollet government, the parliamentary implications of the equivocal election results of 1956 were felt to the full, reminiscent of the decline of the Third Force. With the extremes of the parliamentary spectrum – the Communists, the Poujadists, and various activists, in all roughly 200 deputies – automatically excluded from the calculations, just under 400 deputies remained from which a majority could be formed. Yet no such majority existed: a ministry without the socialists was impossible; so too was one unacceptable to the Independents and Peasants who had just brought down Mollet. Worse, the unity of these already unstable groups was now threatened; for the Algerian problem fragmented opinion, troubled consciences, and sowed discord among the familiar coalitions. As André Siegfried observed, the least disagreement was now sufficient to upset the balance.[2] Always assuming, of course, that a balance was actually possible – for since a governing coalition could no longer be negative the range of choices was further narrowed.

A solution from the Left was more remote than ever. The Communists, still reeling from the shock of Budapest, were trying to limit the damage and restore their credibility. However, faced with the hostility of the SFIO towards all those tainted by the events in Hungary, they had to recognize that hopes for a united front of all the Left had vanished. The Socialists held, then, to their strategic position as the left flank and indispensable element of any parliamentary solution, one which might extend as far rightwards as the Centre. Confident in the strength of this position, Mollet bided his time, comfortably installed as the counsellor to President Coty during the crisis. At the same time, he brutally reasserted his control over the SFIO party machine; after the exclusion of André Philip on 25 January 1958, the left-wing opposition to Mollet within the SFIO was forced to prepare its dissent cautiously. Guy Mollet had become the pivotal figure of the régime; as the crisis of 13 May was to demonstrate, without his support nothing was possible. There remained the chance for the MRP of forcing the hands of the Socialists and wooing the Moderates. But the failure of Pflimlin, presented to the Assembly on 29 May 1957, and the shambles of the MRP congress in June, left no doubt as to the weakness of a party whose only coherence came from the cause of European unity. Invariably denounced by the SFIO for its clericalism, the MRP remained suspect in the eyes of the Right for its variety of Catholic idealism which might endanger *l'Algérie française*. The secular groups of the Centre-Left were in a similar state of flux, absorbed by factional infighting and leadership squabbles. The UDSR expended the last of its energies in the interminable duel between Pleven and Mitterrand, the latter refusing to imperil a promising political future by breaking his silence over Algeria. The Radical Party had split into a number of personal fiefs, definitively rejecting *Mendésisme* in the course of stormy congresses and struggles to control the powerful federations of the South-West, struggles in which *La Dépêche de Toulouse* of Jean Baylet carried more weight than *L'Express*. Party discipline over its parliamentarians was weak, that over ministers weaker still. Edgar Faure controlled the RGR deputies; the dissidents who had broken from Mendès France at the congress of October 1956 were now led by André Morice and Henri Queuille; and within the party organization the Mendésistes were coming under attack from Bourgès-Maunoury, Maurice Faure, and Félix Gaillard, robbing the Radical group in the Assembly of all voting consistency.

Mendès France, isolated and with only a dozen loyal deputies, practically abandoned the Radical Party in June 1957. To complete the confused picture, the remaining Républicains sociaux had abandoned all pretence to consistent action; the Independents, though going from strength to strength, were divided over Algeria; and Poujadism was already receding. The position in the Assembly then was chaotic, with a solution from the Right as improbable as one from the Centre or the Left.

To such weaknesses, however, could be opposed the remarkable capacity of the parliamentary system, demonstrated again in 1957, to neutralize and ultimately absorb developments which challenged its established practices. Thus although the phenomenon was not decisive at the time, with hindsight it is hard not to be struck by the rapid and strikingly parallel failure of *Mendésisme* and *Poujadisme*. The debate begun in 1953 and 1954 over the modernization of France did not find a parliamentary expression, the régime apparently unable to accommodate the issue it had itself helped to raise. Behind this lay the fact that in their helplessness the political parties were keener than ever to act on behalf of specific interests and satisfy particular demands, thus consolidating their electorates and defusing potential threats. The complex web of small interests, powerful pressures, and mutual obligations gradually became stronger and more sophisticated, forming a block to new alignments and suffocating long-term initiatives.[3] Thus, with the return of inflation, the appeal and relevance of Poujadism evaporated; recovered prosperity brought a return to political quiescence and former loyalties; its electorate was won back without difficulty by the Moderates and the Right, while the last militants of the UDCA avidly seized the Algerian theme as a basis for concerted action with the extreme Right. Pierre Poujade, as we have seen, was soundly beaten in the Paris by-election of January 1957; his imprecations and excesses now became just extra ammunition in the larger struggle for *l'Algérie française*; those once enthralled by his 'République des petits' fell back into resignation or traditional politics. A very similar evolution was observable for *Mendésisme*. Its leader was imbued with a strong Republican conviction that politics should not be organized around an individual, however important or necessary the ideas he articulated. Mendès France consistently refused to set up an autonomous political movement, and after the dismal failure to rejuvenate the Radical Party, the energies released by *Mendésisme* were dispersed – some within the Radical Party, some to the 'nouvelle gauche' of the political clubs and small groups, others seeking satisfaction for appetites for modernity in loyalty to de Gaulle – without an attempt by Mendès France to canalize them usefully for the future. The creation of the *Cahiers de la République*, for all their self-confident tone, offered no more than a forum for debate and reflection: the dream of the 'République moderne' did not get a second impetus until the shock of 13 May. Was this general inability to innovate unavoidable, the result of the in-built reflexes of the régime itself? Or could the Fourth Republic, given time, have found a settlement for Algeria, and then returned, successfully perhaps this time, to the debate on modernization? But time, if indeed time is what was needed, was not available. The régime was overtaken by events in Algeria, which swept away the question of renewal and rendered insoluble the problem of authority.

Once again the war in Algeria was at the root of the paralysis. At every point on the political spectrum it fostered contradictions, introduced weakness, and wore down good intentions. On the extreme Left, the Communist Party, having been obliged to abandon its hopes for a common front with the Socialists, at least had greater liberty to develop its opposition to the war. At the Le Havre congress of July 1956, the Party had opportunely abandoned its old position, defended by Thorez since 1936, of the gradual emergence of an Algerian nation that would include the European settlers, coming out in favour of recognition for the bases of Algerian nationalism, though ready to play down the eventuality of an FLN-led independence for fear of alienating part of its electorate. And the Communist militants, if not quite the spearhead of the peace movement they were later to claim,[4] did have an important role in the protest; *L'Humanité* was loud in its denunciation of torture (and was frequently seized); and the PCF did indeed work to encourage popular acceptance of the inevitability of a peaceful solution of the Algerian problem. But it was hard for the Communists to go beyond this, well aware that an avant-garde position over Algeria would merely deepen their isolation in French opinion. Willingly or not, the PCF was forced to adopt a relatively cautious attitude, limiting itself to very conventional forms of protest; unable, for example, to approve openly the initiatives now being proposed by its youth and student organizations in favour of direct support for the FLN.

Inside the SFIO the debate over Algeria had taken an acrimonious tone, with increasingly open allusions by the minorities to the betrayal of ideals, to the disastrously right-wing policies of the Socialists in power, and to the excessive personality cult surrounding the Lacoste–Mollet–Lejeune trio, which blocked discussion.[5] A few of the remaining SFIO student groups, led by Michel Rocard, and workers, academics, and party figures were ready to challenge 'national-molletisme', but made little impression; Jules Moch had no influence in the party, Daniel Mayer and Robert Verdier were suspended, and André Philip was excluded. Despairing of ever being listened to within the SFIO, a Comité socialiste d'études et d'action pour la paix en Algérie was set up; along with the opposition already mentioned, this brought together André Hauriou, Ernest Labrousse, Edouard Depreux, Alain Savary, Charles-André

Julien, and Jean Rous; the split which would lead to the creation of the PSA in 1958 was now openly prepared. Mollet and company reigned supreme at the SFIO, sure of securing three-quarters of the votes in the party congresses, developing their image as men of order, and unaware of – or indifferent to – the hostility of the young and many intellectuals to their particular interpretation of Socialism. Yet whatever the strength of their hold over the SFIO, their capacity for innovation over Algeria was nil: with a solution along the lines of those found for Tunisia and Morocco rejected and independence anathema, all they could offer was the familiar but increasingly doubtful promotion of peaceful co-existence of the two communities in Algeria. This was the pious intention embodied in the *loi-cadre* for Algeria presented in September 1957, preparation of which had been jealously supervised by Lacoste. Confused, and on several points not going as far as the 1947 statute, the *loi-cadre* provoked at best scepticism, at worst rejection. The Left clearly had nothing original to offer; either, as with the PCF, out of prudence, or, in the case of the SFIO, from helpless entanglement in the war.

The MRP was afflicted by the same paralysis. Its leadership was in open disagreement over the Algerian position: Robert Buron had come to favour a liberal solution and speedy negotiations;[6] Georges Bidault had gone in the opposite direction and now favoured the hardline colonialist positions; and Pierre Pflimlin tried to argue for a middle course. What remained of the MRP membership was confused and discouraged, the youth movements protested in vain, and its students went over to join the UNEF's campaign. The warring factions of the Radicals could at least unite in the cause of *l'Algérie française*, the voice of Mendès France drowned out by the unanimous rejection of abandonment from Morice (who was to form his Centre républicain), Queuille and Marie and their band of supporters, and Bourgès-Maunoury and Gaillard within the Radical Party itself. Curiously, the Right was not as united over *l'Algérie française* as might have been expected. True, the Independents prided themselves on being among the most ardent defenders of the French presence; but Pinay and Reynaud were already beginning to lace their support with a cynical liberalism which was to win converts in the more enlightened business circles; they asked whether, in terms of strict economic and political profitability, the war in Algeria was in fact worthwhile, whether the cost for France of holding on to Algeria might not actually outweigh the benefits. Against the background of the newly discovered oil of the Sahara, the opening of frontiers by the Common Market, and the short-term stakes, this fundamental argument made little immediate impact, but it was to re-emerge strongly in 1960. And even at the time, Raymond Aron, to the alarm of his *Le Figaro* readers, gave a skilful presentation of the case for a rational assessment of the real value of Algeria to France.[7]

The general indecision of all the political parties towards the Algerian problem, albeit dressed in a hollow verbosity, favoured the organization of direct pressure on the parliamentarians by the most determined defenders of the French presence. On 15 May 1957, for example, Poujade, Henri Dorgères (erstwhile leader of the 'chemises vertes' Fascist movement of before the war) and Paul Antier, an agrarian Independent not averse to strong-arm methods, concluded a solemn alliance to defend *l'Algérie française* and to uphold the 'valeurs saines' of French civilization. More important by its development and for the closeness with which it monitored proceedings in the Assembly was the Union pour le salut et le renouveau de l'Algérie française (USRAF) founded by Jacques Soustelle. Prominent members of the USRAF included André Morice, the breakaway Radical; Roger Duchet, leader of the Independents; Georges Bidault, the MRP leader; but its appeal was not exclusively to the Right; it also drew the support of Albert Bayet, Paul Rivet, and Mgr Saliège. Groups like these formed the vital link between the politicians and the increasingly emboldened activist minorities of the extreme Right. Georges Sauge, a former Communist turned Catholic militant, had the support of Colonel Lacheroy for a campaign of lectures to army officers; the review *Verbe*, backed by integrist elements in the Catholic hierarchy and General Weygand, preached the virtues of the crusade against the Islamic–Communist fanaticism of the FLN and its 'accomplices' in France; authentic Fascists of 'Jeune Nation', led by Pierre Sidos and Dominique Venner, longed to take control of the streets; they found eager allies among the most violent of Poujade's supporters, led by the deputies Le Pen and Demarquet, inflamed by their experiences with the paras in Algeria; plus of course diehard reactionaries and Pétainistes like Frédéric-Dupont and Tixier-Vignancour. This motley band dreamed of strong action to arrest the decline of France, with General Massu's paratroopers leading a glorious national revival. However, for all the grotesque passion and mindless brutality of these enthusiasts, it is not certain that they were quite the danger that some, notably the left-wing students of the Latin Quarter, took them to be. The more serious and immediate threat lay elsewhere, with the networks of activists discreetly at work in the crucial areas of the ex-servicemen's organizations, the military, and extreme Gaullist circles. Progress here was unobtrusive but sure, cultivating strategic contacts, drawing up plans, making careful preparations: and at the heart of this action was the goal of establishing an indissoluble link between the defence of *l'Algérie française* and a subversion of the Fourth Republic. Men like the indefatigable Biaggi, organizing the military training of a handful of 'patriotes révolutionnaires'; or former *cagoulards* (extreme right-wing conspirators before the war), like Dr Martin, who infiltrated the Indo-China veterans' associations and the ex-students' clubs of the military colleges, building up support in the preparatory classes of Saint-Cyr and in the Law faculties. The same work was continued in Algeria by Robert Martel and Colonel Thomazo, organizing the most ardent of the *pieds-noirs* in paramilitary groups. By the end of 1957, they controlled an ex-serviceman's association, the Comité nationale des anciens combattants (CANAC), where determined Gaullist faithfuls, like Sanguinetti, easily asserted their influence; and orders came from Léon Delbecque, the Algiers agent of Chaban-Delmas; inspiration and encouragement from senator Michel Debré's grandiloquent *Le Courrier de la colère*. Not all those involved had a commitment to Gaullism, far from it; but all could be reached by those who had.

The opposition to the war was somewhat anaemic by comparison, handicapped by the absence of any solid support from the political parties of the Left. Thus it was not until 1960 and the 'manifeste des 121' that the protest against torture recovered the dimensions it had taken at the height of the battle of Algiers. Outside the mainstream of politics and opinion, the leaders of the anti-war protest were as yet unable to organize a sustained pressure. Their movement found support among academics, journalists, students (the minority hostile to the war having taken control of the UNEF in July 1956), and a few young farmers and workers from Action catholique. But its impact on the conscripts and on public opinion as a whole was slight. And in fact the protest tended to swell numerically without developing any real unity. Its audience was highly disparate: post-Budapest breakaways from the PCF; Trotskyists; disenchanted Socialists and Mendésistes; members of the old Ligue des droits de l'homme who had not succumbed to Mollet's charms; Protestants, from a cultural reflex of resistance to authority; militant Catholics, impatient with the prudence of their bishops;[8] missionary priests and former activists of the various Catholic youth movements; teachers and academics; trade union militants, especially from Force Ouvrière and the CFTC; conscripts shattered by personal experience of the war. A vast kaleidoscope of opinion, then, but one united, if at all, only by an awareness of its position as a powerless minority.[9] No more than a tiny handful ever took the decisive step of passing to direct action against the French war by joining the network set up in October 1957 by Francis and Colette Jeanson to organize funds, shelter, and help for the FLN fighters.[10] Like its predecessor this latter-day Dreyfusard movement exhausted itself, but without having produced a giant mobilization of Republican defence on the scale of 1902. Nevertheless, the meetings and demonstrations, the subterranean propaganda, the clandestine distribution of banned books and newspapers did at least help to accelerate the painfully slow awakening of French public opinion. The press which supported the struggle, the object of endless prosecutions and seizures, was, by its circulation, also that of a minority: reviews like *Esprit, Les Temps modernes*, and *Consciences maghrébines* (founded by André Mandouze in 1954); and weeklies such as *Canard enchaîné, France-Observateur* (where Roger Stéphane, Claude Bourdet, and Robert Barrat were at the forefront of the protest), *Témoignage chrétien*, and *L'Express* with Jean-Jacques Servan-Schreiber and Jean Daniel. However, the movement found useful support in some sections of the influential national press, notably *L'Humanité* and *Libération*, but also *Le Monde*, which came out increasingly in favour of negotiations in the course of 1957.[11] And, very gradually, the major organs of French opinion were forced to modify their positions; *Le Figaro, L'Aurore, Paris-Presse* and *France-Soir, Paris-Match* and *Le Parisien libéré* (this last, the privileged vehicle for popular anti-Arab racialism), found it progressively harder, for example, to deny that torture existed or to ignore the insidious damage done to France by the war.

On the other hand, the arguments of the protesters never succeeded in denting the superbly self-confident reporting of the war on French television or national radio, both tightly controlled by the government; and the peripheral radio stations adopted the same unquestioning standpoint. Furthermore, it would be a mistake to imagine the entire French intelligentsia solidly ranged in the anti-war camp. True, the most organized of the Catholic intellectuals were won over, encouraged by the journalist Robert Barrat and by the Centre Catholique des Intellectuels Français,[12] yet as influential a figure as Albert Camus, shattered by the tragedy in his native Algeria, stood back from the orchestrated protest, breaking his pained silence only over particular cases.[13] And the Académie française was unanimously hostile to the 'defeatists', offering forceful denunciations of the FLN from Jules Romains and Thierry Maulnier, plus the persuasive skills of Soustelle, to counter their arguments. But in spite of such hesitations and oppositions, the anti-war movement's basic handicap was internal, the fact that its opposition could never be more than negative: the protesters were so disparate that their views on the future of Algeria were inevitably confused and contradictory. The strict Marxists among them had a vision of the French working class finally opening its arms to its Algerian comrades; others, excited by the imminent victory of the Cuban guerrillas and the success of the Afro-Asian Conference of Cairo, were quick to site the revolutionary combat of the *fellaghas* in the broader context of a Third World liberation struggle; the majority had no commitment to a Socialist future for Algeria and wanted simply to hasten the opening of serious negotiations to end the violence. All, however, were deeply shocked by the crushing indifference of the French people and the resignation of those called upon to fight in Algeria. Indeed, the opposition to the 'dirty war', in many respects akin to a new Resistance, was most in its element, proud and isolated from public opinion at large, as in 1898, in the activities of the Comités d'urgence and the appeals to conscience and justice. This explains the significance for the opposition of a ceremony like that held at the Sorbonne on 2 December 1957, when a doctorate was awarded *in absentia* to Maurice Audin, a young lecturer in Algiers, who had 'disappeared' ten days after being arrested by Massu's men on 11 June. The Comité Maurice Audin, founded in November by Laurent Schwartz and run by Pierre Vidal-Naquet, was to investigate and publicize the atrocities Audin and many others had suffered, work which led in 1958 to the publication of *Nous accusons*, a survey of French torture and repression in Algeria.[14] The same groups were responsible for the clandestine diffusion of Henri Alleg's *La Question*, a terrifying account of French torture by one of its victims, published in February 1958 and immediately seized by the authorities.[15] A protest to President Coty from Mauriac, Martin du Gard, Malraux, and Sartre produced little response. But the question, and its implied accusation, could not be ignored – for many, the régime pleaded guilty by its silence.

## The death-throes of the régime

Government had worked itself, and with it the régime, into a hopeless corner. We have already seen how, at every point of the parliamentary spectrum – Right, Centre, or Left – a stable majority was impossible. Governments were now simply carried along by the increasingly unpredictable course of events in Algeria. That the situation was sliding out of control was clear from the crisis that ended with the forming of the Bourgès-Maunoury government on 11 June 1957, after Pleven and Pflimlin had both refused to pursue their attempts. The change was of personnel rather than policies, for Guy Mollet had strongly recommended to Coty his former Defence Minister, whose loyalty had been demonstrated in the Suez affair. True, once designated Bourgès-Maunoury remained unforthcoming as to what his programme might be or to the profile of the majority he hoped for; but Mollet was backing him, the Radicals were on the whole in favour, the MRP was not actually hostile, and the Right was confident of making its influence felt. In short, with all the other parties refusing power, a collection of circumstances – the 'préjugé favourable' in the jargon of the Assembly – was working for Bourgès-Maunoury. His government was invested by 240 to 194 votes, with 150 abstentions; the Socialists were solidly for; the Communists, Poujadists, and the remaining Mendésistes as solidly against; all the other groups were divided. Premier at the age of forty-three, Bourgès-Maunoury had contrived, in best Radical tradition, to offend no one. The Bourgès-Maunoury ministry had the same Socialist and Radical basis as Mollet's, but with the accent shifted slightly rightwards by the elimination of Mitterrand and Defferre, both unpopular with Lacoste, himself entrenched more solidly than ever in Algeria and now flanked by his colleague Lejeune at Saharan Affairs. And with Pineau remaining at the Quai d'Orsay, Gazier at Social Affairs, and Jacquet moving to Overseas, the Socialists could be certain of seeing their policies continued. The only new developments were the satisfaction given to the partisans of *l'Algérie française* with the appointment of one of their leaders, André Morice, to National Defence, and the arrival at the Finance Ministry of a young and dynamic Radical, Félix Gaillard.

Gaillard responded to the difficult financial situation he inherited by cutting public expenditure, appealing for greater efforts on all sides, and, more importantly, accomplished a disguised 20 per cent devaluation, increasing the value of the franc for exports while reducing it proportionally for imports. Against a background of mounting pressure from various interest groups, and in particular the powerful grain producers, Gaillard managed to hold the situation stable during the summer, though the long-term prospects remained grim. The Bourgès-Maunoury ministry did little more than expedite pending government business, such as the ratification, without difficulty but with no particular credit to itself, of the treaties of Rome in July. As fears for the franc and the external trade balance continued to grow, it was of course over Algeria that Bourgès-Maunoury fell. The *loi-cadre* (whose SFIO antecedents have been mentioned) had finally to go before Parliament. The countless amendments it had undergone satisfied neither side and did not conceal the fundamental contradiction: the status of Algeria as an integral part of France was reaffirmed, yet, and in conflict with this principle, a degree of autonomy in the running of domestic affairs was proposed. Moreover, the real questions – such as over the type of elections for the new Federal Parliament, with or without the single electoral college, and the powers an administration now largely in the hands of the military would in reality be prepared to relinquish to elected representatives – would only be dealt with by subsequent decrees. As complicated as it was anodyne, the project was sufficient nevertheless to unleash the fury of the Europeans and mobilize Soustelle's supporters in the Assembly. But there was an external consideration which could not be ignored indefinitely: international opinion, the United States, and the United Nations were all impatient for a French gesture of good intentions over Algeria. Thus on 17 September Parliament was convened in a special session to discuss and finalize the *loi-cadre*. But on 30 September, the text which had been laboriously drafted and redrafted in committee was rejected by 279 votes to 253. The opponents of all change in Algeria had been organized by Soustelle, knowing that they could count on the automatic hostility of the Communists and Poujadists. The government had lasted just over a hundred days.

Thirty-five days were needed to resolve the crisis brought about by

Bourgès-Maunoury's resignation. The SFIO was now concerned that its mastery of the parliamentary solution might be slipping, for the rejection of the *loi-cadre* had seen the Centre and Right experiment with a coalition. The tentative explorations to find potential majorities, the so-called 'tours de piste', now became far-fetched: Pleven was unable to reconcile the Socialists and Moderates; an increasingly worried Guy Mollet had two unsuccessful attempts to draw the MRP into a similar alliance; Pinay's charm now failed him; long consultations by Robert Schuman came to nothing; and there were persistent rumours of an eventual recourse to de Gaulle. At last, with the franc sliding and the trade deficit yawning, under pressure from the employers, and with the trade unions of the public sector preparing action, a compromise solution was accepted; a return in fact to the Third Force, disguised as a Union nationale and led by Félix Gaillard. Gaillard completed the evolution begun under Bourgès-Maunoury, drawing his support from the Socialists through to the Right, plus some of the Républicains sociaux, and winning the confidence of the employers. The Gaillard government was invested on 5 November by 337 votes to the 173 of the habitual hostile coalition of Communists, Mendésistes, and Poujadists.

This time the Moderates were at the helm. Finance, Economic Affairs, and the Plan went to Pflimlin; Chaban-Delmas was at National Defence; the appointment of an Independent senator, Boscary-Monsservin, to Agriculture appeased the farming lobbies; the MRP also had Lecourt at Justice and Bacon at Labour; while the SFIO retained Lacoste and Lejeune at Algeria and the Sahara. In its favour, the Gaillard team was compact and relatively young; but as Pierre Cot observed to the Assembly, there was every likelihood that it would pursue the old policies. And indeed, on 28 January 1958, a by now completely innocuous *loi-cadre* for Algeria was accepted by 298 votes to 249, and on the firm understanding that it could not be implemented until three months after the end of all hostilities. In the same vein, an offer from Tunisia and Morocco to mediate in the Algerian affair was high-handedly rejected at the end of November. Work was begun on the project for constitutional reform which had been talked about for so long, with the right of automatic dissolution and a legislative contract as remedies for ministerial instability. In his New Year's address, President Coty had spoken of the need to adapt the basic institutions of the Republic to the changed conditions. Yet in January and February, the reform project was torn apart in committee and meetings of the party leaders. René Pleven bluntly identified the reasons for this hostility: parliamentarians were terrified by the prospect of five-year governments, alarmed at the thought that they would no longer be able to pander to their electoral clientele with vote-catching amendments made at the expense of the public purse.[16] Gaillard's efforts to restore financial balance ran up against similar opposition.

The parties were reluctant to impose unpopular new taxes – the issue in fact helped to detach the SFIO from its allies of the Right – and if all wanted to break out of the budgetary impasse, none was ready to sacrifice the defence of its own interests. Consequently, advances had to be sought from the Banque de France, and in January 1958, repeating his mission of twelve years earlier, Jean Monnet was dispatched to Washington to seek American loans. Mendès France, who had suffered his final defeat in the Radical Party on 10 November, spelt out in vain the uncomfortable truth – rejection of which had already cost the life of the Mollet government and the Front républicain – namely that war requires a war economy, that unless accompanied by economic austerity war brings financial, monetary, political, and military disaster.[17]

Developments in France were once again dictated by the situation in Algeria. There, the determined attitude of Lacoste and the victory of Massu's forces in the battle of Algiers were bearing fruit. From January 1957 to the autumn of 1958, military advantage shifted progressively to the French side. The FLN's position was difficult; its urban terrorist networks had gone, and the bloody reprisals against Muslims who co-operated with the French forces alienated popular support. The nationalist leaders were hesitant, continuing too long with the creation of large battalions of 500 men, easily trackable by the French forces; the rebels' arms dumps were discovered or denounced; and FLN activities fell sharply – 4000 incidents in January 1957, 1500 in May 1958. Moreover, the ideological hold of the ALN over the population was weakening; the benefits of the SAS action began to be felt; the peasant fighters deserted; and thanks to the volunteers, the *harkis* or auxiliary forces, and the self-defence groups, France could count on the active military support of approximately 90 000 Muslims. Systematic patrolling of the countryside and tight policing in the towns brought greater order, even if doing little to pacify deep-seated hatreds. This enhanced French mastery of the military situation owed much to the barrier constructed by General Pedron along the frontier with Morocco and, above all, to the one built along the frontier with Tunisia, the Morice line, named after the Defence Minister in the Bourgès-Maunoury government responsible for its construction (by, claimed *L'Express* crying scandal, a company in which Morice had an interest). Begun in the summer of 1957, this imposing barbed wire installation, with guard dogs, search-lights, watch-towers, and minefields giving the region the air of a concentration camp, ran the 300 km along the road from Bône to Tebessa, within firing range of the Tunisian border. The Morice line was massively effective. The FLN forces returning from rest or training in Tunisia, and their arms and supply convoys, all had to surmount this daunting obstacle. And those who did manage to get over, through, or under the Morice line then faced almost certain attack from the five regiments of paratroopers stationed behind it and who controlled all the strategic routes to the interior. At daybreak, alerted during the night by cuts in the electrified fences, the paras descended with often deadly accuracy on the advancing rebels. Increasingly heavy French bombardments and air attacks on the Algerian encampments in Tunisia completed what, by the spring of 1958, was a fierce frontier battle. Approximately three-quarters of the ALN forces were tied down until the summer in an attempt to break through the Morice line, the skirmishes degenerating into pitched battles in the area of Souk-Ahras in April. The tide was turning against the FLN, and with French forces controlling the situation, and the observable beginning of fraternization, a military victory for France against the rebels looked possible. Not surprisingly, this improved position encouraged an upsurge of hope among the Europeans in Algeria, putting them more than ever on their guard for a false move by Paris which might jeopardize the chances for ultimate success.

The drama was set in motion by the intervention of Bourguiba. In addition to being more worried by the presence of ALN troops on Tunisian soil than it was politically possible for him to admit, the Tunisian leader wanted to see Algeria acquire independence without turning her back on the Western camp, and was thus anxious to counter the pan-Arabism of Nasser. It was for these reasons that he sought to act as intermediary between France and Algeria, renewing his offer of negotiations with the announcement on 9 January 1958 that all solution of the Franco-Tunisian dispute was conditional on an end to hostilities in Algeria. However, unwilling to see the initiative pass in this way to Bourguiba, the FLN immediately staged a show of force, engaging a French patrol in a struggle to the death on 11 January near the frontier village of Sakhiet Sidi Youssef. Lacoste noisily invoked the right of legitimate defence; the already strained diplomatic relations between Paris and Tunis crumbled; and on 8 February, with the approval of Gaillard and the cabinet of 29 January, the French forces retaliated. Their air attack on the ALN camp in fact razed the village of Sakhiet, leaving seventy dead, among them many children and civilians. Paris and Algiers had fallen into the trap laid by the FLN, which saw in an internationalization of the conflict, as in Indo-China, a solution to the current difficulties of the rebellion. International opinion was outraged by the French action; Tunisia dramatized the incident, accusing France of aggression at the United Nations, and although France in turn denounced Tunisian belligerence her arguments carried little weight. The foreign press was in uproar, and on 11 April Eisenhower warned that the American loan negotiated by Monnet would be reconsidered if France did not give proof of her good faith. Paris was forced to accept a proposal for United States and British 'good offices', in the form of Robert Murphy, close collaborator of Dulles and former Consul to Algiers in 1942, and Harold Beeley, Under-Secretary of State at the Foreign Office. Gaillard hoped to

Table 14: *The French and the Algerian War*

1 'In your view, should Algeria retain its status as a *département* of metropolitan France, or would you accept a different relationship between Algiera and metropolitan France?' (in %)

|  | French *département* | looser tie | no answer |
|---|---|---|---|
| October 1955 | 47 | 26 | 27 |
| February 1956 | 49 | 25 | 26 |
| April 1956 | 40 | 33 | 27 |
| March 1957 | 34 | 35 | 31 |
| September 1957 | 36 | 40 | 24 |

2 'Have you confidence in the present government to settle the Algerian problem?' (in %)

|  | yes | no | no answer |
|---|---|---|---|
| April 1956 | 37 | 27 | 36 |
| July 1956 | 38 | 30 | 32 |
| March 1957 | 39 | 30 | 31 |
| September 1957 | 26 | 43 | 31 |
| June 1958 | 68 | 11 | 21 |
| July–August 1958 | 68 | 15 | 17 |
| September 1958 | 51 | 25 | 24 |
| September 1959 | 51 | 24 | 25 |

*Source: Sondages, 3, 1956; 3, 1957; 3 and 4, 1958.*

limit the work of the 'good offices' mission to the Franco-Tunisian question, but it was soon quite clear that Murphy and Beeley intended to deal with the root of the issue, the opening of negotiations over Algeria. With little faith in Gaillard's capacity to resist possible pressure, the Right, the Moderates, and the Gaullists, orchestrated by the USRAF under Soustelle, denounced this as a new Munich. The government's majority collapsed, and there were now signs of a weakening in the authority of the State. On 13 March, in an atmosphere reminiscent of 6 February 1934, the Paris police staged a demonstration in open defiance of the government and the deputies – it was time for the Socialists to revise, somewhat belatedly, their judgement of Bourgès-Maunoury's qualities as Interior Minister. The Assembly, reunited on 15 April, brought Gaillard down as soon as the first of the 'good offices' proposals was put before it. The Socialists and the MRP together could not save his government once the familiar opposition coalition of Communists, Poujadists, and Mendésistes had been swollen by 150 deputies of the Right: it fell by 321 to 225 votes, with – as a measure of the gravity of the political situation – no abstentions.

Table 14 (*cont.*)

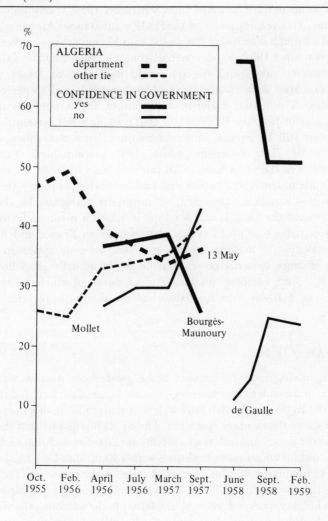

%
70 —

ALGERIA
département
other tie

CONFIDENCE IN GOVERNMENT
yes
no

60 —

50 —

40 —

30 —

13 May

Mollet

Bourgès-
Maunoury

20 —

10 —

de Gaulle

Oct.    Feb.    April    July    March    Sept.    June    Sept.    Feb.
1955    1956    1956    1956    1957    1957    1958    1958    1959

All had ignored the cautionary evolution in French public opinion over the previous months. In fact, confidence in the ability of the politicians to settle the Algerian affair had never been so low. In March 1957, 39 per cent still had confidence in Guy Mollet, but by September, under Bourgès-Maunoury, the figure had slumped to 26 per cent; though, in an unprecedented reversal (Table 14 and diagram), by June 1958, 68 per cent had confidence in de Gaulle. This collapse of consensus must not, however, be taken as a sign of a massive swing in favour of *l'Algérie française*, whatever its increasingly excited partisans were ready to believe. Indeed, it was exactly the opposite. A decisive change in public opinion over the Algerian question seems to have occurred from September 1957; at that point, only 36 per cent of those questioned by the IFOP wanted to see Algeria with the statute of a French *département*, compared with 47 per cent in October 1955; and by September 1957, 40 per cent had gradually been convinced that the links between France and Algeria would inevitably be looser in the future, compared with 26 per cent in October 1955, and 33 per cent in April 1956. A potential majority in favour of negotiation was in fact forming, and in January 1958, 51 per cent no longer felt certain that Algeria would still be French in ten years time. Very clear, then, is the transience of the consensus which had accompanied 'national-molletisme'. On the other hand, with this as a basis it would not be hard for de Gaulle to convince opinion that an honourable solution – the 'paix des braves' – was being prepared, whatever the ambiguity he chose to encourage over the idea. It was a public in which a majority favourable to a negotiated solution of free association between France and Algeria was crystallizing; a majority moreover which not only approved of de Gaulle's advance towards power, but no doubt actually propelled him towards it.[18] And, needless to say, this was a public of which the agitated partisans of *l'Algérie française*, absorbed in their conspiracies, were oblivious.

## The disorders of 13 May

The crisis, arising under the pressure of the 'good offices' mission, was born of a union of irreconcilable extremes – the 170 votes of the Left and the 150 votes of the Right – which left only a slender margin for manoeuvre at the centre of the parliamentary spectrum. The SFIO finally saw that the time had come for it to relinquish responsibility for Algeria, deciding on 2 May that it would no longer enter coalitions with a Right that Guy Mollet now felt free to qualify as 'la plus bête du monde'. The régime was facing its gravest crisis to date, and if the French people, busy preparing for the Whitsun holiday weekend, seemed indifferent to the outcome, the views of the British and American allies could not be ignored. One way out of the deadlock might have been to set up an emergency government of 'Public Safety', led by a strong figure of the Right capable of rallying the *pieds-noirs* and the army in a last chance for the régime, staking everything on an unpopular austerity policy to win the war and the successful integration of nearly 9 million Muslims into France: clearly the Left would never accept such a suicidal risk for the régime it had founded. Alternatively, go to the other extreme, force a showdown with the activists, and content the Americans by preparing for negotiations and possibly for abandonment: yet this would have required a coalition of all the political forces hostile to the war, that is, bring the Communists into the operation, exactly what all the other groups had refused to do since 1947. Finally, have recourse to the supreme arbiter, de Gaulle, whose name was circulating with increasing persistence, and whose supporters had launched a poster campaign for his return as early as 18 April in Paris: but this would antagonize Washington, worried by de Gaulle's attitude to the Atlantic Alliance, putting at risk the alignment that had consolidated the Republic since the terrible year of 1947. With all these logical solutions thus blocked it is not hard to understand the confusion of Coty and the dramatic prolongation of the crisis.

Bidault was the first to try to fill the power vacuum, between the two rounds of the cantonal elections,[19] but was forced to abandon the attempt after his own party, the MRP, refused to follow him in his extreme attachment to the cause of *l'Algérie française*. After Bidault came Pleven, who abandoned his attempt on 8 May after seeing just how little scope remained at the Centre after the withdrawal of the Socialists and the division of the Radicals. Coty, pushed by Mollet and Pinay, now called on Pflimlin; it was thought that this determined and experienced MRP figure might be able to consolidate what remained of government authority, to effect a change of policy and open negotiations – something Pflimlin had called for publicly on 23 April, rejecting the sterile dilemma of intransigence or abandonment in favour of a third way, one of discussion. Pflimlin went ahead with consultations, formed his team, and was to present it to the Assembly on 13 May. What were his chances for success? Lacoste, whom Pflimlin had dared not to reappoint to his place in Algeria, now warned of an approaching diplomatic Dien Bien Phu; and the FLN, through the voice of Ferhat Abbas on 8 May, hinted at a readiness to consider offers of negotiation. In short, Pflimlin quickly became synonymous with all that was totally unacceptable to Algiers.

Once the possibility of negotiation had been raised openly, a reaction from Algiers against the 'régime d'abandon' was of course inevitable. In spite of this, it would be misleading to present the crisis as a neat, mechanical sequence of cause and effect. The 13 May 1958 is an 'event' in the most literal sense of the word, unpredictable and delusive, with an impact at once crucial and ambiguous. In it conspiracy and riot came together, an unstable amalgam of the premeditated and the spontaneous on which the intervention of an individual or a gesture could be decisive. With hindsight the progress of the crisis seems ineluctable; yet for those involved its course was uncertain and hesitant: it is the final outcome which invests it with internal sense and direction.[20] Those who for two years had sought to destroy the Republic were of course present, but neither their ability to manipulate the crowd nor their power to intimidate Paris were as great as they would have liked; thus, for example, the files on the 'Bazooka affair' were destroyed by the activists to whom the Algiers crowd delivered the Government-General building, but success of this sort did not increase their influence on the course of events. Nor, indeed, did the activists have common goals. Those of the 'Groupe des Sept' – which brought together Martel, the UFNA leader; the Poujadists Ortiz and Goutalier; Dr Lefèvre, a fervent admirer of Salazar's Portugal; Pierre Lagaillarde, the students' leader, and a few officers – wanted to break from metropolitan France and set up a fascist Algeria modelled on Franco's Spain or the *corporatisme* of Vichy; they were as vehemently hostile to de Gaulle as they were to Pflimlin. Other activists had cultivated their contacts with the habitual conspiratorial elements of the military, hoping to see the army come to power, under, for example, General Cherrière, an eager Bonapartist. Of course, there was nothing original about these extravagant ambitions and schemes. What was new, however, was that they had begun to win a small but solid audience among senior officers in Algeria and mainland France; not necessarily fervent partisans of *l'Algérie française*, these were nonetheless ready to turn to their own advantage the unease of the army that was now a familiar theme in some quarters. Colonel Thomazo had contacts with all the groups and individuals, informing Cherrière and Crespin, as well as Salan, his immediate superior, who in turn relayed at least some of this to his superior, General Ely, Chief of the General Staff. Indeed, it was Ely who, on 9 May, delivered to Coty a telegram from Salan and his officers in which he declared that the army would consider scandalous an abandonment of Algeria, adding ominously that it would be impossible to predict the reaction of the army if such a thing occurred.

The army's unease had found solid support in political circles. Soustelle, well informed, had ambitions to become the master of the situation, and his USRAF relayed directly the pressure from Algiers. Another key figure was Chaban-Delmas, strategically placed as Defence Minister in the Gaillard government, extremely well informed, with access to secret reports; able, for example, to question Ely and Salan. He had installed a close confidant, Léon Delbecque, in Algiers. Delbecque, a former RPF leader and violently pro-*Algérie française*, aided by another faithful, Lucien Neuwirth, embodied the unexpected in this imbroglio: the presence in Algiers of a handful of determined Gaullists. Delbecque's quasi-official 'antenna' collected information on the European activists of Algiers, developed contacts with the army, winning over men like Colonel Bigeard and Commander Pouget and wooing Massu, organized meetings and set up a Comité de vigilance: Delbecque reported in person to de Gaulle on his progress at the end of April.[21] Meanwhile in Paris, Olivier Guichard and Jacques Foccart multiplied the contacts between Delbecque and Gaullist militants like Michel Debré and the members of the Association des Français libres (responsible in April for the appeals for the return of de

Gaulle), and with politicians like Soustelle and Chaban-Delmas. At this stage, however, the faithful were playing largely by ear; de Gaulle's personal attitude alternated between a bitter pessimism and glimmers of hope, carefully adjusting often contradictory positions over *l'Algérie fran¬ caise* to suit his listeners – though some disciples saw that he was already convinced of the inevitability of independence.[22] But even if he feigned not to be, de Gaulle was in fact perfectly aware of all that was going on, preferring for the moment to foster the ambiguity surrounding his intentions, leaving the preparations to others. Thus, on 26 April, Delbecque's Comité de vigilance successfully organized an important European demonstration in Algiers; and on 11 May, Alain de Sérigny, a former Pétainiste now won over by Soustelle and Delbecque, called in his editorial in *L'Écho d'Alger* for the return of de Gaulle.[23]

However, these manoeuvres by a Gaullist minority had little impact on the demonstrations which took place in Algiers on 13 May. The pretext for these was the announcement of the execution of three French soldiers held prisoner by the FLN. Two demonstrations were planned: one military, led by Salan, as a solemn protest at the executions; the other European, organized by the 'Comité des sept', more interested to oppose Pflimlin in the name of *l'Algérie française*. Colonel Trinquier's Third Parachute Regiment and the CRS were charged with maintaining order. The excited Europeans, many swayed by de Sérigny's call, converged on the war memorial; here the cry went up of 'l'armée au pouvoir' – though it was Massu, the victor of the battle of Algiers, who was cheered, whereas Salan, associated for many with Dien Bien Phu, was booed. The two demonstrations were about to disperse when a group of youths and students, led by Lagaillarde, broke away and headed in the direction of the Government-General building. Here, they encountered little resistance from the forces of order, and in utter confusion stormed and successfully occupied the building, the symbol of the authority of Paris in Algiers. The elated crowd assembled outside, cheering as files and documents streamed from the windows, booing when a by now very uneasy Salan appeared on the balcony. Inside, a Committee of Public Safety was hastily formed; on it were Trinquier, Thomazo, Lagaillarde, members of the USRAF, and Delbecque – the last having hurried to the scene, presenting himself as the emissary of Soustelle, and managing to get himself and a few trusted Gaullists placed on the Committee. It was at this point that Massu, shocked and bewildered by the disorder, agreed to head the Committee; he read to the crowd the list of the members of the Algiers Committee of Public Safety, and the text of a telegram sent to President Coty calling for the creation of a government of public safety in Paris. It was nine o'clock in the evening. With its day of action over, the popular movement of Algiers had nothing more to propose.

The reaction in Paris to events in Algiers was amazement but not despair. With the agreement of Lacoste and Ely, Gaillard, who held interim power until his successor was invested, precipitously delegated all powers in Algeria to Salan, then to Massu, who, for all his known Gaullist sympathies, seemed the only military figure capable of putting a stop to the rising. The *coup de force* of Algiers was thus legalized, but a bloodbath was avoided. The party leaders summoned to Matignon held confused discussions over the action to take next. Should the rising be confronted and a test of strength engaged? Or should the danger be defused by rallying to the cause of *l'Algérie française*? Or, as Massu and Ely wanted, call upon de Gaulle to take charge in order to preserve the unity of the army? The indecision which had marked the first days of the crisis looked likely to prevent the régime from responding to the challenge from Algiers. However, in the afternoon and evening, during the investiture debate, there were signs of a new resolution among the deputies. Pflimlin's performance was impressive. In his speech he roundly condemned the military leaders who had adopted a stance of opposition to the laws of the Republic, calling for a union of Republican defence, while refusing to abandon the idea of negotiation with the FLN. This firm attitude was rewarded with a rallying from the SFIO, the MRP, the UDSR, the Radicals, and roughly a quarter of the Independents, investing Pflimlin by 274 votes, with the Communists abstaining to make his success possible. A total of 129 deputies had refused the call to defend the Republic: the most fervent partisans of *l'Algérie française*, who thus registered their support for the rebels, Georges Bidault, a few Radicals, the bulk of the Independents, the Gaullists, and the Poujadists. During the night, at its first meeting, the Pflimlin cabinet took steps which indicated its resolve to hold firm: all communications with Algeria were suspended, and Salan was named as the sole legitimate authority, thus strengthening the link between Paris and the weakest element of a rebel coalition in Algiers that could subsequently be repudiated. The crisis of 13 May 1958 was not, then, a potentially successful re-run of 6 February 1934, for Pflimlin, unlike Daladier, clearly had no intention of resigning the following day.

Indeed, on 14 May, *Le Parisien libéré* was the only newspaper which thought fit to lead with the possible recourse to de Gaulle. And in Algiers, though the crowd was still mobilized, its leaders began to consider the enormity of their action of the previous day: some now feared the firing-squad for what they had done. Delbecque vacillated, and was pushed aside by the 'Comité des Sept'; Salan refused to break with Paris; and Massu, though making his Gaullist convictions known publicly, maintained his attitude of a faithful soldier of the Republic. The army, then, remained loyal, the activists were losing momentum, and the *pied-noir* population of Algiers became aware of the fact that its action seemed to have produced what it had most wanted to avoid – an authority in Paris resolved to act firmly. Soustelle, who had missed a chance to escape during the night to take his place at the head of the Algiers rebellion, was placed under surveillance by Pflimlin. Pflimlin now called on the Socialists to enter his government; Guy Mollet became vice-premier, while Jules Moch, the strong man of 1947, was appointed to the Interior. At this stage of the crisis, then, with the military rebels disowned but Salan invested with legitimate authority, nothing was settled. The Republic had held firm, de Gaulle had remained silent, and the riot of Algiers had failed. The intrigues could begin again.

### '*Albert, j'ai gagné*'

The developments which laid bare the relative strengths of the principal protagonists and fixed what was really at stake in the crisis occurred on 15 May. In Algeria, Committees of Public Safety were being set up in other towns, and encouragement was given to 'fraternization' between Muslims and Europeans, something quickly invoked by the *putschistes* to justify the failed rising. The real drama, however, was played out between the three men who incarnated the triangle of forces: Salan, de Gaulle, and Pflimlin. The first was swayed by the arguments of Delbecque, who had recovered his sang-froid and was trying to convince the activists of the need for de Gaulle; it was at Delbecque's prompting that he launched a cry of 'Vive de Gaulle' to the crowd from the balcony of the Government-General building. In doing this, by giving de Gaulle the backing of the army, Salan clearly over-reached the legal authority entrusted to him by the government. De Gaulle, closely informed of developments in Paris the previous day, immediately recognized that in not breaking with Salan at this point, Pflimlin had betrayed the fatal indecision afflicting authority. De Gaulle hastened to drive home his advantage, with a brief statement issued at 5.00 p.m. and communicated to Matignon. After condemning the weakness of the party system, the statement ended thus: 'Formerly, the nation from its heart placed confidence in me to lead it to safety. Today, as it faces grave new difficulties, let it know that I am ready to assume the powers of the Republic.' Forgotten, then, were the provisional government and the RPF experience; instead, at the same time as undermining that of the new government, de Gaulle instinctively grounded his legitimacy on his appeal of 18 June 1940. With this, his first pronouncement of the crisis, de Gaulle struck a powerful chord in a people for whom he was identified above all with the famous wartime gesture. The ambiguity was carefully fostered; Algeria was not mentioned; the rebels of Algiers were not repudiated; in short, de Gaulle's hands remained untied. The manoeuvre worked. Pflimlin committed his first two mistakes; in failing to instantly denounce Salan's disobedience, and then by ignoring de Gaulle's statement, he showed that he felt himself too weak to oppose it. Pflimlin still believed, incorrectly, that Salan could serve as the agent of compromise between Algiers and Paris, a solution evoked with insistence on 16 May. Perhaps Pflimlin also sensed the steady erosion of the authority of the State. The new Minister for Algeria, André Mutter, was unable to take up his post; Guy Mollet wrote directly to de Gaulle, calling on him to disown the rebels of Algiers, but also, and more importantly, to find out if de Gaulle would accept an appearance before the Assembly to seek the investiture, and if he would abide by the vote of the Assembly; Ely, Chief of the General Staff, after disagreeing with Chevigné, the new Minister of the Army, had covered himself by resigning. Of course, Pflimlin could, as Jules Moch was urging, play for time in which to reinforce his position; the Assembly had, after all, voted the state of emergency he had called for; the police and prefects, placed on a war alert, were in fact responding better than expected; and Chevigné had exiled the fervently Gaullist General Challe to Brest. Yet these were minor considerations compared with de Gaulle's achievement. In forty-eight hours he had secured his first victory, establishing himself at the intersection of conflicting ambitions; between those of Algiers, powerless to take the initiative, and those of Paris, hesitating to proceed with repression. Knowing that silence and expectation would strengthen this strategic position, de Gaulle announced a press conference for 19 May.

The three days until 19 May were filled with tenebrous manoeuvres, including what was perhaps the decisive episode in the crisis. Since 14 May, disappointed by the failure of the Algiers rising, members of Salan's headquarters had been planning 'Operation Résurrection', whereby para-troops were to be dropped on Paris, backed up by the forces of the South-West under General Miquel, and the armoured forces of Colonel Gribius stationed just outside the capital at Rambouillet. News of the operation, now actually planned for 19 May, reached Delbecque; the Gaullists of the rue de Solferino – Guichard, Foccart, La Malène, and Lefranc – learnt of it, and Debré stepped up his efforts; de Gaulle was informed, and Michel Poniatowski alerted the government and the Elysée. De Gaulle, impassive, let the tension mount, giving no sign of approval or disapproval. And suddenly 'Résurrection' was called off, the 'spontaneous' demonstrations planned for Paris were cancelled, and Sanguinetti pacified the ex-servicemen who were to have joined the action: all, however, without the conspiracy being repudiated.[24] This murky episode was of capital import-ance. For at the same time as adding to the uncertainty over de Gaulle's willingness to use a *putsch* to come to power if all other means proved impossible, it demonstrated, to Pflimlin above all, that the Gaullists were in fact capable of countering an operation of civil war – a vitally important consideration in the increasingly tense situation. On 19 May, with a nervous Paris solidly held by the CRS (personally inspected by Jules Moch), de Gaulle gave his press conference at the Quai d'Orsay. In it he denounced the weakness of the 'system', though promised to save it from the present chaos; he ridiculed the idea that at the age of sixty-seven he intended to embark on the career of a dictator, though added that a crisis might well call for procedures of 'une flexibilité considérable'; he said nothing to condemn the insurrection which gave him a hope of power, and over the Algerian problem offered merely a vague promise to listen to all the interested parties; finally, to calm the Socialist leader, he made flattering references to his 'compagnon' Guy Mollet. With this masterly exercise in studied ambiguity over, de Gaulle returned to Colombey, where he waited, in his words, 'à la disposition du pays'.

From this, de Gaulle's second victory, until 27 May, the situation swung progressively in his favour and against the government. The Assembly now began discussions over constitutional reform, and granted Pflimlin new special powers for Algeria without any allusion being made to de Gaulle's proposals, much to the indignation of Mendès France. Moreover, the embargo on communications with Algiers was partially lifted. For Pflimlin still held out hopes for reasonable negotiations with the military; he dispatched emissaries to them, but immediately ruined any chance for success by establishing the first contacts with the rebels. De Gaulle, meanwhile, was wooing the politicians with reassurances as to his intentions.[25] Antoine Pinay returned from an audience at Colombey on 22 May convinced that de Gaulle would pursue a great policy of national unity; Georges Boris was sounded out on the firmness of Mendès France, and was in turn reassured that the Left had nothing to fear from de Gaulle. However, Soustelle, who had managed to return to Algiers on 17 May, was now at work propagating the 'Révolution du 13 mai', staging processions of Muslims to clamour for the return of de Gaulle. And the 'Résurrection' operation was reactivated, this time with the initial target of Corsica, where the deputy Pascal Arrighi launched a Committee of Public Safety movement. Jules Moch and the other members of the government were now left in no doubt that the State was disintegrating. Commanded from Algiers, 'Résurrection' had an easy triumph in Corsica on 24–25 May, the CRS forces sent to support the prefect having been disarmed without resistance by the local police. The threat of a *coup d'état* was growing; the loyalty of the garrisons in the South-West appeared increasingly suspect; the ministers were divided, with no one prepared to take the risk of spreading civil war by retaliating. The crisis evolved rapidly in the space of a few hours on 25–26 May. Jules Moch, scandalized and powerless, offered his resignation; Guy Mollet wrote secretly to de Gaulle saying that the greatest danger facing France was that of a Bolshevik dictatorship; and an exhausted Pflimlin, pushed by Coty, finally agreed to meet de Gaulle. But their talks, held at Saint-Cloud in the night of 26 May, failed to clarify the situation. De Gaulle rejected Pflimlin's request that he disown the subversion carried out in his name in Corsica, but was in turn not sure of having convinced Pflimlin to accept his conditions.[26]

Consequently, on 27 May, de Gaulle made his third and decisive move. At midday he issued a declaration announcing that the previous day he had initiated the standard process for the formation of a Republican government capable of assuring national unity and independence, adding that he counted on the military, naval, and air forces in Algeria to remain obedient under their leaders. Pflimlin, naturally, was aghast: nothing of this sort had been agreed at his meeting with de Gaulle the previous night. But the declaration was little short of a *fait accompli*: the Socialists were thrown into disarray by Guy Mollet's extraordinary letter; Jules Moch lacked the means to organize resistance to the second and final phase of 'Résurrection', planned for the following day, this time in Paris; and Coty was impatient to call for de Gaulle, whose willingness, however reluctant, to leave Salan 'faire le nécessaire' if the politicians blocked his access to power by the legal channels now looked certain. The Assembly went through the motions of confirming its confidence in the Pflimlin government a last time, but the inevitable could no longer be avoided. Pflimlin, torn between a Right pushing him to resign and a divided and indecisive Left, offered Coty his resignation on the morning of 28 May. The power vacuum now existed, and the only person capable of filling it was de Gaulle.

That afternoon, a solemn procession of several hundred thousand people, with Mendès France, Menthon, André Philip, Mitterrand, and Daladier at its head, took the time-honoured route from Nation to République. Present were politicians, trade-unionists, students, teachers – far more than had responded to the CGT's call of the previous day. The demonstration was peaceful and dignified, directing its hostility more towards the paras and the 'fascists' than towards de Gaulle. But if the Left thus exhibited its loyalty to the Republic, it could do nothing now to alter the course of events. Indeed, the dignitaries of the régime were already busy trying to persuade de Gaulle to accede to power in the normal way. There were letters from Auriol, and efforts by the Presidents of the two Chambers, Le Troquer and Monnerville, to ensure a minimum of disturbance to the cherished parliamentary procedures. In vain. De Gaulle insisted on full powers and a speedy revision of the Constitution. On 29 May, with the paratroop operation menacing, Coty took the initiative and forced the drama to its logical climax by announcing that he had called upon de Gaulle – 'le plus illustre des Français' – to form a government, increasing the pressure on the parliamentarians by threatening to resign if this was rejected. At 7.30 in the evening of 29 May de Gaulle arrived at the Elysée to be formally designated as premier. The following day saw Vincent Auriol, then Guy Mollet and Maurice Deixonne, journey to Colombey to seek assurances that de Gaulle did not intend to break France's Atlantic commitments and that he would abide by the majority verdict of the Assembly. Satisfied on these for them vital points, they now removed the final obstacle in de Gaulle's path by convincing the Socialist parliamentary group (by the narrow majority of 77 to 74) that the choice really was between de Gaulle and a military régime on the lines of Franco's Spain. With the final arbiters of the parliamentary solution having pronounced in his favour, everything was now straightforward for de Gaulle.

On 1 June, the Fourth Republic's last premier-designate appeared before the Assembly. He read a short declaration, evoking the risks of civil war, demanding full powers for his government for six months, and promised to submit a new Constitution to a referendum,[27] and then he departed. After Mendès France, Mitterrand, Isorni, Menthon, and Cot had solemnly protested over a *coup d'état* engineered by the conspirators of Algiers, the new government was invested by 329 to 224 votes. In the opposition were the Communists, half the Socialists, the Mendésistes, plus a few isolated figures. A number of points can be made about the composition of de Gaulle's ministry. First, the political parties were flattered by the presence of many figures of the 'system' – Mollet, Pflimlin, Houphouët-Boigny, and Jacquinot were Ministers of State, Antoine Pinay went to the Ministry of Finance, and Berthoin to Education. Conversely, with the exception of Malraux and Debré, few prominent Gaullists were included; Soustelle, for example, was not given an appointment, and the USRAF leaders were ignored. Instead, the key positions went to reliable top civil servants; Pelletier at the Interior Ministry and Couve de Murville at Foreign Affairs; and de Gaulle himself took the National Defence portfolio. There was, then, a considerable continuity between old and new; indeed, de Gaulle is supposed to have remarked that 'we only need MM Poujade, Maurice Thorez and Ferhat Abbas and we would all be here'. On 3 June, the two Chambers accorded de Gaulle the full powers he had demanded,[28] the relaxed premier acknowledging in return the great confidence being placed in him. Returning that evening to the Hôtel Laperouse, de Gaulle had every reason to sum up the outcome to the hall porter thus: 'Albert, j'ai gagné.'[29]

### A crisis of consensus

After three weeks of open crisis the Fourth republic was dead. Three powers, or rather three legitimacies, each seeking to assert itself, were present at the final agony: the legal authority in Paris, the military authority in Algiers, and the moral authority of de Gaulle. Since none of the principal actors enjoyed an absolute mastery of the situation each had often to wait upon events, something which, amidst widespread popular indifference, opened the way for the conspirators. But if their machinations punctuated the progress of the drama, its final outcome was never in doubt. By their refusal to break out of *immobilisme*, by their consistent rejection of renewal, by their refusal to let Mendès France govern on a genuine consensus, the politicians of the Fourth Republic had long ago placed the régime at the mercy of the sterile arithmetic of the Assembly. Since January 1956 this meant that the balance of parliamentary power was held by the Socialists – divided and hesitant, as jealous of their power as they were weak in its exercise: in spite of a last-minute show of better instincts, the final crisis had laid bare the extent of their impotence. Yet all, whether partisans or opponents of *l'Algérie française* or de Gaulle, were, by their failure to condemn the weaknesses and mistakes of the past, accessories to the equivocations of Mollet and Auriol, to the double-dealings of Coty, who, it was revealed later, had been in contact with de Gaulle as early as 5 May, and whose appeal for order on 13 May had been wretchedly ineffective. The French State had lacked direction for years; the authority of government had been openly flouted since 6 Feburary 1956; the police, administration, and army were of uncertain obedience: not surprisingly, perhaps, for many the choice seemed reduced to one between helpless defeatism or clinging to abstract principles. The procession through the streets of Paris on 28 May had been motivated more by loyalty to the Republic as an ideal than by attachment to the institutional reality of the Fourth Republic. That is why the protest remained solemn, dignified, but, after all, verbal: the crisis of the Fourth Republic provoked no strikes, no popular mobilization, no signs of the enthusiasm of 1944 in which the régime had been born, to arrest the collapse and jolt the politicians from their torpor. At the root of this quiescence lay the fact that the Fourth Republic, from the conflicts of 1947 through the disappointments of 1955 and 1956, had lost the support of a significant section of French society, alienating the masses and driving them into a disenchanted apathy. This indifference to the fate of the Fourth Republic was clear from the feeble response to the calls from the CGT for action during the final crisis, as well, of course, as from the deep isolation of the Communists. In short, part of the French working class stood outside the body politic. Inescapable in the final analysis is the extent to which the political ground rules of the Cold War laid in 1947 had retained their almost obsessional value: thus all could agree to defend the régime, provided that the Communists, accomplices to every Soviet crime, were excluded from participation in it. Hence, too, the unanimous relief when de Gaulle confirmed that he did not intend to break with Washington. The cancer of the Algerian war had certainly done much to erode authority, but the persistence of the cleavages of the years after the war helped to cloud the issues and deepen the paralysis.

The war in Algeria had, nevertheless, set in motion mechanisms strong enough to bring France to the verge of civil war. For a nation where

memories of the bitter conflict which had pitted Frenchman against Frenchman in the recent past were still strong, a nation moreover where the
broadest and most durable consensus was that based on a longing for
stability and prosperity, this was a terrifying and tragic prospect, one which
naturally increased the temptation to pass responsibility to the trusted
figure of de Gaulle. In spite of the anti-EDC hiatus, notions of French
greatness had been severely damaged by Dien Bien Phu and the Suez
adventure. In the wake of these reversals, French nationalism, far more
resigned than was believed at the time, tended to turn in on itself. One
result of this, however, was to arouse a strong defensive reaction as soon as
the territorial integrity of France was menaced: the long indecision of the
mainland over the future of the Algerian territories, finally settled in favour
of a solution no longer that of the French *département*, and the completely
free hand given to de Gaulle, are comprehensible only when seen in this
light. French opinion was genuinely touched by the plight of a million
compatriots in Algeria, and readily accepted that the young conscript
soldiers be used to defend them. But only a tiny handful of activists were
ready to exploit the contradiction which would have made the defence of
*l'Algérie française* a pretext for civil war. Of crucial importance in the outcome had been the climate of fear generated by the conspiracies. It was fear
which paralysed Republican defence, and enabled de Gaulle to keep silent
as to his real intentions. Above all, it was fear which made recourse to the
ultimate weapon, the paras and the army, something to avoid. The threat
from the army and its role in the crisis had in fact been magnified by the
defenders of the Republic themselves: too quick to look for Massu's men in
the skies over Paris, too slow to disown the rebellious chiefs in Algiers, too
hesitant to break with the army and thus risk precipitating France into civil
war. This is not to say that the role of the much publicized and discussed
unease of the army can be dismissed.[30] The French armed forces had slowly
become aware that the nation had unburdened its own hesitations on them,
and they had considerable difficulty adapting to the changed global context
of the years after the Cold War. Partly for these reasons, the war in Algeria
assumed a special importance for the French army, becoming the means to
redeem itself, to save its honour, and, ultimately, to safeguard its own future.
Having said this, outside of a small number of officers linked to the conspirators, and a few élite units, the French army as a whole was much less
deeply implicated in the crisis than was generally believed, certainly less so
than it would be under the Fifth Republic. Pflimlin had been at least partly
correct to believe that the military leaders would hesitate to break with a
régime which, since 1946, had proved so accommodating towards the direct
pressure upon it from the armed forces. The unrest in the French army had
not gone beyond a form of Poujadism; de Gaulle was very far from being the
unanimous choice among former officers of Vichy and followers of Giraud;

and the conscripts had not wavered in their loyalties. At no point in the collapse of the Fourth Republic, then, had there been a military power. What there had been, however, and what proved crucial, was the confluence of civilian and military activists in Algiers; for it was this which provided de Gaulle with a lever to guide the crisis in the direction he wanted.

De Gaulle displayed great subtlety and skill in his manipulation of this lever. He was the only one to see the need to wait, not underestimating Pflimlin's resolve, leaving the army to play out its useful but always subordinate role, and not repudiating the noisy agitators in Algiers and Corsica. De Gaulle was the only one to have immediately grasped that the crisis was one of steady deterioration, to have seen that a conflictual outcome would be unacceptable, and that consequently what mattered was the mastery of time: at each point, on 15, 19, and 27 May, de Gaulle successfully imposed his own chronology on the crisis. Lastly, only de Gaulle had struck the right balance between calls to public opinion and respect for institutions and procedures, winning popular support at the same time as allowing the politicians to save themselves from total humiliation. The great strength of de Gaulle's position lay in having, or appearing to have, two very different options available to him. Consensus or insurrection: a peaceful solution involving everyone, or a more drastic surgical operation. The sincerity of de Gaulle's repeated denials of any direct involvement in the rebellion and conspiracies of Algiers, like that of his professed desire to avoid for France what he termed as 'l'aventure', need not be doubted.[31] Conversely, that he equivocated by not condemning the *putschistes* whose intentions were known to him, that he quite deliberately manipulated a grave danger in order to secure the outcome he wanted, is incontestable. De Gaulle's fautless performance – far superior to those of 1946 or 1968 – was rewarded with massive popular support. In the summer of 1958, and until the triumphant referendum of 28 September which set up the Fifth Republic and when 18 of 22 million citizens were won over, Gaullism once again demonstrated its great capacity for 'rassemblement'; it broke the stalemate of the debate which had opposed *Mendésisme* and *Poujadisme*, settling it by imposing new institutions which favoured modernity. An idea of the depth and profile of the new consensus can be had from the results of an opinion poll conducted in June 1958; this found that 83 per cent (against 4 per cent) had confidence in de Gaulle to secure obedience from the army; 70 per cent (against 8 per cent) in his ability to reform the Constitution; 68 per cent (against 11 per cent) to settle the Algerian question; 67 per cent (against 10 per cent) to improve the international standing of France; and 61 per cent (against 14 per cent) to restore national unity.[32]

It was an impressive rallying to the figure forever identified with 18 June 1940. And in August 1958, 46 per cent hoped de Gaulle would remain in power as long as possible, compared with only 16 per cent who wanted him to leave immediately or after the six months of full power. What did this rallying signify? To what extent was it simply a panic response, a scared and apolitical abdication of responsibility to the proven saviour? It is much more likely that as in 1944 the French people hoped de Gaulle would be the engineer of national unity, capable of reconciling Frenchmen with each other, and healing the divisions in French society. The indifferent, almost contemptuous silence during the crisis a few weeks earlier had translated a rejection of the Fourth Republic's negative consensus based on exclusion: de Gaulle was now the vehicle of longings for a positive consensus based on national unity. At the back of this was the old hope, present in 1944 but subsequently disappointed, for a clear constitutional expression of the deep-seated desire to be governed strongly and well. The same IFOP poll of August 1958 revealed that it was the hope for a good Constitution which most attracted the electorates loyal to the political parties of the Fourth Republic now present in the government: thus 68 per cent of SFIO voters had confidence in the de Gaulle government to construct a new Republic; 79 per cent of Radical voters; 85 per cent for the MRP; 93 per cent for the Moderates; and, not surprisingly, 97 per cent for the Républicains sociaux – compared with just 8 per cent among the electorate of the PCF. Results, then, which clearly prefigure the massive support in the autumn of 1958 and beyond for the institutions of the Fifth Republic. Having suffered a bitter civil war in 1940–5, France refused to be drawn into another over Algeria. The overwhelming support for de Gaulle stemmed not from a sense of helpless resignation, but rather from a cautious but positive desire to see France at last endowed with a strong new Republican democracy. In this respect, the coming to power of de Gaulle marked the continuity of an ambition present since the post-war reconstruction, though repeatedly frustrated, that of adapting an increasingly enfeebled political framework of State and Republic to the needs of a recovering nation. It is to this ambitious and rapidly changing France that attention must now be turned, to appreciate the full failure of the régime she had outgrown.

# PART IV

# Ambitious France

# 16

# The stimulus of growth

After the spectacle of weakness and the final collapse, it is time to look at the other, brighter face of the Fourth Republic. For these years were also those of rising productivity and growing abundance, years when fertility and ambitions acquired new momentum. Does the key to the political experience in fact lie with the economy? Did the materialism of the nascent consumer society foster civic apathy, consolidating the great financial and economic interests while thwarting the efforts of the State? Perhaps. But we must avoid hasty retrospective judgements, and try never to lose sight of the extreme hardships of the years which preceded the return of the longed-for prosperity. The whole troubled existence of the Fourth Republic, like its dismal end, is indissolubly linked to France's experience of economic growth and the profound modernization which resulted. At the threshold of the 1950s, the French economy emerged briskly from the material shortages that weighed so heavily upon the *après-guerre* period; one by one the bottlenecks eased. The way now seemed clear for an expansion which would erase the last traces of the conservatism and *malthusianisme* so often denounced at the time. Nostalgia for the good times before the war, waned; the domestic market expanded with the demographic revival, and an improvement in living standards moved within reach. In fact, a long period of growth and change had begun, the era of the 'trente glorieuses'.[1]

## The French boom

Post-war reconstruction had caused production to soar, reaching its 1929 level by 1949; the external commercial balances had been restored, largely thanks to American aid; at the same time, the purchasing power of French wage-earners had consistently lagged behind. These were the solid bases for the economic growth of the 1950s, one which allowed income and consumption to catch up, while stimulating the most profitable and modern branches of the economy. The Second Plan, covering the period 1954–7, embodied this development, shaping its objectives to the new national and international context. The work of reconstruction had to be brought to completion; provision had to be made for the entry of France to the Common Market; provision was needed also for the new, larger generations, who would soon require education, then jobs; the burden of costly overseas wars had to be supported; above all, appetites for material well-being had now to be satisfied. The basic objective of the Plan thus changed: from the quantity of production the accent now shifted to its quality. Productivity had to rise, with help going to the sectors where demand was strongest, preparing for a modern economy capable of responding to the challenge of free trade and able to offer the consumer a wide choice. The areas selected by the Plan reflected these imperatives: technical and scientific research, the specialization and modernization of industrial firms, better training and retraining of the workforce, and steps to organize markets; priority went to the transformative industries, to the construction of housing, and to regional development. Helped by the strides taken in methods of national income accounting,[2] the Second Plan drew up a series of targets for the economy: gross national product was to rise by 25 per cent, industrial production by 25–30 per cent, and construction by 60 per cent. In the event, all these targets were exceeded comfortably (see Table 15). Between 1950 and 1958, gross national product and national income grew by 41 per cent, the real value of the average hourly wage rose by 40 per cent, the volume of consumption increased by 47 per cent, exports grew by 44 per cent, and gross fixed capital formation was up by 57 per cent. These results were doubly impressive in that they bore witness to more than just a quantitative change: the growth of output could no longer be attributed simply to a catching-up phenomenon due to the war damage and the crisis of the 1930s. The French economy had in fact moved to a higher level of efficiency, for in spite of a contraction of the active population, overall productivity rose by one-third.

Agriculture provides a first example of the ways in which difficulties could be overcome. The buoyancy of agricultural markets immediately after the war was artificial and short-lived. French agriculture, which had recovered its pre-war level of output with the excellent harvest of 1948, was soon confronted with serious problems. It had now to adapt to the structural tendency to falling long-term prices; the challenge of unprotected foreign markets had to be met; and, with dietary patterns slow to change, the future direction of domestic demand was uncertain. An immense effort was required, and a comprehensive agricultural policy now became essential. Not least because the structures of French agriculture were notoriously rigid and slow to evolve: 90 per cent of farms were smaller than 50 hectares; the policy of *remembrement* – the regrouping of scattered or divided and subdivided fields for a more rational and economic use – had stagnated for decades (by 1958, only 29 per cent of the land designated since 1941 as in urgent need of *remembrement* had in fact been dealt with); only a third of the

Table 15: *The general economic movement*

1 On index: 1938 = 100

|  | 1945 | 1950 | 1952 | 1954 | 1956 | 1958 |
|---|---|---|---|---|---|---|
| agricultural production | 61 | 102 | 103 | 116 | 112 | 116 |
| industrial production | 50 | 128 | 145 | 159 | 188 | 213 |
| volume of imports | 34 | 104 | 116 | 126 | 166 | 174 |
| volume of exports | 10 | 161 | 161 | 196 | 202 | 233 |
| volume of national revenue | 54 | 118 | 129 | 140 | 156 | 167 |

2. In milliards of 1956 francs

|  | 1938 | 1950 | 1952 | 1954 | 1956 | 1958 |
|---|---|---|---|---|---|---|
| *Resources* | | | | | | |
| gross national product | 12 200 | 14 400 | 15 700 | 16 900 | 18 800 | 20 400 |
| gross domestic production | 10 710 | 12 620 | 13 740 | 14 940 | 16 640 | 18 180 |
| imports | 1 210 | 1 300 | 1 510 | 1 610 | 2 100 | 2 180 |
| *Uses* | | | | | | |
| consumption | 9 370 | 9 510 | 10 790 | 11 640 | 13 050 | 13 780 |
| gross fixed capital formation | 1 390 | 2 480 | 2 520 | 2 750 | 3 370 | 3 900 |
| stock formation | 150 | 360 | 220 | 210 | 370 | 410 |
| exports and balance on use of services | 1 010 | 1 570 | 1 710 | 1 940 | 1 940 | 2 270 |

*Sources: Annuaire statistique de la France, rétrospectif,* Imprimerie nationale/PUF, 1961, pp. 355 and 365; *Le Mouvement économique en France (1949–1979),* INSEE, 1981, pp. 114 and 310.

agricultural sector was adequately mechanized and using chemical fertilizers in appropriate quantities in 1958. In spite of such daunting 'natural' handicaps, significant progress was made. Between 1949 and 1962, productivity in agriculture rose by an annual average of 6.4 per cent, compared with a rate of 5.2 per cent for the economy as a whole; the yields obtained by French farmers came close to those of the most advanced European agriculture; consumption of fertilizers doubled. Finally, an unprecedented effort was made in the mechanization of farms. The number of tractors rose from 56 000 in 1946 to 136 000 in 1950, then to 560 000 by 1958; in 1958 there was one tractor for 33 hectares, compared with one for 600 hectares in 1938; the production of agricultural machinery doubled between 1954 and 1958. Moreover, this development in agriculture, by freeing labour, albeit still at an uneven rate, indirectly helped progress elsewhere in the economy. Each year after 1950, the decline in the number employed in agriculture represented approximately 1 per cent of the total active population. The new French agricultural revolution had clearly begun.

On a base of 100 for 1938, total agricultural production rose to 102 by 1950, and to 116 by 1958. And the growth was in fact stronger than it appears, since the fastest-rising products inevitably boosted many other less sought-after products. Thus in 1956–7, for agriculture's total earnings of 2550 milliard francs, 60 per cent came from livestock farming and 40 per cent from cultivation – a very modern reversal of the traditional proportions.[3] Cattle farming had become the principal agricultural activity, with its earnings divided between meat (500 milliard) and milk (300 milliard), both productions for which demand was strong. Poultry farming, with total earnings of 300 milliard, displayed a similar progression: the chicken was not yet a totally 'industrial' production, but it was no longer reserved for the better off, or for special occasions. A similar evolution was observed for cultivation, where fruit and fresh vegetables (369 milliard) had definitively overtaken cereals (200 milliard). A basic reorientation was occurring in agricultural production, one which favoured the products now most demanded by consumers – meat, fruit, vegetables, and new cereals such as maize and rice (the latter successfully introduced on a large scale in the Camargue region) – at the expense of wheat, potatoes, industrial plants such as flax, and the oleaginous plants which, after having done well until 1950, were now facing stiff overseas competition. Of course, agriculture's balance sheet included minuses as well as pluses. Production of wine was still too great (220 milliard), and was ineffectively countered by a ruinous official policy based on distillation of the surplus; little was done to tackle the cause of the problem – and if, for example, encouragement was given for the tearing up of vines, nothing was done at the same time to limit imports of Algerian wine. The over-production of alcohol obtained from the distillation of beet (70 per cent), wine, and fruit, was enormous; stocks of such alcohol reached 5 million hectolitres in 1958, this for an already excessive annual national consumption of 2.7 million. We have witnessed the vain attempts by the Mendès France government to curtail the privileges of the *bouilleurs de cru* and the beet-growers.[4] Other well-publicized weaknesses of French agriculture included the extent of dependence on imports of certain meat products, oleaginous crops, and tropical products; progress remained to be made over yields and mechanization; regional disparities were glaring; incomes in agriculture were notoriously low; and farmers were typically the last to taste the fruits of progress.[5] Nevertheless, if the modernization of French agriculture was far from complete, at least it had started, and strongly. Some of the consequences were not slow to be felt by consumers: the penury of the post-war period had gone; not only was the population now assured of the 3000 calories a day of the 'developed' nation, but it was increasingly able to satisfy fuller, richer, and more diverse appetites.[6]

It was, however, from industrial production that the growth derived its greatest force and momentum. The indices here are truly spectacular: for a base of 100 in 1938 they stood at 213 in 1958; for a base of 100 in 1952 they had reached 152 by 1959.[7] Overall, industrial output grew by more than 50 per cent in seven years, at an annual rate of roughly 6 per cent. French industry had never experienced such rapid progress, not during the *belle époque*, nor during the 1920s. A new phase in the history of capitalism was opening, something attested to by the responses observed now from all the relevant indicators – equipment, investment, consumption, and government economic policies. The successes, however, were unevenly distributed (see Table 16 and diagram).

One point to note immediately is that from 1952 to 1958, this expansion was not based on massive increases in energy consumption. The index of energy supplies only rose from 100 to 122, and France was still able to meet two-thirds of her total energy needs, though there were already signs of the important changes of the 1960s. Coal output increased only moderately in this period, rising from 52 to 60 million tonnes between 1952 and 1958. Total coal consumption over the same period rose from 72 to 75 million tonnes; coal would satisfy 54 per cent of French energy needs in 1960, compared with 74 per cent in 1950. But although the Houillères did little more than consolidate the concentration and mechanization introduced under the First Plan, efforts were made in organic chemistry, and plans were already afoot for a drastic reorganization of the small mining basins of the Massif Central. Meanwhile, French membership of the ECSC facilitated the necessary imports of German coke.[8] In contrast to this somewhat sluggish performance of coal, the electricity generating industry increased its output rapidly. On the same index of 100 for 1952, its output passed to 152 in 1958, a progression more closely in line with the changed rhythm of industrial activity, even if still lagging slightly behind a sharp rise in domestic demand. Hitherto highly dependent on the coke of the coal industry, the EDF now concentrated its efforts on a great expansion of the hydro-electric generating network; dams were completed or begun on the Rhine (at Fessenheim and Vogelgrun), the Rhône (Logis-Neuf, Beauchastel, and Pierre-Bénite), the Durance (Serre-Ponçon), and in the Alps. In addition, there were the supplies from the revolutionary tidal power station on the Rance; and nuclear generated electricity was at hand, with the experimental reactors of Châtillon, Saclay, and Grenoble, soon to produce electricity commercially at Marcoule and Avoine – projects realized in co-operation with the Atomic Energy Commission and after the entire national territory

Table 16: *Output of some goods and consumer items*

|  | 1952[a] | 1954 | 1956 | 1958 |
|---|---|---|---|---|
| Meat | | | | |
| million tonnes | 2.06 | 2.46 | 2.58 | 2.56 |
| Milk | | | | |
| thousand tonnes | 150 | 180 | 190 | 205 |
| Wine | | | | |
| million hectolitres | 53.9 | 60.9 | 51.7 | 47.7 |
| Potatoes | | | | |
| million quintals | 110 | 158 | 168 | 127 |
| Tractors | | | | |
| thousands | 26 | 39 | 79 | 93 |
| Synthetic fibres | | | | |
| thousand tonnes | 3.3 | 7.6 | 14.8 | 23.3 |
| Washing powder | | | | |
| thousand tonnes | 8 | 66 | 124 | 164 |
| Plastics | | | | |
| thousand tonnes | 35 | 75 | 130 | 198 |
| Cigarettes | | | | |
| million packets | 1421 | 1502 | 1340 | 1491 |
| Consumer durables | | | | |
| base: 100 in 1949 | 178 | 251 | 455 | 573 |
| Radio sets (declared) | | | | |
| millions | 7.9 | 8.8 | 9.7 | 10.6 |
| Television sets (declared) | | | | |
| thousands | 24 | 125 | 442 | 988 |
| Private cars | | | | |
| thousands | 303 | 352 | 504 | 589 |
| Completed homes | | | | |
| thousands | 84 | 162 | 236 | 292 |

[a] Figures for the period 1938–52 in Table 11 p. 182 above.

*Source: Annuaire statistique de la France, rétrospectif*, Imprimerie nationale/PUF, 1961, *passim.*

had been prospected for fissionable materials. Production of gas had risen to 181 on the index, but the GDF was in fact responding mainly to an extremely strong domestic demand, for only 20 per cent of total gas production was now destined for industrial users. With a comprehensive network of stations in the Nord, Lorraine, and the Basse-Seine, a 350 km feeder linking Paris to Lorraine, yields raised by 52 per cent between 1947 and 1956, and an already extensive use of petroleum products, optimism seemed justified. Symbolizing this proud confidence in the future were the natural gas discoveries at Lacq; the problem of transporting the gas had been solved with a process for eliminating its high sulphur content, and it

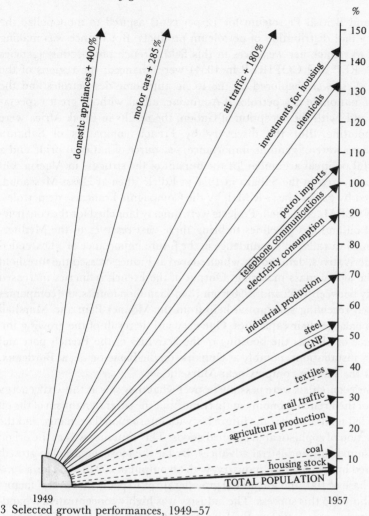

%

- 150
- 140
- 130
- 120
- 110
- 100
- 90
- 80
- 70
- 60
- 50
- 40
- 30
- 20
- 10

domestic appliances + 400%

motor cars + 285%

air traffic + 180%

investments for housing

chemicals

petrol imports

telephone communications

electricity consumption

industrial production

steel

GNP

textiles

rail traffic

agricultural production

coal

housing stock

TOTAL POPULATION

1949                                    1957

3 Selected growth performances, 1949–57

*Source:* based on *Le Mouvement économique en France de 1944 à 1957*, Imprimerie
nationale/PUF, 1958, p. 31.

now began to be distributed throughout the South-West. The most important development, however, concerned the growing role of petroleum, its
contribution to total French energy requirements rising from 16 to 25 per
cent. Of all the forms of energy it was petroleum which carried the greatest
hopes for the future. There were obvious dangers in this: almost all (96 per
cent) of France's supplies of crude oil had to be imported from the Middle
East, and 40 per cent had to pass along the vulnerable Suez Canal artery;
the British and American consortiums were still able to control prices; and
the giant international corporations (Shell for 25 per cent, Esso for 15 per

cent, and British Petroleum for 12 per cent) aspired to monopolize the refining and distribution of petroleum products. But France was making efforts to reduce her weakness in this field. French prospecting agencies (FINA-REP and COFIREP in 1954) were financed; the regions of the South-West were explored by the Régie autonome des pétroles and the Société nationale des pétroles d'Aquitaine, albeit without great expectations; and, with the exception of Gabon, the results in Black Africa were disappointing. But the discovery by French companies of Saharan petroleum were of genuine importance – a source of national pride and a powerful political argument for the pursuit of the struggle in Algeria. Oil was discovered in the Sahara in 1956 at Edjelé, then at Hassi-Messaoud, followed by gas at Hassi-R'Mel, by the Compagnie Française de pétroles, the SNREPAL, and Shell. Projects were quickly launched for the construction of oil and gas pipelines to bring these vast reserves to the Mediterranean. Naturally, this confidence in the future importance of oil extended to its derivatives, demand for which soared as France crossed the threshold into the age of mass motoring. Output of the French refineries increased sharply between 1952 and 1958 from 18 to 33 million tonnes, the companies involved receiving substantial help from the Monnet Plan and Marshall Aid to enlarge their capacities. One very visible result of the growing importance of oil was the boosting of the activities of the French port and estuary installations, notably at Dunkirk, on the Basse-Seine, at Bordeaux, and at the Lavéra complex near Marseille.

Some economists were pessimistic over what they saw as the weak energy bases of the French economy at this time,[9] but the sheer dynamism of the oil sector left no doubt that the future lay with international exchange and the production of sophisticated finished goods. This certainty was at the origin of the important industrial advances. By far the most remarkable growth occurred in the chemical industry, with an output of 209 in 1958 for a 1952 index base of 100, and an annual growth rate of 15 per cent. Several factors contributed to this success. The industry was highly concentrated: a handful of companies – Rhône-Poulenc, Saint-Gobain, Péchiney, Kuhlmann, Air Liquide, and Gillet – alone accounted for two-thirds of its capital and one-third of the total turnover; the research effort was strong; an intelligent policy over patents was pursued; links were built up with the coal and petroleum industries; domestic demand was strong, but external markets were also cultivated. Overall, the output of the industry doubled in six years, while for phosphate fertilizers the increase was three-fold, for synthetic textiles five-fold, and for plastics seven-fold. Production of the major basic materials and organic chemicals increased in volume and multiplied the derivatives. Petrochemistry, dominated by the subsidiaries of the refining companies, the rubber and chemical manufacturers, developed products which met with instant commercial success, such as synthetic detergents (which quickly made inroads on the markets of the traditional fat-based products[10]), solvents and paints, antifreeze, synthetic rubbers, ethylene. The plastics industry, based on organic chemistry and the treatment of plant matter, made startling progress; polystyrene ousted bakelite for moulded objects, vinyl was used for long-playing discs, floor coverings, and paints. The development of polyethylene in particular opened the way for the production of sturdy but light kitchen and household articles, as well as improved insulating materials for the electrical industry. Of special significance were the advances made in the domain of synthetic textiles. These quickly replaced the artificial textiles (rayon and bonded fibre), whose output now reached its peak. The appearance of products such as nylon, orlon, tergal, crylor, and rilsan, a new polyester derived from castor oil, revolutionized the clothing industry and had an immediate impact on everyday life, reducing time-consuming chores such as ironing. French homes were quickly invaded by a whole range of new products, many of which were to become household names – powders and liquids for cleaning and polishing, synthetic sponges, shampoos, new hard surfaces such as formica, cellophane wrapping, the inexpensive ball-point pen. Not without cause did Léo Ferré sing the charms of the 'temps du plastique'.

After chemicals, in the second position on the league table of growth (163 in 1958 for a base of 100 in 1952) came the metallurgical industries. They now consolidated their supremacy in the French economy, both by total turnover (more than 1500 milliard francs in 1956) and by numbers employed (1.15 million at the same time), overtaking definitively the textile industry. The iron and steel industry, integrated into the ECSC since February 1953, expanded its productions: an annual turnover of 560 milliard francs in 1956, with output of cast iron rising from 9.7 to 13 million tonnes between 1952 and 1958, and that of steel from 7.7 to 10.6 million tonnes over the same period, two-thirds of which was produced in Lorraine. The industry had encouraged concentration: in December 1950, the Sidelor group was set up, bringing together several medium-sized companies (the Forges et Aciéries de la Marine et d'Homécourt, Micheville, and the Gironde) around the Société de Rombas and Pont-à-Mousson, and responsible for 13 per cent of French steel; in 1951 the giant De Wendel group was reorganized into a new company, 'De Wendel et Cie' (the de Wendel family retaining control of the operation through a holding company, the 'Petits-Fils de François de Wendel'), and producing roughly 15 per cent of the steel; in 1953, the Lorraine-Escaut group brought together the steel producers of Longwy, and of the valleys of the Escaut and Meuse, producing in all 12 per cent of French steel and assuming an important place in the production of modern tubing and strong steel sheeting; lastly in this movement towards concentration in the industry, the small and vulnerable producers of the Massif Central began their conversion to production of specialized steel products in 1954 by joining the Compagnie des ateliers et forges de la Loire. For the industry as a whole, four groups – Sidelor, Usinor, De Wendel, and the Sollac – with seventeen plants, dominated the market and controlled prices, while 140 small plants scattered here and there were allowed to decline. Concentration favoured technological advance: 60 per cent of steel was now produced by the Thomas method to exploit fully the iron resources of Lorraine;[11] furnaces and plant were modernized, and new plants for the production of laminated steel were set up. Concerted lobbying of governments by the owners resulted in the complete electrification of the Valenciennes–Thionville line, and has-tened work on the Moselle Canal project from 1956. Other encouraging signs included the development of strong links with the Saar, a good use made of help from the Second Plan and the Groupement de l'industrie sidérurgique, and the reduction of operating costs. Lastly, in spite of a lengthening of the working week, the industry was free of serious labour unrest, largely owing to improved salaries after 1954. However, for all the brightness of the immediate picture – the industry's efforts were crowned by a 60 per cent expansion from 1954 to 1960 – clouds were already looming on the horizon. German and Japanese competition was already a cause for concern, the external markets where efforts had been concentrated now seemed to have uncertain long-term prospects. Most serious, perhaps, was that the iron and steel industry was unable to meet an internal demand up by 47 per cent and a demand from the ECSC up by 43 per cent. The French producers had simply failed to anticipate this expansion, and the limits of productive capacity were reached in 1956. Furthermore, they still refused to make extra efforts for their customers among producers of finished metal products. The strategic choices of which the French industry was so proud – such as the concentration of production on the coasts and the use of pure oxygen for making steel (as in the Usinor Dunkirk plant planned from 1956) – were to offer precious little comfort in the cut-throat competition of the 1960s; nor did they provide relief from the chronic financial problems of the industry (the debt of Usinor represented 37 per cent of its total turnover in 1958); nor, of course, did they avoid or ease the regional and social crises of the Nord and Lorraine. To complete this brief survey of the metallurgical industries, it is worth noting that although output of non-ferrous metals remained modest, that of aluminium did progress; drawing on the bauxite reserves of Provence and the inexpensive hydroelectricity of the Alps, and dominated by Péchiney-Ugine, this rose from 106 000 to 168 000 tonnes in the six years after 1952, amply covering French needs.

The metal producers faced strong demand from their major industrial customers. True, the production of railway material fell back once the networks had been reconstructed under the provisions of the First Plan; but machine tools and agricultural machinery were both expanding rapidly, though unable to satisfy needs; the shipyards, modernized and subsidized by the State under the terms of the Defferre law of May 1951, had full order books from 1956, thanks to strong world demand for oil tankers. Two sectors deserve special mention for their future importance: aeronautics and the car industry. The French aircraft industry, particularly weak in the aftermath of the war, required extensive reorganization. In 1958 it still met only 10 per cent of needs, but had managed to achieve a six-fold increase in production of military aircraft, mainly concentrated at the Marcel Dassault Company (the Mystère fighter and Djinn helicopters), and had tried to maintain its place in the construction of medium-sized commercial airliners with the Brégeut-Deux-Ponts. In spite of the overwhelming American supremacy in markets for commercial aircraft, the French constructors had correctly predicted the rapid growth of European air traffic. In May 1955, on a programme begun in 1951, the Société nationale de construction aéronautique du Sud-Est (which became Sud-Aviation in 1957) unveiled the Caravelle, a sturdy, medium-sized jet airliner, delivered to Air France in 1959. The Caravelle was an enormous success, and helped to restore part of the French aircraft industry's former prestige.[12]

However, it is the car industry which monopolizes attention. The French car industry was without doubt the showpiece of the economic growth of these years. Its total turnover in 1956 was 770 milliard francs, its output doubled (500 000 vehicles of all descriptions in 1952; 1 120 000 in 1958), order books were bulging, and a quarter of production was destined for export. The industry was strongly concentrated, attracted high investments, and had an excellent record for productivity increases. And, of course, in the wake of its expansion came a proliferation of suppliers, showrooms, garages, and mechanics. French society now adapted quickly and enthusiastically to the motorized transport revolution. The total stock of private vehicles doubled, going from 1.7 million in 1951 to 4 million in 1958, half of which were less than five years old; by 1958 there was one car for seven Frenchmen. The car was the instantly recognized symbol of material well-being, one whose appeal was universal, rapidly becoming accepted as an instrument of work and leisure. A similar enthusiasm was observed among the younger or more modest clientele for motorized transport of a two-wheeled variety, output of which also doubled, with a total stock of more than 5.5 million machines in 1958. Mobylettes from Motobécane and Peugeot, the famous 'Solex', scooters from Vespa and Lambretta made under Italian licence, motorcycles from Terrot: in all a rapidly expanding market of future car-owners, though one disturbed by the call-up for Algeria in 1956. The production of commercial vehicles remained relatively diversified – with coaches by Chausson and Berliet, lorries from Bernard, Somua, and Berliet – and the domain of motor accessories was international. Production of cars, however, was already highly concentrated. The Régie Renault, led by the dynamic Pierre Lefaucheux until his death in 1955 and then by Pierre Dreyfus, alone accounted for a third of the market, absorbing Salmson in 1955, incorporating the SOMUA into the SAVIEM for heavy-goods vehicles, automating the production lines, improving techniques of pressing and welding, and increasing productivity six-fold. The Renault range was diversified: the 4 CV, then the Dauphine, produced at the new model factory at Flins,[13] ensured for Renault a large slice of the market for small cars, even if its larger Frégate model failed to compete as successfully as was hoped against the prestigious American models. The private sector of the car industry, increasingly forced to act jointly for finance and for manufacture of parts and accessories, had the remaining two-thirds of the market. Citroën, solidly backed by the resources of the Michelin Company, held 28 per cent of the market, with a range extending from the remarkable all-purpose 2 CV up to the innovative DS 19, the latter replacing the 'Tractions' (Citroën saloons) in the dreams of the rising middle classes from 1957. The rest of the market was divided: Peugeot, taking 18 per cent with two robust and successful models, the 203 and the 403; Simca, armed with Ford capital and offering the Aronde range; and Panhard with the Dyna, taking the remainder.

The motor car thus became the potent symbol of aspirations to comfort and leisure. The same criteria were reflected in the development – or non-development – of other branches of industry. The leather industry was relatively stagnant (106 on the index), facing strong competition from plastics; the traditional fat-based products (index 128) were overtaken by synthetic products. A similar evolution befell the textile industry (also 128 on the index), whose turnover was close to that of metallurgy and with a million employees. In spite of the apparent solidity of textile empires such as that of Jean Prouvost in wool, or of Marcel Boussac in cotton,[14] the stagnant internal demand for the industry's traditional products was forcing conversion to synthetics, or increasing its dependence on military customers. International price competition on textiles now became ferocious, French mills were already closing, and the only sector of the industry to benefit from the general shift of public taste in favour of finer and more attractive articles was that of hosiery. The building industry had risen to only 121 on the index, though significant progress was in fact made after 1955. The problems here were manifold: too many firms, often poorly equipped; too slow an industrialization of building components; the end of the priority rebuilding of administrative, industrial, agricultural, and commercial buildings; a shortage of skilled labour; and inadequate investment before the measures of 1953 and the very belated *loi-cadre* for the industry in August 1957. Some progress had been made in the construction of housing, but the industry was quite incapable of meeting demand, which as a result tended to turn towards more readily available products such as the motor car. Or to consumer durables, food, and leisure, something reflected in the spectacular expansions of these sectors, output doubling, tripling, and quadrupling in the six years after 1952. From the food industry came packet soups, confectionery and preserves, fruit juices and aperitifs; in the glass industry, Saint-Gobain launched Pyrex kitchen ware; pharmaceutical products proliferated; the products of the electrical industry were all in great demand, notably lighting, refrigerators, and coffee mills, as were those of the electronics industry, where production quadrupled, 40 per cent of which went to complete the conquest of French households by the wireless, and to start the even more spectacular conquest by the television.

This upsurge of production was paralleled by a comparable, though harder to quantify, expansion in the service sector of the economy. For transport, the railways still handled two-thirds of all traffic, but their supremacy was no longer uncontested. The passenger traffic of the SNCF stagnated,[15] the volume of freight grew only slowly, and in Paris the RATP had reached saturation point. Demand was of course turning in favour of road transport. For the moment, the road network coped more or less well, but the construction of the motorway network was already lagging behind: the Tancarville bridge and the motorway to the south of Paris were the only projects at an advanced stage in 1958. Despite efforts at modernization, the canal network failed to register the true scale of European traffic. Indeed, it was increasingly clear that a coherent transport policy was urgently required if the entire transport system was not to collapse under the weight of the new demands being placed upon it. Nonetheless, there were some signs that the challenge could be met. The number of air passengers doubled; so too did the number of telephone calls, and the volume of mail and postal cheques increased by 50 per cent. Retailing, severely shaken by the trend to concentration and by the hazards of inflation, saw its sales increase by 40 per cent. The beneficiaries of this expansion were not the small shops or even the big stores of Paris, but rather the multiple chain outlets (Uniprix, Casino, Docks Rémois, Damoy, Goulet-Turpin) and the co-operatives, the latter adapting especially well to the new trends in retailing, often encouraged by the work of the Comités d'entreprise. Less specialized retailing, particularly in the towns, with an expanding clientele now prepared to spend more, was handicapped by the proliferation of distributive networks and intermediaries; but even in this sector efforts were being made to improve productivity and modernize points of sale. To conclude with an example of possibly symbolic value, is it not significant that the number employed in hairdressing salons should have tripled in six years?

*The causes of economic growth*

There is abundant evidence, then, of an important movement of economic growth. Is it possible to get an overall view of this process and its mechanism? Can its causes be identified? And, given that awareness tends to follow rather than accompany such changes, to what extent were they actually perceived at the time, not least by those with responsibility for preparing the future? Absorbed in their own lives, acutely sensitive to the most visible inequalities but poorly informed of economic realities, the French people were in fact slow to hail the expansion of this period, not easily swayed by the glowing statistics on the growth of the GNP.[16] For their part, however, the decision-makers, now better informed than ever by the experts of the Plan and ministry officials, were enthusiastic about the progress, eager to point to the virtues of controlled competition, and in some cases already attracted by American management theories. Leaving aside for the moment, then, the social reaction to expansion and to the distribution of its fruits, it is in their arguments and analyses that we must look for an explanation of the growth.[17]

The stock of human resources available to an economy is of obvious importance for its development. The regular annual growth in the population of approximately 0.9 per cent, the arrival of the young on the market-place, the encouragement to the family and to fertility, all contributed no doubt to the increase in demand. But was this a cause or a consequence of the improved economic situation? The question is probably unanswerable, though it is not hard to imagine how hopes of providing a better future for the new generations could stimulate efforts, encouraging acceptance of, even a search for, economic progress in all its forms. But, whatever the possible importance of such considerations, the fact remains that a chronic shortage of labour was a fundamental handicap for the French economy at this time, in spite of recourse to a more than ever necessary immigration – an average of 40 000 each year until 1954, then 155 000 from 1955 to 1961, employed mainly in the construction and metallurgical industries. It was not until 1962 that the population of working age started to grow as fast as the population as a whole. The worst period was the 1950s, when the relative importance of old people doubled, and while those born after the war were still in school. Not only did the active population almost stagnate in absolute terms (19.5 million in 1949, 19.7 in 1954, and 19.9 in 1958), but in relative terms it actually declined (46 per cent in 1949, 45.7 in 1954, and 44.5 in 1958). The decline was particularly marked among women (46 per cent active in 1946, 38 in 1954, and 36 in 1962); and the striking but isolated increases, in the liberal professions and senior management (up by 66 per cent between 1954 and 1962), were obviously no compensation for the stagnation in the number of female workers and the fall in agricultural employment (down by 36 per cent).

However, though the workforce was numerically inadequate it was put to consistently better use. Unemployment was low: with a peak of 310 000 in 1953–4, of which 62 000 were supported (1.6 per cent of the active population), and an irreducible minimum of 160 000 of which 18 000 were helped in 1957 (0.8 per cent of the active population), the prevailing trend was clearly to full employment. The enhanced mobility of labour, almost entirely due to the shake-out from agriculture, sent labour towards the economically most dynamic sectors – chemicals, electricity, engineering, and construction – rather than to textiles and mining, and boosted recruitment to the administration, commerce, and the service sector.[18] The lengthening of the working week, from an average of 45 to 46 hours between 1951 and 1958, off-set the extension of paid holidays after 1956, and provided a very small labour surplus. However, given this extreme inelasticity of the labour market, it is clear that all significant progress was dependent on improvements in the productivity of labour. On a base of 100 for 1949, this in fact rose, albeit at very uneven rate, to 152 by 1958, an overall increase of 5.2 per cent a year. But progress here was in fact general throughout the economy, and did not correspond to the hierarchies of modernization and competition outlined above. Labour productivity increases thus bore little relation to the capacity of new capital equipment, or even to the size of companies: with the exception of textiles and transport, the sectors of low concentration achieved equally impressive increases – those of agriculture have already been seen. The smaller active population thus worked not only harder, maintaining its efforts of the reconstruction period, but now worked better: incontestable evidence of a structural change in the mechanism of economic growth in the 1950s.

The persistent tightness of the labour market points to another possible explanation for growth: investment. To what extent had capital been substituted for scarce labour? Was the economic growth directly linked to an increase in investment, to changes in gross capital formation, and to the levels of savings? There was certainly a major investment effort. Investment (at 1956 values) increased from 24.5 milliard francs in 1952 to 39 milliard in 1958, a total which breaks down into an average of 65 per cent for productive investment, almost 25 per cent in housing, and slightly over 10 per cent for administrative and financial institutions. The progression was not uniform: from 1946 to 1951 it rose by only 2 per cent a year on average, but became much more vigorous after 1953, when the rate of increase rose to 10 per cent a year. This reflected growing demands for equipment, for modernization in industry, and the needs of the service sector, but was in turn stimulated by the policy of fiscal incentives to investment, with the introduction in April 1954 of a value added tax deductible from investment.[19] Especially noteworthy is the way the 'heavy' productive investments which had been given priority under the First Plan – energy, metallurgy, construction, transport, and communications – in fact maintained, thanks to State intervention, a steady growth rate of almost 6 per cent a year from 1955 to 1958. The 'light' investments, in the secondary industries, chemicals, agriculture, housing, services, and commerce, had taken off in 1949, only to stagnate with the rest of the economy in 1952, reviving from 1953 to attain an annual growth rate of 10 per cent the following year.

Overall, investment as a share of the gross national product rose to between 17 and 21 per cent from 1952 to 1958, a much higher level than in the *belle époque* or the 1920s, though inferior to the current levels in Federal Germany and Italy. The State had contributed to this development. The fiscal incentives have been mentioned, but there was also the policy of public tariffs, a consistent orientation of a significant proportion of the resources of the capital markets towards the heavy sectors now judged less profitable, plus the action of the public companies and the nationalized sector to ensure the vitality of these economic infrastructures. Indeed, since the internal investment resources of private companies grew less quickly than their investment needs, the State was in fact obliged to intervene in the capital market as a whole. It did so, however, much less than under the First Plan. A number of agencies had been created to ensure the financing of public projects: the Fonds de modernization et d'équipement was set up in January 1948; others, for construction, rural equipment, economic expansion and productivity, followed in July 1953; finally, that for conversion, decentralization, and labour reorientation was created in September 1954. In an attempt to streamline this aspect of the State's action, Edgar Faure united these in June 1955 in a single Fonds de développement économique et social (FDES), controlled by the Ministry of the Economy and Finance. But this rationalization of the State's intervention was in fact paralleled by a significant reduction of the place of public funds in the general financing of investment, its share falling from 50 per cent in 1950 to 35 per cent in 1952 and 1954, and to 27 per cent in 1956.

In other words, the decisive financial support for the upsurge of investment came from private sources: in as yet insufficient quantities, but an unmistakable sign of the ground being recovered in the economy by free market forces. In the six years after 1950, the share of medium-term bank loans in total investment rose from 3.3 to 14.2 per cent, while the Stock Exchange, recovered from its post-war lethargy, increased its contribution in the form of shares and bonds from 4.4 to 9.2 per cent. This increase in the supply of capital explains the sharp fall in the level of self-financing by companies, dropping from 112 per cent in 1949 to 79 per cent in 1958. Of course, self-financing could still be necessary in difficult periods: in the squeeze which accompanied the Pinay stabilization, for example, its share of total investment rose from 41.7 per cent in 1950 to 50.5 per cent in 1952, only to diminish subsequently, reaching 40 per cent in 1958. Finally, savings, discouraged before 1949 by inflation, and stagnant for a long time afterwards, assumed a growth rate of more than 7 per cent a year after 1953. As a share of the gross national product, savings had dropped from 25.5 to 18.7 per cent between 1949 and 1953, but stabilized at almost 23 per cent in 1958. The administration intervened hardly at all after 1952 in the accumulation of savings, the societies typically offering 45 per cent: the real progress was due rather to an increase in personal savings, rising from 9 per cent in 1950 to 13.6 per cent in 1957. These savings did not gravitate towards the traditional financial outlets – the Stock Exchange and overseas investments never recovered their pre-1914 appeal – nor did they go into the investments of housholds themselves; stocks of clothing and furniture had usually been reconstituted before 1950. Instead, perhaps inevitably, the extra saving was generated by the demand for housing, a result of the scarcity of rented and municipal accommodation. This massive, almost obsessional drive to home-ownership – which had a predictable impact on the housing market – accelerated the reconstitution, after the years of high inflation, of household savings in the form of current accounts or savings deposits, and tripled (from 4 to 12 milliard between 1954 and 1958) medium- and long-term loans. For the expansion of savings was paralleled, indeed complemented, by the appearance of credit in family budget strategies, prompted above all by the demand for accommodation, but also by an appetite for the newer articles, such as cars and consumer durables, particularly if the possibility for home purchase was delayed. To sum up then, capital in all its forms was growing: by 3.9 per cent each year between 1949 and 1954, then by 4.5 per cent until 1960. In this respect France was moving in line with her European neighbours. Yet it is scarcely plausible, albeit in the absence of a detailed analysis of the profits it generated,[20] to suggest that this capital was the primary motive force in the expansion. Capital was certainly better accumulated and better channelled than before; but its substitution for labour was still below what it would be in subsequent decades. On the other hand, however, its inspirational effect is undeniable – the 'myth of investment' contributed to the acceleration of growth.

To this it can be added that a number of other strictly capitalistic economic stimuli appear not to have had a major impact on expansion. True, and as the productivity increases testify, the more intensive use of labour, like the new techniques and machines, ensured that the capital invested was put to good use. But, for example, despite what was often claimed by the Left and by the economists of the PCF in particular,[21] there was no strong push at this time towards more monopolistic forms of production, no dramatic increase in the power of the 'trusts': rather the reverse. Although many firms with fewer than ten employees disappeared, the relative importance of the largest companies was unchanged. The available evidence suggests that it was the medium- and small-sized companies which were the most dynamic elements of the expansion. Between 1950 and 1957, the number of concentrations was limited to sixty a year, of which only half were in industry; these operations were not important for the volume of capital involved, and were confined mainly to the service sectors and to the branches of industry where concentration was a well-established trend (such as metallurgy, electricity, and glass). Indeed, this fact underlines the 'crystallization' discernible in the economic structures at this time:[22] while banks, insurance companies, and commerce were highly responsive to the appeal of concentration, other sectors, notably the industrial, were afflicted by inertia, unable or unwilling to respond in this sense. It was as if the growth was still 'enclavée', confined and isolated to particular sectors of the economy.[23] For the moment at least, investors and industrialists clung to their old habits and preferences, a situation which was not to change significantly until the economic shock that followed the opening of commercial frontiers by the Common Market finally forced them to confront the challenge of international competition.

To sum up then: exploiting opportunities in fact present since the turn of the century, plus the great impetus of reconstruction, the French economy entered a major phase of, for the most part, internally generated growth, thanks notably to productivity increases of more than 5 per cent achieved throughout the economy. These made possible regular increases of national income and household purchasing power; they also stimulated investment and encouraged capital formation, both of which had for a long while been maintained at reasonable levels by means of a systematic recourse to self-financing and public expenditure. In addition, the State could play a counter-cyclical role, and guarantee the vitality of the economic infrastructure. Which factor was determinant? An active population working harder and better? The introduction of new American-style techniques? The advantages of a now unfettered capitalism, or those of the planning and controls which had been retained? Economists, in fact, find it impossible to give clear answers to these questions: no single factor was decisive, no single factor explains the expansion.[24] What one can say is that their unprecedented concurrence established conditions extremely propitious to growth. A schematic explanation would run as follows: the combined effect of a greater effort from an in fact smaller workforce, of the modernization of the infrastructure and the productive machine, plus the action of the State, had been to rejuvenate the country, raising the economy's productive capacity to meet a demand which was potentially large after the successive contractions of crisis, war, and the post-war reconstruction. Boosted and guided by the State, internal demand was, then, the essential factor in French economic growth, much more so than in either Germany or Great Britain. Such a schema, though extreme, is not implausible; yet it rests on

Table 17: *Three growth rates compared*

| | France | | | Federal Germany | | | UK | | |
|---|---|---|---|---|---|---|---|---|---|
| | 1950 | 1954 | 1958 | 1950 | 1954 | 1958 | 1950 | 1954 | 1958 |
| Population millions | 41.6 | 42.8 | 44.5 | 48.4 | 50.5 | 52.1 | 50.3 | 50.7 | 51.8 |
| Volume of GNP index 1950 = 100 | 100 | 117 | 141 | 100 | 138 | 179 | 100 | 110 | 118 |
| Per capita GNP index 1950 = 100 | 100 | 113 | 131 | 100 | 133 | 164 | 100 | 108 | 116 |
| Industrial production index 1953 = 100 | 98 | 110 | 150 | 85 | 112 | 151 | 98 | 107 | 113 |
| Exports index 1950 = 100 | 100 | 122 | 146 | 100 | 208 | 332 | 100 | 97 | 107 |
| Consumer prices index 1953 = 100 | 77 | 100 | 93 | 100 | 110 | 110 | 81 | 102 | 119 |

*Source: Annuaires statistiques des Nations Unies.*

basically non-economic elements. And indeed, in his analysis of the phenomenon, Harvard economist Charles P. Kindleberger came to the conclusion that the fundamental change in the French economy was one of personnel and attitudes.[25] In short, there was a sense in which growth occurred because it was actively sought after, because behaviour had changed, because knowledge had increased: thus the French were prepared to accept growth even before they could actually promote it. A new-found confidence in the future, a taste for education, possibly a less deferential attitude to the status quo, were all changes as important as the rate of capital formation or the intensity of competition. In the final analysis then, an explanation of the economic leads us back to the domains of the social and the mental.

The French renovation appears less remarkable, of course, when considered in its European context;[26] with all the other capitalist countries of Europe, France participated in the economic 'miracles' of the post-war period. Her performance was an honourable one – superior to that of Great Britain and Belgium, different to that of Italy, though no match for German dynamism (see Table 17). The great originality of the French growth, however, was that it occurred without an increase in the labour force and without apportioning more than 18 – 20 per cent of the national income to investment. And it was achieved without the economy being fully opened up to international competition: in response rather to a strong internal demand. This vigorous and exclusive exploitation of purely national resources in perhaps the surest hallmark of the French experience.

*The role of the State*

Another characteristic of the French experience since the Liberation was the active intervention by the State in the general development of the economy. In spite of the return of the liberals (see Chapter 11) and the massive re-emergence of capitalist forces in the productive circuits, did the State continue to act as arbiter in the general interest? Was there a serious attempt to realize a controlled and equitable growth? Did the public authorities intervene successfully in the economy, watching out for possible problems ahead, maintaining the economy on a sound course while working to promote an '*économie concertée*'?[27]

The statistical profile of the expansion of these years appears to offer a triumphant vindication of the benefits of planning. Not only did the Second Plan make up the accumulated shortfalls of the First Plan and correct the imbalance created by its rigorous concentration on capital equipment, but almost all its targets were reached a year ahead of schedule: preparations for the Third Plan began in 1957. National output was 29 per cent higher than in 1952, for a planned increase of 25 per cent; the index of industrial production stood at 145 instead of the 130 originally hoped for; agricultural output was up to 117, narrowly short of the 120 planned; and investment targets were exceeded by an average of 10 per cent. The successes, then, were incontestable, even if consumer goods output continued to grow faster than that of equipment, to the consternation of the public authorities determined to encourage this sector. In the period 1954–7, public investment accounted for between 26 and 29 per cent of the total, and was distributed following the guidelines set by the Plan: 30 per cent for construction, 15 per cent for industry, 15 per cent for energy, 14 per cent for overseas, 13 per cent for transport, 9 per cent to agriculture and the food industry, and 4 per cent to social action. These investments help to explain the excellent results in chemicals (where targets were reached at 142 per cent), housing and educational building (111 per cent), electricity (105 per cent), wheat (116 per cent), while the Suez Canal blockade was responsible for the stagnation of fuel oils (85 per cent); and the advance was rapid in the dynamic sectors already mentioned: cars, electrical constructions, synthetic textiles. Yet these ostensibly exciting results did not produce enthusiasm among the senior officials of the Plan – one of them, Jean Ripert, was even to speak of planning's 'traversée du désert' after 1952.[28] One handicap may have been leadership: whatever his other qualities, the Plan's new General Commissioner, Etienne Hirsch, did not carry the same authority as Jean Monnet. Moreover, the eager enthusiasm of the heroic period of reconstruction seemed to be wearing thin: the Plan was no longer the object of political unanimity – the CGT had withdrawn from its commissions after 1948. Another handicap lay in the fact that the planners were arguing against the weight of received opinion, especially that of the parliamentarians, few of whom were convinced of the virtues of competition and who, along with ministers, often obstructed their projects. Hirsch, influenced by Gruson, had reached the conclusion that the fundamental problem for the future of the national economy was that of the balance of payments, particularly in the European context. Yet over agriculture, for example, he had to wage a long struggle against the protectionists at the Ministry of Agriculture, and it was not until 1955 that the French agricultural trade balance with foreign economies at last became positive. Similar resistances held up the attempts to merge Cail and Fives-Lille, who were competing against each other in the European market for engineering products; or the creation of companies to promote and sell French techniques abroad.

The Plan was changing. It was becoming more intellectual, more sophisticated (owing, for example, to the national income material at its disposal), less preoccupied with short-term needs, able to look further ahead; and less subject to democratic discussion, despite the growing numbers who participated on its modernization commissions. With the accent now on encouragement and incentives, French planning was more liberal and less compulsory. A new division of economic responsibility was in fact taking shape: to the State went responsibility for the economic infrastructure and for helping the ailing sectors, plus tentative steps towards a policy of decentralization; to a reinvigorated capitalism went the major share of industrial production, and a freedom to exploit all the profitable possibilities of the market. One reason for this change was, quite simply, that many of the Plan's ideas on modernization had been successfully diffused – under its encouragement – throughout the areas of economic decision-making. The American model of company management, and the obsession with constantly changing products and techniques, had been observed at first hand by the young managers and employers sent on the 'productivity missions' organized by Jean Monnet. The more forward-looking members of the employers' organizations were gradually persuaded to provide more honest and useful figures to the national income experts, receiving in return advice on how to improve management and accounting techniques; the Bureau d'information et de prévision économique (BIPE) was set up to this end by the SEEF. The officials of the Plan won converts in companies and at the CNPF; they enlarged their political audience, particularly thanks to *Mendésisme*, with which they had obvious affinities. The efforts of the productivity missions were now focused openly on ways to increase free competition; a close co-operation, often smacking strongly of corporatism, developed between officials, employers, and engineers. At the same time as its greater complexity and sophistication tended to distance the Plan from the public as a whole, so its place in the political consensus contracted, with the failure

of *Mendésisme* and the decline of the régime. For a time under the Fifth
Republic, the Plan led by Massé was to recover some of its former dynamic
interventionist role; but before that, between 1952 and 1958, it gradually
became fixed in a role of a public agency working to promote efficiency in
the economy, offering the best information and advice for the steady progress of growth, but a growth in which the Plan was an intermediary agent
rather than an active participant in its own right.[29]

As a result of this change and the absence of ambitious programmes of
economic development, the impact of the State must be sought also in the
ordinary economic and financial policies of governments. Many of the most
dramatic aspects of these policies have been described in the preceding
chapters, but it is worthwhile attempting now to give an overall view. The
point of departure, as we have seen, was the Pinay experiment of 1952. With
its mixture of calls to confidence and rigour, this established a number of
basic principles for government policy: in future the State would not hinder
the action of private capital; savings were to be protected; 'good housekeeping' was to be the golden rule for budgetary policy; and the tax burden
was not to be increased. With his highly empirical approach, Pinay
succeeded in the main thing, namely, convincing the French people that
their own efforts were the key to greater well-being, and, above all,
stabilizing prices by fostering a latent recession and curbing demand. The
risk of galloping inflation had not been eliminated, however. When
economic activity slowed down in 1952–3, exports declined, the foreign
trade deficit started to grow again, and French prices were stabilized at a
level 15–20 per cent higher than world prices. And the quick devaluation in
fact necessary to remedy this was precluded by the attachment to the
currency, an attachment which Pinay had reinforced. France thus embarked on growth by drawing on her currency reserves, and with price
levels which until 1957 allowed her to live beyond her means. In spite of the
mediocre level of production, 1953 saw the start of recovery: the Plan was
reactivated, loans for the construction of housing were unfrozen; the strikes
of the summer showed that improvements in the standard of living could be
delayed no longer; the Plan's productivity missions began again.

Now began the astonishing period of 'expansion in stability' of 1953–4,
with Edgar Faure responsible for economic policy, first as Minister of
Finance, then as premier. Indeed, this was close to being a 'golden age',[30]
when private initiatives coincided with skilful public intervention, in an
international context favourable to European and Japanese producers,
thanks to the relaxation of the American economy under the Republican
administration. Working in co-operation with Laniel, then with Mendès
France, Faure made the most of the opportunities. He favoured, as we have
seen, an expansion of private investment with the introduction of the value
added tax (TVA); by an improved use of public support through the

creation of the FDES; and by making credit cheaper, the discount rate being reduced from 4 to 3 per cent between September 1953 and December 1954. Investment was thus freed of control – potential investors could seek funds where they wanted; the Treasury limited its role to the providing of guarantees to lenders, but refused now to fuel investment automatically from tax revenues. There was greater competition on the capital markets, from personal savings, from companies themselves (such as the Groupement des industries sidérurgiques, whose financing role was encouraged), and from all the public and semi-public credit agencies – the Caisse des dépôts, the Crédit national, the Crédit foncier, and the Crédit agricole. This suppleness bore fruit: in 1954, investments were up by 8.5 per cent compared with the previous year, by 13 per cent in 1955, and by 8.5 per cent in 1956, while industrial production rose annually by 7 per cent. These measures were completed with a policy to encourage industrial reconversion and regional development, the start of a revived policy for housing, and an application of the 1952 law on collective bargaining which favoured a much freer negotiation of wages. Only the SMIG remained tightly controlled, often by recourse to a manipulation of the price indices.

This success was due to the generally improved international economic context and to the revival of savings, especially those of households. Evidence of the favourable concurrence of circumstances abounded. For the first time expansion did not push up prices, which in fact remained exceptionally stable: France seemed cured of her inflation, and Pinay retrospectively justified. True, since the government refused to devalue while gradually freeing prices, systematic recourse to advances from the Banque de France was unavoidable. But the prosperity was visible to all, Treasury bond issues were taken up, and military expenditure was reduced after the defeat in Indo-China (before the war in Algeria had become a massive burden). So much so that the deficit – the 'impasse' in Faure's phrase – settled at below 700 milliard francs, and at the end of 1955 the Treasury was even able to repay 122 milliard to the Banque de France. Expansion and stable prices in turn helped exports. The structure of French foreign trade was still flawed: France continued to import too much energy and machinery, while exporting too many primary materials, notably iron from Lorraine, and agricultural produce. Nonetheless, the overall commercial balance was solidly positive in 1955: the dollar deficit shrank – 328 million in 1952, 325 in 1953, 180 in 1954, a surplus of 84 in 1955, before plummeting into a deficit of 800 million in 1956, 950 in 1957, and 300 in 1958. Moreover, America helped the French balance of payments in a number of ways: by shouldering the burden of Indo-China; through the off-shore contracts negotiated at the Lisbon Conference in February 1952 and made in France by the United States with funds from the Export–Import bank; and by earnings from the construction of American military bases in France. As a result of this amelioration in the balance of payments, French reserves of gold and strong currencies were reconstituted, growing from 204 milliard in 1953 to 680 at the end of 1955. France now began to repay some of the heavy debts contracted at the Liberation. One especially promising sign was the changed response to international trade: as European expansion started in earnest, France threw herself more wholeheartedly than ever before into the system of unhindered international exchanges, suppressing part of the import quotas, helping exporters, keeping her OEEC commitments (freeing, for example, 75 per cent of her exchanges in April 1955, and 82 per cent the following April). And an elaborate system of special customs duties on the decontrolled products and multiple exchange rates amounted in fact to a devaluation. However, if the French economy could not now afford to forgo the stimulus of recovered economic liberty, currently gal-vanizing all the Western economies, the national bases of French external trade remained fragile, and the old protectionist and isolationist instincts were likely to reappear at the first sign of trouble.

And indeed, the situation was brutally reversed in 1956 and 1957, when the growth rate entered a period of crisis and the economy over-heated. The difficulties resulted from a combination of structural weaknesses and circumstantial factors. At the root of the crisis lay the tragic and inescap-able fact that France could not afford the war in Algeria *and* expansion in the mainland. The economic and financial costs of political commitment to an all-out war in Algeria were now felt to the full: the 400 000, then 500 000 young soldiers called to serve in Algeria were an intolerable loss to an economy already suffering from a scarcity of labour and an extremely long working week. True, immigration compensated for this to some extent; but the familiar North African sources were in turn dislocated by the Algerian crisis and its repercussions. The sectors worst affected by the labour shortages were textiles, metallurgy, and construction. Meanwhile, the Suez crisis deprived France at a stroke of 90 per cent of her usual petroleum supplies, exhausting stocks, and forcing a recourse to costly imports of refined products without which the economy would have suffocated. This increase was naturally reflected in the average price of imports, which rose by 50 per cent in 1956. When the shortage of petrol products was overcome, their price had risen by 23 per cent; industrialists, meanwhile, had tried to combat the anticipated increases by switching energy demands to coal and electricity, thus setting up inflationary tensions. The problem of inflation was in turn accentuated by the structural shortcomings. We have already seen how the productive capacity of the iron and steel industry was saturated: supply and demand of basic metallurgical products were no longer matched, delivery delays lengthened, and the unsatisfied demand caused prices to rise. Against the background of labour scarcity pushing up wages, the Mollet government's social policy caused the wage bill and charges of companies to rise by 12 per cent in 1956, then by 12.5 per cent in 1957. Not only did cost-push inflation take off, but, with the economy slowed down, demand-pull pressures also built up. The official response to this difficult situation was piecemeal and inadequate, treating symptoms rather than causes: interest rates were raised (the discount rate going from 3 to 5 per cent in August 1957); all prices were blocked; the promised freeing of external exchange was abandoned; and subsidies were multiplied to produce an artificial stabilization of the prices of the 213 items on the general price index, a rise in which would set in motion the sliding scale mechanism of across-the-board wage increases. With this response governments failed on every front. Wage-earners were disappointed by the failure of their real incomes to rise, while producers were suffocated by the general blockage: 16 per cent of firms reported cash-flow difficulties in November 1955, 19 per cent in October 1956, and 44 per cent in October 1957. On top of these difficulties came poor harvests in the aftermath of the severe frosts of 1956, and the extra imports of war materials with the intensification of the conflict in Algeria. Exports, meanwhile, were damaged by the rise in French prices, the recession of the American economy, and increases in freight and service charges. Finally, capital fled the country after the victory of the Front républicain. Given this catalogue of difficulties, it was scarcely surprising that in eighteen months the currency reserves were exhausted, nor that the deficit for 1956–7 reached 2 milliard dollars. The situation was humiliatingly close to that of 1947–8, with the crucial difference that there was hardly any American aid to ease the crisis this time. Drastic remedies were needed. Jean Monnet, as we have seen, was sent to Washington in January 1958, negotiating loans of 650 million dollars, in return for a promised reduction of the budget deficit. In the short term, however, the gold reserves had to be used, while in June 1957 came Gaillard's 'vérité des prix' operation, readjusting the exchanges and, in effect, devaluing the franc by 20 per cent.

The picture was an alarming one: with generalized price increases (retail prices rose by 14 per cent between June 1957 and January 1958), public finances in a deplorable condition, and the long-term prospects for growth increasingly compromised. The necessary surgical operation finally came in 1958 with de Gaulle's appointment of Antoine Pinay to Finance. As in 1952, Pinay imposed the only realistic solution, a provisional stabilization of demand, but this time accompanied by a devaluation and, in January 1959, the creation (by shifting the decimal point) of the 'franc lourd'. But the way for this solution had in fact been prepared by Gaillard's policy, and since 1956 the clear intention had been to avoid serious damage to the productive capacity of the economy. There were some encouraging signs of resilience. The level of company investment remained high throughout these months of financial and political turmoil, actually increasing from 11 to 13 per cent a year; and the indices of output had held firm. Of course, this is not to absolve the Fourth Republic's leaders of their grave policy mistakes: the crushing burden of the war in Algeria and the repercussions of the Suez adventure on petrol costs speak for themselves. And their financial incompetence was inescapable: by 1958 France was left without reserves! Having said this, however, they had been consistently concerned to minimize the dislocation of the economy's productive structures. They had, moreover, shown considerable dexterity in their handling of variables as diverse as the public sector, private savings, competition, and controls. Credit must also go to the courage, real enough at the time of Poujade's threat, with which they accepted the social implications of modernization. In this respect at least they had responded successfully to the challenge of their time. Ramadier, an old-time Socialist convinced of the benefits of economic growth, illustrates perfectly this attitude: in September 1956, launching a State loan whose prospects for success looked slight, he had the idea of indexing it to property values: the loan in fact brought in 320 milliard, a striking example of the intelligent recognition by an SFIO leadership in so many other respects lamentable, of the virtues of neo-capitalism and the advantages of expansion – even if, in reverse, the same example could be cited as evidence of submission to vested interests! In fact, and as many authors have concluded,[31] the economic intervention practised by the final governments of the Fourth Republic was on balance genuinely effective. Of course, their policies undoubtedly exacerbated the social and political tensions from which the régime would perish. Yet they had managed to preserve the best features of the mixed economy set up in 1945, an economy, moreover, in which the workforce was no longer treated merely as another factor of production. Their policies had helped to maintain the capitalist economy on its path of recovery and expansion. For this they had armed themselves with serious means of action: subsidies to production and investment, the intervention of the nationalized sector,[32] fiscal and budgetary instruments, a panoply of social aids; the total financial resources thus mobilized and redistributed increased by 188 per cent between 1952 and 1957, representing 22 per cent of the gross industrial product in 1952, 31 per cent in 1954, 40 per cent in 1956, and 32 per cent in 1958. And considerable flexibility, if not eclecticism, was displayed in the deployment of these policy instruments, whether for the struggle to limit the deficit, or for efforts to boost expenditure, or to severely restrain prices and incomes, while after 1952 the unconditional defence of the franc had been abandoned in the interests of consumers. Governments succeeded, then, in channelling a boisterous demand constructively, accepting in the process imbalance and the evils of inflation, in order that the economic growth might develop to the full.

The achievement went unacknowledged by the French public. For achievement it was: the political leaders and senior officials of the Fourth Republic, acutely aware of the disastrous way in which the French economy had fallen behind since 1930, had responded intelligently to the new development: in doing so they created an invaluable heritage for the Fifth Republic. Important in their success, however, was the essentially autarkic character of the French economy until 1958. The development of these years was almost entirely an internal phenomenon; as a result, the intervention by the State, however fragmentary or incoherent, was at no point rendered completely ineffective by shifts in the external balances or by changes in the international context: after all, between 1950 and 1958, French exports had never exceeded 6 per cent of the gross industrial product. Until the shock produced by the opening of commercial frontiers in the Fifth Republic, this expansion of the French economy was fuelled by domestic energies and was orientated to the satisfaction of domestic demand. At this stage, then, the French economy was still one in which external demand could neither compensate for the fluctuations of internal demand, nor offset the errors of public policy and the effects of inflation. In such an economic closed circuit, imbalances of supply and demand could quickly cause spectacular ravages, complicating decision-making and eroding the consensus: some of the consequences were felt in the final crisis of May 1958. The least one can say, in conclusion, is that by its efforts – multiple, unappreciated, and certainly uneven in benefits – the French State established for itself a valuable and legitimate role in fostering and guiding a dynamic though circumscribed movement of economic growth, by means of policies as empirical as they were broadly effective.

## New life for the 'désert français'

On 17 March 1950, the Bidault government approved a policy from its Minister of Reconstruction and Town Planning, Claudius-Petit, the stated aim of which was: 'to check the current which is tending to concentrate all the resources of the nation in its major centres; to recreate life in the regions whose resources are underexploited, regions which, for all their rich potential, are becoming deserted'. This far-sighted policy and the action it produced was evidence of the widespread awareness in governmental, administrative, and economic circles of the massively destabilizing impact economic growth was having on the French regions. One of the first to draw attention to the phenomenon was Jean-François Gravier, a geographer attached to the Plan. In his famous book *Paris et le désert français* (first published in 1947, republished with additions in spring 1958), Gravier showed how the combined effects of Napoleonic centralization, the industrial revolution, and the decline of the 1930s had institutionalized regional imbalance in France, creating and reinforcing a dangerous concentration of capital, knowledge, and power in Paris. Gravier pointed to the current developments – new demographic vitality, greater mobility of labour, narrowing of regional disparities in incomes, and new taste for initiatives among local élites – to argue that the time was ripe for concerted action to begin to restore a geographical balance between the regions. He saw deconcentration as the first step towards a real decentralization, though he was careful to avoid any technocratic simplification of the problem, or an exaggerated faith in purely economic solutions. The profitable use of the entire French territory would have to draw on a wide range of civic, social, and political energies, mobilizing the resources of the basic units of collective life in France, the communes and the local communities and their bodies. Gravier's book found a wide and influential audience among the politicians, decision-makers, and the first technocrats of the 1950s;[33] its message recalled the spirit of the Liberation period, when regional initiatives, co-ordinated by the commissaires de la République, had expressed themselves so strongly, as well as echoing the ideas of the *planistes* of the 1930s. Indeed, the cause of regional development marked a continuity of hopes which were common to Vichy, the Resistance, and the period of reconstruction. Its appeal was manifold: offering a new chance for previously dissipated energies, a springboard for democratic local initiatives against administrative authority, an inexhaustible subject for political speeches and high-powered symposia, as well, of course, as providing a fresh alibi for *immobilisme*. With this theme, the new national and regional élites were to tap a potentially rich source of energy, one, moreover, to which the public at large was well disposed.

The statistical dimensions of the regional problem, now made familiar by the work of the INSEE, notably using the results of the 1954 census, were certainly grim. To begin with there were startling disparities in population densities. The national average was 78 inhabitants per square kilometre, but this average masked an enormous range: 1100 in the Paris region, 363 in the Nord, and 336 in the Rhône regions, yet only 16 in the Lozère, 15 in the Hautes-Alpes, and 12 in the Basses-Alpes. Only a quarter of the country had population densities above the average, concentrated mainly in the Paris region, the North, Alsace-Lorraine, the regions of Lyon and Grenoble, the coastal zones of Provence and the Languedoc, the Haute-Garonne and the Gironde, plus a few Breton and Norman *départements*. Many of these areas had a high birth-rate. All the others, however, suffered in varying degrees from an ageing population, departure of the young, collapse of the social structure, numerical weakness of *cadres*, exodus from the countryside, and crippling preponderance of agricultural activities. Two regions were particularly badly affected: the Massif Central, also handicapped by poor communications and the decline of its traditional industries; and the South-West, the region of polyculture and a historically falling birth-rate, where the only hopes for the future were the gas from Lacq, and the large urban centres of Bordeaux and, especially, Toulouse, with its chemical and aeronautical industries. All the other criteria – output, productivity, added value, and income – revealed a France cut in two, bisected by a line from Le Havre to Marseille, or, more striking still, from Le Havre to Grenoble. At one extreme, the regions to the west-south-west: the poorest, the most rural, where wages were lowest, knowledge and opportunities scarcest, able only to export their human resources to the dynamic regions. At the other extreme, the east-north-east: accounting for two-thirds of the population, three-quarters of the wealth, containing all the major industries, the centres of research and decision-making, and, of course, Paris. Everything pointed to a widening of the gulf in the future, as the most dynamic French regions became more closely linked with their counterparts in the Europe of the Six, the plain of the Po and the Rhine axis. And at the centre was Paris – the 'tête monstrueuse d'un corps exsangue' as René Pleven described it; with 8 million inhabitants in its agglomeration, absorbing 150 000 immigrants each year, alone responsible for generating a quarter of the national income, and the centre of all the networks of distribution, communication, economy and finance, administration, and intelligence.

It would, of course, be misleading to present the situation in completely black-and-white terms. On each side of the dividing line, the medium-sized towns were a considerable force, tending to soften the contrast between archaism and modernity; the *exode rural* was not always an unmitigated disaster, at least not if it increased opportunities for the farmers who remained; and the appetite for immediate consumption observed in the disadvantaged regions could indicate a readiness for renewal as well as a simple attempt at compensation.[34] Nonetheless, the most sophisticated economic studies always revealed the same disturbing cartography of imbalance, the same inescapable logic of localization. Synthesizing all the available material, F. Coront-Ducluzeau established a distinction between three types of region (see Map 6). First, the 'evolved' regions: here participation in primary economic activities was low, but a developed secondary sector was concentrated in the most dynamic fields (metallurgy, chemicals, electricity), and had a stimulative effect on the entire regional economy. Next came the regions of 'imbalance': here, in contrast to the 'evolved' regions, either the industrial sector had simply failed to take off compared with agriculture, or else was not concentrated in the most profitable sectors; these regions were often those with a declining textile industry or a heavy metallurgical industry without local customers in the processing sector, regions where agricultural produce was not processed locally. Lastly, there were the 'underdeveloped' regions: in spite of often thriving micro-regions or towns, these lacked a sufficiently strong pole of economic growth; their tertiary sectors were plethoric and inefficient, agriculture was poorly

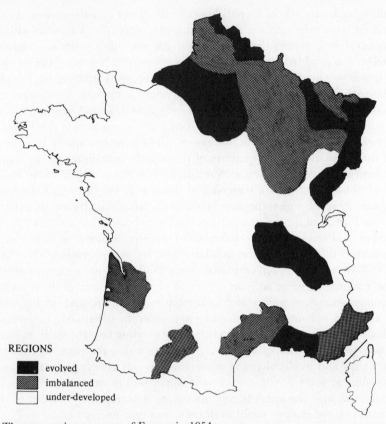

REGIONS

▮ evolved
▨ imbalanced
☐ under-developed

6 The economic structure of France in 1954

*Source:* F. Coront-Ducluzeau, *La Formation de l'espace économique national,* Colin, 1964, p. 125.

modernized, the industries were those of stagnant technology and bleak prospects, energy and mineral resources were inadequately exploited, and there was little manufacturing industry. The criteria of industrial development point, then, to a steep hierarchy of the French regions. The map of disposable incomes (see Map 7) reflects these inequalities, and in fact accentuates them by taking into account profitable services and well-exploited agricultural productions. From this map it is clear that the Le Havre–Marseille line also separates rich from poor; the regional variation around the national average of 100 extends from 148 for the Paris region down to 73 for the Centre-South. Only four regions attained or exceeded the average annual income of 252 000 francs: the East (250 000), the North (255 000), the Lyon conurbation (261 000), and the Paris region (375 000): and these four of course pushed up the national average considerably. At

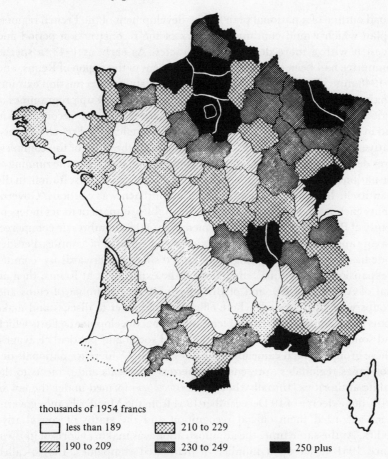

thousands of 1954 francs

| | | |
|---|---|---|
| ☐ less than 189 | ▨ 210 to 229 | |
| ▨ 190 to 209 | ▨ 230 to 249 | ■ 250 plus |

7 Disposable per capita income in 1954

*Source:* N. Delefortrie and J. Morice, *Les Revenus départementaux en 1864 et en 1954*, Colin, 1959, p. 121.

the other end of the scale, twenty-five *départements* had incomes 40 per cent inferior to the average.[35] Here again, of course, the handful of exceptional cases – Seine and Seine-et-Oise at one extreme, Corsica and Lozère at the other – stretched the range: when they are excluded from the calculations, it is clear that the dispersal around the national average was in fact much weaker, whichever criterion is used. However, even thus corrected, the overall dispersal remained between 65 and 125 per cent of all the national averages. Disparities of this magnitude were what formed the basis for arguments and policies in favour of a better use of national territory and resources and for a reduction of inequalities.

The policy presented by Claudius-Petit in 1950 in fact contained the broad outline of a national plan for the development of the French regions, a plan which would continue the work of the reconstruction period and invest it with a more democratic character. As early as 1943, a special committee had been set up for the development of the region of Reims, and in 1948 nine inspecteurs généraux de l'administration en mission extraordinaire (IGAME) were appointed with powers to draw up programmes of regional action. Yet the imperatives of the task of post-war reconstruction had in fact led to a strengthening of the Jacobin reflexes in French administrative life – something clear, for example, from the work of the commissaires de la République, or in the close control from Paris over the running of the nationalized industries, and, for all the emphasis on consultation, in the Plan itself. In the early stages, then, the approach was cautious. Governments encouraged initiatives from local notables, impatient to act independently of Paris, from industrialists, members of the chambres de commerce, mayors and conseillers généraux. As a result, a number of 'comités d'études et de liaison régionaux' sprang up, followed shortly afterwards by 'comités d'expansion économique', modelled on the experiment at Reims, then on that of Alsace in 1950, and of Brittany in 1951. A number of clubs and groups were also formed, where officials could meet to discuss and make plans for tackling concrete problems of regional development, efforts which had some success in surmounting the usual social and political cleavages. These groups, which came together in 1952 at a 'Conférence nationale des économies régionales', presented numerous proposals and projects to the public authorities. Initially they were *associations* formed under the law of 1901, but a decree of 19 Dececember 1954 from the Mendès France government accorded them official recognition and the status of consultative bodies. At the same time, the administration was making efforts of its own. Since 1951 it set up a number of mandated companies, the so-called Sociétés d'économie mixte, each charged with the development of a specific urban or rural zone or even an entire region. The companies were eventually placed under a *loi-cadre* of 7 August 1957, the outcome of an exhaustive parliamentary debate during which were exposed and examined all the means of action available for a comprehensive policy embracing regional development, town planning, and construction.[36] One of the first of the Sociétés d'économie mixte launched an irrigation scheme for the interior of the Languedoc using the water of the lower Rhône; the project, the brainchild of Philip Lamour, gave the region its first opportunity to loosen the stranglehold of the vine, encouraging reconversion to production of fruit and vegetables.

In spite of such efforts, it soon became clear that to be effective regional development would have to be based on an active policy of industrial decentralization. True, such a policy could do little to restrict the free circulation of capital and labour between the regions; but the State, acting in the general interest and at the expense of the tax-payer, could certainly encourage industrialists not to neglect the disadvantaged regions. For this the public companies could set an example, and the FDES could assume responsibility for the funding. Decrees taken under Mendès France and Edgar Faure (5 January and 30 June 1955), forbade the siting of new factories in an 80 km radius of Paris, while firms ready to set up production in the zones of under-employment and stagnation were offered tax relief, attractive loans, support from the FDES, and help from the State for the training of the workforce. Incentives to decentralization now proliferated: improved returns for joint stock companies, efforts by communes and local authorities to attract firms to their industrial zones, grants for reconversion and decentralization, encouragement, then official status, for the private companies charged with regional development.[37] A recognition, albeit still cautious, of the imperatives of regional development and planning, of the legitimate ambitions of local interests, plus the old issue of administrative reform, were enshrined in the decree of 28 October 1956. Under this, the work of a study group organized by the Planning Commissariat, France was divided into twenty-two economic regions, within which the planning efforts and the various incentives available would be organized and co-ordinated. With this, in fact, were laid the foundations of a policy which, under the Fifth Republic, was to lead to the creation of the Circonscriptions d'action régionale in 1960, and the setting up of a government department for regional development (DATAR) in 1963.

For the moment, however, the gap between aims and achievements remained considerable. The real beneficiaries at this early stage were the urban centres around the Paris basin, receiving roughly half the total aids to decentralization: with Renault at Flins, Le Mans, Cléon, and Caen; Citroën at Rennes; Chausson at Reims; Motobécane at Saint-Quentin; Radiotechnique at Chartres; and Cadum at Compiègne. As yet no order of priority had been established of the areas to industrialize; and there was still no central agency in Paris to co-ordinate regional development. Nor, on the other hand, was there a regional power strong enough to maintain the momentum of the first beneficial effects.[38]

# 17

# An unequal prosperity

The stimulus of growth had shaken up society, exciting new dynamisms as well as provoking defensive reactions. This of course was the point at which the forces of change confronted the weight of the past. Unfortunately, the ambitious and concrete historical analyses it merits are, for the most part, lacking. It is for this reason that a number of important themes are barely explored below: having, so far, been ignored by research, any attempt to do them justice now would necessarily have been either impressionistic or pretentious and misleading. Nevertheless, a range of statistics drawn from the impressive battery of contemporary inquiries makes it possible to avoid the worse excesses of wordy supposition or ideologically guided discussion: the statistical material provided below is intended then to serve as a basis for further reflection. Yet in this domain, more than in any other, the figures tell only a part of the story: what was actually perceived by the population, frequently bordering on resentment, by no means always corresponded to the verdict of the statistics. For the problems involved were vast and the solutions often contradictory. Economic expansion had certainly multiplied opportunities, but at the same time it had favoured the most qualified and talented: is this to say that by placing a heavy premium on competence and competion it had actually increased social disparities? The debate over this question began before 1958 among the experts, those involved with the Plan, and with the works of Jean Marchal and Jacques Lecaillon, who, for their part, show the range of social hierarchies to have in fact narrowed in all the industrial nations.[1] It is very clear, however, that at a time when appetites for consumption were being so vigorously whetted and when an alternative way of life was being constantly exhibited by the media and being incorporated into the nascent mass culture, the question of inequalities, starting with the most familiar ones, acquired a singular social significance: one translated by the phenomena of the *'jardin du voisin'* and *'toujours plus'*.[2] On the other hand, when the crucial role of human and psychological factors in the economic growth of these years is considered, does the population not have to be credited with the reduced importance it now attached to the status quo and to entrenched social positions? And credited also with its greater appetite for education, change, and a better future for its children? The social imbalances were still enormous, irreducible even: but there was a greater awareness of them. Could this be considered as progress?

### 'Douze millions de beaux bébés'

These were the terms used by de Gaulle in 1945 to define the duty of French couples for the coming decade. His patriotic and paternal wish was largely answered: 9 million births by 1955, more than 11 million by May 1958. With just over 40 million inhabitants in the mainland in 1946, France's population had been at a virtual standstill for fifty years, all signs of demographic vitality lacking. In 1958, a population of 44.5 million placed France demographically among the most dynamic nations of Western Europe. Not only had the lost ground been made up, but the growth was sustained, stronger than in previous centuries.

The new vitality was due to the strong rise in the birth-rate, based on the increase in fertility after 1942: more than 800 000 births a year and a birth-rate of between 21 and 18 per thousand, compared with just over 600 000 and 15 per thousand before the war (see Table 18). The active population policy launched in 1939 and pursued since then had undoubtedly contributed to this development. Governments had recognized that in the struggle for reconstruction and prosperity the demographic front was to be as important as those of energy and the economy, and had acted accordingly. In addition to antenatal allowances, a wide range of measures made it possible to protect and encourage childbirth and the family. In November 1945, the Ministry of Public Health and Population had set up welfare services for mothers and babies, concentrating their efforts on premarital tests and antenatal and nursing consultations (approximately half the mothers were covered thus). The provision of crèches, nursery and child-minding facilities, on the other hand, remained scandalously inadequate: the Paris region had 480 or one-third of the national total, whereas the Nord and the Pas-de-Calais had only 9, a total of just 400 places for 3.5 million inhabitants in 1958! In the towns, care of pre-school-age children was still a serious problem, a major obstacle for mothers wishing to work on a regular basis. Social Security made efforts in this domain, reimbursing the cost of care for the children of working parents by paying allowances to nursing mothers and by extending maternity leave to fourteen weeks: the total represented more than a third of all benefits paid in 1958. Families were also helped through the tax system, with the application of a system under which allowances were to be made according to the number of children and irrespective of income levels, with additional relief for low incomes and a reduction of rates of income tax. Above all there was the law of 22 August 1946 which created the system of family allowances: all sick

Table 18: *Natural movement of the population*

|  | 1913 | 1936 | 1946 | 1950 | 1954 | 1958 |
|---|---|---|---|---|---|---|
| Total population millions | 41.6 | 41.1 | 40.1 | 41.6 | 42.8 | 44.5 |
| Marriages thousands | 312 | 279 | 516 | 331 | 314 | 312 |
| Marriage rate (‰) | 15 | 13.4 | 25.7 | 15.9 | 14.6 | 14 |
| Births thousands | 790 | 630 | 840 | 858 | 807 | 808 |
| Birth rate (‰) | 19 | 15 | 20.9 | 20.6 | 18.8 | 18.1 |
| Net rate of reproduction for 100 women | 92 | 80 | 128 | 133 | 125 | 126 |
| Deaths thousands | 731 | 642 | 541 | 530 | 515 | 496 |
| Death rate | 17.5 | 15.3 | 13.5 | 12.7 | 12 | 11 |
| Infant mortality (‰) | 114 | 71 | 77.8 | 51.9 | 40.8 | 31.5 |
| Natural increase thousands | 59 | −12 | 299 | 328 | 292 | 312 |
| Under 20 (%) | 33.2 | 28.9 | 29.5 | 30.1 | 30.8 | 31.6 |
| 20–64 (%) | 57.7 | 60.2 | 59.4 | 58.4 | 57.7 | 56.9 |
| 63 and over (%) | 9.1 | 10.9 | 11 | 11.3 | 11.5 | 11.5 |

workers, handicapped or unemployed persons, or single mothers, would receive an allowance after the second dependent child; this system, paid for by extra contributions from employers, was conditional only on acceptance by the parents of the principle of compulsory education and medical check-ups. A so-called 'salaire unique' allowance, initiated by the legislation of 1938, and completed by that of 1955 for the 'mère au foyer' (mother at home) for non-earners, a housing allowance established in September 1948, holiday allowances, cheap transport on the SNCF and RATP; large numbers of 'travailleurs sociaux' – social workers, home helps, nursery minders, therapists for handicapped and abandoned children – were re-cruited. In all, the concerted efforts to encourage child rearing and the family – by the public authorities, local authorities, employers, and a strong network of family associations[3] – came to absorb more than 4 per cent of the gross national product each year.

But policy alone does not explain the demographic revival, even if the steady depreciation of the family allowances (inadequately indexed to the cost of living and prices) may indeed have been responsible for the fall in the birth-rate between 1950 and 1953. The fundamental reasons for the increase in births were psychological and social, a combination of the new enthusiasm for marriage (the marriage-rate remained high even after the 'catching up' of the immediate post-war period), and the shift of attitudes in favour in children, bordering on idolization. Above all, however, there was the general rise in levels of fertility, and it was the mechanism of this change which monopolized the attention of the demographers. The fact that the figure of 800 000 babies a year was reached owed most to the acceptance, by a significant number of families, of the third child. For in spite of selfish criticisms from some quarters that the official policies were encouraging '*lapinisme*', the demographic upsurge did not take the form of sprawling families, but rather a greater readiness to form average-sized families: thus the number of children per couple stood at 2.35 in 1943, 2.45 in 1950, 2.33 in 1954, and 2.42 in 1960. This regular and sustained fertility was not uniform; it was more vigorous in the economically dynamic regions, and in 1954 was at its strongest of 3.43 among farmers, at its average of 2.57 among workers and officials, while lagging behind among the self-employed, the shopkeepers (1.96) and the manufacturers (2.2). This was the extremely favourable demographic context in which the family welfare legislation could have such a strategic impact, convincing in effect two in five couples with two children that they could afford a third, in some cases a fourth, child. There was another side to this: from 1956 the first impassioned debates over the question of birth-control and family planning began, the 1920 law forbidding all advertising of contraceptives and abortions was strictly enforced, and 800 000 is a realistic estimate of the number of back-street abortions carried out each year.[4] On balance, however, the prospects for the future were now brighter than they had been for many years.

No less encouraging was the fact that the rise in fertility was accompanied by a decline in mortality rates. France now took her place with the other developed nations striving to improve and safeguard the health of their populations. Infant mortality was the first area to register the beneficial effects of the collective efforts, dropping sharply by one-half up to 1952, by another third up to 1958. Overall mortality rates responded more slowly but nonetheless significantly, falling from 13 to 11 per thousand between 1946 and 1958. These advances were of course uneven, both geographically – infant mortality in 1958 was 39 per thousand in the Nord compared with 18 per thousand in Paris – and socially. But the average life expectancy of the population grew by six years between 1946 and 1958: from 61.9 to 67 years for men, from 67.4 to 73.4 for women, compared with 55.9 and 61.6 respectively in 1938.[5] With a sharp diminution of deaths in the first five years of life, and a halving of those in the 20–50 age group, death was, quite logically, now taking a heavier toll among the over-60 age group. The way of death was also changing. Medical progress, compulsory vaccination, and Social Security measures all helped to reduce the ravages of the old killers – pneumonia, child illnesses, gastro-enteritis among nursing mothers, nephritis, and, above all, tuberculosis, which was now responsible for five times fewer deaths than at the beginning of the century. And respiratory diseases and infant meningitis were now more firmly under control, though influenza remained a serious menace, with major epidemics in 1949, 1953, and 1957. On the other hand, however, the French now suffered more from the evils of a developed society: accidents–for the most part those on the roads – cardiac trouble, cancer, and not forgetting of course the dismal world record for alcoholism, cirrhosis of the liver, and related mental disorders.[6]

Once again progress owed most to collective efforts, with the State responding to the strong demand for improved health. Although the number of doctors increased (29 000 in 1946; 44 000 in 1958), the medical profession as a whole could claim little credit for the improvements. The profession's division between practitioners and consultants was rigidly upheld; its Order (set up by Vichy) and the doctors' unions jealously guarded its privileges, fighting a bitter struggle against the Social Security to defend its liberal status and refusing all socialization of its work. Thus of doctors in practice in 1958, less than one in ten was salaried, barely three in ten worked in public service medicine; group medicine was slow to develop, and the multiplication of practices occurred with little regard for regional needs. True, Social Security now reimbursed 80 per cent of medical charges, but treatment could still be very costly given that doctors would not respect the tariffs, or refused to sign agreements with the Social Security which would have meant disclosing their real incomes to the tax inspectors. In the Paris region and the major urban centres the agreement between doctors and the Social Security was a dead letter, though social pressure had imposed its adoption in rural areas and small towns.[7] The position inside the profession was scarcely encouraging: medical teaching was moribund, élitist, and divorced from hospital experience; research was weak, and innovations (notably in antibiotics) came almost exclusively from the United States. Lastly, entry to the associated professions was tightly controlled, with the tacit agreement of the State – 9000 dentists in 1946, 15 000 in 1958; 12 000 and 14 500 chemists over the same period. This gloomy professional background makes it easier to appreciate the extent and value of the public effort.

This was particularly important in the hospitals, where numbers and equipment were seriously deficient. Not all the problems had been overcome by 1958: overcrowding was common in Paris and the major cities; and while, happily, 7 per cent of beds in the sanatoriums were empty after 1955, the provision of psychiatric services was sadly inadequate; buildings were often outdated or unsuitable; the staff were poorly paid. Nonetheless, the hospital services, armed with 400 000 public beds and 200 000 private ones, embarked on energetic action to shake off the unfortunate public image inherited from the nineteenth century. Technical progress and experimentation were given a privileged place, consultations were multiplied, and the training of doctors was improved. The results obtained reflected the effort: between 1946 and 1958 the level of hospitalization rose from 37 to 52 per thousand. Organized preventitive medicine was also making strides: measures were taken for schoolchildren in October 1945, for babies under the ordinance of November 1945, and in the workplace by the law of 11 October 1946. Stricter town planning regulations imposed higher standards of hygiene and water supplies in new buildings. These improvements in public health were, of course, strongly helped by financial aid to health care and prevention – it was now that the fruits of the Social Security system began to be reaped. In 1958 this covered more than 40 per cent of medical expenses (455 milliard francs of a total of 1133 milliard); medical aid for those not covered by the national insurance scheme affected 1.5 million people, and reimbursed 9 per cent of the total expenses (104 milliard); while the development of mutual insurance schemes provided a sizeable reimbursement of the 574 milliard left for individuals to pay.[8] Nor, finally, must one overlook the contribution made by the population itself to improved health. With 50 per cent of charges now guaranteed by the various schemes, the spending on hygiene and health care by the people rose by 8 per cent a year, growing from 344 milliard in 1950 to 1288 milliard in 1958, or from 4.7 to 8 per cent of their budgets: the fastest growth, in fact, of all their expenditure.[9]

This double movement of rising fertility and receding mortality resulted in a net natural increase in the population of the order of 300 000 individuals each year, with a peak between 1946 and 1950. In addition, nearly 700 000 foreigners entered France to work, the influx remaining modest until 1956, and certainly much lower than before the war: Italians accounted for almost half this number, followed by Spanish, Portuguese, and North Africans. In all, the total population of France increased by roughly 4 million under the Fourth Republic, a record figure which marks a decisive rupture with a century of demographic difficulties. An unfortunate consequence of this renewal was the creation of imbalance, owing to the distortions it produced in the age structure of the population. One manifestation of this was the chronic shortage of labour which so handicapped the economy. The adult working population was now compressed at both ends of the 20–65 age group; there were more young people, remaining longer in education; there were also more old people, tending for their part to retire earlier.

Although the special problems posed by the old were recognized, no completely satisfactory solution was found. The old – between 4.5 and 5 million people in all – found it increasingly hard to find a place in a rapidly changing France: their experience is one of the less engaging aspects of the modernization. Not that they had ceased to make a contribution to society: a third, for the most part men, continued to work or took an undeclared job after 65, while one in two farmers were still active at 70. Yet retirement, so desired but so feared, always came as a great shock, one for which those involved were usually ill-prepared, and not least financially. Hasty attempts were made at the Liberation to generalize old age insurance with the law of 22 May 1946, completed by that of 17 January 1948 for non-earners, plus that of 10 July 1952 for the farmers. But many defects remained: the legislation on retirement and pensions was of a daunting complexity; Social Security provided a minimum, but the incoherence of the pre-war systems and the insouciance of employers and wage-earners themselves made the calculations highly arbitrary; inflation eroded real values of pensions as fast as they could be revised; and there was an anarchic and senseless proliferation of insurance schemes (more than 5000 in May 1957 when the CNPF, the CFTC, and FO, at the prompting of the CGT, at last reached an agreement to limit the number!). Faced with the loosening of traditional family solidarities, the impossibility of saving, and with their nest-eggs wiped out by inflation, the old were penalized on every side. There was only the Fonds national de solidarité set up in 1956 to provide some help for the worst off. That year, 77 per cent of individual old people and 82 per cent of retired couples had incomes below 200 000 francs,[10] compared with a proportion of one-third for the population as a whole: the Fonds national in fact provided assistance to 2.7 million, that is, approximately half of all old people – whatever the possibilities for extra help or support from children, this figure leaves no doubt as to the widespread tragedy of France's old people in the 1950s. Victims of developments which left them perplexed and vulnerable, benefiting much less than other social groups from the policies over housing, the family, and leisure, and facing often uncertain futures (the number of places in nursing and old people's homes did not rise above 35 per thousand), the old, isolated in housing which, though its rent might be blocked by the law of 1948, was usually of poor quality, were forced to tighten their belts, reducing expenditure on clothing and holidays, economizing even on diet and health. The old seemed increasingly out of place, their experience and wisdom, like their means, progressively devalued in a society where all eyes were turned to the young.

For the other side of the plight of the old was the care and attention lavished on babies and the younger generation. The signs of French society's infatuation with the young were everywhere: the Salon de l'Enfance was set up, the nation readily accepted the extra costs of education (see Chapter 19), expenditure on toys increased more than three-fold, advertisers discovered that babies were now as effective as film stars for promoting products: May 1968 was to come as a rude shock to a society which had placed so much confidence and so many hopes in its young. Those already in their youth, born in the difficult years before and during the war, were also favoured by this shift in attitudes: their ambitions, loves, and anxieties now filled the pages of magazines, and generation-spotting became almost a national pastime: the '*nouvelle vague*' was awaited with impatience.[11]

Not only was the population younger but it was markedly more mobile, both geographically and professionally. Particularly revealing of this change was the sustained growth of the urban population:[12] from 52 per cent of the total in 1936 and 53.2 per cent in 1946, this rose to 56 per cent in 1954 and 61.7 per cent in 1962. The towns gained most from the population growth, received the bulk of the immigrants, displayed the highest birth-rates, and made the biggest strides to combat disease and death. This new-found urban dynamism dissipated the last traces of the nine-teenth-century image of the French town as unhealthy and lugubrious: the town was now the showcase of modernity. The optimism and confidence which accompanied this development had solid economic and human bases, for progress was in fact concentrated in the most robust sections of the nation's urban fabric. In the twelve major cities of more than 250 000 inhabitants, and in particular Paris, Marseille, and Lyon, which alone had absorbed the newcomers during the long period of demographic stagnation, the gains now were very slight. Indeed, the most densely populated actually regressed: the Paris agglomeration accounted for 28.8 per cent of the total urban population at its zenith in 1936, but had fallen back to 28.1 per cent by 1954, and to 25.8 per cent by 1962; and the regional metropolises also stagnated, with 18.6, 18.4, and 17.5 per cent respectively at the same dates; as for the small towns with fewer than 50 000 inhabitants, they just about maintained their positions. It was, then, in the agglomerations of between 50 000 and 250 000 inhabitants that the strongest gains were concentrated. In 1936 these contained 23 per cent of the total urban population, a proportion which had risen to 30.4 per cent by 1962, after a brutal change in the rate of expansion after 1952. The very large urban centres were thus maintained, but the increases associated with modernization were chiefly in the medium-sized centres; changes which left France still less urbanized than her European neighbours, however.

These gains by the towns were exactly mirrored by losses from the countryside. Growth brought a vastly increased mobility and *déracinement* (literally uprooting) of the population. The census results show that 7

million French changed commune between 1954 and 1962.[13] This
unprecedented flux saw 2.4 million leave the countryside – for the most
part the young, in search of work – and 1.3 million return to it for retirement: a continuing haemorrhage, then, of 1.1 million individuals
from the rural communes, at a rate of 130 000 each year. And the *exode
rural* had in fact started again at the end of the war, at a rate of 90 000
each year before 1954, exacerbating the qualitative impact of these massive losses. Shopkeepers, artisans, and labourers disappeared from the
countryside; services declined, the structures of rural communities
became imbalanced, and their social life collapsed. Moreover, the *exode*
was now agricultural as well as rural: young and determined farmers,
unable to modernize their farms, now moved to the nearest medium-
sized town, just as their predecessors of before the war had gone to Paris
or a regional metropolis. Between 1949 and 1954, one farmer in ten left
the land; from 1954 to 1962 the figure was three in ten. The contraction
of the rural population was at the origin of the profound modification in
the overall distribution of the active population – as long as the number
of economically active remained static, the countryside was of course the
only reservoir from which mobility could come. The primary sector declined, accounting in 1936, 1954, and 1962, for 37, 27.4, and 20.6 of the
active population; in parallel, the secondary sector was reinforced, with
30, 36.2, and 38.6 per cent respectively; while the tertiary sector now
moved ahead to establish its predominance, rising from 33 to 36.4, then
to 40.8 per cent. These figures, for all their shortcomings,[14] point clearly
to the general evolution in the economy: first, an increased industrialization; secondly, the advance of the service and administrative sectors.
Indeed, by the 1950s, the efforts of four in every ten members of the
active population went to administering in one way or another what the
others produced (see Table 19).

*Patrimony, income, and consumption*

Money in all its forms – inherited, earned, spent, saved; of individuals,
families, or groups – though more important than ever as French society
entered the age of mass consumption, remains a largely uncharted area.
The available information is deficient. An accurate social breakdown of
incomes, savings, and profits is impossible: given the known extent of tax
avoidance and evasion and fiscal injustice, it is clear that the tax figures,
even when adjusted by the INSEE, afford little serious indication; information from companies on their earnings, when it could be obtained
and when not obviously fraudulent, remains highly suspect – the administration was reduced to estimating; comparisons between wage-earners
and the self-employed have little meaning; inheritances were rarely

Table 19: *The active population*

### 1. By sectors

| | 1938 thousands | % | 1949 thousands | % | 1954 thousands | % | 1963 thousands | % |
|---|---|---|---|---|---|---|---|---|
| agriculture and forestry | 5900 | 31.4 | 5580 | 28.9 | 5030 | 26.1 | 3650 | 18.4 |
| industry | 5280 | 28.1 | 5610 | 29.1 | 5550 | 28.8 | 5920 | 30 |
| services | 5180 | 27.6 | 5360 | 27.8 | 5750 | 29.8 | 6780 | 34.3 |
| administration | 1450 | 7.7 | 1890 | 9.8 | 2130 | 11 | 2620 | 13.2 |
| total of the active population occupied | 18 760 | | 19 260 | | 19 250 | | 19 730 | |

### 2. By socio-professional categories

| | 1954 thousands | % | 1962 thousands | % |
|---|---|---|---|---|
| farmers | 3966 | 20.7 | 3044 | 15.8 |
| agricultural workers | 1160 | 6 | 826 | 4.3 |
| industrial and commercial employers | 2301 | 12 | 2044 | 10.6 |
| liberal professions and executives | 553 | 2.9 | 765 | 4 |
| middle managers | 1112 | 5.8 | 1501 | 7.8 |
| employees | 2066 | 10.8 | 2396 | 12.4 |
| workers | 6492 | 33.8 | 7060 | 36.7 |
| service personnel | 1017 | 5.3 | 1047 | 5.4 |
| other categories | 513 | 2.7 | 564 | 2.9 |
| | 19 184 | 100 | 19 251 | 100 |

*Sources:* 1. J.-J. Carré, P. Dubois and E. Malinvaud, *La Croissance française*, Seuil, 1972, p. 122.
2. *Le Mouvement économique en France*, 1949–1979, INSEE, 1981, p. 21.

declared in full. Fortunately, a series of surveys by the INSEE and the CREDOC, in particular that of 1956–7 on household consumption, do allow a cross-section to be made, though extrapolating back from this is hazardous.

The increases in material prosperity are of course incontestable. And a glance at a few indices leaves no doubt as to their relationship with the economic expansion:

| | 1949 | 1952 | 1954 | 1956 | 1958 | 1965 |
|---|---|---|---|---|---|---|
| Industrial production | 57 | 68 | 74 | 88 | 100 | 141 |
| Per capita GNP | 71 | 82 | 87 | 96 | 100 | 132 |
| Per capita consumption | 71 | 81 | 89 | 96 | 100 | 130 |

Broadly speaking, consumption and incomes grew by one-third between 1949 and 1958,[15] before increasing by another 30 per cent up until 1965. This rhythm, superior to that of the general movement of the economy, allowed consumption to make up the losses it had suffered during the period of reconstruction.

In spite of the difficulties of its estimation, not to mention the dangers of making comparisons between the different sets of statistics, the examination of the national fortune or patrimony confirms this generally broader access to higher living standards. It seems certain that, after two wars, the crisis, and two reconstructions, the French patrimony had recovered its 1914 level by 1954.[16] From then until 1963 its total grew sharply: by approximately 50 per cent for companies, 20 per cent for households, and 60 per cent for the administration; the resources available to these categories each year increased by 50, 50, and 14 per cent respectively over the same period. However, not only was the patrimony thus swollen by economic growth, but its structures were evolving. In 1954, private fortunes, which represented 64 per cent of the national patrimony, were divided thus: 28 per cent in land, 28 per cent in industrial and commercial capital, 22 per cent in buildings, and 15 per cent in movable property and personal wealth (gold and financial assets are excluded from the calculations).[17] Deducting the capital of companies, one can estimate at 32 per cent the share of the national patrimony held by households, divided between land (35 per cent), buildings (33 per cent), and movable and personal property (24 per cent). One important development after 1954 was the collapse, brutal in the 1960s, of the place held in fortunes by rents, interest, stocks and shares, farm tenancies and livestock: their place was taken by land, more secure an investment than ever, by buildings, highly attractive in a period of housing shortage, and, though to a much lesser extent, by home equipment. Decisive choices were now being made in family strategies, opting in favour of consumption at the expense of accumulating capital, savings, or financial investments.[18] After 1954, while companies and the administration continued to add to their capital, up by 50 per cent until 1963, household fortunes in the form of capital progressed at less than half this rate. The reasons for this relative withdrawal are not hard to identify: rents were too low to justify investing more capital in buildings, the speculation on building land made construction less profitable, and the feeble appeal of the capital market deterred investment in stocks and bonds;[19] while on the other hand there was the growing place taken by the State, local authorities, and companies in the formation and channelling of savings and investment. This development in fact reflected a profound change occurring in social attitudes. Not only did patrimony lose part of its function as an income-earning capital in order to be more actively mobilized for useful and pleasure-giving purposes, but the population was less concerned to add to it than formerly, preferring instead visible consumption and more liquid forms of investment. In short, the old notion of the patrimony was being challenged, with the emphasis shifting away from the careful accumulation of past generations towards a more immediate enjoyment.

This change was only reinforced by the threat to the stable transmission and use of the patrimony posed by the greater geographical and, to some extent, social mobility of the population. As the constraints imposed by the traditional endogamy weakened, so the patterns of inheritance were disrupted and established fortunes were broken up. True, geographical homogamy remained strong: of the couples who married in 1958, 52 per cent had been born and 82 per cent lived in the same *arrondissement*. And social homogamy was also resilient: one worker in two, and two farmers in three, chose a spouse from within their own social group.[20] In contrast, however, endogamy declined spectacularly, even in the most isolated upland and rural regions of the Hautes-Alpes, Corsica, and the Corrèze: by 1956–8 endogamy had fallen on a base of 100 in 1926 by between 6 and 54, an average fall of 34. In other words, a third of all marriages were now made without regard for the old rules of isolated and tightly knit communities, rules which had for so long contributed to the patient formation of family fortunes. The patrimony of French households was entering a period of rapid change: the effects on it of social and above all geographical mobility were felt more keenly; its holders were now faced with a choice between sacrificing it by immediate consumption or adding to it by continuing to honour the old virtues of savings and frugality. Inequalities surrounding its acquisition and distribution were no doubt as strong as ever, but the notions of security and refuge of which it was the tangible expression were increasingly open to change.[21]

This less solid and somewhat more confused picture of the patrimony suggests in turn that the origins of increased well-being lay elsewhere. That it is in production and income from work that one must look is confirmed by an examination of household income.[22] This is in fact the best indicator available, because from 1949 it accounted for a highly stable 94 per cent of national income. The breakdown by proportions of its sources and uses (Table 20), prepared on the basis of the *Comptes de la nation*, reveals some important changes over time.

Wages had accounted for only 37 per cent of total household income in 1949, on a par with the gross income of individual entrepreneurs. After 1951, however, the former edged ahead, establishing a lead of eight points by 1958, and of fifteen points by 1963: this was a two-fold movement, for not only was the share of wages growing but that of incomes to entrepreneurs was contracting. At the same time, the various social allowances, more important among wage-earners, were also growing, whereas interest payments, transfers, and diverse sources of income stagnated. The 1950s

Table 20: *Household income (in percentages)*

|  | 1949 | 1952 | 1954 | 1956 | 1958 | 1963 |
|---|---|---|---|---|---|---|
| *Sources* | | | | | | |
| wages | 37 | 38 | 39 | 39.5 | 40.5 | 42.5 |
| social transfers | 11.5 | 13.5 | 14 | 14.5 | 15 | 17 |
| interest, dividends, | | | | | | |
|   farm rents | 4.5 | 4.5 | 4.5 | 4.5 | 4 | 3 |
| transfers | 4.5 | 4 | 4 | 4 | 3.5 | 4 |
| foreign earnings | 2 | 2 | 2 | 2 | 2 | 2 |
| gross income of | | | | | | |
|   individual | | | | | | |
|   entrepreneurs | 37 | 35 | 32.5 | 32 | 32 | 27.5 |
| gross income of | | | | | | |
|   households (rents etc.) | 3.5 | 3 | 4 | 3.5 | 3 | 4 |
| *Uses* | | | | | | |
| consumption | 81 | 81.5 | 80 | 79.5 | 79 | 78.5 |
| social contributions | | | | | | |
|   and wages | 1.5 | 2 | 2 | 2 | 2 | 2 |
| taxes | 4 | 3.5 | 4 | 4 | 5 | 5 |
| diverse | 2.5 | 3 | 3 | 3 | 3 | 3.5 |
| gross saving | 11 | 10 | 11 | 11.5 | 11 | 11 |

witnessed then a decisive change: the late but now incontestable victory of wages – wage-earners and officials accounted for 65 per cent of the active population in 1958 – over all other forms of income, whether from firms or property, capital, profits, or investments. Two in three households now drew their resources solely from wages and salaries, becoming in one sense more dependent on those who paid them or distributed social payments, yet reaping more fully the fruits of an effort whose supremacy had at last found expression in terms of income. To this striking change in the way income was obtained has, however, to be opposed the no less striking stability in the uses to which it was put: over this period consumption hovered around the 80 per cent level, savings were more or less stable at 11 per cent, and the weight of taxation scarcely increased. Here is concrete evidence of a social characteristic as important in its way as the progress of growth and wages: expenditure, savings, and consumption – mainly social and mental factors – evolved more slowly than incomes, a more strictly economic factor. In short, radical changes in income, but conservatism in the uses to which it was put. This generalization has, it is true, to be nuanced in the light of what is known about the responses of different groups. The INSEE survey of declared income in 1956 makes it possible to divide households into three categories:[23] the first, of workers, agricultural labourers, service personnel, white-collar workers, middle managers, and those not active, consumed 85 per cent of their income, saving only 6 per cent. The second category is made up of the groups still influenced by the older attitudes, and whose needs were less immediate than those of the first groups – farmers, and owners of shops and businesses, consuming respectively 79 and 54.5 per cent, while saving 16 and 31.5 per cent of their income. Lastly, senior managers and members of the liberal professions, now gaining in every respect, consumed 62 per cent and saved 20 per cent.

To what extent is it possible to reply to the fundamental question evoked at the outset: did economic growth reduce or magnify income inequalities? There are serious lacunas in our information about the resources of several important groups: farmers, for example, were subject to little pressure from the tax authorities, could consume their own produce and make un-declared sales; the liberal professions were rarely forthcoming over the size of their incomes; and the figures are inaccurate or incomplete for artisans, shopkeepers, and small business men. In short, information is lacking for all those whose incomes did not come in the form of wages, yet who together received 43–50 per cent of total distributed income – a shortcoming which makes difficult all meaningful comparison with the advances, real or supposed, of the wage-earners. However, intermittent broad breakdowns can be obtained, using the surveys carried out by the INSEE and the CREDOC, plus the works of Lecaillon and Marchal: Table 21 offers a cross-section for 1956. Important inequalities obviously existed within each of the groups represented here, but an overall comparison between the share of total income received and demographic importance can be made. From this emerges a severe hierarchy of inequality: highly privileged in the share-out are industrial and commercial employers, senior executives, and members of the liberal professions; next, bunched around the average or only reasonably distanced from it, come the middle managers, the service personnel, employees, and agricultural workers; lastly, and clearly dis-advantaged, are the workers and the farmers. With the tertiary sector thus favoured, and the major groups of the primary and secondary sectors lag-ging behind, the result mirrors closely the new economic developments and the perennial social penalties. The same surveys also show, with a strong consistency for 1956, then for 1962, that the curves for the relative dispersal of income to households headed by a wage-earner or whose head was self-employed are in fact parallel.[24] In other words, the blockage was more social than economic: the hierarchy remained as strict as ever, even if the scale was a little shorter or if, for some, the levels were lower.[25]

This observation can be confirmed statistically only for the wage-earners, for whom the figures on income, transfers, and taxation can be manipulated with confidence. There is clear evidence to begin with that the average disparity between wages in different branches of the economy was reduced between 1952 and 1962 – probably since 1946 – chiefly owing to

Table 21: *Distribution of disposable incomes between the socio-professional categories in 1956*

|  | % of active population 1954 | income | |
|---|---|---|---|
|  |  | milliards of 1956 francs | % of total |
| farmers | 20.7 | 1723 | 10.3 |
| agricultural workers | 6 | 303 | 1.8 |
| industrial and commercial employers | 12 | 2613 | 15.7 |
| liberal professions and executives | 2.9 | 1169 | 7 |
| middle managers | 5.8 | 974 | 5.9 |
| employees | 10.8 | 919 | 5.5 |
| workers | 33.8 | 3455 | 20.8 |
| service personnel | 5.3 | 216 | 1.3 |
| other categories | 2.7 | 400 | 2.4 |
| non-active and non-resident |  | 2015 | 12.1 |
| total disposable income of households |  | 13 787 | 82.8 |
| disposable income of the administration |  | 790 | 4.8 |
| gross savings of companies |  | 1569 | 9.4 |
| disposable incomes of financial institutions |  | 191 | 1.1 |
| balance of distributive transactions with the exterior |  | 311 | 1.9 |
| total income |  | 16 648 | 100 |

*Source:* based on J. Lecaillon, *Croissance et politique des revenus,* Cujas, 1964, p. 169.

the advance of middle incomes: the general range had thus narrowed slightly. Yet such a change was too abstract, too remote from everyday life to be easily or widely perceived, or, as a result, to have tangible social repercussions: wage-earners were most sharply aware of the inequality closest to them. And, with equal statistical certitude, only this time verifiable on a day-to-day basis, one sees that the disparities of wages within each of the non-agricultural branches were actually increasing: the average absolute difference here rose from 15.8 in 1947 to 18.1 in 1952, and to 20.3 in 1962. Thus was set up a durable and tense social contradiction. The total of wages increased regularly with economic growth, all wage-earners experienced an improvement in their purchasing power – the gain was in the order of 43 per cent from 1949 to 1957, the average hourly wage rising on the index from 100 to 228, while the cost of living rose only to 159 (see Fig. 6).

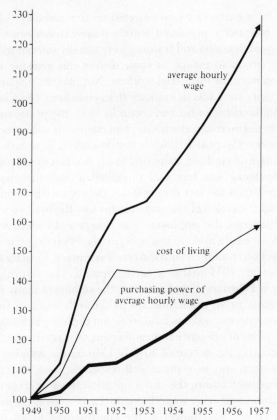

4  Wages, cost of living, and purchasing power, 1949–57
   (base 1949 = 100; whole of France)
   *Source:* based on *Le Mouvement économique en France de 1944 à 1957*, Imprimerie
   nationale/PUF, 1958, p. 31.

Yet this positive consequence of growth was simultaneously negated by the
widening inequality between adjacent wage levels, with the general
upward movement actually accelerating the hierarchical dispersal. The
explanation for this is simple: faced with labour shortages, employers now
put a premium on the technical competence of the work-force, while the
training and personal competitiveness of the wage-earners themselves
scrupulously respected the inherited hierarchies. Indeed, in this competitive context the higher the initial income, the greater its subsequent increase: thus between 1956 and 1964, the real income of managers increased
by 39.5 per cent, that of employees by 32 per cent, for skilled workers by 25
per cent, and for *smigards* (minimum wage earners) by just 3.8 per cent.
There is, in addition, an interesting chronological inflexion in this trend,
with the rule applying less severely before 1954: after 1954, when the State
relaxed its surveillance of wages, the demand for qualified labour in-

creased, a freer enterprise now selected more rigorously. Moreover, this very basic inequality penalized female wage-earners especially heavily, since their qualifications and training were usually inferior to those of men.

The only group to escape to some degree this growing inequality by qualification were the industrial workers. Not that the disparities between types of activity were less in industry than elsewhere. On a base of 100 for wages throughout the industrial sector in 1954, the print-workers were at 131, those in engineering, electricity, and chemicals were around 115, construction workers were at 102, while textile workers were at 90, and those in leather, skins, and clothing stagnated at 81. Nor is it to suggest that professional competence was less well rewarded in industry than elsewhere. Rather, it reflected the fact that this was the sector where intervention by the State and the action of the trade unions was the most effective; here too that surveillance of the employers was closest and collective wage agreements the least easily broken: it was here in fact that negotiation, vigilance, and strike action combined with the greatest impact. Even for the industrial sector, however, 1954 marks a turning-point. The return to free wage bargaining in February 1950 had led to the signing of many sturdy collective agreements; at the same time, the public authorities created the SMIG to guarantee a decent wage to labourers and the low paid, and encouraged its use as a point of reference in negotiations over revisions of higher wage levels. Moreover, the decree of 30 July 1946 on the equality of wages for men and women was in general well respected; and, as the start of the policy of decentralization, the real wage allowances in certain parts of the provinces compared with wage levels in Paris were implemented by the employers. After 1954, however, the controls lost much of their effectiveness. The State had, it is true, endeavoured to set an example after the strikes in the summer of 1953 by improving the wage scales in the public sector, and by narrowing the range of salaries in 1956 from 1:8 to 1:6. But a strong liberal current was at work in the private sector, and the allowances no longer had tangible effects. The SMIG gradually became divorced from economic reality; we have already seen how it was the object of dubious manipulations of the indices, when maintaining it at a low level made it possible to hold back a rush to negotiate wage increases throughout the economy. The list of 213 'necessities' the basic wage was supposed to purchase and on which the index was calculated, steadily became obsolete or irrelevant (a struggle was needed, for instance, before the plastic bowl or the washing-up cloth were included on it), and was the target for numerous opportune subsidies. Above all, the spurts of inflation and the attitude of the private sector meant that the value of the SMIG became derisory – by 1952 it was already trailing 35 per cent behind the cost of living. Indeed, what had started out in 1950 as a courageous and effective measure gradually lost its original significance, becoming merely a source of friction, the

permanent object of trade union demands, and an alibi for stubborn
employers. By 1956, the 25 000 francs a month of the SMIG were the wage
for two in ten workers, one employee in three – notably the young before
military service – women, and workers in small firms and in the already
disadvantaged regions.[26]

A system of free wage bargaining, one in which confrontation was an
ever-present possibility, was thus allowed to gradually re-establish itself,
and this while the public authorities tightened up controls and, after 1955,
encouraged the signing of agreements on the basis of the one at Renault to
ensure peace in specific sectors. Would it be fair to see this as the bankruptcy
of a policy, given after all that the socialist Left returned to power in 1956?
Or did it result from the absence of a social pressure strong enough to
impose a continuous surveillance? A mixture of the two no doubt, though
the role of the second should not be underestimated. What seems likely is
that the State preferred to exercise its pressure through more modern and
efficient means: notably by increasing transfer payments. This was certainly the solution adopted by the Mollet government, raising them to the
unprecedented level of 18.1 per cent of gross national product in 1956,
against a level of 14.6 in 1958, and 17.6 in 1960. Table 22 shows the
breakdown of this effort by category and relative importance. At the head of
the list naturally come the areas where need was the most urgent: old age
and illness; also present, however, were those whose future importance had
not been perceived or which were for the moment impossible to develop:
housing and education. Almost 60 per cent of them were in fact continu-
ations of older policies, launched at the Liberation or during the time of the
Popular Front, such as policy over the family or health, and paid holidays.
Overall, social allowances and transfers of one sort or another constituted
16 per cent of household incomes in 1958, compared with barely 2 per cent
in 1938. They were especially important to wage-earners (37 per cent of
income for agricultural workers, 23 per cent for all other low-wage groups);
but they also went now to less needy groups, coming to represent 7.5 per
cent of the income of senior managers and members of the liberal professions, 5 per cent in the case of industrial and commercial employers; and, as
we have seen, the retired were often dependent on them for up to half their
incomes; once again, however, farmers were disadvantaged, receiving only
8 per cent of their income in this form. In all, when expenditure by the
State and the local authorities is added to these social allowances, the
public sector is found to have controlled a total of 35 per cent of the gross
national product in 1954, and 37 per cent in 1957: a striking contrast with
the impecunious liberal State of the nineteenth century! The 1950s in fact
saw develop a public power which distributed annually in the form of
welfare payments a sum almost equal to that earned by workers, with, at its
disposal, a broad range of sophisticated interventionist instruments to

Table 22: *The social effort of the State in 1956* (*in milliards of 1956 francs*)

| | milliards | % of total | % of GNP |
|---|---|---|---|
| Help to families | 873 | 26.3 | 4.6 |
| of which: | | | |
| Social Security family allowances | 754 | | |
| supplementary family allowances | 45 | | |
| Health insurance and accidents at work | 678 | 20.4 | 3.6 |
| of which: | | | |
| health insurance payments | 453 | | |
| accidents at work | 128 | | |
| sickness allowances | 73 | | |
| Old age/disablement | 986 | 29.8 | 5.3 |
| Help to wage-earners | 456 | 13.7 | 2.4 |
| of which: | | | |
| paid holidays | 397 | | |
| help to *œuvres sociales* of companies | 53 | | |
| Housing | 83 | 2.5 | 0.4 |
| Education | 244 | 7.3 | 1.8 |
| | 3 320 | 100 | 18.1 |

This table does not include help from local authorities, the professions, or companies.

*Source:* N. Questiaux, in P. Laroque, *Succès et faiblesses de l'effort social français*, Colin, 1960, p. 72.

redistribute more than one-third of the wealth produced by the nation. The effects of this action were felt at every level of French society. Against a background of greater freedom for private companies, an acceptance by the workforce of longer hours and a system in which the largest rewards went to skills, and the visible resilience, indeed strengthening, of hierarchies and inequalities before the movement of growth – against this background, social transfers initiated by the State were the only means for realizing what social pressure had not imposed: the reduction, at least for the low wage earners, of the range of average incomes from 5.7 to 5 after family allowances, to 4.6 after tax. A modest but nonetheless significant reduction then, for the least well off, of almost one-fifth of the inequality generated by the economy. In this respect the Fourth Republic had not betrayed the hopes of the Liberation.

After the size of income it is the use to which it was put which allows the scale and implications of prosperity to be gauged and understood. Households, as we have seen, devoted roughly 80 per cent of their outgoings to consumption.[27] From the comprehensive surveys carried out by the

CREDOC it emerges that total household consumption grew by 40 per cent between 1950 and 1957 – and possibly by 45 per cent between 1949 and 1958 – at an annual rate of 6 per cent, a stronger increase than for investment, production, and income. In this respect France outdistanced all the developed countries (Italy 4.6 per cent, United States 3.8 per cent, Great Britain 1.1 per cent), with the exception of Federal Germany where the annual increase was 8.4 per cent. This buoyancy of demand cannot be explained solely in terms of the regular growth of purchasing power and financial resources. A proliferation of credit for consumption, something on which we are still poorly informed, had accompanied the growth in demand, fostering the development of anticipatory reflexes. Henceforth, credit was to be as much a social as an economic phenomenon; it touched all occupational groups, though was obviously more accessible at higher and, most important, more stable incomes; its great appeal lay of course in allowing immediate access to the fruits of economic growth, satiating appetites without delay. The three-fold increase in the volume of loans between 1954 and 1958 is particularly revealing of the evolution in attitudes: as people adjusted to living with inflation and a greater abundance of consumer goods, so traditional values of caution and frugality crumbled; debt was no longer considered something to be ashamed of, its potential usefulness could be admitted more easily. Only the farmers' households resisted this change – the very ones so often forced to contract heavy debts to purchase machinery and to save their farms: in 1957, when they formed 27 per cent of the population, they represented only 1 per cent of credit purchasers. But all the other social categories were succumbing to the appeal of credit: worker households participated in close proportion to their importance (32 per cent of credit purchasers, 33 per cent of the population), households of employers and shopkeepers in proportion (14 and 12 per cent), those of the liberal professions and senior managers with greater eagerness (6 and 4 per cent), and the households of employees and middle managers with massive enthusiasm, in an explosive combination of frustration and social ambition (26 and 15 per cent for the former, 10 and 5 per cent for the latter[28]). France was not yet, however, on a par with her European neighbours or the United States: the average Frenchman contracted debts of 3000 francs in 1957, compared with 5000 and 9000 for his Belgian and British counterparts.

Consumption did not develop uniformly, and its structural analysis offers some valuable social information. Food, for example, was advancing only very slowly, going on a base of 100 in 1950 to 129 in 1957, though it remained one of the principal elements in household budgets. It grew by a steady 3.7 per cent a year, reflecting the average price fall of 6 per cent over this period, a trend reversed only by the violent but short-lived movements of panic buying and hoarding when international tension rose, as during the Korean War and the Suez crisis. The general trend was towards the substitution of superior and sophisticated products from the food industry for the older and simpler foodstuffs: pasteurized industrial butters and margarines ousted farm butter and dripping, the traditional home-made soups were abandoned in favour of cubed and packeted preparations, refined bread, biscuits, and cakes took over from the coarse bread sold by weight. Demand was growing for beef for grilling or roasting, veal, poultry, and fish; whereas consumption of tripe, pork, and the inferior cuts requiring long cooking grew more slowly. This shift in dietary ambitions – those of a nation turning from the *pot-au-feu* to the steak – were still frustrated by the insufficient output of meat which kept prices high. Similarly, an increase of 70 per cent in the price of fruit and vegetables reflected the combination of a very strong demand and an inadequate output and distribution. Less startling increases in consumption were registered for clothing (index 145 in 1957), shoes (133), and expenditure on hotels, bars, and restaurants (137); but lingerie, shirts, and baby clothes progressed rapidly (178). With the demand for necessities now satisfied, choice was increasingly shaped by fashion.

The consumer goods for which demand was rising fastest are the most revealing of the social model taking shape between 1950 and 1957. This would include all the items related to health and personal hygiene, up by 86 per cent. Those involving the home – less by higher expenditure on rent and charges, up by only 29 per cent, and rather by the irresistible expansion, guided by advertising, of everything related to home equipment – rose by 110 per cent, at an annual rate of 15 per cent from 1955, and was especially strong for cleaning materials and, above all, household machines. The latter were solidly established as the new symbols of a legitimate and useful domestic comfort since the great success of the Salon des Arts ménagers of 1950, though the most dramatic expansion really came after 1954 (see Table 23). Indeed, in 1954 only 7.5 per cent of households had a refrigerator, barely a quarter were equipped with hot water, 18 per cent had a vacuum cleaner, and just 10 per cent a washing-machine; on the other hand, nearly 90 per cent had both an electric coffee mill and a radio. In other words, and as a poll conducted by the IFOP for the Plan in summer 1954 confirmed, satisfaction of aspirations to well-being began at home, with a greater comfort in everyday domestic life rather than with items of visible and prestigious consumption. Among the extra purchases those questioned said they would make if they had 20 per cent more income, household equipment (32 per cent of new purchases) came far ahead of the purchase of a house, flat, or car (5 per cent), while as yet little importance was attached to holidays and television sets (2 per cent). After this increased domestic comfort, however, everything pointed to the car as the next dream to be realized. By 1954, 21 per cent of households owned one. In spite of the

Table 23: *Level of equipment of households (in % of households in the category)*

| | motor car | | | television set | | | refrigerator | | | washing machine | | |
|---|---|---|---|---|---|---|---|---|---|---|---|---|
| | 1954 | 1959 | rank[a] | 1954 | 1959 | rank | 1954 | 1959 | rank | 1954 | 1959 | rank |
| farmers | 29 | 35.5 | 7 | 0.2 | 3.3 | 8 | 2.4 | 9.6 | 3 | 7.3 | 15.4 | 6 |
| agricultural workers | 3 | 12.1 | 1 | – | 2.1 | 7 | 0.5 | 3.2 | 1 | 1.8 | 13.4 | 1 |
| industrial and commercial employers | 52 | 50.1 | 8 | 2 | 15.6 | 4 | 18 | 34.7 | 7 | 13.2 | 32.8 | 5 |
| liberal professions and executives | 56 | 74.3 | 6 | 4.7 | 24.8 | 6 | 42.8 | 66.7 | 8 | 23.4 | 45 | 8 |
| middle managers | 32 | 57.8 | 3 | 2.5 | 16.1 | 5 | 15.5 | 39.7 | 6 | 16.4 | 33.1 | 7 |
| employees | 18 | 30.1 | 4 | 1.3 | 13.1 | 2 | 9.9 | 31 | 5 | 6.7 | 25.3 | 2 |
| workers | 8 | 21.5 | 2 | 0.9 | 9.7 | 2 | 3.3 | 16.8 | 2 | 8.5 | 23.2 | 4 |
| non-active | 6 | 9.8 | 5 | 0.4 | 5.8 | 1 | 3.7 | 12.1 | 4 | 3.8 | 11.2 | 3 |
| | 21 | 28.4 | | 1 | 9.5 | | 7.5 | 20.5 | | 8.4 | 21.4 | |

[a] By the rate of increase in equipment between 1954 and 1959.

petrol shortages of 1956–7 and the extra cost of the *vignette*, the purchase of new cars – leaving aside the flourishing and anarchic secondhand market – surged forward between 1950 and 1955, slowing down slightly afterwards, increasing overall by 2.53, expansion being especially strong in sales of economical small cars. There was one car for seventeen inhabitants in 1951, one for ten in 1955, one for seven in 1958. Finally, leisure and culture were already identifiable as the next stage after the car in the pursuit of better standards of living, expenditure on them rising by 42 per cent. Sales of radios and television sets, records – 78s and microgrooves – games, photographic and sporting equipment also grew by 2.5, considerably more than those of books or theatre tickets, which rose by only 40 per cent.[29]

Overall, the French displayed a clear preference for consumption at the expense of investment or saving, and in general more so than their European neighbours.[30] This is not to suggest that the consumption born of the economic growth was equitably distributed, nor that it eased social tensions. As in the case of income, the general progress was overshadowed by inequalities. Table 24, which summarizes the most reliable information available for 1956, reveals the extent of disparities in consumption. The differences of income are fundamental: average per capita resources for all households were 304 000 francs a year, yet an industrial labourer, his wife and child disposed of only 190 000 francs, compared with 526 000 for the senior manager: around the average of 100 the index of income dispersal ranges from 62 to 173. However, and this is a social and behavioural factor of great importance, the financial inequality was accentuated by the existing and new patterns of consumption: for the index of disparity for total consumption in fact stretched from 74 to 202. The range thus widened, with the better-off increasing their lead in terms of consumption by a group response which underlined their successful integration in the new society. In other words, consumption added a new socio-cultural dimension to economic inequality: the disadvantaged were thus further penalized, and this in a society where the media, publicity, and the agents of popular culture were increasingly geared towards encouraging consumption, fostering the myths of an equal accessibility to goods and an equal social prestige for their purchasers. The social breakdown of differing consumption reveals the full magnitude of the inequalities, ranging from the irreducible patterns of the low-paid, up through a variety of registers of consumption more intimately linked to social pressures and fashion. For food the differences come as little surprise and are close to the general average – there were limits to how much roast beef even the wealthiest could consume, just as there were limits to the shades of social differentiation it was possible to give to pasteurized butter! For clothing, however, the disparities start to appear, with an effort over personal appearance already marking the managers off from the simple employees. Housing remains

Table 24: *Principal household expenditures in 1956*

| | annual per capita resources in each household | total expenditure | | groceries | | clothing | | housing | | transport holidays | | hygiene health | | culture leisure diverse | |
|---|---|---|---|---|---|---|---|---|---|---|---|---|---|---|---|
| | francs | 2[b] | 2 | 1[a] | 2 | 1 | 2 | 1 | 2 | 1 | 2 | 1 | 2 | 1 | 2 |
| liberal professions and executives | 526 600 | 173 | 202 | 27.2 | 118 | 12.2 | 211 | 20.3 | 203 | 16.7 | 384 | 5.8 | 241 | 16.3 | 377 |
| industrialists and merchants | 418 000 | 137 | 161 | 35.6 | 117 | 12.9 | 175 | 20 | 126 | 16.2 | 311 | 6.3 | 207 | 8.7 | 201 |
| middle managers | 365 000 | 120 | 143 | 36.6 | 111 | 13.1 | 159 | 19.1 | 190 | 13.6 | 225 | 5.5 | 195 | 12.1 | 200 |
| small shopkeepers | 334 500 | 110 | 133 | 39.6 | 112 | 11.1 | 124 | 12.1 | 105 | 14.1 | 213 | 6.6 | 154 | 7.7 | 126 |
| employees | 272 300 | 89 | 107 | 45 | 102 | 13.3 | 120 | 18.3 | 120 | 7.5 | 87 | 6.1 | 112 | 9.8 | 125 |
| artisans | 256 600 | 84 | 101 | 44.3 | 97 | 11.3 | 96 | 11.3 | 93 | 10.8 | 142 | 5.4 | 101 | 8.5 | 92 |
| workers | 231 200 | 76 | 90 | 50.4 | 97 | 12.4 | 93 | 17 | 102 | 6 | 61 | 5 | 89 | 9.2 | 88 |
| retired and non-active | 224 500 | 70 | 90 | 50.6 | 99 | 10.5 | 79 | 9.1 | 71 | 4.7 | 47 | 6.5 | 64 | 7.5 | 69 |
| farmers | 214 700 | 70 | 85 | 49.2 | 106 | 10.5 | 75 | 16 | 67 | 5.7 | 68 | 5.6 | 106 | 6.2 | 44 |
| labourers | 190 000 | 62 | 74 | 54.2 | 87 | 11.8 | 73 | 16 | 64 | 3.9 | 35 | 5.2 | 94 | 8.9 | 68 |
| average for all households | 304 000 | 100 | 100 | 46.3 | 100 | 11.9 | 100 | 10.8 | 100 | 8.4 | 100 | 5.8 | 100 | 9 | 100 |

[a] 1 percentage of annual expenditure of households.
[b] 2 index of disparity (ratio of resources or expenditure per capita of each category/resources or average expenditure per capita overall = 100).

*Source:* based on *Consommation. Annales du CREDOC*, April–June, 1960, pp. 106–9.

close to the average, though once again the tertiary sector confirms its relatively privileged position. Conversely, social penalties and privileges assert themselves strongly in the category of culture and leisure, where the index shows a disparity of 1 to 8 in propensity to consume, reproducing with crushing accuracy the social hierarchy. And the inequality is more brutal still for holidays and motoring, where the range extends from 1 to 11. The selection was severe: senior managers, executives, and members of the liberal professions enjoyed the fruits of consumption to the full; farmers, labourers, and the non-active lost out in every category; the workers, though in general maintaining an average position, were seriously penalized over culture and leisure; finally, the tertiary sector and the self-employed all consumed more and better in proportion to their income.

Each social category, acutely aware of marginal inequalities and hungry for the most immediately accessible goods, was thus drawn into the generalized movement to greater well-being. And the least privileged at the outset showed the most determination to catch up their backwardness. At the top of the league table of households accelerating their purchases of cars, television sets, refrigerators, and washing-machines were those of agricultural labourers, workers, employees, and the non-active, closely followed by middle managers, but outdistancing employers, senior managers, and members of the liberal professions, all already well equipped, plus of course the farmers, left far behind: in this respect at least consumption based on social prestige and domestic comfort was a genuinely popular one. Yet the results went largely unacknowledged: in 1956, when average per capita real income had increased by almost 6 per cent, 92 per cent of those questioned considered their standard of living to have declined or remained stationary.[31] Improvements and frustrations co-existed; indeed, they fuelled each other.

*Frustrations and demands*

Access to consumption, though more open, was thus far from being democratic. Indeed, the generalized upward movement of income actually set up new tensions, arising from the way each category earned its share and the widespread conviction that adjacent social groups were increasing their prosperity without difficulty. In 1954, 45 per cent of households claimed to have difficulty making ends meet.[32] No doubt the range of efficient social transfers eased some of these tensions, but it was impossible to ignore the combination of traditional injustices and new demands which lay behind the complaints. Since every demand for consumption represented a call on the energies of the active population, on companies, and on the public authorities, it was not surprising that the appeal of economic growth should have been so strong in the 1950s: expansion was widely recognized as the key to prosperity. Yet this awareness in no way precluded the same economic groups from making efforts to protect their own income: the other side of the productive dynamism of this period was a brake on growth in the form of organized pressure to defend existing positions and privileges. France under the Fourth Republic became a vast forum for pressure groups directing their efforts at companies, other professions, and the public authorities. For 1956–7, Jean Meynaud has catalogued nearly 300 such groups, associations, and trade unions,[33] acting for a kaleidoscope of disparate interests – young barristers and ex-parachutists, surveyors and soft-drinks sellers, wardens of blocks of flats, and the victims of agricultural calamities – but all engaged in the serious business of pressure and self-publicity, seeking recognition for their grievances and status. In the last resort this pressure always converged upon the State, to which the ultimate appeal could be addressed. True, it is not hard to understand that the producers of household goods, for example, had little need for such action, or that the lack of organization among the fruit-growers might explain their silence. On the other hand, the iron and steel producers, or the major grain-growers, were past masters at pressuring the administration, at perfecting their lobbying tactics, and at engineering for themselves an advantageous place in fiscal legislation: in the process, they set a powerful example to other groups, contributing in this way to stifle newer energies and productive sectors; sooner or later the consequences of their action were felt throughout production and distribution. Paradoxically then, the same determination was the agent of both progress and retardation, implicated in both expansion and frustration. And inevitably this contradiction rebounded on the State, at once the scapegoat for all the defects of the market economy and ceaselessly attacked for its own shortcomings: here were the origins of much of the popular indifference of May 1958. This is not to absolve the governments of the Fourth Republic of their failure to build enough schools or hospitals; merely to recognize that they cannot be held resonsible for something beyond their powers to remedy.

The sensitive question of housing provides a perfect illustration of these phenomena and points up the contradictions present in the transition to modernity. There was widespread awareness of the problem's vital importance for the future; reports and studies multiplied; the public authorities had long made efforts; and yet no overall solution was found: the problem was tenacious, penalizing, for a long time after the hardships of the war, those described by Claudius-Petit as the 'victims de la vie'. The statistics of the housing situation were grim. True, on paper there were 14.5 million homes for 13.5 million households in 1954. But this housing was very unevenly distributed; three-quarters of the unoccupied homes were in rural communes where they were no longer required, whereas in the towns 35 per cent of homes with between one and five rooms were overcrowded, 50 per cent in the case of one- and two-room homes. With an average of more than one person per room, France had the worst housing record in Europe, an acute shortage that the various legal measures taken between 1945 and 1948 had failed to alleviate. Moreover, the housing stock was badly run down: 85 per cent of housing in Paris dated from before 1914, and the figure was 63 per cent in all the other towns of more than 50 000 inhabitants. Many towns contained entire quarters of quite exceptionally bad housing: 80 per cent of flats in the second *arrondissement* of Paris were without running water, and similar cases existed at Rouen, Grenoble, Lille, Roubaix, and Vienne. In 1959 there were still more than 350 000 slums, 41 per cent of homes still had no running water, 73 per cent had no toilets of their own, and almost 90 per cent were still without either a shower or bath. These dismal statistics make it easy to understand the obstinacy with which the population continued to pressure the administrations, why the waiting-lists for municipal housing lengthened inexorably, why the presence of old people in large flats was a cause of resentment; and why kowtowing to officials, housing managers, and concierges, having recourse to family help and depressing makeshift, and scrutinizing the classified advertisements, all became a way of life for so many families. In 1955, 27 per cent of households wanted to move as quickly as possible (52 per cent where the head of the household was under 30), 38 per cent among workers compared with 25 per cent for members of the liberal professions.[34]

The reasons for this desperate situation are not hard to identify. Scarcely any housing had been built in France between the wars; rents had been blocked since August 1914, and the new moratorium imposed by the law of 1948 served to discourage investment by individuals in buildings. The damage of 1939–45 and the demographic and urban upsurge created a strong demand for new housing, one to which the construction industry responded inadequately. Finance for building was insufficient, with the State limiting its help to the HLM – Habitations à loyer modéré, the equivalent of council housing in Britain. The result of these cumulative shortcomings was an estimated shortage of 3 million new homes: by 1954 the construction of more than 300 000 homes each year for twenty years was needed in order to provide decent housing for all the population. Against this background, the first benefit of growth, the foundation of well-being for all, clearly had to be housing.

The measures taken since 1945 had dealt with the most serious emergencies, but had not avoided the creation of bottlenecks. Behind the law of 1948 lay the ambition of introducing an orderly upwards revision of rents, and the hope of persuading households to devote more than the present 2 per cent of their expenditure on consumption to housing. There were signs of progress in the construction industry, with a beginning of the introduction of American methods allowing homes to be built cheaper and quicker –

3600 man hours for one home in 1952, less than 2000 in 1959. Yet with the Plan giving absolute priority to other sectors, the economy could not satisfy the demand; and the State refused to assume full financial and human responsibilities by according budgetary priority to housing. As a result reconstruction simply duplicated the old forms, with no attempt to define an urban policy to impose a new approach. There were a few model schemes for particular quarters – Le Havre, Caen, Marseille, Lyon, and Maubeuge – but overall the results were disappointing: for one prestige project based on Le Corbusier's revered ideas there were thousands of soulless boxes; for a few town centre redevelopments – uninspired, monotonous, designed for the motor car, and with high rents – there were hundreds of poorly planned suburban developments, with houses sprouting wherever land was available, reinforcing social segregation. Above all there was the simple but inescapable fact that not enough homes were being built: fewer than 40 000 a year until 1949, 56 000 that year, the 100 000 figure finally reached with great difficulty in 1953. In short, barely one-sixth of needs were covered, and this at a time when large families and young couples were engaged in a desperate hunt for literally any accommodation. There were signs that the discontent might boil over. A squatting movement, invoking the ordinance of 19 October 1945 that allowed for the requisition of vacant housing, and organized by the Mouvement populaire des familles, made many commando operations up until 1950; impatient workers, like those at Pessac in the Gironde, seized the initiative and built their own homes. And massive public attention was focused on the plight of the homeless by the campaign launched by Abbé Pierre in the depths of winter 1954. Backed by local helpers and making effective use of the radio, Abbé Pierre exposed the scandal of the *bidonvilles* (shanty towns) of Nanterre and Saint-Denis. The vast national response to his crusade was evidence of widespread tension and readiness to act. The public had received a shock; yet this groundswell of unrest did not acquire a political colouring: the housing crisis was too general and touched social groups that were too disparate for a Poujadism of the poorly housed to develop.

This absence of coherent political expression may have owed something to the launching of a public policy which for the first time looked likely to tackle the housing problem from all angles – a striking demonstration of the capacity of French society at this time to defuse its internal conflicts and tensions! The financial obstacle was overcome: the *décret-loi* of 9 August 1953, immediately after the wave of strikes, imposed on employers a charge of 1 per cent of the wage bill to finance the housing of their workforce, a measure which resulted in an extra 60 000 homes a year. A system of incentives and savings indexed to the price of buildings was created, and the Caisse des dépôts was mobilized by Bloch-Lainé to finance the sociétés d'économie mixte de construction et d'aménagement. And the State no longer limited its efforts to the construction of HLMs – a decree of 16 March 1953 defined the 'Logéco', low-cost housing aimed at middle-income families. The other stumbling-block to be tackled was that of land. A law of 6 August 1953 increased the scope for expropriation of land in the public interest, making it easier for municipalities and promoters to find vacant land for building purposes. Lastly, there were improvements in construction methods and technology, notably through standardization: costs fell, space was used more intelligently, a highly successful 'F3' or three-room flat of 52 square metres was established as the model for the typical household; this policy favoured the construction throughout France, usually in the suburbs, of the so-called Grands Ensembles housing developments – a solution to the housing problem which, it should be remembered, was widely considered at the time to be the summit of rational modernity. From now on the position began to improve significantly. Finance for the HLMs rose from 53 milliard francs in 1953 to 130 milliard in 1955; the total of public aid grew by 120 milliard a year; and, realizing the dream of the Liberation, the target of 300 000 homes a year was almost reached in 1958, before being passed in 1959. The number of homes built within the official framework of credits and norms was far superior to that of individual new homes offered by the private sector, a position which was to remain unchanged for over a decade. The public policy was completed in 1954 with the 'Plan Courant' which offered generous advances (up to 80 per cent of the total cost) through the channel of the Crédit foncier to would-be home purchasers, giving a great boost to joint-ownership of new and older properties.

To see the problem as conquered, however, would be to underestimate the social dimension of the housing question. For the new opportunities tended in fact to work to the advantage of the more affluent, encouraging them to embark on the purchase of a home or to apply pressure in order to jump the queue. Thus, of the new homes allocated in the five years prior to 1960, 40 per cent had gone to executives and salaried staff, members of the liberal professions, and businessmen, 40 per cent to employees, artisans, small retailers, and qualified workers, compared with only 20 per cent to labourers, unskilled workers, service personnel, and the non-active. The hierarchy of inequality faithfully reproduced itself. Promoters and local authorities were readier to offer the 'Logécos' to young couples willing to assume debts; the HLMs accumulated a dense and socially disparate population – genuinely needy low-income and 'problem' families to be sure, but also middle-income families waiting for alternative housing, teachers or engineers, plus all those who had secured an HLM through influence or pressure on local officials and politicians. And while 'social' housing did not always go to the most needy, speculation was a growing problem in the private sector, attracted by the easy profits made possible by the shortage. Many households were ready to devote more than 4 per cent of their expenditure to housing: they spent 90 milliard in 1957 simply to remain as they were; they were prepared to spend 200 milliard for something better. In vain: the cost and the means of financing were such that they had to abandon the attempt; impatient and disappointed they turned their expenditure to other forms of consumption.[35] Housing remained a major source of frustration; the sovereignty of money was undisputed, and the weakest were left behind.

With serious unrest defused by the timely improvement in public policy, and a coherent articulation of demands impossible given the diversity of interests involved, the dissatisfied were left with a choice between individual *débrouillardise* (resourcefulness) or organized pressure in favour of specific groups. The housing problem multiplied the conflicting and energetic interest groups. For the tenants the old Confédération nationale des locataires (CNL) founded in 1916 was challenged by the new Confédération générale du logement (CGL) which issued from the campaign of Abbé Pierre; the Communists were active in both; action took the form of systematic harassment of elected officials and the media. For their part, the owners, grouped in the Union de la propriété bâtie de France and in the *chambres syndicales*, adopted a calmer approach, stressing civic responsibilities. Trade unions, family associations, and employers' associations swelled the chorus of argument and pressure; while the construction industry cast itself in the role of a social service. A united front over housing was thus excluded. Yet the various pressure groups could not but find audiences among the political parties, eager to harness their energies, or in Parliament, or among the ministers intimidated by their action, or in the municipalities mindful of their electoral weight. In short, this noisy movement of discontent posed few overall questions and inhibited general solutions; what it did do was obtain satisfaction for a number of particular cases and work up indignation against the State.[36]

The example of housing points up a major weakness in French society: the difficulty encountered in transforming frustrations into tangible demands which could then be negotiated and pursued to eventual success. There were numerous signs, however, that French society was becoming less conflict-ridden, and that the mechanism of social integration was operating more efficiently. The example of the choice of spouse shows how the old allegiances to clan or locality were being broken down; crimes and offences were in steady regression – 360 000 cases in 1948, 197 000 in 1958; juvenile delinquency, a major problem at the Liberation, declined – though it reappeared after 1955 with the 'blouson noir' motorcycle gangs from underprivileged backgrounds or the overcrowded conditions of the Grands Ensembles. Broadly speaking, social deviation became concentrated among the groups that were least favoured economically and least integrated into the society of consumer growth; violence decreased, or found an outlet in Algeria. Nevertheless, the imperative of group membership already observed after the war remained powerful: not only did individuals want to be submerged in a group, but all the 'social partners' thus constituted preferred to look to the supreme authority of the State rather than engage in constructive dialogue and effort between themselves. This reflected the profound mutations occurring in French society: the decomposition of rural communities was more than compensated for by the solidarities of the workforce; the growing importance of the tertiary sector encouraged prompt action to integrate and organize the newcomers. Having said this, the failure of collective action to articulate widespread frustration inevitably raises questions about the relationship between these groups and the organizations which claimed to represent them; one example merits particular attention, that of the trade unions.

One commentator has spoken of a 'piétinement dans l'impasse' to sum up the position in this domain.[37] The trade-unionism of the workers and state employees – the oldest, most lucid, and strongest of all the organized social groups, whose powers had been extended at the Liberation – in fact had great difficulty recovering from the trauma of the Cold War, and now failed to measure the full implications of the economic expansion. It was uncertain of the course to be adopted or approved; direct action, like that at Saint-Nazaire in 1955? Branch-by-branch negotiation with the employers, and defence of a framework of collective agreements? Or should efforts be focused on the State, marrying the methods of a pressure group to the status of a privileged social partner, in preparation perhaps for a future role as an integral part of a generalized dialogue overseen by a true Welfare State? Without clear answers to these questions the paralysis deepened. Local and sectorial conflicts remained sharp in 1953, 1955, and 1957 – yet the unions displayed an uncharacteristic torpor in October 1954 when the Mendès France government increased the SMIG but refused to take the place of the trade unions in determining the repercussions of this increase on wage levels throughout the economy. The CNPF for its part adopted a wait-and-see attitude, and the confederations of wage-earners hesitated: the militancy of the trade union base was blunted by the palpable increase in living standards. This inability to come to terms with the changes at work in the economy and society aggravated the internal divisions of the trade union movement. After 1953, a metallurgical section of Force Ouvière was active, the left-wing 'Reconstruction' group launched its bid to take control of the CFTC,[38] while in the CGT the 1955 congress saw the civil servants and printworkers led by Le Brun argue in vain with Frachon and the leadership against a dogmatic adherence to the thesis of the absolute pauperization of the working class and against irresponsible, doctrinally motivated action.

Divided and powerless, French working-class trade-unionism was stagnant. In the 1955 elections of the administrators of the Social Security, the CGT failed to advance beyond 43 per cent of the votes, the CFTC and Force Ouvrière stagnated at 20 and 16 per cent, whereas a collection of narrowly corporatist lists made important gains. The optimism of the Liberation period had evaporated: working-class trade-unionism now represented no more than 15 per cent of the wage-earners it aspired to lead. A call for the unity of the trade union movement made in June 1957 by Denis Forestier of the Syndicat national des instituteurs failed miserably, and unity of action remained a hollow good intention at the national level.

In contrast, a trade-unionism based on the defence of highly specific interests was going from strength to strength, thus accelerating the fragmentation of energies. The 'autonomous' and 'independent' groups multiplied, hostile to the Communists, and quick to invoke the apoliticism of the Charter of Amiens (1906). Separate unions were organized for the engineers of the SNCF, policemen, university teachers, journalists, the *routiers*, drivers on the métro, doctors; the Confédération générale des cadres quickly put down solid roots; the CGPME had no trouble absorbing the Poujadists; the teachers of the FEN continued to call for more funds, without serious reflection as to objectives. Meanwhile, the CNPF leader Georges Villiers had quickly grasped the usefulness to employers of agreements like that signed at Renault in September 1955, and won over his members – fifty-odd contractual agreements were signed in July 1957, chiefly in the metallurgical industry. A general rule was emerging, one alien to the traditions of a working-class trade-unionism which, since the nineteenth century, had aspired to take responsibility for the broadest aspects of social transformation: the more pronounced a frustration and the narrower the scope of the demands, the more unity was possible and pressure effective, and the more the trade unions became fixed in the role of simple pressure groups – the least favoured, the farmers for example, were attracted on this new basis. With the exception of small and isolated groups, such as 'Reconstruction' in the CFTC, often with affinities to *Mendésisme*, which did attempt to come to terms with the evolution of social values, the trade union movement now abandoned the broader, educative aspects of its action, responsibilities now taken on by other associations, the Comités d'enterprise, and the public authorities. The trade unions were in fact being reduced to vehicles for the articulation of narrowly economic frustrations, devoid of long-term projects or ambitions. Working-class trade-unionism in particular paid a heavy price for its political divisions, with the CGT suffering by association from the isolation of the PCF. In addition, it now had to contend with the role of modern media and the weight of public opinion in the conduct of industrial action. Badly weakened, working-class unionism stood still in a rapidly evolving society.[39]

This dissipation of energies and aimless abdication by the groups supposed to represent the dynamic social forces left the way clear for the exercise of other pressures, consolidating existing positions and inhibiting change. The generalized offensive of particular interests against an already weak and vulnerable political authority aggravated the imbalances: how, after all, could the public authorities correct social shortcomings in which, via the party system, they themselves participated? This was the stark dilemma posed by the Armand-Rueff report in 1959: the absence of a consensus on the future and the fragmentation of general interest were obstacles to economic expansion and social progress.[40] French society remained, then, profoundly marked by social hierarchy and authority; and while face-to-face dialogue was shunned, the State was held responsible for problems beyond its powers to resolve.[41] That the incontestable improvement in living standards should have brought appeasement but not a durable peace to French society was no doubt because the development was too recent. One point, however, is certain: all, whether winners or losers, were deeply affected by it.

# 18

# The fluid society?

Greater prosperity had not narrowed inequalities, and social distance remained considerable. Is this observation, made for individuals and households, also valid for the established groups in French society? In the new mixture of dynamism and discontent, were the stakes those of the class struggle, or rather of competing categories? That economic change should have favoured some while penalizing others was to be expected; but to what extent did the losses suffered now in fact aggravate long-standing handicaps and, likewise, the gains serve merely to enhance existing advantages? In short, had change and progress brought new opportunities for social mobility?

*Peasants under threat*

The statistics leave no doubt that the principal losers in the expansion were the peasants: though accounting for 25 per cent of the active population they received only 12 per cent of the national income; on a base of 100 for 1949 their per capita income reached a ceiling of 123 in 1958, compared with 141 for the population as a whole. They fared consistently badly in the league table of disparities in consumption, trailing behind for every category except food; and they were both victims and agents of the sharpest regional inequalities. And the statistics convey only a part of the bitterness present throughout rural society. The village grocer bearing the cost of long van journeys to his dispersed customers, the rural *instituteur* isolated with a single class, the young dreaming of escape from the drudgery of the farms to the towns, and of course the farmers themselves, bitterly aware that working fourteen hours a day without a holiday brought in just enough to service the bank loans and allow their families to survive – all suffered a sense of deepening isolation from the rest of society, of being 'citoyens à part' rather than 'citoyens à part entière' as the frustration and ambition were commonly summed up at the time, a widespread sense of exclusion that only a few privileged groups participating more fully in the general prosperity – doctors, vets, lawyers, chemists, agricultural counsellors –

could escape. The hopes encouraged by Vichy for a renaissance of the countryside had proved illusory, and even the relative prosperity of the period of the black market and scarcities had been short-lived. The stark fact had to be faced: the land no longer supported everyone, increased competition hastened the disintegration of rural civilization; with progress the old values, like the patrimonies, crumbled. In the steadily emptying countryside, the peasants, or *agriculteurs* as they were now referred to, experienced to the full the pains of modernization.

Yet they had made strenuous efforts to increase output and productivity. We have witnessed the scale of the productivity increases realized in agriculture owing to mechanization, improved methods of stocking, and heavy use of chemical fertilizers. The symbol of these efforts to modernize was without doubt the tractor, now replacing the horse or cow, initially running on petrol but soon turned over to diesel and able to benefit from the substantial tax reliefs on fuel oils that governments of all persuasions maintained. Although often unsuited to upland regions or heavily subdivided land, and not always of sufficient power – manufacturers like Massey-Ferguson flooded the French market with small machines – the tractor nonetheless established itself everywhere as the indispensable instrument. With the possibility of attachments and extra equipment it became a mobile power-house in the fields, adapted to all tasks and types of farm. An individual tool, the tractor freed the farmer from the most crushing of his labours, making him master of the land, and boosting his self-confidence. The triumph of the tractor was complete, not seriously challenged by other machines, the press, milking machine, or combine harvester, which required more labour; it was an obvious sign of rural social promotion, a source of satisfaction for the farmer, a source of admiration or envy for his neighbours. Yet the purchase of a tractor typically led the farmer into debt, absorbing funds which could have gone to other investments. A very visible status symbol, the tractor encouraged competitiveness, stimulating demand for better and more powerful models; more than anything else, it was the tractor which drew the French peasant farmer into the remorseless system of credit and profitability. The agencies for the collective use of agricultural machinery and equipment (CUMA), though launched before the war, developed little until after 1955: apart from the harvester, it was individual ownership of the motor reaper, the cultivator, and above all the tractor which stood as the sign of independence and determination.

This highly individualistic mechanization of agriculture is the best indicator of the so-called 'silent revolution' whose effects were starting to be felt in the French countryside.[1] Henceforth, all the variables in agriculture – technology, the structure of farms, labour, the quality, scale, cost, and price of output – were linked in a strongly capitalistic interdependence. The great irruption of the tractor brutally posed the question of the optimum size of farms: over 15–20 hectares to the south of the Loire, over 50 hectares in the fertile plains of the North, and with the land rationally organized in large fields, were now the basic conditions for profitability. Marginal farms unable to meet these criteria began to be squeezed out; slowly to begin with, then more ruthlessly after 1955, at a rate of 30 000 fewer farms each year. From a total of 2 454 000 farms in 1942, 170 000 had disappeared by 1955, and nearly 400 000 more by 1963. Farms of less than 10 hectares declined steadily at first, still accounting for 16 in every 100 hectares in 1955, compared with 22 in 1942, then collapsed abruptly; those of between 10 and 20 hectares seemed more solid, accounting for 25 hectares in every 100 in 1955, but then disappeared in their turn, absorbed into other farms when their owners died or retired after a decade of struggle to survive. On the other hand, farms of over 20 hectares experienced a continuous growth, accounting for 57 per cent of farmed land in 1942, 60 per cent in 1955, and 66 per cent in 1963; they ranged from the great cereal 'factory' farms of the North and the Paris basin, down to the 'typical' farm of 20–50 hectares, now specialized and well equipped, and established as the model for 'dynamic' farmers in all regions. Mechanization thus initiated a phase of rapid change in agriculture; disturbing, though perhaps not sufficiently redistributing, ownership of land. Moreover, it operated a form of natural selection: the ineluctable depopulation of the countryside, at a rate of 130 000 a year after 1955, could be viewed more calmly if it was the weakest who left, while bolstering the hopes of those who remained that they were safely over the threshold of profitability.

The only solution for those who did stay was to adopt the approach of the entrepreneur and bow to the laws of the market. The old responses of autarky and frugality had to be abandoned; the wider range of products to grow taught the farmers to respond to the fluctuations of prices and markets, to conceive of their efforts in a national and European context, one increasingly influenced by the agro-food industries, the general growth of the economy, and the new demands of urban consumers. Maize, hitherto confined to the South, now conquered the regions to the north of the Loire, while new wheat varieties spread into the South; and around 1950 the major changes began which were to impose fodder cultivation everywhere; efforts were concentrated on the produce most in demand – meat, dairy produce, fruit, and vegetables. But with these developments came two potential dangers: first, from the fact that markets could soon become saturated, resulting in surpluses; secondly, they placed the farmers at the mercy of prices. Their position was indeed a vulnerable one. For purchases of fertilizers, materials, livestock feeds, and even land (for the speculation remained strong), the farmers were faced with high and uncontrolled prices. Conversely, the presence of numerous intermediaries, the vigilance of the public authorities over food prices, soon the European controls, competition, and the weakness of distributive co-operatives, all served to drive down regularly the prices obtained by the producers. The unrest of 1953 was a direct result of this. Caught between costs tending to rise and income tending to fall, with irreducible financial requirements to pay or amortize the cost of material bought on credit, and wanting to participate like other groups in the consumer society, the farmers could only count on their labour and on being able to increase productivity. This posed little problem for the large semi-industrial farms specializing in the production of grain, maize, or beet, with strong pressure groups to defend prices, and able to respond quickly over investment and planting policies to maximize profits. But it was an increasingly difficult course for the smallest farmers, burdened with debts, often still locked into a family based polyculture with just a few surplus productions to bring in ready cash. For a time, however, the pressure of prices actually favoured the medium-sized farms, where unremitting toil, the participation of the farmer's wife in all the tasks of the farm, and adoption of a range of modern animal productions and a relatively light mechanization, allowed significant productivity gains to be realized quickly. But the mechanisms of economic strangulation were already in place. Technical and managerial skills were increasingly as important as the quality of the soil itself; the farmer had to become a businessman and technician; the working capital of the farm outweighed the capital tied up in the land; and the financial needs added to the demands on individual or family effort. The hopes and relative prosperity were fragile: bad prices could easily spell crisis.

Another, related, sign of change was the growing appetite of the farmers for a way of life modelled on that of the urban population. The process took many forms, was slower in some areas than in others, but was everywhere irreversible. Each rural commune had its own small group of innovators to set the example: go-ahead notables, militants of the JAC or the unions, shopkeepers, artisans. And the external pressures were multiple: publicity on radio and later on television, the regional press, holiday-makers, relatives from Paris or a regional metropolis, retired people from the towns, purchasers of second homes. All were agents of change, all served to whet rural appetites for a different way of life, one synonymous with electric coffee mills and shavers, smart clothes, the bath and shower, central heating. The speed of the changes must not be exaggerated, however. In 1958, even if electricity had completed its conquest of the countryside, only one rural home in four was equipped with running water, one in six an indoor toilet; and the regional inequalities were striking – 45 per cent of rural homes in Brittany had earth floors, while in the Limousin 15 per cent were lit only by petrol lamps or a single low-powered electric bulb over the dining-table. Old habits died hard, and for a long time only what were judged essential needs were met. The car or van to begin with, usually bought secondhand, often driven by the wife, and valued as an instrument of economic and human relations more than as a source of social prestige: after the Paris region, the prosperous Vaucluse had the highest number of cars on the roads in 1958. The car was typically followed by the introduction of running water to the kitchen, a cooker working from bottled gas, a formica-topped table, tiles or linoleum on the floor in the main room, the purchase of the first toys for the children. Later came the refrigerator and household equipment, central heating and bathrooms; the old-fashioned farm furniture was relegated to the attic to make way for modern mass-produced articles; for the young came the Mobylette and records; clothing was bought from mail order catalogues or at the nearest town, rather than from the local store or at the fair. New articles were accompanied by new attitudes and patterns of behaviour, with the young at the forefront of the change. Young couples preferred to set up home away from their parents; the radio now rivalled village gossip as a source of information; rural diet began to move closer to that of the town-dwellers; the focus of social life was as likely to be the meeting as it was the *veillée*; there was more mobility, with children being taken to school by car or in the first coaches of the new school bus services, the possibility of organized excursions, visits to the Salon d'agriculture; the telephone arrived; basic mechanics had to be learnt. A long list of ostensibly minor changes in everyday life, yet which together amounted to a major cultural upheaval in the countryside. The rural family was increasingly nuclear, rural horizons were expanding, and the traditional forms of organized social intercourse were disappearing.

This revolution of taste and expectations made a return to the past impossible for those who accepted the gamble of modernization, just as it threw into confusion all those who refused it. Rural society, traditionally diverse, was now deeply divided, torn between the old and new civilizations, though inescapably subject to the profit imperative of the latter. Caught by the contradictions of progress, the farmers managed nonetheless to find themselves new organizational élites who took seriously the national choice between modernization or decline. The social group whose future was the most compromised by the economic growth in fact made an important effort to master its own mutation. The first step in this process was the gradual challenge to the élites who for so long had monopolized representation of the farming interest. With the CGA having failed to realize its ambitions for unity and greater democracy, and institutionalized from 1953 in an anodyne consultative role, the old corporatist leaders of the FNSEA had reasserted their authority, finally making peace with the Republic at the beginning of the 1950s. Under their president, René Blondelle, they committed the farmers to a policy of '*action civique*' by electing parliamentarians carrying the '*agricole*' label – that is, Independents and Peasants of various right-wing hues – and by organizing the chambres d'agriculture, re-established in 1949, as pressure groups. In spite of the decree of December 1954 empowering them to raise levies to finance a number of concrete services, the chambres d'agriculture and their presidents gradually settled into the role of campaign machines for candidates of the Centre and Right in elections to the Senate, apparently oblivious to the upheavals affecting French agriculture. It was in response to this failure of the established agrarian élites that a new generation of militants and agricultural leaders sprang up.[2] In its ranks were men committed to responding positively to the challenge of the new technology; agricultural engineers and enthusiastic young farmers, responsible for setting up several hundred Centres d'études techniques agricoles (CETA) to train groups of go-ahead farmers. Also present were those who had a vision of the peasants as politically mature and freed from the tutelage of the notables and dependence on public funds, and with an original contribution to make to development in a wider sense. For the most part these were members of the JAC (Jeunesse agricole chrétienne), young and energetic, often working in pairs, well aware of broader problems, such as Third World famine, and with an understanding of the mechanisms of capitalism and techniques of management. These currents, present in the CGA, came together in 1954 to form the Centre national des jeunes agriculteurs (CNJA). Under the strong leadership of figures like Michel Debatisse, the CNJA quickly emerged as the only force likely to inject new life into the moribund world of the agricultural trade unions. Its militants accepted modernization as inevitable, recognizing that it would help to restore the prestige of agriculture as a profession; they had deep personal commitment to technical innovation from experience on their own farms; they accepted the *exode rural* and the demise of the old family-based agriculture, but argued in return that the land should go to the most competent professionals; they defended the need for such changes, but wanted them to be accomplished without sacrificing the independence and dignity of the farmer, at once opposed to many aspects of capitalism yet wishing to harness its strengths. With these demands for an extensive reform but not destruction of the existing system, the militants of the CNJA became the strident voice of the countryside in transition.

Their message found an audience among the troubled farmers. Not the large specialized grain producers of the Paris basin, capable of holding stocks and waiting for prices to rise: for them a good pricing policy and the activities of the Office national interprofessionnel des céréales and the various pressure groups operating within the FNSEA were sufficient. But the other farmers, those who had pinned their hopes on the development of fodder and livestock, who had attempted modernization on frequently mediocre land, struggling to assemble the 20–40 hectares necessary for economic viability, were no longer satisfied with price protection alone. They wanted to see markets organized and international agreements honoured, and training and respect for their profession. Government, however, had shown itself incapable of providing a coherent agricultural policy adapted to their needs. After the Comité de Guéret, led by Socialists and Communists, had organized the road-blocks in 1953 to protest over low prices for meat and livestock, seriously embarrassing the FNSEA leadership, a Société inter-professionnelle du bétail et des viandes (SICBEV) was set up in December 1953 under the Laniel government. And similar moves were made in 1954 and 1955 for milk producers. Yet these attempts at concerted action by producers and the public authorities to organize markets were in vain: after a few peaceful months, grasping middlemen and industrial dairy companies reasserted their domination as strongly as ever. From now on, propelled by a hunger for improvement, the farming profession was steadily seized by an agitation which foreshadowed the violent protests of the 1960s. In March 1956, the CNJA became part of the FNSEA, upsetting the powerful agrarian interests and the older generation of union leaders (70 per cent of whom were over 50); and in 1957, Debatisse, the former General Secretary of the JAC, took control of the CNJA and began to prepare the strategy for the young farmers' takeover inside the FNSEA. The final governments of the Fourth Republic offered a general indexation of agricultural prices by the decrees of September 1957, and negotiated French agriculture a reasonable place in the Treaty of Rome framework. But while they knew how to respond to familiar pressures from the grain and beet producers, the new voices in the agricultural unions were demanding action over structures rather than simply over prices, along with measures to ease the social integration of a struggling minority. True, these new representative élites did not have the backing of a majority of the farmers, but they were developing themes which in the long run could not fail to find an important audience. An animated conflict had begun, one that only the far-reaching Pisani law on agriculture of 1964 would calm. For the old habit of looking to the State for a remedy was as deeply ingrained in the rural areas as elsewhere. In the crisis now gathering force, the State was believed to have a responsibility to come to the aid of a section of society which had lost its unity and seemed to be heading for impoverishment. Very considerable financial help had in fact been given to agriculture,[3] but the leaders of the Fourth Republic had merely tried to cushion the fall in prices, without undertaking a major structural reorganization of markets. They had failed to impose the modern agricultural policy which might have secured them the support of the countryside.

## The workers at the margin

The 1950s were also a period of profound mutation for the workers, though one whose impact varied with the size of companies, the industrial sector involved, and the region. But whereas the dificulties of the peasants serve to focus attention on their efforts to come to terms with modernization, the experience of the working class raises a different central question, one present in all the studies carried out at the time: to what extent did the progress of technology, income, and consumption favour the integration of the workers into the national community? Was working-class consciousness being modified? In other words, of course, did the new abundance turn the workers from the class struggle, a struggle in which they were no longer certain to be the decisive force?

The first point to note is that the definition of the working class was less clear cut than in the past. Indeed, a number of sociologists now began referring to a '*nouvelle classe ouvrière*' that was springing up alongside the older one. Manual labour was certainly no longer adequate as a criterion. New machines capable of carrying out a sequence of complicated operations, the first computers, and the advances of robot technology and remote control systems permitted a switch from assembly line methods to automated production in several large companies; tasks were allocated within self-contained production teams; developments in chemicals, electronics, petroleum, and metallurgy did much to promote an image of the white-coated modern worker guiding production by pushing buttons on a control desk, his work demanding nervous energy and concentration rather than brute force and manual dexterity. Between repetitive tasks on pre-set machines and jobs involving the exercise of initiative and decision-making responsibilities, the frontiers drawn by Taylorism at the start of the century were no longer as rigid. Those involved in production – punch card operators, foremen, technicians, supervisors, skilled and unskilled workers – were no longer as tightly compartmentalized. True, the organization of work was still hierarchical, but its character was changing, with the wage-earners acquiring a greater mastery of the whole of production and competition. And not only was manual work less monotonous, capable of offering a degree of personal satisfaction, but it looked to be less of a dead end than in the past. Did the young, now more educated, with qualifications, and better integrated socially and culturally, have a greater chance of avoiding the brutalizing impact of work on the assembly line? The inquiry conducted by Pierre Naville in 1957–9 revealed little cause for such optimism: 80 per cent of those working on automated equipment were OS (*ouvriers spécialisés* or unskilled workers), and companies often had difficulty in mastering the changes.[4]

Not, however, that the notion of a new category of wage-earning producers was false. But the sheer confusion of French industrial structures and the technological conservatism of many companies meant that it was a very marginal phenomenon. For although the small workshop-style factories were tending to disappear, large factories employing more than 500 workers and capable of adopting the technology of automation were still rare. In contrast to the experience in the United States, the development and dynamism of French industry at this time came from the medium-sized factories with between 100 and 500 workers, possibly integrated into a group or dependent on sub-contracting work, but usually retaining their autonomy in the methods of production and the use of the workforce. Whether large- or medium-sized, French companies automated only a small fraction of their production. Indeed, far from breaking up under the shock of automation, the old system of production based on specialization was actually strengthened. What was witnessed in the 1950s was the perfection and extension of production using a rational division of labour, the system whereby different components were produced simultaneously ready for subsequent assembly on the line. In short, the components were designed by experts, made by unskilled workers helped by labourers, on equipment looked after by the machine setters. The extent of this development varied from sector to sector. In the industries of glass, food, paper, and wood, the labourer still accounted for more than 40 per cent of the workforce in 1954, skilled workers between 20 and 30 per cent, and unskilled workers 30 per cent; in textiles, iron and steel, and engineering, the labourers had fallen to below 30 per cent, skilled workers accounted for 25 to 40 per cent, whereas the proportion of OS had risen to 45 per cent; only a few sectors requiring considerable manual dexterity, such as construction, clothing, and printing, conserved roughly 50 per cent of skilled workers. The general distribution for the total of companies employing more than ten people in 1954 was: 29 per cent labourers, 36 per cent OS, and 35 per cent skilled workers. The OS now became the most typical worker: forced to keep up with the speed of the line, with little or no opportunity for personal initiative, working the parts as demanded, the results liable to rejection by the foreman, timed and paid on piece-rates, with the bonus system as an incentive to still greater efforts. Closely supervised, dispensable, ready to slow down the rate of production imposed on them, though in reality snared by a system of overtime which boosted pay packets but lengthened an already long working week; close to the labourers, eager to keep on good terms with the machine setters, but detesting the '*petit chef*' who timed and scrutinized their work – the unskilled workers formed the reservoir of consciousness and revolt. Not, however, that they were always a coherent group in the factory: the hazards of recruitment and company restructuring meant that the OS could often find himself working alongside former skilled workers or future technicians. This diversity of ranks and status complicated working relations and social conflicts, often to the point of paralysing class action. Such differences were even more noticeable in the case of women OS. In addition to the hierarchies and rivalries faced by the men they suffered other vexations, some of them serious, and were paid less for equal work. The dismal condition of the unskilled workers set the tone for the whole profession, weakening the combative reflexes of some, notably the immigrants, inciting others to greater militancy, and humiliating for all. More than ever, it was in the workplace that consciousness was shaped.

In fact, the workers remained very much a closed, subordinate, and barely mobile group. The 1954 census showed an 'industrial population', that is, the secondary sector, of 6.8 million individuals; 36 per cent of the active population compared with 34 per cent in 1931. To this number have to be added various wage-earners of the tertiary sector, notably in transport, and from it subtracted the foremen, closer to the *cadres*, as well as a number of public sector workers whose attitudes were those of civil servants. In all, the broadest definition of the workers covered just about 6 million individuals; for whom consciousness was rooted less in the fact of manual work than in the submission to orders and rules, in an economic dependence on wages inferior to those of the white-collar workers and, as we have seen, often close to the SMIG, plus of course in the daily experience of social exclusion. Considerable allowance has to be made for attitudes of group membership when trying to assess the impact of prosperity on the lives of the workers. Of those questioned in an INED survey in 1956, 36 per cent considered life to be harder than before the war, and 63 per cent of those asked by the IFOP in December 1955 felt that there was too much injustice in the current state of affairs.[5] Nonetheless, according to the calculations of Jean-Marcel Jeanneney,[6] the purchasing power of the net weekly wage of a metal-worker in Paris was still actually lower in 1955 than in 1937, and this despite a growth of production in this sector of industry by 75 per cent over the same period. Furthermore, the general improvement of wages in 1956 and 1957, still lagging behind the productivity increases in industry and the incomes of higher social categories, was slowed down until 1961 by the return of inflation. This observation for a sector whose social record had frequently been held up as exemplary since the Renault agreement helps to place in some perspective the notion of the *'embourgeoisement'* of the working class.

However, the incontestable rise in its living standards, linked to the long-term increases for wage-earners (6.3 per cent on average each year between 1949 and 1957), albeit highly sensitive to variations in the economy despite the greater number of collective agreements signed after 1955, the sliding scale, the greater willingness of employers to raise wages in expansionary periods, a stable and tight market for labour which reduced the threat of unemployment, the social transfers, and the start of an incomes policy – all contributed to the irresistible upward movement of working-class income. Those who profited most from the developments were workers in very large companies with a workforce of over 1000: their hourly wages in 1958 were 28 per cent higher than those of comparable workers in companies employing less than twenty. On the other hand, the old industrial regions were susceptible to disparities, with the Nord conserving lower wage levels than in Lorraine or the Paris region; new, decentralized factories could sometimes offer higher wages than those in traditional industrial sites. And the income of workers in the provinces and of heads of large families now caught up with those of other workers.[7] The abundance of material and cultural goods available on the market could not but tempt the workers as it did other groups. Yet their access to consumption was restricted. To begin with, it was less important among the workers than other groups; it was only solidly obtained on credit; it disrupted existing ways of life less than among the peasants; and above all, the stark fact on which a basic class consciousness could be nourished, in contrast to the peasants or self-employed who could at least gamble on increasing their productivity, the workers exercised no control over their own future. Exploitation was common, and technological progress was by no means certain to be translated as wage increases. Improvements in income had to be fought for by negotiation or industrial action, protected against the ravages of inflation, continually threatened and reconquered. In the system in which they existed, the workers were more than ever dependent on selling their labour, forced to defend what was grudgingly conceded in return.

An awareness of this fact, and the patience necessary to support it, were the ever-present facts of daily life. Only newcomers entertained serious hopes for change. Workers who had taken the momentous step of leaving the countryside tended to have more faith than others in the possibility of surmounting the social barriers and hierarchies of work through tenacious individual effort.[8] For them, entering the factory as a labourer or unskilled worker constituted a first victory, and the optimism this generated was transferred to their children, in turn strenuously 'pushed'. Mobility here retained some of the impetus of the initial rupture with the countryside. Conversely, for all the established sections of the working class the opportunities for mobility, even for children, were slight: in 1958, the son of a worker had a 4 in 5 chance of remaining a wage-earner, and 3 in 5 of remaining a worker. Many potential openings were in fact blocked. The centres for the occupational training of adults stagnated miserably, with 23 000 students in 1949, 27 000 in 1958; technical training was apathetic, and the results achieved through the evening courses of the Conservatoires des arts et métiers were modest in the extreme. The trade union movement, as we have seen, no longer aspired to take the place of the public authorities in meeting the educational and cultural needs of its members, while for their part the employers were usually reluctant to grant the educational leave planned by the law of 1957. But it would be a mistake to imagine that this social cul-de-sac produced a hopeless resignation. For as Andrieux and

Lignon show,[9] whatever the claims of those eager to fix the proletariat in its historic mission, a fundamental characteristic of the working class as a whole was a stubborn desire for social self-improvement: either for oneself or for the next generation, by earning more, setting up on one's own, through more or less profitable leisure activities, through absenteeism, gardening, or odd-jobbing, all in the hope that change really was possible.

At the level of everyday life, however, there remained solid social barriers. The investigation conducted by the team under Paul-Henry Chombart de Lauwe in 1950–4 revealed frequently appalling conditions.[10] In the workplace, where the major strikes of 1947–8 had left bitter disappointment, a tighter control by the employers added to the sense of deterioration and uncertainty surrounding employment. One worker in two wanted professional promotion, only to run up against the hierarchies, while three unqualified workers in four, unhappy or frustrated, would have preferred to change occupation completely. In the great majority of cases the lack of opportunities in the firm or sector made this impossible, while conflict was always latent with wife and family, looking to a low but at least stable income in order to consume more, equip the home or buy a car. And the virtual absence of unemployment did not resolve the problem of jobs: two out of three workers questioned had changed job between four and eleven times in their working lives; when a promotion had been refused or the displeasure of a superior incurred, or when a feeling of humiliation or helplessness or a quarrel had led to a sudden departure. Similarly, although varying with the strength and activity of the unions in the factory, the poorly qualified workers all pointed to the gulf separating them from their trade union representatives and delegates. The militants, with their routine of meetings and threats to employment, often had a difficult time, especially if not strongly supported by their wives. Many had become deeply disenchanted with the Comités d'entreprise, considering them to be little more than social alibis.[11] Indeed, with their economic and consultative powers slowly eroded, these were gradually reduced to organizing a range of useful *oeuvres sociales*: providing Christmas trees and holiday camps for the children in large firms, running small co-operatives, libraries, and mutual aid funds. In short, work was still the basic point of reference which marked, and no doubt ruined, daily life.

The other pole of existence remained of course that of the home, family, and leisure, to which on average no more than three hours a day could be devoted. In many young households, the wife also went to work, even more sensitive to the noise, rhythms, and rivalries of the factory, or badly exploited if she worked at home. And if she kept her job when children arrived, the extra housework was a constant source of worry and could easily result in a working week of over eighty hours; the upkeep of the home became an intolerable burden, frequently leading to the abandon of work outside if a part-time job was not available. The pace of work was more relentless for women than for men, broken only by the occasional coffee or chat. Children under school age condemned their parents to a social life based on the home, and often grew up under far from ideal conditions, lacking privacy, exposed to tensions, and subjected to a crude system of rewards and punishments. Many couples strove to maintain hospitality and good humour, but poor housing conditions inevitably militated against even the best intentions. Housed 'normally', a labourer's family in the Paris region disposed of only seven square metres per person; wretched lodging houses, run-down housing, and, worse still, the *bidonvilles* for immigrants, were the typical experience of many working-class families before 1954. In 1956, 36 per cent of housing occupied by workers was overcrowded, compared with 24 per cent for employees and 16 per cent for lower salaried staff. True, the situation did begin to improve later, with the policy over the Grands Ensembles and contributions from firms; but finding decent housing at reasonable rents – home purchase was out of the question for the vast majority – remained the fundamental preoccupation. In the urban centres the working-class quarters were still solidly segregated; and in most cases the only alternative was to move to the new suburbs, thus increasing the time spent travelling to work, and aggravating, in spite of the efforts by local authorities, isolation from adequate educational and collective services. As in the past, the segregation of the workers was strong, and only the most privileged fringes could hope to break it down.

Against this background it is not hard to understand the strength of desires for leisure and distraction – the car already summed up aspirations to Sunday outings and the development of social relations. And not least since holidays were still rare: 90 per cent of workers received a paid holiday in 1958, yet only 30 per cent actually left their homes during it. One can appreciate also how the often meagre home could be the repository of class habits as well as a mirror of changing tastes in consumption. True, its contents were progressively standardized by mass production: utensils, machines, furnishings, and decoration distinguished the homes of workers less than in the past. Yet traditional everyday diet, even if partially abandoned on Sundays and special occasions, had evolved less. Although the working-class family tended to devote less of its income to food than other social groups, at least until 1955, its preferences were well established. Pride of place went to red meat, the indispensable source of strength in the workplace; dried vegetables were valued for their staying powers; relatively little fruit and green vegetables, but plenty of salads, sugar, and wine, all believed to fortify. In short, diet was dictated by the imperatives of work, and their satisfaction was a time-honoured source of pride. Likewise, exposed to the invasion of mass culture, a number of groups marked by long-standing cultural particularisms managed to conserve some original forms of leisure, identified with the status of the manual worker but providing considerable social compensations. The regions of the North, East, and Centre were the heartlands of historic working-class customs. Brass bands, *cercles*, pigeon fancying clubs, sports clubs, a multitude of associations in decline, control of which was slipping into the hands of teachers and the middle classes, were evidence, however erratic, of the resilience of a specifically working-class culture of leisure.[12] Even at the centre of their private lives, then, the workers are seen to have been in transition in the 1950s. Their group was becoming more diversified under the impact of changes in the nature of industrial work and the relative prosperity which brought internal divisions and a greater integration into society as a whole. At the same time, however, the mechanisms of economic and socio-cultural exclusion still operated to isolate it behind redoubtable barriers. Undeniably better off, but poorly integrated, the workers could not benefit fully from the fruits of the growth.

## The expansion of the middle classes

Mobility and progress were generally more successfully combined in the experience of the amorphous middle classes. The evolution of the economy and the new organization of society favoured their expansion: the multiplication of services, the extension of bureaucracy throughout production, the rise of information, welfare services, administration, technology, and the advance of wage-earners. This widespread extension of tertiary activities had major repercussions on this fluid section of the social hierarchy. Traditionally, of course, the middle classes constituted a far from homogeneous group, mixing wage-earners with the self-employed, productive and service sectors, manual and intellectual work. What they did have in common – security, qualifications defining skills and competence, opportunities to exercise personal choice and competence – was too general to bestow a real unity: indeed, the diversity of their material interests faced with the vagaries of production, inflation, and policy was the obvious lesson to be drawn from the gradual collapse of the 'Comité national de liason et d'action des classes moyennes' set up in 1947 to resist the imposition of a uniform system of social security. The 'petite' and 'moyenne' bourgeoisie, so problematic for Marxist social analysts,[13] defied neat classification more vigorously than ever in the 1950s. Yet its expansion gave it an important place in social change; its doubts and difficulties following the euphoria of the aftermath of the war had immediate political repercussions, visible in the public sector or in the Poujadist movement; the State continued to acknowledge its autonomy and particularity, advancing gingerly outside the public sector. Although less well known than the workers and peasants, the middle classes in fact reflect more clearly than other groups the dynamism of the

French experience of these years. But their ranks included winners and losers. Of the four main social groups which made up the middle classes – the artisans and small industrial and commercial businessmen, the bulk of the employees, the liberal professions, and the *cadres* – only the last two were unequivocally favoured by the expansion, as registered in their income and consumption. For the others, the adaptation was confused and even difficult.

Of the 2.3 million businessmen of industry and commerce covered by the INSEE definition in 1954, from which have to be deducted the major industrial and commercial figures who belong in a superior social category, the notion of middle class can only be applied usefully to approximately 1 450 000 small- and medium-sized tradesmen and 750 000 self-employed artisans and producers. They accounted in all for 11.5 per cent of the active population. After 1950, this group was buffeted by the crisis whose political expression was Poujadism. Small shops and workshops faced sharper competition from the chain stores, production of many formerly artisan products was industrialized, the general trend was to concentration, the period of shortages ended, and inflation slowed down. By 1962, this category had 300 000 fewer members, the losses divided equally between small re-tailers and artisans. With the ending of controls, the abundance of goods, and the new tastes among consumers, these sellers were thrown into a generalized movement of capitalistic competition for which the easy sales of the years of controls and shortages had not prepared them. They were loud in their complaints and protests; but were not necessarily all victims, dragged along in spite of themselves in the expansionist choices after 1953–4, adapting with varying degrees of effort and success. More than the superior classes or the workers, this troubled group, 38 per cent of whose members questioned in 1964 had succeeded their fathers in the business, feared being swept away by economic change. These anxieties showed up in an accentu-ation of efforts to favour the social mobility of their children, vigorously propelled towards higher education, the liberal professions, or the ranks of the *cadres*. But such efforts could not compensate for the descent into the proletariat which already touched nearly four in ten of them in 1959, destined to become workers or employees. This traditional but now unstable group was thus deeply involved in the risks and opportunities which accompanied the nation's progress, its solidarity increasing the chances of both success and failure. It became a turbulent zone of the social landscape, one characterized by strenuous self-defence, as well as by more discreet but no less strenuous efforts to acquire social mobility.

The position was reversed but equally fluid for employees, for the most part shop and office workers.[14] Their numbers were growing rapidly – 2 million wage-earners in 1954, 2.4 million in 1962; or from 10.7 to 12.4 per cent of the active population. By numerical importance they now became the third occupational group behind the peasants and workers, and ousted the small businessmen as the largest single element of the middle classes. In the past, restricted numbers had allowed them the luxury of social emulation: shop workers dreamt of opening their own shop, commercial travellers and representatives aspired to become managers. But employees in the commercial sector now experienced the same mutations as their employers, and were heavily outnumbered by office workers in firms and the administration. The evolution in the nature of work and the implications for social mobility this change testified to did not go unrecognized at the time, and awareness was deepened by a number of sociological studies.[15] The range of office work in companies was enormous. The place of the typist in the middle classes may be questioned, but the trained punch-card operator, the accounting clerk, the computer operator, the statistician and draughtsman all clearly belonged, by attitudes and status as much as by income. Parallel developments were occurring in the public sector with the extension of the Welfare State and the work of local authorities: the Social Security system, town planning, and the nationalized industries all engendered a similar proliferation of jobs calling for literacy, numeracy, and clerical skills. Of course, many of these jobs consisted merely of carrying out orders; the use of new techniques did not always bring competence, while the strictly hierarchical definition of jobs and the structure of office life posed serious obstacles to internal promotion. And with over half the jobs in these areas going to women, wages tended to be low and opportunities for promotion to management were limited to men. This high proportion of women could be taken as both a sign and consequence of a loss of professional prestige; and indeed, as far as incomes were concerned, many employees had lost part of their traditional edge over the qualified workers.[16] Yet if this appears to raise doubts over their exact place in the social hierarchy, there was certainly no shortage of factors pushing them to adopt the behaviour and share the status of the middle classes. Everything in fact tended to distance them from the workers: levels of education and cultural capital, leisure and holidays, their homes, well equipped with consumer durables, clothing, and cars, and 50 per cent less crowded. Relatively comfortable in their work, however monotonous, ambitious for their careers, with secure monthly salaries and less exposure to unemployment, and well equipped to integrate into the education system and dominant culture, the employees were at once demarcated from the workers and eager to identify with their social superiors: the characteristics, in fact, of an intermediate social category. The world of the employees acted as an efficient social sieve, with a greater degree of social mobility than any other socio-professional group, and formed the fertile lower stratum of the new middle classes.

The *cadres* – broadly speaking, trained and salaried staff, with administrative and decision-making functions – accounted in all for approximately

40 per cent of the diverse middle range categories. Their sheer mass allowed them to modify the internal equilibria, to display a greater self-confidence, and to impose themselves as the model for all the other categories. They carried considerable responsibilities, though without actually controlling the direction of the company or service. Their relative importance in firms was, however, proportional to the modernity of the sector: 3 per cent of the wage-earners in the mining industry, 5 per cent in textiles, compared with 15 per cent in engineering, and almost 20 per cent in electricity, petroleum, and the banks. They owed their position to the knowledge and technical expertise they brought to the running of productive and managerial units, one from which the 'technostructure' already taking shape in the United States was as yet absent. Everything favoured them in the race for promotion and social prestige: a detachment *vis-à-vis* established property and professional traditions (still so strong among the artisans and retailers, for example), an ostentatious consumption moulded by fashion, a sense of management influenced by the American model,[17] and, above all, the determination they showed in protecting the security of their income and collective guarantees of social risks. Their income was an obvious source of prestige: in 1957, 82 per cent of executives and 37 per cent of trained personnel had monthly incomes in excess of 85 000 francs, compared with 3 per cent among the employees and 2 per cent among the workers. It was the CGC (Confédération générale des cadres) set up in 1954, more than the weak managerial sections within the working-class trade unions, which had led the successful struggle against the State to obtain separate systems of Social Security and retirement pensions in 1947 and 1948 for the *cadres*. This was in contrast to other middle-class groups, notably the artisans and retailers, who defended their interests feebly and remained outside the system of minimal health insurance, or the employees, who joined other wage-earners in the general scheme. Armed with prestigious qualifications and a generous cultural capital, able to employ domestic help and perhaps a maid, with a car to avoid public transport, magazines and records, bridge and tennis, soon the television, a second home, ownership already of the main home, and the telephone: by their culture, leisure, and life style, *cadres* enjoyed an enviable isolation. They presented the rest of the middle classes with a seductive model of a successful new wage-earning bourgeoisie.

Although united by a strong sense of status and shared identity, the ranks of the *cadres* nonetheless embraced a number of different categories. The lower salaried staff were expanding rapidly: 1.1 million in 1954, 1.5 million in 1962. And they were concentrated in the newest areas of production: technicians, supervisors, and foremen accounted for the bulk of the increase, doubling their numbers from 280 000 to 560 000 over the same period. Less dramatic but still appreciable was the expansion among the administrative *cadres* (520 000 to 590 000), *instituteurs*, and the various para-medical and intellectual professions (from roughly 300 000 to 350 000), forming a disparate group, strictly salaried and hierarchical, often more attached to the company but receptive to the challenge of competition and training schemes. Lastly, the executives advanced at the same pace: 430 000 in 1954, 630 000 in 1962. These figures all bear witness to the determination of both the public and private sectors to equip themselves with adequate and competent administrative and managerial staff. They also point to the efforts being made to provide a good standard of higher education (from 77 000 to 120 000 teachers and members of the literary and scientific professions over the same period, and from 353 000 to 510 000 engineers and senior administrative officials). Even allowing for the crudeness and even incoherence of the classifications established by the INSEE, that the number of engineers, directors, planners, holders of the *agrégation* and researchers, ENA graduates, and senior civil servants grew proportionally four times faster than that of workers and members of the liberal professions is a clear indication of the scale of the management revolution in the private sector and the dynamism of public administration in France at this time. True, the fact that 55 per cent of these new decision-makers lived in the Paris region raises obvious questions over the prospects for decentralization; but that they alone received 10 per cent of the total of earned income leaves no doubt as to the willingness to reward them handsomely.

It would be misleading, however, to present the position of the *cadres* as an entirely untroubled one. They too could face the shifting priorities and sometimes brutal adaptations which accompanied modernization; and the defence of long-standing privileges and positions could still foster a sterile *malthusianisme*. Professional status was sometimes uncertain and vulner-able, which was the case for journalists. Re-established at the Liberation on the bases of the flimsy 1935 statute, the profession experienced considerable difficulty adjusting to changed conditions. Amateurism and plurality were rife, and the profession was poorly protected – almost 12 000 individuals claimed membership in 1954, whereas the total of salaried and freelance journalists was barely 8000 in 1958. The unity of the profession was pre-carious, 50 per cent of its members had been recruited since 1945; income and responsibilities varied greatly between Paris and the provinces, between the press and radio and television; standards of training were uneven (with the gulf growing between the old school of gifted amateurs and the young generation of professionals trained by the new Centre de formation des journalistes), and the unions were weak: in short, the jour-nalists were still faltering between the old and the new.[18] Nor were such groups immune from drops in social prestige, particularly in the civil service. The magistrature, for example, retained a high degree of social and geographical coherence – of its 5000 members in 1954, 80 per cent were from middle- or upper-class backgrounds, and more than half came from the Midi. The officer corps, on the other hand, was exposed to all the difficulties of the period. Recruitment was socially narrow (almost 60 per cent were sons of soldiers or civil servants) and of a more mediocre level; careers were blocked after the war, real incomes declined, family and social lives were disrupted by the hazards of postings, and of course there were the moral and psychological traumas resulting from the colonial wars and isolation in the nation.[19] Finally, the new needs of society were not always understood or answered. By 1956, for example, in addition to the existing 110000 engineers, a further 28000 were in fact required in order to staff and expand the various development, marketing, and production services. Yet the 4000 engineers who graduated each year from the Grandes Ecoles and the Conservatoire des arts et métiers were just sufficient to replace those retiring: at this rate more than thirty years would have been needed to meet the national requirements. The profession was ageing (nearly 60 per cent of engineers were over 45 and had received their training in the 1920s) and stagnant, with numbers barely superior to those in 1937. Of course, the shortage ensured handsome incomes for the engineers, but betrayed their profession's poor assumption of its new responsibilities and the sterile impact of the socially selective entrance examinations.[20]

Selection, corporatism, and privilege were frequently encountered in the world of the liberal and chartered professions. These last had roughly 125000 members in 1954, just about 135000 in 1962 – not many more than in the 1930s. The weight of the past combined with strong group loyalties to produce a vigorous defence of existing advantages. The unsatisfactory response of the medical profession to the social demand for improved health care has been examined in Chapter 17. Fifteen other professions had been organized along similar lines under Vichy. The Fourth Republic inherited and accepted this development, delegating considerable powers over organization, recruitment, and discipline to these almost feudal professional bodies; offering their members all the advantages of welfare protection while turning a blind eye to the extensive fiscal fraud which probably accounted for a quarter of incomes – and this while subjecting salaried *cadres* of a similar status to a much stricter control. This, then, was the comfortable and secure position of the 37000 members of the liberal professions in 1954 – lawyers, barristers, and accountants, their numbers stationary; legal and fiscal experts, the technical professions, surveyors, and architects, all just beginning their expansion. These privileged groups all enjoyed the benefits of growth, but did not always contribute to increase them.

The cross-section of the middle classes reveals then the clear impact of modernity, but also the weight of established privileges. Whether advantaged or not, the middle classes, though readier to identify with the new norms of a society of expansion and prosperity than any other group, in fact reproduced the old rules of the bourgeois mentality: those of barriers and levels of status. All of their members believed in the value of qualifications, for themselves or for their children, and were highly sensitive to status, existing advantages, and standing. They had, however, to adapt these old imperatives to the newer forms of social gratification. For with the exception of the liberal professions, the criterion of salary now sharply separated winners from losers: a victory of the collective urge to expansion. Their force as a group enabled them to stand firm against the encroachments of the State: a recognition of competence. Yet at the same time, it was their mentality and style of life which so successfully conquered the public service; employment there was stable (1.3 million in 1956, the same as in 1947) but better directed to the areas of training and education and the organization of production, solidly protected by the statute of 1946, and more dependent on qualifications even if material rewards had progressed little. Finally, they had adapted rapidly and enthusiastically to mass consumption, but without sacrificing a vital sense of social distinction. The supple and dynamic middle classes, with few values of their own but offering a powerful model for generalized tastes and aspirations, could, for the most part, envisage the future with confidence.

## Social mobility and the élites

This so far static description of the different socio-professional categories obviously needs to be animated: one would like to be able to measure the rhythm and extent of long-term movements of social mobility, and gauge the contribution to them of the economic expansion. Unfortunately, for the period before 1958 we dispose of only a few isolated cross-sections – essentially an INED survey of 3000 men in 1948, another by the INSEE on 6000 individuals in 1953 – whereas the growth of the 1960s led to some broader-based surveys, in 1964 and 1970, again by the INSEE.[21] The making of comparisons is complicated by the fact that these infrequent cross-sectional views do not all use the same classifications, and were not conducted with the same objectives. The results should be treated as no more than approximate indications of size, and pointers to the general direction of slow and extremely diversified movements. The most reliable figure in each case concerns the proportion of sons exercising the same profession as their father or belonging to the same category. The mobility illustrated is thus confined to very crude classifications, based uniquely on the criterion of occupation, and makes no allowance for all the nuances of respectability, socio-cultural factors, family relations, for the membership

Table 25: *Social mobility in 1953*

| Socio-professional category of sample | Profession of fathers (in percentages) | | | | | | | | |
|---|---|---|---|---|---|---|---|---|---|
| | industrialists and liberal professions | executives | middle managers | employees | artisans and small shopkeepers | workers | peasants | agricultural workers | service personnel |
| industrialists and liberal professions | 41 | 7 | 4 | 7 | 19 | 9 | 10 | 1 | 0 |
| executives | 11 | 22 | 10 | 17 | 15 | 11 | 6 | 1 | 4 |
| middle managers | 3 | 6 | 9 | 14 | 16 | 33 | 11 | 0 | 6 |
| employees | 3 | 4 | 6 | 13 | 17 | 33 | 13 | 4 | 5 |
| artisans and small shopkeepers | 2 | 1 | 2 | 3 | 49 | 20 | 15 | 6 | 1 |
| workers | 1 | 0 | 1 | 5 | 11 | 53 | 15 | 9 | 4 |
| peasants | 0 | 0 | 0 | 1 | 3 | 3 | 88 | 4 | 1 |
| agricultural workers | 1 | 0 | 0 | 0 | 6 | 13 | 32 | 45 | 2 |
| service personnel | 1 | 2 | 4 | 4 | 12 | 44 | 19 | 8 | 5 |

*Source:* P. Laroque, *Succès et faiblesses de l'effort social français*, Colin, 1961, p. 299.

of networks, all no doubt as important as incomes and occupations for an appreciation of the mobility of an individual or group. Until other research becomes available, the results are to be treated with an appropriate caution.

Table 25 gives the breakdown for 1953. The least permeable strata of the social landscape are easily identifiable. The farmers break all the records for social immobility, with more than 90 per cent of sons following their fathers into agriculture; after the farmers come the agricultural and industrial workers, the artisans and retailers, for whom the proportion is approximately 50 per cent. The *exode rural* and the crisis of distribution were still not bringing major upheaval to these traditionally closed categories, though the artisans and retailers were already recruiting 40 per cent of their members from the agricultural or working classes, no doubt owing to the proliferation of small retail outlets immediately after the Liberation. At the other extreme, the industrialists and liberal professions, with a rate of social reproduction of over 40 per cent, already constituted something of a closed group, drawing significant numbers only from the sons of artisans and retailers. At the centre of the breakdown, with the broadening in the range of figures, the importance of the tertiary sector in mobility is apparent: the service personnel were in a state of flux, recruited from artisans and retailers, and workers and farmers; three-quarters of lower salaried staff were recruited from the closest categories, such as employees, artisans, retailers, and workers, and in 90 per cent of cases were redistributed at the next generation; like them, employees had the role of a social sieve, slightly more effectively still, since in 90 per cent of cases they came from immediately adjacent categories; the executives were beginning to display the same hermetic characteristics as the liberal professions, though were still capable of recruiting from distant categories, agriculture excepted. Overall then, mobility was low, since on average for all the categories 42 per cent of sons remained in the same category as their father; furthermore, such mobility as did occur was weak in extent, limited essentially to shifts to neighbouring categories, superior or inferior, with the middle classes contributing most to the general movement.

These rules of social mobility were not rendered obsolete by economic expansion. The blockages in French society so often observed and criticized towards 1968 were already present in outline.[22] True, an overall comparison of the proportion of sons having the same occupation as their fathers in 1953, with the results from the inquiry of 1964 dealing with men aged 30–40 already working in 1959, and with those for 1970, does reveal an acceleration of mobility, linked to economic growth. From 42 per cent in 1953, the proportion of sons in the same occupation or category as their fathers fell to 34 per cent in 1964, and was the same in 1970. Mobility had increased by 8 per cent, and now affected two in three members of the active population. However, while the scope of mobility was thus enlarged, its magnitude actually decreased; that is to say, the greatest change was now confined to a few sectors of social transit, not disrupting the overall structure of society as much as might have been expected. Two reasons account for this blockage. The first relates to the persistent handicap of the working classes: 53 per cent of sons of workers would in turn become workers in 1953, 68 per cent in 1959–64, and 61 per cent in 1970, thus perpetuating the severe exclusion. The second reason lies in the increasing rigidity of the executives, who now followed the industrialists and liberal professions in a hereditary and almost dynamic consolidation of their social superiority: 41–42 per cent in 1953, 35 per cent in 1959–64 (with the renewal of the second wave of modernization), then up to 52 per cent in 1970. And the same phenomenon of consolidation was already visible in the ranks of the lower managerial and administrative staff, with 9, 32, and 30 per cent at the same dates: whereas nine in ten of them had come from other social groups in 1953, the figure had fallen to seven in ten by 1970. Indeed, although affecting greater numbers, the mobility was very likely to have no more than a slight impact on the lower reaches of the middle classes and the inferior categories. The employees continued to push their offspring without being able to retain them (with remarkably stable rates of 13, 15, and 13 per cent), while artisans and retailers (49, 24, and 29 per cent), agricultural workers (45, 24, and 14 per cent), and above all farmers losing half their capacity of social retention (88, 41, and 40 per cent), fuelled the current of mobility with large numbers of individuals who could now only hope for a limited social movement. The risk of stagnation was considerable; the new élites stabilized quickly; a vigorous movement from the lower classes was accommodated by the existing middle classes only at a minimum cost to themselves; their promotion was weak, whereas social demotion became more common from one end of the scale to the other. But of course, these remarks apply only to occupations. Perhaps there were compensations to be found in consumption and appearances? Social structures had certainly been shaken up by the growth, yet by 1958 the old hierarchical reflexes were ready to operate again. And it is plausible, after all, that the growth of income and greater well-being actually added to the exasperation of all those who fell foul of the redoubtable socio-professional blockages. Ten years later, the events of May 1968 would reveal the depth of the disappointment and frustration.

It comes as no surprise, then, that despite the rise of mass consumption and a greater prosperity for most of the population the rules for social success differed little from those of the past. The inquiry conducted under Alain Giraud from 1955 to 1958 on a sample of 3000 persons confirmed the existence of mechanisms of social promotion which had changed little since Balzac's day.[23] For if attitudes and behaviour had evolved, the acquisition of power and status still obeyed the well-established norms of the bourgeoisie. The strong candidate's profile was thus: a male member of an average-sized family, preferably one of the older children, aged over forty-five, who had grown up and matured in a large city in a dynamic region – above all in Paris – rather than in some sleepy *bourgade* of the provinces, if possible with a father who had raised himself to the category just below the one now aimed for, and better still for the upward mobility to have started with the grandparents, to be equipped intellectually and culturally to perform well in the education system, and, finally, to be ambitious. More than ever, then, success was the fruit of accumulated effort and inherited socio-cultural capital. With, however, one significant new factor: by 1958, the typical candidate was likely to be a graduate of the ENA. These practically unchanged rules of social success helped to attenuate still further the already hesitant mobility of the 1950s, and even accentuated some of the more stubborn imbalances of French society: Paris was favoured, the world of labour was disadvantaged, and, as we shall see, education did little to improve the prospects of the weakest categories.

Can one conclude then that social authority had, after all, remained in the same hands, and that the chances for redistributing it were actually diminishing? In other words, did the growth and reconstruction produce a transformation within the ruling classes, was their supremacy now challenged, and were new élites emerging? The carnage of 1914–18 and the turmoil of the crisis of the 1930s had left the traditional bourgeois élites of power, knowledge, and advancement in a state of shocked collapse, inadequately renewed from the middle classes in disarray, numerically reduced and incapable of overcoming the absence of national consensus which led to the defeat of 1940. In their different ways, the 'non-conformistes des années 1930',[24] the men of Vichy, and those of the Resistance, had all aspired to replace them with new service élites working for the general good, and competent to lead a regenerated democracy and State. But as we know, the urgent problems of the aftermath of the war and the Gaullist imperative of the higher interest of the State in fact obliged the slender forces of the Resistance to collaborate with the traditional élites in the work of restoring the shattered nation.[25] The return to power of the Moderates and the Right, and the euphoria of the economic expansion cemented this disenchanted compromise. Is this to say that France had not changed her masters? In the absence of a serious general study of this problem one can only make a number of observations. Taken together, however, they point to plausible conclusions.

To begin with, there is no doubt that the political and moral criterion of membership of the Resistance was of lasting significance. This was clear for the political élites: 80 per cent of the parliamentarians elected in 1945–6, and two-thirds until 1958, had issued directly from the clandestine struggle. The change was thorough, felt at the topmost levels of government, and was part moreover of a long-term social evolution, with the Liberation accelerating the steady advance, under way since the start of the Third Republic, of the middle classes to the control of political power.[26] The isolation of the Communists after 1947 quickly stifled the zeal of the new working-class élites, the failure of Vichy's Corporation was a lasting setback to the ambitions of the agrarian élites, and the traditional bourgeoisie was disqualified with the Right until 1952. The way was thus clear for the '*couches nouvelles*' to consolidate their positions, solidly protected by the umbrella of the Resistance. The same label, a mark of civic merit and a sign of recognition, also favoured the advancement of careers in the State's services, notably in the army and the Grands Corps, but seems to have been less important for those of executives, owners of firms, and members of the liberal professions.[27] With the exception of the political and administrative classes, membership of the Resistance did not supplant high social origins and cultural capital as a passport for the élite. Similarly, the Liberation appeared for a time to have thrown up vigorous trade-unionist élites, participating on the commissions of the Plan and the Conseil économique, running the Social Security system and the Comités d'entreprise, contributing to victory in the battle for output; élites in agriculture, as we have seen; and similar developments in the worlds of communication and culture, with the rise of the press and radio, the prestige of science and the authority of intellectuals identified with progress. Yet it quickly became clear that their ambitions were limited to the renewal of personnel and organization rather than to major changes in powers of decision or structures, so strong still was the upward thrust of the middle classes. Most of all, however, because the work of reconstruction had in fact facilitated the re-emergence of the traditional élites, justified on the criterion of proven competence and effectiveness. The hopes of 1944 faded. New faces had indeed appeared, but the necessity of an élite of excellence and authority was no longer disputed.

Is this to say that there was a return to the supremacy of wealth, that a traditional bourgeoisie recaptured control under cover of the neo-capitalist development of the economy? The answer is not as clear-cut as it seems. The great bourgeoisie of industrial and financial capital did of course recover its positions: the Gillet, Michelin, Peugeot, and Wendel families adjusted to the changed conditions, dissimulating their authority behind the juridical anonymity of the limited company but holding onto the key posts in their empires. Likewise the owners of the great commercial banks, having escaped nationalization, reasserted their power and influence, in Europe or in Indo-China, as in the past. True, many heads of companies in the economically dynamic regions were aware that their responsibility now was to pursue modernization, oversee the prosperity, and exercise their authority in relative harmony with the '*partenaires sociaux*': the CNPF's contractual strategy marked their solid determination throughout the 1950s. But many others, often those lesser figures who had taken the plunge at the height of the reconstruction, retained the reflexes of power and wealth, ferociously defending their interests and privileges, not hesitating to manipulate the politicians. Marcel Boussac offers, in this respect, a perfect example of this timeless *patronat* now rejuvenated by the expansion (see note 14, chapter 16). These remarks all require, of course, statistical confirmation and local studies.

Nevertheless, the great bourgeois dynasties could no longer perpetuate their positions on the criteria which, the Left claimed, had placed the destiny of France in the hands of the '*200 familles*' and their scions. The State had enlarged its role, the socio-professional groups were better organized and more effective in their pressure, and the workforce aspired to representation and even control. And in fact, to the naked power of wealth and great names was joined a third and very different force, that of management. For companies now began to experience the revolution of directors and managing directors. The new men, half of whom held top engineering qualifications, were more mindful of investment than patrimony, interested in long-term productivity more than in assuring punctual dividend payments, assertive of their authority *vis-à-vis* the shareholders, readier to make contractual agreements with the workforce: the directors of large- and medium-sized firms were as much wage-earners as they were capitalists, as much managers as *patrons* in the old sense. Social authority was no better distributed than before, and its exercise could be as brutal as ever: in a period of expansion, however, a legitimacy founded on managerial and technical competence had a better chance of being accepted than had the tyrannies or paternalism of pure capital still observed in many companies. This new development, occurring against the background of the slow evolution of the 1950s, stirred up a furious competition among the candidates for power, from the impatient middle classes in general, and from the executives in particular. Accompanied already by a number of top civil servants, they provided almost all the new recruits to the ruling classes, more than the liberal professions whose relative stagnation has been seen, or the retailers and middle managers unable to climb so high in a single generation. In 1954, on the sample taken by Pierre Birnbaum, 59 per cent of the executives listed in *Who's Who* finished their careers at the level of director, managing director, or employer, and the proportion was still 51 per cent in 1964. These '*emplois de direction*' – in all, roughly 300 000 in 1954 – constituted authentic new economic élites. Among them were *polytechniciens*, financiers, a few academics (Georges Pompidou, for example, who in 1956 went from the Conseil d'État to a directorship with Rothschild), economists; all of whom now encroached upon positions usually acquired in the past by personal fortunes, the manipulation of capital, or marriage: the crowning victory of salaried knowledge.

Indeed, already distinguishable in outline were the developments which in the 1960s would bring these new managerial élites into close contact and co-operation with the most dynamic elements in the civil service. For the topmost echelons of the public administration had also attracted established and new élites: of the students of the ENA between 1945 and 1954, 60 per cent were sons of *cadres*, liberal professions, or high officials, 34 per cent of employees, artisans, or retailers, and 6 per cent of farmers or workers. From 1955 to 1962, however, these proportions underwent a significant modification, shifting to 67, 26, and 7 per cent respectively. In short then, not only were the most modest categories still excluded but, after a period of relative flexibility, even the access of the lower reaches of the middle classes was now severely limited. The result of this blockage at the highest level was the creation of an élite whose characteristics closely resembled those of its managerial counterpart in the private sector. Throughout the administration of the public sector, the graduates of the ENA were already bringing change to established methods and hierarchies. As yet, these *énarques* did not occupy the summit of the administration, but their conquest of the State had clearly begun: still without major political influence or even absolute authority in their own domain, they formed an unfinished élite. Was this already the age of the technocracy? Was André Siegfried correct to assert in 1956 that 'France is administered by an aristocracy of technical competence'?[28] The answer has to be no. At least until 1958 it is anachronistic to speak of a union of technocracy and power: the administration was far from totally subjected to the technocracy's imperatives and the politicians were not openly won over to its views. Having said this, 40 per cent of the *énarques* had worked at the Ministry of Finance, and others were present in strength at Labour and in the nationalized companies. Professional and personal links were developing between them and the worlds of commerce and industry. In future, many public projects were to have extensive ties with the private sector. Gradually then, a strong caste spirit, a concern with progress, managerial competence, and similar social backgrounds helped form the group whose commitment to a shared perception of the general interest would, in the 1960s, bring together top civil servants, leaders of the public sector, and managers of the private sector. The identification of outlook and approach was not complete under the Fourth Republic, but the personnel was in place and eager.

In many respects the members of this group personify the outcome of the ambitions and failures since 1944. The power élite was still in place. It had to a large extent been renewed, however, with competence replacing the possession of capital as a more efficient basis for recruitment. But established wealth had not surrendered its authority. Against the background of economic expansion, old and new elements of the ruling élite had settled for co-existence. That the administrators were already challenging the leaders pointed to a victory for the organization of groups rather than to a general progress of social mobility.

# 19

# Towards the 'polyculture'

Could renewal have occurred without a recognition by individuals and groups that cultural capital was also important, and as rich in potential as were productivity, incomes and statutes? Growth and relative abundance stimulated reflection about the nature of the established values currently responsible for mobilizing energies, as well as about the knowledge and beliefs that might provide new ones. For the expansion of goods, services and ambitions was inevitably matched by one of cultural needs. In this fertile tumult, profound questions were posed; over the transmission of public and private spiritual heritages, and over alternative ways of life and different sensibilities. With conflict and resistances, modern France became a 'polycultural' society.[1]

## The hunger for education

The change was felt first at the point where collective needs and the ambitions of individuals and families intersected: the education system.[2] It was of course only to be expected that the post-war demographic renewal would create strains here. The 800 000 children born on average each year after 1946, 250 000 more than in the difficult years before the war, would arrive at kindergarten and nursery school in 1949–50, at primary school in 1951–2, in the secondary schools in 1957–8, before reaching higher education around 1964. It would be a mistake to imagine that this foreseeable development took the nation unawares and that a negligent and impecunious administration simply ignored the inevitable. Yvon Delbos, Pierre-Olivier Lapie and, above all, André Marie, Ministers of Education between 1948 and 1954, were all aware of the facts; but, and their responsibility is all the greater, along with many of the politicians and the social and economic élites they failed to grasp in time that the new dynamism had an educational dimension, to see that modernization would stimulate demand for education. For the populations in fact anticipated on and added to the foreseeable additional burden the education system would have to bear: numbers in nursery schools were rising at a regular rate from 1945, that is,

411

completely independently of the demographic boom; likewise, the number of children entering the first year of *lycées*, *collèges* (secondary modern schools), and *cours complémentaires* (intermediate secondary schools) at the start of the 1956 school year had almost doubled since 1950, that is, before those born in 1946 were eleven. The brutal combination of a natural increase in numbers and a spontaneous growth in demand for both earlier and longer education crushed the French education system, overwhelmed by what in the early 1960s was commonly referred to as an 'explosion' or even 'revolution',[3] though these two terms were not widely used before 1958. Increased demand from demographic change then, but increased demand also as a result of social change: the resulting shortages and problems, though ultimately damaging, were at the time evidence of generalized ambitions and optimism.

The crisis of education was in reality several things at once: aspirations to a new learning of social roles, the sign of an evolution in mentalities, a reflection of the strength of the economic take-off and the premium now attached to the development of capacities. As such, it was a structural as well as circumstantial phenomenon. Having said this, the pressure which set it off came without any doubt from families. We have witnessed the extra care society now lavished on its young (see Chapter 17). Generally speaking, though with considerable variation from one social category to another, attitudes to children were becoming less authoritarian; the young were treated differently, their confidence and consent were more actively sought; the accent was increasingly on a fuller development of their gifts. Mothers were ready to accept the ideas of Dr Spock, and fathers to admit that their authority was perhaps no longer natural or absolute, that the young needed advice and encouragement, and that knowledge and social relations could contribute to success. The traditional division of roles continued to be respected. Yet the family was changing – more isolated from the workplace by the growth of wage labour, at least in the towns, more stable thanks to the prosperity, despite the housing problems, and more tightly organized around the model of the couple and two children: as a result it now sought a fuller development of its members and attached a greater importance to their education. A longer time spent at school was no longer seen as a burden but as a vital investment in the future. With the ambitions of the family thus better aligned with society's dominant values, the education system was now expected to discharge the parents of some of their educative responsibilities, while reflecting more closely the choices of the parents themselves.[4] This was a transitional period, when the contradiction between these wishes was not yet apparent: parents still chose the type of school and education they wanted for their children, but were already prepared to accept a socialization of the choices according to aptitude, to acknowledge the supposed profitability and wisdom of an

orientation beyond their control. The revolution of streaming and selection, the imposition of a hierarchy of merit by society – in reality uniquely
by the education profession – was occurring in the minds of parents well
before it received official expression in the Berthouin reforms of 1959. It is
worth noting also that while this blind confidence in the merits of advancement and education by the school no doubt comforted the old Republican
ideal of education as second only to bread among the needs of the people,
the sheer size of the new needs in fact made it harder to defend a public
monopoly of education; families were more interested in acquiring knowledge than a particular morality. This helps to explain the easing of the old
quarrel over the secular principle after the set-to in 1951: nearly half the
population were now favourable to the *école libre*, and the hostility of the
other half had softened; the contrived agitation of 1956 did not have a major
impact on public opinion as a whole.[5] With this relaxing of ideological
tensions and the desire to share the benefits offered by all the schools,
private ambitions in fact coincided with national needs. For the progress of
economic and scientific knowledge and longer and better studies had been
considerable assets for all the active population in the battles for output and
mobility.[6] With the extension of tertiary employment, and the greater call
for responsibility, communication and information in firms and administration as a result of the spread of technology, the modernized economy
required a wholesale improvement in the quality of human capital in order
to profit fully from new equipment and to favour a balance between
production and social progress. It was to the education system that the
population addressed the formidable challenge of social mobility.

And that challenge began with the youngest, now entering the education
system sooner and in greater numbers: the reflexes needed for subsequent
academic and social success had to be acquired early. The infant classes in
the primary schools in fact declined, responding poorly to the new demands
and not adapting their pedagogy to the special needs of the two to fives. On
the other hand, the nursery classes held in distinct and purpose-built
schools, systematically constructed in the new urban suburbs of the Grands
Ensembles, doubled their intake from 400 000 to 800 000 between 1945 and
1958. The secret of their success lay in honouring the new cult of the child
while gently but firmly imposing the rules for eventual social integration.
Their equipment was actually designed for very small children; they
adopted a more flexible approach in the classroom, introducing new and
livelier teaching methods, with singing, drawing and play, and were staffed
by enthusiastic mistresses, typically from more comfortable backgrounds
than their colleagues in the primary schools. At the same time of course,
they familiarized the children with the routine of the near future: uniforms
and satchels, timetables, compulsory siestas, reading and maths for the
most advanced. These '*jardins d'enfants*' – the very apt name was adopted by

the law after 1950 – made play educational, structured social relations, and inculcated the behaviour and norms of the adult world. Their success was complete. Although its methods were little copied by other levels of teaching, the nursery school had won a secure place for itself: and without particular efforts by the State, for it was to the action of families and municipalities that it most owed its development. The demographic pressure cemented this triumph after 1949, and by 1958 the pre-school education of the under-sixes exceeded 40 per cent of each generation. Regional inequalities remained strong, however, and once again favoured the town-dwellers, for *ramassage scolaire* was not introduced on a large scale in rural areas until after 1959.

Conversely, primary education, public or private, had hardly changed. Since it was compulsory it merely registered the arrival of larger generations after 1953, with the total number of pupils, not counting the pre-school classes, rising from 4.3 million in 1945 to 5.7 million in 1959. It retained a useful task of orientation, taking the strain off other areas, since its *classes de fin d'études* were supposed to prepare their pupils – more than 900 000 in 1959 – for work or apprenticeship: the extension of schooling to age fourteen introduced by the Popular Front government had not been a complete success. But the primary sector lacked resources: new schools were rare, and the typical solution was simply to cram more pupils into existing or hastily built prefabricated classrooms. Moreover, there was little evidence of a readiness to rethink its role or methods. The primary classes of the *lycées* and *collèges* persisted until 1962, despite the fact that their suppression had been imposed by an ordinance of 1945, continuing thus to ensure the automatic passage of the children of the better-off into the *lycées*. Coeducation made little progress, pedagogy was stagnant, and the followers of Freinet were without influence; the old syllabuses, very demanding and considerably ahead of those in other European countries, were hardly modified, teaching hours retained their almost military strictness, and physical education was still neglected. Indeed, primary education gradually became an area where failures accumulated; repeated years were more common, with only roughly half the children able to keep up with the required rhythm. That the primary school teachers resisted so strenuously and successfully the ministerial instruction of December 1956 suppressing homework is an indication of their disarray and the extent of the impasse. The problems were not helped by the fact that the body of *instituteurs* had lost much of its former coherence. It was marked by a strong professional mobility: numbers grew in line with those of pupils, becoming younger and with a higher proportion of women, with the pressure from families leading to more appointments at both extremes of the chain, in the nursery classes and in the *cours complémentaires*, and a large contingent of 140 000 hastily trained *auxiliaires* or assistants now rubbed shoulders with established and highly qualified teachers. The primary school's teachers, the once proud 'hussards noirs de la République', were slowly losing part of their social prestige, particularly in the towns, and had a less certain grip on the effects of their teaching. Locally they could often still play a valuable role as mediators, but at the national level they became locked into narrow group demands and complaints. They incarnated the school of Jules Ferry, one which, though still strong, was less sure of itself as it faced the new problems.[7]

The real surprise came from the massive expansion of secondary education, where numbers in the two cycles almost doubled from 740 000 to 1 350 000 between 1948 and 1958. The larger post-1946 generations arrived in its first cycle as an unprecedented tidal wave from 1957 to 1961. And not until 1959–60 did the reformed *cours complémentaires* ease the burden on the *lycées* and *collèges* by taking the bulk of the newcomers. A demand mounting steadily since 1945 now became acute: that of giving the greatest number of young people the opportunity to follow a common course of study until sixteen, thus training a large and qualified workforce. Between 1945 and 1958 the proportion of the twelve to fifteen age group receiving education soared from 20 to 45 per cent of each generation. Never before had the education system taken such a shock at a particular point of its structure. Unfortunately, it proved incapable of steering this upsurge towards the real needs of the nation. The apprenticeship centres and technical schools were still neglected, considered as second-rate establishments for working-class children: technical training doubled its intake, but was not the object of the kind of expansionist policy which would have enabled it to train a higher proportion of technicians and blue-collar workers. As a result, it was the first cycle of general secondary education which had to bear the burden of the numbers, completely without preparation. The Vichy régime, albeit with the intention of reinforcing the classic humanities, was in fact responsible for the first breach here. In August 1941, under Carcopino, the old *écoles primaires supérieures* were transformed into *collèges modernes* and brought into the secondary system where their pupils were allowed to prepare for the *baccalauréat*: between 1936 and 1946, the proportion of sons of artisans, farmers, or workers in this enlarged secondary sector rose from 8 to 31 per cent. Consequently, with the return to free education at the Liberation, the expansion encountered no obstacles. Until 1951 this was divided fairly equally between the technical schools, the *cours complémentaires*, the *lycées* and the *collèges*. But from 1952, when the school population of these ages ought to have decreased, almost 300 000 pupils entered the first secondary cycle and the higher primary sector; in other words, a massive increase of 46 per cent compared with 1950. In the crisis after 1957, when the increased social demand was compounded with the effects of the demographic change, there began a stiff competition between the *instituteurs* of the primary sector and the *professeurs* of the secondary schools for the task of educating these young people. The primary school, where material needs were lighter and the training of teachers shorter, finally won in 1963, but by then the first cycle of secondary education had been seriously shaken up.

Essentially, of course, the problem was that of how a secondary system conceived for the élite was to cope with the irruption of the masses. The *cours complémentaires* managed to postpone the hour of reckoning by mechanically applying the methods and discipline of the primary schools. But in the *lycées* and *collèges* the contradictions between the ambition of the syllabuses and the recruitment of the pupils began to appear. Latin, vigorously defended, continued to operate its selection in the prestigious classical options, protected from being swamped by large numbers of pupils, directed instead to the modern options, with mathematics not yet established as the supreme criterion for selection; meanwhile, physical education, the arts disciplines, and modern languages were neglected. An archaic pedagogy based on the values of a humanist culture that pupils were assumed to acquire from their families failed to reform itself. Yet so strong was the demand for secondary education that the failings and weaknesses went largely unnoticed: the second cycle of secondary education, swollen in the modern sections with the pupils from the *cours complémentaires*, grew without any change to its structures from 120 000 to 270 000 between 1945 and 1958, with the increase accelerating after 1952–3. The number of *bacheliers* passed the 40 000 figure in 1956, but with the philosophy-based option still massively outnumbering the others, the mathematics-based option actually starting to contract, regardless of the nation's scientific and technical needs, while the new science-based options remained stable. The *professeurs*, still recruited by the *agrégation* and the *licence*, to which was added the CAPES examination in 1950, retained most of their very considerable prestige. But a massive recruitment (their numbers in *lycées* and *collèges* rose from 17 400 in 1945 to 22 000 in 1955, but to 30 000 by 1959), an insufficient pedagogical training, and the large numbers of *auxiliaires* were already producing a disturbing fall in standards. Overall, with the heavy increase in numbers of pupils, the *baccalauréat* overcharged, its methods static, and the competence of its personnel increasingly open to question, secondary education underwent a steady deterioration. That in 1957, when the pressure mounted still further, the old examination for *lycée* entrance had to be suppressed, and good students recruited from the Instituts de préparation à l'enseignement du second degré (IPES) to be hastily directed towards the *professorat* was clear evidence of the difficulties it was now experiencing.

The only area to escape for the moment was higher education. Even here, however, the effects of the imbalance in the numbers obtaining the *baccalauréat*, the passport to university entrance, were beginning to be felt. Thus in 1958 the faculties of letters accounted for almost 30 per cent of university students, whereas numbers in the faculties of science (33 per cent) were not growing fast enough; and the first-year foundation courses failed to resolve all the problems of orientation, technology was neglected, the training of medical personnel lagged behind, and the law faculties still had not come fully to terms with the ascendancy of economics. But the world of the universities seemed insulated from the turmoil affecting the rest of the education system: student numbers progressed moderately (123 000 in 1946, 180 000 in 1958),[8] and the buoyant demand for teachers and *cadres* guaranteed them jobs at the end. In addition, the carefully controlled expansion of the preparatory classes and the Grandes Ecoles ensured a satisfactory reproduction of élites. With the qualifications they awarded still valued, the universities did not depart from their traditional certitudes. Such complacency was ill-adapted to the imperatives of modernization. The research effort, so strong after the Liberation, had slowed down. Apart from the success of the CEA in the domain of atomic energy, the latest technologies were in fact developing poorly; the CNRS stagnated and the faculties failed to expand their laboratories, reacting unfavourably to the creation in 1954 and 1958 of a shorter doctoral thesis to complete the third cycle of studies; and the recommendations from the technological ministries and from the Plan's experts were often misinterpreted. Improvement in this field, when it came at last, was a result of private initiatives and encouragement from government. The spectacular results obtained in the Grenoble region, where the relationship between university and industry had been particularly fruitful, served as the model. Against a background of warnings from the Plan over the shortages of engineers and researchers, a number of political figures close to *Mendésisme*, high officials, industrialists, and scientists, began to meet and exchange ideas, receiving encouragement from Mendès France and Henri Longchambon, the Secretary of State for Scientific Research. This movement in favour of a national policy over science, instituted as a pressure group in the Association d'études pour l'expansion de la recherche scientifique (AEERS), led in 1954 to the creation of the Conseil supérieur de la recherche scientifique et du progrès technique which worked on the guidelines of the Third Plan. It also lay behind the publication in 1956 of the pessimistic Landucci report which pinpointed the urgent need for investment in human capital to assure the future, and in the holding of two symposia, the first at Caen in November 1956, the other at Grenoble in October 1957, where the bases were laid for the policy of expansion that the Fifth Republic was to activate.[9] The financial problems of 1957–8 delayed action here, but public opinion had at least been alerted for the first time to the importance of this crucial area of national interest.

The entire education system was under pressure. An increasingly complex modern society with rising expectations looked to it for much: equality of opportunity and model success, the teaching of norms and behaviour, the full development of the young, and an assumption of new responsibilities. How could this incoherence be translated into policy? Could a new consensus be founded on a basically competitive imperative? There is absolutely no doubt that by leaving too great a responsibility for shaping the future with the teachers themselves, the Fourth Republic allowed this rich opportunity for change to be missed. Not, however, that it had been particularly niggardly with resources, even if the two Plans had given little priority to an examination of their vital future development. Between 1952 and 1958, the education bill grew from 7 to 10 per cent of total public expenditure, an increase which at least allowed the necessary building programme to proceed.[10] And the authorities had even grasped that the heart of the problem lay at the conclusion of primary education, at the entry to the first cycle of secondary education where demand was now so urgent. Yet despite this certainty they failed to impose the necessary structural reforms.

This refusal to confront the need for a drastic overhaul of the education system was not without antecedents.[11] Under Vichy, a social demand concentrated above all at the top end of the primary sector had instead been channelled into the unreformed secondary system. At the Liberation, René Capitant had appointed a commission headed by Paul Langevin, then by Henri Wallon, to examine the problem. But its report, known as the Langevin–Wallon plan, which became the basis for all subsequent reform proposals from the Left, was not presented until June 1947, by which time the Cold War and reconstruction had drawn attention and scarce resources elsewhere; with the exception of the teachers, no one paid great attention to its conclusions, which were, moreover, statistically uncertain and with an inadequate definition of the demand for education. The Langevin–Wallon plan in fact developed themes first put forward in the 1930s. There was to be a single school, with education compulsory between six and eighteen, and divided into three cycles. The first, from seven to eleven, would be the same for all pupils; the second, for the eleven to fifteens, was to be split between two general years and two years of options, taught by general and specialized teachers, all of them degree-holders; the third, for the fifteen to eighteens, split into three sections – practical, professional, and theoretical – would determine the final orientation of the pupils; finally, at the summit, the Grandes Ecoles were to be attached to the universities. The school itself was to be remodelled, with the introduction of a new pedagogy, a better training for teachers, shorter hours, and modernized syllabuses: in short, all the ambitions of Jean Zay's famous period as Minister of Education during the time of the Popular Front.[12] Not surprisingly, the governments of the Third Force, then of the Right, concerned above all to survive in power, were in little hurry to implement this project, made controversial thanks to the left-wing commitment of its advocates, though less revolutionary in reality than has been claimed since. André Marie, for example, did nothing to alter the structures of education during the whole of his four years as Minister of Education: nor, indeed, was he under any pressure to do so. The quarrel over the *école libre* in 1951, and its threatened resurgence in 1956, served to convince politicians, sensitive to pressure from teachers of all persuasions, that it was still impossible to dissociate the debate over the democratization of the school from the old clerical–anticlerical conflict. After 1956 the Ministry of Education became a fief of Radicals and Socialists, reduced to the role of an administrative service managing its vast personnel, practically an annex of the FEN, rather than a great ministry serving society.

Here too, 1955 brought a glimmer of hope. Well aware of the new needs, Mendès France and his Education Minister, Jean Berthoin, proposed a reform which focused the debate on the creation of a middle school. And the following year, under the Mollet government, René Billères adopted the main points of this proposal, with a two-year middle cycle in separate establishments and with teachers of varying levels: a serious attempt in fact to reconcile satisfaction of the demand for education with the need for an orientation of pupils. But the Billères project was rejected, and it was not until January 1959, in the first months of the Fifth Republic, that Berthoin managed finally to impose a reform which salvaged the principle of the middle school in the form of a two-year cycle of observation, exploiting for this end a strong public consensus which prevailed for a time over the views of the teachers.

For this was the crux of the problem. The Fourth Republic had proved incapable of resisting the pressure from a teaching profession quick to set itself up as the sole judge of the future of the school.[13] When the question of a common core syllabus was raised, it was natural that the competence of the teachers to implement it should also come under discussion. But after 1948, with the all-powerful Fédération de l'éducation nationale dominated by the SNI established as the privileged interlocutor of the authorities, the issue became hopelessly clouded. So much so that what should have been a truly national debate over the future of education was reduced to a quarrel between primary and secondary teachers acting through their respective pressure groups. The SNI aspired to control the common core, and insisted that the best students of the *écoles normales* be directed towards the *baccalauréat* and thence to the *cours complémentaires*. Opposing the primary school was the Syndicat national de l'enseignement secondaire (SNES), backed by the

Table 26: *Population in education (in thousands)*

|  | 1948–1949 | 1953–1954 | 1958–1959 |
|---|---|---|---|
| nursery schools | 962 | 1266 | 1335 |
| elementary and junior classes of primary schools | 3411 | 3819 | 4886 |
| senior and 'fin d'études' classes of primary schools | 881 | 763 | 864 |
| first cycle of secondary education | 583 | 674 | 1066 |
| second cycle of secondary education | 156 | 184 | 269 |
| apprenticeship centres | 166 | 257 | 330 |
| technical and professional training schools | 120 | 145 | 179 |
| preparatory classses for the 'Grandes Écoles' | 11 | 15 | 18 |
| students of the 'Grandes Écoles' | 33 | – | 40 |
| university students | 120 | – | 167 |
| education of the 12–15 age group (in percentage) | 24 | 32.8 | 44.3 |
| holders of the baccalauréat | 30 | 34 | 46 |
| holders of university degrees | 8 | 8.8 | 10.1 |
| State education personnel | – | 276 | 393 |
| of which: |  |  |  |
| primary teachers | 158 | 170 | 214 |
| secondary teachers | 18 | 21 | 29 |

*Source:* based on A. Prost, *Histoire générale de l'enseignement et de l'éducation en France*, Nouvelle Librairie de France, 1981, vol. 4, p. 23.

Société des agrégés and the Association des professeurs de lettres classiques, all determined to fight for the retention of Latin and the elimination of the *instituteurs* from the middle school. On the one side then, the teachers of the *lycées* and *collèges*, self-appointed defenders of humanist culture, eager to force even more pupils into its mould; on the other, the teachers and methods of the primary school, claiming for themselves the exclusive right to educate the children of the people. This sterile quarrel between old and new, with its narrowly corporatist aspects and obvious political repercussions (the SFIO, where the teachers were so numerous, was, predictably, split by the issue), caused France to miss a unique opportunity. The ideal would have been to ignore the self-interested claims of the teachers, shaking them from their intellectual complacency, to have identified clearly the needs of society and proceeded to reform firmly while the school still enjoyed popular confidence. As it was, of course, the régime no longer possessed the political will necessary to impose such a solution.

The extent of the distortions and blockages, like the repeated procrastinations, comes therefore as no surprise. The access to education for the over-elevens was a vast collective waste. The economically backward regions south of the Loire pushed their children into secondary education (see Map 8), accepting the risk of losing them later when the dynamic

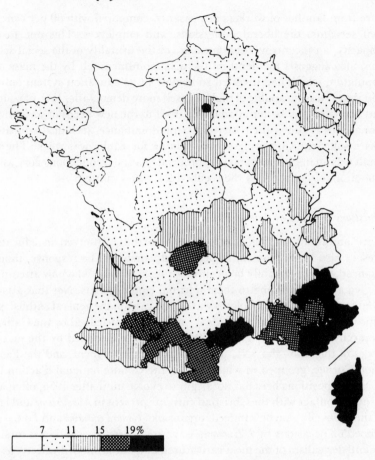

7    11    15    19%

8 Entry to the first cycle of secondary education in 1956

> Source: adapted from A. Prost, *Histoire générale de l'enseignement et de l'éducation en France*, Nouvelle Librairie de France, 1981, vol. 4, p. 243, from a map by Christiane Peyre.

regions of the North attracted the well qualified. The social hierarchy was faithfully reproduced: in 1958, the proportion of sons of workers decreased from the *cours complémentaires* (33 per cent) to the modern sections (19 per cent) and down to the classical sections (9 per cent), while the same proportions were inverted for the liberal professions and executives (2, 10, and 25 per cent respectively). For those who did make it over the barrier, failure before reaching the final year claimed four in five sons of workers, compared with one in ten for those of *cadres*. And as a result the democratization of higher education did not descend below the children of artisans, retailers, and employees. Only 6.5 per cent of university students in 1956 were from families of workers or peasants, compared with 60 per cent for civil servants, the liberal professions, and employers. This one to ten disparity, an incontrovertible measure of the brutality of the social selection, also suggests the depth of the disappointment felt by the mass of a population which had invested so heavily in its education system only to find that it was incapable of making itself more democratic. Nor, of course, had it proved any better at adapting itself to the new needs of society: the humanities retained their sacrosanct predominance, technical education was insufficient, and professional training for adults was weak. The net result was an inadequate and inappropriate national education effort, and a school unable to serve as the seedbed for a new culture.

*Christians in search of their century*

Were ambitions and blockages similar to those observed in education present also in the domain of belief and worship? The response, though nuanced, would certainly be positive for most of those who now attempted to give a fuller meaning to their spiritual commitments. Not that attachment to the familiar shibboleths was swept away in the general enthusiasm. This was clear for the secular ideal – at last acknowledged by the Catholic hierarchy in 1945 and again in 1958 – ardently defended by the massed forces of the FEN, the SNI, the Ligue de l'enseignement, and the Fédération Cornec, grouped in what became the Comité national d'action laïc (CNAL): positions here did not begin to evolve until after 1956, often as a result of contact with the Christian currents present in *Mendésisme* and later in the 'nouvelle gauche'. Indeed, organs like *Canard enchaîné* and *La Calotte*, echoed on occasions by *L'Humanité* or *L'Ecole libératrice*, continued to distil an anticlericalism of the most caricatured and old-fashioned variety, as for example during the affair of the Finaly children in 1953, or in the scandal over the alleged deathbed repentance of Herriot in 1957.[14] But to what extent had private attitudes to the divine been modified? In fact, belief, hostility, and doubt were as equally divided as before: questioned in 1950 over the addition of an allusion to God to the preamble to the Constitution, 37 per cent were in favour, 33 per cent disapproved, and 30 per cent were indifferent or without an opinion.[15] In a country where 92 per cent of the population had been baptized, a lethargic indecision seemed to be establishing itself as the norm.

What was in fact occurring was an easing of the old religious quarrels and a gradual secularization of problems: the imperatives of modernization obliged all the spiritual communities to modify or update their positions. This explains why minorities traditionally cemented by persecution now either lost part of their former coherence or turned in upon themselves. This was clearly the case for the Jewish community, tragically reduced to less than 1 per cent of the population, and where only a small proportion practised the religion. In the aftermath of the Holocaust, the traditional commitment of Jews to the struggles for liberty and justice was much less in evidence. The obsessive memory of genocide and the conviction that it had not been just a ghastly accident of History seemed to contradict the wisdom of the older humanist positions. Henceforth, the priority was that of self-assertion as Jews and the formulation of a specifically Jewish political stance – something complicated in the French context by the victory of Zionism and the creation of Israel. Among intellectuals a common response was to deny these developments and retreat into Marxism or cling to the positions advanced by Sartre in his *Réflexions sur la question juive* of 1946. But the Jewish religious community felt the need for vigilance and the creation of a united front: in 1945, a collective organization, the Conseil réprésentatif des Israélites de France (CRIF), was set up, and the rabbinate showed a greater readiness to take up a position on moral and political issues. The only new contributions to this debate came from *Mendésisme* and the campaign against torture in Algeria, before the posing of new problems with the influx of French Jews from North Africa in 1962.

Diametrically opposed but with similar results, the evolution of the Protestants also reduced their capacity for initiatives and pressure, which had been so valuable in forming the national consensus under the Third Republic. The faithful numbered roughly 800 000, 60 per cent of them members of the Reformed Church, accounting for 1.5 per cent of the population; three-quarters were from the bourgeoisie or middle classes, implanted, notably in the towns, in the East, the Rhône valley, Languedoc, the Charente and Vendée in the West, and in the Paris region. The Fédération Protestant de France did not succeed in reducing the religious particularisms, notably among the Lutherans of Alsace, but its authority was growing, and Protestant pastors were typically ready to make concessions to lay opinion. In short, alignment on the general model, a combination of organization and initiative. The political evolution of the community confirms this definitive reinsertion of Protestants into society as a whole. In the elections of 1951, and even more so in 1956, Protestants, with the exception of those in the Cévennes, abandoned the left-wing electoral preference which had so strongly characterized them in the past: their votes were now scattered over the whole of the political spectrum. A solid following for Poujadism in the Gard, a strong Gaullist vote everywhere, and a more critical support for the Front républicain all testified to the breakdown of their original political identity. True, the Protestant élite still displayed solidarity at the level of the administration or in the world of business; and the weekly *Réforme* did not hesitate to invoke a specifically Protestant experience to justify the position it took at the height of the battle of Algiers. But the general tendency was clearly towards participation in the broader consensus and to the abandonment of the traditional positions: that the role of the Protestant *Le Temps* had passed to the more obviously Catholic *Le Monde* is significant in this respect. This rallying should not, however, be dissociated on the religious level from the progress of the ecumenical movement, still diffuse, conflictual, and limited mainly to theological circles, but which experienced a promising development in the early 1950s.[16]

So what, then, of French Catholicism? The 1930s had been a particularly fertile period for the Catholic Church in France, bringing the definitive reconciliation with the Republic, the removal of the political stumbling-block of the Action française, a conviction that the general crisis, by exciting a revival of Christian values, would broaden its appeal, the realization, thanks to the work of the JOC (Jeunesse ouvrière chrétienne), of the rich potential of the Action catholique movement, and, with *Quadragesimo Anno*, an updating of the Church's social doctrine. Signs in fact of a Catholic renewal, one which drew fresh militants for the struggle on behalf of a common good now held to be inseparable from the evangelization of the masses.[17] These hopes for a more modern and democratic Church, one attuned to the real problems of the age, all found a rich field for experiment in the Second World War. In spite of the hierarchy's compromise with Vichy, the revival of religious zeal and practice, the importance of Christians in the Resistance, even the terrible logic of the new paganisms, cemented the conviction that the Catholics could no longer remain isolated within French society and that they had a positive contribution to make to the new era. The decisive changes were practically complete by 1945.[18]

It was then a Catholic Church with a resolute sense of mission which entered the post-Liberation period. The positions consolidated during the war were maintained. In the parishes there were processions, sermons, pilgrimages to Lourdes or to Rome for Holy Year in 1952, and fêtes, to perpetuate the forms of a popular religion, one already suspect in the eyes of many younger members of the clergy, along of course with the inevitable ceremonies of baptism, first communion, marriage, and burial. The youth fellowships and holiday camps, though showing signs of stagnation, were kept going by energetic chaplains and young enthusiasts. Charitable works and the youth movements maintained their momentum, and the *école libre* was the object of constant attention. In their different areas, the success of the Secours catholique founded in 1946 and the campaign of Abbé Pierre in 1954 showed the extent of charitable capacities, while their Boy Scout movement, which grouped more than 400 000 youths, demonstrated the effectiveness of new forms of mass organization. Modern means of communication were employed with considerable success: thriving publishing activities, a Catholic press headed by the major newspaper *La Croix*, a variety of quality publications from religious orders and Christian movements, plus a readiness to use cinema, radio, television, and records. Yet whatever the signs of vitality, the Church had no grounds for complacency. There were serious financial problems, with the level of collections failing to keep pace with inflation. After a catching-up at the Liberation and a few conversions in the prison camps, vocations were at a virtual standstill, and seminaries were already having to be regrouped in the large towns. The priests were ageing and numbers were stagnant: 48 000 in 1946, 50 200 ten years later – but the slight increase came from among members of orders, and in fact ordinations no longer compensated for deaths. Only the regions of the West and the southern Massif Central remained as strong sources of candidates for the priesthood, but it was still not possible to distribute their small surplus over the rest of the parishes. The Church faced the prospect of soon not being able to meet the needs of the rural regions, while its presence in the towns risked becoming patchy in the extreme, despite efforts, like those in the Paris region by the 'Chantiers du cardinal' launched in 1931, to construct new places of worship.

But these problems paled into insignificance compared with the crisis of the Christian faith itself. Religious sociology, its methodology perfected by Gabriel Le Bras, had done much to create an awareness of the problem in the 1940s, producing statistics and maps which left no doubt as to the scale of the disaster, and helping to stimulate reflection and a desire for action. In 1943, two chaplains of the JOC, the abbés Godin and Daniel, exposed the pagan condition of the French proletariat in their *La France, pays de mission*. And in 1945, a *jaciste*, Canon Boulard, in his *Problèmes missionnaires de la France rurale*, then with the map of rural religious practice (see Map 9) published by the *Cahiers du clergé rural* in November 1947, showed how the regions of apparently strong practice were in reality surrounded by an ocean of indifference, purely customary practice, or, above all in the Paris region and the Limousin, the complete absence of religious life. Boulard's *Essor ou déclin du clergé français* published in 1950 added to the dismal picture by drawing attention to the growing cost of the Church's action and the urgent need for a major effort over recruitment to the priesthood. Finally, in January 1956, in the new *Archives de sociologie des religions* run by this group of Christian sociologists, Jacques Petit revealed the magnitude of the problems posed for the Church by urban growth.[19]

In all it was a remarkable exercise in painful self-examination, and one whose findings were translated into determined action. For the exposure of the disastrous state of Catholicism produced a major effort to redress the balance; it was an effort which attached more importance to practice than to belief, one too obsessed, perhaps, by the need to increase the Church's presence among the working-class masses, yet one whose principles and methods formed much of the basis for a renewal of the Church along the

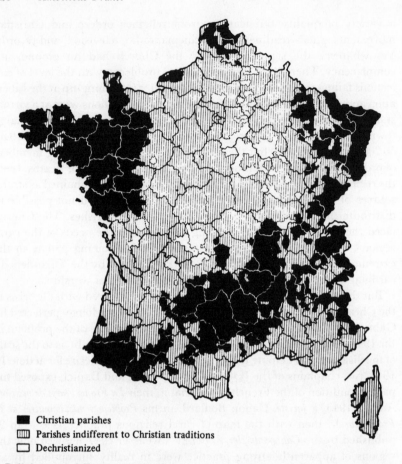

Christian parishes
Parishes indifferent to Christian traditions
Dechristianized

9 Religious rural France, 1947–50

*Source:* adapted from F. Boulard, *Essor ou déclin du clergé français?*, Editions du Cerf, 1950, p. 169.

lines recognized by the Vatican Council II in 1962. This began with attempts to revive religious life within the framework of the parish. The imperatives of reconstruction and the apostolate galvanized a generation of energetic priests, some of whom were not afraid to modernize ecclesiastical art and architecture, even if the results did not always come up to the standard of the successes obtained at Ronchamp, Assy, or Vence. A similar modernizing zeal was brought to bear on the liturgy, the style of services, and sermons. Following the example of a few pioneers – Fathers Michonneau and Rétif at Colombes, Father Conan at Saint-Séverin de Paris, and the team of Saint-Alban at Lyon – the accent shifted from the parish as the fold for the faithful to the parish as the centre and source of initiatives and activities; there were efforts to reach all the social groups in the community and to develop the work of Action catholique; less importance was attached to the traditional good works than to organizing meetings of neighbour-hoods and residents; a more flexible attitude was adopted over doctrine and practice, with encouragement for the laity, the suppression of collections, and the opening of dialogue. The results were uneven. In spite of a good co-ordination after 1951 by the Centre pastoral des missions de l'intérieur, the new approach met with a very mixed reception. Many conservative priests resisted, and the bigots were outraged; worse, the urban masses remained indifferent, while in the rural areas the most urgent needs could now be met only by recourse to the merging of parishes. In short, only the already convinced were encouraged to multiply their efforts.

This difficulty, that of mobilizing the Catholic community as a whole, became even more apparent when attempts were made to use a framework other than the parish to achieve radical change. Before the war, the various movements of the Action catholique, though aware of the imbalances and tensions their work could set up, had proved the effectiveness of their methods. Consequently, they persevered after 1945, with, however, the difference that they now encountered increasing difficulties in the domain of the workers. In fact, the Action catholique movements maintained their presence and role only in the areas where other organizational structures were lacking. This accounts for the very real success of the JAC (Jeunesse agricole chrétienne) after the war, which brought together more than 70 000 young people by 1950; it acted as a fertile seedbed for new élites in the agricultural trade unions, established itself as the only mass organization capable of articulating a coherent ideology of rural modernization, and was ready in practice to show considerable flexibility over many explicitly Christian positions. In 1957, when the Church hierarchy was already becoming worried over its activities, the JAC obtained what was indirectly its most resounding success, the creation of the CNJA. An equally promising development was experienced by the Mouvement familial rural, with its monthly *Clair foyer* magazine diffusing 250 000 copies in 1958. Among the workers, on the other hand, where the presence of well-estab-lished political parties and trade unions left little room for alternative organizations, the stagnation was alarming. True, the Mouvement populaire des familles, with 140 000 members in 1946, was extremely active over the food shortages and in support for the squatters; yet such action, whatever its intrinsic merits, offered no direct solution to the problem of the evangelization of the masses. Likewise, some *jocistes* were very deeply in-volved with militants of the Communist Party, many of its former leaders were now active in the CFTC, and the chaplains saw their pre-war prestige evaporate. In 1950, when the MPF significantly turned itself into the Mouvement de libération du peuple, the Church hierarchy launched a new

Action catholique ouvrière on strictly religious bases. Even the Scouts were troubled by the controversy when their magazine *La Route* attempted to give the movement a more overtly political dimension: and the war in Algeria increased the friction after 1957. In short, the Action catholique movement was in crisis, one whose stakes the problems of the JOC exposed clearly. In order to reach the working class, or indeed any other self-aware group, was it possible to avoid a fragmentation of energies through specialization, and could a predominance of the spiritual over the temporal be maintained? The dissolution of the Association catholique de la jeunesse française (ACJF) in 1956 highlighted the contradictions and weaknesses. Its leaders, often former activists of the JAC and JEC, were struggling for autonomy of the movements: they were brutally repudiated by the hierarchy, which proceeded to purge the organizations, imposing a return to the strictly spiritual aspects of their work.

The crisis was even more spectacular in the affair of the worker-priests. As early as 1941, a Dominican, Father Lœw, had taken a job as a docker in Marseille in order to acquire a personal understanding of the workers to be converted.[20] Cardinal Suhard, deeply impressed by a report on the problem by the abbés Godin and Daniel, authorized the creation of a group of special mission priests with the task of exploring the world of the proletariat from within: in January 1944 the Mission de Paris was set up.[21] By 1953 a hundred worker-priests were active in factories and on sites in Paris and the major provincial cities. Observers like Mauriac and Mounier were profoundly impressed by the informal community of new Christians from the working class they witnessed at Montreuil where Father Depierre was based. And a best-selling novel, Gilbert Cesbron's *Les saints vont en enfer*, focused massive public attention on the experiment in 1952. The worker-priests co-ordinated their activities, arguing openly that the proletariat's ignorance of religion could not be dissociated from the capitalist exploitation of which it was the victim; some joined and were militant in the CGT; in 1950 they had worked with the Mouvement de la Paix to obtain signatures for the Stockholm appeal; two of their number were arrested during the demonstrations against Ridgway in 1952. Not surprisingly, such action made them enemies within the Church – in Rome, Cardinal Ottaviani had for some time been compiling hostile reports. The storm broke in 1953, with a brutal condemnation from the Vatican of the worker-priest experiment. In France, where the integrist press, *Rivarol* and *Aspects de la France* were railing against the 'Stalinist' Christians, the Jesuits of Lyon, led by Father de Lubac, were forbidden to teach. And in January 1954 French bishops called on the worker-priests to cease all trade union and political activities, and forbade them to work more than three hours a day: only forty-odd complied. The effort to reach the working class in this form had failed.[22]

And not only did the Catholics seem powerless to go out to the dechristianized masses, but the divisions within their own ranks had rarely been so deep as they were in 1958. Indeed, it was as if there was no longer a basic Catholic consensus. Even Christian morality was not always the object of unanimity: that articulated by the films from the Centrale catholique du cinéma, or the rigidity of the arguments against birth control,[23] delighted some and angered others. The ardour of the Dominicans and Jesuits, the theological prowess of Fathers de Lubac, Congar, and Chenu, even the renewal of Bible studies and the emergence in the pages of the *Aneau d'Or* of a new conjugal spirituality – all infuriated the integrists while enthusing their opponents. The divisions were hardened by politics. At the Liberation, many of the younger generation of Christians had believed in the possibility of leading both an evangelical and political transformation of the established order, injecting a new morality into the civic debate, hopeful of transcending the Left–Right cleavage.[24] The electoral and ideological collapse of the MRP served to discourage many, and only *Mendésisme* and the struggle against the war in Algeria sustained the activism of the others until the debate was revived with the arrival of the new generation at the end of the 1950s. In parallel, however, the colonial wars and the Cold War had facilitated the resurgence of a hardline integrist current, violently anti-Marxist, admiring of the army, fanatical in its defence of the Christian West; a current that was sustained by the war in Algeria as much as by the condemnation of the worker-priests. And the Catholic hierarchy remained silent over this revival of the extreme Right, which occurred as it was reasserting its authority over the Action catholique movements. As a result, a part of Catholic energies were henceforth running against the stream. For like that of the Protestants, the traditional Catholic vote had, thanks to the MRP and *Mendésisme*, settled mainly at the centre and left of the political spectrum. This meant of course that the integrist reaction had little long-term future, but it was not enough at the time to silence the extremists.[25]

To what extent was this deep division the sign of an inevitable abdication of the Church faced with what Boulard had described as 'cette civilisation urbaine, fascinante et déchristianisante'? Was it evidence of an irreversible contraction of the place occupied by religious belief in French society? The answers to these questions lay in the future. For the moment, however, it is worth recalling the richness of such periods of transition and the value of the new men they help to bring to prominence. The effort to reach and convert the masses had failed: in this sense the Church remained shut in its ghetto. Yet from a majority Catholicism based on the weight of custom and the force of habit had sprung a minority Catholicism based on the conviction and dedication of the militants,[26] a Catholicism which, having shed many of its more narrowly clerical aspects, was better able to come to grips with modern society. The balance-sheet, an intermediate rather than final one, has to include the success of this minority. And it was with this minority that lay Catholicism's contribution to modernity. For men issued from the Scouts and the Action catholique, often influential in the ACJF, had been absorbed into the new national élites, bringing with them their concern for coherence and concrete problems, their organizational abilities and sense of teamwork. All were not yet in positions of authority, but all were confident of their moral qualification to assume such responsibilities. Three names indicate the quality and diversity of the contribution they were already making: François Bloch-Lainé at the Ministry of Finance and the Caisse des dépôts, Michel Debatisse at the CNJA, and Eugène Descamps at the CFTC.[27]

## The intellectuals and commitment

'Politics determine everything', affirmed Mounier in 1945. The same year Sartre observed that the intellectual 'embraces his epoch. He is its only chance: he is made for it; it is made for him.' Ambitiously, earnestly, sometimes self-importantly, a generation of intellectuals set itself the task proudly announced in the first number of *Les Temps modernes* in October 1945: to seek only a practical truth, to 'unmask in order to change'.[28] The cultural shock produced by the war was immense: art forms evolved rapidly and the established schools broke up. In future, it seemed, the artist would have to live in, with, and for his era, assuming fully his responsibilities before History.

For more than a decade, from the Liberation to Budapest, it is the *maître à penser*, the intellectual as mentor and message-bearer, who dominates the stage. From the autumn of 1945, in the excitement of recovered liberty, the artistic and intellectual turmoil of Saint-Germain-des-Prés captivated all who believed that the war had swept away the older beliefs. The major pre-war writers were eclipsed or turned to new themes: Malraux, for example, threw himself into Gaullist activism with the RPF and into meditation on art in *Les Voix du silence*. The Saint-Germain-des-Prés scene of jazz, American writing, animated discussions in bars and cafés, quickly fastened on and made famous by the press,[29] was the colourful setting for the emergence of a new philosophy: existentialism. At its head was Sartre, whose key philosophical work *L'Etre et le néant* had been published in 1943. At this level Sartre was a follower of Heidegger, in revolt against academic philosophy; but at another, through his drama, novels, and journalism, he was a *maître à penser* for an entire generation. His political commitments – including that in the short-lived Rassemblement démocratique révolutionnaire (RDR) he founded with Rousset in 1948 – were intended to be the outcome of a personal reflection which went far deeper than the superficial formulas picked up by the press. In the space of a few months the new doctrine, the Hegelian dialectic corrected by Marx, was popularized; a highly abstract justification of action established its legitimacy, seeming to offer solutions to problems of personal choice and responsibility. Thus apart from its intrinsic merits as a philosophy, accessible only to a small number, existentialism had the important role of providing a new language and assuring the necessary transition between the political commitments of the Resistance and those of the post-war period.

As such it quickly had to come to terms with institutionalized and partisan Marxism in the form of the Communist Party. The *engagé* or committed intellectual could scarcely ignore the PCF, now firmly installed for the first time at the heart of the debate over ideals, able to dispense letters patent in its capacity as the *parti des fusillés* and fount of wartime heroism. Personal reactions to the Party among intellectuals varied greatly – from the absolute loyalty of Aragon, Eluard, and Vailland, and the members of the literary group of *Les Lettres françaises*, to the fellow-travelling of Vercors and the conflicting sympathies of the group at *Esprit*, through to outright rejection by Raymond Aron and Mauriac. But whatever the range of personal positions, the power of the PCF to arbitrate was undeniable. Consequently, just as mastery of a new democratic culture in the service of all could no longer be dissociated from the Revolution, so its hopes and disappointments were intimately linked to the twists and turns of official Communist policy. Once again the experience of Sartre, and with him that of *Les Temps modernes*, provides the clearest illustration of this. Definitive rupture with the Party came with the success of *Les Mains sales* in 1948, Sartre having refused to consider as more than a 'querelle de famille' the hostility of Kanapa and Courtade that was mounting, in fact, since 1946. In a ferocious anti-Americanism produced by the Cold War and the Korean War, and brought to a climax by the execution of the Rosenbergs, Sartre became a loyal fellow-traveller, his indulgent attitude towards the Party paralleled by a conviction that dialogue was impossible with the anticommunists, the lackeys of the White House. The campaign in favour of Henry Martin in 1952 strengthened these links. In a long article on 'Les Communistes et la paix', Sartre argued that a position between the two blocs was untenable, that the PCF was indeed the true and necessary expression of the French working class, and that Marxism was the root of all culture. It was at this point that Etiemble, a neutralist, and Merleau-Ponty broke with the team of *Les Temps modernes*. The Krushchev report and events in Budapest imposed a painful reappraisal in 1956: in an important interview in *L'Express* of 9 November, Sartre denounced 'the total failure of socialism as a model imported from the USSR', and developed his hostility in the special number of *Les Temps modernes* of January 1957 devoted to Hungary with an article on 'Le fantôme de Staline'. Yet the bases of the debate were unchanged: the task for the future was to maintain a united front against the deviations of the 'nouvelle gauche' influenced by *Mendésisme*; the French Communists had of course to be destalinized, but the time had not yet come when they would be repudiated.[30]

The sacrifices necessary for cohabitation with the Soviet version of the praxis had reached caricatured proportions on a number of occasions: the Kravchenko affair and the Rousset case produced an enthusiastic mobilization of the French intelligentsia to deny the existence of Soviet prison camps and show solidarity with the French Stalinists.[31] Nevertheless, the right to alternative expression and different moralities had its champions. Merleau-Ponty, in *Sens et non-sens* of 1948 and in *Les Aventures de la dialectique* of 1955, while not renouncing any commitments, outlined the principles of a philosophy of contingency which challenged those of conscience and history. Claude Lefort, then the members of the 'Socialisme ou barbarie' group were vigorous in their denunciations of Stalinism; others, closer to a libertarian current – Louis Guilloux, Etiemble, and above all Albert Camus from *L'Homme révolté* of 1951 – refused to accept the dictatorship of History's laws, resisting ideologies in order to acquire a more probing and less self-assured vision of the world; Lacan, defying the official Communist ukase against Freud, tried through his writings to render the analytical process intelligible. A generation of non-committed writers was emerging, those of the irreverent Right or the young writers grouped at the *La Parisienne* review in 1953: their reaction of style and sensibility against the quest for meaning could be felt clearly in Nimier's *Le Hussard bleu* of 1950, or in Gracq's *Le Rivage des Syrtes* of 1951, as well as in the dialogues of death and eroticism of Bataille and Genet. And the members of the *nouveau roman* group based at Jérôme Lindon's Les Editions de Minuit were already making their flight from rhetoric and message to develop a different language – intimate, elliptical, disjointed, abandoning even the narrative form. This right to follow a different creative itinerary, one whose risks of introspection the public quickly sensed, was asserted in 1949 by Sarraute's *Portrait d'un inconnu*, and by Beckett's *Molloy* in 1951, before being triumphantly recognized with the Renaudot Prize for Michel Butor's *La Modification* in 1957. And Ionesco's *La Cantatrice chauve*, solidly installed at the La Huchette theatre from 1950, delighted in its proclamation of the metaphysical void and rejection of plot: the dramatic situation itself became a treacherous hazard rather than a setting for the combat of ideologies.

A parallel development was occurring in the visual arts. The established masters, dominated by Picasso, honoured in his lifetime by both the general public and the PCF, retained their importance, with Braque, Chagall, and Derain continuing on their personal itineraries, or Matisse developing in the work on the chapel at Vence or in the *Nu Bleu* series of 1952. The influence of Kandinsky, Mondrian, and Klee could operate unhindered, and at least until 1950 Paris continued to dominate the artistic world, before seeing the role pass finally to New York. But the new Ecole de Paris did not establish itself without a struggle. The social realism of Fougeron, Pignon, or Taslitzky, followed at a distance by the young 'misérabilistes' like Buffet and Lorjou, and strongly backed by Kanapa and Marcenac at *Les Lettres françaises*, looked for a time likely to impose itself as the new Soviet-style orthodoxy. Fougeron's 'Les Pays des Mines' exhibition of 1951 marked the apogee of this current. The furore in March 1953 provoked by the appearance in *Les Lettres françaises* of Picasso's portrait of Stalin, judged to be disrespectful to the memory of the Soviet leader by the PCF leadership, served as an eye-opener for some.[32] But in fact the debate over abstract versus figurative art lost much of its pertinence around 1950, for the group of young painters who during the Occupation had exhibited under the label of 'de la tradition française' to escape Nazi censorship of 'degenerate' art, had won recognition. Manessier, Bissière, Estève, Bazaine, and Le Moal were at the height of their powers, and had already opened the way for the geometrical abstraction of Vasarely, Poliakoff's compositions, and the turbulence of the 'abstraction lyrique' group, where Mathieu poured scorn on the self-satisfaction of the consumer society. Indeed, from now on all experimentation was permissible to throw off the mantle of message: informal art, signs, paint drips, new relationships with raw materials and objects, kinetics. From this exuberant cocktail of styles and – once the influence of the United States began to be felt – continents, came Michaux, Fautrier, Wols, and, above all, Nicholas de Staël and Dubuffet, in an artistic flowering which rendered meaningless the abstract or non-abstract argument.

This survival of free experimentation was of course reinforced by the gradual fading of the progressive hopes and ambitions of the immediate post-war period. In 1954, when Simone de Beauvoir's *Les Mandarins* presented a sombre balance sheet of the weaknesses of the Liberation and Cold War periods, the Algerian conflict was already imposing a painful and cruelly practical transition from an ethic sprung from conviction to one based on responsibility. The following year, in his *L'Opium des intellectuels*, Raymond Aron castigated intellectuals for their lack of contact with reality and their infatuation with History. The struggles of 1956 against torture in Algeria and for destalinization completed this evolution: as at the time of Dreyfus, intellectuals discovered that moral protest and the service of truth were the bases for the only worthwhile commitment. Not that the hegemony of the Marxist logic was ruined – some were still ready to believe that the Algerians would at last accomplish what the French proletariat had failed to do. But such comfortable positions became less tenable once Lacoste had attacked the self-satisfied and posturing intellectuals, and the nascent Third World movement had raised doubts over the validity of the familiar schemas of revolution. In short, culture became *désengagée* or non-committed. Intellectuals recovered at least part of their former prophetic role by finally deciding to examine reality, and to abandon the false lucidity and universality synonymous with Saint-Germain-des-Prés.[33] The change was opportune: for the traditional humanist culture, even when bolstered with existentialism, was reeling under the shock of social change, and the status of intellectuals had already been modified.

Taking shape and acquiring self-consciousness was a new social class of technocratic intellectuals with new responsibilities, technical intellectuals whose task was to open up fresh fields of knowledge and multiply their application. Experts were taking over from the literati, the distributors of culture started to overshadow its creators, and the 1954 census revealed more than a million individuals who by their work could reasonably be described as intellectuals.[34] The autonomy of scientific and technical knowledge was already apparent in industry and in offices; the extension of tertiary activities in the most advanced areas of the economy placed a premium on knowledge, thereby integrating the intellectuals into the middle classes and making them the vital accessories to economic growth and social mobility. There was a gradual decline in the vain self-criticism and defensive provincialism of general ideas which had sought to hold off new currents at a time when many observers were convinced of the inevitability of French stagnation.[35] This discovery of new horizons, a waking-up to the crucial role of research and Anglo-Saxon culture, of an appetite for exchange ready to concede that Paris was not the hub of the universe – all owed much to the astonishing development of the social sciences.[36] The universities and new research institutes had opened their doors to demography, economics, social psychology, and war studies before 1947; they trained a new breed of intellectual, one no longer dismissive of the exact and natural sciences, ready to explore new avenues of research, and to make contracts with enterprises in the private and public sectors. Sociology made particularly rapid advances into virtually every field of human activity, investigating the suburbs and rural areas, beliefs and consumption, work and mass communications, borrowing the methods and language of its American counterpart, and subjecting industry, academe, and the Plan to the scrutiny of its researchers. Lastly, from ethnology came the new interest for unknown and exotic cultures and civilizations: Lévi-Strauss's *Tristes Tropiques* of 1955 heralded the structuralist movement of the 1960s, and through anthropology, history rediscovered a concern for the local. These developments came as a further blow to the unwieldy intellectual constructions of the recent past, still handicapped by their inability to resolve the question of Stalinism. At the same time, they encouraged the making of individual and independent commitments over the war in Algeria. But perhaps most importantly, they led the intellectuals gently back to the tasks and positions that were really theirs, those of observing and explaining social change, assessing its impact by their own participation in it, exposing the ideologies which shored up their own material and cultural privileges, and, finally, to try, in an attitude of humility, to equip modern France with a new style of thought, one which would help all involved to master their own experience of the change in their society.

## Mass culture

Whatever its negative aspects, the commitment of the intellectuals could at least find justification and legitimacy in its links with the strong urge to a democratization of culture that had seized France at the Liberation. In the line traced by the CNR programme, a new movement of cultural democracy, based on the notion of popular education, looked, for a time, set to triumph. Its collective ambitions, which were given juridical expression in the Preamble to the 1946 Constitution where the right to culture was proclaimed, took concrete form in the associations, clubs, film societies, maisons de jeunes et de la culture (MJC),[37] and the training centres for organizers that now proliferated, seeking to provide a framework for a 'cultural revolution' of national proportions. To their credit, both the provisional government and the young Fourth Republic gave timely help and encouragement to this development, providing funds and personnel, often hastily trained. At the time of the Langevin–Wallon plan, a department for Youth Movements and Popular Education was created at the Ministry of Education. The choice of person to head it was symbolic: Jean Guéhenno, the son of a shoemaker, who had gone on to the prestigious Ecole Normale, had an unshakeable and sincere faith in the virtues of education for the people. Far from seeing the new action of his department as a challenge to the traditional school and its work, Guéhenno dreamt of seeing France covered by a dense network of educational centres whose task was to complement, not to challenge, the work of the school in the awakening of the people. In a similar spirit, and under Parodi's influence, the comités d'entreprise were charged with undertaking a far-reaching cultural action, and encouragement was given to the work of the cultural associations. Present in these efforts was a firm conviction that popular enlightenment constituted the surest democratic safeguard; the new approach to culture, one that owed much to the antifascist struggle of the recent past, was seen as having an important contribution to make to the work of national reconstruction. However, it was not totally free from the temptation to paternalism that was currently exciting message-bearing intellectuals. The enthusiasts in fact gave themselves the mission of 'improving' popular taste, of introducing the masses to highbrow culture; moreover, they were

ready to update the latter if necessary, adding Brecht to Racine, Shos-
takovitch to Mozart, and Picasso to Delacroix. Indeed, links with the
school system remained strong, while the needs of popular culture itself
were neglected. More original, however, were the long-term ambitions:
those of mobilizing young people (by 1958, almost one in three young
people had been involved in the various secular and confessional movements), of considering cultural organizations as the natural interlocutors of
the public authorities, and, above all, of favouring the creation of merito-
cratic élites constantly renewed from the ranks of the people.

Yet these generous ambitions necessarily meant exposing the projects of
a handful of dedicated *animateurs* to the judgement of society as a whole. The
implications of this became painfully apparent after 1947, and by 1952 the
common reaction was increasingly one of bitterness. For efforts to modernize and generalize access to culture were inevitably left at the mercy of
broader political developments. The enthusiastic progressive unanimity of
1944 did not survive the Cold War and Budapest, and the Fourth Republic's own fractures and weaknesses turned it from its early ambitions.
The appointment in January 1947 of the young and energetic Pierre Bourdan (UDSR) as the new Minister of Youth, Arts and Letters in Ramadier's
ministry in fact marked the high point for the hopeful. The Third Force
governments, deeply suspicious of the impact on the people of this brand of
militancy, did not repeat the experiment; this was, after all, the time when
the Queuille government instigated proceedings against the French pub-
lisher of Miller's *Tropic of Cancer*. Thus, and with the approval of the *laïcs*
and the political parties of the Left, responsibility for action over youth and
culture returned to the Education Ministry, with predictable results. A
Secretariat to the Beaux-Arts was re-established and given by Pleven in
July 1951 to an innocuous senator from the Côtes-du-Nord, André Cornu.
The Secretariat, which had no autonomous budget, simply returned to the
banal and uninspired policy of the past – mounting a noisy operation of
safeguard for Versailles, or moving the statue of Gambetta from the place
du Carrousel – before breaking with the administrators who had worked
enthusiastically with Guéhenno, notably Jeanne Laurent, responsible for
dramatic art and instigator of the policy of decentralization.[38] By 1950, the
national budget for the arts was actually below its 1938 level, and stagnated
at 0.1 per cent of public expenditure. Of course, the established 'humanist'
positions were content; but a dynamic cultural action never recovered. This
was not least since those involved at the grass-roots, who were less strongly
supported by the public authorities, now measured the extent of social
change. Their optimistic cultural populism – which had postulated a neat
progression from the *quarante-huitards* to the maquis, from Michelet to Jean
Vilar – was increasingly fragmented by political divisions, caught between
the education system back on the offensive, and the rising mass culture

which threatened to submerge all classes. And with this, the established notions of culture, creation, and even that of 'the People' were less and less appropriate. The initial hope had been to enrich the lives of all by the diffusion of a genuinely democratic culture: yet what the enthusiasts in fact encountered in their associations, clubs, and theatres was not the masses – for whom other forms of leisure appeared to suffice – but rather the members of the new middle classes, hungry for a culture with which to embellish their social mobility. Cultural action gradually became the domain of experts armed with specialized techniques of *animation*, catering essentially for the needs of the products of social promotion; a seedbed for the new organizational élites and a testing-ground for cultural products created elsewhere, rather than the crucible of a common and democratically shared culture as originally hoped for. In short, cultural action had become technical, like society itself.

A few individual and remarkable successes testified, nonetheless, to the strength of the original commitments, and served to pave the way for the cultural policy initiated by André Malraux under the Fifth Republic. Two examples, startling and fruitful, can be cited. The first is that of the 'Peuple et culture' association, set up in Grenoble in December 1944, then at Annecy in the following spring, by the education commissions of the Liberation Committees of the Isère and Haute-Savoie. It was organized by personnel from the Uriage school and members of the Vercors maquis, such as Dumazedier, Thisse, and Cacérès.[39] They were determined not to become stuck in the old debate over 'bourgeois' versus 'proletarian' cultures, wanting instead to 'restore culture to the people and the people to culture'. The movement built up strong links with the trade unions of the region, and was staffed with competent *animateurs* who received financial support from Guéhenno and local authorities. From its inception, the 'Peuple et culture' movement combined the original revolutionary hopes with a serious, almost managerial approach to their realization, aspiring to 'produce education as others produce bread, steel, or electricity'. The entire 'Peuple et culture' experiment was marked by this unusual dichotomy: with the establishment of Dasté's theatre company at Grenoble in 1945, training of proficient organizers (soon to call for a social statute), and a publishing venture distributed by Editions du Seuil; on the other hand, however, there was the steady centralization of activities on Paris, and serious conflicts with the Communists at the time of the Korean War and the Stockholm appeal. The 'Peuple et culture' experiment was a faithful mirror of all the difficulties and traumas of the cultural effort: the decline of the early populist hopes, the increasingly technical character of the action, the steady *tertiarisation* of cultural consumption, and the rise of mass culture.

The Fourth Republic's second great success in the cultural domain came over the decentralization of theatre. Having begun at Colmar in 1946, the idea was quickly seized by Pierre Bourdan and Jeanne Laurent; in 1952, new dramatic centres were opened at Strasbourg, Saint-Etienne, Aix, Toulouse, and Rennes. At stake was not simply a sop to regionalism, but rather a serious attempt to break with the theatrical tyrannies of fashion, the critics, and Paris (in 1945, for example, the capital had fifty-two theatres compared with fifty-one for the rest of France), as well as a determined effort to seek out a new theatre-going public, continuing the work of Gémier, Copeau, and Chancerel; those involved saw the theatre as having a contribution to make to national reconstruction in the fullest sense and to the construction of a new democracy, becoming, in the words of Jean Vilar, a public service like any other. The success was not total – municipalities were often alarmed by the new developments – but the policy did succeed in awakening a public hitherto anaesthetized by the mediocre and banal touring productions of *théatre du boulevard*; it helped to promote the generation of Dasté and Planchon, encouraged moreover since 1946 by the concours des jeunes compagnies and financial assistance towards the cost of producing new plays. Development was completed by the festivals, in particular by that of Avignon, launched in summer 1947 and soon to acquire international fame. Its founder, a former pupil of Dullin, was Jean Vilar, who had toured the provinces during the Occupation with the company of the 'Jeune France' association, then with his own company. Vilar had staged and played Molière, Eliot, and Strindberg, astonishing Paris with his production of *Murder in the Cathedral* in 1945. In fact, like Baty, Jouvet, and Barrault, who were also breaking from the traditional 'digestif' theatre, Vilar was putting into practice the advances of the previous fifty years, motivated by a strong spirit of civic responsibility, promoting a regenerated theatre, one that would not be a prisoner of class or doctrinaire commitments. The venture of course was helped greatly by the rich and unique style developed at Avignon, with a radical approach to the notion of scene; stunning costumes, lighting, music, and colour, and with a minimum of decor other than the superb setting of the Palais des Papes itself. Enthusiastic audiences were treated to Shakespeare and Claudel, with the definitive success coming in the summer of 1951 with Gérard Philipe's memorable incarnation of Rodrigue in Corneille's *Le Cid*. In September 1951, Vilar and his company were chosen by Jeanne Laurent for the Théâtre national populaire, charged with continuing the work begun by Gémier in 1920. First at Suresnes in a marquee, then at the Palais de Chaillot, the TNP succeeded in breaking down some of the barriers which, in the past, had prevented the theatre from finding a genuinely popular audience: the late hours of performances, high prices, sumptuous seats, and other trappings of bourgeois theatre. Working in close collaboration with the comités d'entreprise and associations like 'Travail et culture', offering weekends and greatly reduced subscriptions, the TNP introduced a new public – drawn for the most part from the upwardly mobile sections of the lower classes, officials, students, office workers, technicians, and even some qualified workers – to programmes of the great classics, Molière, Hugo, Musset, and von Kleist, as well as to a more modern repertoire of Brecht and Pichette. Gradually, the élite and the critics were won over. In spite of the open hostility of the Right, clear from the parliamentary debate on the arts budget in December 1951, Vilar's work created roughly two million new theatre-goers: a unique ambition and triumph.[40]

Yet it is important not to forget that Gérard Philipe, although a key figure for the development and success of the TNP, was also a film star: he, in fact, personifies the interpenetration of the 'classic' and 'mass' cultures which marks the 1950s. A new culture, based on the American model, was taking shape; one produced on an industrial scale using industrial methods, requiring heavy capital investments, adapted to reach the largest possible audience, and distributed by the mass media; alien, finally, both in its conception and diffusion, to the intellectuals, whatever their commitments. New cultural products were becoming available, the results of crossing national cultures with international technologies, selected on the sole criterion of consumption, and without reference to the notions of Art and Culture familiar to the intellectuals or to the popularizers of the humanist values. Creation was increasingly synonymous with production, imagination carried a higher premium than reason, and standardization substituted the backer for the author. The 'lonely crowd',[41] this vast anonymous public formed by the expanding class of wage-earners, found in economic growth a new capacity to consume average values. The shock of this development dislocated the traditional points of cultural reference; the mass media democratized and homogenized according to the laws of supply and demand, and, with their passive consumers, even founded a new form of social communication, one based more on leisure than on work. The ubiquity of the mass culture in fact imposed a dynamic 'polyculture'. New, all-embracing mythologies of high technology began to establish a commanding place in social consciousness, and new socio-cultural practices invaded public and private life.

The cinema offers the best example of this evolution. It had undoubtedly improved its cultural standing. The crude, almost amateurish pre-war cinema, though still present, gradually made way for a sophisticated and professional cinema, one more attentive now to dialogue than to mere spectacle, exploiting the skill of the director as well as the charm of the star. This development was fostered by the film festivals (Cannes was its apogee), by the film clubs, the first 'art et d'essai' cinemas, and by the growth of film criticism, where André Bazin led the field.[42] The 'seventh art' won over the aesthetes, the intellectuals, and above all, the young. As a result it was honoured by the public authorities; a Centre national du cinéma was hastily set up in 1946 to resist the invasion of American films that Blum had short-sightedly accepted in return for the first dollars for reconstruction; considerable financial aid was given to encourage quality French productions, such as Bresson's *Un condamné à mort s'est échappé* of 1956, or the *Montparnasse 10* from Becker the following year. What was thus gained in artistic terms, however, afforded little protection from the damaging effects of the laws of the cultural market-place. True, the cinema had certainly conquered the younger generation – the 15–20 age group accounted for 43 per cent of its audience in 1954; but its penetration into rural areas and small communities was weak – thus, at the same date, 95 per cent of its audiences were from localities with over 2000 inhabitants. Worse, cinema-going experienced a steady decline – 230 million visits each year on the eve of the war, a peak of 420 million in 1947, then stable at around 380 million, before dropping to 350 million in 1959. With an average annual output of 130 films, and a low concentration of production companies after the dismantling of the Pathé empire, French cinema was in a weak position, unable to hold off the American invasion, and already facing competition from television. But its difficulties in fact went deeper than this: for the staple output of the French film industry was no longer capable of satisfying a new public, one made more demanding by its contact with other media. The film-making effort of the Liberation period, responsible for productions like *Antoine et Antoinette* and *La Bataille du rail*, had run out of steam, and the established industry, content with its traditional approach and standards, was unable to come up with anything new to arrest the slide. People went to the cinema as much to be entertained as to see a particular film, and although 60 per cent of them may have preferred to watch French productions, from 1950 they actually saw more American than French films, without counting the enthusiasm for Italian neo-realism. The box office successes of 1954, for example, reveal a strong eclecticism, mixing, pell-mell, films as different as *Le Salaire de la peur* and *La Strada, Tant qu'il y aura des hommes* and *Si Versailles m'était conté, Sissi* and *Porte des Lilas*. But the repetitive and conservative offerings from the established film-makers, like Borderie, Le Chanois, Duvivier, or Christian-Jaque, using performers like Jean Gabin and Martine Carol, even when in colour or cinemascope, were unlikely to satisfy audiences indefinitely. Meanwhile, gifted new figures like Tati, Resnais, Clément, Melville, and Astruc could not find the financial and commercial structures which would have allowed their talents to flower sooner. However, at the *Cahiers du cinéma*, launched in April 1951 by a group of young enthusiasts impassioned by westerns and new film techniques, and that ousted *L'Écran français* in the analysis of what was wrong with French film-making, Truffaut, Godard, and Chabrol were already preparing the onslaught of the '*Nouvelle Vague*', which began with *Le Beau Serge* early in 1958. The period of psychological realism and humanistic clichés, with its domestic dramas, likeable villains and silence over the problems of modern France, came to a close: a new generation, with new techniques, imposed itself: the crisis of talent had been overcome. But the cinema evolved rapidly. In the United States, James Dean had already usurped Bogart, and the naturalism of Marilyn Monroe was supplanting the platinum glamour of the Hollywood queens. In 1956 came a film which provoked a scandal in France: *Et Dieu créa la femme* brought to fame Brigitte Bardot, a provocative young dancer who, in May 1949, had done a cover for *Elle* magazine, opportunely launched by Vadim and Raoul Lévy. Her unprecedented success and pouting sensuality made 'BB' an obvious symbol of change, a powerful demonstration that moral codes were evolving, and that a less inhibited younger generation was ready to assert itself. And even cultural mutations had a silver lining: back in office after 13 May, Antoine Pinay was to inform Bardot personally that she was a bigger currency earner for France than the Régie Renault!

The media were also obliged to adapt to the new and volatile rhythms of mass consumption. After the euphoria of the Liberation, the press had achieved a temporary stabilization of its circulation – more than 15 million copies a day in 1946, 9.6 million in 1952, and 11.4 million in 1958 – but was still waiting for a definitive statute after the provisional ordinances of 1944. The quality political, and general daily press, with its outdated approach to publicity, was in decline (180 titles in 1947, 123 in 1958), losing ground to the radio.[43] On the other hand, concentrations accelerated and the groups extended their hold over production. The old-style provincial press of the Third Republic could not keep up; *Ouest-France*, *La Dépêche*, and *Le Dauphiné libéré* dominated their regions; and the savage takeovers and mergers multiplied, with Robert Hersant providing the best-known example, building his fiefs in Picardy and from Poitiers to Rodez with *Centre-Press*, definitively organized in 1959. It was a difficult period for the Parisian press: the contraction in the Communist audience led to the disappearance of *Ce Soir* in 1953; *Le Monde* was rocked by major crises in 1951 and 1956; an entrepreneur of the romantic press, Cino del Duca, made a racy tabloid, *Paris-Journal*, of the once proud *Franc-Tireur* which had issued from the Resistance; *Le Populaire* lost nine in ten of its readers between 1947 and 1958, and *L'Humanité* almost half its readership; and *Le Parisien libéré*, *Le Figaro*, and *L'Aurore* owed the very slight improvements in their circulations only to important financial support from industrialists like Amaury, Prouvost, and Boussac. In the press, clearly, whether through political struggles or cynical restructuring, money had reasserted its authority. Not, however, that the outcome was openly deplored by the public: new popular tastes were responsible for the success of weekly magazines modelled on the American formula: *Paris-Match* from March 1949, *L'Express* in May 1953, as well as other, more discreet organs, aimed at specific audiences and with commercially sound contents. And in fact, the most durable successes were in the realm of the women's press which, with more than 200 titles, now touched all the popular social classes: *L'Echo de la mode*, *Nous deux*, and *Confidences* sold over a million copies each week, followed at a distance by *Marie-France*, *Elle*, and *Marie-Claire*. With articles on household equipment, romance stories, beauty care advice, and modern publicity, this women's press was a powerful instrument of alignment on the dominant social models.[44] The rise of a specialized press bore witness to new affluence and the growth of leisure: cultural relaxation, with the *Sélection du Reader's Digest*; practical interests, with *Le Chasseur français* and knitting and gardening magazines; sporting, with the success of *L'Équipe*, *Miroir-Sprint*, and *Paris-Turf*; the growing cult of the car ensured an audience for *Auto-Journal*; while *France-Dimanche* and *Détective* responded to appetites for titillation. As a clear sign of the times, the children's press, already well-established before the war, now triumphed. It imposed the strip cartoon in the collective imagination: for the first time, a generation of children and adolescents grew up with *Tintin*, *Spirou*, *Le Journal de Mickey*, and *Vaillant*; a generation unaware that it was the object of a fierce battle, one in which the offensive from the United States was held off for a long time by the strength of French cartoon production and by the quality of the cartoonists of the 'Ecole Belge'.[45]

The same development was confirmed for the audio-visual media, now competing victoriously with the press. Here too an inherited conformism was threatened by the cultural explosion. At the Liberation, however, by the ordinances and decrees of March and November 1945 establishing the Radio-télévision française (RTF), everything had been done to impose a very rigid conception of the State's monopoly in this domain. The familiar cultural ambitions of the period, widely shared by the up-and-coming younger broadcasters, weighed heavily upon radio programmes at all levels; and political news was tightly controlled by governments. But in vain. A hugely swollen public (5.3 million radio sets in 1945, 10.7 million in 1958) imposed its tastes, making clear its preference for light entertainment and lively reporting rather than strident militant drama and dreary bulletins. Some broadcasters, like Vital Gayman, the much-criticized director of the 'Journal parlé' from 1945 to 1958, and Vladimir Porché, were responsive to this evolution; but the public authorities stifled all innovation. The national radio was enlisted in the anticommunist offensive at the time of 'Paix et liberté', and used with a complacent cynicism for the defence of the Algerian policy; only the Saturday evening *causeries* of Mendès France brought some relief from this systematic abuse. The final months of the Fourth Republic were the most wretched in this sense, with the War Ministry itself preparing the commentaries on the Suez adventure, while in Algeria, Lacoste personally selected the sounds and images from his fief; indeed, after the departure of Penchenier in 1955, the radio no longer had a special correspondent in Algiers! In short, a monopoly of the State had become a monopoly of the government. This development helps of course to explain the great popular success achieved by the revived commercial radio stations, over which this sort of control was harder to achieve, despite the strong participation of the State through the Sofirad, set up in 1945. Radio-Luxembourg, back on the air in November 1945, quickly won a large following thanks to attractive and popular programmes conceived by Louis Merlin, with quiz programmes, singing competitions, serials, and sponsorship by manufacturers. Radio-Andorre and Radio-Monte-Carlo also recovered their audiences. The launching in 1955, after a vigorous political and financial battle, of Europe Number One, transmitting from the Saar, accelerated the evolution in broadcasting; games and publicity were exploited to support a lively and reliable news service, one that proved itself to the mass of the population by its coverage of the events in Budapest. Maurice Siegel introduced reporting based on sound documents, brief commentaries, and a less formal style of presentation; and younger singers, jazz and the first Anglo-American rock were now offered as alternatives to the familiar sugary pap and accordion airs.[46] The young, the middle classes, and the popular audience, tired of being patronized by the national radio, were enthusiastic.

Likewise for television, whose irruption (60 000 sets in 1954, 680 000 in 1958) announced the crumbling of the last resistance to 'polyculture'. Here, the monopoly of the State was preserved, though governments still had not taken stock of the full power of the image. But the new medium had a vitality of its own which enabled it to adjust well to the needs of the period. In the 'Journal télévisé', created by Pierre Sabbagh in April 1949 and constantly supported by Jean d'Arcy, the future formula of Europe Number One took shape, often with the same personnel; the effects were multiplied, soon using reporter cars and regional stations, offering on-the-spot reactions to events, and backed up by innovative improvisation in the studios, with attractive *speakerines* to bring calm and continuity. On a single channel, but with greater production capacities after the transfer to the Buttes-Chaumont studios in 1957, a new balance was struck, between serious documentaries, light entertainment, games, popular sports, solid cultural programmes – that in their way realized the ambitions of 1944 – children's drama and science series. After 1952, the establishment of the Eurovision network, with great spectacles such as the coronation of Elizabeth II and the Five Nations rugby tournament, accelerated the massive rallying of the population to this new and total form of communication.[47]

Many other examples could be given of the great advance of mass culture. It had an important role in extending the diffusion of the classic culture: the 'Livre de poche' collection, launched in 1953 and inspired by the American model, completed the success of authors like Camus, Sartre, and Prévert. Publishing for children developed, representing 12 per cent of the total turnover of the French publishing industry in 1957, compared with 5 per cent a decade earlier. Overall expenditure on books followed the general trend in consumption, climbing at a rate of 6 per cent a year.[48] And records, 78s and then microgrooves, sold in shops and through mail order clubs, diffused classical as well as light music. In the latter category, moreover, there was now an alternative to the usual banalities in the form of the fresher successes of 'chanson française', currently experiencing something of a golden age thanks to artists like Montand, Greco, Ferré, Brassens and Brel, Aznavour and Bécaud, albeit one menaced already by Bill Haley and Elvis Presley. Sport, though poorly popularized among the young and little practised, was closely covered by the mass media; both collective games like football and rugby and the cult of the champion triumphed now: sport established an important place for itself at the intersection of culture and leisure.[49] Fashion, at last shedding its social exclusivity of the post-war years, and advertising, changed beyond recognition; both also contributed to the growing cultural homogeneity. A multitude of signs heralded what Dumazedier was soon to baptize as 'the leisure civilization'.[50]

As yet, however, the development was incomplete. France in fact succumbed more slowly than her European neighbours to the invasion of mass culture, often due as much to a diffuse anti-Americanism as to economic backwardness. The glaring social inequalities and the great length of the working week clearly make it unrealistic to speak of a rapid generalization of this cultural consumption. At its simplest level, that of taking holidays, much progress remained to be made. In spite of the development of various forms of tourism, with, for example, the creation of the Club Méditerranée in 1950, which sent its first contingent of 'gentils membres' to the beaches of the Baleares the same year, going away on holiday remained a privilege of Parisians (51 per cent of expenditure on holidays in 1957) or the inhabitants of other cities. And it is worth remembering that just a few dozen kilometres from the bright lights of Saint-Tropez, 69 per cent of the inhabitants of Marseille still took no holiday. Nevertheless, and with the obvious reservations, the leisure ethic was extending its hold, already organizing the mass culture that was its expression. In a mixture of game and spectacle, of traditional *sociabilités* and more modern temptations that, for all the problems, give to the 1950s a rich and exuberant tonality, the new 'polyculture' offered a vast and exciting landscape, one in which the social classes mixed as they had never done before. New and questionable 'mythologies', which promoted a social model of youthfulness at the expense of the old and, soon, of parents, now underpinned the efforts of the people to come to terms with modernity.[51] Rarely had the process of acculturation been so brutal and so intense. Rarely had an old society been so constrained to partake of the present and to protect its historical, religious, and political values from the onslaught of the standardized norms of the age of mass communications. Already tempted, it was still hesitating. The next chapter belonged to Brigitte Bardot and General de Gaulle.

# Conclusion

'Here you are, freed of a silly prejudice that cost you dear!' This slogan, originally used to end an advertisement for margarine, could, as Roland Barthes observed at the time,[1] be applied to cover all the material, moral, and political consumption of the French people in the 1950s. To a population tired of repeated disappointments and soured hopes, modernization – symbolized of course by the irresistible success of margarine – provided a new panacea, at once effective and accessible. It was as if the people had arrived at the same conclusion as the advertisement: in May 1958, more mindful of the exciting advantages it had already obtained by its own efforts, and without even sampling what the Fifth Republic might have to offer, it had not stirred in defence of the Fourth Republic. The prejudice which had gone was the Liberation's blind faith in the virtues of a just democracy run by powerful and honest political parties; gone too was the obstinacy with which, from one election to another, it had been believed that the ballot-box could produce durable majorities, and that the parliamentary régime was capable of enlarging the consensus rather than fragmenting it. The Assembly-based régime was ridiculous, inefficient in decision-making, a prisoner of events, governing little and badly, while attempting to mask its incompetence with moralizing. And the cost of the myopia of its leaders was only too obvious: handicapped by the traumas of 1947, defeated in Indo-China and caught in their Algerian War, at a time when French society wanted, unanimously, simply to partake of prosperity. A crippled régime and an impatient France: powerless to resolve this contradiction, the Fourth Republic was condemned by a population which opted, blandly but without regrets, for the safeguard of its comfort, and change without risks.

Described thus, bordering on caricature, the issue goes far beyond the debate which animated many who experienced 13 May 1958 at close hand: suicide or assassination? The Republican old guard, which had performed its ritual of protest in the streets of Paris on 28 May, that of Daladier but also of Mendès France and Mitterrand, fulminated for a long while against those responsible for a *coup d'État*, before succumbing in their turn to the

446

charm of the institutions it had created. To their defence of principles in a void, and to the routine denunciations of 'bonapartism' and 'fascism', other voices, persuasive but disparate, replied by insisting on a diagnosis of methodical suicide. To listen to them, the Fourth Republic's entire existence had been a protracted agony. For the Gaullists, it was condemned from birth by depriving itself of de Gaulle in 1946, and by refusing to heed the advice of the Bayeux discourse. For the Communists, the régime had become unbalanced and hysterical in 1947, when it handed France over to American imperialism and spurned the support of the strongest battalions of the working classes. Unpopular, divided, bearing the scars of the 'années noires' and the Cold War, immobilizing the nation as it faced the challenge of modernity, a shadowy continuation of the Third Republic, mortally wounded by Dien Bien Phu and the failure of the EDC, brought down by Algiers, and interred to popular indifference: political commentators and journalists were quick to write the obituary of the Fourth Republic. In *Le Monde* of 29 May 1958, Sirius concluded that it 'died much less from the blows it received than from its unfitness to live'.[2]

The historian is tempted to intervene cautiously in this debate, one still far from settled in the national conscience. Moreover, much material is still inaccessible and many key witnesses have yet to give their evidence. But if judgement has to be reserved, the chronology has, nonetheless, to be indicated, and the positive achievements, as well as the tragic crises, detailed. There is a place also for scepticism about explanations whose outcome is too neatly inevitable. Is it realistic to hold the régime responsible for the collection of national and international constraints which shattered hopes and stifled enthusiasms in the immediate post-war period? That an already weakened régime then, and until 1952, found the strength to set up the Third Force on the ruins of the tripartite alliance, blocked the aggression of the Communists and Gaullists, launched the Plan, fostered economic growth, and encouraged European unity while preserving an authentic if uninspired democracy: these were, after all, considerable achievements for an organism supposedly bent on self-destruction. And that, after the disaster in Indo-China and the troubles in North Africa, in a social climate made tense by the unequal access to economic prosperity, a new optimism even reigned for a few months in 1955 thanks to Mendès France and Edgar Faure, suggests that the régime could, perhaps, have held on for longer. In short, and until more is known, it seems wise to beware of lazy interpretations in terms of insidious torpor, of the fragility of 'transitional' régimes, or of the weakness of 'interim' periods.

But is this to abandon the destiny of the Fourth Republic to the hazard of the event, the perennial spanner in the ideological works of History? It is obvious, of course, that the régime was thrown hopelessly off balance by the Algerian conflict; obvious too, that the death blow was delivered on 13 May

1958. With hindsight, moreover, it is not hard to discern the disturbing symmetry of the failure of renewal after 1953, when the appetites of modern France and the problems of decolonization swept away the solutions – too mediocre or too demanding – offered by the Centre-Right and then by the Centre-Left. But although the direction and force of the underlying movements is easy to gauge retrospectively, we must not forget that at the time they were visible only through events. Nor should we forget, for example, that the Algerian War held several unpleasant surprises for the men of the Fifth Republic. Indeed, when even their opponents hesitated, and when the people decided but in silence, perhaps the leaders of the Fourth Republic could, like their predecessors and successors, reasonably invoke the historical right to error. It is incontestable that the Algerian drama had forced the nation to make a choice, and sooner than was generally realized: from September 1957 onwards, public opinion refused to give its confidence to political leaders to settle the affair, preferring the fruits of expansion to the sacrifices of a war economy. And on 13 May, when the stakes were fixed and the issue forced by de Gaulle, this hitherto latent choice was revealed: by the passivity of the citizens and by the isolation of the political class, the latter stuck in its hollow protests and pathetic recantations. That the reflexes of 1947, those of elemental anticommunism and the sacrosanct nature of the Atlantic alignment, then operated again, merely added to the paralysis of the parliamentarians. Here, no doubt, lay the secret vice of the régime, for, as Raymond Aron observed, 'When men fail to choose, events choose for them.'[3]

The consideration of the causes of the failure has then another formulation, just as classic in the historiography of the period:[4] did responsibility rest with the institutions or with the men? The former have been too abused since 1958 for one not to be tempted to try in turn to judge the views of their detractors. Half-heartedly but, for the first time in their history, in the full exercise of their democratic liberty, the French people had adopted a workable Constitution. The great role in it of Parliament could be rationalized by the power of three strong political parties capable of expressing accurately the popular will. Two Presidents of the Republic, Auriol and Coty, had been able to exercise their moral authority and their right of opinion and choice: their action cannot be dismissed simply as a hiatus between two assumptions of power by de Gaulle. The decline into a tyrannical *régime d'assemblée* is incontestable; but, and whatever has been claimed to the contrary, the fault stemmed not from the omnipotence of the political parties which had allowed them to exploit and pervert the 'system', but rather from their weaknesses. None of the political parties, new or old, was capable of responding to the new aspirations of society; they submitted to the pressure from the electorate without, in return, managing to inculcate a new civic pedagogy; they used the old methods to exercise a new sovereignty; they decayed as society prospered. The political parties fell victims to the short-sightedness of their views, to their own archaic structures and outmoded ideologies, and, above all, to their naive confidence in the regenerative qualities of a spirit of the Resistance which was supposed to renew the élites and mobilize the people indefinitely. We have witnessed the results of these failings: the political parties incapable of articulating the popular will in Parliament, and abdicating responsibility for decisions to the leadership of the groups; the deputies imposing their conditions on governments without proposing a policy; and the destiny of the nation settled in the corridors of the Assembly. Under these conditions, two tacit rules, absurd and dangerous, were gradually established. Firstly, elections had significance uniquely as pressure on the régime, since the elector knew that he was voting neither for a government nor for a particular policy: the frustration after the elections of 1956, when the deputies robbed the electorate of its choice by preferring Guy Mollet to Mendès France, was in fact a severe warning. Secondly, the repeated ministerial crises, which left France without a government for a total of 348 days between 1946 and 1958, acquired almost institutional legitimacy, becoming the most practical means of settling problems while the outgoing ministry expedited 'pending business' with decrees: policy 'à la sauvette', less ineffective than it was immoral.[5]

It was, then, the men and their mediocre partisan groupings which undermined the institutions they were meant to serve. True, Pinay, Mendès France, and Edgar Faure had held office, capable of restoring confidence, of securing peace in Indo-China, of relaunching European unity and encouraging modernization, of resisting the demagogy of Poujadism, and emerging intact from the scandals. Yet they were sadly atypical. Events had remorselessly exposed too many little chiefs of the MRP, SFIO potentates, Gaullist activists, servants of powerful interests, and young Turks mindful of the main chance. The Republic was weakened by their divisions, so visible, for example, in the reversal of majorities over the EDC, and was torn apart by their rancour and exclusion. It was with a cruel irony that de Gaulle had deplored the absence at the decisive moment of Thorez, Poujade, and Ferhat Abbas. Yet how, after all, could a consensus have been constructed without the backing of an important section of the working class, of the casualties of change, and of the Algerian people? Those responsible claimed that these ostracisms had saved the Republic. But they had also thinned the ranks of its defenders to an alarming degree. So much so that in the final crisis the ruling political class found itself alone, no longer in control of its power, an 'infernal machine abandoned at the centre of a large circle of fear'.[6] In their defence has to be cited the endless succession of crises and the proliferation of adversaries. Credit is also due for their capacity to make a virtue of their own weaknesses, letting the modern

Welfare State develop without allowing its administrators to dictate their conduct. In contrast to their successors, even if like them they experienced brutal pressure from the military, the men of the Fourth Republic managed to establish a healthy relationship with the top administration, for its part well protected, that avoided a confusion of powers, at the same time as letting take shape – in the structures of the Plan, at the ENA, in the public sector, and in the ministries – the advent of technocracy. In the final analysis, however, this 'République des députés' had supported a political class that was too remote from social change to be able to perceive and respond to the national needs. As before 1940, the extreme dissociation of political, administrative, economic, and social power – statistically demonstrable[7] – was responsible for making the parliamentarians and the party machines dangerously isolated from the nation itself.

Is this to say that the crisis of the régime was simply a reflection of a larger national crisis? The question has often been posed.[8] Depoliticization, an underdeveloped civic sense, and indifference, all causes for concern well before 1958, were without doubt rooted in the widespread and powerful desire for social organization which had failed to find satisfaction among the trade unions, professional and cultural groups capable of contributing to the political debate. In spite of the shake-up of the Liberation, sharpening of appetites by the economic expansion had taken a chronically feeble civil society by surprise: the old national shortcomings now became a new source of tensions. And for this structural inaptitude for dialogue and consultation in French society, the political leaders had little or nothing to offer. They abandoned themselves to the contradictory pressures of the best organized groups, and to the unstable aggregate of sectorial demands. Isolated from the other organizational élites, they failed to make use of new opportunities – prosperity, hunger for education, social mobility, the rise of the wage-earners, and cultural effervescence – to build a new consensus. Parliament and its version of democracy was increasingly isolated from a changing society, yet came under assault from the discontent generated by the change: this brutal contradiction was not, perhaps, insurmountable, but the war in Algeria made it insupportable.

Yet for all its powerlessness and problems, the Fourth Republic was not sterile. The achievements and projects it left behind, too often ignored by the Fifth Republic, deserve to be recalled. Social Security and insurance, help for the family, an identification of the crucial role of the middle school, aspirations to a sharing of culture, all the panoply of the Welfare State in its early vigour; planning, regional development, and empirical economic policies which had failed to control inflation and the deficit but safeguarded future chances, the potential of European unity, and without neglecting the collective imperatives; policies for scientific research, for the development of atomic energy, and an alliance with Black Africa which augured well for the preservation of sovereignty. The Fourth Republic had not held back the work of modernization and rejuvenation, nor, above all, had it hindered improvement in living standards. Against these pluses, however, have immediately to be set its limitations and failures. The powerful mechanisms of inequality and social exclusion remained: workers, peasants, and too many of the old suffered the consequences daily. The gangrene of Algeria sapped the morale of the nation, and badly tarnished the image of the birthplace of the Rights of Man. Above all, since 1945 France had given a faltering performance on the international stage, apparently unsure if she was the smallest of the great powers or the greatest of the small powers. Dazed, yet attached to every element of her sovereignty, living no doubt beyond her means but shot through with dynamism, this ambitious nation was worth more than the dismal end of its political régime.

The people decided. To de Gaulle they delegated the task of providing a more solidly structured democracy, one which would repair, they believed, the dialogue between the governed and the governing, reconciling the defence of interests and national ambitions. The Fourth Republic was condemned for a failure of authority: its successors took great care to justify their alternative by giving periodic warnings against the weaknesses of the defunct régime. Indeed, for a long while the Fourth Republic was simply a fleshless argument, without historical consistency. Thirty years on, however, as new generations face the economic crisis, and pose questions about the Welfare State, democracy, power and the masses, without going as far as total rehabilitation, given that the institutions of the Fifth Republic enjoy such broad national approval, perhaps the French people can at last admit that this weak and despised régime was not, after all, completely unworthy. Retrospectively, one is even tempted to credit it precisely for a perserverance in governing little, which left France to develop her new energies unhindered. Better still, might the lesson of these years not be that the risk of shaping the future can, indeed, be taken, and that while failure is never insurmountable, ambition has no price?

# Chronology

## 1944

| | |
|---|---|
| *2 June* | The CFLN became the GPRF. |
| *6 June* | Allied landings in Normandy. |
| *10 June* | Massacre at Oradour. |
| *14 June* | De Gaulle at Courseulles. |
| *26 June* | Cherbourg taken. |
| *1–22 July* | Bretton–Woods Conference and agreements. |
| *6 July* | Decrees at Algiers on the commissaires de la République and on the re-establishment of democratic liberties. |
| *6–10 July* | De Gaulle's visit to the United States and Canada. |
| *11 July* | The United States recognized the *de facto* authority of the GPRF over the liberated areas. |
| *17–23 July* | Battle of the Vercors. |
| *27 July* | Ordinance abolishing Vichy's *Chartre du travail*. |
| *31 July* | American breakthrough at Avranches. |
| *1 August* | The 2ᵉ DB land in Normandy. |
| *5 August* | Liberation of Rennes. |
| *9 August* | Ordinance re-establishing Republican legality. |
| *10 August* | Ordinance on the Patriotic Militia. |
| *15 August* | French–American landings in Provence. |
| *17 August* | Final meeting of the Vichy cabinet. |
| *19–25 August* | Liberation of Paris. |
| *20 August* | Toulouse liberated. |
| *23 August* | Liberation of Aix and Grenoble. |
| *26 August* | De Gaulle walks down the Champs-Élysées. |
| *29 August* | Liberation of the Mediterranean littoral. |
| *30 August* | Liberation of Rouen and Reims. |
| *2 September* | First meeting of GPRF ministers in Paris. |
| *7 September* | Pétain and Laval leave for Germany. |
| *9 September* | Government of 'unanimité nationale' formed. |
| *12 September* | De Gaulle's speech at the Palais de Chaillot. |
| *14–18 September* | De Gaulle's first visit to the provinces. |
| *15 September* | Setting up of the special courts of justice. |
| *19–28 September* | Failure of the British raid on Arnhem. |
| *23 September* | Decree incorporating the FFI to the army. |
| *5 October* | Ordinance on female suffrage. |
| *18 October* | Decree on illicit profits. |
| *23 October* | Formal Allied recognition for the GPRF. |

| | |
|---|---|
| *23–25 October* | Congress of MLN leaders. |
| *28 October* | Suppression of the Patriotic Militia. |
| *3–20 November* | The 'Liberation Loan'. |
| *7 November* | Meeting of the enlarged Consultative Assembly. |
| *9–12 November* | Special congress of the SFIO. |
| *21 November* | Rail traffic over the Loire restored. |
| *23 November* | Entry of Leclerc's forces to Strasbourg. |
| *26 November* | Founding congress of the MRP. |
| *27 November* | Return of Maurice Thorez to Paris. |
| *28 November* | Ordinance on the chambres civiques. |
| *8 December* | Paris–Brest line reopened. |
| *10 December* | Franco-Soviet Pact signed in Moscow. |
| *14 December* | Ordinance setting up the Houillères nationales du Nord et du Pas-de-Calais. |
| *15–17 December* | National meeting of the CDLs. |
| *18 December* | First issue of *Le Monde*. |
| *20 December* | Comité d'entente PCF–SFIO. |
| *26 December* | Ordinance on the *indignité nationale* punishment. |

## 1945

| | |
|---|---|
| *1–5 January* | The Germans threaten Strasbourg. |
| *3 January* | Free secondary education restored. |
| *16 January* | Ordinance nationalizing the Renault factories. |
| *21–23 January* | Central Committee of the PCF at Ivry. |
| *23 January* | General retreat of the Germans in the Ardennes. |
| *23–28 January* | First national congress of the MLN. |
| *25 January* | France not invited to Yalta. |
| *27 January* | Maurras sentenced to life imprisonment. |
| *28 January* | Congress of the Front national. |
| *2 February* | Taking of Colmar by de Lattre. |
| *6 February* | Execution of Brasillach. |
| *12 February* | Yalta agreements. |
| *14 February* | Bombing of Dresden. |
| | Ordinance on the family associations. |
| *21 February* | De Gaulle refuses to meet Roosevelt. |
| *22 February* | Ordinance on the Comités d'entreprise. |
| | First American shipments of supplies for civilian use. |
| *28 February* | Lend-lease agreements signed in Washington. |
| *2 March* | De Gaulle's speech on reconstruction. |
| *4 March* | The Allies reach the Rhine. |
| *9 March* | Japanese takeover in Indo-China. |
| *11 March* | Proclamation of independence of Vietnam and Cambodia. |
| *13–18 March* | First trial before the High Court of Justice. |
| *5 April* | Resignation of Mendès France. |
| *9 April* | Nationalization of Gnome et Rhône and Air France. |
| *12 April* | Truman succeeds Roosevelt. |
| *13 April* | Ordinance on the municipal statute of Paris. |
| *25 April* | American and Soviet forces meet on the Elbe. |
| *26 April* | Pétain returns to France. |
| | Opening of the San Francisco conference. |

|              |                                                                          |
|--------------|--------------------------------------------------------------------------|
| *29 April and* |                                                                        |
| *13 May*     | Municipal elections.                                                     |
| *8 May*      | German surrender.                                                        |
| *8–12 May*   | Insurrection and repression in Petite Kabylie.                           |
| *10–30 May*  | Return of large numbers of deportees and prisoners.                      |
| *16 May*     | France a permanent member of UN Security Council.                        |
| *30 May*     | Ceasefire in Syria.                                                       |
| *4–15 June*  | Exchange of banknotes.                                                    |
| *5 June*     | France obtains a zone of occupation in Germany.                          |
| *7–25 June*  | Breakup of the MLN and the creation of the UDSR.                         |
| *12 June*    | Suppression of press censorship.                                         |
|              | Article in *L'Humanité* by Duclos on organic unity.                     |
| *22 June*    | Reform of the Civil Service; creation of the ENA.                       |
| *26 June*    | Close of the San Francisco conference, and the United Nations Charter.  |
| *26–30 June* | Tenth congress of the PCF.                                                |
| *28 June*    | Ordinance on rents.                                                       |
| *30 June*    | Ordinance on control of prices.                                          |
| *10–14 July* | The 'États généraux de la Renaissance française'.                       |
| *21 July*    | Speech by Thorez at Waziers.                                              |
| *23 July–15 August* | Trial and condemnation of Marshal Pétain.                         |
| *2 August*   | End of the Potsdam Conference.                                           |
| *6 August*   | American atomic bomb on Hiroshima.                                       |
| *8 August*   | USSR declares war on Japan.                                              |
| *9 August*   | American atomic bomb on Nagasaki.                                        |
| *12–15 August* | Thirty-seventh congress of the SFIO.                                   |
| *15 August*  | Japanese surrender.                                                       |
|              | Launching of the tax of 'solidarité nationale'.                         |
| *16 August*  | Ho Chi Minh calls for a national insurrection.                          |
| *17 August*  | Ordinance on the October elections.                                     |
| *20 August*  | Proclamation of the Republic of Vietnam.                                |
| *23 August*  | End of the lend-lease operations.                                       |
| *5 September* | Frachon General Secretary of the CGT.                                   |
| *11–20 September* | Failure of the London Conference.                                  |
| *23 and 30 September* | Cantonal elections.                                            |
| *4–15 September* | Trial and execution of Laval.                                        |
| *4 and 19 October* | Ordinances on the Social Security.                                 |
| *5 October*  | Leclerc and an expeditionary force arrive in Saigon.                    |
| *11 October* | Ordinance on the housing crisis.                                        |
| *17 October* | Ordinance on the *fermage* statute.                                     |
| *21 October* | Referendum and legislative elections.                                    |
| *30 October* | Creation of the Fédération syndicale mondiale.                          |
| *2 November* | Ordinance on the conditions of residence for foreigners.                |
| *7 November* | Programme of the Délégation des gauches.                                |
| *8 November* | Gouin President of the Constituent Asembly.                             |
| *20 November* | Start of the Nuremberg Trials.                                         |
| *21 November* | Formation of de Gaulle's government.                                    |
| *2 December* | Nationalization of the Banque de France and the principal deposit banks. |
| *12 December* | Strike by civil servants.                                              |

| 13–16 December | Second congress of the MRP. |
| 21 December | Creation of the General Commission of the Plan. |
| 22 December | Creation of the PRL. |
| 26 December | Ratification of the Bretton–Woods agreements; devaluation of the franc. |
| 28 December | Bread rations reintroduced. |
| 31 December | Difficult vote over military credits in the Assembly. |
| | Removal of controls on the opening of new businesses. |

## 1946

| 10 January | First General Assembly of the UNO. |
| 20 January | General de Gaulle resigns. |
| 24 January | Tripartite agreement MRP–SFIO–PCF. |
| 26–29 January | Gouin government. |
| 26 January–1 February | Strike in Paris press. |
| 31 January | Auriol President of the Constituent Assembly. |
| 21 February | Re-establishment of the 40 hours law. |
| 22 February | Agreements with China over Indo-China. |
| 5 March | Speech by Churchill at Fulton. |
| 6 March | Agreements between Sainteny and Ho Chi Minh. |
| 16-19 March | First meeting of the Council of the Plan. |
| 26 March | Commissaires de la République abolished. |
| 6 April | Law on proportional representation in the legislative elections. |
| 8 April | Gas and electricity nationalized. |
| 8–14 April | Twenty-sixth congress of the CGT. |
| 13 April | Marthe Richard law. |
| 16 April | Law on staff representatives. |
| 19 April | Assembly votes on constitutional project. |
| 25 April | Nationalization of principal insurance companies. |
| 30 April | Law setting up the FIDES. |
| 5 May | Victory for 'No' in the referendum. |
| 16 May | Law on the Comités d'entreprise. |
| 17 May | Law creating the Charbonnages de France. |
| 28 May | Blum–Byrnes agreements. |
| 29 May | The CGT calls for a general wage increase. |
| 2 June | Elections to the second Constituent Asembly. |
| 12 June | Creation of the CNPF. |
| 16 June | De Gaulle's Bayeux discourse. |
| 23–26 June | Bidault government. |
| 25 July | Dalat conference. |
| 27 July | Palais-Royal conference. |
| 30 July–3 August | Postal workers' strike. |
| 6 August | Law on family allowances. |
| 29 August | Thirty-eighth congress of the SFIO. |
| 4 September | Mollet becomes SFIO General Secretary. |
| 12 September | Law on old-age pensions. |
| 14 September | End of the Fontainebleau conference. |
| 19 September | Churchill's Zurich speech. |
| 22 September | De Gaulle's Epinal speech. |

| | |
|---|---|
| *29 September* | Constituent Assembly adopts the new constitutional project. |
| *13 October* | Referendum on the Constitution. |
| *15 October* | End of the Paris Conference. |
| *19 October* | Law on the statute for state employees. |
| *23 October* | The episcopate expresses its fears over a new secular conflict. |
| *29 October* | Law on compensation for war damage. |
| *October* | Success of the Renault 4 CV at the Salon de l'Auto. |
| *October* | Scandals over wines and textiles. |
| *10 November* | Legislative elections. |
| *18 November* | Interview with Thorez in *The Times*. |
| *23 November* | Bombardment of Haiphong. |
| *24 November and* | |
| *8 December* | Elections to the Council of the Republic. |
| *27 November* | Adoption of the Monnet Plan. |
| *3 December* | Auriol President of the National Assembly. |
| *16 December* | Formation of the Blum government. |
| *19 December* | Insurrection at Hanoi. Economic annexation of the Saar to France. |
| *23 December* | Law on collective bargaining. |

## 1947

| | |
|---|---|
| *1 January* | Social Security plan comes into effect. |
| *2 January* | Decree imposing 5 per cent price reduction. |
| *8–15 January* | Strike of the Paris press. |
| *8–9 January* | Moutet and General Leclerc leave Indo-China. |
| *16 January* | Auriol elected President of the Republic. |
| | Resignation of the Blum government. |
| *21 January* | Herriot elected President of the National Assembly. |
| *24 January* | French plan on the future of Germany. |
| *28 January* | The Ramadier government. |
| *1 February* | Creation of an autonomous trade union for the Paris metro. |
| *5 February* | Strikes in the ports. |
| *10 February* | Signature in Paris of the peace treaty with Finland, Bulgaria, Hungary, Rumania, and Italy. |
| *11 February–17* | |
| *March* | Strike of the Paris press. |
| *24 February* | Second 5 per cent price reduction. |
| *4 March* | Franco-British alliance treaty. |
| *5 March* | Bollaert appointed High Commissioner in Indo-China. |
| *10 March* | Moscow Conference on Germany. |
| | Meeting of the CGPME. |
| *12 March* | Truman's speech to Congress on American aid. |
| *18 March* | Monnerville elected President of the Council of the Republic. |
| | The PCF rejects the Indo-China policy of Ramadier. |
| *22 March* | Vote on military credits for Indo-China. |
| *30 March* | Bruneval speech by de Gaulle. |
| | Outbreak of insurrection in Madagascar. |
| *31 March* | De Gaulle–Ramadier meeting. |
| | Creation of the 'minimum vital wage'. |
| *2–12 April* | Repression in Madagascar. |

| | |
|---|---|
| *7 April* | Founding of the RPF. |
| *9 April* | French protectorate denounced by the Sultan in Tangier. |
| *21 April* | Anglo-Franco-American agreement over the Ruhr. |
| *24 April* | Elections of the Social Security and Family Allowance administrators. |
| | Failure of the Moscow Conference. |
| *25 April* | Strike at Renault. |
| *29 April* | The CGT recovers the initiative in the Renault strike. |
| *1 May* | Bread rations at 250 g a day. |
| | Demonstrations in Paris for May Day. |
| *4 May* | Communist ministers dismissed. |
| *6 May* | The SFIO continues to support the Ramadier government. |
| *10–21 May* | Incidents in Lyon and Dijon. |
| *13 May* | General Juin becomes Resident General in Morocco. |
| *14 May* | Start of the campaign for grain collection. |
| *16 May* | Return to work at Renault. |
| *25 May* | Requisition of EDF–GDF staff. |
| *4 June* | Ramadier denouces a 'chef d'orchestre clandestin'. |
| *5 June* | Speech by Marshall at Harvard. |
| | Meeting of the overseas representatives at the Vel' d'Hiv'. |
| *6 June* | Transport strike. |
| | Parliamentary immunity of the Malagasy deputies lifted. |
| *10 June* | Beginning of a wave of strikes. |
| *17 June* | France and Great Britain accept Marshall Aid. |
| *25 June* | Eleventh Congress of the PCF at Strasbourg. |
| *2 July* | Failure of the Three's conference. Refusal of Marshall Aid by the USSR. |
| *9–12 July* | Czech about-turn on Marshall Aid. |
| *16 July* | CGT–CNPF agreement on an 11 per cent wage increase. |
| *27 July* | De Gaulle denounces the Communists as 'séparatistes'. |
| *1 August* | New CGT–CNPF agreement on wages. |
| *6 August* | Government rejects the CGT–CNPF agreement. |
| *13 August* | Law on municipal elections. |
| *14 August* | SFIO congress at Lyon. |
| *15 August* | Independence for India and Pakistan. |
| *27 August* | Statute for Algeria adopted. |
| | Bread ration at 200g. |
| *28 August* | New CGT–CNPF agreement. |
| *29 August* | Temporary suspension of imports paid for in dollars. |
| | Strikes in the car industry. |
| *September* | Wave of strikes, marked by incidents. |
| *10 September* | Bollaert's Hadong speech. |
| *18 September* | Proclamation of Bao Dai to the Vietnamese people. |
| *25 September* | Conference of the Communist Parties at Szklarska-Poreba. |
| *2 October* | Speech by Thorez against the 'parti américain'. |
| *5 October* | Creation of the Cominform. |
| *13–21 October* | Transport strikes. |
| *16 October* | Blum's speech on the 'Troisième Force'. |
| *19 and 26 October* | Municipal elections. |
| *27 October* | Call from de Gaulle for the dissolution of the Assembly and the revision of the Constitution. |
| *29–30 October* | Autocritique by Thorez before the Central Committee. |

| | |
|---|---|
| *November* | Wave of strikes and demonstrations. |
| *12 November* | The MRP advocates a 'Troisième Force'. |
| | Incidents at Marseille. |
| *15 November* | General strike in the mines. |
| *19 November* | Resignation of the Ramadier government. |
| *22 November* | Schuman's government. |
| *26 November* | Creation of a 'Central Strike Committee'. |
| *28 November* | Death of General Leclerc. |
| *29 November* | Vote of measures of 'Republican Defence'. |
| *30 November* | Government–CGT negotiations fail. |
| *1 December* | Expulsion of the deputy Calas from the National Assembly. |
| *4 December* | Visit of Dulles to Paris. |
| | Law on the freedom to work; reservists called up. |
| *6 December* | Along Bay meeting of Bollaert and Bao Dai. |
| *7 December* | Meeting between Daniel Mayer and the CGT. |
| *9 December* | The return to work. |
| *10 December* | Inaugural session of the Assembly of the French Union. |
| *15 December* | Failure of the conference of the Four over Germany. |
| *18 December* | Vote of the law on rents. |
| *19 December* | The 'Force ouvrière' national conference breaks from the CGT. |
| *29 December* | Vote of the UNO on Palestine. |
| *31 December* | Vote of a fiscal reform. |

## 1948

| | |
|---|---|
| *2 January* | Franco-American agreement on interim aid. |
| *3 January* | France recognizes the autonomy of the Saar. |
| *4 January* | De Gaulle launches the association of capital and labour at Saint-Etienne. |
| *5 January* | Adoption of the Mayer plan against inflation. |
| *7 January* | Creation of the Fonds de modernisation et d'équipement. |
| | Geneva talks between Bao Dai and Bollaert. |
| *19 January* | Génissiat dam inaugurated. |
| *25–30 January* | Devaluation of the franc, banknotes blocked, and a return to free holding of gold. |
| *28 January* | Western agreement on the coal of the Saar. |
| *5 February* | Spanish frontier reopened. |
| *7 February* | First congress of the Alliance démocratique. |
| | Reclassification of civil servants. |
| *9 February* | Anglo-American joint-zone in Germany. |
| *11 February* | Naegelen appointed Governor-General in Algeria. |
| *20–27 February* | Communist takeover in Prague. |
| *23 February* | Start of the London Conference. |
| *28 February* | Creation of the GDR. |
| *7 March* | At Compiègne, de Gaulle announces that he is ready to govern. |
| *10 March* | Laos joins the French Union. |
| *17 March* | Brussels Pact signed. |
| *20 March* | Franco-Italian economic agreement. |
| *23 March* | Founding of the FEN. |
| *3 April* | The Marshall Plan adopted by the American Congress. |
| *4 and 11 April* | Elections in Algeria. |

| | |
|---|---|
| *7 April* | Appointment of the first 'super-préfets'. |
| *12 April* | Constitutive congress of CGT–FO. |
| *13 April* | Strike of Paris metal-workers. |
| *14 April* | PCF Central Committee at Gennevilliers. |
| *16 April* | First congress of the RPF at Marseille. |
| | Conference of the Sixteen at Paris: birth of the OEEC. |
| *22 April* | Strike of the miners of Nord-Pas-de-Calais. |
| *7–10 May* | The Hague congress on Europe. |
| *14 May* | Proclamation of the State of Israel. |
| *15 May* | Vote of the Deixonne law. |
| *20 May* | General Xuan President of the Vietnamese government. |
| *21 May* | Creation of the IGAMES. |
| *22 May* | Poinsot–Chapuis decree on help to the *école libre*. |
| *1 June* | Bread rations at 250 g. |
| | London Agreement on the future of Germany. |
| *13–14 June* | Incidents at Nevers and at Clermont-Ferrand. |
| *19 June* | CGT strike call. |
| *22 June* | Start of the Berlin blockade. |
| *24 June* | Vote of the law on rents. |
| *26 June* | Airlift for Berlin. |
| *28 June* | Franco-American agreements on Marshall Aid. |
| | Tito condemned by the Cominform. |
| *6–13 July* | Strike of civil servants. |
| *19 July* | Resignation of the Schuman government. |
| *24–27 July* | Marie government. |
| *1 August* | The French zone of occupation in Germany united economically to the joint zone. |
| *25–28 August* | Congress of Wroclaw: birth of the Mouvement de la Paix. |
| *27 August* | Resignation of the Marie government. |
| | Strikes in the metal industry. |
| *31 August* | Investiture of Schuman. |
| *1 September* | Law on rents. |
| *11 September* | Investiture of Queuille. |
| *15 September* | Strikes in the metal and aircraft industries. |
| *18 September* | Incidents at Grenoble. |
| *20 September* | Law on the renewal of members of the Council of the Republic. |
| *25 September* | Cantonal elections postponed. |
| *26 September* | The Berlin affair at the United Nations. |
| *1–15 October* | Wave of strikes. |
| *4 October* | Creation of the permanent military committee of the Western Union. |
| *7 October* | Strike of the miners. |
| *9 October* | Queuille denounces the 'caractère insurrectionnel' of the strikes. |
| *11 October* | Call-up of reservists. |
| *2 November* | Troops clear the mine shafts. |
| | Election of President Truman. |
| *7 November* | Elections to the Council of the Republic. |
| *13 November* | General strike in the Paris region. |
| *17–24 November* | Parliamentary debate on the activities of the Communists. |
| *29 November* | End of the strikes. |
| *10 December* | Universal declaration of the Rights of Man. |
| *15 December* | The starting-up of 'Zoé', France's first atomic pile. |

| 16 December | Members of the Council of the Republic take the title of senator. |
| 29 December | First project for the Atlantic Pact. |

## 1949

| 12 January | Price freeze. |
| 22 January | Communist forces enter Peking. |
| 24 January | Launching of the loan for reconstruction. |
| | First hearing in the Kravchenko trial. |
| 29 January | The Five set up the Council of Europe. |
| 8 February | Condemnation of Cardinal Mindszenty. |
| 22 February | Bao Dai–Queuille–Coste–Floret talks. |
| 22–23 February | Thorez: 'La France ne fera jamais la guerre à l'URSS'. |
| 2 March | Parliamentary debate on the school. |
| 4 March | Molotov succeeded by Vychinski. |
| 8 March | Franco-Vietnamese agreements signed. |
| 24 March | Picasso's *Colombe de la paix*. |
| 31 March | Petrol goes on free sale. |
| 2 April | Mission of inquiry of General Revers in Indo-China. |
| 4 April | Atlantic Pact signed in Washington. |
| 8 April | Agreement of the Three over Germany. |
| 20–25 April | World Peace Congress in Paris. |
| 27 April | Devaluation of the franc. |
| 28 April | London Agreements on the Ruhr. |
| 5 May | Statute of the Council of Europe voted in London. |
| 8 May | Constitution of Federal Germany. |
| 12 May | Lifting of the Berlin blockade. |
| 23 May | Parliamentary debate on the economic and financial projects of Reynaud. |
| 30 May | Constitution for the GDR. |
| 3 June | Voting of a statute for Cochin China. |
| 13 June | Bao Dai enters Saigon. |
| 27 June | Forward market of the Bourse de Paris reopened. |
| 6 July | Suppression of the courts of justice. |
| 13 July | Communism condemned by the Holy Office. |
| 20 July | Laos becomes an Associated State in the French Union. |
| 27 July | Ratification of the Atlantic Pact. |
| 8 August | First session of the Strasbourg Assembly. |
| 15 August | Mgr Feltin Archbishop of Paris. |
| 24 August | Atlantic Pact operational. |
| 29 August | First atomic explosion by the Soviet Union. |
| September | Trade union campaign over prices and wages. |
| September | The 'Affaire des généraux'. |
| 8 September | The French cardinals clarify the sense of the decree of the Holy Office. |
| 15 September | Adenauer becomes Chancellor of Federal Germany. |
| 19 September | Devaluation of the pound and the franc. |
| 21 September | Birth of the People's Republic of China. |
| 22 September | Rajk condemned in Hungary. |
| 6 October | Resignation of the Queuille government. |
| 7 October | Proclamation of the GDR. |

| | |
|---|---|
| *16 October* | End of the civil war in Greece. |
| *27–29 October* | The Bidault government. |
| *8 November* | Franco-Cambodian agreements. |
| *11 November* | The Three bring the GFR into the Western bloc. |
| *30 November* | Abolition of the High Commission for food supplies. |
| *7 December* | General Revers discharged. |
| *14 December* | Kostov condemned to death. |
| *30 December* | Franco-Vietnamese agreements. |

## 1950

| | |
|---|---|
| *17 January* | Parliamentary debate on the 'Affaire des généraux'. |
| *19 and 31 January* | Ho Chi Minh's government recognized by China and the Soviet Union. |
| *27 January* | Ratification of Indo–Chinese agreements. |
| *4 February* | Resignation of Socialist ministers. |
| *7 February* | Ministerial reshuffle. |
| *11 February* | Law freeing the fixing of wages. Adoption of the SMIG. |
| *21 February* | Strike in the metal industry. |
| *3–20 March* | Wave of strikes. |
| *3 March* | General convention on the Saar. |
| *18 March* | Stockholm Appeal. |
| *27 March* | Strike of dockers at Marseille. |
| *30 March* | Death of Blum. |
| *2–6 April* | Twelfth Congress of the PCF at Gennevilliers. |
| *11 April* | March of Saint-Nazaire metal-workers on Nantes. |
| *13 April* | Arrival in France of American war material. |
| *23 April* | Mgr Gazauz advocates a tax strike. |
| *28 April* | Dismissal of F. Joliot-Curie. |
| *7 May* | Speech by General Clay on the European army. |
| *9 May* | Announcement by Schuman of the coal and steel plan. |
| *27 May* | Battle of Dong Khé. |
| *8 June* | Elections of Social Security administrators. |
| *24 June* | Resignation of the Bidault government. |
| *25 June* | Start of the Korean War. |
| *30 June* | First shipment of American war material to Indo-China. Investiture of Queuille. |
| *1 July* | American intervention in Korea. |
| *4 July* | Resignation of Queuille. |
| *7 July* | Creation of the European Payments Union. |
| *13 July* | The GFR joins the Council of Europe. The Pleven government. |
| *21 July* | Law on construction. |
| *12 August* | Encyclical *Humani generis*. |
| *17 August* | France borrows 225 million dollars from the International Bank. |
| *23 August* | Sending of a French battalion to Korea. |
| *9 September* | Expulsion of foreign Communists. |
| *12 September* | J.-P. David launches 'Paix et liberté'. |
| *14–18 September* | Meeting of the Twelve in Washington. |

| | |
|---|---|
| *19 September* | The UNO refuses to admit China. |
| *29 September* | Counter-attack by MacArthur in Korea. |
| *3–8 October* | French defeat at Cao Bang. |
| *8 October* | Start of visit to France by the Sultan of Morocco. |
| *18 October* | Langson evacuated. |
| *26 October* | Pleven Plan on the European army. |
| *27 October* | Law extending military service from 12 to 18 months. Setting up of SHAPE. |
| *3 November* | Parliamentary debate on the amnesty and the *épuration*. |
| *4 November* | European Convention of the Rights of Man signed. |
| *28 November* | Auriol refuses the resignation of the Pleven government. |
| *29 November* | Chinese forces in North Korea. |
| *6 December* | De Lattre appointed High Commissioner in Indo-China. |
| *10 December* | Speech by de Gaulle at Lille. |
| *19 December* | Eisenhower in command of SHAPE. |
| *27 December* | Recognition for Franco's Spain from the United States. |

## 1951

| | |
|---|---|
| *1–4 January* | Sino-Korean offensive on South Korea. |
| *5–26 January* | Crisis in Morocco between the Sultan and Juin. |
| *9 January* | Demonstrations in Paris against Eisenhower. |
| *11 January* | Deixonne law on the teaching of regional languages. |
| *12 January* | Vietminh offensive in north Tonkin. |
| *18 January* | First number of *Rivarol*. |
| *8 February* | Franco-Tunisian agreements. |
| *15 February* | Founding of the Centre national des indépendants et paysans. |
| *19 February* | SHAPE set up at Rocquencourt. |
| *22 February* | American counter-offensive in Korea. |
| *26 February* | Strike of public transport in Paris. |
| *28 February* | Resignation of Pleven government. |
| *9–13 March* | Queuille government. |
| *9 March* | Naegelen, Governor-General in Algeria, resigns. |
| *15 March* | De Lattre calls for fresh reinforcements in Indo-China. |
| *23–30 March* | General increase of prices and wages. |
| *4 April* | End of the Paris transport strike. Léonard appointed Governor-General in Algeria. |
| *5–28 April* | Parliamentry debate on electoral reform. |
| *18 April* | Treaty of Paris: birth of the ECSC. |
| *7 May* | Adoption of the electoral law. |
| *12 May* | First American H-bomb explosion. |
| *16 May* | Demonstration by the Comité d'action pour la liberté scolaire. |
| *17 June* | Legislative elections. Franco-Vietnamese offensive in Indo-China. |
| *20 June* | Mossadegh nationalizes Iranian petrol. |
| *8 July* | Opening of armistice negotiations in Korea. |
| *10 July* | Resignation of the Queuille government. |
| *16 July* | Death of Pétain on the Ile d'Yeu. |
| *19 July* | Condemnation of Henri Martin. |
| *8 August* | Pleven government. |
| *28 August* | General Guillaume replaces Juin in Morocco. |

|                   |                                                            |
| ----------------- | ---------------------------------------------------------- |
| *8 September*      | Peace treaty with Japan at San Francisco.                  |
| *13–24 September*  | De Lattre's visit to Washington.                           |
| *20 September*     | Adoption of sliding scale for wages.                       |
| *21 September*     | Marie and Barangé laws.                                    |
| *7–14 October*     | Cantonal elections.                                        |
| *25 October*       | Conservative victory in Great Britain.                     |
| *1–16 November*    | Wave of price increases.                                   |
| *14 November*      | Hoa Binh taken.                                            |
| *15 November*      | Miners' strike.                                            |
| *16 November*      | René Mayer presents his austerity plan.                    |
| *26 November*      | Loan 'bons-kilometres' by the SNCF.                        |
| *27 November*      | Ceasefire agreement in Korea.                              |
| *12 December*      | Decree on the Plan of modernization and equipment.         |
| *13 December*      | Parliament ratifies the Schuman Plan.                      |
| *19 December*      | Gas discovered at Lacq.                                    |
| *28–29 December*   | Conference of the Six on the European army.                |

## 1952

|                  |                                                            |
| ---------------- | ---------------------------------------------------------- |
| *7 January*      | Fall of the Pleven government.                             |
| *11 January*     | Death of General de Lattre.                                |
| *17–22 January*  | Faure government.                                          |
| *18 January*     | Repression at Cap Bon.                                     |
| *7 February*     | Strike of miners in the Cévennes.                          |
| *19 February*    | Vote of confidence in the Assembly on the European army.   |
| *24 February*    | Evacuation of Hoa Binh.                                    |
| *29 February*    | Resignation of Faure government.                           |
| *6 March*        | Investiture of Pinay.                                      |
| *14 March*       | Memorandum of the Sultan of Morocco.                       |
| *26 March*       | Tunisian ministers arrested.                               |
| *12 April*       | Vote on financial projects.                                |
| *28 April*       | SHAPE commanded by Ridgway.                                |
| *9 May*          | *Le Monde* publishes the 'Fechteler report'.               |
| *26 May*         | Launching of the Pinay loan.                               |
| *27 May*         | EDC treaty signed in Paris.                                |
| *28 May*         | Communist demonstration against Ridgway.                   |
| *10 June*        | Dissidence of RPF deputies.                                |
| *24 June*        | Electrified line Paris–Lyon inaugurated.                   |
| *1 July*         | Duclos, arrested on 28 May, released.                      |
| *3 July*         | Law-programme on the development of atomic energy.         |
| *8 July*         | Sliding wage scale.                                        |
| *12 September*   | Hirsch becomes General Commissioner for the Plan.          |
| *16 September*   | Sanctions against Marty and Tillon.                        |
| *25 October*     | Donzère-Mondragon dam inaugurated.                         |
| *1 November*     | American H-bomb.                                           |
| *4 November*     | Eisenhower elected President of the United States.         |
| *9 November*     | Grants for pupils of private schools.                      |
| *22 November*    | Labour code for the overseas territories.                  |
| *5 December*     | Ferhat Hached assassinated.                                |
| *7–8 December*   | Riots in Casablanca.                                       |
| *23 December*    | Resignation of the Pinay government.                       |

**1953**

| | |
|---|---|
| *7 January* | Investiture of René Mayer. |
| *12 January* | The 'Oradour trial' opens at Bordeaux. |
| *14 January* | Courant Plan for construction. |
| *10 February* | Common market for coal and steel (ECSC) opened. |
| *25 February* | De Gaulle rejects the EDC. |
| *5 March* | Death of Stalin. |
| *11–13 March* | Law of amnesty and suppression of the High Court of Justice. |
| *19 March* | EDC treaty ratified by the Bundestag. |
| *10 April* | Thorez returns to France. |
| *14 April* | Vietminh offensive in Laos. |
| *15 April* | Strike at Renault and of public transport. |
| *26 April–3 May* | Municipal elections. |
| *6 May* | De Gaulle gives freedom of action to the RPF deputies. |
| *8 May* | Navarre appointed Commander-in-Chief in Indo-China. |
| *14 May* | First number of *L'Express*. |
| *21 May* | Resignation of the Mayer government. |
| *26 May* | The parliamentary Gaullists found the URAS. |
| *4 June* | Mendès France fails to secure the investiture. |
| *16 June* | Riots in East Berlin. |
| *19 June* | Execution of the Rosenbergs. |
| *26 June* | Investiture of Laniel. |
| *21 July* | Adoption of the 'Navarre Plan' in Indo-China. |
| *22 July* | Poujade launches his movement at Saint-Céré. |
| *27 July* | Armistice in Korea. |
| *7 August* | General strike of public services. |
| *12 August* | Laniel announces his hostility to the strike action. |
| *20 August* | Sultan of Morocco deposed. |
| *25 August* | Return to work in the public services. |
| *7 September* | Krushchev becomes First Secretary of Soviet Party. |
| *15 September* | Worker-priests condemned by Rome. |
| *11 October* | Roads blocked by the peasants. |
| *17–27 November* | Debate on the EDC. |
| *20 November* | Camp of Dien Bien Phu set up. |
| *4–8 December* | Western summit in Bermuda. |
| *23 December* | Coty elected President of the Republic. |
| *25 December* | Vietminh offensive in Laos. |

**1954**

| | |
|---|---|
| *1 February* | Abbé Pierre begins his campaign. |
| *4 February* | Plan for economic recovery. |
| *5 February* | Dien Bien Phu encircled by the Vietminh. |
| *4 April* | Laniel and Pleven booed at Place de l'Étoile. |
| *10 April* | Law instituting the TVA. |
| *26 April* | Geneva Conference opens. |
| *29 April* | American refusal of military aid in Indo-China. |
| *7 May* | Dien Bien Phu falls. |
| *30 May* | The SFIO pronounces, not without difficulty, in favour of the EDC. |

| | |
|---|---|
| *3 June* | Ely appointed Commander-in-Chief in Indo-China. |
| *12 June* | Fall of the Laniel government. |
| *18 June* | Investiture of Mendès France. |
| *20 July* | Geneva settlement. |
| *22 July* | Geneva settlement ratified by the Assembly. |
| *30 July* | Boyer de Latour becomes Resident-General in Tunisia. |
| *31 July* | Carthage declaration. |
| *1–7 August* | Ceasefire in Vietnam, Cambodia, and Laos. |
| *13 August* | Vote of special economic powers. Resignation of Gaullist ministers hostile to the EDC. |
| *22 August* | Conference of the Six in Brussels. |
| *6 September* | Creation of SEATO. |
| *18 September* | Beginning of the 'affaire des fuites'. |
| *28 September* | Government measures against the beet-growers. |
| *3 October* | London Agreements. |
| *9 October* | Evacuation of Hanoi. |
| *21 October* | Agreement with India over the French trading-posts. |
| *23 October* | Paris Accords over Germany and the Saar. |
| *1 November* | Beginning of the Algerian insurrection. |
| *22 November* | Mendès France advocates détente at the United Nations. |
| *30 November* | Vote on the 'réformette'. |
| *3 December* | Parliamentary debate on the 'affaire des fuites'. |
| *30 December* | Ratification of the Paris Accords. |

## 1955

| | |
|---|---|
| *5 January* | Programme of reforms in Algeria. |
| *8 January* | Decree on industrial decentralization. |
| *20 January* | Ministerial reshuffle. |
| *25 January* | Soustelle appointed Governor in Algeria. |
| *6 February* | Fall of Mendès France. |
| *20 February* | Poujade holds a mass meeting at the Vel' d'Hiv'. |
| *25 February* | Investiture of Edgar Faure. |
| *2 April* | State of emergency voted for Algeria. |
| *18–24 April* | Conference of Bandoeng. |
| *15 May* | Peace treaty with Austria. |
| *21 May* | Call-up of reservists in Algeria. |
| *27 May* | Second Plan adopted. |
| *1 June* | Bourguiba returns to Tunis. |
| *1–3 June* | Messina Conference. |
| *20 June* | Grandval Resident-General in Morocco. |
| *22 June* | Start of strikes at Saint-Nazaire. |
| *30 June* | Creation of the FDES. |
| *18–24 July* | Conference of the Four at Geneva. |
| *29 July* | State of emergency maintained in Algeria. |
| *1 and 17 August* | Incidents at Saint-Nazaire and Nantes. |
| *20 August* | Wage settlement at Saint-Nazaire. |
| *21 August* | Massacre by the FLN at Guelma. |
| *24 August* | Call-up of reservists for Algeria. |
| *12 September* | General strike in the Nantes region. |
| *15 September* | Renault agreements. |

| 27–30 September | Algerian affair debated at the UN. |
| 1 October | Wage settlement at Nantes. |
| 13 October | Monnet launches a Comité d'action pour l'Europe. |
| 23 October | Referendum in the Saar. |
| 5 November | Restoration of Mohammed V. |
| 15 November | Lecœur excluded from the PCF. |
| 17 November | Elections of Social Security administrators. |
| 29 November | Fall of the Faure government. |
| 2 December | Dissolution of the National Assembly. |
| 8 December | Front républicain formed. |
| 12 December | Adjournment of elections in Algeria. |

## 1956

| 2 January | Legislative elections. |
| 7 January | Marcoule atomic pile goes into action. |
| 14 January | Committee for the defence of *l'Algérie française* set up in Algiers. |
| 5 February | Investiture of Mollet. |
| 6 February | Mollet in Algiers. Catroux resigns. |
| 9 February | Lacoste becomes Resident-General in Algeria. |
| 25 February | Krushchev report to the Twentieth Congress of the Soviet Communist Party. |
| 28 February | Three weeks of paid holiday. |
| 7 March | Independence for Morocco. |
| 12 March | Special powers in Algeria voted. |
| 20 March | Independence for Tunisia. |
| 23 March | Defferre *loi-cadre* for the overseas territories. |
| 4 April | Desertion of Maillot. |
| 12 April | Algerian Assembly dissolved. |
| 5 May | Creation of the Fonds national de solidarité. |
| 15–19 May | Mollet and Pineau visit the USSR. |
| 18 May | Palestro massacre. |
| 6 June | Krushchev report published by *Le Monde*. |
| 28 June | Poznan riots. |
| 5 July | General strike by the Algerians in France and at Algiers. |
| 18–21 July | Congress of the PCF at Le Havre. |
| 25 July | Billères project for education reform. |
| 26 July | Suez Canal nationalized by Nasser. |
| 8 August | Franco-British military contacts. |
| 1 September | Secret contacts with the FLN at Rome. |
| 10 September | Ramadier loan launched. |
| 14 September | France and Great Britain take the Suez affair to the United Nations. |
| 28 September | First nuclear-generated electricity at Marcoule. |
| 16 October | Searching of the *Athos*. |
| 22 October | Ben Bella aircraft captured. |
| 23–30 October | Budapest rising. |
| 29 October | Israeli forces invade Sinai. |
| 30 October | Franco-British ultimatum to Nasser. |
| 3 November | Gaza taken by the Israelis. |

| | |
|---|---|
| *4 November* | Soviet repression in Hungary. |
| *5 November* | Franco-British raid on the Canal and Port Said. |
| *5–6 November* | Ultimatums from Soviet Union and United States. |
| *7 November* | End of the operations in Egypt. |
| | Anticommunist demonstration in Paris. |
| *29 November* | Petrol rations. |
| *24 December* | Froger assassinated in Algiers. |
| *28 December* | European reprisals. |

## 1957

| | |
|---|---|
| *7 January* | Massu made responsible for order in Algiers. |
| *16 January* | Bazooka attack on Salan's headquarters. |
| *22 January* | Assembly favourable to the Common Market. |
| *27 January* | Paris by-election. |
| *23 March* | Death of Ali Boumendjel. |
| *25 March* | Treaty of Rome signed. |
| *31 March* | Territorial elections in Black Africa. |
| *5 April* | Setting up of the 'Commission de sauvegarde' for Algeria. |
| *9 May* | Autonomous government for the Cameroons. |
| *21 May* | Fall of the Mollet government. |
| *28–31 May* | Massacres of Melouza and Wagram. |
| *12 June* | Investiture of Bourgès-Maunoury. |
| *21 June* | Death of Maurice Audin. |
| *10 July* | Treaties of Rome ratified. |
| *25 July* | Bourguiba President of the Tunisian Republic. |
| *12 August* | Disguised devaluation of the franc. |
| *15 September* | Morice Line completed. |
| *30 September* | Fall of Bourgès-Maunoury government. |
| *4 October* | Launching of Sputnik 1. |
| *7 October* | Nobel prize to Camus. |
| *5 November* | Investiture of Gaillard. |

## 1958

| | |
|---|---|
| *1 January* | Opening of the Common Market. |
| *11 January* | First crude oil from the Sahara arrives at Philippeville. |
| *30 January* | American loan to France. |
| *31 January* | Adoption of the *loi-cadre* for Algeria. |
| *8 February* | Sakhiet bombed. |
| *17 February* | Anglo-American 'good offices'. |
| *13 March* | Policemen demonstrate outside the National Assembly. |
| *23 March* | The Républicains sociaux call for de Gaulle. |
| *27 March* | Seizure of Alleg's *La Question*. |
| *9 April* | Failure of the 'good offices'. |
| *15 April* | Fall of the Gaillard government. |
| *26 April* | Demonstration in Algiers for 'Algérie française'. |
| *13 May* | Investiture of Pflimlin. |
| *15 May* | Salan shouts de Gaulle's name to the crowd on the Forum. |
| *19 May* | Press conference by de Gaulle. |

| | |
|---|---|
| *24 May* | Success of 'Resurrection' in Corsica. |
| *28 May* | Pflimlin resigns. Antifascist demonstration in Paris. |
| *29 May* | Coty summons de Gaulle. |
| *1 June* | Investiture of de Gaulle. |
| *2 June* | Vote of full powers. |
| *4–7 June* | De Gaulle in Algiers: 'Je vous ai compris.' |
| *28 September* | Referendum on the new Constitution. |
| *23–30 November* | Legislative elections |
| *21 December* | De Gaulle becomes the first President of the Fifth Republic and the French Community. |

# Notes

The figures in brackets refer to the bibliography

## 1 Victory

1 By a decision of General Revers on 19 September, ratified by de Gaulle on 24 September, the B Army received tactical autonomy, on a par with the American Army, and took the name of First French Army. A change of detail, of course; but one largely imposed by the enthusiasm of the French forces.

2 In *La Force des choses* (Gallimard, 'Folio', 1963), vol. 1, p. 51. 'Indifférence et angoisse', added J.-P. Sartre, in *Situations III* (Gallimard, 1949), p. 63.

3 See Ch.-L. Foulon, 'Les Etats-Unis et la France combattante, 1942–1945', *Espoir*, 26 (March 1979), 62–78.

4 See J.-P. Azéma (13), chapter 6.

5 For example, the writer Louis Guilloux. See *Solido*, followed by *O. K. Joe* (Gallimard, 1976), the second story of this collection dealing with these little-known questions.

6 Some opinion polls show that in November 1944, 44 per cent of Parisians thought the American aid to be insufficient, a view held by 55 per cent of the population at large in January 1945. Other polls, however, show that at the beginning of December 71 per cent were satisfied with the conduct of the American forces. True, figures from the South and the towns influenced this result, and the complaints would in fact multiply; the sense, however, is clear. See *Bulletin de l'IFOP*, 10–25 January 1945, and *Sondages du Service de sondages et statistique (SSS)*, 7, 1 January 1945.

7 For de Gaulle's comments on the affair see Ch. de Gaulle (55), pp. 181 *et seq.* The final settlement came with the peace treaty with Italy of 10 February 1947, and in February 1948 the Italian Parliament accorded the Val d'Aosta a statute of relative autonomy.

8 See J.-M. d'Hoop, 'De Gaulle et l'affaire de Strasbourg', in (104), pp. 286–93.

9 For Eisenhower's account see D. D. Eisenhower, *Crusade in Europe* (New York, Doubleday, 1948), pp. 362–3.

10 See *Sondages SSS*, 7, 9, and 12, 1 January, 1 February, and 1 April 1945. See chapter 6 below.

11 Three roughly equal parts can be identified: individual enlistments – for the duration of the war or longer – those arriving in an existing FFI unit, and FFI reinforcements sent by the central administration. With our present knowledge, classing them politically is extremely difficult. One thing is certain, however: all the political currents of the Resistance were present at the front. On these

little-explored questions see the reports of Colonels le Goyet and Michalon in (51), pp. 559–704.

12 On this brigade, relatively well known owing to the personalities of its leaders, see J. Lacouture, *André Malraux* (Seuil, 1973), pp. 290–303.

13 For example, de Lattre managed to bring together the last 'grandes compagnies' of FFI in the 14ᵉ Division, which Salan would lead with success on the Alsacien front. But it was already late – February 1945 – and the General Staff was made up uniquely of career officers. See R. Salan, *Mémoires*, vol. 1, *La Fin d'un empire* (Presses de la Cité, 1970), p. 149.

14 See J. Chauvel (195), p. 73.

15 This figure is certainly too high. The failure of the Scapini mission, the confusion of the final combat, and the improvisation of the new administration – all help to make it imprecise. See J.-P. Azéma (13), pp. 174 and 212, who settles for 940 000.

16 See O. Wormser-Migot, *Quand les Alliés ouvrirent les portes* (Laffont, 1965), and his contribution in (51), pp. 721 *et seq.*, and Frenay's own account in *La Nuit finira* (Laffont, 1973).

17 The first accounts by deportees came as warnings, and presented the camps as the mirror-image of the breakdown of the society of Nazi Germany. One of the most important, written in August 1945, is that of D. Rousset, *L'Univers concentrationnaire* (Le Pavois, 1946). He concluded that the deportees 'are separated from other people by an experience impossible to communicate', and that the evil contaminated 'beyond the ruins'. Attention turned afterwards to other camps. From 1948, Rousset collected material against Vichy, published as *Le Pitre ne rit pas*, new edn (Ch. Bourgois, 1979), and launched the debate on the Soviet camps.

18 Even the best studies, such as P. Gascar, *Histoire de la capitivité des français en Allemagne* (Gallimard, 1967) and J. Evard, *La Déportation des travailleurs français dans le IIIᵉ Reich* (Fayard, 1972), have almost nothing to say on the return; and nor do the two most famous novels, *Les Grandes Vacances* of F. Ambrière and *Le Caporal épinglé* of J. Perret.

19 'We felt just like Martians', reported Pierre Daix, on his return from Mauthausen, in (168), p. 143.

## 2 Survival

1 Ch. de Gaulle (55), p. 1.

2 From (11), p. 197. A. Sauvy advances slightly lower figures in *La Vie économique des Français de 1939 à 1945* (Flammarion, 1978). In (55), p. 235, de Gaulle suggests 635 000 killed. H. Michel (76), p. 433, proposes 600 000, explaining how civilian losses and desertion make reliable figures hard to establish.

3 P. Delouvrier and R. Nathan (256), p. 215.

4 Thus R. Debré and A. Sauvy, although well-informed observers, did not mention it in *Des Français pour la France* (Gallimard), a vigorous plea for a policy to favour a higher birth-rate published in March 1946. See J.-P. Azéma (13), pp. 165–6.

5 At the age of fourteen, compared with their elders of 1935, the adolescents of 1945 had lost between 7 and 11 cm in height and between 7 and 9 kg in weight: the averages had fallen back to the levels of 1900. School doctors reported many cases of rickets and a general fall in the red blood cell count due to vitamin deficiency. Infant mortality had gone from 65 per thousand in 1936–9 to 77 per thousand in 1944. At Tourcoing, for example, it stood at 99 per thousand in

1945, before falling back to 72 per thousand and 57 per thousand in 1946 and 1947 when milk supplies were re-established. See (51), pp. 281–321.

6 During the war the population was split into categories: E (0–3 years), J1 (3–6), J2 (6–13), J3 (13–21, plus pregnant women), A (21–70), T (labourers), and V (over 70). Each category had its own food coupons and rations.

7 On 1 January 1950, when the last compensation claims and loans for war losses were settled, the final figure stood at 460 000 buildings destroyed and 1 900 000 damaged, compared with 345 000 and 541 000 respectively in 1918. Worst affected was Normandy – 52 000 dead, of which 20 000 buried in the ruins, 40 000 wounded and injured; 280 000 victims for 438 000 inhabitants in the Manche, and a total of more than 500 000; Caen was 75 per cent destroyed, Saint-Lô 77 per cent, Rouen 50 per cent, Le Havre 82 per cent; roughly 600 000 mines had to be removed, and the beaches and ruins cleared; economic life was at a standstill; the region had lost approximately 40 per cent of its productive capital. The victims in the large towns spent a very hard winter of 1944–5 in wooden emergency housing; some were to remain in it for over a decade. See (462), pp. 292–347.

8 For the whole of this period of hyper-inflation, statistical comparisons with the pre-war years are obviously imprecise and open to question. In most cases no more than broad estimates are given; but their scale remains significant. For an attempt to convert to current values see R. Sédillot (90), pp. 293–4.

9 See E. Dejonghe, 'Pénurie charbonnière et répartition en France (1940–1944)', *Revue d'histoire de la Deuxieme Guerre Mondiale, RHDGM*, 102 (April–May 1976), 21–55.

10 Hence the ordinance of 2 November 1945 laid down relatively free conditions for the entry and residence of foreign workers. That it then remained in force until 1979 is clear evidence of this permanent and irreducible need of the French economy.

11 See J. Bouvier, 'Sur la politique économique en 1944–1946', in (51), pp. 835–56.

12 Under the terms of the agreements signed there in July 1944 by forty-four nations (the French delegation was led by P. Mendès France), currencies were henceforth to be defined in gold or in dollars. In fact, the dollar became the exchange standard and the strongest international currency. Now the International Monetary Fund (IMF) for short-term loans, and the International Bank for Reconstruction and Development (IBRD) for long-term aid were set up.

13 The figure is higher still if, to the budget of the State, are added the accounts of the Treasury, the Caisse autonome d'amortissement, and the local authorities.

14 See J.-M. Jeanneney in (51), pp. 305–8, and the analysis of Gaëtan Pirou, 'Le problème monétaire en France depuis la Libération', *Revue d'économie politique*, 1–2 (1946), 12–49. The total money supply rose from 264 milliard francs in 1939 to 1035 at the end of 1944. An increase of 3.9 compared with one of 4.8 for banknotes.

15 See J.-P. Azéma (13), pp. 160 *et seq.*

16 S. P. Kramer (87), p. 27; Ch.-L. Foulon (52), pp. 185–94; A. Sauvy, *La Vie économique*, chapters 10 and 11.

17 See the remarks in this vein made in July 1945 by J. Mairey, commissaire de la République at Dijon, in S. P. Kramer (87), p. 31.

18 See (11), p. 80. In the same official publication it is moreover discreetly revealed (p. 69) that the most minor officials of the Service national de la statistique in sixteen cities, including Paris, had between 1840 and 2540 calories a

day in May–June 1944, and between 2050 and 2870 in September–October, thanks to 'ressources d'appoint'.

19 See J. Dutourd, *Au bon beurre* (Gallimard, 1952).

20 See E. Dejonghe and D. Laurent (73), p. 190. On these little-known questions, the first serious reflections are those of M. Cépède (86), P. Verley, 'Quelques remarques sur l'agriculture française de 1938 à 1945', *Recherches et travaux de l'Institut d'histoire économique et sociale de l'université de Paris-I*, 5 (July 1977), and I. Boussard (85).

21 The *exode rural* had remained strong during the war; there were 500 000 dead, prisoners or labour conscripts to the STO, in higher proportions than in the towns. In spite of the courageous efforts of women, the old, and adolescents, and despite the temporary help of German prisoners, the balance remained negative; a clear sign of the failure of Vichy's 'retour à la terre', and of the persistence of an agricultural crisis that had begun in the 1930s. Between 1936 and 1945, 726 000 were lost from the active population. I. Boussard (85), p. 80.

22 On those shortages of materials and on the subterfuge necessary to overcome them in the Beauce, see E. Grenadou and A. Prévost, *Grenadou, paysan français* (Seuil, new edn 'Points-Histoire', 1978), pp. 225 *et seq.*

23 The last items were painfully missed. In October 1944, the population wanted to see reappear, in descending order, chocolate, coffee, tea, bananas, oranges, and lemons. Many of the young had either not experienced or had forgotten these delights. *Sondages IFOP*, 3, 1 November 1944.

24 M. Cépède estimates the 'friendly' price at double the official price and the black market price at triple or quadruple (86), p. 334. Yet in the Nord, for example, a cow worth 25 000 francs at the beginning of 1945 would be purchased for only 5000 francs by the administration. Slaughtered and sold clandestinely, it would fetch at least 70 000 francs.

25 See P. Verley, 'Quelques remarques sur l'agriculture française', pp. 40–1.

26 Little is known about the other voices in this chorus of complaint, those of the small shopkeepers and middlemen. There is no doubt, however, that the provisions crisis posed the question of an urgent modernization of distributive networks and of stronger control by the public authorities. Thus were shaped many of the themes that Poujadism would develop ten years later.

27 See I. Boussard, *Vichy et la corporation paysanne* (Presses de la Fondation nationale des sciences politiques, 1980), pp. 347–70.

28 See S. P. Kramer (87), pp. 32–3.

29 See E. Dejonghe and D. Laurent (73), p. 194; F. Rude (70), p. 209; R. Bourderon (64), pp. 232–6; P. Guiral (66), p. 137. In Montpellier, where the announcement of a visit by Tanguy-Prigent led to agitation by the Union des femmes françaises, the commissaire de la République presented its representatives with the menu of the planned 'feast': 'carottes râpées avec un rond de saucisson, ragoût immangeable, fromage approximatif', in J. Bounin (65), p. 204. For Toulouse see P. Bertaux (61), pp. 207–10 and Ch.-L. Foulon (52), p. 191.

30 The official daily bread ration per day (estimated at 500 g before the war) was: 350 g for 1 October 1944 to 1 November 1945; free sales from 1 November to 28 December 1945; 300 g from 29 December 1945 to 1 May 1947; 250 g from 1 May to 1 September 1947; 200 g from 1 September 1947 to 31 May 1948; 250 g from June 1948 to the end of rationing in autumn 1949.

31 Thus in February 1945, 39 per cent wanted a return to a free market, 31 per cent the retention of full controls, and 25 per cent a mixed system. See *Sondages SSS*, 9 and 11, 1 February and 1 March 1946; *Sondages IFOP*, February 1946.

32 The most famous of these was the 'affaire des vins', launched in summer 1946 by Y. Farge, which implicated the entourage of F. Gouin (see Y. Farge, *Le Pain de la corruption*, Editions du Chêne, 1947, and G. Elgey (19), pp. 172 *et seq.*). The figure of four million dealers, large and small, is sometimes advanced. A 'specialized' press informed over the political implications (see *Le Crapouillot*, 27 and 28, 1955), but the history of this aspect remains to be written.

33 See F. Caron, in (51), pp. 861–86.

## 3 The purges

1 See J.-P. Rioux, 'L'épuration en France, 1944–1945', *L'Histoire*, 5 (October 1956), 24–32.

2 Y. Durand and R. Vivier (59), pp. 226–9.

3 Ch. de Gaulle (55), p. 38, and P. Novick (97).

4 M. Baudot, in (51), p. 769.

5 See F. L'Huillier (71), pp. 176–81.

6 For a specific example, see J. Larrieu, 'L'épuration judiciaire dans les Pyrénées-Orientales', *RHDGM*, 112 (October 1978), 29–45.

7 At Lyon, for example, where rival demonstrators clashed in December for or against the death penalty for Vichy's former regional prefect, Alexandre Angeli. See F. Rude (70), pp. 190 *et seq.*

8 See L. Noguères (100).

9 See E. Dejonghe and D. Laurent (73), pp. 182–5.

10 *Bulletin de l'IFOP*, 8, February 1945.

11 *Bulletin de l'IFOP*, 2, 16 October 1944.

12 *Journal officiel, Débats de l'Assemblée nationale constituante*, 6 August 1946, 3016–17.

13 These are the conclusions of J.-P. Azéma (13), pp. 353–9.

14 Summary of all their themes in *Le Livre noir de l'épuration, lectures françaises*, 89–90 (August–September 1964).

15 *Les Crimes masqués du 'résistantialisme'* (L'Elan, 1948).

16 A. Camus (387), pp. 212–13.

17 Originally published by Editions de Minuit. New edition, with a dossier of the controversy, published by J.-J. Pauvert in 1968.

18 Pétain was condemned to death by the High Court on 15 August 1945. In accordance with the wishes of the jurors, de Gaulle commuted the sentence. The prisoner was transferred to Portalet, then to the Ile d'Yeu, where he died on 23 July 1951. The trial was often confused and without great dignity. After making an introductory statement, Pétain retreated into silence, invoking History as his judge. The proceedings, which heard evidence from the former accused of the Riom trial, and from the great names of Vichy and the Occupation, failed to establish a clear distinction between the responsibilities of the Vichy régime and those of the dying Third Republic. Against the background of a noisy and polemical press campaign, the debate became bogged down over the armistice of 1940 and on the delicate period between 1942 and 1944. From the vast literature on this spectacular episode of the *épuration* can be consulted, apart from the complete transcript of the trial (*Le Procès du maréchal Pétain*, 2 vols. Albin Michel, 1945), two extreme points of view, treason and sacrifice: A. Bayet, *Pétain et la Cinquième Colonne* (Editions Franc-Tireur, 1944), and J. Isorni, *Souffrances et mort du maréchal* (Flammarion, 1951). Isorni, one of the counsel at the trial, subsequently specialized in an untiring campaign for the rehabilitation of Pétain and his memory.

19 *Situations III* (Gallimard, 1949), p. 41.

20 Pascal Ory, *Les Collaborateurs, 1940–1945* (Seuil, 1977), p. 273. A new edition 'Points-histoire' in 1980.
21 'Y a-t-il une justice en France?', *Esprit* (August 1947), 191.

## 4 Restoration

1 F. Coulet, *Vertu des temps difficiles* (Plon, 1967), p. 231, and Ch. de Gaulle, *Mémoires de guerre*, vol. 2, *L'Unité* (Plon, 1956), pp. 710 and 712.
2 See R. Rémond, 'Les problèmes politiques au lendemain de la Libération', in (51), pp. 815–34.
3 Namely the ordinances of: 17 September 1943, creating the Provisional Consultative Assembly; 10 January 1944, creating the commissaires de la République; 14 March, on the delegation of power and the exercise of military authority during the fighting; and, the most important, 21 April, concerning the organization of civil powers after the Liberation (text in G. Dupeux (15), pp. 70–2).
4 See D. de Bellescize, *Les Neufs Sages de la Résistance* (Plon, 1979), R. Hostache, *De Gaulle 1944, victorie de la légitimité* (Plon, 1978), and M. Debré, *Une certaine idée de la France* (Fayard, 1972), pp. 30 *et seq.* The members of the Comité général d'études were, in order of appointment, F. de Menthon, P. Bastid, R. Lacoste, A. Parodi, P.-H. Teitgen, R. Courtin, M. Debré, J. Charpentier, and P. Lefaucheux. All held key posts after the Liberation.
5 See L. Hamon in (51), p. 947; R. Bourderon, 'Une question clé, celle de l'État', *Cahiers d'histoire de l'Institut Maurice-Thorez*, 24 (1978), 135, and J.-P. Scot, 'La Restauration de l'Etat', *ibid.*, 20–21 (1977), 167–87. Careers, legal training, social backgrounds, absence of action in mass organizations–all tended to make these top administrators lean towards 'vigilance républicaine'. According to Ch.-L. Foulon (52), the prefects were drawn in equal proportions from among the existing prefectoral corps, the private sector, and top officials; the commissaires de la République counted eight members of the liberal professions, six top officials, and three parliamentarians.
6 See F. Closon, *Le Temps des passions* (Presses de la Cité, 1974), p. 193.
7 See J.-P. Azéma (13), pp. 308–22, and J.-P. Rioux, 'La dynamique unitaire de 1944 à 1947', *Politique aujourd'hui* (February 1973), 41–51.
8 See D. Hostache, *Le Conseil national de la Résistance* (PUF, 1958), and J. Debû-Bridel, *De Gaulle et le Conseil national de la Résistance* (France-Empire, 1978), who minimizes the tensions between the two parties.
9 F. Billoux (108), p. 56.
10 With just one commissaire de la République, two prefects and two ministerial general secretaries. Yet 26 per cent of the members of the CDLs in the former northern zone, and 35 per cent in the former southern zone, were Communists.
11 In addition to: A. Lepercq at Finance, P. Mendès France at National Economy, R. Lacoste at Industrial Production, F. de Menthon at Justice, P.-H. Teitgen at Information, R. Pleven at Colonies, R. Capitant at Education, A. Parodi at Labour. The extent of the destruction led to the creation on 13 November of a new Ministry of Reconstruction and Town Planning, under Raoul Dautry. A complete list can be found in (4) 1944–45, p. 32.
12 The formula is that of P.-H. Teitgen, in (51), p. 103.
13 On Limoges, see J. Chaintron (51), pp. 531–43, and G. Guingouin (62),

pp. 220–30; on the Auvergne, H. Ingrand (63), chapters 12 to 18; special pleading from H. Romans-Petit (69), pp. 157 *et seq.*, and P. Bertaux (61) – the book's appearance in 1973, coupled with a television programme, re-kindled passions over the issue. On the Languedoc, see J. Bounin (65) and R. Bouderon (64), 3rd section.

14 See M. Baudot (58), p. 172.

15 See, for example, Ch.-L. Foulon, 'L'opinion, la résistance et le pouvoir en Bretagne à la Libération', *RHDGM*, 117 (January 1980), 75–114.

16 See M. Agulhon and F. Barrat (67), pp. 27 *et seq.* In Provence and at Lyon, the situation was further complicated by the creation, on the initative of the commissaires de la République, of Forces républicaines de sécurité, the first stage in bringing the militia under control.

17 The decision by the government was approved by 63 per cent of those questioned, compared with 24 per cent against and 13 per cent without an opinion. *Bulletin de l'IFOP*, 5, 1 December 1944.

18 See J.-P. Azéma (13), pp. 314–22.

19 See (116) 4th section. An excellent regional example in B. Montergnole, *La Presse grenobloise de la Libération* (Presses Universitaires de Grenoble, 1974).

20 The Parisian daily press had 3 500 000 copies in January 1948. With 370 copies for 1000 inhabitants in 1946 (compared with 261 in 1939 and less than 200 in 1978), the national press was at its apogee.

21 See P. Miquel (120), pp. 171–9.

22 See J.-N. Jeanneney and J. Julliard (117), pp. 47–66.

23 Publication had been held up for several months by the paper shortage. On a related review, *Esprit*, see M. Winock (384), chapter 8.

24 As examples, two books, very different but that share this spirit: A. Ferrat, *La République à refaire* (Gallimard, 1945), and R. Aron, *L'Age des empires et l'Avenir de la France* (Editions Défense de la France, 1945).

25 See E.-F. Callot (115), p. 225.

26 See S. P. Kramer, 'La stratégie socialiste à la Libération', *RHDGM*, 98 (April 1975), 77–90.

27 As Léon Blum wrote to Félix Gouin in October 1942, the party's task was to push de Gaulle 'to do what we would do in his place and that he will be infinitely better placed to accomplish than we shall be'. The tactic had not changed.

28 236 000 membership cards were distributed in 1945. In addition to conserving a strong worker base, the SFIO attracted many State employees, notably among the schoolteachers. Thus in Meurthe-et-Moselle, the SFIO Federation counted 59 per cent workers and 17 per cent white-collar recruits. Overall, however, its militants were too few faced with the Communists. In the Ariège, for example, for 2000 Socialists there were 7000 Communists, 4000 Members of the Front national, and 5000 Femmes françaises.

29 The MLN minority was organized around Pierre Hervé, Maurice Kriegel-Valrimont, Emmanuel d'Astier, Albert Bayet, and Pascal Copeau.

30 The UDSR brought together individuals as diverse as Jacques Baumel and René Capitant, Gaullists, Socialists like Francis Leenhardt, and Moderates like René Pleven, Eugène Claudius-Petit, and François Mitterrand.

31 *Sondages SSS*, 8, 15 January 1945, 12, 1 April 1945, and 13, 1 May 1945. The second poll is revealing of the degrees of disparity between Paris and the rest of France. To the question 'Do you approve, yes or no, the CNR programme?', the answers were:

|              | yes  | no   | no opinion |
|--------------|------|------|------------|
| France       | 40%  | 7%   | 53%        |
| Paris        | 48%  | 12%  | 40%        |
| Other towns  | 40%  | 7%   | 53%        |
| Countryside  | 35%  | 3%   | 62%        |

32 On the other hand, strict Bolshevik methods made little progress. The cells within firms, which represented roughly a third of all cells in 1937, accounted for barely a fifth in 1945–6. See G. Willard, 'Les cellules d'entreprise du PCF en 1944–1945', *Cahiers d'histoire de l'institut Maurice-Thorez*, 24 (1978), 72.

33 A figure of 75 000 'fusillés' is sometimes advanced. It is clearly an exaggeration, since the Reistance as a whole, all tendencies mixed and including hostages, had roughly 40 000 victims of executions.

34 In November 1944, 61 per cent of those questioned thought that the Soviet Union was playing the principal role in the defeat of Germany, compared with 29 per cent for the United States and 12 per cent for Great Britain. *Bulletin de l'IFOP*, 1 October 1944.

35 See M. Agulhon, 'Les communistes et la Libération de la France', in (51), pp. 88–9, many of whose analyses we follow here.

36 See R. Rémond, in (51), p. 826.

37 Moreover, the presence of American troops in France made an alternative hypothesis implausible. Indeed, on this basis J. Elleinstein minimizes the role of Stalin in the elaboration of the strategy. See *De la guerre à la Libération* (Editions sociales, 1977), pp. 95 *et seq.*

38 In *L'Humanité* of 12 September 1944, echoing Radio-Moscow. See J.-P. Scot, 'Les pouvoirs d'État et l'action des communistes pour la "démocratie agissante", août 1944–juillet 1945', *Cahiers d'histoire de l'institut Maurice-Thorez*, 8–9 (1974), and R. Bourderon, 'Une question clé', 128–32.

39 See A. Lecœur, *Le Partisan* (Flammarion, 1963), pp. 207–8; Ch. Tillon (109), chapter 27. With a similar approach, the Trotskyist extreme Left was able to recruit some new militants and obtained encouraging results in the municipal elections. See Y. Craipeau, *La Libération confisquée* (Savelli/Syros, 1979).

40 See Ph. Robrieux (107), chapter 6, and Ch. Tillon (109), p. 408. 'Pensons au retour de Maurice!', was urging Duclos from August 1944.

41 Is this to say that several strategies were not in fact combined? For the period from November 1944 to 1947, A. Kriegel identifies three, in *Communismes au miroir français* (Gallimard, 1974), pp. 163–76. For his part, S. Courtois offers many texts which point to an underlying strategy of offensive against the bourgeoisie, without a civil war, to prepare the way for the Red Army and set up a Popular Democracy. *Le PCF dans la guerre* (Ramsay, 1980), chapter 16.

42 Appeals to reason were rare. See, for example, H. Chatreix, *Au-delà du laïcisme* (Seuil, 1946), written in May–August 1945. Public opinion followed, but slowly and with hesitation: 54 per cent of those asked in January refused the maintenance of the subsidies, 61 per cent in April. But a majority rejected the suppression of the *école libre*: the issue was not dead! *Sondages SSS*, 12 and 14, March and May 1945, and *Bulletin de l'IFOP*, 1 May 1945, 99.

43 Thus on 5 February, in the course of a curt interview with Daniel Mayer, he refused to receive a delegation of the SFIO Committee of direction. See R. Quilliot (110), pp. 53 and 778, and *Les Cahiers Léon-Blum*, 6–7–8 (1980).

44 P.-M. de La Gorce (26), pp. 96–7.

45 'Se sortir de Mauthausen pour tendre la main à Herriot!', sighed Pierre Daix (168), p. 154.

46 This occurred in the framework of the *département* and by the system of the highest average – something which favoured the large parties locally but disadvantaged them in the overall national result. In order to obtain fairer representation of the cities, there were 103 constituencies for 90 *départements*.

47 See the analysis by F. Goguel, 'Géographie des élections', *Esprit* (1 December 1945), 956, and R. Rémond, in (51), pp. 827–34.

48 See Ch. de Gaulle (55), pp. 642–4.

49 A poll of January showed the division of opinion: 41 per cent felt that de Gaulle had succeeded well in his task, 36 per cent disagreed; and 23 per cent were without an opinion, *Sondages IFOP*, 51, 16 February 1946. His departure left 40 per cent discontented, 32 per cent were satisfied, and 28 per cent were indifferent. And 21 per cent thought he would return to power, 36 per cent were without an opinion, while 43 per cent condemned him to retirement. This last percentage was hardly to vary from now on: it corresponded to the proportion of the population for whom de Gaulle was a man of the Right, *ibid.*, 1 March 1946.

50 See Ch. de Gaulle (55), p. 8. Overall balance-sheet by Ch.-L. Foulon, in (104), pp. 60–71, and M. Cointet, 'Le général de Gaulle et la reconstruction de la France à la Libération', *Etudes gaulliennes*, 21 (1978), 25–71. On his popularity, see the reminiscences of his private secretary Cl. Mauriac, *Aimer de Gaulle* (Grasset, 1978). The case for a 'restoration' and of 'dynastic' ambitions, is pleaded with talent – and sometimes confusion – by Ph. Tesson, *De Gaulle I^er, la révolution manquée* (Albin Michel, 1965).

## 5 Production

1 *Une leçon, un devoir* (October 1945), Bibliothèque nationale, 16° Lb[59] 269.

2 See his speech of 24 May 1945 in Ch. de Gaulle (56), p. 590.

3 See B. Frachon, *Au rythme des jours* (Editions sociales, 1967), vol. 1, pp. 32–47. Indeed, Gaston Monmousseau was soon to denounce 'la grève, arme des trusts'; see his preface to B. Frachon, *La Bataille de la production* (Editions sociales, 1946).

4 See J.-P. Scot, 'Le programme de gouvernement du PCF (novembre 1946)', *Cahiers d'histoire de l'institut Maurice-Thorez*, 17–18 (1976), 169–201.

5 See R. F. Kuisel, 'Vichy et les origines de la planification économique (1940–1946)', *Le Mouvement social*, 98 (January–March 1977).

6 On this struggle of the winter, see the transcript of his Saturday radio broadcasts, edited by the Comité d'histoire de la Deuxième Guerre mondiale, 1979, 104pp.

7 Ch. de Gaulle (55), pp. 120 and 435.

8 See J. Bouvier in (51), p. 846.

9 The Pleven franc had a value corresponding to 7.6 mg of gold (against the 21 mg of the Reynaud franc of February 1940), or 119 francs to the dollar (against 43.8 since 1940, but in reality 233 francs on the 'parallel market'). That is, in terms of gold, $\frac{1}{39}$ of the Germinal franc. Given the real value of the dollar, this devaluation was not very combative: in fact, the government hoped to curb exports. In addition, a franc zone was created, one that favoured speculations with the Empire: the metropolitan franc was legal tender in North Africa, the West Indies, and Guiana; a CFA (Colonies françaises d'Afrique) franc, advantageously fixed at 1.70 francs for the metropole, was imposed in Black Africa, Madagascar, and Reunion Island. And in Indo-China, the piastre was also fixed at a low price.

10 See J. Le Bourva (89), pp. 366 *et seq.*

11 R. Courtin, *Rapport sur la politique économique d'après guerre* (Algiers, Editions Combat, 1944).

12 See G. Declas, 'Berliet sans Berliet (1944–1949): une expérience autogestionnaire?', *Recherches et travaux de l'Institut d'histoire éconmique et sociale de l'université de Paris-I*, 7 (December 1978), 71–105.

13 See J. Domenichino, 'Marseille: les usines requisitionnées', *Cahiers d'histoire de l'institut Maurice-Thorez*, 4 (July–September 1973), 161–77, and R. Bourderon (64), pp. 225–32.

14 See P. Fridenson, in (51), pp. 867–72, and 'La bataille de la 4CV Renault', *L'Histoire*, 9 (February 1979).

15 See J. Bouvier, in (51), p. 853.

16 See E. Fajon, 'Les communistes et les nationalizations', *Cahiers du communisme* (February 1945).

17 See B. Georges, D. Tintant, and M.-A. Renauld, *Léon Jouhaux dans le mouvement syndical français* (PUF, 1979), p. 304. At the Congress of April 1946, the first since the war, the Communists disposed of roughly 80 per cent of the votes and controlled the seven largest federations (Metals, Building, Textiles, Rail, Mining, Food, Agriculture).

18 More accurately by the Union des fédérations de fonctionnaires de la CGT, brought together in March 1946. See the reminiscences – highly partisan – of R. Bidouze, *Les Fonctionnaires, sujets ou citoyens?* (Editions sociales, 1979). The statute – that did not apply to those employed by local and municipal authorities – brought protection from arbitrariness, and set up representative bodies and a Conseil supérieur de la fonction publique, thus favouring trade union pressure. However, it froze the existing categories and hierarchies. In future, any change to wages for one category automatically led to a revision for all the others: governments found in this a strong reason for neglecting wage revisions. Article 32, stipulating that the minimum wage be equal to 120 per cent of the vital minimum, was hardly applied.

19 A brainchild of the Socialists, the CGA, whose complex structure was elaborated by the congresses of March 1945 and February 1950, brought together general trade unions (the Féderation nationale des syndicats d'exploitants agricoles – FNSEA – set up in March 1946), agricultural co-operatives, mutual benefit and credit agencies, technicians and managers, and agricultural workers, for their part also attached to the working-class unions. The young farmers of the CNJA formed in 1947 did not join until 1954. In spite of the return to free trade unions on 6 June 1945, only the CGA received official recognition. However, by the end of 1946 the former leaders of Vichy's Corporation Paysanne, often using the MRP label, had recovered control.

20 See J.-N. Jeanneney, 'Hommes d'affaires au piquet. Le difficile intérim d'une représentation patronale (septembre 1944–janvier 1946)', *Revue historique* (January–March 1980), 81–100.

21 To this general survey have to be added a number of complementary measures: help for the 'economically weak' (for the most part small *rentiers*, victims of the inflation) in September 1946; the ordinance of 28 June 1945 setting up a national housing service, and, in 1948, housing allowances; advantages to the complementary mutual benefit schemes under the terms of the statute of 19 October 1945.

22 For Paris, see (12), pp. 118–20. H. Brousse, in *Le Niveau de vie en France* (PUF, 1949), gives the following table, open to criticism but whose general sense is clear:

| | length of working week index | hourly wage index | retail price index | purchasing power index |
|---|---|---|---|---|
| October 1944 | 100 | 100 | 100 | 100 |
| April 1945 | 103 | 121 | 112 | 111 |
| October 1945 | 107.7 | 131 | 158 | 89 |
| April 1946 | 107.9 | 140 | 169 | 89 |
| October 1946 | 108.7 | 184 | 295 | 67 |
| April 1947 | 109.9 | 200 | 288 | 76 |
| October 1947 | 111.7 | 252 | 436 | 68 |
| April 1948 | 112 | 335 | 517 | 71 |

## 6 France in the world

1 See J. Chauvel (195), pp. 147 *et seq.*
2 See the analyses, very untypical of the period, of R. Aron, *L'Age des empires et l'Avenir de la France* (Editions Défense de la France, 1945), especially pp. 337 *et seq.*
3 (55), pp. 60 *et seq.*
4 (55), p. 88.
5 In Syria and Lebanon, vulnerable to a nationalist offensive backed by the Arab League formed in March 1945, and closely watched by the British, France was quickly isolated, despite an ostentatious sending of reinforcements. On 31 May, de Gaulle gave way; in December the evacuation began that was to be concluded in autumn 1946. The Near East was henceforth part of a global strategy dominated by the United States and the Soviet Union, the subject of violent debates at the United Nations, and in which France had few means of intervening. Her petroleum interests in Iraq were absorbed into a consortium dominated by the American companies. In the preparations for the founding of Israel, despite a stirring of opinion in the Exodus affair, she could not match the determination of the British.
6 Allowance made for exceptions: see J. Rovan, 'L'Allemagne de nos mérites', *Esprit* (November 1945 and December 1946).
7 A. Grosser (32), p. 216.
8 Significantly, the Blum–Byrnes agreements opened the way for a massive diffusion of American films, thus delighting the long-deprived cinema enthusiasts, and accelerating – at the time of the 'Série noire' and *Reader's Digest* – the Americanization of the nascent mass culture. On the political consequences, see the letter from Robert Blum in G. Elgey (19), pp. 140–1.
9 See Ch.-R. Ageron (200), pp. 259–92.
10 See Ch.-R. Ageron, 'De Gaulle et la Conférence de Brazzaville', in (104), pp. 243–51.
11 In January 1946, in the Gouin cabinet, Moutet inaugurated the new Ministry of Overseas France, which replaced the old Ministry of the Colonies the de Gaulle cabinets had retained.
12 See J. Julliard (21), p. 89.
13 Half the Assembly was made up of representatives of the metropole (article 66), in contradiction therefore with the principles of collective equality, proclaimed moreover in the text.

14 See J.-P. Azéma (13), pp. 277 *et seq.*
15 Ch.-A. Julien (220), pp. 263 and 379, R. Aron *et al.*, (226), pp. 91–169, and Ch.-R. Ageron (224), pp. 564–75, all hold to these figures. The civilian authorities announced a maximum of 1500 dead, whereas American sources rashly advanced a figure of at least 35 000 victims.
16 See his articles in *Combat* between 13 and 23 May 1945, in part republished in *Actuelles III* (Gallimard, 1958).
17 Ch.-R. Ageron (224), p. 587.
18 Quoted by G. Elgey (19), p. 152.
19 Quoted by G. Elgey (19), pp. 161–2.
20 See *Le Populaire*, 11 December 1946.
21 See Ph. Devillers (209), p. 359.


## 7 The parties take charge

1 Text of this letter in G. Elgey (19), pp. 102–6.
2 See G. Vedel, 'Les institutions de la IVᵉ République', in (25), pp. 13–25; J. Julliard (21), chapter 2, and 'La Constitution de la IVᵉ République: une naissance difficile', *Storia e Politica*, 1–2 (1975), 140–62.
3 It is included, along with the final text of the Constitution and many annexes, in the collection edited by G. Burdeau, 'Les institutions de la IVᵉ République', *Documents d'études*, 10 (October 1970), La Documentation française.
4 Ch. de Gaulle (55), p. 644.
5 In *Le Populaire*, 21 June 1946.
6 See F. Goguel, 'Géographie du référendum du 13 octobre et des élections du 10 novembre 1946', *Esprit* (February 1947), 237–64.
7 The electoral law of 5 October 1946 closely followed the terms of the ordinance of 17 August 1945: a system of full proportional representation, with electors voting for lists of candidates in each *département*, and redistribution of the remainder by the highest average.
8 Two hundred were elected by the deputies, the conseillers généraux, and 'grands électeurs' in each *département*. The others were elected by the National Assembly and its groups. The aims of the law were clear: maintain proportionality, sacrifice local representation to the strategic and national interests of the major political parties.
9 V. Auriol (8), 1947, pp. 38–9.


## 8 The double fracture of 1947

1 The Communists had made their participation in the Ramadier government conditional on obtaining one of the three major ministries – Foreign Affairs, Interior, Defence – de Gaulle had refused them in 1945. François Billoux thus received the Defence portfolio; but, to quell the fears of the other parties, his ministry was split up and short-circuited: all important questions were the reserve of Ramadier, War went to Paul Coste-Floret (MRP), the Navy to Louis Jacquinot (Independent), and Air to André Maroselli (Radical).
2 See the text of his memorandum presented to Bidault at the end of July in V. Auriol (8) 1947, pp. 695–9, and the commentary of P. Nora, pp. xlii–xliii.
3 France, Great Britain, Italy, Portugal, Ireland, Greece, the Netherlands, Belgium, Switzerland, Turkey, Austria, Denmark, Sweden, and Norway.

France had insisted that Spain – where Franco remained in power – not be included.

4 See J. Tronchon (208), pp. 70–1. On 27 March, the MDRM had called on its militants to stay calm.

5 Not forgetting the crises of conscience of the officers who condemned these methods: see *Réforme*, 9 October 1948. In short, a dress rehearsal for the Algerian War.

6 See P. Stibbe, *Justice pour les Malgaches* (Seuil, 1954).

7 See L. Chevalier (221), a model study of the three Maghreb countries.

8 See F. L'Huillier, 'Les gaullistes et l'Union française: action et réflexion (1943–1953)', *Études gaulliennes*, 22 (April–July 1978), 71–9.

9 See E. Sivan, *Communisme et nationalisme en Algérie* (Presses de la Fondation nationale des sciences politiques, 1976), pp. 154 *et seq.*

10 On the eve of the election, 32 of the 59 MTLD candidates were imprisoned; at Guelma and Sétif the results were not made known; voting was rigged and carried out under police supervision; some communes were placed under virtual military occupation. The second round of the election 'corrected' the result of the first: at Bône, for example, the MTLD obtained 6544 votes on 4 April and 96 on 11 April, the UDMA respectively 4186 and ... nil. See R. Aron *et al.* (226), pp. 275 *et seq.*

11 See Ph. Fallachon, 'Les grèves de la Régie Renault en 1947', *Le Mouvement social*, 81 (October–December 1972), 111–42.

12 The CGT feared a decline in its influence. On 24 April, in the first elections of the Social Security and Family allowance administrators, it had obtained only 59 and 61 per cent, whereas original estimates had given it at least 75 per cent. The CFTC had 26 and 25 per cent. In addition, many CGT electors had split their votes and penalized prominent Communist trade-unionists.

13 The opinion polls, however, moderate this apparent triumph: 43 against 34 per cent (and 23 per cent without an opinion) in fact disapproved the founding of the RPF. See J. Charlot, *Les Français et de Gaulle* (Plon, 1978), p. 76.

14 That is, taking responsibility for the organization and defence of the popular classes excluded from the political and cultural system. On this 'fonction tribunicienne' see G. Lavau in *Le Communisme en France* (Colin, 1969), p. 18.

15 V. Auriol (8), 1947, p. 441.

16 Ch. de Gaulle (158), pp. 108 and 135.

17 See J. Fauvet (17), p. 163.

18 See (4), 1947, p. 222.

19 See M. Agulhon and F. Barrat (67), part 3, and their debate with R. Gallissot in *Le Mouvement social*, 92 (July–September 1975), 49–91.

20 See J. Moch (182), chapters 14 and 15.

21 A good regional example analysed by J. Merley and M. Luirard, 'Les grèves de 1947 à Saint-Étienne', in *Histoire, économies, sociétés* (Presses Universitaires de Lyon, 1978), pp. 151–85.

22 This 'historic' debate, which covers 250 pages of the *Journal officiel*, saw the Communist deputy of the Hérault, Raoul Calas, expelled from the chamber, after having occupied the tribune for a whole night and led the hymn celebrating the mutineers of Béziers of 1907. See G. Elgey (19), pp. 365–72.

23 See R. Gallissot, 'Les leçons de l'année 1947', *Politique aujourd'hui*, 3–4 (1978), 59–80.

24 See A. Bergounioux (180), and J. Kantrowitz, 'L'influence américaine sur Force ouvrière', *Revue française de science politique* (August 1978), 717–39.

25 D. Sapojnik, 'La FEN choisit l'autonomie', *Le Mouvement social*, 92 (July–September 1975), 17–47.

## 9 France under the American umbrella

1 A. Grosser (32), pp. 95 *et seq.*
2 See P. Mélandri, *Les États-Unis et le 'Défi européen' 1955–1958* (PUF, 1975), pp. 21–32.
3 'In government circles the dominant attitude was one of self-satisfaction in the role of esteemed and privileged friend of the United States', notes R. Massigli in (197), p. 143.
4 On 28 March, permission was given to the United States to establish an important air base at Châteauroux. From July, seven bases were conceded in Morocco.
5 Regrouped in the Union progressiste, which brought together Emmanuel d'Astier, founder of 'Libération', Pierre Le Brun of the CGT, Pierre Cot, former Radical, Gilbert de Chambrun, and a number of *résistants*.
6 See H. Claude, *Le Plan Marshall* (Editions sociales, 1948).
7 *Sondages* 1–2, 1958.
8 See J.-N. Jeanneney and J. Julliard (117), chapter 3. The special issue of *Esprit* (April 1948) on *Le Plan Marshall et l'Avenir de la France* contains a broad spectrum of opinion. Neutralism was at the origin of the launching of the weekly *L'Observateur* from 13 April 1950.
9 See R. Schuman, *Pour l'Europe* (Nagel, 1963), pp. 153 *et seq.* For a good portrait of the man, see L. Noël, *La Traversée du désert* (Plon, 1973), pp. 63 *et seq.*, and R. Rochefort, *Robert Schuman* (Editions du Cerf, 1968).
10 See P. Gerbet, 'La genèse du plan Schuman', *Revue française de science politique*, 3 (1956); the account by J. Monnet in (187) chapters 12, 13 and 14; and of P. Uri in *Le Monde* of 9 May 1975. A full dossier in *30 jours d'Europe*, 202 (May 1975).
11 See P.-J. Schaeffer, 'Recherche sur l'attitude de la SFIO à l'égard de l'unification européenne', *Travaux et recherches du Centre des relations internationales de l'université de Metz*, 5 (1973/2).
12 See P. Mélandri, 'Les Etats-Unis et le plan Pleven', *Relations internationales*, 11 (autumn 1976), 201–29.
13 He explains his efforts in *Présence française et abandon* (Plon, 1957). Thanks to him, however, the idea developed that evolution in Black Africa would not necessarily favour Communism.
14 See L. Périllier, *La Conquête de l'indépendance tunisienne* (Laffont, 1979).

## 10 The Third Force

1 Eight ministries in all: R. Schuman (24 November 1947–19 July 1948), A. Marie (24 July–28 August), R. Schuman (5–7 September), H. Queuille (11 September 1948–6 October 1949), G. Bidault (28 October 1949–24 June 1950), H. Queuille (2–4 July), R. Pleven (12 July 1950–28 February 1951), and H. Queuille (10 March–10 July 1951).
2 In July 1947, 35 per cent of the population believed a war to be close, 14 per cent in July 1949 (*Sondages*, 3, 1956, p. 40).
3 See F. Fejtö, *Le Coup de Prague, 1948* (Seuil, 1976), pp. 255–9, quoting *L'Humanité* of 28 February 1948.
4 Such as the violent exchanges between Lecœur (who cried 'CRS–SS') and

Moch on 18 December. This flared up again in March 1950 during the vote on measures against 'sabotage'.

5  As always, the statistics on PCF membership are questionable: not all the cards sent from Paris to the federations were actually distributed to members. The press controlled by the PCF suffered a decline of similar proportions: between 1946 and 1956, its total output fell from 7.5 to 3.8 million copies. For its part, *L'Humanité* fell from 380 000 to 180 000 copies daily.

6  See B. Legendre, 'Quand les intellectuels partaient en guerre froide', *L'Histoire*, 11 (April 1979), and D. Caute (381).

7  The French delegation, which included Communists (Picasso, Eluard, Joliot-Curie, Léger, Daquin, Daix etc.) and fellow-travellers (Vercors, Autant-Lara, J.-L. Barrault, Martin-Chauffier), there accepted without protest the attack of the Soviet novelist Fadeiev on Sartre, 'cette hyène dactylographe'. See D. Desanti (166), pp. 112 *et seq.*

8  The Mouvement de la paix et de la liberté, more proletarian in its recruitment and launched by the PCF on its own initiative, had been shelved again. See the regrets of its prime mover Ch. Tillon (109), pp. 474 *et seq.*

9  See *L'Affaire Henri Martin, textes commentés par J.-P. Sartre* (Gallimard, 1953).

10  See D. Lecourt, *Lyssenko* (Maspero, 1976), pp. 23–44.

11  See, more than thirty years on, the divergent recollections of the two accused, Claude Morgan, director of *Les Lettres françaises*, in *Le Don Quichotte et les Autres* (Roblot, 1979), and André Wurmser, leader writer of *L'Humanité*, in *Fidèlement vôtre* (Grasset, 1979). Among those giving evidence against Kravchenko: F. Grenier, P. Courtade, Vercors, J. Cassou, J. Baby, E. d'Astier, A. Bayet, W. Pozner, R. Garaudy, P. Cot, J. Bruhat, Y. Farge, F. Joliot-Curie, and the Archbishop of Canterbury ... *J'ai choisi la liberté* was republished in 1980 (O. Orban), with a penitent preface by D. Daix.

12  See M. Winock (384), chapters 9–12, and D. Caute, *The fellow travellers: a postscript to the Enlightenment* (London, Weidenfeld and Nicolson, 1973). On Sartre and *Les Temps modernes*, see M.-A. Burnier (383).

13  See A. Astroux (161), for the North-East.

14  See P. Guiol, 'L'association capital-travail: le projet de loi, genèse et destinée', *Espoir*, 28 (October 1979), and his thesis on 'L'Action ouvrière du RPF'. CNRS, 1980 (microfilm).

15  A Siegfried (40), p. 157.

16  For the bitter reminiscences of one of the founders of the MRP, see F. Gay, *Les Démocrates d'inspiration chrétienne à l'épreuve du pouvoir* (Bloud and Gay, 1950). *L'Aube*, run by Gay, folded in October 1951.

17  Against the background of a vigorous anticommunist witch-hunt, 'Paix et liberté' was launched on 8 September 1950, backed discreetly by the Pleven government and probably by the FBI. It brought together ex-Communists and politicians of the Right, and had important contacts in the police. Although given access to the national radio and allowed to distribute its propaganda, 'Paix et liberté' made little impact on public opinion, with the exception of its skilful poster campaign on themes like 'Jo-Jo la colombe' and 'Passez vos vacances en URSS'. 'Paix et liberté' disappeared in 1954, but the same handful of militants were to be found behind other causes, notably in 1958.

18  The revival of *maréchalisme* rocked the RPF. Colonel Rémy was forced to leave the Rassemblement after having praised Vichy's 'double game' in an article in *Carrefour* on 11 April 1950. In practice, however, the struggle against the 'system' was to throw many Gaullists and Vichyites together.

19  See R. Rémond, 'Droites classiques et droite romantique', *Terre humaine* (June 1951), 60–9.
20  See the broad view given by non-Marxist intellectuals in the special *Ordre et désordre de la France, 1939–1949* number of *La Nef* (December 1949–January 1950).
21  See G. Elgey (19), p 467 *et seq.*
22  The RPF made only thirteen *apparentements*, above all in the West – in order not to fragment the Moderates or disperse the Catholic vote. Elsewhere, in the Yonne, for example, where an exception was made for Léon Noël, the RPF gained nothing.
23  The often cited example of the second constituency of Lille makes clear the highly undemocratic consequences of the *apparentement* system. With 240 000 of roughly 440 000 votes. the Third Force took all the seats. The SFIO had five deputies for 107 000 votes and the MRP had four for 84 000; yet the RPF and the PCF with, respectively, 90 000 and 106 000 votes had none.
24  Estimates put the losses at 9 per cent of the vote for the PCF, 15 per cent for the SFIO, 11 per cent for the Radicals, 44 per cent for the MRP, and 12 per cent for the Independents. See C. Leleu (102a), p. 74.
25  See F. Goguel, 'Géographie des élections du 17 juin 1951', *Esprit* (September 1951).
26  See R. Rémond, 'Laïcité et question scolaire dans la vie politique française sous la IVᵉ République', in *La Laïcité* (PUF, 1960), pp. 381–400.
27  See J. Fauvet (17), p. 245.

## 11  Reconstruction and modernization

1  Text in Ch. de Gaulle (55), pp. 634–7. See also J. Monnet (187), chapter 10.
2  See M. Volle, 'Naissance de la statistique industrielle 1930–1950', in *Pour une histoire de la statistique* (INSEE, 1977), vol. 1, pp. 352–61, and 'L'organisation des statistiques industrielles françaises dans l'après Deuxième Guerre mondiale', *RHDGM*, 116 (1979), 1–25. On the ambitions and experiments of the period, see F. Perroux, *Les Comptes de la nation* (PUF, 1949), and F. Bloch-Lainé (142), chapter 4.
3  See R. Gilpin, *La Science et l'État en France* (Gallimard, 1970), chapter 6.
4  See, for example, its inquiry by poll (93), and A. Sauvy, 'La création de l'INED, 24 octobre 1945', *Espoir*, 21 (1977) 18–20.
5  This notion, common in 1947, is disputed today. See M. Lévy-Leboyer, 'Le patronat français a-t-il été malthusien?', *Le Mouvement social*, 88 (July–September 1974).
6  This broad consensus vanished of course with the Cold War and the triumph of the Third Force. From 1948, the Treasury distributed its aid to metallurgical companies on the criterion of profitability, and the CGT refused to participate in the modernization commissions. From now on public opinion was increasingly indifferent to questions of planning.
7  For an example of these very considerable ambitions, see J.-F. Gravier, *Mise en valeur de la France* (Le Portulan, 1949), p. 378.
8  See F. Bloch-Lainé (142), pp. 106–7, who expresses it thus: 'On a foncé les yeux fermés'.
9  See (12), p. 90. On this still little-known subject, however, this conclusion will no doubt have to be strongly nuanced in the light of the current research of Jean Bouvier.
10  See M. Freyssenet, *La Sidérurgie française, 1945–1979* (Savelli, 1979), chapter 1.
11  In 1952 (on a base of 100 for 1938), the index of industrial production stood at 145,

that of energy at 156, and that of capital equipment at 164, whereas output of consumption goods stagnated at 109.

12 See the chapter by M.-A. Brier in (462).

13 See (426).

14 We follow here some of the new ideas on economic policy presented by F. Caron at the symposium on the Fourth Republic organized by Paris-I/CNRS in February 1979.

15 See H. W. Ehrmann (367), pp. 246–9.

16 After a 'combative' devaluation of sterling, the franc was worth only 2.54 mg of gold at 20 September 1949 (that is, a devaluation of 22 per cent). But the free market in currencies was re-established in France.

17 Not without misgivings in orthodox quarters. See the letter of 29 February 1952 from W. Baumgartner, Governor of the Banque de France, to E. Faure in J. Autin, *20 ans de politique financière* (Seuil, 1972), pp. 16–17.

18 It is important not to forget that the effort for reconstruction and modernization had to come from an appreciably smaller active population: roughly 19 500 000 active members between 1946 and 1952, compared with 20 500 000 in 1931. The level of 20 million was not passed until after 1962.

## Conclusion to Parts 1 and 2

1 See J. Borgé and N. Viasnoff, *La 2CV* (Balland, 1977), pp. 78–9.

2 F. Bloch-Lainé (142), p. 124, and Cl. Bourdet, *L'Aventure incertaine, de la Résistance à la Restauration* (Stock, 1975), pp. 431 *et seq.*

3 See F. Caron, in (51), p. 865.

4 In *La Nef*, 60–62 (December 1949–January 1950), 81.

5 See J.-P. Scot, 'La restauration de l'État, juin 1944–novembre 1945), *Cahiers d'histoire de l'institut Maurice-Thorez*, 20–21 (1977), 207.

6 See J. Bouvier, '1944–1948: de la Résistance à la Restauration, du malthusianisme à la croissance', *Histoire, économie, sociétés* (Presses Universitaires de Lyon, 1978), pp. 205–14.

7 F. Mitterrand, *Ma part de vérité* (Fayard, 1969), p. 24.

8 See P. Hervé, *La Libération trahie* (Grasset, 1945), and Cl. Bourdet, *l'Aventure incertaine.*

9 See J.-P. Azéma (13), p. 354.

10 G. Bernanos (386), p. 226.

## 12 Governing without choosing

1 In *Le Figaro* (24 April 1951), F. Mauriac denounced 'une assemblée sans visage'. In 1953 and 1954, Joseph Laniel became the whipping-boy of Mauriac's 'bloc-notes' column in *L'Express* (244), 'il y a du lingot dans cet homme-là', 'la dictature à tête de bœuf', and Mendès France his hero: a sign of the times. On this question, see R. Rémond, 'Les grands leaders', in (29).

2 See V. Auriol (8), 1952, pp. 152–88.

3 See G. Elgey (20), p. 50.

4 In (4), 1952, p. 60.

5 See *Sondages*, 3, 1951; 3, 1956; 3, 1958.

6 See M. Catinat (307), 28–30.

7 The index of industrial production (on a base of 100 for 1938) went from 151 to 145 between January and December 1952.

8 The principle of indexation was a source of controversy among the experts, notably François Bloch-Lainé who, on this occasion, left the Ministry of

Finance where he had been since 1947 to take charge of the Caisse des dépôts. See F. Bloch-Lainé (142), pp. 120 *et seq.*

9  See *Sondages*, 1953, 3. There were 56 against 21 per cent who had not wanted Pinay's fall. The figures were respectively 47 and 25 per cent for de Gaulle, 40 and 26 per cent for Blum. Even the popularity of Mendès France experienced stronger fluctuations than that of Pinay.

10  Antoine Pinay has himself deliberately fostered the myth. See S. Guillaume (153).

11  See R. Sommer, 'Paix et liberté: la IV$^e$ République contre le PC', *L'Histoire*, 40 (December 1981), 26–35.

12  See *Le Monde* of 30 May 1952. For this in many respects mysterious episode, see Ph. Robrieux (164), p. 304.

13  In addition to Duclos, André Stil, editor of *L'Humanité*, was also arrested in May; then in September it was the turn of Alain Le Léap, second secretary of the CGT, and the leaders of the Union des Jeunesses républicaines de France (P. Laurent, L. Baillot, J. Elleinstein).

14  See A. Marty, *L'Affaire Marty* (Editions Norman Béthune, 1972) and Ch. Tillon, *Un 'procès de Moscou' à Paris* (Seuil, 1971). Accused of 'travail fractionnel', they were denounced as 'flics'. The affair can be sited in the long list of trials occurring at the same time in Budapest and Prague.

15  See R. Aron and D. Lerner (192), p. 9. Complete the findings of their remarkable sociological study with J.-P. Rioux, 'L'opinion publique française et la CED: querelle partisane ou bataille de la mémoire?', *Relations internationales*, 37 (1984), 37–53.

16  Diethelm, leader of the Gaullist group in the Assembly, cried: 'We are not dead, since we can still destroy!'

17  R. Aron and D. Lerner (192), p. 13.

18  *Le Monde* now successfully weathered two crises. That following its publication of the false Fechteler report in May 1952 which purported to show that the United States had no faith in the EDC, and that of *Le Temps de Paris*. See J.-N. Jeanneney and J. Julliard, (117), chapter 5.

19  See P. J. Schaeffer, 'Recherches sur l'attitude de la SFIO à l'égard de l'unification européenne', *Travaux et recherches, Université de Metz*, 1973–2, 107–29.

20  See P.-M. de La Gorce (27), pp. 128–35.

21  See R. Aron and D. Lerner (192), p. 153.

22  *Sondages*, 4, 1954. Hostile views were in the majority only in August–September, at the time of the project's rejection.

23  An additional proof: the provincial press, closely attuned to the views of its readers, maintained a great prudence over the EDC, and was much less divided than the Parisian press over the issue.

24  See R. Rémond, 'Quand la CED divisait les Français', *L'Histoire*, 13 (June 1979).

25  The Vietnamese currency, the piastre, was worth 10 francs in Saigon and 17 at Paris: officials, soldiers, businessmen, and members of the underworld were implicated in the lucrative traffic this disparity made possible. A journalist, Jacques Despuech, exposed the extent of the abuse in 1953 in *Le Trafic des piastres* (Éditions des Deux Rives). The subsequent parliamentary quarrel, in which the Communists were especially incisive, helped to convince public opinion in France that the war was corrupt; and this as the Soviet thaw favoured a minimizing of the Vietminh threat.

26  In Tunisia, for example, between 1946 and 1956, the total population grew from 3 200 000 to 3 800 000, and the proportion of Europeans fell from 7.4 to 6.7 per

cent. Yet just 4000 European farmers produced 20 milliard francs of the 65 milliard total in 1953, the remaining 45 milliard being divided between 500 000 *fellaghas*. In Tunisia as in Morocco, mining interests, industry, transport, and modern services were in European hands.

27 *L'Observateur* of 1950 became *France-Observateur* on 15 April 1954. See C. Estier, *La Gauche hebdomadaire* (Colin, 1962), chapters 6 to 8.

28 See J. Lacouture, *François Mauriac* (Seuil, 1980), chapter 18, and R. Barrat, *Justice pour le Maroc* (Seuil, 1953).

29 See E. Cohen-Hadria, 'Du protectorat français à l'indépendance tunisienne', *Cahiers de la Méditerranée*, Université de Nice, 1976.

30 As well as the sympathetic press. Thus, Raymond Cartier revealed details of the future conspiracy in *Paris-Match* on 7 February.

31 Juin's fellow Academician, Mauriac, replied with a biting article entitled 'Un coup de bâton étoilé' in *Le Figaro* of 30 June. For the Moroccan crisis in general, see J. Lacouture (203), pp. 217–32, and *Le Maroc à l'épreuve* (Seuil, 1958).

32 Bidault was in fact highly in favour of the deposition of the Sultan. For the detail of the telegrams between Paris and Rabat, see G. Elgey (20), pp. 407–21.

33 Quoted by A. Grosser (32), p. 286.

34 See, on its preparation and defeat, the report of the commission of inquiry presided over by General Catroux, published by G. Elgey (20), pp. 551–662.

35 These are estimates. In fact, the figures given by Navarre (214a), Roy (215), Bergot (216), Gras (210), and Giap (217), do not agree. This painful question will soon be settled by the opening of the relevant military archives.

36 In 1956, in *Agonie de l'Indochine 1953–1954* (Plon, p. 315), General Navarre absolved the army of responsibility, arguing that the humiliation of France dated not from Dien Bien Phu but from Geneva, and that the politicians rather than the soldiers were answerable. He concludes (p. 335) with a call 'au grand chirugien'. For the same views twenty years later, see Navarre (214a), chapter 7. Compare this attitude with that of J. Laniel, *Le Drame indochinois* (Plon, 1957).

37 See J. Lacouture, 'La défaite de Diên Biên Phu', *L'Histoire*, 12 (May 1979), 14–23, and his film with Ph. Devillers and J. Kanapa, *La République est morte à Diên Biên Phu*, 1974.

38 Of those questioned by the IFOP in July 1947, 48 per cent were in favour of negotiation or abandon, against 52 per cent determined to pursue the war to victory. In October 1950, the two positions had respectively 52 and 38 per cent, 50 and 15 per cent in May 1953, and 60 and 7 per cent in February 1954. The level of non-response rose, the sign of a clear indifference.

39 *Le Monde*, 3 November 1953.

40 Quoted by G. Elgey (20), p. 170.

41 See J.-P. Rioux, 'La révolte de Pierre Poujade', *L'Histoire*, 32 (March 1981).

42 See J.-F. Noël (362). The post office workers had to deal with a growth in traffic (128 in 1954 for an index base of 100 in 1948) and an extension of financial operations (13 million savings accounts and 3 million cheque accounts in 1952), whereas financial resources had fallen, on a base of 100 in 1948, to 96 by 1955, and their wages had dropped 50 per cent behind the private sector since 1948. On the impact of technological change, see the description of C. Bertho, *Télégraphes et téléphones, de Valmy au microprocesseur* (Le Livre de poche, 1981), chapter 7.

43 J.-F. Noël (362), pp. 97–8.

44 Herriot in fact ceased to open his mail once the number of deputies demanding a recall reached 209. On 15 September, the Oppostion forced him to admit that he had received 214 demands, sufficient for an extraordinary session, See J.-F. Noël (362), p. 120, and G. Elgey (20), p. 163.

45 Between 1947 and 1953, the RPF fell from 26 to 10 per cent of the places on muncipalities, losing half its votes to the Right and Centre. A year later, just after Dien Bien Phu, de Gaulle drew only a small crowd at the Arc de Triomphe.

46 In (4), 1953, pp. x–xi.

47 In fact, by a manoeuvre on the part of Le Troquer, President of the Congress, Joseph Laniel's election was annulled at the eighth round: the ballot papers did not carry his Christian name and could thus be attributed to his brother, the senator René Laniel. See J. Laniel, *Jours de gloire et jours cruels, 1908–1958* (Presses de la Cité, 1971).

## 13  The impossible renewal

1 See J. Chapsal (28), p. 247.

2 Ambitions honoured by the creation of a Secretary of State for Scientific Research and Technical Progress, to which Longchambon was appointed.

3 See the texts of his two investiture speeches in (4), 1953, p. 490, and 1954, p. 521.

4 Where he received the loyal support of the existing officials, Alexandre Parodi, René Massigli, and Jean Chauvel. A number of other major figures of the administration adopted the same attitude: Gabriel Ardant, Claude Gruson, François Bloch-Lainé, Paul Delouvrier, Louis Armand, and Alfred Sauvy.

5 Edgar Faure also surrounded himself with young talent, such as Jacques Duhamel and Valéry Giscard d'Estaing.

6 See Chauvel's account in (219), pp. 39–89.

7 See the detailed narrative of J. Lacouture (155), chapters 11 and 12, and J. Lacouture and Ph. Devillers (218).

8 See S. M. Bao Dai, *Le Dragon d'Annam* (Plon, 1980).

9 To which have to be added 114 000 wounded and 28 000 prisoners. See *Le Monde*, 21 July 1954.

10 See Boyer de Latour's memoirs, *Vérités sur l'Afrique du Nord* (Plon, 1956).

11 See *Sondages*, 4, 1954. In August the results of another poll, this time not taking party preferences into account, gave 62 per cent satisfied against 7 per cent: an absolute record in the history of the Fourth Republic.

12 As a further sign of her lack of interest in Asia, France ceded the last of her trading posts to the Indian Republic on 21 October. Is this to say that the policy of Mendès France over the Far East was in fact complementary to that of Dulles, and hence favourable to American imperialism? For an interpretation in this sense, see A. Ruscio, 'Le mendésisme et l'Indochine', *Revue d'histoire moderne et contemporaine* (April–June 1982), 324–42.

13 Public opinion, however, though not abandoning its familiar indecision, resigned itself to the inevitable. The Paris Accords were approved by 36 per cent of those questioned, disapproved by 32 per cent, and 32 per cent did not reply. (See Table 12 and diagram).

14 F. Mauriac (244), p. 158.

15 See J. Mons, *Sur les routes de l'histoire* (Albatros, 1981). Some caution is required when using the lively book by C. Clément, *L'Affaire des fuites, objectif*

*Mitterrand* (Olivier Orban, 1980). For a contemporary narrative, J.-M. Théol-leyre, *Le Procès des fuites* (Calmann-Lévy, 1956). On the role of the secret service (DST), see the questionable account by Ph. Bernert, *Roger Wybot et la bataille pour la DST* (Presses de la Cité, 1975).

16 The six Socialists proposed were Alain Savary, Albert Gazier, Gaston Defferre, Marcel David, Robert Lacoste, and Augustin Laurent.

17 See J. Georgel, 'La réforme constitutionelle sous la IV$^e$ République', in (25), pp. 95–109, and C. Poutier, *La Réforme de la Constitution* (Sirey, 1955).

18 Indeed, it was in this domain that the Mendès France government did least well in the opinion polls. In December 1954, 32 per cent of those questioned, against 38 per cent, thought it had a good policy on prices, 22 against 48 per cent a good incomes policy, and 22 against 27 per cent a good handling of the budget, while the number without an opinion increased. See *Sondages*, 1, 1955.

19 Was this also the start of research towards the atomic weapon, research which began in earnest with the announcement of a five-year programme on 30 November 1956? Mendès France has always denied this (see *Le Monde*, 29 September 1973), but General Ailleret argues that it was in *L'Aventure atomique française* (Grasset, 1968).

20 On the scale of the disaster, see M. Querlin, *Les Chaudièrs de l'enfer* (Gallimard), which appeared in December 1955 and describes the battle.

21 See (4), 1954, p. 277. These declarations, for which their authors have subse-quently been reproached, at the time shocked only a minuscule fraction of opinion. Only the use of torture in police stations and prisons now began to provoke protests: on 13 January, Claude Bourdet entitled an article in *France-Observateur*: 'Votre Gestapo en Algérie'.

22 Mostefa Benahmed, SFIO deputy for Constantine, gave a moving denunciation of this hysteria and provided a grim account of French exactions in Algeria. See (4), 1955, p. 12, and F.-O. Giesbert, *François Mitterrand* (Seuil, 1977), pp. 142–3.

23 *Sondages*, 1, 1955. Only 3 per cent thought it had done less well than its pre-decessors, while 20 per cent thought it had done more or less the same. For 79 per cent the best work was peace in Indo-China. On all the other questions, the popularity of Mendès France was declining, but remained exceptional. That his political image and personality had a future was clear from the 10 000-odd letters of support he received after his defeat.

24 For a lively account of the conflict and a description of the conditions of workers in the region, see L. Oury (348).

25 At the same time, an agreement of 10 August with Libya withdrew French troops from the Fezzan, which they had entered in 1942 under Leclerc, while preserving for France an influence in this strategic zone.

26 See S. Hoffmann (170), whose inquiry began in February 1955. The first publi-cations have been listed and commented upon by J. Touchard, 'Bibliographie et chronologie du poujadisme', *Revue française de science politique* (January–March 1956).

27 A. Siegfried (41), p. 235.

28 See P.-H. Simon, 'L'appel du vide', *Le Monde*, 25 January 1956.

29 An opinion poll published by *L'Express* on 10 December found that 66 per cent were dissatisfied with the work accomplished by the dissolved Assembly.

## 14 The Algerian snare

1 See B. Blin, 'La radiodiffusion et la télévision' in (192), pp. 165–81.

2 His pamphlet on *La Situation économique de la France* originally appeared in *Les*

*Cahiers du communisme* of March 1955. See Ph. Robrieux (164), pp. 368–9. Its publication provoked a lively debate, with replies from Ramadier, Mendès France, academics, and journalists. See *Le monde*, 30 June 1958.

3  This bitter conclusion was drawn by P. Rimbert for 1951 in *La Revue socialiste* of February–March 1952, and he confirmed it in 1955 in (129), pp. 195–207. See L. Bodin, 'L'âge mûr de la SFIO', *Esprit* (May 1956).

4  See R. Quilliot (110), chapter 33.

5  See E.-F. Callot (115), p. 226. Between 1950 and 1955, MRP membership among workers and employees fell from 20 to 14 per cent, and among students from 3 to 0.3 per cent, whereas among the non-active and retired it climbed from 24 to 31 per cent.

6  See *Sondages*, 4, 1955.

7  A national survey conducted by the IFOP and published by *L'Express* on 16 December 1955. The results were in response to the question of the most important issue of national interest to be dealt with by the new government after the elections. Economic expansion, ministerial stability and constitutional reform, retirement for the old, the education question and the European problem, were the priority for only 2–3 per cent of those questioned.

8  Poujade, however, declared that his band did not intend to act as saboteurs. In theory, his deputies, more than 60 per cent of whom were artisans or retailers, were committed to 'defend the Republic, that of the little men and the hard-working'.

9  In addition to Mauriac, Catholic intellectuals like R. Rémond, G. Suffert, R. Barrat, P.-H. Simon, and H. Marrou had stressed in the course of the campaign that the Catholics 'peuvent voter à gauche'.

10  Maurice Duverger, for example, protesting against this corruption of the electorate's wishes by the politicians, published a series of influential articles in *Le Monde* between 12 April and 12 June 1956, in which he argued for the direct election of the head of the executive.

11  On the dealings and the final outcome, see J. Lacouture (155), pp. 411–16.

12  In order to obtain the support of the MRP – necessary to avoid dependence on PCF votes but which broke the Front républicain agreement–Guy Mollet in fact refused Mendès France the Foreign Ministry, appointing instead a Socialist, the highly pro-European Christian Pineau. Mendès France, after having refused Economy, which then went to Lacoste, became simply a Minister of State. Mitterrand was the Garde des Sceaux, and Chaban-Delmas the Minister of State responsible for ex-servicemen.

13  The Poujadists were increasingly worried. In a tumultuous atmosphere and on dubious grounds of irregularities in the making of their *apparentements*, eleven Poujadist deputies were invalidated during February, and replaced by their defeated opponents.

14  See Guy Mollet's defence of his policy as a whole, *Bilan et perspectives socialistes* (Plon, 1958).

15  See the 'official' texts, especially that of J. Duclos, in *Le Parti communiste français dans la lutte contre le colonialisme* (Éditions sociales, 1962), pp. 119–21, introduced by M. Lafon.

16  See Ph. Robrieux (164), p. 439.

17  The opinion polls reveal a division in the metropole into three more or less stable blocks. Between April 1956, July 1956, and March 1957, mobilization of opinion was developing only very slowly. Thus on the question of confidence in the government to settle the difficulties in Algeria, the proportion of undecided fell only from 36 to 32 and 31 per cent. Opposition stabilized, going from 27 to 30

and 30 per cent. On the other hand, confidence in Guy Mollet's policy did not suffer, on the contrary: 37, 38 and 39 per cent. See Table 14 and diagram in Chapter 15.

18 Text in M. Harbi (234), pp. 160 *et seq.*

19 The strength of the FLN lay in arguing that the conflict was in fact between states, hence international, and that the civil war was a consequence of this. It was a position never fully grasped by the French leadership. On these problems of definition, see the excellent analysis of G. Pervillé, 'Guerre étrangère et guerre civile en Algérie (1954–1962)', *Relations internationales*, 14 (1978), 171–96. And the official viewpoint of K. Mameri, *Les Nations unies face à la question algérienne* (Alger, SNED, 1969).

20 They were launched by Soustelle, who underlined their affinities with the 'bureaux arabes'. See his article in *Combat*, 28 April 1955.

21 See P. Milza, 'La relève des impérialismes au Proche-Orient', *L'Histoire*, 38 (October 1981), and the rest of the dossier devoted to Suez. Critical analysis of the accounts by J.-Cl. Allain in *Relations internationales*, 20 (winter 1979), 511–16.

22 See his defence, *1956, Suez* (Laffont, 1976), p. 76; but this is completely contradicted by some of his declarations at the time.

23 See the strongly pro-Israeli reminiscences of Thomas, *Comment Israël fut sauvé* (Albin Michel, 1978).

24 The French *paras* were acclaimed as victors on their return to Algiers. Many officers considered themselves to have been betrayed by 'un gouvernement de lâches'. See General Beauffre, *L'Expédition de Suez* (Grasset, 1967).

25 See A. Grosser (32), pp. 367 *et seq.* For a more nuanced analysis, see Ch.-R. Ageron, 'L'opinion publique française pendant la crise de Suez', *Cahiers de l'Institut d'histoire de la presse et de l'opinion*, 5 (Tours, Université François-Rabelais), and J.-P. Rioux, 'L'opinion publique dans l'affaire de Suez', *L'Histoire*, 38 (October 1981), 35–7.

26 See *Sondages*, 4, 1956, and 3, 1957.

27 See *Sondages*, 4, 1958.

28 Of those questioned for an IFOP poll in December 1956, 65 per cent had a bad or very bad opinion of the Soviet Union, compared with 13 per cent with an average view and 5 per cent with a good or very good opinion. A year previously the figures were, respectively, 36, 27, and 13 per cent. A year later, the distribution was almost the same again, at 39, 26, and 11 per cent. See *Sondages*, 1, 1958, 46–7.

29 See the texts presented by P. Kende and K. Pomian, *1956, Varsovie-Budapest* (Seuil, 1978), and in particular those of A. Kriegel, M. Winock, and G. Martinet on the repercussions within the French Left.

30 See B. Lazitch, *Le Rapport Krouchtchev et son histoire* (Seuil, 1976), and the texts compiled by R. Martelli, *1956, le Choc du XX<sup>e</sup> Congrès du PCUS* (Éditions sociales, 1982).

31 See Ph. Robrieux (107), chapter 8. The PCF was not informed of the crimes cited in the report until October 1961, and the communication of its text to the French delegation was not openly admitted in *L'Humanité* until 13 January 1977, during a press campaign launched by J. Elleinstein.

32 A negotiation was also opened with the bishops and the Vatican. Until May 1957 this explored the possibility of a new Concordat, under which the Church would surrender its privileges in education, the military chaplaincies, religious orders, Opus Dei, and the statute of Alsace-Lorraine. See R. Lecourt, *Entre l'Église et l'État. concorde sans concordat, 1952–1957* (Hachette, 1978).

33 By 342 to 239 votes. Mendès France invoked the weakness of the French economy to vote against the treaty.

34 Petrol had in fact just been discovered at Hassi-Messaoud. See J.-L. Quermonne, *L'Organisation commune des régions sahariennes* (Librairie générale de droit et de jurisprudence, 1957).

35 At the end of 1956, Paul Teitgen had no trouble in using the police to thwart the plot of General Faure. More disturbing was the 'Bazooka affair', in which few steps were taken to apprehend those in Algiers and the metropole responsible for a bloody attack on Salan's headquarters in January 1957. See the account by R. Salan himself, *Mémoires* (Presses de la Cité, 1974), vol. 3, pp. 115–34.

36 Through the channel of the Dispositif de protection urbaine (DPU) created on 4 March 1957, Massu's forces received help, with Lacoste's approval, from the European counter-terrorist militia groups, who established their own torture centre of the Villa des Sources.

37 See the 'candid' defence of J. Massu, *La Vraie bataille d'Alger* (Plon, 1971), which justifies the use of torture, and the indignant reply of J. Roy, *J'accuse le général Massu* (Seuil, 1972).

38 On 12 September 1957, after a first letter of resignation had been refused on 24 March. In all, Paul Teitgen had authorized 24 000 house arrests; according to him, 3000 individuals subsequently died, were tortured, executed, or disappeared. See Y. Courrière (228), vol. 2, p. 289. Likewise, after having publicly repudiated the methods of Massu, General de Bollardière was condemned to sixty days' confinement. See his account, *Bataille d'Alger, bataille de l'homme* (Desclée de Brouwer, 1972).

39 In reality, the political authorities were informed after the Mairey report on the use of torture by the police, made to Edgar Faure in March 1955 and completed in December 1956. And they now refused to divulge the incriminating reports. The purpose of the 'Commission de sauvegarde' was thus not to inform the government, but rather to appease the protesters.

40 Spring 1957 was indeed tumultuous. At the end of February a letter appeared – for which they were imprisoned – from fifty-two Algerian officers of the French army expressing their anguish to René Coty. See A. Rahmani, *L'Affaire des officiers algériens* (Seuil, 1959). In March came the call of P.-H. Simon, *Contre la torture*, one echoed by H. Beuve-Méry in *Le Monde* of 13 March: 'From now on, French people must realize that they no longer have the full right to condemn in the same terms as a decade ago the atrocities of Oradour and the torturers of the Gestapo.' In April, *Esprit* published 'La paix des Nementchas', a chilling account by a young historian, Robert Bonnaud, who had returned horrified from his zone of operations. The academics began to organize; a Comité pour la défense des libertés et la paix en Algérie alerted the secondary school teachers; at its head were four women: Bianca Lamblin, Madeleine Rebérioux, Andrée Tournès, and Geneviève Tremouille. On 27 March, General de Bollardière congratulated J.-J. Servan-Schreiber for his *Lieutenant en Algérie*, serialized in *L'Express*. And in *Sur ce rivage*, Vercors attempted to describe a former deportee who became a torturer in his turn: the collective memory had come a full and tragic circle.

## 15  The collapse

1 Quoted by P. Vidal-Naquet (239), p. 89.

2 Preface to (4), 1957, p. ix. Silence betrays the anguish: Siegfried, although so well-informed, elaborated his entire text without a single substantial reference to the situation in Algeria!

3 See J. Meynaud (370).
4 See in particular the collective work edited by H. Alleg (229). For a more nuanced account of the Communists' contribution to the struggle, see E. Sivan, *Communisme et nationalisme en Algérie, 1920–1962* (Presses de la Fondation nationale des sciences politiques, 1976), and J. Moneta, *Le PCF and la question algérienne, 1920–1965* (Maspero, 1971).
5 See A. Philip, *Le Socialisme trahi* (Plon, 1957), the extreme position in the polemic with the leadership. In a more muted key, *La Revue socialiste* of January 1957 catalogues the arguments for and against, with the opposing articles of E. Weill-Raynal and E. Cohen-Hadria.
6 See Buron's *Carnets politiques de la guerre d'Algérie* (Plon, 1965).
7 In *La Tragédie algérienne* (Plon, 1947). J. Soustelle quickly replied to Aron with *Le Drame algérien et la décadence française* (Plon, 1957).
8 See A. Nozière, *L'Algérie, les chrétiens dans la guerre* (Éditions Cana, 1979), and the texts of Mgr Duval, *Au nom de la vérité* (Éditions Cana, 1982), for the reactions in Algeria.
9 See the analyses of M. Crouzet, 'La bataille des intellectuels', *La Nef* (October 1962–January 1963), and of M. Winock (246).
10 See H. Hamon and P. Rotman (240).
11 See J.-N. Jeanneney and J. Julliard (117), pp. 232–3.
12 Their first major mobilization occurred in November 1956 to demand the freeing of André Mandouze, charged with 'attempted demoralization of the army and the nation'. See the skilful defence by Georges Suffert in *Le Monde* of 5 December 1956.
13 See *Actuelles III, Chroniques algériennes, 1939–1958* (Gallimard, 1958), and H. R. Lottman, *Albert Camus* (Seuil, 1978), parts 4 and 5.
14 See M. Winock (246), pp. 156–66. Complete with P. Vidal-Naquet, *L'Affaire Audin* (Éditions de Minuit, 1958).
15 Published by Éditions de Minuit, which, with Éditions du Seuil, took considerable risks at this time by publishing such material.
16 See (4), 1958, p. 16.
17 On 16 November 1957. See (4), 1957, p. 118.
18 In December 1955, just 1 per cent of the population wanted de Gaulle to form the next government. The figure had risen to 5 per cent by April 1956, to 9 per cent in July 1956, and stood at 11 per cent in September 1957. This last date is once again a crucial one, since at this point de Gaulle was ahead of Mendès France (9 per cent), Pinay (8 per cent) and the Communists (7 per cent), and was himself outdistanced only by Guy Mollet, now declining, with 14 per cent. The curves actually crossed at the beginning of the winter. In January 1958, 13 per cent wanted to see de Gaulle leading the country: from now on he easily outdistanced all the political figures of the Fourth Republic. Informed Gaullists, Marie-Madeleine Fourcade and André Astoux, sensed the change; they now launched a campaign for the sending of letters to Coty calling for de Gaulle's recall. See J. Ferniot (248), p. 123.
19 Elections which seem, moreover, to have preoccupied the parliamentarians. The Poujadists were dispersed, and the Communists, Gaullists, and Radicals all declined appreciably. The SFIO held up. The real victors were the MRP and the Moderates. However, as always with this type of election, the diversity of local coalitions and conditions makes it hard to give the results a national interpretation.
20 See R. Rémond, 'Le 13 mai 1958', *L'Histoire*, 1 (May 1978), 26–34.
21 See his interview in *L'Express* of 3 May 1962, and J. Ferniot (248), p. 201.

22  See the illuminating account by J. Touchard (105), pp. 147–63.

23  See A. de Sérigny, *La Révolution du 13 Mai* (Plon, 1958).

24  See P.-M. de La Gorce (27), p. 541, E. Jouhaud, *Ce que je n'ai pas dit* (Fayard, 1977), pp. 90–110, and his letter in *Le Monde* of 13 June 1978.

25  The world of finance was already won over. On 20 May, *La Vie française* headlined with 'La Bourse attend de Gaulle'.

26  De Gaulle is reported to have said to Pflimlin: 'I prefer to use my authority to re-establish order rather than to repudiate disorder.' See the account by G. Monnerville, *Vingt-deux ans de présidence* (Plon, 1980), p. 72.

27  The authority to prepare a new Constitution, like the temporary full powers, were accorded to de Gaulle's government, not to de Gaulle alone: a fundamental difference, then, from the vote of 10 July 1940 to Pétain, the memory of which was, naturally, still strong. To introduce constitutional change, de Gaulle had to keep his ministers: and the major parties of the Fourth Republic were well represented in his government.

28  On 2 June, the National Assembly and the Council of the Republic voted three laws giving the new government a free hand, and that were promulgated the following day. The first of these confirmed the new government in the use of the special powers in Algeria enjoyed by its predecessors. The second accorded it full powers for six months. And the third was a constitutional law modifying the procedures for revision laid down in article 90 of the 1946 Constitution, in particular by the addition of the referendum. These measures had long been planned and announced by the Gaullists. See the communiqué from the Républicains sociaux drawn up by Roger Frey and published by *Le Monde* on 5 May 1956, and to be faithfully applied two years later.

29  See J. Ferniot (248), p. 480. And to Delbecque, come to be congratulated, de Gaulle confirmed, 'You have played well', adding after a silence, 'But you will admit that I have also played well.'

30  See, for example, J. Planchais, *Le Malaise de l'armée* (Plon), published in February 1958.

31  See de Gaulle's *Mémoires d'espoir* (Plon, 1970), pp. 21–34.

32  Although only 44 against 18 per cent to solve the economic questions. The percentage of 'abstentions' for these questions is, in order, 13, 22, 21, 23, 25, and 38 per cent for the economy. See *Sondages*, 4, 1958.

## 16  The stimulus of growth

1  The expression was popularized by Jean Fourastié with *Les Trentes Glorieuses ou la Révolution invisible de 1946 à 1975* (Fayard, 1979). His name belongs at the head of this chapter: for the unequivocal affirmation of *homo œconomicus*, for the optimism of *La Civilisation de 1960* (his famous 'Que sais-je?', constantly republished since its appearance in 1947), and of *La Productivité* (PUF, 1947), *Grand espoir du siècle* (PUF, 1949 and 1958), *Machinisme et bien-être* (Éditions de Minuit, 1951 and 1962). On the threshold of the 1950s, no one better than he expressed the ideology of progress and modernity, or wrote the history of a future which was to be that of comfort and work.

2  Owing in particular to the creation at the Ministry of Finance of a Service des études économiques et financières (SEEF), that liaised constructively with the Plan. François Bloch-Lainé appointed Claude Gruson to lead it. Meanwhile, the INSEE, directed by Francis Closon, launched economic inquiries with firms, and established the socio-occupational classification in 1951.

3 See 'Le revenu de l'agriculture en France en 1956–1957', *Études et conjoncture* (December 1957).

4 The decrees of August 1953 and September 1954 attempted to tackle the root of the problem: to reduce the annual quota of alcohol bought by the State, and force the beet-growers to convert their production and direct a larger share to sugar production. However, their beneficial effects were practically annulled by decrees of May 1955 and September 1957 introduced under pressure from the alcohol lobby.

5 One example: the electrification of isolated areas had certainly reduced the number of country people without electricity from 2 500 000 in 1946 to 800 000 in 1956, yet in 1958 only 15 per cent of farms were equipped with high current facilities.

6 A general survey in *Économie rurale* (January–June 1959), special number on 'L'économie agricole française 1938–1958'.

7 More exactly, on a base of 100 for 1952, 57 in 1946, 88 in 1950, 99 in 1951, 101 in 1953, 110 in 1954, 119 in 1955, 130 in 1956, 141 in 1957, 147 in 1958 and 152 in 1959. What is clear is the 'Korean boom' of 1950–1, the stagnation of 1952–3, and the strength of expansion since 1953.

8 See Ph. Saint-Marc, *La France dans la CECA* (Colin, 1961).

9 See J. Chardonnet (306), vol. 1, chapter 1, and vol. 2, chapter 23.

10 One example: the Unilever giant and its French subsidiaries marketed – with a great publicity effort – both traditional (soaps, margarine, and oils) and synthetic products (washing and cleaning powders).

11 Between 1950 and 1958, the extraction of iron ore doubled, going from 30 to 60 million tonnes. A growing proportion, however, was exported in its crude state, the French metallurgical industry being without the means, and considering it less profitable, to transform all of this iron into steel.

12 Not to mention a number of opportune diversifications: the SNCASO produced refrigerators and the SNECMA creamers.

13 Opened on 2 October 1952, this 'factory in the fields' spread over the 200 hectares of the communes of Aubergenville and Flins that the Régie Renault had bought in 1947. The 'most modern factory in Europe', to which visiting heads of State were taken, employed 2300 in 1952 and 8300 in 1958. There, the 'Juvaquatre' and the 'Frégate' were produced, then the 'Dauphine', sales of which soared after its victory in the Monte Carlo Rally in January 1958.

14 See M.-F. Pochna, *Bonjour, Monsieur Boussac* (Laffont, 1980). With a fortune made between the wars, Boussac adapted admirably to penury – he bought – and to affluence – he sold. He received most of the important figures of the Fourth Republic at his château de Mivoisin. His social passions – race horses, the Dior fashion house – were matched by his political ambitions: he was a confidant of Auriol and Mollet, gave 'advice' during the Suez affair, and funded loyal parliamentarians. A press magnate, Boussac strengthened *Le Populaire*, participated in the *Le Temps de Paris* operation against *Le Monde*, and bought *L'Aurore* in 1951.

15 A development that in no way detracted from the technical achievements of the SNCF, with the world train speed record for the BB9004 locomotive, and the 'Mistral' train, which from December 1955 linked Paris and Marseille at an average speed of over 100 km per hour.

16 Thus, in September 1953, *Réalités* denounced 'le grand sommeil de l'économie française', and on 3 January 1958 in *La Vie française*, R. Sédillot affirmed that 'la France vivote au jour le jour'. Monetarism, and fears of investment and of over-production were still causing damage.

17 And in particular in the classic interpretation of J.-J. Carré, P. Dubois, and E.

Malinvaud (301), themselves practitioners of national accounting as much as analysts.

18  Thus the number of wage-earners in 1957 stood, on a base of 100 for 1938, at 177 in the petroleum industry, 129 in chemicals, 126 in banking and insurance, 115 in metallurgy, compared with 90 in coal mining, 86 in textiles and 71 at the SNCF.

19  The value added tax (TVA) replaced the production tax established in 1936 which penalized manufacturers by its application both to their finished product and to their purchases of supplies, loans, and raw materials. The TVA is an *ad valorem* tax levied on the extra value acquired by a product at each stage of its manufacture, after deduction of the depreciation of the investments used to produce it.

20  In fact, it seems that the rate of profit actually fell, and that it was uniquely the effects of competition which had stimulated the entrepreneurs. According to fiscal statistics, the overall profit margin for firms fell from 8.9 to 7.7 per cent between 1951 and 1958. See J.-J. Carré, P. Dubois, and E. Malinvaud (301), pp. 381–8.

21  See, for example, the apocalyptic special number of *Économie et politique*, 1954, 5–6, on 'La France et les trusts', presented by J. Duclos and J. Baby.

22  See J.-M. Jeanneney (303), p. 261, and F. Caron (265), pp. 211–13 and 227–8.

23  See J.-P. Gilly and F. Morin, 'Les Groupes industriels en France, concentration du système productif depuis 1945', *Notes et études documentaires* (La Documentation française, 1981), 4.605–4.606, 30–2. The 500 largest companies accounted for less than 30 per cent of the productive system in 1958, compared with 60 per cent in 1980.

24  The debate on the root causes of economic growth was a lively one from the 1950s. For a good summary of the arguments, see F. Caron (265), pp. 170–4.

25  In (42), p. 184.

26  See J.-P. Mockers (304) and the remarks of R. Aron in the epilogue to J. Lecerf (294), p. 310.

27  F. Bloch-Lainé, *A la recherche d'une économie concertée* (Éditions de l'Épargne, 1964).

28  See F. Fourquet (291), p. 233.

29  See J. Boissonnat, 'La planification indicative en France', *Revue de l'action populaire* (December 1958).

30  See J. Guyard (260), p. 50.

31  See M. Catinat (307), p. 36, and J.-J. Carré, P. Dubois, and E. Malinvaud (301), pp. 321 and 622.

32  Overall, public companies and services remained highly competitive: in 1956 they employed 8.5 per cent of the productive sector labour force and were responsible for 12.3 per cent of the gross industrial product.

33  See, for example, G. Dessus, P. George, and J. Weulersse, *Matériaux pour une géographie volontaire de l'industrie française* (Colin, 1949), and the classic article of F. Perroux, 'Les espaces économiques', *Économie appliquée. Archives de l'ISEA*, 1950.

34  The car provides the clearest example of this desire to catch up. The highest national rates of increase in the number of cars (less than 5 years old) by *département* between 1955 and 1959 bring together declining rural regions (Basses-Pyrénées and Ardèche) and regions where modernization had begun (Alpes, Rhône valley, Brittany, Loire valley). See the maps published in *Études statistiques* (July–September 1959), 258.

35  The ten lowest (in thousand francs) are: Corsica (133), Lozère (156), Morbihan

(167), Ardèche (169), Mayenne (171), Vendée and Haute-Loire (174), Gers and Aveyron (175) and Ariège (180). Of the ten highest, nine are to the east of a Le Havre-Marseille line: Seine and Seine-et-Oise (383), Rhône (304), Nord (277), Moselle (272), Seine-Maritime (271), Bouches-du-Rhône (267), Meurthe-et-Moselle (262), Seine-et-Marne (262), and Pyrénées-Orientales (258). Many such series of figures with analyses are to be found in N. Delefortrie and J. Morice (313).

36 See J.-E. Godchot, *Les Sociétés d'économie mixte et l'Aménagement du territoire* (Berger-Levrault, 1966), and Ph. Lamour, *L'Aménagement du territoire* (Éditions de l'Epargne, 1964).

37 See P. Poplu, *Les Sociétés de développement régional* (Berger-Levrault, 1973).

38 Except in Brittany, thanks to the work and suggestions (often taken up by Paris) of the Comité d'études et de liaison des intérêts bretons (CELIB), founded in November 1951. See M. Philipponeau, *Le Problème breton et le programme d'action régionale* (Colin, 1960), and R. Pleven, *Avenir de la Bretagne* (Calmann-Lévy, 1961). In this struggle against isolation and dependence, a Breton cultural movement built up a new and strong action. See M. Nicolas, *Histoire du mouvement breton* (Syros, 1982), part 2.

## 17 An unequal prosperity

1 See P. Massé (297), p. 24, and J. Marchal and J. Lecaillon (322).

2 See J. Fourastié and B. Bazil, *Le Jardin du voisin. Essai sur les inégalités en France* (Le Livre de Poche, 'Pluriel', 1980), and F. de Closets, *Toujours plus!* (Grasset, 1982).

3 And in particular the Union nationale des associations familiales (UNAF) which represented the interests of families in the courts. It was weakened after a split by the family groups close to the PCF in 1949.

4 See J. Derogy, *Des enfants malgré nous* (Éditions de Minuit, 1956), which puts at 20 000 the number of deaths each year as a result of back-street abortion. *L'Express* now embarked on a lively campaign against the law of 1920: see Françoise Giroud's editorial on 15 February 1956. In vain. On the other hand, Pius XII now finally abandoned his condemnation of painless childbirth methods.

5 With appreciable social disparities. Studies dealing with three-quarters of the male population aged 30–69 in 1954 showed that at 35 years, a primary school teacher had a life expectancy of a further 40.8 years, a member of the liberal professions or a senior manager 40.3, a farmer 37.2, a white-collar worker, artisan, or retailer 37.7, a skilled worker 35.2, an unskilled worker 34.9, an agricultural worker 34.9, and a labourer 33.5. See P. Longone, 'L'inégalité devant la mort', *Population et société*, 64 (December 1973). Likewise, there were strong regional disparities, with (still for the men) the regions south of the Loire making up for their economic backwardness: in 1952–6, the average male life span was 61.2–62.9 years in Brittany, 61.5 in the Pas-de-Calais, 63.1 in the Nord, an average of 62.4 throughout Normandy, compared with 67.7 in Limousin and the southern Alps, 67.9 in Ariège and Tarn, with all the records for longevity being broken by Vendée and Languedoc, led by Aude at 68.4 years. The same disparities were present in 1967–9. See P. Longone, 'Relief régional de la mortalité', *Population et société*, 72 (September 1974).

6 Thirty-nine litres of alcohol per adult a year, well in excess of the 14 litres of the Italians; almost 16 000 deaths due to alcohol in 1958, against 3000 in 1946 after the enforced abstemiousness of the war years; an annual social cost of 200 milliard francs. Plus, of course, all the accidents and the mental disorders, for

which France had no remedy: 1 psychiatrist in 4400 doctors, 5000 beds for 10 000 cases in 1958; 10 000 alcohol-induced psychoses in 1957, compared with 1000 in 1947. Clearly, the legislative measures of 1954 had had only a very limited impact.

7 See the inquiry 'Les médecins vous parlent de la médecine', *Esprit* (February 1957).

8 The mutual benefit insurance schemes were also at the forefront of the new effort over provision for convalescence, controlled by the decree of 9 March 1956: almost all of the 4500 places in convalescent homes today were, in fact, created before 1958.

9 See G. Rösch, 'Les dépenses médicales en 1956', *Consommation. Annales du CREDOC* (July–September 1958), 47–66.

10 Sixty-four per cent according to an INSEE survey in 1955 based on tax returns.

11 See the IFOP inquiry on the young, aged 15–29 years, published by *L'Express* in October–December 1957, and R. Kanters and G. Signaux, *Vingt ans en 1951, enquête sur la jeunesse française* (Julliard, 1951).

12 Urban in this context – and until the census of 1962 – refers to communes with an agglomerated population of at least 2000.

13 The geography of this movement is a predictable one. The areas of repulsion were the countrysides of the Massif Central (with the exception of the Clermont-Ferrand region), Aquitaine, Poitou and Vendée, Brittany, Normandy, the Paris basin and the plateaux of the East. The zones of attraction were, in addition to the Paris region, the Rhône-Alpes region and the Côte d'Azur (for retirement!), and, of course, all the dynamic average-sized towns. See the map in P. Sorlin (262), p. 24.

14 They can be no more than broad estimates. The classification of branches of activity and socio-professional categories by the INSEE used in the *Tableau économique de l'année 1951* differ from those in the *Code* of 1954 and from those in the 1956–7 inquiry conducted with the CREDOC; the information is deficient for the immediate post-war period; the disputed figures for unemployment are not free of ambiguities; the retrospective calculations use bases whose comparison is hazardous.

15 The figures of the CREDOC study published in 1958 in fact make it possible to conclude that consumption increased by 40 per cent between 1950 and 1957.

16 See F. Divisia, J. Dupin, and R. Roy (321), p. 82.

17 Other estimates give the following breakdown, in percentages:

| | 1929 | 1950 | 1960 |
|---|---|---|---|
| land | 26.5 | 22.8 | 22 |
| housing | 20 | 24.7 | 23.5 |
| other buildings ⎫ | 37.8 | 20.5 | 16.4% |
| equipment ⎬ | | 16.2 | 19.3 |
| consumer durables | 4.2 | 4.2 | 6.1 |
| stocks | 6.8 | 10.2 | 11 |
| livestock | 4.1 | 1.4 | 1.7 |

The additional patrimony represented by gold and financial assets in terms of these real assets is estimated at 80 per cent for 1929, 103 per cent in 1950 and 125 per cent in 1960. See the figures in *Le Mouvement économique en France, 1949–1979* (INSEE, 1981), p. 37.

18 Hesitation over the choices to be made now is clear from a 'guide' of the period, R. Truptil, *L'Art de gérer sa fortune* (Hachette, 1957), which uses a survey of *La Vie française* of June 1953.

19 A decline which, according to Ch.-A. Michalet (318), p. 232, explains the parallel expansion of the place in private patrimonies of real estate: 44 per cent in 1941–5, 59 per cent in 1951–5. In the portfolios of stocks and shares, bonds fell more rapidly (50 per cent of portfolios in 1945, 18 per cent in 1957–9) than shares which progressed steadily. These figures are confirmed by P. Cornut (319) for the structure of inheritances: in 1934, 1949, and 1953, the place of securities represented respectively 31, 20, and 16 per cent, whereas that of real estate climbed from 42 to 54, then to 59 per cent of the inheritances examined.

20 See A. Girard, *Le Choix du conjoint* (PUF, 1954), p. 189.

21 See J. Cuisenier, 'Accumulation du capital et défense du patrimoine', in Darras (270), pp. 350–81.

22 That is, in the definition now established by national income accounting, 'all the people present on the metropolitan territory carrying out operations linked to their domestic life'.

23 See J. Cuisenier in (270), pp. 358–9.

24 See G. Seibel and J.-P. Ruault in Darras (270), pp. 96–7.

25 As indications, here are some gross monthly incomes (male) in 1956; they are average figures for the whole of France and in the course of working lives or careers (in thousands of 1956 francs); senior manager 175, salary of a deputy 151, senior civil servant 145, colonel 89, middle manager 85 (woman 56), teacher *agrégé* 85, justice of the peace 60, white-collar worker 50 (woman 40), miner (face worker) 49, tax collector 46, skilled worker 43, primary school-teacher 38, unskilled worker 36, labourer 29, farm worker 25, cleaning woman 23. The SMIG then stood at roughly 25 000 francs a month.

26 The chaotic evolution of the SMIG was thus: 100 francs an hour in February 1954; under the governments of Laniel, Mendès France, and Faure it was raised by, respectively, 15, 6.50 and 4.50 francs, taking it to 126 francs in April 1955, when the trade unions and the Commission des conventions collectives were calling for 157 francs; after nine removals of tax from items on its index between March 1956 and March 1957, and after 28 months of freeze and against a background of rising prices, its revision could be postponed no longer, to 133 in August 1957, 139 in January 1958 and 144 in March. In October 1956, moreover, 74 per cent of workers and 63 per cent of employees earned less than 40 000 francs a month for 200 hours of work. *Études et conjoncture* (January 1957).

27 It was now that the notion of 'consumers' developed. See Cl. Quin, J. Boniface, and A. Ganssel, *Les Consommateurs* (Seuil, 1965).

28 See P. Thibaud and B. Cacérès (325), p. 153, and M. Drancourt, *Une force inconnue, le crédit* (Hachette, 1961).

29 See the special number of *Consommation. Annales du CREDOC*, 1958–2, from which these figures are taken.

30 According to an OEEC inquiry of 1955, for a base of 100 for the French, the Germans were at an index of 97 for consumption and 133 for investment or saving, the Belgians at 103 and 143, and the Italians at 56 and 64.

31 (245), p. 743. See also L.-A. Vincent, *Études et conjoncture* (February 1959), pp. 143–50.

32 For the households of labourers the figure was 71 per cent, and 49 per cent for those of workers, compared with 34 and 12 per cent for employees and engineers respectively. See P. Thibaud and B. Cacérès (325), p. 28.

33 See J. Meynaud (369).

34 See *Consommation. Annales du CREDOC* (1962–3), and the special number 'Nos maisons et nos villes', *Esprit* (October–November 1953), which contains many concrete examples.
35 See (245), p. 744.
36 See J. Meynaud and A. Lancelot, 'Groupes de pression et politique du logement', *Revue française de science politique* (December, 1958), pp. 821–60.
37 See G. Lefranc (178), pp. 115–45 and 201–24.
38 See P. Vignaux (361), and G. Adam (360).
39 The fall in numbers was particularly marked for the CGT, which distributed 3 million membership cards in 1951, 2.1 in 1954 and 1.6 in 1958. Force ouvrière stabilized at roughly 500 000 members in 1958. Only the CFTC progressed, rising from 350 000 paid-up members in 1952 to 415 000 in 1958.
40 See S. Hoffmann (42).
41 See M. Crozier, 'La France, terre de commandement', *Esprit* (December 1957), 779–97.

## 18  The fluid society?

1 See M. Debatisse, *La Révolution silencieuse: le combat des paysans* (Calmann-Lévy, 1963).
2 See P. Muller, 'La naissance d'une nouvelle idéologie paysanne en France, 1945–1965', *Revue française de science politique* (February 1982), 90–108.
3 See P. Alphandery *et al.*, *Les Concours financiers de l'Etat à l'agriculture de 1945 à 1980* (report INRA–CORDES, 1982), 3 vols.
4 See P. Naville (343).
5 *Sondages*, 2, 1956.
6 See J.-M. Jeanneney (303), p. 187. Was this, then, the 'absolute' pauperization of the working class even under 'enlightened capitalism' as the Communists and the CGT insisted, basing their argument uniquely on the case of the single metalworker? The polemic continued; but social transfers and wage increases had already invalidated the argument for workers with children. See the case for and against in P. Montjoie, 'La paupérisation absolue et la classe ouvrière', *Économie et politique* (June 1956), and N. Jacquefont, 'La paupérisation: dogme ou réalité?', *Esprit* (December, 1955).
7 For workers as a whole, the evolution in the index of the purchasing power of net monthly incomes was the following (base 100 in 1962):

|  | 1949 | 1956 |
|---|---|---|
| *Paris* | | |
| single | 56 | 86 |
| father of 2 children | 66 | 91 |
| father of 5 children | 74 | 94 |
| *Provinces* | | |
| single | 57 | 84 |
| father of 2 children | 67 | 84 |
| father of 5 children | 72 | 93 |

8 See A. Touraine and O. Ragazzi (339), p. 117.
9 See A. Andrieux and J. Lignon (344).

10 See P.-H. Chombart de Lauwe (342).

11 See M. Montuclard (282), and M. Combe (283).

12 See, for example, J. Frisch-Gauthier, *La Colombophilie chez les mineurs du Nord* (CNRS, 1961). This resistance was certainly stronger than in the countryside, where the traditional *sociabilités* and folklore declined, abandoned to the notables and *érudits*, and despised by the modernized peasants; before, however, experiencing a revival in the 1960s. See M. Agulhon and M. Bodiguel, *Les Associations au village* (Actes Sud, 1981).

13 See the best attempt of C. Baudelot, R. Establet, and J. Malemort, *La Petite Bourgeoisie en France* (Maspero, 1974).

14 See R. Sainsaulieu, 'Les employés à la recherche de leur identité', in Darras (270), pp. 296–308.

15 In particular those of Michel Crozier. See (349).

16 Like the workers, they now proved capable of strong action in support of their claims. For example, the strike in June–July 1957 of bank employees, organized by the CFTC, FO, and the CGT, which ended in partial victory: a 5.5 per cent salary increase for the 12 per cent demanded.

17 See L. Boltanski, 'America, America ... Le plan Marshall et l'importation du management', *Actes de la Recherche en sciences sociales* (May 1981), 19–41, and (352).

18 See B. Voyenne, 'Les journalistes', *Revue française de science politique* (December 1959), 901–34.

19 See R. Girardet (247).

20 See F. Jacquin (353), and A. Thépot, 'Quels ingénieurs pour la modernisation?', in (30).

21 See M. Bressard and A. Girard, 'Mobilité sociale et dimension de la famille', *Population*, 1950, no. 3, and 1951, no. 1; *Bulletin mensuel de statistique* (October–December 1954), supplement; M. Praderie, R. Salais, and M. Passagez, 'Une enquête sur la formation et la qualification des Français (1964)', *Études et conjonctures*, 1967, no. 2, and M. Praderie, 'Héritage social et chances d'ascension', in Darras (270), pp. 330–48; R. Pohl, C. Thélot, M.-F. Jousset, 'L'enquête formation-qualification professionnelle de 1970', *Démographie et emploi* (INSEE, 1974).

22 See in particular M. Crozier, *La Société bloquée* (Seuil, 1970).

23 See A. Girard (356).

24 See J.-L. Loubet del Bayle, *Les Non-conformistes des années 30* (Seuil, 1969).

25 See J.-P. Rioux (358).

26 See J. Charlot, 'Les élites politiques en France de la III$^e$ à la V$^e$ République', *Archives européennes de sociologie* (1973–1), 78–92.

27 At least in the sample, necessarily incomplete, drawn from *Who's Who* by P. Birnbaum (357), pp. 156–9. The proportion of former *résistants* was, in 1954, between 33 and 48 per cent for the military and top administrators, around 20 per cent for employers in insurance and banking and members of the liberal professions, and roughly 10 per cent for employers in industry and commerce, and senior executives. These proportions had changed little by 1964, but by 1974 the replacement of this generation was well under way.

28 A. Siegfried (41), p. 220.

## 19 Towards the 'polyculture'

1 See E. Morin (411), p. 13.

2 See A. Prost (392), many of whose analyses we follow here.

3 See J. Natanson and A. Prost, *La Révolution scolaire* (Éditions ouvrières, 1963).

4 The parents did not, however, manage to organize the expression of their wishes

outside of the religious quarrel (the APELs were mobilized for the defence of the *école libre* in 1950–1) or independently of the teachers themselves (the Fédération Cornec, created in 1947, was very closely linked to the FEN).

5 See pp. 167–8 and 277 above. Private education was, moreover, in decline. In 1938, it accounted for 16 per cent of the primary school population, and 32 per cent of that of secondary schools; in 1958, the proportions were, respectively, 14.9 and 29 per cent. It remained strong, however, in technical education (44 per cent of pupils in 1958), due chiefly to the weakness of the public sector effort in this field. The West, South-East, and the Massif Central were the regions where the *école libre* was strongest. But, and in spite of the Marie and Barangé laws, its mounting financial difficulties meant that it was increasingly favourable to the idea of an associative contract with the State.

6 See J.-J. Carré, P. Dubois, and E. Malinvaud (301), pp. 87–94.

7 See the 1954–5 inquiry in I. Berger, *L'Univers des instituteurs* (Éditions de Minuit, 1964).

8 The students, mobilized and divided by the war in Algeria, were not immune to the widespread desire for collective organization. Hence the spectacular growth of the Union nationale des étudiants de France (UNEF): from 18 000 student members in 1948 to 100 000 in 1958. In addition to the traditional functions (running canteens and insurance schemes), the UNEF also developed a political consciousness, due to the minority groups which won control of it in summer 1956. It contributed to the political and organizational apprenticeship of a generation of students, and, because of the presence within its ranks of many Christians, to a more positive experience of *laïcité*. See P. Gaudez, *Les Étudiants* (Julliard, 1961), and M. de La Fournière and F. Borella, *Le Syndicalisme étudiant* (Seuil, 1957).

9 See 'Le colloque de Caen', *Les Cahiers de la République* (January–February 1957).

10 See J.-C. Asselain, *Le Budget de l'Education nationale, 1952–1967* (PUF, 1969).

11 See J.-M. Donegani and M. Sadoun, 'La réforme de l'enseignement secondaire en France depuis 1945, Analyse d'une non-décision', *Revue française de science politique* (December 1976), 1125–46.

12 The text was republished in *L'Enseignement public*, the organ of the FEN, in June 1968. See *Le Plan Langevin–Wallon de réforme d l'enseignement* (PUF, 1964).

13 See, for example, the criticism of the Billères project by J. Marchais, president of the Société des agrégés, very influential in the SNES, in *L'Éducation nationale* of 8 November 1956. And F.-G. Dreyfus, 'Un groupe de pression en action: les syndicats universitaires devant le project Billères', *Revue française de science politique* (April 1965), 213–50.

14 See R. Rémond, *L'Anticléricalisme en France de 1815 à nos jours* (Fayard, 1976), chapter 8, and *La Laïcité* (PUF, 1960).

15 See A. Coutrot and F. Dreyfus (372), p. 131.

16 See E. Fouilloux, *Les Catholiques et l'Unité chrétienne du XIX$^e$ au XX$^e$ siècle* (Le Centurion, 1982).

17 See R. Pucheu, 'Ceux qui ont cru réussir', *Esprit* (April–May 1977), 11–27.

18 See R. Rémond, 'Le Catholicisme français pendant la Seconde Guerre mondiale', *Revue d'histoire de l'Eglise de France* (July–September 1978), 203–13.

19 See also E. Poulat, 'La découverte de la ville par le catholicisme français contemporain', *Annales ESC* (November–December 1960), 1168–79. An inquiry by the IFOP (*Sondages*, 1952, 4, republished in *Réalités* of November 1952) asked the question: 'La France est-elle encore catholique?' Although 85 per cent of the population considered themselves as Catholics, only a third

thought it necessary to practise. These figures have been criticized by Boulard, but the inquiry is revealing of the unease.

20 See J. Lœw, *Journal d'une mission ouvrière, 1941–1959* (Editions du Cerf, 1959).

21 See J. Vinatier, *Le Cardinal Liénart et la mission de France* (Le Centurion, 1978).

22 See the dossier of *Les Prêtres-ouvriers* (Éditions de Minuit, 1954); E. Poulat, *Naissance des prêtres-ouvriers* (Casterman, 1965), and (376), chapters 5–9.

23 See S. de Lestapis, *La Limitation des naissances* (Spes, 1959).

24 See F. Bédarida, 'Les Jeunes chrétiens face à la politique (1944–1945)', in *Églises et chrétiens dans la Seconde Guerre mondiale* (Presses Universitaires de Lyon, 1982), pp. 493–500.

25 See R. Rémond, 'Droite et gauche dans le catholicisme français contemporain', *Revue française de science politique* (1958), 3–4.

26 See Y. Tranvouez, in (371), p. 479.

27 See also F. Varillon, *Beauté du monde et souffrance des hommes* (Le Centurion, 1980), G. Suffert, *Les Catholiques et la Gauche* (Maspero, 1960), *Aimé Savard interroge René Rémond* (Le Centurion, 1976), E. Descamps, *Militer* (Stock, 1971), F. Krumnow, *Croire ou le feu de la vie* (Editions ouvrières, 1975). See R. Pucheu, *Esprit* (April–May 1977), 11–27, and, for the next generation, R. Chapuis, *Les Chrétiens et le Socialisme* (Calmann-Lévy, 1976). This informal group has yet to be the subject for a study.

28 See J.-P. Sartre (391).

29 On this cultural tumult see, in addition to studies like H. R. Lottman's *The Left Bank* (1982), the works of Boris Vian and, above all, published in 1952, Gaston Criel's *La Grande Foutaise* (Plasma, 1979).

30 See M.-A. Burnier (383).

31 See pp. 154–6 above, and G. Malaurie and E. Terrée, *L'Affaire Kravchenko* (Laffont, 1982). On the general appeal of Communism, see N. Dioujeva and F. George (eds.) *Staline à Paris* (Ramsay, 1982).

32 See J. Verdès-Leroux, 'L'art de parti. Le parti communiste français et ses peintres (1947–1954)', *Actes de la recherche en sciences sociales*, 28 (June 1979), 35–55.

33 See J.-F. Revel, *Pourquoi des philosophes?* (Julliard, 1957).

34 See 'Les intellectuels dans la société française contemporaine', *Revue française de science politique* (December 1959), L. Bodin, *Les Intellectuels* (PUF, 1962), F. Bon and M.-A. Burnier, *Les Nouveaux Intellectuels* (Seuil, 1966).

35 See M. Crozier, 'Les intellectuels et la stagnation française', *Esprit* (December, 1953), 771–82.

36 See A. Drouard, 'Réflexions sur une chronologie: le développement des sciences sociales en France de 1945 à la fin des années soixante', *Revue française de sociologie* (January–March 1982), 55–85.

37 The first MJC was launched by André Philip, at Lyon in October 1944. They became federated in 1948, and had already reached 200 in number by 1958, before multiplying fivefold under Malraux.

38 See J. Laurent, *La République et les beaux-arts* (Julliard, 1955), and A. Cornu, *Mes Républiques indiscrètes* (J. Dullis, 1976). For an overall view of arts policy, see A.-H. Mesnard, *L'Action culturelle des pouvoirs publics* (Librairie générale de droit et de jurisprudence, 1969). In 1954–5, only the Mendès France and Faure governments attempted to co-ordinate an overall policy on youth, but without linking it to the arts.

39 See J.-P. Rioux, 'Une nouvelle action culturelle? L'exemple de "Peuple et culture"', in (30).

40 See J. Vilar, *De la tradition théatrale* (L'Arche, 1955, and Gallimard, 1963),

G. Leclerc, *Le TNP de Jean Vilar* (UGE '10–18', 1971), and Ph. Wehle, *Le Théatre populaire selon Jean Vilar* (Alain Barthélemy/Actes Sud, 1981).

41 See D. Riesman, *The Lonely Crowd*, published in the United States in 1950 (Yale), but – and the delay is revealing of the resistance in France – not translated and published in French (Arthaud) until 1964.

42 See *Regards neufs sur le cinéma* (Seuil, 1953), and A. Bazin, *Qu'est-ce que le cinéma?* (4 vols., Éditions du Cerf, 1958–62).

43 See the IFOP inquiry on 'La presse, le public et l'opinion', *Sondages*, 3, 1955.

44 See E. Sullerot, *La Presse féminine* (Colin, 1963).

45 See E. Morin, 'Tintin, héros d'une génération', *La Nef*, 13 (January 1958).

46 The innovation was a daring one, since 60 per cent of the population was still hostile to jazz in 1958. See *Sondages*, 1–2, 1958, 78.

47 See E. Lalou, *Regards neufs sur la télévision* (Seuil, 1957).

48 See 'Ce que lisent les Français', *Réalités* (July 1955), 54–9.

49 See G. Magnane, *Sociologie du sport* (Gallimard, 1964).

50 See J. Dumazedier (409).

51 See R. Barthes (412).

**Conclusion**

1 See R. Barthes (412), pp. 46–8.

2 See Sirius (46), p. 106.

3 See R. Aron, (39), p. 256.

4 See for example (*Le Monde*, 23 February 1979) the divergence during a recent symposium between academics, stressing the institutional weakness, and Mendès France, passing a severe judgement on the men.

5 See J. Fauvet in *Le Monde*, 20 June 1958, and F. Bouyssou, 'L'activité des gouvernements démissionnaires sous la IV^e République', *Revue française de science politique* (August 1970), 645–80.

6 Sirius (46), p. 43.

7 See P. Birnbaum (138), chapter 3.

8 See 'La France, crise du régime, crise de la nation', *Cahiers d'économie humaine* (Éditions ouvrières, September 1956), and (147).

# Bibliography

This bibliography does not aspire to be exhaustive. The vastness of the printed output on the period, and the size of this book, preclude such an ambition. It attempts simply to help those wishing to pursue their reading on the Fourth Republic. Priority has been given to works of clarification, eyewitness accounts, and instruments of research, where possible of recent publication. Further references are provided in the notes to each chapter, and most of the works listed feature an additional bibliography. Section 1 contains instruments of research, and general and introductory works on the period. The contents of sections 2, 3, and 4, have, as much as is practical, been grouped according to the themes dealt with in the chapters. Section 5 contains suggestions to correct an overly national perspective on the period. Section 6 contains a short supplementary bibliography, compiled specifically for this English-language edition.

## GENERAL

### Tools for research

1 *Atlas historique de la France contemporaine (1800–1965)*, R. Rémond (ed.), Colin, 1966.
2 *La France contemporaine, guide bibliographique et thématique*, R. Lasserre (ed.), Tübingen, Niemeyer/PUF, 1978.
3 *Bibliographie annuelle de l'histoire de France*, Éditions du CNRS. (Since 1975 this lists books and articles concerning the period 1944–58)

### The facts

4 *L'Année politique*, Éditions du Grand Siècle, then PUF. (For each year since 1944–5. A chronological survey of the principal political, diplomatic, economic and social facts in France and the French Union; with prefaces by André Siegfried. Fundamental)
5 *Le Monde: index analytique*, Saint-Julien-du-Sault, Editions F.-P. Lobies and Le Monde. In publication. (An annual classification since 1944 of all the subjects treated in France's principal daily newspaper. Inexhaustible)
6 G. Vincent, *Les Français 1935–1975, chronologie et structure*, Masson, 1977. (The salient facts, tables, and incisive commentaries)
7 M. Belloc *et al.*, *Chronologies 1946–1973*, Hachette, 1974.

8  V. Auriol, *Journal du septennat* (1947–1953), Colin.
   1947, edited by P. Nora, 1970.
   1948, edited by J.-P. Azéma, 1974.
   1949, edited by P. Kerleroux, 1977.
   1950, edited by A.-M. Bellec, 1980.
   1951, edited by L. Theis, 1975.
   1952, edited by D. Boché, 1978.
   1953–1954, edited by J. Ozouf, 1971.
   (The scope and quality of the critical apparatus which accompanies Auriol's
   text make these volumes solid tools of research for all aspects of the period)


   *Statistics and official publications*

9  *Annuaire statistique de la France, rétrospectif,* Imprimerie nationale/PUF, 1966.
10 *Les Institutions sociales de la France,* La Documentation française, 1963.
11 *Mouvement économique en France de 1938 à 1948,* Imprimerie nationale/PUF, 1950.
12 *Mouvement économique en France de 1948 à 1957,* Imprimerie nationale/PUF, 1958.
   (Indispensable)


   *Periodical publications*

   *Bulletin d'information de l'IFOP,* then, from September 1945, *Sondages.*
   *Études et conjoncture* (the INSEE review).
   *Notes et études Documentaires,* La Documentation française.
   *Population,* PUF (the INED review).
   *Revue d'histoire de la Deuxième Guerre mondiale* (*RHDGM*), PUF.
   *Revue française de science politique,* Colin, then Presses de la Fondation nationale
   des sciences politiques.


## General works on France from 1944 until 1958


   *The weight of the 'années noires'*

13 J.-P. Azéma, *De Munich à la Libération (1938–1944)*, Seuil, 'Nouvelle histoire de
   la France contemporaine', vol. 14, 1979. English translation, Cambridge
   University Press, 1985.


   *Introductory*

14 P. Courtier, *La Quatrième République,* PUF, 1975.
15 G. Dupeux, *La France de 1945 à 1965,* Colin, 1969. (A good collection of documents with commentaries)


   *Basic works concerned chiefly with political questions*

16 A. Werth, *France, 1940–1955,* Hale, London, 1956.
17 J. Fauvet, *La IVᵉ République,* Fayard, 1959, and Le Livre de Poche, 1971.
   (Unequalled for its analysis of parliamentary life)
18 J. Barsalou, *La Mal-aimée, histoire de la IVᵉ République,* Plon, 1964.
19 G. Elgey, *La République des illusions (1945–1951),* Fayard, 1965.

20  G. Elgey, *La République des contradictions (1951–1954)*, Fayard, 1968. (Lively and detailed, with unpublished documents. A work of reference)
21  J. Julliard, *La IV^e République (1947–1958)*, Calmann-Lévy, 1968, and 'Pluriel', 1980. (A solid historical analysis. Bibliography)
22  P. Williams, *Politics in Post-War France*, 2nd edn, Longmans, London, 1958. (The best synthesis on the subject)
23  H. Claude *et al.*, *La IV^e République*, Éditions sociales, 1972. (Concise, selective, and partisan)
24  P. Limagne, *L'Éphémère IV^e République*, France-Empire, 1977.
25  *La Quatrième République*, Actes du colloque de Nice, 1977, Librairie générale de droit et de jurisprudence, 1978. (A symposium of political scientists and jurists. Essential for political life and decolonization)
26  P.-M. de La Gorce, *L'Après-guerre (1944–1952)*, Grasset, 1979.
27  P.-M. de La Gorce, *Apogée et mort de la IV^e République*, Grasset, 1979.
28  J. Chapsal and A. Lancelot, *La Vie politique en France depuis 1940*, PUF, 5th edn, 1979. (A clear textbook. Rich bibliography)
29  *La IV^e République*, Actes du colloque de l'Université de Paris-I/CNRS, 1979.
30  *La France en voie de modernisation (1944–1952)*, Actes du colloque de la Fondation nationale des sciences politiques (FNSP), 1981.

*Basic works on French international relations*

31  A. Grosser, *Les Occidentaux; les pays d'Europe et les États-Unis depuis la guerre*, Fayard, 1978.
32  A. Grosser, *La IV^e République et sa politique extérieure*, Colin, 1967. (Belies its somewhat narrow title. Fundamental)
33  G. de Carmoy, *Les Politiques étrangères de la France (1944–1966)*, La Table ronde, 1967.
34  J.-B. Duroselle, *Histoire diplomatique de 1919 à nos jours*, Dalloz, 1978. (A comprehensive textbook)

*To capture the 'spirit of the age'*

G. Guilleminault, *Le Roman vrai de la IV^e République*:
35  *Les Lendemains qui ne chantaient pas (1944–1947)*, Denoël, 1969, and Le Livre de poche, 1970.
36  *La France de Vincent Auriol (1947–1953)*, Denoel, 1970, and Le Livre de Poche, 1970.
37  *De Bardot à de Gaulle*, Denoël, 1972. (Anecdotal but instructive. Chronologies unreliable)

*Some essays*

38  R. Aron, *Espoir et peur du siècle*, Calmann-Lévy, 1957.
39  R. Aron, *Immuable et changeante, De la IV^e à la V^e République*, Calmann-Lévy, 1959.
40  A. Siegfried, *De la III^e à la IV^e République*, Grasset, 1956.
41  A. Siegfried, *De la IV^e à la V^e République*, Grasset, 1958.
42  S. Hoffmann *et al.*, *France: Change and Tradition*, Harvard University Press and Gollancz, 1963.
43  S. Hoffmann, *Essais sur la France, déclin ou renouveau*, Seuil, 1974.
44  S. Hoffmann, *Sur la France*, Seuil, 1976.

45  J. Fauvet, *La France déchirée*, Fayard, 1957.
46  Sirius, *Le Suicide de la IV<sup>e</sup> République*, Éditions du Cerf, 1958. (Incisive commentaries by the two editors of *Le Monde*)
47  D. Schoenbrun, *As France Goes*, Gollancz, London, 1957.
48  H. Lüthy, *The State of France*, Secker and Warburg, London, 1955.
49  F. Fonvieille-Alquier, *Plaidoyer pour la IV<sup>e</sup> République*, Laffont, 1965. (An attempt at rehablilitation)


THE LIBERATION


**The Liberation and its aftermath: general works**

50  C. Lévy, *La Libération, remise en ordre ou révolution?*, PUF, 1974. (A good introduction, with a selection of documents)
51  *La Libération de la France*, Éditions du CNRS, 1976. (A symposium of 1974. Exhaustive)
52  Ch.-L. Foulon, *Le pouvoir en province à la Libération*, Presses de la Foundation nationale des sciences politiques, 1975. (Invaluable for the work of the commissaires de la République)
53  G. Madjarian, *Conflit, pouvoir et société à la Libération*, Union générale d'édition, 1980. (Based on unpublished prefectoral sources)
54  R. Aron, *Histoire de la Libération de la France*, Fayard, 1959, and Le Livre de poche (2 vols.), 1967.
55  Ch. de Gaulle, *Mémoires de guerre*, vol. 3, *Le Salut (1944–1946)*, Plon, 1959 (all notes refer to this edition), and Le Livre de poche, 1961.
56  Ch. de Gaulle, *Discours et messages*, vol. 1, *Pendant la guerre (1940–1946)*, Plon, 1970, and Le Livre de poche, 1974. (All the main texts, presented by F. Goguel)


**The Liberation and its aftermath: regional studies**

57  M. Baudot, *Libération de la Normandie*, Hachette, 1974.
58  M. Baudot, *Libération de la Bretagne*, Hachette, 1973.
59  Y. Durand and R. Vivier, *Libération des pays de la Loire*, Hachette 1974.
60  P. Bécamps, *Libération de Bordeaux*, Hachette, 1974.
61  P. Bertaux, *Libération de Toulouse et sa région*, Hachette, 1973. (By the former commissaire de la République in this 'hot spot')
62  G. Guingouin, *Quatre ans de lutte sur le sol Limousin*, Hachette, 1974. (Another 'hot spot', seen by one of the main participants, though curiously discreet on the aftermath of the liberation of Limoges)
63  H. Ingrand, *Libération de l'Auvergne*, Hachette, 1964.
64  R. Bourderon, *Libération du Languedoc méditerranéen*, Hachette, 1974. (A good account, even if the Socialists of the Aude are somewhat absent)
65  J. Bounin, *Beaucoup d'imprudence*, Stock, 1974. (By the commissaire de Montpellier)
66  P. Guiral, *Libération de Marseille*, Hachette, 1974. (Clear with a long preface by Gaston Defferre)
67  M. Agulhon and F. Barrat, *CRS à Marseille (1944–1947)*, Colin, 1971. (Invaluable on the Pariotic Militia and on 1947)
68  'La Libération des Alpes-Maritimes', *Cahiers de la Méditerranée*, 12, June 1976. (A symposium held at Nice in 1974)
69  H. Romans-Petit, *Les Maquis de l'Ain*, Hachette, 1974.

70  F. Rude, *Libération de Lyon et de sa région*, Hachette, 1974.
71  F. L'Huillier, *Libération de l'Alsace*, Hachette, 1975.
72  G. Grandval and A.-J. Colin, *Libération de l'Est de la France*, Hachette, 1974.
73  E. Dejonghe and D. Laurent, *Libération du Nord et du Pas-de-Calais*, Hachette, 1974.
74  'La Libération du Nord-Pas-de-Calais (1944–1947), *Revue du Nord*, July–September and October–December 1975.
75  F.-L. Closon, *Commissaire de la République du général de Gaulle, Lille, septembre 1944–mars 1945*, Julliard, 1980.

### The military victory

76  H. Michel, *La Seconde Guerre mondiale (1939–1945)*, PUF, 1968, vol. 2. (A good textbook)
77  B. H. Liddel Hart, *History of the Second World War*, Cassell, London, 1970.
78  J. Robichon, *Le Débarquement de Provence*, Laffont, 1962.
79  J. Nobécourt, *Le Dernier Coup de dés de Hitler*, Laffont, 1962.
80  'L'armée française à la fin de la guerre', *Revue d'histoire de la Deuxième Guerre mondiale*, 110, April 1978.
81  J. Planchais, *Une histoire politique de l'armée*, vol. 2, *1940–1967*, Seuil, 1967.
82  J. de Lattre de Tassigny, *Histoire de la I$^{re}$ armée française*, Plon, 1949, and Presses de la Cité, 1971.
83  E. de Larminat, *Chroniques irrévérencieuses*, Plon, 1962.
84  R. Nimier, *Le Hussard bleu*, Gallimard, 1950.

### Penury and inflation

85  I. Boussard, 'État de l'agriculture française aux lendemains de l'Occupation (1944–1948)', *Revue d'histoire de la Deuxième Guerre mondiale*, 116 (October 1979), 69–95. (A good survey, followed by a useful bibliography)
86  M. Cépède, *Agriculture et alimentation en France durant la Deuxième Guerre mondiale*, Génin, 1961. (Goes in fact up to 1951)
87  S. P. Kramer, 'La crise économique de la Libération', *Revue d'histoire de la Deuxième Guerre mondiale*, 111 (July 1978), 25–44. (Clear, and solidly based on the reports from the commissaires de la République)
88  J.-P. Mockers, *L'Inflation en France (1945–1975)*, Cujas, 1976.
89  J. Le Bourva, *L'Inflation française d'après-guerre (1944–1949)*, Colin, 1952. (The only study)
90  R. Sédillot, *Histoire du franc*, Sirey, 1979.
91  M. Rist, *La Federal Reserve et les Difficultés monetaires d'après-guerre (1945–1950)*, Colin, 1952. (The origin and significance of the dollar-gap)
92  J.-L. Guglielmi and M. Perrot, *Salaires et revendications sociales en France (1944–1952)*, Colin, 1953. (Indispensable)
93  *Désirs des Français en matière d'habitation urbaine*, PUF, 1947. (One of the first studies by the INED in 1945. The private and, in most cases, unrealizable dream of a majority of Frenchmen)

*Three balance sheets of the period*

94  Ch. Bettelheim, *Bilan de l'économie française (1919–1946)*, PUF, 1947.
95  P. George, *Géographie économique et sociale de la France*, Éditions Hier et Aujourd'hui, 1946.

96 J. Chardonnet, *Les Conséquences économiques de la guerre (1939–1946)*, Hachette, 1947.

**The purges**

97 P. Novick, *The Resistance versus Vichy. The purge of collaborators in liberated France*, Columbia University Press, New York, 1968. Published as *L'Épuration française*, Ballard, 1985, with a preface by Jean-Pierre Rioux. (Fundamental)

98 R. Aron, *Histoire de l'épuration*, Fayard:
   1. *De l'indulgence aux massacres (nov. 1942–sept. 1944)*, 1967.
   2. *Des prisons clandestines aux tribunaux d'exception (sept. 1944–juin 1949)*, 1969.
   3. Vol. 1, *Le Monde des affaires (1944–1953)*, 1974.
      Vol. 2, *Le Monde de la presse, des arts et des lettres … (1944–1953)*, 1975.
   (To be used with caution)

99 M. Baudot, 'La Résistance française face aux problèmes de répression et d'épuration', *Revue d'histoire de la Deuxième Guerre mondiale*, 81 (January 1971), 23–47. (The best French survey. To be completed with the same author's report in (51), pp. 759–813)

100 L. Noguères, *La Haute Cour de la Libération (1944–1949)*, Éditions de Minuit, 1965. (By the President of the High Court)

101 A. Latreille, *De Gaulle, la Libération et l'Église catholique*, Éditions du Cerf, 1978. (An excellent study of the *épuration* among the clergy and of the fears of the *laïcité*)

## POLITICAL LIFE

### Under the provisional governments

102 F. Goguel, *Géographie des élections françaises sous la Troisième et la Quatrième République*, Colin, 1970. (A collection of maps with commentaries)

102a C. Leleu, *Géographie des élections françaises depuis 1936*, PUF, 1971. (A work of reference)

103 J. Fauvet, *Les Partis Politiques dans la France actuelle*, Le Monde, 1947. (A useful handbook)

104 *'L'Entourage' et de Gaulle*, Plon, 1979. (A symposium of the Institut Charles-de-Gaulle on de Gaulle's methods and decision-making between 1940 and 1969)

105 J. Touchard, *Le Gaullisme (1940–1969)*, Seuil, 1978. (Clear and acute. Indispensable)

106 J. Fauvet and A. Duhamel, *Histoire du parti communiste français*, Fayard, 1977. (The best general study to date)

107 Ph. Robrieux, *Maurice Thorez, vie secrète et vie publique*, Fayard, 1975. (A detailed portrait)

108 F. Billoux, *Quand nous étions ministres*, Éditions sociales, 1972.

109 Ch. Tillon, *On chantait rouge*, Laffont, 1977.

110 R. Quilliot, *La SFIO et l'Exercice du pouvoir (1944–1958)*, Fayard, 1972. (Indispensable)

111 B. D. Graham, *The French Socialists and Tripartism, 1944–1947*, Weidenfeld and Nicolson, London, 1965. (Exhaustive)

112 *L'Œuvre de Léon Blum*, vol. 6, *1945–1947*, Albin Michel, 1958. (The principal texts)

113 D. Blume *et al.*, *Histoire du réformisme en France depuis 1920*, Éditions sociales, 1976, 2 vols. (An exercise in revisionism by Communist historians)

114 J. Vaudiaux, *Le Progressisme en France sous la IV<sup>e</sup> République*, Cujas, 1968. (Useful on the 'rêve travailliste')
115 E.-F. Callot, *Le Mouvement républicain populaire*, Rivière, 1978. (The only accessible synthesis)


**On the information battle**

116 *Histoire générale de la presse française*, vol. iv, *De 1940 à 1958*, C. Bellanger *et al.*, PUF, 1975. (Fundamental)
117 J.-N. Jeanneney and J. Julliard, *'Le Monde' de Beuve-Méry ou le métier d'Alceste*, Seuil, 1979.
118 J. Thibau, *'Le Monde', histoire d'un journal, un journal dans l'histoire*, Simoën, 1978. (More chronological than the above, which it completes)
119 A. Chatelain, *'Le Monde' et ses lecteurs sous la IV<sup>e</sup> République*, Colin, 1962. (A useful sociology)
120 P. Miquel, *Histoire de la radio et de la télévision*, Richelieu-Bordas, 1972. (General, but the first attempt at synthesis)
121 R. Duval, *Histoire de la radio en France*, Alain Moreau, 1979. (A confused but useful chapter 5)


**The system of the Fourth Republic**

122 P. Miquel, *La IV<sup>e</sup> République, hommes et pouvoirs*, Bordas, 1972. (A short introduction)
123 F. Goguel, *Le Régime politique français*, Seuil, 1955.
124 F. Muselier, *Regards neufs sur le Parlement*, Seuil, 1956.
125 D. Macrae, *Parliament, parties and society in France (1946–1958)*, Macmillan, London, 1967.
126 J. Théry, *Le Gouvernement de la IV<sup>e</sup> République*, Librairie générale de droit et de jurisprudence, 1950.
127 S. Arné, *Le Président du Conseil des ministres sous la IV<sup>e</sup> République*, Librairie générale de droit et de jurisprudence, 1962.
128 G. Lavau, *Partis politiques et réalités sociales*, Colin, 1953.
129 M. Duverger (ed.), *Partis politiques et classes sociales en France*, Colin, 1955. (Two indispensable studies)
130 R. Rémond, A. Coutrot and I. Boussard (eds.), *Quarante ans de cabinets ministériels*, Presses de la Fondation nationale des sciences politiques, 1982. (A quantitative study)
131 P. Williams, *War, plots and scandals in post-war France*, Cambridge University Press, 1970. (The accumulation of problems which sapped the authority of the régime)
132 G. Vedel (ed.), *La Dépolitisation, mythe ou réalité?*, Colin, 1962.


**The administration**

133 F. de Baecque, *L'Administration centrale de la France*, Colin, 1973.
134 B. Gournay, 'Technocratie et administration', *Revue française de science politique*, (October–December 1960), 881 ff.
135 M.-C. Kessler, *La Politique de la Haute fonction publique*, Presses de la Fondation nationale des sciences politiques, 1978. (A good history of the ENA)
136 P. Lalumière, *L'Inspection des finances*, PUF, 1959.

137 J. Siwek-Pouydesseau, *Le Corps préfectoral sous la Troisième et la Quatrième République*, Colin, 1969.
138 P. Birnbaum, *Les Sommets de l'État*, Seuil, 1977. (The gulf between politicians and the administration)
139 R. Catherine, *Fonction publique*, Segep, 1952 (2 vols.), and Sirey, 1958.
140 E. N. Suleiman, *Les Hauts Fonctionnaires et la Politique*, Seuil, 1976.
141 Ph. Bauchard, *Les Technocrates et le Pouvoir*, Arthaud, 1966.
142 F. Bloch-Lainé, *Profession: fonctionnaire*, Seuil, 1976. (An exceptional personal account, and a solid study of the key figures)

## Men and parties in power

143 F.-G. Dreyfus, *Histoire des gauches en France (1940–1974)*, Grasset, 1975.
144 R. Rémond, *Les Droites en France*, Aubier, 1982. (Fundamental)
145 'La gauche', *Les Temps modernes*, special number, 1955.
146 'Tableau politique de la France', *La Nef*, April–May 1951.
147 'Pouvoir politique et pouvoir économique', *Esprit* (June 1953).
148 M. Duverger, F. Goguel, J. Touchard (eds.), *Les Elections du 2 janvier 1956*, Colin, 1957.
149 F. de Tarr, *The French Radical Party from Herriot to Mendès France*, Oxford University Press, London, 1961.
150 J.-Th. Nordmann, *Histoire des radicaux (1820-1973)*, La Table ronde, 1974.
151 V. Auriol, *Mon septennat (1947–1954)*, Gallimard, 1970. (A selection from the scholarly edition (8). Indispensable)
152 P.-O. Lapie, *De Léon Blum à de Gaulle, le caractère et le pouvoir*, Fayard, 1971. (The memoirs of a Socialist minister)
153 S. Guillaume, *Antoine Pinay*, Presses de la Fondation nationale des sciences politiques, 1983.
154 P. Rouanet, *Mendès France au pouvoir (1954-1955)*, Laffont, 1965. (The best narrative account)
155 J. Lacouture, *Pierre Mendès France*, Seuil, 1981.
156 P. Mendès France, *Gouverner, c'est choisir*, Julliard, 1953, 1955, 1958 (3 vols.). (Collection of the essential texts)

## The opposition

### (a) The RPF

157 Ch. Purtschet, *Le Rassemblement du peuple français*, Cujas, 1965. (The only general study)
158 Ch. de Gaulle, *Discours et messages*, vol. 2, *Dans l'attente (1946–1958)*, Plon, 1970, and Le Livre de poche, 1974.
159 P. Lefranc, *... avec qui vous savez*, Plon, 1979.
160 J. Soustelle, *Vingt-huit ans de gaullisme*, La Table ronde, 1968. (The former General Secretary of the RPF)
161 A. Astoux, *L'Oubli, de Gaulle, 1946-1958*, J.-Cl. Lattès, 1974. (A former regional delegate of the RPF)

### (b) The PCF

162 A. Kriegel, *Les Communistes français, essai d'ethnographie politique*, Seuil, 1968. (The best description of the Communist 'counter-society')

163  J. Duclos, *Mémoires*, vol. 4, *1945–1952*, Fayard, 1971.
164  Ph. Robrieux, *Histoire intérieure du parti communiste*, vol. 2, *1945–1972*, Fayard, 1981.
165  R. Bourderon *et al.*, *Le PCF, étapes et problèmes 1920–1972*, Éditions sociales, 1981.
166  D. Desanti, *Les Staliniens (1944–1956), une expérience politique*, Fayard, 1975.
167  E. Morin, *Autocritique*, Seuil, 1970 and 1975. (The best account of the mechanisms of exclusion in 1951)
168  P. Daix, *J'ai cru au matin*, Laffont, 1977. (Aragon's second-in-command at *Les Lettres françaises*)
169  R. Pannequin, *Adieu, camarades*, Le Sagittaire, 1977. (For the bureaucracy of the Party and for the strikes in the Nord)

*(c) Poujadism*

170  S. Hoffmann, *Le Mouvement Poujade*, Colin, 1956.
171  D. Borne, *Petits-bourgeois en révolte? Le Mouvement Poujade*, Flammarion, 1977.

**The crises of 1947 and the Cold War**

172  D. Yergin, *La Paix saccagée, les Origines de la guerre froide et la Division de l'Europe*, Balland/France Adel, 1980. (Richly documented and acute)
173  C. Delmas, *Armements nucléaires et guerre froide*, Flammarion, 1971.
174  A. Fontaine, *Histoire de la guerre froide*, Fayard, 2 vols. 1965 and 1967.
175  F. Fonvielle-Alquier, *La Grande Peur de l'après-guerre (1946–1953)*, Laffont, 1973. (A good narrative account)
176  D. Desanti, *L'Année où le monde a tremblé*, 1947, Albin Michel, 1976.
177  R. Aron, *Le Grand Schisme*, Gallimard, 1948. (Scintillating contemporary analysis)
178  G. Lefranc, *Le Mouvement syndical de la Libération aux événements de mai–juin 1968*, Payot, 1969. (Good narrative account of the CGT/FO split)
179  J. Bruhat and M. Piolot, *Esquisse d'une histoire de la CGT*, CGT, 1966. (The official version)
180  A. Bergounioux, *Force ouvrière*, Seuil, 1975.
181  É. Depreux, *Souvenirs d'un militant*, Fayard, 1972.
182  J. Moch, *Une si longue vie*, Laffont, 1976. (Explanations from the two Ministers of the Interior)

**The Atlantic alignment and European unity**

183  P. Mélandri, *L'Alliance atlantique*, Gallimard/Julliard, 1979. (Indispensable. Useful bibliography and chronology)
184  C. Delmas, *L'OTAN*, PUF, 1960.
185  M. Marantz, *Le Plan Marshall, succès ou faillite?* Rivière, 1980.
186  F. Perroux, *Le Plan Marshall, ou l'Europe nécessaire au monde*, Librairie des Médicis, 1948.
187  J. Monnet, *Mémoires*, Payard, 1976. (Essential for an understanding of the period)
188  P. Gerbet, *La Politique d'unification européenne*, Institut d'études politiques de Paris, 1975.
189  *La France et les Communautés européennes*, J. Rideau *et al.*, Librairie générale de droit et de jurisprudence, 1975.

190 J. Freymond, *La Sarre (1945–1955)*, Institut de sociologie Solvay, Brussels, 1959. (A good case-study)
191 J. de Soto, *La CECA*, PUF, 1958.
192 R. Aron and D. Lerner (eds.) *La Querelle de la CED*, Colin, 1956. (Fundamental)
193 Ph. Pondaven, *Le Parlement et la Politique extérieure sous la IVᵉ République*, PUF, 1973.


   *Four diplomats, four different analyses*

194 A. Bérard, *Un ambassadeur se souvient, Washington et Bonn (1945–1955)*, Plon, 1978.
195 J. Chauvel, *Commentaire, d'Alger à Berne (1944–1952)*, Fayard, 1972.
196 J. Dumaine, *Quai d'Orsay (1945–1955)*, Julliard, 1955.
197 R. Massigli, *Une comédie des erreurs (1943–1956)*, Plon, 1978.

## The French Union

*(a) The general context*

198 H. Grimal, *La Décolonisation (1919–1963)*, Colin, 1965. (A good textbook)
199 X. Yacono, *Les Étapes de la décolonisation française*, PUF, 1971.
200 Ch.-R. Ageron, *France coloniale ou parti colonial?*, PUF, 1968. (On the durability of the basic questions, an important book)
201 F. Borella, *Évolution juridique et politique de l'Union française depuis 1946*, Librairie générale de droit et de jurisprudence, 1958. (Fundamental)
202 P. Mus, *Le Destin de l'Union française, de l'Indochine à l'Afrique*, Seuil, 1954. (A particularly well-informed observer)
203 J. Lacouture, *Cinq hommes et la France*, Seuil, 1961. (Ho Chi Minh, Bourguiba, Mohammed V, Ferhat Abbas, and S. Touré)
204 C. Paillat, *Vingt ans qui déchirent la France*, vol. 1, *Le Guêpier*, Laffont, 1969.


*(b) Black Africa*

205 R. Cornevin, *Histoire de l'Afrique contemporaine, de la Deuxième Guerre mondiale à nos jours*, Payot, 1972.
206 J. Suret-Canale, *Afrique noire, de la colonisation aux indépendances (1945–1960)*, Éditions sociales, 1972, vol. 1. (A Marxist analysis of economic exploitation)
207 H. Deschamps, *Histoire de Madagascar*, Berger-Levrault, 1972. (The general context)
208. J. Tronchon, *L'Insurrection malgache de 1947*, Maspero, 1974.


*(c) Indo-China*

209 Ph. Devillers, *Histoire du Viet-Nam de 1940 à 1952*, Seuil, 1952. (Fundamental)
210 Y. Gras, *Histoire de la guerre d'Indochine*, Plon, 1979. (Strictly military)
211 L. Bodard, *La Guerre d'Indochine* (5 vols.), Gallimard, 1963–7, and Gallimard 'Folio', 1973.
212 J. Sainteny, *Histoire d'une paix manquée, Indochine 1945–1947*, Amiot-Dumont, 1953. (The testimony of a crucial participant)
213 J. Doyon, *Les Soldats blancs d'Hô Chi Minh*, Fayard, 1973.
214 J. Lacouture, *Hô Chi Minh*, Seuil, 1967.

214a  H. Navarre. *Le Temps des vérités*, Plon, 1979.
215  J. Roy, *La Bataille de Diên Biên Phu*, Julliard, 1963. (Many documents and a chronology)
216  E. Bergot, *Les 170 jours de Diên Biên Phu*, Presses de la Cité, 1979. (The voice of the French expeditionary force)
217  V. N. Giap, *Diên Biên Phu*, Éditions en Langues étrangères, 1964. (The voice of the victor)
218  J. Lacouture and Ph. Devillers, *La Fin d'une guerre, Indochine 1954*, Seuil, 1960.
219  J. Chauvel, *Commentaire*, vol. 3, *De Berne à Paris (1952–1962)*, Fayard 1973.

*(d)  North Africa*

220  Ch.-A. Julien, *L'Afrique du Nord en marche, nationalisme musulman et souveraineté française*, Julliard, 1972. (Important)
221  L. Chevalier, *Le Problème démographique nord-africain*, PUF, 1947. (A magnificent study by the INED)
222  R. Le Tourneau, *Évolution politique de l'Afrique du Nord musulmane (1920–1961)*, Colin, 1962.
223  Ch.-A. Julien, *Le Maroc face aux impérialismes (1415–1956)*, Éditions Jeune Afrique, 1978.
224  Ch.-R. Ageron, *Histoire de l'Algérie contemporaine*, vol. 2, *1871–1954*, PUF, 1979. (Fundamental)
225  A. Nouschi, *La Naissance du nationalisme algérien (1914–1954)*, Éditions de Minuit, 1962. (Documents)

*(e)  The Algerian War*

226  R. Aron *et al.*, *Les Origines de la guerre d'Algérie*, Fayard, 1962.
227  B. Droz and É. Lever, *Histoire de la guerre d'Algérie (1954–1962)*, Seuil, 1982. (Indispensable)
228  Y. Courrière, *La Guerre d'Algérie*, Fayard, 1968–71 (4 vols.), and Le Livre de poche, 1974. (An excellent account, solidly researched)
229  H. Alleg (ed.), *La Guerre d'Algérie*, Temps actuels, 1981 (3 vols.). (Favourable to the Communists, but richly documented)
230  A. Horne, *A savage war of peace*, Macmillan, London, 1978.
231  H. Elsenhans, *Die Französische Algerienkrieg (1954–1962)*, C. Hauser, Munich, 1974. (The best study of French policy)
232  B. Étienne, *Les Européens d'Algérie et l'Indépendance algérienne*, CNRS, 1968.
233  M. Harbi, *Le FLN, mirages et réalités, des origines à la prise du pouvoir (1945–1962)*, Éditions Jeune Afrique, 1980. (Critical and well-informed)
234  M. Harbi, *Les Archives de la révolution algérienne*, Éditions Jeune Afrique, 1981. (The best collection of documents)
235  J.-P. Vittori, *Nous les appelés d'Algérie*, Stock, 1977.
236  E. Bergot, *La Guerre des appelés en Algérie*, Presses de la Cité, 1968.
237  G. Perrault, *Les Parachutistes*, Seuil, 1961.
238  R. Girardet, *L'Idée coloniale en France (1871–1962)*, La Table ronde, 1972.
239  P. Vidal-Naquet, *La Torture dans la République*, Éditions de Minuit, 1972. (Powerful. Important bibliography)
240  H. Hamon and P. Rotman, *Les Porteurs de valise. La résistance française à la guerre d'Algérie*, Albin Michel, 1979, and Seuil, 1982.
241  J. Cahen and M. Pouteau, *Une resistenza incompiuta. La guerra d'Algéria e gli anticolonialisti francesi (1954–1962)*, Il Saggiatore, Milan, 1964 (2 vols.).

## Taking leave of the Fourth Republic

242 R. Buron, *Les Dernières Années de la IV<sup>e</sup> République, Carnets politiques*, Plon, 1968.
243 R. Massigli, *Sur quelques maladies de l'État*, Plon, 1958.
244 F. Mauriac, *Bloc-notes (1952–1957)*, Flammarion, 1958.
245 'La France des Français', *Esprit*, December 1957.
246 M. Winock, *La République se meurt. Chronique 1956–1958*, Seuil, 1978, new edn, Laffont, 1985.
247 R. Girardet (ed.), *La Crise militaire française (1945–1962)*, Colin, 1964.
248 J. Ferniot, *De Gaulle et le 13 mai*, Plon, 1965.
249 A. Debatty, *Le 13 Mai et la Presse*, Colin, 1960. (Two reliable studies)
250 J.-P. Buffelan, *Le Complot du 13 mai 1958 dans le Sud-Ouest*, Librairie générale de droit et de jurisprudence, 1966.
251 M. and P. Bromberger, *Les 13 Complots du 13 mai*, Fayard, 1959.
252 *L'Établissement de la Cinquième République. Le référendum de septembre et les élections de novembre 1958*, Colin 1960.
253 J. Chapsal, *La Vie politique sous la V<sup>e</sup> République*, PUF, 1981.
254 P. Viansson-Ponté, *Histoire de la république gaullienne*, vol. 1, *La Fin d'une époque (mai 1958–Juillet 1962)*, Fayard, 1970.

## ECONOMY AND SOCIETY

### General works on the economy and society

255 *La Civilisation quotidienne*, P. Breton (ed.), vol. 14 of the *Encyclopédie française*, Société nouvelle de l'Encyclopédie française, 1954.
256 P. Delouvrier and R. Nathan, *Politique économique de la France*, Les Cours de droit, 1958. (Indispensable)
257 A. de Lattre, *Politique économique de la France depuis 1945*, Sirey, 1966.
258 P. Laroque, *Succès et faiblesses de l'effort social français*, Colin, 1961.
259 *Cent ans d'esprit républicain*, vol. 5 of the *Histoire du peuple français*, L.-H. Parias (ed.), Nouvelle Librairie de France, 1964. (For the chapters by J.-L. Monneron)
260 J. Guyard, *Le Miracle français*, Seuil, 1965.
261 *Tendances et volontés de la société française*, J.-D. Reynaud (ed.), SEDEIS/Futurible, 1966. (Sociological studies of reactions to the change)
262 P. Sorlin, *La Société française*, vol. 2, *1914–1968*, Arthaud, 1971. (A good synthesis)
263 M. Parodi, *L'Économie et la société française de 1945 à 1970*, Colin, 1971.
264 M. Gervais, M. Jollivet, and Y. Tavernier, *La Fin de la France paysanne, de 1914 à nos jours*, vol. 4 of the *Histoire de la France rurale*, Seuil, 1976.
265 F. Caron, *Histoire économique de la France, XIX<sup>e</sup>–XX<sup>e</sup> siècle*, Colin, 1981.
266 *Histoire économique et sociale de la France*, F. Braudel and E. Labrousse (eds.), vol. 4,
ii *(1914–vers 1950)*, PUF, 1980.
iii *(années 1950 à nos jours)*, PUF, 1982. (Indispensable)
267 A. Prost, *Histoire sociale de la France au XX<sup>e</sup> siècle*, FNSP, 1975–6.
268 A. Armengaud, *La Population française au XX<sup>e</sup> siècle*, PUF, 1970.
269 J. Beaujeu-Garnier, *La Population française*, Colin, 1969.
270 Darras, *Le Partage des bénéfices. Expansion et inégalités en France*, Éditions de Minuit, 1966. (The position at the beginning of the 1960s)
271 G. Rotvand, *L'Imprévisible Monsieur Durand*, Pierre Horay, 1956. (Identikit picture from polls and surveys)

## Nationalization and social policy

272  B. Chenot, *Organisation économique de l'État*, Dalloz, 1965.
273  B. Chenot, *Les Entreprises nationalisées*, PUF, 1956. (The authoritative view of the former director of the Houillères du Nord-Pas-de-Calais)
274  Ph. Brachet, *L'Etat-Patron, théories et réalités*, Syros, 1973. (A good introduction to long-term comparisons)
275  J.-M. Six, 'Nationalisations et environnement capitaliste', unpublished thesis, Université de Paris X–Nanterre, 1977, 3 vols.
276  G. Bouthillier, *La Nationalisation du gaz et de l'électricité en France*, Microéditions universitaires AUDIR-Hachette, 1973.
277  R. Gaudy, *Et la lumière fut nationalisée: naissance d'EDF–GDF*, Éditions sociales, 1978.
278  O. Hardy-Hemery, 'Permanences et mouvements dans un pôle industriel: Le Valenciennois de septembre 1944 à 1947', *Revue d'histoire de la Deuxième Guerre mondiale*, 102 (April 1976), 83–108. (A good regional example)
279  J. Bouvier, *Un siècle de banque française*, Hachette, 1973. (Clear on the failed nationalization)
280  J.-J. Dupeyroux, *Droit de la sécurité sociale*, Dalloz, 1975.
281  H.-C. Gallant, *Histoire politique de la sécurité sociale française (1945–1952)*, Colin, 1955. (Fundamental)
282  M. Montuclard, *La Dynamique des comités d'entreprise*, Éditions du CNRS, 1963. (The only sound study)
283  M. Combe, *L'Alibi, vingt ans d'un comité d'entreprise*, Gallimard, 1969. (The experience of a worker-priest in the metallurgical industry of Saint-Étienne)
284  A. Bockel, *La Participation des syndicats ouvriers aux fonctions économiques et sociales de l'État*, Librairie générale de droit et de jurisprudence, 1965. (On its developmente up to 1948 and subsequent decline)
285  A. Tiano, *Les Traitements des fonctionnaires et leur détermination (1930–1957)*, Génin, 1957. (Technical, but shows the new importance of state employees in the social struggle)

## Planning, modernization, and the role of the State

286  P. Bauchet, *L'Expérience française de planification*, Seuil, 1958.
287  J. and A. M. Hackett, *Economic Planning in France*, Allen and Unwin, London, 1965.
288  P. Corbel, *Le Parlement français et la planification*, Cujas, 1969.
289  J. Fourastié and J.-P. Courthéoux, *La Planification économique en France*, PUF, 1968.
290  J. Benard, *Comptabilité nationale et modèles de politique économique*, PUF, 1972.
291  F. Fourquet, *Les Comptes de la puissance. Histoire de la comptabilité nationale et du Plan*, Recherches, 1980.
292  C. Gruson, 'Les comptes de la nation, 1949–1959', *Études et conjoncture*, December 1963.
293  R. F. Kuisel, *Capitalism and the State in Modern France. Renovation and Economic Management in the Twentieth Century*, Cambridge University Press, 1981. (Fundamental)
294  J. Lecerf, *La Percée de l'économie française*, Arthaud, 1963.
295  J. MacArthur, R. B. Scott and A. T. Sproat, *L'Industrie française face aux plans. Harvard ausculte la France*, Les Editions d'organisation, 1970.
296  P. A. Bélanger, *Bibliographie générale sur la planification nationale en France*, Presses Universitaires de Grenoble, 1974.

297  P. Massé, *Le Plan ou l'Anti-Hasard*, Gallimard, 1965.
298  C. Gruson, *Origines et espoirs de la planification française*, Dunod, 1968.
     (Two personal reflections to complete those of F. Bloch-Lainé (142) and Jean
     Monnet (187))
299  G. Friedmann, *Où va le travail humain*, Gallimard, 1950. (The irruption of the
     American model)
300  A. Sauvy, *La Montée des jeunes*, Calmann-Lévy, 1959.

**Economic growth**

301  J.-J. Carré, P. Dubois, and E. Malinvaud, *La Croissance française, un essai
     d'analyse économique causale de l'après-guerre*, Seuil, 1972. (Monumental)
302  J.-J. Carré, P. Dubois, and E. Malinvaud, *Abrégé de la croissance française*, Seuil,
     1973. (More accessible than the above)
303  J.-M. Jeanneney, *Forces et faiblesses de l'économie française (1945–1959)*, Colin,
     1959. (Essential)
304  J.-P. Mockers, *Croissances économiques comparées, Allemagne, France, Royaume-Uni
     (1950–1967)*, Dunod, 1969.
305  P. Maillet, *La Structure économique de la France*, PUF, 1960. (Clear on the years
     1956–8)
306  J. Chardonnet, *L'Économie française. Étude géographique d'une décadence et des
     possibilités de redressement*, Dalloz, 1958 and 1959 (2 vols.). (A pessimism
     common at the time)
307  M. Catinat, 'La production industrielle sous la IV$^e$ République', *Economie et
     statistique*, January 1981.
308  J.-J. Carré, 'Évolution de la productivité en France depuis 1939', *Notes et
     études documentaires*, March 1967.
309  Ph. Herzog, 'Comparaison des périodes d'inflation et de récession de l'éc-
     onomie française entre 1950 and 1965', *Etudes et conjoncture*, March 1967.
     (Three important articles)

**The regional question**

310  J.-F. Gravier, *Paris et le désert français*, Le Portulan, 1947, and Flammarion 1958
     and 1972. (The book which launched the debate)
311  M. Bourjol, *Les Institutions régionales de 1789 à nos jours*, Berger-Levrault, 1969.
312  F. Coront-Ducluzeau, *La Formation de l'espace économique nationale*, Colin, 1964.
313  N. Delefortrie and J. Morice, *Les Revenus départementaux en 1864 et en 1954*, Colin,
     1959.
314  P. Madinier, *Les Disparités géographiques de salaires en France*, Colin, 1959.
315  J. Labasse, *La Planification régionale et l'organisation de l'espace*, Les cours de droit,
     1960.
316. J.-P. Jobard, *Les Disparités régionales de croissance*, Presses de la FNSP, 1971.
     (The Centre-East region from 1802 to 1962)
317  M. Philipponneau, *Le Problème breton et le programme d'action régionale*, Colin,
     1960. (The most significant example)

**Patrimony, income, and consumption**

318  Ch.-A. Michalet, *Les Placements des épargnants français de 1815 à nos jours*, PUF,
     1968.
319  P. Cornut, *Répartition de la fortune privée française, par département et nature des biens
     au cours de la première moitié du XX$^e$ siècle*, Colin, 1963.

320 R. Pupin, 'La fortune privée en France au 30 juin 1958', *Statistique et études financières*, May 1959.

321 F. Divisia, J. Dupin, and R. Roy, *A la recherche du franc perdu*, vol. 3, *Fortune de la France*, SERP, 1956.

322 J. Marchal and J. Lecaillon, *La Répartition du Revenu national*, 3 vols. Génin, 1958.

323 'Données statistiques sur l'évolution des rémunérations salariales de 1938 à 1963', *Etudes et conjoncture*, August, 1965.

324 'La consommation des ménages français en 1956', *Consommation, Annales du CREDOC*, 1906, 2 and 3.

325 P. Thibaud and B. Cacérès, *Regards neufs sur les budgets familiaux*, Seuil, 1958. (Documents)

326 J. Morice, *La Demande d'automobiles en France*, Colin, 1957. (The breakdown by *départements* in 1954)

## Rural society

327 H. Mendras, *Sociologie de la campagne française*, PUF, 1959. (An excellent introduction)

328 D. Faucher, *Le Paysan et la machine*, Éditions de Minuit, 1954.

329 H. Mendras, *Les Paysans et la modernisation de l'agriculture*, CNRS, 1958. (The impact of technological change)

330 P. Merlin *et al.*, *L'Exode rural*, PUF, 1971. (Comparisons for the period 1954–62)

331 R. Dumont, *Voyages en France d'un agronome*, Génin, 1951 and 1956.

332 'Paysans d'hier, agriculteurs de demain', *Économie et humanisme, cahier 1*, 1951. (Typical of the period)

333 H. Roussillon, *L'Association générale des producteurs de blé*, Colin, 1970.

334 Y. Tavernier, *Le Syndicalisme paysan. FNSEA et CNJA*, Colin, 1969.

335 P. Barral, *Les Agrariens français de Méline à Pisani*, Colin, 1968.

336 J. Fauvet and H. Mendras (eds.), *Les Paysans et la politique dans la France contemporaine*, Colin, 1958. (The new organizational élites)

## The workers

337 A. Touraine, 'La civilisation industrielle', vol. 4 of the *Histoire générale du travail*, Nouvelle Librairie de France, 1961.

338 A. Touraine, *L'Évolution du travail ouvrier aux usines Renault*, CNRS, 1955.

339 A. Touraine and O. Ragazzi, *Ouvriers d'origine agricole*, Seuil, 1961, and Éditions d'aujourd'hui, 1975.

340 A. Touraine, *La Conscience ouvrière*, Seuil, 1966.

341 M. Collinet, *L'Ouvrier français. Essai sur la condition ouvrière (1900–1950)*, Éditions ouvrières, 1951. (A comparison of 1938 and 1948)

342 P.-H. Chombart de Lauwe, *La Vie quotidienne des familles ouvrières*, CNRS, 1956 and 1977. (Exemplary)

343 P. Naville, *L'Automation et le travail humain*, CNRS, 1961.

344 A. Andrieux and J. Lignon, *L'Ouvrier d'aujourd'hui*, Rivière, 1960, and Gonthier/Méditations, 1966. (Interviews)

345 P. Belleville, *Une nouvelle classe ouvrière*, Julliard, 1963.

346 M. Aumont, *Monde ouvrier inconnu. Carnets d'usine*, Spes, 1956.

347 D. Mothé, *Journal d'un ouvrier (1956–1958)*, Éditions de Minuit, 1959.

348 L. Oury, *Les Prolos*, Denoël, 1973. (Three testimonies)

## The middle and upper classes

349 M. Crozier, *Le Monde des employés de bureau*, Seuil, 1965.
350 M. Crozier, *Petits fonctionnaires au travail*, CNRS, 1956.
(Two pioneering studies)
351 F. Gresle, *L'Univers de la boutique*, Presses universitaires de Lille, 1981. (The *petits patrons* of the Nord from 1920 to 1975)
352 L. Boltanski, *Les Cadres. La formation d'un groupe social*, Éditions de Minuit, 1982. English translation, Cambridge University Press, forthcoming.
353 F. Jacquin, *Les Cadres de l'industrie et du commerce en France*, Colin, 1955.
354 M. Penouil, *Les Cadres et leurs revenus*, Génin, 1957.
355 M. Perrot, *Le Mode de vie des familles bourgeoises*, Colin, 1961, and Presses de la Fondation nationale des sciences politiques, 1982. (A comparison over a century)
356 A. Girard *et al.*, *La Réussite sociale en France*, PUF, 1961. (An inquiry of 1955–7)
357 P. Birnbaum, *La Classe dirigeante française*, PUF, 1978. (An analysis of *Who's Who* since 1954)
358 J.-P. Rioux, 'A changing of the guard? Old and new elites at the Liberation', in J. Howorth and P. G. Cerny (eds.) *Elites in France: Origins, Reproduction and Power*, Frances Pinter, London, 1981.

## Trade unions and pressure groups

359 R. Mouriaux, *La CGT*, Seuil, 1982.
360 G. Adam, *La CFTC (1940–1958), histoire politique et idéologique*, Colin, 1964.
361 P. Vignaux, *De la CFTC à la CFDT: syndicalisme et socialisme. 'Reconstruction' (1946–1972)*, Éditions ouvrières, 1980.
362 J.-F. Noël, *Les Postiers, la grève et le service public*, Maspero, 1977. (The social crisis of summer 1953)
363 R. F. Hamilton, *Affluence and the French worker in the Fourth Republic*, Princeton University Press, 1967. (Prosperity and the stability of the Communist vote)
364 S. Mallet, *La Nouvelle Classe ouvrière*, Seuil, 1963 and 1969.
365 G. Lefranc, *Les Expériences syndicales en France de 1939 à 1950*, Aubier-Montaigne, 1950.
366 G. Lefranc, *Les Organisations patronales en France*, Payot, 1976.
367 H. W. Ehrmann, *La Politique du patronat français (1936–1955)*, Colin, 1959. (Fundamental)
368 B. Brizay, *Le Patronat français, histoire, structure et stratégie du CNPF*, Seuil, 1975. (For the adoption by the CNPF of the contractual policy)
369 J. Meynaud, *Les Groupes de pression en France*, Colin, 1958.
370 J. Meynaud, *Nouvelles études sur les groupes de pression en France*, Colin, 1962.

## Religion

371 F. Lebrun (ed.), *Histoire des catholiques en France*, Privat, 1980. (A good chapter 7, up to date and with a bibliography)
372 A. Coutrot and F. Dreyfus, *Les Forces religieuses dans la France contemporaine*, Colin, 1965.
373 A. Latreille *et al.*, *Histoire du catholicisme contemporain*, vol. 3, Spes, 1962.
374 A. Dansette, *Destin du catholicisme français (1926–1956)*, Flammarion, 1957. (The first synthesis. Dated)

375 G. Le Bras, *Études de sociologie religieuse*, 2 vols., PUF, 1955 and 1956.
376 É. Poulat, *Une Église ébranlée*, Castermann, 1980. (A collection of pioneering articles)
377 P. Toulat, A. Bougeard, J. Templier, *Les Chrétiens dans le monde rural*, Seuil, 1962.
378 A. Latreille and A. Siegfried, *Les Forces religieuses et la vie politique*, Colin, 1951.
379 R. Rémond (ed.), *Forces religieuses et attitudes politiques dans la France contemporaine*, Colin, 1965.
380 *Histoire des protestants en France*, Privat, 1977. (Chapters 7 and 8)

**The *engagement* of the intellectuals**

381 D. Caute, *Communism and the French Intellectuals, 1914–1960*, London, André Deutsch, 1964.
382 R. Aron, *L'Opium des intellectuels*, Calmann-Lévy, 1955.
383 M.-A. Burnier, *Les Existentialistes et la Politique*, Gallimard, 1966.
384 M. Winock, *Histoire politique de la revue 'Esprit' (1930–1950)*, Seuil, 1975.
385 S. de Beauvoir, *Les Mandarins*, Gallimard, 1954, and Gallimard 'Folio', 1972.
386 G. Bernanos, *Français, si vous saviez*, Gallimard, 1961.
387 A. Camus, *Actuelles, chroniques 1944–1948*, Gallimard 1950.
388 F. Mauriac, *Mémoires politiques*, Grasset, 1967.
389 M. Merleau-Ponty, *Les Aventures de la dialectique*, Gallimard, 1955, and Gallimard, 'Idées', 1977.
390 E. Mounier, *Les Certitudes difficiles*, Seuil, 1951.
391 J.-P. Sartre, *Qu'est-ce que la littérature?*, Gallimard, 1948, and Gallimard, 'Idées', 1964.

**Education**

392 A. Prost, *L'École et la famille dans une société en mutation (1930–1980)*, vol. 4 of the *Histoire de l'enseignement et de l'éducation en France*, Nouvelle Librairie de France, 1981. (An excellent synthesis. Rich bibliography)

**Culture**

393 V. Descombes, *Le Même et l'Autre. Quarante-cinq ans de philosophie française (1933–1978)*, Éditions de Minuit, 1979.
394 G. Picon (ed.), *Panorama des idées contemporaines*, Gallimard, 1957.
395 D. Hollier (ed.), *Panorama des sciences humaines*, Gallimard, 1973. (Selections)
396 'Chroniques des années froides (1947–1956)', *Silex*, 20, 1981.
397 J. Bersani *et al.*, *La Littérature en France depuis 1945*, Bordas, 1970.
398 R. Escarpit, *Sociologie de la littérature*, PUF, 1958.
399 *Paris-Paris (1937–1957)*, exhibition catalogue, Centre Georges-Pompidou, 1981. (A mine of information on all the subjects)
400 J. Cassou, *Panorama des arts plastiques contemporains*, Gallimard, 1960.
401 B. Voyenne, *La Presse dans la société contemporaine*, Colin, 1962.
402 S. Siritzky and F. Roth, *Le Roman de 'l'Express' (1953–1978)*, Atelier Marcel-Jullian, 1979.
403 E. Morin, *Le Cinéma ou l'Homme imaginaire*, Éditions de Minuit, 1958.
404 J. Durand, *Le Cinéma et son public*, Sirey, 1958.
405 F. Courtade, *Les Malédictions du cinéma français*, Alain Moreau, 1978.
406 P. Albart and A.-J. Tudesq, *Histoire de la radio-télévision*, PUF, 1981.

407  H. Spade, *L'Album de famille de la télévision française (1950–1959)*, Laffont, 1978.
408  'Le loisir', *Esprit*, June 1959.
409  J. Dumazedier, *Vers une civilisation du loisir?* Seuil, 1962.
410  F. Giroud, *La Nouvelle Vague*, Gallimard, 1958.
411  E. Morin, *L'Esprit du temps*, Grasset, 1962.
412  R. Barthes, *Mythologies*, Seuil, 1957.
      (Two superb essays)


A TOUR DE FRANCE

413  P. Georges, P. Randet and J. Bastié, *La Région parisienne*, PUF, 1964.
414  P.-H. Chombart de Lauwe, *Paris, essais de sociologie (1952–1964)*, Editions ouvrières, 1965.
415  J. Lojkine, *La Politique urbaine dans la région parisienne (1945–1972)*, Mouton, 1972.
416  J. Bastié, *La Croissance de la banlieue parisienne*, PUF, 1964.
417  P. Georges et al., *Études sur la banlieue de Paris*, Colin, 1950.
418  G. Pourcher, *Le Peuplement de Paris*, PUF, 1964.
419  Ph. Bernard, *Économie et sociologie de la Seine-et-Marne (1850–1950)*, Colin, 1953.
420  C. Bettelheim and S. Frère, *Une ville française moyenne: Auxerre en 1950*, Colin, 1950.
421  M.-C. Pingaud, *Paysans en Bourgogne. Les gens de Minot*, Flammarion, 1978.
422  P. Nistri and C. Prêcheur, *La Région du Nord et du Nord-Est*, PUF, 1964.
423  *Histoire du Nord-Pas-de-Calais de 1900 à nos jours*, Privat, 1981.
424  R. Gendarme, *La Région du Nord, essai d'analyse économique*, Colin, 1954.
425  A. Blanc et al., *Les Régions de l'Est*, PUF, 1960.
426  *Histoire de la Lorraine de 1900 à nos jours*, Privat, 1979.
427  C. Prêcheur, *La Lorraine sidérurgique*, SABRI, 1959.
428  S. Bonnet, *Sociologie politique et religieuse de la Lorraine*, Colin, 1972.
429  *L'Alsace de 1900 à nos jours*, Privat, 1979.
430  M. Rochefort, *L'Organisation urbaine de l'Alsace*, Les Belles Lettres, 1960.
431  R. Blanchard, *Annecy, essai de géographie urbaine*, Les Amis du vieil Annecy, 1957.
432  J. Dumazedier and A. Ripert, *Loisir et culture*, Seuil, 1966 (Annecy culturel).
433  C. Marie, *Grenoble (1871–1965), évolution et comportement politique d'une ville en expansion*, Colin, 1966.
434  J. Labasse and M. Laferrère, *La Région lyonnaise*, PUF, 1966.
435  M. Laferrère, *Lyon ville industrielle*, PUF, 1960.
436  M. Luirard, *La Région stéphanoise dans la guerre et dans la paix (1936–1951)*, Presses Universitaires de Saint-Étienne, 1980.
437  J. Labasse, *Les Capitaux et la région*, Colin, 1955.
438  J. Lojkine, *La Politique urbaine dans la région lyonnaise (1945–1972)*, Mouton, 1974.
439  P. Clément and N. Xydias, *Vienne sur le Rhône*, Colin, 1955.
440  L. Wylie, *Village in the Vaucluse*, Cambridge, Mass., 1957.
441  P. Carrère and R. Dugrand, *La Région méditerranéenne*, PUF, 1960.
442  *La Provence de 1900 à nos jours*, Privat, 1978.
443  B. Kayser, *Villes et campagnes de la Côte d'Azur*, Éditions du Rocher, 1960.
444  A. Olivesi and M. Roncayolo, *Géographie électorale des Bouches-du-Rhône sous la IVᵉ République*, Colin, 1961.
445  R. Dugrand, *Villes et campagnes en bas Languedoc*, PUF, 1963.
446  *Histoire du Languedoc de 1900 à nos jours*, Privat, 1980.
447  S. Moscovici, *Reconversions industrielles et changements sociaux. Un exemple: la chapellerie dans l'Aude*, Colin, 1961.

448  P. Barrère *et al.*, *La Région du Sud-Ouest*, PUF, 1962.
449  J. Coppolani, *Toulouse au XX<sup>e</sup> siècle*, Privat, 1963.
450  M. Preuilh, *L'Évolution de l'industrie dans l'agglomération bordelaise*, Bordeaux, Bière, 1964.
451  P. Estienne and R. Joly, *La Région du Centre*, PUF, 1961.
452  H. Mendras, *Études de sociologie rurale, Novis et Virgin*, Colin, 1953. (A village in the Aveyron)
453  A. Fel, *Les Hautes Terres du Massif central*, PUF, 1962.
454  J. Bonnamour, *Le Morvan, la terre et les hommes*, PUF, 1966.
455  F. Jarraud, *Les Américains à Châteauroux (1951–1967)*, 1981.
456  L. Wylie, *Chanzeaux, a Village in Anjou*, Cambridge, Mass., 1966.
457  P. Flatrès, *La Région de l'Ouest*, PUF, 1964.
458  W. Diville and A. Guilcher, *Bretagne et Normandie*, PUF, 1951.
459  S. Berger, *Peasants against politics*, Cambridge, Mass., 1972.
460  E. Morin, *Commune en France. La métamorphose de Plodémet*, Fayard, 1967.
461  A. Burguière, *Bretons de Plozévet*, Flammarion, 1975.
462  G. Désert (ed.), *La Normandie de 1900 à nos jours*, Privat, 1978.
463  J. Gouthier, *Naissance d'une grande cité: Le Mans au milieu du XX<sup>e</sup> siècle*, Colin, 1953.
464  M. Quoist, *La Ville et l'homme: Rouen*, Éditions ouvrières, 1952.
465  J.-Ph. Damais, *La Nouvelle Ville du Havre*, CNRS, 1963.
466  L. Bernot and R. Blanchard, *Nouville, un village français*, Musée de l'Homme, 1953.

## SUPPLEMENTARY BIBLIOGRAPHY

### General works

A. M. Earle, *Problems of the Third and Fourth Republics*, Princeton, 1951.
J. M. Gaillard, *Le Jeu de l'oie. Troubles et passions dans la France contemporaine*, Lattès, 1985.
Dorothy Pickles, *France: the Fourth Republic*, Methuen, 1958.
Michel Winock, *La Fièvre hexagonale*, Calmann-Lévy, 1986.
Gordon Wright, *The reshaping of French democracy*, Boston, 1970.

### Some essays

Raymond Aron, *Mémoires: 50 ans de réflexion politique*, Julliard, 1983.
Raymond Aron, *Histoire et politique. 1905–1938. Commentaire*, Julliard, 1985.

### The Liberation and the purges

Pierre Assouline, *L'Épuration des intellectuels*, Brussels, 1985.
Pierre Bourget, *Paris: Année 44*, Plon, 1984.

**Basic works concerned chiefly with political questions**

D. L. Hartley, A. P. Kerr, and N. H. Waites, *Contemporary France*, Routledge, 1979.
R. W. Johnson, *The long march of the French Left*, Macmillan, 1980.
P. M. Williams, *French politics and elections 1951–1969*, Cambridge University Press, 1970.


**On political parties**

M. Adereth, *The French Communist Party*, Manchester, 1984.
N. Dioujera and F. George, *Staline à Paris*, Ramsay, 1982.
Edward Mortimer, *The rise of the French Communist Party*, Faber, 1984.
Ronald Tiersky, *French Communism 1920–1972*, Columbia, 1974.
Irwin M. Wall, *French Communism in the era of Stalin 1945–1962*, Connecticut, 1983.
J. Charlot, *Le Gaullisme d'opposition 1946–1958*, Paris, 1983.
L. Terrenoire, *De Gaulle 1947–1954*, Plon, 1981.
R. E. M. Irving, *Christian democracy in France*, Cambridge University Press, 1970.


**On the Algerian War**

J. S. Ambler, *The French army in politics 1945–1962*, Ohio, 1966.
G. Kelley, *Lost soldiers: the French Army and Empire in crisis*, Boston, 1965.
John Talbott, *The war without a name*, Faber, 1981.


**Problems of Europe and the French Union**

P. Gerbet, *La Construction de l'Europe*, Imprimerie nationale, 1984.
D. B. Marshall, *The French Colonial myth and Constitution-making in the Fourth Republic*, New Haven, 1973.
P. Melandri, *Les États Unis face à l'unification de l'Europe (1945–1954)*, Pedone, 1980.
Alan S. Milward, *The reconstruction of Western Europe 1945–1951*, Methuen, 1984.


**The economy and society**

A. Lacroix, *CGT et revendications ouvrières face à l'État* (September 1944–December 1947), University of Paris I.
G. Labrevote, *Les Écoles normales primaires en France*, 1879–1979, Presses Universitaires de France, 1985.
G. Lavan, G. Grundberg and N. Mayer, *L'Univers politique des classes moyennes*, Presses de la Fondation nationale des sciences politiques, 1983.
Frances M. B. Lynch, Resolving the paradox of the Monnet Plan, *Economic History Review*, 2nd series, vol. XXXVII, 1984.
Jane Marceau, *Class and status in France; economic change and social immobility 1945–1975*, Oxford, 1977.

P. Mioche, 'Le démenage du Plan Monnet', *Revue d'histoire moderne et contemporaine*, 9, 1984.

Ezra N. Suleiman, *Elites in French society*, Princeton, 1978.

**On 1958**

Jean Lacouture, *De Gaulle*, vol. 2, Seuil, 1984.

René Rémond, *Le Retour de de Gaulle*, Brussels, 1984.

# Index

526